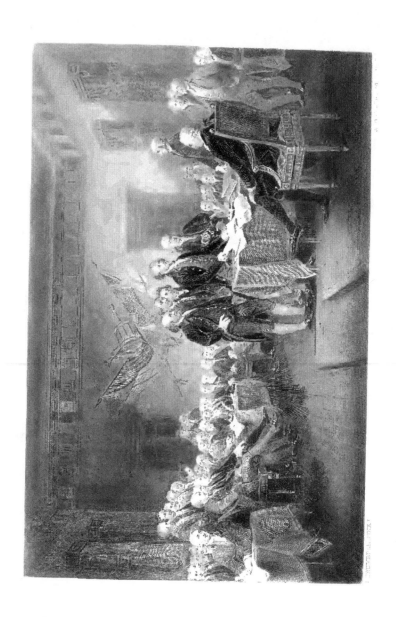

THE

CENTENNIAL HISTORY

OF THE

UNITED STATES.

FROM

THE DISCOVERY

OF THE

AMERICAN CONTINENT

TO THE

CLOSE OF THE FIRST CENTURY

OF

AMERICAN INDEPENDENCE.

BY

JAMES D. McCABE,

AUTHOR OF "A MANUAL OF GENERAL HISTORY," "PATHWAYS OF THE HOLY LAND," "HISTORY OF THE WAR
BETWEEN GERMANY AND FRANCE," "THE GREAT REPUBLIC," ETC., ETC.

EMBELLISHED WITH 442 FINE HISTORICAL ENGRAVINGS AND PORTRAITS.

Issued by subscription only, and not for sale in the book stores. Residents of any State desiring a copy should
address the Publishers, and an Agent will call upon them. See page 957.

PUBLISHED BY

THE NATIONAL PUBLISHING COMPANY,

PHILADELPHIA, PA., CHICAGO, ILL., ST. LOUIS, MO., AND COLUMBUS, OHIO.

PREFACE.

HERE is nothing more worthy of a man's study than the history of his country In our own land, however, the means of pursuing such a study are limited. Our great cities contain large and valuable public libraries, and the collections of our historical societies are rich and very complete, but these are accessible only to the communities in which they are located, and are practically useless to the majority of the American people The great works of Bancroft and Hildreth cover but a portion of our history, and are removed from the reach of the masses by reason of their costliness Besides these, the larger number of the works treating of American history are compendiums, or outlines intended for the use of schools, and are therefore unsatisfactory to the adult reader.

The demand for a popular History of the United States which shall fill a place between these greater and smaller works has led the author to the preparation of this volume. He has endeavored to popularize the story of the nation, and at the same time to neglect nothing that could in the least contribute to a clear and comprehensive understanding of the subject He has sought to trace the history of the Republic from the discovery of the American continent to the present day, and has endeavored especially to fix the attention of the reader upon the various influences which have aided in moulding our national character, and have produced those distinctive political and moral national traits which we call "American Institu-

3

tions." He has endeavored to write from a broad national standpoint, and to cultivate in the minds of his readers that feeling of national patriotism which must ever be the safeguard of our country.

It is a fitting time to consider the story of the past, to learn the lessons which it teaches, and to ponder the warnings which it conveys for the future. On the 4th of July, 1876, the United States of America will complete the first century of their national existence The people of this country can look back upon this period with pride, and in this feeling may justly embrace the whole course of our history. Less than four hundred years ago America was an unknown wilderness Less than three centuries ago it passed into the hands of England, and was thus secured for the language and the free influences of the all-conquering Anglo-Saxon race. It was a precious heritage which was thus secured for liberty; a land stretching from the frozen regions of the north to the sunny skies of the tropics, from the stormy Atlantic to the calm Pacific; a land embracing every variety of climate, and a soil capable of producing almost every product of the earth, from the stunted herbage of the frozen regions to the luxuriant fruits of the tropics. The earth is rich in mineral deposits, from the homely, but invaluable, veins of coal, to beds of the most brilliant and precious minerals It pours out in streams, oil for burning, gas that may be used fresh from the natural springs, salt that requires but the heat of the sun for its perfection, and beds of pure soda that cover the earth like the dust in the highways In short, all that is needed for the preservation and comfort of animal and human life exists in this favored land in the greatest profusion.

Such is the land designed by God for the home of liberty. The people to whom He has intrusted it have not abused His

goodness   In the short space of two centuries, the American
people have grown from a small handful of hardy adventurers
to a "mighty continental nation," increasing with a rapidity
that is almost marvellous   They have built up their country
on a scale of magnificence of which they are justly proud
They have covered it with powerful and free States, and splendid cities, connected by a network of railways, telegraphs,
navigable rivers. and canals. which bind all the scattered parts
into one solid whole   They have made a commerce and a
system of manufactures before which the fabled wealth of Tyre
sinks into insignificance.   They have created a literature
which commands the respect of the world, they have illustrated their history with deeds of arms not less splendid than
their more peaceful achievements, and have given to the world
names in every walk of life that will never die.   They have
shown that liberty and power can go hand in hand, they have
made themselves a nation in which God is feared. and of which
Christianity is the basis, in which ignorance and vice are
despised, and in which the great lesson that liberty is possible
only to an educated and virtuous people is being practically
demonstrated

  This is a grand history—a record of the highest achievements
of humanity—the noblest, most thrilling, and glorious story
ever penned on earth.   Yet the fact remains that the great
mass of the American people are but imperfectly acquainted
with it.   There is a real need that we should know better than
we do what we have done   It is only by a thoughtful study of
our past that we can safely provide for the perils of the future
We have triumphed over adversity. and we are now called
upon to bear the test of success   He can be no good citizen
who is ignorant of his country's history

  In the preparation of this volume no authority of importance has been overlooked; the author has carefully searched every source of information open to him; and has availed himself of every fact that could throw new light upon, or impart additional interest to, the subject under consideration

In the narration of military events, he has preferred to give each campaign as a whole rather than to mingle several by presenting the events in chronological order. At the same time he has sought to preserve the inter-relation of events in one field of operations to those in the others.

An honest effort has been made to do justice to both sections in the relation of the events of the civil war, and it is believed that each will admit the fairness and accuracy of the narrative. The author has made no attempt to intrude his own political views upon the reader, and has constantly kept in mind the purpose which has guided his labors—to write a national history free from sectional or partisan bias, which shall be acceptable to the whole country.

The book is offered to the public in the sincere hope that it may induce its readers to take to heart the lessons which our history teaches, and to set a higher value upon the precious heritage of constitutional liberty which our fathers won for us with their blood, and handed down to us in trust for our children's children.

October 19th, 1875.

A. Lincoln

CONTENTS.

CHAPTER I.

PRIMITIVE INHABITANTS.

CHAPTER II.

THE VOYAGES OF COLUMBUS.

CHAPTER III.

ENGLISH AND FRENCH DISCOVERIES.

CHAPTER IV.

THE SPANIARDS IN AMERICA.

CHAPTER V.

THE FIRST ENGLISH COLONY.

CHAPTER VI

THE SETTLEMENT OF VIRGINIA.

CHAPTER VII.

PROGRESS OF THE VIRGINIA COLONY.

CHAPTER VIII.

VIRGINIA AFTER THE RESTORATION.

CHAPTER IX.

THE COLONIZATION OF MARYLAND.

CHAPTER XIII.

THE UNION OF THE NEW ENGLAND COLONIES.

CHAPTER XIV.

NEW ENGLAND AFTER THE RESTORATION.

CHAPTER XV.

WITCHCRAFT IN MASSACHUSETTS.

CHAPTER XVI.

THE SETTLEMENT OF NEW YORK.

CHAPTER XVII.

COLONIZATION OF PENNSYLVANIA.

CHAPTER XVIII.

SETTLEMENT OF THE CAROLINAS.

CHAPTER XIX.

SETTLEMENT OF GEORGIA.

CHAPTER XX.

THE FRENCH IN THE VALLEY OF THE MISSISSIPPI.

CHAPTER XXI.

THE ENGLISH AND FRENCH COME IN CONFLICT.

CHAPTER XXII

THE FRENCH AND INDIAN WAR.

CHAPTER XXIII.

THE FRENCH AND INDIAN WAR—CONTINUED.

CHAPTER XXIV.

THE FRENCH AND INDIAN WAR—CONCLUDED.

CHAPTER XXV

CAUSES OF THE AMERICAN REVOLUTION.

CHAPTER XXVI.

THE AMERICAN REVOLUTION.

CHAPTER XXVII.

THE DECLARATION OF INDEPENDENCE.

CHAPTER XXVIII

THE YEAR 1777.

CHAPTER XXIX

AID FROM ABROAD.

CHAPTER XXX.

THE CLOSE OF THE WAR.

CHAPTER XXXI.

THE ADOPTION OF THE CONSTITUTION—WASHINGTON'S ADMINIS-
TRATION.

CHAPTER XXXII.

THE ADMINISTRATIONS OF JOHN ADAMS AND THOMAS JEFFERSON.

CHAPTER XXXIII.

THE ADMINISTRATION OF JAMES MADISON—THE SECOND WAR WITH ENGLAND.

CHAPTER XXXIV

ADMINISTRATIONS OF JAMES MONROE AND JOHN QUINCY ADAMS

CHAPTER XXXV.

ADMINISTRATIONS OF ANDREW JACKSON AND MARTIN VAN BUREN.

CHAPTER XXXVI.

ADMINISTRATIONS OF WILLIAM HENRY HARRISON AND JOHN TYLER.

CHAPTER XXXVII

ADMINISTRATION OF JAMES K. POLK—THE WAR WITH MEXICO.

CHAPTER XXXVIII.

ADMINISTRATIONS OF ZACHARY TAYLOR AND MILLARD FILLMORE.

CHAPTER XXXIX.

THE ADMINISTRATION OF FRANKLIN PIERCE.

CHAPTER XL.

THE ADMINISTRATION OF JAMES BUCHANAN

CHAPTER XLI.

THE ADMINISTRATION OF ABRAHAM LINCOLN—THE CIVIL WAR

CHAPTER XLII.

THE ADMINISTRATION OF ABRAHAM LINCOLN—THE CIVIL WAR— CONCLUDED.

CHAPTER XLIII

THE ADMINISTRATION OF ANDREW JOHNSON

CHAPTER XLIV.

THE ADMINISTRATION OF ULYSSES S GRANT.

CHAPTER XLV.

APPENDIX.

LIST OF ILLUSTRATIONS.

FRONT VIEW OF THE CAPITOL

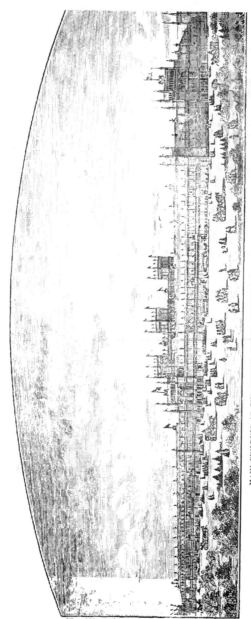

MAIN BUILDING OF THE INTERNATIONAL CENTENNIAL EXHIBITION, PHILADELPHIA, 1876.

1880 feet in length and 464 feet in width.

THE

CENTENNIAL HISTORY

OF THE

UNITED STATES.

CHAPTER I

PRIMITIVE INHABITANTS

Earliest Inhabitants of the United States—The Mound Builders—Remarkable Works constructed by them—Evidences of a Primitive Civilization—Indications of the Antiquity of this Period—The American Indians—Divisions of the Country among the Tribes—Names and Location of the various Tribes—Organization and Government of the Indians—Their Dress, Manners, and Customs—Villages—Indian Inventions—The War Dance—Legends of the Norsemen respecting the Discovery of America.

E do not know who were the inhabitants, or what was the history of North America previous to its discovery and settlement by the Europeans That it was at some remote period occupied by a more civilized and powerful race than the Indians found by the first explorers, is very certain ; but who they were, what was their history, or what the cause of their extinction, are among the profoundest mysteries of the past. Traces as distinct as those which mark the various physical changes which the continent has undergone, exist to show that these primitive inhabitants were both numerous and far advanced in civilization ; but this is all that we know concerning them.

In various parts of the country, and especially in the valley of the Mississippi, large mounds and other structures of earth and stone, but chiefly of earth, remain to show the magnitude of the works constructed by these people, to whom the name "Mound Builders" is generally applied. Some of these earth-works embrace as much as fifteen or sixteen miles of embankment. As no domestic animals existed in this country

3   3

at this period, these works must have been constructed by bringing the earth used for them by hand, a fact which shows that the primitive population was a large one. The construction of the works proves that they had considerable engineering skill. The square, the circle, the ellipse, and the octagon are all used in these structures, being all combined in a single system of works in some places. The proportions are always perfect. The square is always a true square, and the circle a true circle. Many implements and ornaments of copper, silver, and precious stones—such as axes, chisels, knives, bracelets, beads, and pieces of thread and of cloth, and well-shaped vases of pottery—have been found in these mounds, and show the extent of the civilization of the "Mound Builders." In the region of Lake Superior are found old copper mines worked by these ancient people. In one of these mines there was discovered an immense block of copper weighing nearly six tons. It had been left in the process of removal to the top of the mine, nearly thirty feet above, and was supported on logs of wood which were partly petrified. The stone and copper tools used by the miners were discovered lying about as they had been left by their owners ages before. At the mouth of this mine are piles of earth thrown out in digging it, and out of these embankments trees are growing which are nearly four hundred years old. At Marietta, Ohio, there is a mound bearing trees eight hundred years old. The age of the mounds is necessarily equal to that of the trees. How much older they are is unknown.

This mysterious race had perished long before the discovery of the continent by Columbus. Whether the "Mound Builders" were the ancestors of the American Indians is uncertain, but it is not likely that they were. The two races were unlike in habits, and the Indians neither constructed such works as the mounds, nor gave any evidence of the skill or industry necessary to their construction. The Indians themselves had no recollection of any previous race in this country, although they preserved their traditions with care. Various conjectures have been made as to the origin and character of the "Mound Builders," but it is useless to give them here. We have no means of arriving at a definite or satisfactory conclusion concerning this lost race. We only know that they existed and erected the great works which alone attest their presence in this country, perhaps more than a thousand years ago.

At the time of its discovery by the whites the Indians were the sole human occupants of the continent, which was covered with vast woods and plains abounding with game of every description, the pursuit of which formed the principal occupation of the natives, and furnished them with food and clothing.

INDIAN VILLAGE IN WINTER.

35

Though nominally divided into tribes and "nations," the Indians were really one great family in physical appearance, manners, customs, religion, and in the observance of their social and political systems. The division into tribes was the result of their difference in language. Each tribe had a dialect peculiar to itself and distinct from those of the others. The tribes were for the most part hostile to, and were constantly engaged in war with, each other. They were generally divided into eight nations, speaking eight radically distinct languages. These were:

I. *The Algonquins,* who inhabited the territory now comprised in the six New England States, the eastern part of New York and Pennsyl-

vania, New Jersey, Delaware, Maryland, Virginia, North Carolina as far south as Cape Fear, a large part of Kentucky and Tennessee, and nearly all of Ohio, Indiana, Illinois, Michigan, Wisconsin, and Minnesota. This nation was subdivided into the following tribes: the Knistenaux, Ottawas, Chippewas, Sacs and Foxes, Menomonees, Miamis, Piankeshaws, Potawatomies, Kickapoos, Illinois, Shawnees, Powhatans, Corees,

NAVAJO BOY.

Nanticokes, Lenni-Lenapes or Delawares, Mohegans, Narragansetts, Pequods and Abenakis.

II. *The Iroquois,* who occupied almost all of that part of Canada south of the Ottawa, and between Lakes Ontario, Erie, and Huron, the greater part of New York, and the country lying along the south shore of Lake Erie, now included in the States of Ohio and Pennsylvania. This territory, it will be seen, was completely surrounded by the domains of their powerful and bitter enemies, the Algonquins. The nation was subdivided into the following tribes: the Senecas, Cayugas, Onondagas, Oneidas, and Mohawks. These five were afterwards called by the English the "Five Nations." In 1722, they admitted the Tuscaroras

MEMORIAL BUILDING OR ART GALLERY—INTERNATIONAL EXHIBITION.

365 feet in length and 210 feet in width.

into their confederation, and were afterwards called the "Six Nations." The nation called itself collectively the Konoskioni, or "Cabin Builders." The Algonquins termed them Mingoes, the French, Iroquois; and the English, Mohawks, or Mingoes

III. *The Catawbas,* who dwelt along the banks of the Yadkin and Catawba rivers, near the line which at present separates the States of North and South Carolina.

IV *The Cherokees,* whose lands were bounded on the east by the Broad river of the Carolinas, including all of northern Georgia

V. *The Uchees,* who dwelt south of the Cherokees, along the Savannah, the Oconee, and the head-waters of the Ogeechee and Chattahoochee. They spoke a harsh and singular language, and are believed to have been the remnant of a once powerful nation

VI. *The Mobilian Nation,* who inhabited all of Georgia and South Carolina not mentioned in the above statements, a part of Kentucky and Tennessee, and all of Florida, Alabama and Mississippi Their territory was next in extent to that of the Algonquins, and extended along the Gulf of Mexico from the Atlantic ocean to the Mississippi river. The nation was divided into three great confederations—the Creeks or Musco-gees, the Choctaws, and the Chickasaws—and was subdivided into a number of smaller tribes, the principal of which were the Seminoles and Yemassees, who were members of the Creek Confederation

VII. *The Natchez,* who dwelt in a small territory east of the Missis-sippi, and along the banks of the Pearl river They were surrounded on all sides by the tribes of the Mobilian language, yet remained until their extinction a separate nation, speaking a distinct language peculiar to themselves, and worshipping the sun as their God. They are believed to have been the most civilized of all the savage tribes of North America.

VIII *The Dacotahs or Sioux,* whose territory was bounded on the north by Lake Winnipeg, on the south by the Arkansas river, on the east by the Mississippi, and on the west by the Rocky mountains. The nation was divided into the following branches : the Winnebagoes, living between Lake Michigan and the Mississippi; the Assiniboins, living in the extreme north ; the Southern Sioux, living between the Arkansas and the Platte; and the Mintarees, Mandans, and Crows, who lived west of the Assiniboins.

The great plains, the Rocky mountains, and the Pacific coast were held by the powerful tribes of the Pawnees, Comanches, Apaches, Utahs, Black Feet, Snakes, Nezpercees, Flatheads, and California Indians.

Each tribe was divided into classes or clans, which were distinguished by a mark tattooed on the breast. This mark was called the *totem,* and was generally the representation of an animal or bird. The Indians believed that all animals had protecting spirits, and each class was supposed to be protected by the spirit of the animal it chose for its totem. Over each class was a chief, and the head of the tribe was a chief or sachem, who was usually a man, but sometimes a woman. The Indians had no written laws, but the customs and traditions of the Indians took the place of these. The religious belief of the Indians was simple. They adored a Great Spirit—some tribes had many gods—and believed in a future state. The brave were admitted to the happy hunting-grounds of the spirit world, but cowards were excluded from them. The weapons of a warrior were buried with him that he might use them in his spirit

PUEBLO INDIAN AT PRAYER.

home. Their heaven lay far beyond the mountains of the setting sun. It was a land rich in game, and abounding in fertile meadows and sparkling streams. There the warrior, released from the cares and hardships of life, passed the ages of eternity in the chase; and there parting from friends, suffering, fatigue, hunger, and thirst were unknown. The Indian heard voices of spirits in the wind, and saw them in the stars. The shades of his ancestors were constantly hovering over him, stimulating him to brave deeds, and keeping fresh in his mind the duty of avenging them upon the enemies they had left behind.

The dress of the savages consisted of the skins of animals, which were prepared by smoking them. After the settlement of the colonies they added a blanket to this dress. Their garments were decorated with skins and feathers, and on special occasions they painted their faces with various bright colors. In the warm weather they wore scarcely any clothing. Their houses or wigwams were formed of poles set firmly in the ground and bent toward each other at the top. These were covered with chestnut or birch bark. Some of the tribes had large houses, often thirty feet high and over two hundred feet long, which accommodated a number of families. Some of the Indian villages were laid off regularly and were permanent; others were broken up with each migration of the tribe.

PENN'S TREATY WITH THE INDIANS.

38

All the Indians, however, pursued a roving life, passing from point to point in search of game and the means of subsistence. Some of the tribes lived by hunting only; others added to this pursuit the cultivation of maize or Indian corn, beans, tobacco, hemp, and pumpkins. The food of the Indians was coarser and less nourishing than that of the Europeans, and they were consequently inferior to the latter in bodily strength. They surpassed them in endurance, however, and could bear tests which the whites could not. They were swift runners, and could accomplish long distances in this way. It was a common thing for a good runner to run seventy or eighty miles in a single day. They were thoroughly proficient in the craft of the woodsman. Sounds and sights which had no meaning to the white man were eloquent to them; and they surpassed

the latter in keenness of hearing and of vision. They communicated with each other by signs or marks on rocks and trees. For money they used wampum beads; and belts made of this wampum were used to record treaties and other important events. They had no intoxicating drinks before the arrival of the whites; but used tobacco, which they smoked in pipes made of clay. They were expert marksmen with the bow until they learned the use of fire-arms from the whites, when they lost much of their ancient skill with this weapon.

CONVERTED INDIAN WOMAN.

"The most ingenious inventions of the Indians," says Colonel Higginson, "were the snow-shoe and the birch canoe. The snow-shoe was made of a maple-wood frame, three or four feet long, curved and tapering, and filled in with a network of deer's hide. This network was fastened to the foot by thongs, only a light, elastic moccasin being worn. Thus the foot was supported on the surface of the snow; and an Indian could travel forty miles a day upon snow-shoes, and could easily overtake the deer and moose, whose pointed hoofs cut through the crust. The peculiar pattern varied with almost every tribe, as did also that of the birch canoe. This was made of the bark of the white birch, stretched over a very light frame of white cedar. The whole bark of a birch tree was stripped off and put round the frame

A DEAD TOWN OF THE MOQUIS INDIANS.

without being torn. The edges were sewed with thongs cut from the roots of the cedar, and were then covered with pitch made from the gum of trees. If torn, the canoe could be mended with pieces of bark, fastened in the same way. The largest of these canoes was thirty feet long, and would carry ten or twelve Indians. They were very light, and could be paddled with ease. They were often very gracefully shaped, and drew very little water. . . . .

"The Indians had great courage, self-control, and patience. They were grave and dignified in their manners on important occasions; in their councils they were courteous to one another, and discussed all important questions at great length. They were often kind and generous, and sometimes even forgiving; but they generally held sternness to be a virtue, and forgiveness a weakness. They were especially cruel to captives, putting them to death with all manner of tortures, in which women took an active part. It was the custom among them for women to do most of

the hard work, in order that the bodies of the men might be kept supple and active for the pursuits of the chase and war. When employed on these pursuits, the Indian men seemed incapable of fatigue; but in the camp or in travelling the women carried the burdens; and when a hunter had carried a slain deer on his shoulders for a long distance, he would throw it down within sight of the village, that his squaw might go and bring it in.

INDIAN OF THE PLAINS.

"Most of the Indian tribes lived in a state of constant warfare with one another. When there was a quarrel between tribes, and war seemed ready to break out, strange ceremonies were used. Some leading chief would paint his body black from head to foot, and would hide himself in the woods or in a cavern. There he would fast and pray, and call upon the Great Spirit; and would observe his dreams to see if they promised good or evil. If he could dream of a great war-eagle hovering before him it would be a sign of triumph. After a time he would come forth from the woods and return among his people. Then he would address them, summon them to war, and assure them that the Great Spirit was on their side. Then he would bid the warriors to a feast at his wigwam. There they would find him no longer painted in black, but in bright and gaudy colors, called 'war paint.' The guests would also be dressed in paint and feathers, and would seat themselves in a circle Then wooden trenchers, containing the flesh of dogs, would be placed before them, while the chief would sit smoking his pipe, and would not yet break his long and exhausting fast

"After the feast, the war-dance would follow, perhaps at night, amid the blaze of fires and lighted pine knots. A painted post would be driven into the ground, and the crowd would form a wide circle round it.   The war chief would leap into the open space, brandishing his hatchet, and would chant his own deeds and those of his fathers, acting out all that he described and striking at the post as if it were an enemy. Warrior after warrior would follow, till at last the whole band would be dancing, shouting, and brandishing their weapons, striking and stabbing at the air, and filling the forest with their yells

"Much of the night would pass in this way In the morning the warriors would leave the camp in sing'e file, still decorated with paint and feathers and ornaments ; and, as they entered the woods, the chief would fire his gun, and each in turn would do the same. Then they would halt near the village, would take off their ornaments and their finery, and would give all these to the women, who had followed them for this purpose. Then the warriors would go silently and stealthily through the forest to the appointed place of attack. Much of their skill consisted in these silent approaches, and in surprises and stratagems, and long and patient watchings. They attached no shame to killing an unarmed enemy, or to private deceit and treachery, though to their public treaties they were always faithful. They were desperately brave, and yet they saw no disgrace in running away when there was no chance of success."

At the time of the discovery of America the Indians were rapidly disappearing. Their relentless wars and frequent pestilences were sweeping them away Contact with the white race has hastened the work of destruction Many of the tribes exist now but in name, and those which remain are growing smaller in numbers with each generation ; and it would seem that the time is not far distant when the last trace left of the red man in America will be his memory.

Whether any white men ever trod the shores of America previous to the coming of Columbus is a disputed question. It would seem, however, that, several centuries previous to his discovery, a Norwegian vessel from Iceland to Greenland was driven out of her course by storms to the coast of Labrador or Newfoundland The national pride of the Icelanders and the Danes has led them to accept as literal history the

GROUP OF INDIANS OF NEW MEXICO.

43

traditions of their race concerning this voyage, and they have given it a
definite date. According to them this voyage took place in A. D. 986,
and was followed in 1001 by a voyage of Lief Erickson, an Icelandic
navigator, who is said to have discovered America, reaching Labrador
first, and then sailing southward to Newport and New York harbors.
This voyage is said to have led the way to the further exploration of the

LOWER FALLS OF THE YELLOWSTONE, WYOMING,
(350 FEET IN HEIGHT.)

coast as far south as the capes of Virginia, and to the planting of colonies,
which soon perished, in Newfoundland and Nova Scotia. That some
Icelandic voyagers visited the American continent previous to the expedition of Columbus is most likely; but we cannot accept the definite and
explicit statements of the writers in question; at least in the present state
of our knowledge respecting these.

WOMEN'S PAVILION.—INTERNATIONAL CENTENNIAL EXHIBITION.

CHAPTER II

THE VOYAGES OF COLUMBUS

THE fifteenth century witnessed a remarkable awakening of human
thought and enterprise, one of the most important features of
which was the activity in maritime undertakings which led to
the discovery of lands until then unknown to the civilized world
The invention, and the application to navigation, of the mariner's
compass, had enabled the seamen of Europe to undertake long and distant
voyages   The Portuguese took the lead in the maritime enterprises of
this period, the chief object of which was to find a route by water from
Europe to the Indies   The equator had been passed , Bartholomew Diaz
had even doubled the Cape of Storms, and had established the course of
the eastern coast of Africa , and it was hoped by some of the most daring
thinkers that the distant ports of India could be reached by sailing
around this cape.   Others, still bolder, believed that although the earth
was really a sphere, it was much smaller than it is, and that the central
portion of its surface was occupied by a vast ocean which washed the
shores of what they regarded as its solitary continent, on either side, and
that by sailing due west from Europe, the shores of India, China, or
Japan would be reached

Among those who held this opinion was Christopher Columbus.   He
was a native of Genoa, in Italy, was born about the year 1435, and was
the son of a weaver of cloth   His ancestors had been sailors, for which
calling he at an early age evinced a preference.   He received a common-
school education, and afterwards went to the University of Pavia, where
he studied geometry, astronomy, geography, and navigation   He stayed

at Pavia but a short time; only long enough to gain a decided relish for the mathematical studies in which he afterwards excelled. At the age of fourteen he went to sea with a relative, and followed the calling of a sailor until he had completed his thirtieth year. During this period he had married, and by this marriage he had become possessed of the papers of the former husband of his wife, who had been a distinguished Portuguese navigator. He had learned but little at school, but he had been a close student all his life, and had stored his mind with a valuable fund of information. This habit of study he never abandoned, and his

CHRISTOPHER COLUMBUS.

extensive knowledge, added to his years of practical experience, made him one of the most learned navigators of his day.

In 1470, being then about thirty years old, Columbus took up his residence in Portugal, which was then the centre of maritime enterprise in Europe. He continued to make voyages to the then known parts of the world, and while on shore engaged in the work of making and selling maps and charts. The papers given him by his wife were now of the greatest service to him. He entered eagerly into the speculations of the day concerning the shortest passage to the Indies, and his studies, fortified by his experience, induced him to believe that there was land beyond the western seas, which could be reached by sailing in that direction. This land he believed to be the eastern shores of Asia. He was confirmed in his belief by his correspondence with the learned Italian Toscanelli, who sent him a map of his own projection, in which the eastern coast of Asia was laid down opposite the western coast of Europe, with only the broad Atlantic between them. Other things also confirmed him in what had now become the profoundest conviction of his life. Sailors who had been to the Canary islands told him they had seen land far to the westward of those islands. A piece of wood strangely carved had been thrown by the waves upon the Portuguese coast after a long westerly gale, and had been seen by the brother-in-law of Columbus. An old pilot related to him the finding of a carved paddle at sea, a thousand miles to the westward of Europe. Pine trees had been cast ashore at Madeira, and at the Azores he learned that the bodies of two men, whose features and dress showed that they belonged to no nation of Europe, had been thrown on the land by the waves.

Having settled it in his own mind that there was land to the westward, Columbus was eager to go in search of it. He was not possessed of sufficient means to accomplish this at his own expense, and began his efforts to interest some European state in the enterprise. His first application was addressed to his native country, the Republic of Genoa. He met with a refusal, and then turned to Venice, with a like result. His next effort was to enlist the Portuguese king, John II, in his scheme. Here he was subjected to delays and vexations innumerable, and once the Portuguese sovereign attempted to make a dishonorable use of the information given by Columbus in support of his theory. Disgusted with the conduct of this sovereign, Columbus, after years of waiting, abandoned the hope of obtaining his assistance, and applied to Henry VII. of England, from whom he received a decided refusal.

Quitting Lisbon in 1484, Columbus went to Spain, intending to lay his plans before Ferdinand and Isabella, the sovereigns of that country. He could scarcely have chosen a more unpropitious time. The Spanish nation was engaged in the Moorish war, which had exhausted the treasury, and which absorbed the attention of the sovereigns to the exclusion of every other matter. He spent seven years in endeavoring to interest the government in his plans. "During this time Columbus appears to have remained in attendance on the court, bearing arms occasionally in the campaigns, and experiencing from the sovereigns an unusual degree of deference and personal attention." At last, wearied with the long delay to which he had been subjected, he pressed the court for an answer, and was told by the sovereigns that, "although they were too much occupied at present to embark in his undertaking, yet, at the conclusion of the war, they should find both time and inclination to treat with him." He accepted this answer as a final refusal, and prepared to go to France to ask the assistance of the king of that country, from whom he had received a friendly letter.

Travelling on foot, he stopped at the monastery of Santa Maria de Rabida, near Palos, to visit the Prior Juan Perez de Marchena, who had befriended him when he first came to Spain. The prior, learning his intention to quit Spain, persuaded him to remain until one more effort could be made to enlist the government in his plans.   Leaving Columbus at the convent, Juan Perez, who had formerly been the queen's confessor, mounted his mule and set off for the Spanish camp before Granada   He was readily granted an interview by Queen Isabella, and he urged the suit of Columbus with all the force of eloquence and reasoning of which he was master.   His appeal was supported by several eminent persons whom Columbus, during his residence at the court, had interested in his project, and these represented to the queen the impolicy of allowing Columbus to secure the aid of a foreign power which would reap the benefits of his discoveries, if he were successful   The result was that the sovereigns consented to reopen the negotiation, and Columbus was invited to return to the court, and was furnished with a sum of money to enable him to do so

Columbus promptly complied with the royal mandate, and reached the camp in time to witness the surrender of Granada   Amidst the rejoicings which attended this event, he was admitted to an audience with the king and queen, and submitted to them the arguments upon which he based his theory   Isabella was favorably disposed toward the undertaking, but Ferdinand looked coldly upon it.   Columbus demanded, as the reward of his success, the title and authority of admiral and viceroy over all lands discovered by him, with one-tenth of the profits, and that this dignity should be hereditary in his family   The archbishop of Granada advised the king to reject the demands of Columbus, which he said "savored of the highest degree of arrogance, and would be unbecoming in their highnesses to grant to a needy foreign adventurer"   Columbus firmly refused to abate his pretensions, and abruptly left the court, "resolved rather to forego his splendid anticipations of discovery, at the very moment when the career so long sought was thrown open to him, than surrender one of the honorable distinctions due to his services."   His friends, however, remonstrated with the queen, and reminded her that if his claims were high, they were at least contingent on success.   By representing to her the certainty of his being employed by some other potentate, and his peculiar qualifications for success, and by reminding her of her past generous support of great and daring enterprises, they roused her to listen to the impulses of her own noble heart.   "I will assume the undertaking," she exclaimed, "for my own crown of Castile, and am ready to pawn my jewels to defray the expenses of it, if the funds in the treasury shall be found inadequate."   Louis de St Angel, the receiver who had been chiefly instrumental in bringing about this decision of the queen, offered to advance the necessary funds from the

THE BRONZE DOOR IN THE NATIONAL CAPITOL, COMMEMORATING THE EVENTS
OF THE LIFE OF CHRISTOPHER COLUMBUS.

revenues of Aragon That kingdom, however, was indemnified against loss, and all the charges and profits of the expedition were reserved exclusively for Castile.

A messenger was despatched in haste after Columbus. He overtook him a few leagues from Granada, and delivered the royal order to return. On the 17th of April, 1492, a formal agreement was signed between Columbus and the Spanish sovereigns Ferdinand and Isabella, "as lords of the ocean-seas, constituted Christopher Columbus their admiral, viceroy, and governor-general of all such islands and continents as he should discover in the Western ocean, with the privilege of nominating three candidates, for the selection of one by the crown, for the government of each of these territories. He was to be vested with the exclusive right of jurisdiction over all commercial transactions within his admiralty. He was to be entitled to one-tenth of all the products and profits within the limits of his discoveries, and an additional eighth, provided he should contribute one-eighth part of the expense. By a subsequent ordinance, the official dignities above enumerated were settled on him and his heirs forever, with the privilege of prefixing the title of Don to their names, which had not then degenerated into an appellation of mere courtesy."

A fleet of three vessels was assembled in the little harbor of Palos in Andalusia Two of these were furnished by the government, and one by Columbus, aided by his friend, the Prior of La Rabida, and the Pinzons, "a family in Palos, long distinguished for its enterprise among the mariners of that active community." The admiral had some difficulty in equipping his vessels, for his voyage was regarded by the sailors of the country as rash and perilous in the extreme At length, however, a sufficient crew was obtained One hundred and twenty persons were enlisted in the expedition. The three vessels were all small The "Santa Maria," the largest, was ninety feet long, was decked all over, had four masts, and carried a crew of sixty-six seamen The "Pinta" and "Nina" were smaller, and were without decks. All the vessels were provisioned for a year. The admiral was instructed to keep clear of the African coast, and other maritime possessions of Portugal.

At length all things were in readiness, and, Columbus and his whole crew having confessed themselves and received the sacrament, the fleet sailed from Palos on the morning of Friday, the 3d of August, 1492. A month later the Canary islands were reached A brief delay was made there to refit, and then the vessels turned their prows to the westward, and sailed out into the unknown seas. As the night came on, the sailors, imagining they had seen the land for the last time, gave way to tears Columbus soothed their fears and held his course At length he fell in with the trade winds, which wafted him steadily toward the west. The sailors were greatly alarmed at this, and declared that if the wind did not change it would be impossible for them to reach home again. The variation of the compass also alarmed them, and their murmurs increased to almost open mutiny. It required all the firmness of the admiral to restrain them, and to keep them from abandoning the enterprise and returning to Europe.

Ten weeks of anxiety and disappointment had passed since the departure of the fleet from Palos; but still no land was seen. There were unmistakable signs that land was near, such as the flight of land birds

THE LANDING OF COLUMBUS.

around the ship, the finding of a bush floating on the waters with fresh berries upon it, and the frequent discovery of land weeds upon the waves. Often the lookout would startle the fleet by the cry of land, but as often the supposed shore would prove to be only a bank of clouds low down upon the western horizon. Still the ships held their westward course, and at length the sailors broke into open mutiny, and demanded that the fleet should return home. They were even ready to throw the admiral overboard if he refused to grant their demands.

Columbus alone had been calm and hopeful throughout the voyage. He was resolved to succeed or perish in the attempt to find the land

The success of the mutiny would have destroyed all his hopes, and as the events of each succeeding day strengthened him in his conviction that they were rapidly approaching land, he condescended to plead with his men, and obtained from them a promise to obey him for a few days longer. The next night the land breeze, laden with the rich perfumes of tropical flowers, convinced the weary crews that the admiral was right, and that the long wished-for shore was indeed near. The ships were ordered to lie to for the night lest they should go ashore in the darkness. No one slept on board that night. About ten o'clock, Columbus saw a light moving along the shore, as if it were a torch carried in a man's hand. He called Martin Alonzo Pinzon, one of his captains, and pointed it out to him. Pinzon confirmed the admiral's opinion, and all waited in the most intense eagerness for the approach of the morning.

With the first light, on the morning of Friday, the 12th of October, 1492, a gun from one of the vessels announced that land was indeed in sight, and the rising sun revealed to the delighted seamen a large island, luxuriant in foliage and of very beautiful appearance, lying about six miles away, with crowds of natives running along the beach. As the great admiral stood with folded arms, and heaving breast, gazing upon the world which his genius had discovered, the penitent sailors crowded about him, and, kissing his garments, implored his pardon for their rebellious conduct during the voyage.

The fleet stood in and anchored near the shore. The boats were manned, and the admiral, clad in rich scarlet, and bearing the royal banner of Spain, and accompanied by his captains, each of whom bore a green banner inscribed with a cross, went ashore. As he set foot on the land, Columbus knelt reverently and kissed the ground, and then rising and drawing his sword, took possession of the island in the name of Ferdinand and Isabella, King and Queen of Spain. The island was one of the Bahama group, and was called by the natives Guanahani. Columbus named it San Salvador. He explored the island, and then sailing on discovered Cuba, Hayti, and other West India islands. He believed these islands to be off the coast of Asia and to form a part of the Indies. For this reason he called the natives Indians, a name which they have since borne.

Having built and garrisoned a small fort called La Navidad, in Hayti, Columbus took on board seven of the natives, and laid in a stock of fruits, plants, and a number of animals, as proofs of his success and specimens of the products of the country, and then set sail on his return to Spain. A storm compelled him to seek refuge in the Tagus. He was received with distinguished courtesy by John II, who was now not

SIGNATURES OF THE SIGNERS OF THE DECLARATION OF INDEPENDENCE.

a little mortified at having thrown away so glorious an opportunity in rejecting the application of the admiral years before. Leaving Lisbon Columbus sailed to Palos, where he arrived on the 15th of March, 1493, seven months and eleven days after his departure from that port. His arrival was greeted with enthusiasm. From Palos he set out for the court at Barcelona.

Every step of the journey to Barcelona was a triumphal progress. Multitudes thronged the way, eager to gaze upon him. He was received with the most distinguished honors by the sovereigns, and the whole court joined in a *Te Deum* of thankfulness for the success of his voyage. The king and queen confirmed his appointment of viceroy or governor-general of all the countries he had discovered, or should discover, and conferred titles of nobility upon his family, with permission to use a coat of arms. These honors, though conferred with a lavish hand, had all been fairly won; but they aroused the jealousy of the Spanish nobility, and made for Columbus enemies who filled the remainder of his life with sorrow and care.

A second expedition, consisting of seventeen ships and fifteen hundred men, was now fitted out, and sailed from Cadiz, under the command of Columbus, on the 25th of September, 1493. On this voyage he discovered Jamaica and many of the Caribbee islands. He found that his colony in Hayti had been destroyed by the savages in revenge for their outrages; but, undismayed by this, he planted a new town, which he called Isabella, in honor of the queen. From this time the permanent settlement of the island continued without interruption.

In 1498 Columbus made a third voyage, and in this expedition discovered the mainland of the American continent near the mouth of Orinoco, and explored the coast of the provinces since called Paria and Cumana. He was not aware of the true nature of his discovery, however, but supposed that the South American coast was a part of a large island belonging to Cathay or Farther India.

In the meantime gold had been discovered in Hayti, which island the Spaniards had named Hispaniola, or Little Spain. The colonists neglecting all the more useful avocations, applied themselves to the search for gold, and crowds of worthless adventurers were drawn over from Spain by the hope of acquiring sudden wealth. They inflicted the greatest hardships upon the natives, and when Columbus arrived at Hispaniola from the South American coast, he found the affairs of the colony in the most deplorable state. The whole settlement rebelled against him, and the rebels, not content with refusing to acknowledge his authority, sent numerous complaints to Spain, charging him with tyranny and misgovernment. The sovereigns at length sent over a commissioner named Bobadilla, to investigate the affairs of the colony. He was a narrow-minded and incompetent man, and instead of investigating the charges against the admiral, arrested him, and sent him back to Spain in irons. When the officers of the ship which bore him back home wished to remove his fetters, he refused to allow them to do so, saying, "I will wear them as a memento of the gratitude of princes." The news of this outrage filled the people of Spain with honest indignation "All seemed to feel it as a national dishonor," says Prescott, " that such indignities should be heaped upon the man, who, whatever might be his indiscretions, had done so much for Spain, and for the whole civilized world." Queen Isabella at once ordered his fetters to be struck off, and he was summoned to court, reinstated in all his honors, and treated with the highest consideration Isabella gained from the king a promise to aid her in doing justice to the admiral, and in punishing his enemies; but Ferdinand, who could never bear to do a generous or noble act, evaded his promise, and the admiral failed to receive the recompense he was justly entitled to.

In 1504 Columbus sailed on his fourth voyage; his object this time being to find a passage from the Atlantic to the Pacific ocean, by which he might reach India. He explored the Gulf of Honduras, and saw the continent of North America, but was compelled by a mutiny of his crew and by severe storms to abandon his attempt and return to the northward He was shipwrecked on the coast of Jamaica, where he remained more than a year. Returning to Spain in November, 1505, he found his best friend, Queen Isabella, on her death-bed. The enemies whom his great success had raised up for him were numerous and powerful, while he was now old and broken in health. He vainly sought from Ferdinand a faithful execution of the original compact between them; but though he received fair words and promises in abundance from the king, Ferdinand steadily refused to comply with the just demands of the admiral At last, worn out with care and disappointments, Columbus died at Valladolid, on the 20th of May, 1506, being about seventy years old He was buried with great pomp in the convent of St. Francis, at Valladolid In 1513 his remains were removed to the monastery of Las Cuevas, at Seville, and Ferdinand caused this inscription, which cost him nothing and expressed his excuse for his conduct towards the dead man, to be placed upon his tomb "To Castile and Leon Columbus gave a New World!" In 1536 the body of the great admiral was conveyed with appropriate honors to St. Domingo. Upon the cession of that island to France in 1795, the body was removed to Cuba, and buried in the cathedral of Havana. Not yet have the ashes of the Discoverer of America found their true rest-

THE UNITED STATES TREASURY, WASHINGTON CITY.

ing place. That place is under the great dome of the Capitol of the Republic, for whose existence he prepared the way

Though Columbus reached the continent of South America on his third voyage, he was not the first European who beheld the mainland of the western world. In the winter of 1497–98, Amerigo Vespucci, or Americus Vespucius, a Florentine navigator, made a voyage to the West Indies and the South American coast, thus reaching the mainland of the continent nearly a year before Columbus. Returning to Europe he published an account of his discoveries. This was the first account of the new world published in Europe, and some years later a German geographer gave to the continent the name of "*Americi Terra*," or the land discovered by Americus. From this time the name AMERICA was applied to the western continent *

* In the *Atlantic Monthly* for March, 1875, Mr Jules Marcou gives some very striking reasons for regarding the name America as derived from an indigenous word originally applied to a range of mountains in Central America. "*Amerie, Amerrique, or Amerique,*" he says, "is the name in Nicaragua for the highland or mountain range that lies between Juigalpa and Libertad, in the province of Chontales, and which reaches on the one side into the country of the Caracas Indians, and on the other into that of the Ramas Indians.

The names of places in the Indian dialects of Central America often terminate in *ique*, or *ie*, which seems to mean 'great,' 'elevated,' 'prominent,' and is always applied to dividing ridges, or to elevated mountainous countries, but not to volcanic regions.

"The question to be decided is, whether the word Amerie or Amerrique, designating a part of the *terra firma* discovered by Cristoforo Colombo, on his fourth and last voyage to the new world, was known to the great navigator, and consequently could have been repeated by him or by the companions of his voyage. There is no certainty of this, for the word is not found in the very brief account he has left us. But as the origin of the word Amerie has been until now an enigma, in spite of the different interpretations of it that have been given, and as Vespuchy had nothing to do with this name, entirely unknown to him—the inventor of the word Amerie or America being a printer and bookseller in a small town in the Vosges mountains—it is perhaps well to review the facts, and to show where lies the greatest probability for a true solution of the origin of this word America

"There is the strongest evidence that this word, denoting the range and the rocks of Amerrique, Amerique, or Americ, is an indigenous word, the terminal *ique* or *ic* being common for the names of locality, in the language of the Lenca Indians of Central America, a part of Mexico, and that this name has been perpetuated without alteration since the discovery of the new world, by the complete isolation of the Indians who live in this part of the continent who call their mountains by the same word to-day as they did in 1502, when Colombo visited them, Amerrique, Amerique, or Americ. These mountains are auriferous, at their foot lie the gold mines of Libertad and Santo Domingo, and further the gold of the alluvium or the placers is entirely exhausted, which can only be explained by a previous washing by the Indians themselves; at present the gold is to be found only in the veins of the quartz rock.

"Colombo says the Indians named several localities rich in gold, but he does not give the names in his very curtailed account, contenting himself with citing the name of the province of Cariai ... that the ... ique was often pronounced by the Indians in answer to the pressing demands of the Europeans of the expedition   The eagerness for gold was such among the first navigators that it formed their chief preoccupation everywhere, and it is almost certain that to their continual questions as to the place where the gold was found that the Indians wore as ornaments, the reply would be from Amerie, this word signifying the most elevated and conspicuous part of the interior, the upper country, the distinguishing feature of the province of Cimba.   .

We may suppose that Colombo and his companions on their return to Europe, when relating their adventures, would boast of the rich gold mines they had discovered through the Indians of Nicaragua, and say they lay in the direction of Amerie   This would make popular the word Amerie, as the common designation of that part of the Indies in which the richest mines of gold in the new world were situated

"The word Amerie, a synonym for this golden country, would become known in the seaports of the West Indies and then in those of Europe, and would gradually penetrate into the interior of the continent, so that a printer and bookseller in St Dié, at the foot of the Vosges, would have heard the word Amerie without understanding its true meaning as an indigenous Indian word, but would become acquainted with it in conversations about these famous discoveries, as designating a country in the New Indies very rich in mines of gold.

'Hylacomylus of St Dié, ignorant of any printed account of these voyages but those of Albericus Vespucius—published in Latin in 1505, and in German in 1506—thought he saw in the Christian name Albericus the origin of this for him, altered and corrupted word, Amerie or Amerique, and renewing the fable of the monkey and the dolphin who took the Piræus for a man, called this country by the only name among those of the navigators that had reached him, and which resembled the word Amerie or Amerique

"In order to accomplish this it was necessary to change considerably the Christian name of Vespucius, and from Albericus, Alberico, Amerigo, and Morigo—which are the different ways of spelling the first name of Vespuzio, or Vespuchy, or Vespucci—he made Americus' thus, according to my view, it is owing to a grave mistake of Hylacomylus that the aboriginal name of the new world, Amerie or Amerique, has been Europeanized and connected with the son of Anastasio Vespuzio '

The reader is referred to the article in question for the arguments by which the writer sustains his very ingenious theory, which we have given in substance in his own words in the above extract

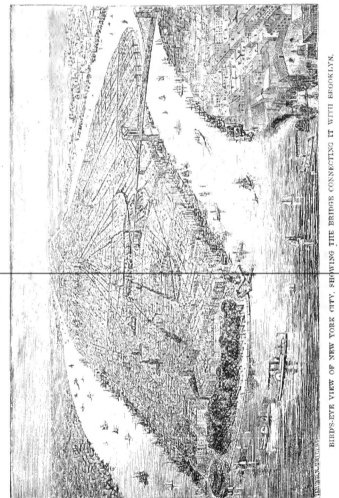

BIRDS-EYE VIEW OF NEW YORK CITY, SHOWING THE BRIDGE CONNECTING IT WITH BROOKLYN.

CHAPTER III.

ENGLISH AND FRENCH DISCOVERIES

Discovery of the North American Continent by John Cabot—Voyages of Sebastian Cabot —The English fail to follow up these Discoveries—Efforts of the French to explore America—Voyage and Discoveries of Verrazzani—Cartier explores the St Lawrence— Reaches Montreal—Efforts to found a Colony on the St Lawrence—Failure—Roberval's Colony—Trading Voyages—Explorations of Champlain—Colonization of Nova Scotia —Founding of Quebec—Discovery of Lake Champlain— ..al of the Jesuits in Canada—Death of Champlain

IN the meantime the success of the first voyage of Columbus had stimulated other nations to similar exertions. The English court had experienced a feeling of keen regret that the petition of Columbus had been refused, and when John Cabot, a native of Venice, then residing at Bristol, applied for leave to undertake a voyage of exploration his request was readily granted. On the 5th of March, 1496, a patent or commission was granted to him and his three sons by Henry VII., authorizing either of them, their heirs or their agents, to undertake with a fleet of five ships, at their own expense, a voyage of discovery in the eastern, western, or northern seas Though they were to make the attempt at their own cost, they were to take possession of the countries they should discover for the king of England. They were to have the exclusive privilege of trading to these countries, but were bound to return to the port of Bristol, and to pay to the king one-fifth of the profits of their trade.

Early in 1497 Cabot sailed from Bristol, accompanied by his son, Sebastian The object of his voyage was not only the discovery of new lands, but the finding of a northwest passage to Asia He sailed due west, and on the 24th of June, 1497, reached the coast of Labrador. He thus discovered the mainland of the North American continent, fully fourteen months before Columbus reached the coast of South America, and nearly a year before Amerigo Vespucci made his discovery. He explored the coast to the southward for over a thousand miles, made frequent landings, and took possession of the country in the name of the English king. Returning home, he was received with many marks of honor by Henry VII , and was called the "Great Admiral" by the people.

57

GENERAL VIEW OF THE YOSEMITE VALLEY, CALIFORNIA.

Towards the close of the year 1497, the Cabots undertook a new voyage, and the king, pleased with the success of the first venture, became a partner in the enterprise, and assumed a portion of the expense. The object of this voyage was to trade with the natives, and to ascertain if the country was suited to colonization. The expedition sailed from Bristol in May, 1498, and was commanded by Sebastian Cabot, who reached the Labrador coast about four hundred miles north of the point discovered by his father. He found the country cold and barren, though it was but the beginning of the summer, and sailed southward. "The coast to which he was now borne was unobstructed by frost. He saw there stags larger than those of England, and bears that plunged into the water to take fish with their claws. The fish swarmed innumerably in such shoals they seemed to affect even the speed of his vessels, so that he gave to the country the name of Bacallaos, which still lingers, on the east side of Newfoundland, and has passed into the language of the Germans and the Italians, as well as the Portuguese and Spanish, to designate the cod. Continuing his voyage, according to the line of the shore, he found the natives of those regions clad in skins of beasts, but they were not without the faculty of reason, and in many places were acquainted with the use of copper. In the early part of his voyage he had been so far to the north that in the month of July the light of day was almost continuous, before he turned homewards, in the late autumn, he believed he had attained the latitude of the Straits of Gibraltar and the longitude of Cuba."[*] On his homeward voyage he noticed the Gulf Stream.

This was the last voyage from England made by Sebastian Cabot. On the death of Henry VII, he took service with Ferdinand of Spain, and under him and his grandson, Charles V, he made many voyages, and was for nearly sixty years the foremost man in Europe in maritime enterprises. He explored the eastern coast of South America, and in his efforts to find the northwest passage sailed within twenty degrees of the North Pole, and explored the eastern coast of North America from Hudson's straits to Albemarle sound. He was in many things one of the most remarkable men of his day, and besides his own discoveries contributed generously by his advice and encouragement to those of others. "He gave England a continent, and no one knows his burial place."

The English made no effort to take advantage of the discoveries of the Cabots. They sent a few vessels every year to fish on the banks of Newfoundland, but pursued even this industry without vigor. The other nations were more energetic and showed a keener appreciation of the value of the new lands. The French were especially active in this

---

[*] Bancroft

THE NEW DEPARTMENT OF STATE, WASHINGTON, D. C.

87

respect. Their vessels engaged in the fisheries far outnumbered those of the English, and many plans were proposed in France for the colonization of these regions. In 1523, Francis I. employed a Florentine named John Verrazzani, an experienced navigator, to undertake the discovery of a northwest passage to India. Verrazzani sailed on the 17th of January, 1524, and, after a stormy voyage of fifty days, reached the American coast in the latitude of Wilmington, North Carolina. Failing to find a good harbor, he sailed southward for 150 miles, and then turned northward, examining the coast as he proceeded. Verrazzani was surprised and delighted by the appearance of the new country and its inhabitants. The latter welcomed with hospitality the strangers whom they had not yet learned to fear, and the Europeans, on their part, regarded with wonder the "russet"-colored natives in their dress of skins ornamented with feathers. Judging from the accounts which they carried to Europe, the voyagers regarded the country as a sort of terrestrial paradise. "Their imagination could not conceive of more delightful fields and forests; the groves spreading perfumes far from the shore, gave promise of the spices of the East; and the color of the earth argued an abundance of gold." The harbors of New York and Newport were carefully explored, and in the latter the voyagers remained fifteen days.

SENTINEL ROCK, YOSEMITE VALLEY.

They then proceeded along the New England coast to Nova Scotia, and still farther to the north. They found the natives here less friendly than those farther south. A Portuguese commander, Gaspar Cortereal, had visited their coast a few years before, and had carried away some of their number and sold them into slavery.

Returning to France, Verrazzani published an account of his voyage. This narrative forms the earliest original description now in existence of the American coast, and added very much to the knowledge of the Europeans concerning this country. France at a subsequent period based upon Verrazzani's discoveries her claim to the whole coast of America from Newfoundland to South Carolina.

The struggle in which Francis I. was engaged with the Emperor Charles V. prevented him from taking advantage of these discoveries, and nothing was done with regard to them by the French until ten years later, when Chabot, Admiral of France, induced King Francis to make another effort to explore and colonize America. An expedition was fitted out, placed under the command of James Cartier, a mariner of St. Malo, and despatched in April, 1534, for the purpose of exploring the American coast with a view to colonizing it. A quick voyage of twenty days carried Cartier to Newfoundland. Having passed through the Straits of Belleisle, he crossed the gulf and entered a bay which he named Des Chaleurs, from the extreme heats he experienced there. He proceeded along the coast as far as the small inlet called Gaspé, where he landed and took formal possession of the country in the name of the king of France. Leaving Gaspé bay, Cartier discovered the great river of Canada, and sailed up the stream until he could see the land on either side. His explorations consumed the months of May, June and July. Being unprepared to pass the winter in America, the fleet sailed for Europe early in August, and reached St. Malo in safety in about thirty days.

The reports of Cartier concerning America aroused the deepest interest in France, and it was determined by the government to proceed at once to the founding of a colony in the new world. A fleet of three well-equipped ships was fitted out, and volunteers from some of the noblest families in France were not lacking. The whole company repaired to the cathedral, where they received the bishop's blessing, and on the 19th of May, 1535, the expedition sailed from St. Malo. The voyage was long and stormy, but Newfoundland was reached at length. Passing through the Straits of Belleisle, they entered the gulf lying west of Newfoundland on the 10th of August, the festival of St. Lawrence the Martyr, and gave to the gulf the name of that saint, which was subsequently applied to the great river emptying into it. The voyagers ascended the stream to the island since called Orleans. There the fleet anchored, while Cartier proceeded farther up the river to the chief Indian settlement on the island of Hochelega. It was the delightful season of September, and the country was beautiful and inviting. Cartier ascended a hill at the foot of which the Indian settlement lay, and gazed with admiration at the magnificent region which spread out before him He named the hill Mont Real, or Royal mount, a name which is now borne by the island and by the great city which marks the site of Indian village

The balminess of the autumn induced Cartier to hope that the climate would prove as mild as that of France; but a rigorous winter, which was rendered horrible by the prevalence of scurvy among the ships' crews, disheartened the whole expedition The winter was spent at the Isle of Orleans, and in the early spring Cartier erected a cross on the shore, to which was affixed a shield inscribed with the arms of France and a legend declaring Francis I. the true and rightful king of the country. The fleet then sailed for France, and arrived at St. Malo on the 6th of July, 1536 Cartier published a truthful account of his voyage, setting forth the severity of the Canadian climate and the absence of mines of precious metals. His report checked for the time the enthusiasm with which the French had regarded America, and for four years the plan of colonizing the new country was laid aside

Some ardent spirits, however, still believed in the possibility of planting successful colonies in the new world and bringing that vast region under the dominion of France. Among these was Francis de la Roque, lord of Roberval, a nobleman of Picardy. He was appointed, by King Francis, Viceroy of the territories on or near the gulf and river of St. Lawrence, to which the high-sounding name of Norumbega was given, and was empowered to colonize it. The assistance of Cartier was necessary to such an undertaking, and he had the additional advantage of possessing the entire confidence of the king Roberval was forced to employ him, and Cartier was given authority by the king to search the prisons and take from them such persons as he needed for the expedition. Roberval and Cartier, however, failed to agree, and their dissensions defeated the object of the undertaking. Cartier sailed from St Malo in May, 1541, and ascended the St. Lawrence to a point near the present city of Quebec, where he built a fort. The winter was passed in idleness and discord, and in the spring of 1542 Cartier abandoned the attempt, and sailed away for France with his ships just as Roberval arrived with a large reinforcement.

Roberval was unable to accomplish more than Cartier His new subjects had been largely drawn from the prisons, and they gave him considerable trouble, if we may judge from the efforts resorted to to keep them quiet. One of them was hanged for theft during the winter, several were put in irons, and a number of men and women were whipped

FIRST WINTER OF THE FRENCH IN CANADA.

After remaining in Canada for a year, Roberval became disheartened, and re-embarked his subjects and returned to France.

Nearly thirty years passed away, during which the French made no effort to secure to themselves the region of the St. Lawrence. Their fishermen, however, continued to frequent the American waters By the close of the sixteenth century one hundred and fifty vessels were engaged in the fisheries of Newfoundland, and voyages for the purpose of trading with the Indians had become common In 1598, the Marquis de la Roche, a nobleman of Brittany, attempted to plant a colony on the Isle of Sable. The colonists consisted of criminals from the prisons of France, and the effort proved a failure

In 1600, Chauvin obtained a patent from the crown, conferring upon him a monopoly of the fur trade, and Pontgravé, a merchant of St Malo, became his partner in the enterprise Two successful voyages were made to Canada, and Chauvin intended founding a colony there His death, in 1602, prevented the execution of this plan

In 1603, a company of merchants of Rouen was organized, and Samuel Champlain, an able and experienced officer of the French navy, was placed in charge of an expedition, and sent to Canada to explore the country He was in every way qualified for the task committed to him, and after making a thorough and systematic examination of the region of the St. Lawrence, and fixing upon Quebec as the proper site for a fort, returned to France and laid before his employers his report, which is still valuable for its accurate description of the country and the manners of the natives.

Soon after Champlain's return to France a patent was issued to Des Monts, conferring upon him the sole right to colonize the vast region lying between the fortieth and forty-sixth parallels of latitude. As this territory embraced the St. Lawrence region, the Rouen company were unable for the present to accomplish anything Des Monts proceeded with his preparations, and in March, 1604, an expedition consisting of two ships was sent out to Acadie or Nova Scotia The summer was passed in trading with the Indians and exploring the coast, and in the autumn the colonists made a settlement on the island of St Croix, at the mouth of the river of the same name. In the spring of 1605, they abandoned this settlement and removed to Port Royal, now known as Annapolis. Efforts were made to find a more southern location in the latter part of 1605 and 1606, but the expeditions sent out for this purpose were driven back by storms or wrecked among the shoals of Cape Cod, and the colonists decided to remain at Port Royal. Thus the permanency of the colony was established Some years later a number of Jesuit

5

ROCK PINNACLES ABOVE TOWER FALLS, YELLOWSTONE RIVER.

missionaries were sent out to Port Royal. These labored diligently among the tribes between the Penobscot and the Kennebec, and not only spread the Christian faith among them, but won for the French the constant affection of the savages. During all her contests with the English in America, these tribes remained the faithful and unwavering allies of France. In 1613, a French colony was planted on the eastern shore of Mount Desert. The settlement was named St. Sauveur, and became another centre of missionary enterprise among the savages of Maine.

In the meantime the French merchants had succeeded in obtaining a revocation of the impolitic monopoly of Des Monts. A company of merchants of St. Malo and Dieppe was formed, and an expedition was

SCENE ON THE ST. LAWRENCE.

sent out to Canada under Champlain, who "aimed not at the profits of trade, but at the glory of founding a state." On the 3d of July, 1608, the city of Quebec was begun by the erection of one or two cottages. In 1609, Champlain, with but two Europeans, joined a party of Hurons from Montreal, and Algonquins from Quebec, in an expedition against the Five Nations. He ascended the Sorel, explored the lake which is now called by his name, and examined a considerable part of northern New York. The religious disputes of France spread to the colony, and Champlain was obliged to use all his energy and authority to overcome the evils which these inflicted upon the infant settlement. He succeeded in overcoming them, and by his energy and perseverance the fortunes of Quebec were placed beyond the reach of failure. Champlain died in 1635, and was buried in "New France," of which he is justly called "the father."

CHAPTER IV.

THE SPANIARDS IN AMERICA

WHILE the French were seeking to obtain a footing in the north,
the Spaniards were busy in the south. In the first years of the
sixteenth century the more important of the West India islands
were subdued and colonized, and from these expeditions were
from time to time sent out to explore the shores of the Gulf of
Mexico The southern part of the peninsula of Yucatan was explored,
and a colony was established on the Isthmus of Darien. One of the
governors of this colony was Vasco Nunez de Balboa In 1513, while
searching the isthmus for gold, he discovered the Pacific ocean, and took
possession of it in the name of the king of Spain In 1520, a Portuguese navigator named Magellan, employed by the king of Spain,
passed through the straits south of Cape Horn, which bear his name, and
entered the Western ocean, which he named the Pacific because it was so
calm and free from storms He died on the voyage, but his ship reached
the coast of Asia, and returned thence to Spain by the Cape of Good
Hope, thus making the first voyage around the world, and establishing
its spherical form beyond dispute.

In 1513, Juan Ponce de Leon, who had been a companion of Columbus
on his second voyage, and had been governor of Porto Rico, fitted out
three sh   He had

heard the reports which were then commonly believed by his country-men, that somewhere in the new world was a fountain flowing in the midst of a country sparkling with gold and gems, whose waters would give perpetual youth to the man who should drink of and bathe in them. Ponce de Leon was an old man, and he longed to taste again the pleasures and the dreams of youth. He gave a willing ear to the stories of this wonderful fountain, and in March, 1513, set sail from Porto Rico in search of it. He sailed among the Bahamas, but failed to find it, and on Easter Sunday, which the Spaniards call *Pascua Florida*, land was dis-covered. It was supposed to be an island, but was in reality the long

THE COAST OF FLORIDA.

southern peninsula of the United States. De Leon gave it the name of Florida—which it has since borne—partly in honor of the day, and partly because of the beauty of its flowers and foliage. The weather was very bad, and it was some days before he could go ashore. He landed near the site of St. Augustine, and took possession of the country for Spain on the 8th of April, 1513. He remained many weeks on the coast, exploring it, and sailing southward, doubled Cape Florida and cruised among the Tortugas. He failed to find the fountain of youth,

and returned in despair to Porto Rico   The king of Spain rewarded his
discovery by appointing him governor of Florida, on condition that he
should colonize the country   A few years later he attempted to plant a
colony in Florida, but was attacked by the Indians, who were very
hostile, and driven to his ships with the loss of a number of his men
Ponce de Leon himself received a painful wound, and returned to Cuba
to die   He had staked his life upon the search for perpetual youth , he
found only a grave

Between the years 1518 and 1521, the expeditions of Hernando Cortez
against Mexico, and of Francesco Pizarro against Peru, were despatched
from Cuba   They resulted in the conquest of those countries and their
colonization by Spain. These expeditions, however, form no part of this
narrative, and we cannot dwell upon them.

The native population of the West Indies died out rapidly under the
cruel rule of the Spaniards, and it soon became necessary to look elsewhere for a supply of laborers for the plantations and the mines.   In
1520, Lucas Vasquez de Ayllon, at the head of a company of seven
Spaniards, fitted out a fleet of two slave-ships from St. Domingo or Hispaniola, for the deliberate purpose of seizing the natives of the mainland
and selling them as slaves.   The vessels went first to the Bahamas, from
which they sailed to the North American coast, reaching it at or near St
Helena sound, in the present State of South Carolina   The Indians had
not yet learned to fear the whites, and were utterly unsuspicious of the
fate which awaited them   They were timid at first, but this feeling was
soon overcome by the distribution of presents among them   Their confidence being won, they received the Spaniards with kindness, and at their
request visited the ships in great numbers   When the decks of the vessels were covered with the unsuspecting natives Vasquez made sail, and
standing out to sea steered for the West Indies, regardless of the entreaties
of the natives who were thus torn from their friends and relatives on the
shore.   A retributive justice speedily avenged this crime.   A violent
storm arose and one of the ships foundered with all on board.   A pestilence broke out in the remaining vessel, and swept away many of the
captives   Returning to Spain, Vasquez boasted of his infamous deed,
and even claimed a reward for it at the hands of the Emperor Charles
V , who acknowledged his claim, and appointed him governor of Chicora,
as South Carolina was called, with authority to conquer that country
Vasquez spent his entire fortune in fitting out an expedition, and reached
the coast of Chicora in 1525   There he met with nothing but misfortune.
His largest ship was stranded in the Combahee river, then called by the
whites the River Jordan and so many of his men were killed by the

Indians that he was obliged to abandon the undertaking. He returned to Europe to die of grief and mortification for his failure "It may be," says Bancroft, "that ships sailing under his authority made the discovery of the Chesapeake and named it the Bay of St Mary, and perhaps even entered the Bay of Delaware, which in Spanish geography was called Saint Christopher's."

In 1526, Pamphilo de Narvaez obtained from the Emperor Charles V. authority to explore and conquer all the country between the Atlantic and the River of Palms He was very wealthy, and spent his entire estate in preparations for the expedition. There was no lack of volunteers, and many younger sons of nobles joined him, hoping to find fame and fortune in the new world. Among the adventurers was Cabeza de Vaca, the historian of the expedition, who held the second place in it as treasurer Narvaez sailed from the Guadalquivir in June, 1527, touched at St. Domingo, and passed the winter in Cuba In the spring of 1528, he was driven by a strong south wind to the American coast, and on the 14th of April his fleet cast anchor in Tampa bay A week later, he landed and took possession of the peninsula of Florida in the name of Spain

The natives showed unmistakable signs of hostility, but they exhibited to the governor samples of gold, which he believed, from their signs, came from the north In spite of the earnest advice of Cabeza de Vaca, he determined to go in search of the precious metal. He directed his ships to meet him at a harbor with which his pilot pretended to be acquainted, and then, at the head of three hundred men, forty of whom were mounted, set off into the interior of the country. No one knew whither he was going, but all believed that each step led them nearer to the land of gold The beauty of the forest, the richness of its vegetation, and the size of its gigantic live-oaks, filled them with wonder and admiration, and the variety and abundance of the birds and wild beasts of the country excited their surprise, but they found neither the gold nor the splendid cities they had fondly believed they were about to discover The forest grew denser and more intricate at every step, and the rivers were broad and deep, with swift currents, and could be crossed only by means of rafts, which were constructed with great difficulty The march lay through swamps, in which the Indian warriors harassed the strangers painfully, and, their provisions becoming exhausted, they began to suffer with hunger. Late in June they reached Appalachee, which they had supposed was a large and wealthy city They found it only a hamlet of some forty poor wigwams, but remained there twenty-five days, searching the neighboring country for gold and silver, and finding none, suffering all the while from hunger, and the attacks of the Indians.

It was plain now even to the governor that there was no gold to be found in this region, and every nerve was strained to hasten the march to the harbor where they had appointed to meet the ships There was but one impulse now in the whole expedition—to escape from the terrible country which was proving so fatal to them. After a painful march they reached a bay which they called the Baia de Caballos, now the harbor of St. Marks The ships could not be seen, and it was resolved at once to build boats and attempt to reach some of the Spanish possessions by sea. The horses were slain to furnish food, and several hundred bushels of corn were seized from the Indians. Subsisting upon these supplies, the Spaniards beat their spurs, stirrups, cross-bows, and other implements into saws and axes and nails, and in sixteen days built five boats, each more than thirty feet long. Pitch for the calking of the boats was made from the pine trees, and the fibre of the palmetto served as oakum. Ropes were made of twisted horse-hair and palmetto fibres, and the shirts of the men were pieced together for sails Fifty men had been lost on the march, and on the 22d of September the survivors, two hundred and fifty in number, began their perilous voyage They followed the shore, encountering many dangers, and suffering greatly from hunger and thirst On the 30th of October they discovered one of the mouths of the Mississippi, and on the 5th of November a storm scattered the little fleet Cabeza de Vaca's boat was wrecked upon an island which is believed to be that of Galveston. Castillo's boat was driven ashore farther to the east, but he and his crew were saved alive. Of the fate of the other boats nothing is known with certainty Of those who were cast ashore, all but Cabeza de Vaca, Dorantes, Castillo, and Estevanico, a negro, died of exposure and hardship. These four were detained captives among the Indians for nearly six years

At the end of this period, Cabeza induced his companions to join him in an attempt to escape In September, 1534, they set out, naked, ignorant of the way, and without any means of sustaining life. In this condition these men accomplished the wonderful feat of traversing the continent. The journey occupied upwards of twenty months, and extended from the coast of Texas to the Canadian river, and thence into New Mexico, from which they continued their way to the village of San Miguel, in Sonora, near the Pacific ocean. They reached this village in May, 1536, and found themselves again among their countrymen. They were escorted to Compostella by Spanish soldiers, and from that place were forwarded to the City of Mexico by the authorities

The reports of Cabeza and his companions made the viceroy Mendoza anxious   New Mexico which was

SPANIARDS ENSLAVING THE INDIANS.

SPANISH

73

THE SPANIARDS EXPLORING THE VALLEY
OF THE COLORADO.

believed to be richer in wealth and splendid cities than Mexico itself. A Franciscan friar boasted that he had visited a region in the interior named Cibola, the Land of Buffaloes, in which were seven splendid cities. He declared that the land was rich in silver and gold, and that his Indian guides had described to him a region still wealthier. The friar's story was religiously believed, and an expedition set out in 1539, under command of Francisco Vasquez Coronado, the governor of New Galicia. The expedition explored the region of the Colorado, examined the country now known as New Mexico, and penetrated as far east as the present State of Kansas. Coronado found neither gold nor precious stones, and the only cities he discovered were the towns of the Zuni Indians of New Mexico. He reported to the viceroy on his return to Mexico that the region was not fit to be colonized, and his description of the country through which he marched is so accurate as to challenge the admiration of every succeeding traveller.

Still the Spaniards refused to abandon the belief that fabulous wealth was to be found in the interior of the continent; and even those who had borne a part in the conquest of Mexico and Peru gave credit to the wild stories that were told concerning the undiscovered regions. Among those who gave such implicit faith to these stories was Ferdinand de Soto, of Xeres, a veteran soldier, who had served with distinction with Pizarro in the conquest of Peru, and had amassed a considerable fortune from the spoils of that province. The fame and wealth acquired by him in this expedition opened the way to other successes in Europe. He was honored with the favor of the Emperor Charles V., and received the hand of a noble lady in marriage. Eager to distinguish himself still further, he determined to attempt the conquest of Florida. He demanded and received from the emperor permission to undertake this at his own cost, and was also made governor of Cuba and of all the territories he should conquer. As soon as he made known his intentions applications for leave to serve in the expedition poured in upon him.

Many of the volunteers were of noble birth, and sold their lands and other property to equip themselves for the undertaking. De Soto selected six hundred well-equipped men from the number who had volunteered, and in 1538 sailed from Spain to Cuba, where he was welcomed with great rejoicings. A vessel was despatched from Cuba to find a harbor in Florida suitable for the landing of the expedition. On its return it brought two Indian captives, who perceiving what was wanted of them, told by signs such stories of the wealth of the country as greatly delighted the governor and his companions. Volunteers in

FERDINAND DE SOTO.

Cuba swelled the ranks of the expedition to nearly one thousand men, of whom three hundred were horsemen.

In May, 1539, leaving his wife to govern the island, De Soto sailed with his fleet for Florida, and a fortnight later landed at Espiritu Santo, now Tampa bay. Everything had been provided which the foresight of an experienced commander deemed necessary, and De Soto, in order to remove any temptation to retreat, sent his ships back to Cuba. He never dreamed of failure, for he believed that at the most the task before him would not be more difficult than those which had been accomplished by Cortez and Pizarro. After a brief halt at Tampa bay the march into the interior was begun. It was long and tedious, and was full of danger. The Indians were hostile, and the guides constantly led the Spaniards astray, and plunged them into difficult swamps. The guides were instantly given to the bloodhounds, and torn in pieces by the ferocious animals; but not even this dreadful punishment was sufficient to prevent a renewal of such acts   Before the close of the first season the whole company, save the governor, had become convinced that their hope of finding gold was vain, and they besought De Soto to return to Cuba   He sternly refused to abandon the effort, and pushed on to the country of the Appalachians, east of the Flint river, and not far from the Bay of Appalachee.   The winter was passed in this region, and a scouting party during this season discovered· Pensacola

In the spring of 1540 the march was resumed   An Indian guide promised to conduct the Spaniards to a country abounding in gold and governed by a woman, and he described the process of refining gold so accurately that De Soto believed his story.   It is possible that the Indian may have referred to the gold region of North Carolina.   One of the guides told the governor plainly that he knew of no such country as his companion had described, and De Soto had him burned for what he supposed was his falsehood.   The Indians, terrified by his fate, from this time invented all manner of fabulous stories to excite the cupidity of the Spaniards   De Soto, with a singular perversity, held to his belief that he would yet realize his hopes, and continued to push on long after his men had become disheartened ; and so great was his influence over them that in their deepest despondency he managed to inspire them with something of his own courage and hopefulness

Instead of conciliating the Indians, the Spaniards seized their provisions, and provoked their hostility in numberless ways   They treated their captives with the greatest cruelty   They cut off the hands of the poor Indians, burned them at the stake, or turned them over to the bloodhounds, who tore them in pieces   They were chained together by the neck, and forced to carry the baggage and provisions of the troops.   The march was now into the interior of Georgia, as far as the headwaters of the Chattahoochee, from which the Spaniards passed to the headwaters of the Coosa   Here they turned to the southwest, and marched through Alabama to the junction of the Alabama and Tombigbee rivers.   At this point there was a large and strongly fortified town called Mavilla, or Mobile, a name which has since been given to the river and bay   The town consisted of "eighty handsome houses, each sufficiently capacious to contain a thousand men.   They were encompassed by a high wall made of immense trunks of trees, set deep in the ground and close together, strengthened with cross-timbers and interwoven with large vines"   It was the middle of October when Mavilla was reached, and the Spaniards, tired of living in the open country so long, wished to occupy the town.   The Indians resisted them, and a desperate battle ensued, which was won by the Spanish cavalry The victory cost the whites dear, however, for the town was burned during the battle, and with it all the baggage of the Spaniards was consumed. The Indians fought with a desperate bravery, and numbers of them were slain and burned to death in the town. The Spaniards had 18 killed and 150 wounded; 12 horses were killed, and 72 wounded.

Ships had arrived in the meantime, according to appointment, at Pensacola, and by them De Soto received letters from his wife. He would send no news home, however. He had not yet realized the objects of the expedition, and he determined to send no news of himself to his countrymen until he had found or conquered some rich country. Turning his back resolutely upon the ships, the governor resumed his march to the northwest By the middle of December he reached the north-western part of the State of Mississippi, and finding a deserted village in the country of the Chickasaws, occupied it as the winter quarters of the expedition. December, 1540, the winter was severe, and the ground was covered with snow, but the corn was still standing in the fields, and this furnished the Spaniards with food. Their force was now reduced to five hundred men, and it was evident to all, except the governor, that they would never find the cities or the wealth they had set out to seek.

With the opening of the spring of 1541 a new disaster befell the Spaniards De Soto, as had been his custom with the other tribes, demanded of the Chickasaw chief two hundred men to carry the baggage of the troops The demand was refused, and that night the Indians, deceiving the sentinels, set fire to the village. The bewildered Spaniards were aroused from their slumbers to meet a fierce attack of the savages. The latter were repulsed after a hard fight, but the whites were left in an almost helpless condition. The little they had saved from the flames at Mavilla was destroyed in the burning village. Armor and weapons were rendered worthless, and scarcely any clothing was saved. The troops were forced to resort to dresses of skins and of the long moss of the country woven into mats. In this condition, they suffered greatly from the cold. To supply the weapons destroyed forges were erected, and the swords were retempered, and new lances made.

Renewing their march the Spaniards pushed on still farther west, and about the 2d of May reached the banks of the Mississippi, at a point a short distance below the present city of Memphis. They were the first white men to gaze upon the mighty flood of this noble river, but De Soto had no admiration to express for it. It was only an obstacle in his west-ward march, and would require greater efforts for its passage than any stream he had yet encountered. A month was passed on the banks of the river in constructing barges large enough to hold three horsemen each. At length they were completed, and the Spaniards were transported in safety to the opposite shore. The natives received them kindly, and presented them with food, and regarding them as the children of their god, the sun, brought to them their sick to be healed, and their blind to be restored to sight. The blunt soldier, cruel as he had been to the savages, shrank from claiming the power of heaven "Pray only to God, who is in heaven, for whatsoever ye need," he answered

De Soto remained forty days on the western bank of the Mississippi, and during this time an exploring party was sent to examine the country to the north. They reported that this region was thinly inhabited by hunters, who lived by chasing the bison, which abounded in this region The governor then turned to the west and northwest, and advanced 200 miles farther into the interior of the continent, probably to the highlands of the White river. Then turning southward, he passed through a succession of Indian tribes who lived by cultivating the soil, and who enjoyed a civilization superior to that of their nomadic brethren. The winter was passed near the Hot Springs of Arkansas. The Indians west of the Mississippi were treated with the same cruelties that had marked the conduct of the Spaniards towards the savages east of that stream "Any trifling consideration of safety would induce the governor to set fire to a hamlet He did not delight in cruelty, but the happiness, the life, and the rights of the Indians were held of no account."

In the spring of 1542, De Soto determined to descend the Washita to its mouth, and endeavor to reach the sea At last, after a most arduous march, in which he frequently lost his way amid the swamps and bayous of the region, he reached the Mississippi The chieftain of this region could not tell him the distance to the sea, but informed him that the country along the lower river was a vast and uninhabited swamp. An exploring party was sent to descend the banks of the river, and returned, after penetrating about thirty miles in eight days, to confirm the Indian's report. Reaching the vicinity of Natchez, the governor found the Indians prepared to contest his occupation of that town. He attempted to overawe them by claiming to be the child of the sun, their chief deity. The chieftain answered him scornfully: "You say you are the child of the sun. Dry up the river, and I will believe you Do you desire to see me? Visit the town where I dwell. If you come in peace, I will receive you with special good will; if in war, I will not shrink one foot back." The savages were becoming more dangerous every day, and the Spaniards less able to resist their assaults.

De Soto was now conquered It was at last as plain to him as it had been all along to his followers that the expedition was a failure. He had spent three years in roaming over the continent, and he had found neither the cities nor the wealth he had hoped for. His magnificent anticipations had disappeared; his little army was reduced to a mere handful of the splendid force that had left Cuba; and he was in the midst of a region from which he could see no escape. A deep melancholy took the place of the stern pride that had hitherto marked his demeanor, and his heart was torn by a conflict of emotions. His health gave way rapidly, and he was seized with a violent fever. When informed by his medical attendant that his end was at hand, he expressed his resignation to the will of God, and at the request of his men appointed Louis de Mocoso his successor, and advised him to continue the expedition. He

NATCHEZ IN 1875.

died on the 5th of June, 1542. In order to conceal his death from the savages, who had come to regard him as immortal, his body was wrapped in a mantle, and in the silence of midnight was rowed out into the middle of the Mississippi. There, amid the darkness and the wailing requiems of the priests, the mortal remains of Ferdinand de Soto were committed to the great river he had discovered.

The Spaniards at once prepared to disregard the advice of their dead leader, and resolved to set out across the country for Mexico, believing it less dangerous to go by land than by sea. They roused the whole country against them by their barbarous treatment of the people, and, having proceeded upwards of 300 miles west of the Mississippi, were driven back to that stream by the savages. It now became necessary to build vessels and descend the river. Seven of these were constructed

THE SPANIARDS DESCENDING THE MISSISSIPPI AFTER THE DEATH OF DE SOTO.

with great difficulty, and amidst the constant hostility of the Indians. They were frail barks, without decks, and in order to construct them the Spaniards were obliged to beat their weapons, and even their stirrups, spurs and bridles into saws, axes and nails During this period they suffered greatly from the lack of clothing, for it was the winter season They obtained provisions by plundering the granaries of the neighboring tribes, and thus dooming many of the savages to death by starvation. On the 1st of July, 1543, they embarked in their vessels, their number being now reduced to about 250, and began the descent of the river. Their progress was harassed at every mile by the Indians, who covered the stream with their canoes and kept up an almost constant assault upon the fleet. On the 18th of July, the vessels entered the Gulf of Mexico, and by the 10th of September the Mexican coast was reached. The vessels succeeded in gaining the Spanish settlement of Panuco, where the survivors were hospitably received by their countrymen

The failure of Narvaez and De Soto prevented the Spaniards from making any further attempt for many years to colonize the Florida coast. The next effort to found a settlement in that region was by the French. The religious wars which had distracted France for so many years made the great Huguenot leader, Coligny, Admiral of France, anxious to provide in the new world a refuge to which his persecuted brethren of the faith might fly in times of danger, and be free to worship God after the dictates of their own conscience. He succeeded in obtaining authority for this undertaking from Charles IX, and in 1562 an expedition was despatched to America under the command of Jean Ribault, a Protestant. Ribault was instructed to avoid the more rigorous climate of Canada, and to select a southern location for the colony. Land was made in May, 1562, in the vicinity of St Augustine, Florida, and the fleet proceeded along the coast and anchored in what is now Port Royal harbor, in the State of South Carolina. Ribault was delighted with the noble harbor, which he believed to be the outlet of a large river, and with the beauty and richness of the country A fort was built on an island in the harbor, and called Carolina, which name was also applied to the country, in honor of Charles IX. of France. A force of twenty-five men was left to garrison the fort, and Ribault returned to France to report his success and bring out reinforcements for the colony. He reached France in the midst of the civil war, which prevented any attention being paid to the colony. The garrison of Fort Carolina waited in vain for the promised reinforcements and supplies, and at last, becoming disheartened, built a brigantine and set sail for their own country. Their provisions soon gave out and they began to suffer the horrors of famine.

6

When they were nearly exhausted, they were rescued by an English vessel, which set the most feeble upon the coast of France, but carried the remainder to England. In both countries the colonists spread their accounts of the beauty and fertility of Carolina.

In 1564, there was a lull in the struggle between the contending parties in France, and Coligny took advantage of it to renew his efforts to colonize America. Three ships were furnished by the king, and were placed in command of Laudonniere, who had accompanied Ribault in the first expedition. Emigrants volunteered readily, and the required number was soon completed. In order to obtain reliable information concerning the country, Coligny sent out with the expedition a skilful painter, James le Moyne, called Des Morgues, with orders to make accurate colored sketches of the region. The fleet sailed on the 22d of April, 1564, and on the 22d of June reached the coast of Florida. Avoiding Port Royal, the site of the first colony, the colonists chose a location in Florida, on the banks of the St. John's, then called the River May. A fort was built, and called, like the first, Carolina.

The colony was begun with prayers and songs of thanksgiving, but the bulk of the colonists were by no means religious men. Their true character soon began to appear. They wasted the supplies they had brought with them, as well as those they succeeded in extorting from the Indians, whom they alienated by their cruelties. Mutinies were frequent. The majority of the men had joined the enterprise in the hope of acquiring sudden wealth, and, finding their hopes vain, resolved to abandon the colony. They compelled Laudonniere to sign an order allowing them to embark for New Spain, under the pretext of wishing to avoid a famine, and at once equipped two vessels and began a career of piracy against the Spaniards. Their vessels were soon captured, and the pirates were sold as slaves. A few escaped in a boat and took refuge at Fort Carolina. Laudonniere caused them to be hanged; but their outrages had already drawn upon the colony the bitter hostility of the Spaniards.

Famine now began to be felt by the little settlement, and as month after month passed by the sufferings of the colonists increased. The natives, who were at first friendly, had been rendered hostile by the cruel treatment they had received from the French, and no provisions could be obtained from them. On the 3d of August, 1565, Sir John Hawkins, an English commander, arrived with several ships from the West Indies, where he had just sold a cargo of negro slaves whom he had kidnapped in their native Africa. He is said to have been the first Englishman who engaged in this infamous traffic. He proved himself a generous friend to the suffering colonists, however, and supplied them with provisions and gave them one of his own ships. They had suffered too much to be content with this, and were resolved to abandon the settlement. They were on the point of embarking in the ship furnished them by Sir John, when a fleet of several vessels was discovered standing into the river. It was the squadron of Ribault, with reinforcements and all the supplies necessary for founding a permanent settlement. The despair of the colonists was changed to rejoicing, and all were now willing to remain in the colony.

When the news of the planting of the French colony in Florida reached Philip II. of Spain, he was greatly incensed. Florida was a part of his dominions, and he not only resented the intrusion of the French, but could not tolerate the idea of allowing a Protestant colony to enjoy its settlement in peace. He determined at once to exterminate the heretics, and for this purpose employed Pedro Melendez de Avilès, an officer who had rendered himself notorious for his cruelty when engaged against the pirates and in the wars of Spanish America. His son and heir having been shipwrecked among the Bermudas, Melendez desired to return to America to search for him. Philip, who knew his desperate character, suggested to him the conquest of Florida, and an agreement was entered into between the king and Melendez, by which the latter was to invade and conquer Florida within three years, and establish in that region a colony of not less than 500 persons, of whom 100 should be married men, twelve priests of the Catholic Church and four members of the order of the Jesuits. Melendez also agreed to transport to Florida all kinds of domestic animals, and 500 negro slaves. All this was to be done by Melendez at his own cost, and he was secured by the king in the government of the province for life with the privilege of naming his successor, and was granted large estates in the province and a comfortable salary. Though the destruction of the French colony was not named in the agreement, Philip and Melendez understood each other on that point. The cry was at once raised in Spain that the heretics must be exterminated, and Melendez had no trouble in obtaining recruits. Twenty-five hundred persons gathered under his orders, "soldiers, sailors, priests, Jesuits, married men with their families, laborers and mechanics, and, with the exception of 300 soldiers, all at the cost of Melendez."

The expedition sailed in June, 1565, but the vessels were parted by a storm, and Melendez reached Porto Rico in August with but a third of his force. Unwilling to lose time, however, he sailed at once to the mainland, and arrived off the coast of Florida on the 28th of August.

On the 2d of September he discovered a fine harbor and river, and selected this place as the site of his colony. He named the river and bay in honor of St. Augustine, on whose festival he had arrived off the Florida coast Ascertaining from the Indians the position of the French, he sailed to the northward, and on the 4th of September arrived off Fort Carolina, where a portion of Ribault's fleet lay anchored in the roadstead The French commander demanded his name and the object of his visit. He was answered "I am Melendez of Spain, sent with strict orders from my king to gibbet and behead all the Protestants in these regions. The Frenchman who is a Catholic I will spare, every heretic shall die." The French fleet being unprepared for battle, cut its cables and stood out to sea. Melendez gave chase, but failed to overtake it. Returning to the harbor of St. Augustine, he went on shore on the 8th of September, and took possession of the country in the name of Philip II. of Spain, who was proclaimed monarch of all North America. A solemn mass was said, and the foundations of the town of St. Augustine were laid Thus was established the first permanent town within the limits of the United States This task accomplished, Melendez prepared to attack Fort Carolina by land

Ribault had returned with his ships to Fort Carolina after escaping from the Spaniards A council of war was held, and it was debated among the French whether they should strengthen their works and await the approach of the enemy, or proceed to St Augustine and attack them with the fleet. Ribault supposed that Melendez would attack the fort by sea, and favored the latter plan, but his officers opposed his design. Disregarding their advice Ribault put to sea, but had scarcely cleared the harbor when a violent storm wrecked his entire fleet on the Florida coast. Nearly all the men reached the shore unharmed, about one hundred and fifty miles south of Fort Carolina.

The wreck of the French fleet was known to Melendez, and he resolved to strike a blow at once at the fort, which he knew to be in a defenceless state. Leading his men through the forests and swamps which lay between the two settlements, he surprised and captured the fort on the 21st of September Every soul within the walls, including the aged, the women and children, was put to death. A few escaped to the woods before the capture of the fort, among whom were Laudonniere, Challus, and Le Moyne Their condition was pitiable They could expect no mercy from the Spaniards, and death awaited them in the forest A few gave themselves up to the Spaniards, and were at once murdered; the remainder succeeded in gaining the sea-shore, where they were rescued by two French vessels which had remained in the harbor, and escaped the storm. This ... m that ly ... ...

The number of persons massacred by the Spaniards at Fort Carolina amounted to nearly two hundred. When the victims were all dead, mass was said, a cross raised, and a site selected for a church. Then Melendez set out to find the survivors of the shipwrecked fleet. They were discovered in a helpless condition, worn out with fatigue, hunger, and thirst. Melendez promised to treat them with kindness if they would surrender to him, and trusting to his plighted word, they placed themselves in his hands. They were at once seized and bound, and marched towards St Augustine. As they approached the settlement a signal was given, and the Spaniards fell upon them and massacred all but a few Catholics and some mechanics, who were reserved as slaves. French writers place the number of those who perished in the two massacres at nine hundred. The Spaniards give a smaller number. On the scene of his barbarity Melendez set up this inscription "I do not this as unto Frenchmen, but as unto Lutherans."

In 1566 Melendez attempted to plant a colony on the shores of the Chesapeake bay, but the vessel despatched for this purpose met such contrary winds that the crew abandoned the effort to reach the bay, and sailed for Spain. Melendez the next year returned to Spain, having spent his fortune in establishing the colony of St Augustine, from which he had derived no benefit.

The massacre of the French and the destruction of the colony at Fort Carolina excited not even a remonstrance from the French court, which was blinded to its true interests by its religious bigotry. The Huguenots and the better part of the nation felt keenly the wrong the country had suffered, and Dominic de Gourges, a gallant gentleman of Gascony, determined to avenge it. Selling his ancestral estate, he equipped three vessels, and with one hundred and fifty men sailed for Florida, in August, 1567. He surprised and captured a Spanish fort near the site of Fort Carolina, and took the garrison prisoners. He spent the winter here, and finding himself too weak to maintain his position sailed for France in May, 1568. Before doing so, however, he hanged his prisoners, and set up over them the inscription: "I do not this as unto Spaniards or mariners, but as unto traitors, robbers, and murderers." His expedition was disavowed by the French government, and he was obliged to conceal himself to escape arrest after his return to France.

France now abandoned her efforts to colonize the southern part of North America, and relinquished her pretensions to Florida. Spain, on the other hand, gave more attention to this region, and emigrants from her dominions were encouraged to settle, and new colonies were formed within its limits. In the West Indies, and in Mexico, Central and South America, Spain during the sixteenth and seventeenth centuries was supreme.

CHAPTER V.

THE FIRST ENGLISH COLONY.

The English Claim to America—Voyages of Frobisher—Exploits of Sir Francis Drake—Sir Humphrey Gilber—Intends to found a Colony in America—Is lost at Sea—Sir Walter Raleigh obtains a Patent of Colonization—Discoveries of Amidas and Barlow—Raleigh sends out a Colony to Virginia—Settlement on Roanoke Island—Its Failure—Arrival of Grenville—Second Effort of Raleigh to Colonize Virginia—Roanoke Island again Settled—The "City of Raleigh"—Virginia Dare—Fate of the Colony—Death of Raleigh—Other Voyages of the English

THOUGH England had made no effort to colonize America during the long period we have been considering, she never abandoned her claims to that region, claims which were based upon the discoveries and explorations of John and Sebastian Cabot. The voyages of her fishermen to Newfoundland kept the country fresh in the minds of the seafaring Englishmen, and from time to time voyages were made to the American coast for the purpose of trading with the savages. Under Elizabeth, who pursued the wise policy of fostering her navy, a race of hardy and daring sailors grew up in England, and carried the flag of their country into every sea. In this reign Martin Frobisher with two small ships made a voyage to the frozen regions of Labrador in search of the northwest passage. He failed to find it, but penetrated farther north than any European had yet gone, A. D 1576. His second voyage was made the next year, and was undertaken in the hope of finding gold, as one of the stones he had brought home on his first cruise had been pronounced by the refiners of London to contain the precious metal. The fleet did not advance as far north as Frobisher had done on his first attempt, as a large mass of yellow earth was found which was believed to contain gold. The ships were loaded with this, and all sail was made for home, only to find on reaching England that their cargo was but a heap of worthless dirt. A third voyage with fifteen ships was attempted in 1578, but no gold was found, and the extreme northern latitudes were ascertained to be too bleak for colonization.

Between the years 1577 to 1580 Sir Francis Drake sailed to the Pacific and made descents upon the Spanish settlements on the western coast of America acquired an immense treasure. As Bancroft well observes, this part of Drake's career "was but a splendid piracy against a nation with which his sovereign and his country professed to be at peace." Having acquired this enormous wealth Drake applied himself to the more useful task of discovery. Crossing the equator he sailed northward, as far as the southern part of Oregon, in the hope of finding a northern passage between the oceans. The cold seemed very great to voyagers just from the tropics, and he abandoned his attempt and returned southward to a harbor on the coast of Mexico. Here he refitted his ship, and then returned to England through the seas of Asia, having circumnavigated the globe, a feat which had been accomplished only by the ship of Magellan.

It was not the splendid but demoralizing achievements of Drake which led the way to the establishment of the English power in America. That was the work of the humble fishermen who sailed on their yearly voyages to the banks of Newfoundland. The

progress of this valuable industry was closely watched by Sir Humphrey Gilbert, who believed that a lucrative trade might be opened with the new world by the planting of a colony within its limits. He obtained authority from Queen Elizabeth to establish such a colony in the vicinity of the fisheries. In 1578 he sailed to America on a voyage of discovery, and in August of that year landed at St. Johns, Newfoundland, and took formal possession of the country for England. He then sailed to the southward, exploring the coast, but lost his largest ship with all on

SIR WALTER RALEIGH.

board. This made it necessary for him to return home, as the two vessels which remained to him were too small to attempt a protracted voyage. One of them, called the "Squirrel," was a mere boat of ten tons. Unwilling to expose his men to a danger which he would not face, Sir Humphrey took passage in the "Squirrel" instead of in the larger and safer vessel. On the homeward voyage the ships encountered a terrific storm. In the midst of the gale the people on the "Hind," the larger ship, saw Sir Humphrey sitting at the stern of his little vessel, which was laboring painfully in the heavy seas. He was calmly reading a book, perhaps that sublimest of books, from which he had drawn the pure principles which guided his whole life. As the "Hind" passed him he called out to those on board of her, "We are as near to heaven by sea as by land." That night the lights of the "Squirrel" suddenly disappeared, and the good Sir Humphrey was seen no more. The "Hind" continued her voyage, and reached Falmouth in safety.

Sir Walter Raleigh, Gilbert's half brother, had been interested in this expedition, but its ill success did not dishearten him   He was one of the noblest spirits of his age, and has laid the world under heavy obligations to him by his many noble services in the cause of humanity   He had served in the army of the Huguenots of France under Coligni, and had heard from the voyagers sent out by that leader of the richness and beauty of Carolina   Undaunted by the sad fate of Sir Humphrey Gilbert, Raleigh determined to plant a colony in the region from which the Huguenots had been driven.   He had no difficulty in obtaining from the queen a patent as liberal as that which had been granted Sir Humphrey Gilbert   He was given ample powers over the region he proposed to colonize, as its feudal lord, and was bound to maintain the authority of the queen and church of England in his possessions   He fitted out two vessels commanded respectively by Philip Amidas and Arthur Barlow, and sent them to explore the region granted to him, and to obtain accurate information concerning it.   They reached the coast of North Carolina at Ocracock inlet, and took formal possession of the country.   They partially explored Albemarle and Pamlico sounds, together with the neighboring coast and islands   It was the month of July, and the climate was delightful, the sea was calm, the atmosphere clear, and the heat was tempered by the delicious sea-breeze.   The woods abounded with birds and echoed with their carols, and wild grapes were found in the greatest profusion   The explorers were enchanted with this delightful region, and returning to England, published glowing accounts of it   They took with them two Indians, named Wanchese and Manteo, the latter of whom afterwards did good service to the colonists as an interpreter.   Queen Elizabeth deemed her reign honored by the discoveries of Amidas and Barlow, and gave to the new region the name of Virginia in honor of England's virgin queen

Raleigh at once set to work to organize a colony   Emigrants volunteered readily, and in a short time a fleet of seven vessels, containing one hundred and eight persons, apart from the crews, was in readiness.   Sir Richard Grenville, a friend of Raleigh, and a man of tried skill and bravery, was given the command of the fleet, and Ralph Lane, who was also a man of considerable distinction, was made governor of the colony.   The fleet sailed from Plymouth on the 9th of April, 1585, and after a long and trying voyage reached Ocracock inlet in June.   Passing through the inlet, a settlement was established on Roanoke island, lying between Albemarle and Pamlico sounds.   Expeditions were sent out to explore the

surrounding country, and in one of these a silver cup was stolen by an
Indian, and its restoration was delayed. With thoughtless cruelty Grenville punished this fault by the destruction of the village to which the
culprit belonged, and also of all the standing corn. This inconsiderate
revenge made the Indians the enemies of the whites, and brought great
future suffering upon the colony. A little later, having seen the colonists
successfully established on Roanoke island, Grenville returned to England with the fleet, capturing a rich Spanish prize on the voyage home.

Left to themselves the colonists began to explore the country, and to

THE COAST OF NORTH CAROLINA.

observe the productions of the soil, and the character of the inhabitants.
Many of the plants were strange to them. Among these were the Indian
corn, tobacco, and the sweet potato. Hariot, "the inventor of the system
of notation in modern algebra, the historian of the expedition," observed these plants and their culture with great minuteness, and became a
firm believer in the healing virtues of tobacco. He has left an interesting account of the natives of the country and their manners and customs.

The Indians, alarmed by the superiority of the whites, began to plot
their destruction, as they believed their entire country would be overrun

by the new-comers. Lane on his part became suspicious of the savages, and this feeling of mutual distrust had the most unhappy consequences Being informed by the savages that there was a splendid city, whose walls glittered with gold and pearls, on the upper waters of the Roanoke, Governor Lane made a boat voyage up that stream, but failed to find anything He returned to the colony just in time to disconcert the plan of the savages for attacking the whites during the absence of the exploring party. Lane now determined to outrival the savages in perfidy. He visited Wingina, one of the most active of the neighboring chiefs, and, professing to come as a friend, was received with confidence by the Indians At a given signal from the governor the whites fell upon the chief and his warriors, and put them to death Lane proved himself utterly unfit to govern such a colony, and his people soon lost confidence in him Their discontent was increased by the failure of their provisions, and they began to entertain the idea of abandoning the colony and returning home.

On the 8th of June, 1586, Sir Francis Drake, with a fleet of twenty-three ships, anchored in the roadstead off Roanoke island. He had been cruising in the West Indies, and had called on his homeward voyage to visit the plantation of his friend Raleigh. He at once set to work to remedy the wants of the colony, and supplied the settlers with such things as they needed They were thoroughly disheartened, however, with their year's experience, and begged Drake so earnestly to take them back to England that he received them on board his ships and put to sea Thus the first effort of the English to settle America resulted in failure. Drake's fleet had scarcely disappeared when a ship loaded with supplies, which had been despatched by Raleigh, reached the island. Finding the place deserted, the commander returned to England A fortnight later, Grenville arrived with three ships Finding the colonists had gone, he too returned to England, leaving fifteen men to hold the island.

Raleigh was greatly disappointed by the failure of his colony, but he did not despair of success; for, notwithstanding the gloomy stories of Lane and his followers, the conclusive testimony of Hariot convinced him that the country could be made to yield a rich return for the trouble and expense of its settlement, and he set to work to form another colony. With the hope of giving the settlers a permanent interest in the plantation, he selected emigrants with wives and families, who should regard the new world as their future home, and endeavor to found a permanent state in that region Everything was provided which could contribute to the success of the colony, and agricultural implements were furnished for the proper cultivation of the soil. All the expense of the undertaking was borne by Raleigh, for though Queen Elizabeth greatly favored the venture, she declined to contribute anything toward it. John White was appointed governor of the colony. A fleet of transport vessels was equipped, also at Raleigh's expense, and on the 26th of April, 1587, the expedition sailed from England. The coast of North Carolina was reached in July.

The approach to Roanoke island was both difficult and dangerous, and Raleigh ordered the new settlers to select a site for their colony on the shores of the Chesapeake bay. The expedition proceeded first, however, to Roanoke island to search for the men left there by Grenville. They could not be found. The island was deserted, the fort was in ruins, and the human bones which lay scattered over the field told plainly that the unfortunate garrison left by Grenville had been murdered by the Indians. Governor White was now anxious to sail to the Chesapeake, but Fernando, the commander of the fleet, refused to proceed any farther, as he wished to go to the West Indies for purposes of trade. The instructions of Raleigh were thus disregarded, and the colonists were compelled, to go ashore on Roanoke island. The old settlement of Governor Lane was rebuilt, and another effort was made to establish the "city of Raleigh." The Indians were bitterly hostile to the settlers, and a friendly tribe was offended by an unfortunate attack upon them, made upon the supposition that they were hostile Indians. The settlers becoming alarmed, implored the governor to return to England and exert himself to hasten the sending out of reinforcements and supplies to them. He was unwilling to do this, as he deemed it his duty to remain among them, but at length yielded to their unanimous appeal. Just before his departure his daughter, Mrs Dare, the wife of one of his lieutenants, gave birth to a daughter, the first child born of English parents within the limits of the United States, and the little one was named Virginia from the place of its birth.

White sailed for England in August, 1587. He found the mother country greatly excited over the threatened invasion of the Spaniards. Raleigh, who was energetically engaged in the efforts for the defence of the country, did not neglect his colony. He fitted out two ships with the needed supplies, and despatched them under White's orders in April, 1588. The commanders, instead of proceeding direct to the colony, undertook to make prizes. At last one of them fell in with a man-of-war from Rochelle, and after a sharp fight was plundered of her stores. Both ships were obliged to return to England, to the anger and disgust of Raleigh. The approach of the Invincible Armada and the exertions demanded of the nation for its defeat, made it impossible for anything more to be done for the colonists at Roanoke until after the Spanish fleet had been destroyed. Even then Raleigh, who had spent over forty thousand

pounds without return, was unable to send aid at once to the colony, and
a year elapsed before a vessel could be sent out under White. In 1590,
the governor reached Roanoke, but no trace of the colony could be found.
The settlers had either died, or been massacred, or had been taken prisoners
and carried by the Indians into the interior of the continent. "The con-
jecture has been hazarded," says Bancroft, "that the deserted colony,
neglected by their own countrymen, were hospitably adopted into the
tribe of Hatteras Indians, and became amalgamated with the sons of the
forest. This was the tradition of the natives at a later day, and was
thought to be confirmed by the physical character of the tribe, in which
the English and the Indian race seemed to have been blended." The generous heart of Raleigh could not bear to leave his countrymen unaided
while a single hope of finding them remained, and he is said to have sent
to America as many as five expeditions at his own cost, to search for them.

With the failure of the settlement at Roanoke Raleigh relinquished
his hope of colonizing Virginia. He had expended nearly his entire
fortune in the undertaking, and the remainder of his life was passed
under the cloud of undeserved misfortune. His career as a statesman
was honorable to himself and to his country, and he proved himself in
all his acts a loyal subject and a devoted patriot. His zeal in behalf of
knowledge made him a generous friend of the learned, and he merits the
gratitude of the American people, not only for his efforts to colonize our
shores with his countrymen, but for the liberality with which he spread
a knowledge of America throughout England by his publication of the
reports of Hariot and Hakluyt. He opened the way for the dominion
of the English in the new world, and his memory is preserved in the
name of the capital city of the great State which he sought to make the
seat of an English empire.

Upon the accession of James I, Raleigh, broken in health and fortune,
but still the most illustrious Englishman of his day, was arraigned on a
charge of high treason, of which not even his enemies believed him
guilty, and was sentenced to the Tower, as the king did not yet dare to
order his execution. During this period Sir Walter beguiled the weari-
ness of his imprisonment by composing his "History of the World"
He remained a prisoner for thirteen years, and was then released on
condition of making a voyage to Guiana in search of gold. His failure
to accomplish the object of the voyage sealed his doom, and on his return
to England he was beheaded, not upon any fresh charge, but on his old
sentence His real fault was that he was too true an Englishman to
sustain the sacrifice of the national honor by King James to the demands
of Spain, and he was generally regarded by the nation as the victim of

the king's cowardice. He met his fate with the calm bravery which had marked his whole life

Until now the voyage from England to America had been made by way of the Canary islands and the West Indies. In 1602, Bartholomew Gosnold conceived the idea of proceeding direct from England to Virginia, as the whole region north of Florida was called by the English. Sailing directly across the Atlantic, he reached Cape Elizabeth, on the coast of Maine, after a voyage of seven weeks. Proceeding southward along the coast he reached Cape Cod, to which he gave the name on the 15th of May, and went ashore there. He was thus the first Englishman to set foot in New England. He continued his voyage along the coast and entered Buzzard's bay. To the westernmost of the islands of this stately sound he gave the name of Elizabeth—a name which has since been applied to the entire group. Loading his ship with sassafras root, which was then highly esteemed for its medicinal virtues, Gosnold sailed for England, and arrived home safely after a voyage of less than four weeks. He gave the most favorable accounts of the region he had visited, and other adventurers were induced by his reports to undertake voyages for the purpose of trading with the natives. Among these was George Waymouth, who reached and explored the coast of Maine in 1605. On his return voyage Waymouth kidnapped five Indians and carried them to England, "to be instructed in English, and to serve as guides to some future expedition."

The voyages of Gosnold and Waymouth to the coast of New England were followed by those of numerous other English adventurers. In 1614, Captain John Smith, who had already distinguished himself by his services in Virginia, made a voyage to America with two ships, furnished at the expense of himself and four merchants of London. The voyage was for the purpose of trading with the natives, and was very successful. Smith took advantage of the opportunity to explore the coast from the Penobscot to Cape Cod. He prepared a map of the coast, and named the country New England—a title which was confirmed by the Prince of Wales, afterwards Charles I. After Smith's return to England, Hunt, the commander of the other vessel, succeeded in inducing twenty of the natives, with their chief Squanto, to visit his ship, and as soon as they were on board put to sea. He sold the savages as slaves in Spain. A few of them, Squanto among the number, were purchased by some kind-hearted monks, who instructed them in the Christian faith in order to send them back to their own people as missionaries of the cross. Squanto escaped to England in 1619, and there learned the language, and was afterward an interpreter between the English settlers and his people.

CHAPTER VI.

THE SETTLEMENT OF VIRGINIA

THE favorable reports which had been brought back to England by the voyagers to the new world had prevented the interest of Englishmen in America from entirely dying out, and some ardent spirits still believed it possible to make that continent the seat of a prosperous dominion dependent upon England. The former assistants of Raleigh, in particular, held to the convictions which their chief had entertained to the day of his death. The selfish and timid policy of King James having made it impossible for men to acquire distinction by naval exploits, as in the days of Elizabeth, the more adventurous classes lent a willing ear to the plans for colonizing America, which were discussed in various parts of the kingdom. Bartholomew Gosnold, who had explored the New England coast, was especially active in seeking to induce capitalists to send out a colony to it. Sir Ferdinand Gorges, a wealthy gentleman and Governor of Plymouth, had been greatly interested in America by the accounts of Waymouth, who had given him two of the Indians he had brought to England. These succeeded in interesting others in their plans, and the result was, that early in the reign of King James two companies were formed in England for the colonization of America. One of these was the "London

94

Company," composed chiefly of noblemen and merchants residing in London. The other was the "Plymouth Company," composed of "knights, gentlemen, and merchants," residing in the west of England. King James divided Virginia into two parts. To the London Company he granted "South Virginia," extending from Cape Fear, in North Carolina, to the Potomac. To the Plymouth Company he gave "North Virginia," stretching from the Hudson to Newfoundland. The region between the Potomac and the Hudson he left as a broad belt of neutral land to keep the companies from encroaching upon each other's domains. Either was at liberty to form settlements in this region within fifty miles of its own border.

The London Company was the first to settle the country assigned it. A liberal charter was granted the company: the lands in the new world were to be held by it on the simple conditions of homage and the payment to the crown of one-fifth of the gold and silver and one-fifteenth of the copper that should be discovered. A general council, residing in England, was to have authority over the whole province, and the members of this council were to be appointed and removed by the king at his good pleasure. Each separate colony was to be under the control of a colonial council residing within its own limits, and the king retained

COAT OF ARMS OF VIRGINIA.

the right to direct the appointment or removal of the members of these councils at his pleasure. The king also reserved the supreme legislative authority over the colonies, and framed for their government a code of laws—"an exercise of royal legislation which has been pronounced in itself illegal." The colonists were placed by this code under the rule of the superior and local councils we have named, in the choice of which they had no voice. The religion of the Church of England was established as that of the colony, and conformity to it was secured by severe penalties. Death was the punishment for murder, manslaughter, adultery, dangerous seditions and tumults. In all cases not affecting life and limb offenders might be tried by a magistrate, but for capital offences trial by jury was secured. In the former cases the punishment of the offender was at the discretion of the president and council. The Indians were to be treated with kindness, and efforts were to be made for their conversion to Christianity. For five years at least the affairs of the colonists were to be conducted in a joint stock. The right to impose future legislation upon the province was reserved by the king. Such was the form of government first prescribed for Virginia by England, in which, as Bancroft truly says, there was "not an element of popular liberty" "To the emigrants themselves it conceded not one elective franchise, not one of the rights of self-government. They were to be subjected to the ordinances of a commercial corporation, of which they could not be members, to the dominion of a domestic council, in appointing which they had no voice, to the control of a superior council in England, which had no sympathy with their rights, and finally, to the arbitrary legislation of the sovereign."

Under this charter the London Company prepared to send out a colony to Virginia. It was to be a commercial settlement, and the emigrants were composed altogether of men. One hundred and five persons, exclusive of the crews of the vessels, joined the expedition. Of these not twenty were farmers or mechanics. The remainder were "gentlemen," or men who had ruined themselves at home by idleness and dissipation. A fleet of three small ships, under command of Captain Newport, was assembled, and on the 19th of December, 1606, sailed for America.

The emigrants sailed without having perfected any organization. The king had foolishly placed the names of those who were to constitute the government in a sealed box, which the adventurers were ordered not to open until they had selected a site for their settlement and were ready to form a government. This was most unfortunate, for during the long voyage dissensions arose, and there was no one in the expedition who possessed the authority requisite for controlling the unruly spirits. These quarrels grew more intense with the lapse of time, and when the shores of Virginia were reached the seeds of many of the evils from which the colony afterwards suffered severely had been thoroughly sown. There were among the number several who were well qualified to direct the affairs of the expedition, but they were without the proper authority to do so, and there was no such thing as voluntary submission to be seen among the adventurers. The merits of the deserving merely excited the jealousy of their companions, and the great master spirit of the enterprise found from the first his disinterested efforts for the good of the expedition met by a jealous and determined opposition.

Newport was not acquainted with the direct route, and made the old passage by way of the Canaries and the West Indies. He thus consumed the whole of the winter, and while searching for the island of Roanoke, the scene of Raleigh's colony, his fleet was driven northward by a severe storm, and forced to take refuge in the Chesapeake bay on the 26th of April, 1607. He named the headlands of this bay Cape Henry and Cape Charles, in honor of the two sons of James I., and because of the comfortable anchorage which he obtained in the splendid road-tead which enters the bay opposite its mouth, he gave to the northern point the name of Point Comfort, which it has since borne. Passing this, a noble river was discovered coming from the westward, and was named the James, in honor of the English king. The country was explored with energy, and though one small tribe of Indians was found to be hostile, a treaty of peace and friend-hip was made with another at Hampton. The fleet ascended the river, and explored it for fifty miles. A pleasant peninsula, on the left bank of the stream, was selected as the site of the colony, and on the 13th of May, 1607, the settlement was definitely begun, and was named Jamestown, in honor of the king.

The leading spirit of the enterprise was John Smith, one of the truest heroes of history, who has been deservedly called "the father of Virginia." He was still a young man, being but thirty years of age, but he was old in experience and knightly deeds. While yet a youth he had served in Holland in the ranks of the army of freedom, and had travelled through France, Egypt, and Italy. Burning to distinguish himself, he had repaired to Hungary, and had won a brilliant reputation by his exploits in the ranks of the Christian army engaged in the defence of that country against the Mohammedans. He repeatedly defeated the chosen champions of the Turks in single combat, but being at length captured was sent to Constantinople and sold as a slave. The wife of his master, pitying his misfortunes, sent him to a relative in the Crimea, with a request to treat him with kindness, but contrary to her wishes he was subjected to the greatest harshness. Rendered desperate by this experience, he rose against his task-master, slew him, and seizing his horse, escaped to the border of the Russian territory, where he was kindly received. He wandered across the country to Transylvania, and rejoined his old companions in arms. Then filled with a longing to see his "own sweet country" once more, he returned to England. He arrived just as the plans for the colonization of Virginia were being matured. He readily engaged in the expedition organized by the London Company, and exerted himself in a marked degree to make it a success. He was in all respects the most capable man in the whole colony, for his natural abilities were fully equal to his experience. He had studied human nature under many forms in many lands, and in adversity and danger had learned patience and fortitude. His calm, cool courage, his resolute will, and his intuitive perception of the necessities of a new settlement, were destined to make him the main stay of the colony of Virginia, but as yet these high qualities had only excited the malicious envy of his associates, and

7

the efforts he had made to heal the dissensions which had broken out during the voyage had made him many enemies.

When the box containing the names of those who were to constitute the colonial government was opened, it was found that the king had appointed John Smith one of the council. Smith was at this time in confinement, having been arrested on the voyage upon the frivolous charges of sedition and treason against the crown, and his enemies, notwithstanding the royal appointment, excluded him from the council. Edward Wingfield, "a grovelling merchant of the west of England," was chosen

CAPTAIN JOHN SMITH.

president of the council and governor of the colony. The services of Smith could not be dispensed with, however, and he was released from his confinement, and sent with Newport and twenty others to explore the river. They ascended the James to the falls, where the city of Richmond now stands, and visited Powhatan, the principal chief of the Indian nation holding the country into which they had come. He was

then dwelling at his favorite seat on the left bank of the river, a few miles below the falls. Powhatan received them kindly, and silenced the remonstrances of his people by saying: "They hurt you not; they only want a little land." The chief was a man of powerful stature, "tall, sour and athletic." He was sixty years of age, and had under him a population of six or eight thousand souls, two thousand being warriors. Having carefully observed the river, Smith and Newport returned to Jamestown.

Their presence there was needed, for Wingfield had proved himself utterly unfit to govern the colony. He would not allow the colonists to build either houses for themselves or a fortification for the common defence against the savages While they were in this helpless condition, they were suddenly attacked by a force of four hundred Indians, and were saved from destruction only by the fire of the shipping, which filled the savages with terror and put them to flight It is believed that the cause of Wingfield's singular conduct was his jealousy of Smith, whose talents he feared would attract the support of the settlers. The fort was now built without delay, cannon were mounted, and the men trained in the exercise of arms When the ships were in readiness to sail to England, it was intimated to Smith that he would consult his own interests by returning in them, but he refused to do so, and boldly demanded a trial upon the charges which had been preferred against him. The council did not dare to refuse him this trial, and the result was his triumphant acquittal More than this, he succeeded so well in exposing the malice of his enemies that the president, as the originator of the charges against him, was compelled to pay him two hundred pounds damages, which sum Smith generously applied to the needs of the colony His seat in the council could no longer be denied him, and he took his place at the board to the great gain of the colony.

Newport sailed for England about the middle of June, leaving the settlement in a most pitiable condition. The provisions sent out from England had been spoiled on the voyage, and the colonists were too indolent to cultivate the land, or to seek to obtain supplies from the Indians. Sickness broke out among them, owing to the malarious character of their location, and by the beginning of the winter more than half their number had died. Among these was Bartholomew Gosnold, the originator of the London Company, who had come out to Virginia to risk his life in the effort to settle the country. He was a man of rare merits, and, together with Mr. Hunt, "the preacher," who was also one of the projectors of the company, had contributed successfully to the preservation of harmony in the colony In the midst of these sufferings it was found that Wingfield was preparing to load the pinnace with the remainder of the stores and escape to the West Indies He was deposed by the council, who appointed John Ratcliffe in his place.

The new president was not much better than his predecessor He was incapable of discharging the duties of his office, and was perfectly satisfied that Smith should direct the affairs of the settlement for him. From this time Smith was the actual head of the government Food was the prime necessity of the colony, and as it was now too late to raise it, Smith exerted himself to obtain it from the Indians. He purchased of

supply, and towards the close of the autumn the wild fowl which frequent
the region furnished an additional means of subsistence.

The danger of a famine thus removed, Smith proceeded to explore the
country. In one of these expeditions he ascended the Chickahominy as
far as he could penetrate in his boat, and then leaving it in charge of two
men, struck into the interior with an Indian guide. His men disobeyed
his instructions, and were surprised and put to death by the Indians.
Smith himself was taken prisoner, and deeply impressed his captors by
his cool courage and self-possession. Instead of begging for his life, he
set to work to convince them of his superiority over them, and succeeded

POCAHONTAS RESCUING CAPTAIN SMITH.

so well that they regarded him with a sort of awe. He astonished them
by showing them his pocket compass and explaining to them its uses, and
excited their admiration by writing a letter to his friends at Jamestown
informing them of his situation, and of the danger to which they were
exposed from a contemplated attack of the Indians. One of the savages
bore the letter to its destination.

Smith had been captured by Opechancanough, a powerful chieftain of
the Pamunkey Indians; but as the curiosity of the neighboring tribes
was greatly aroused by his presence, he was led in triumph from the
Chickahominy to the villages on the Rappahannock and the Potomac,

and then taken through other towns to the residence of Opechancanough, on the Pamunkey Here the medicine men of the tribe held a three days' incantation over him to ascertain his character and design All this while his demeanor was calm and fearless, as if he entertained no apprehension for his safety He was regarded by the savages as a superior being, and was treated with kindness, though kept a close prisoner. His fate was referred to Powhatan for decision, as the other tribes feared to bring the blood of such an extraordinary being upon their heads. Powhatan was then residing at Werowocomoco. which lay on the north side of Fork river, in what is now Gloucester county, Virginia. He received the captive in great state, surrounded by his warriors "He wore," says Smith, "such a grave and majestical countenance as drove me into admiration to see." Brought into the presence of Powhatan, Smith was received with a shout from the assembled warriors A handsome young squaw brought him water to wash his hands, and another gave him a bunch of feathers to dry them Food was then set before him, and while he applied himself to the repast a consultation was held by the savages as to his fate Smith watched the proceedings closely, and was aware from the gestures of the council that his death had been determined upon Two great stones were then brought into the assembly and laid before the king. The captive was seized and dragged to the stones, forced down, and his head laid upon them Two brawny savages stood by to beat out his brains with their clubs. During these proceedings, Pocahontas, a child of ten or twelve years, "dearly loved daughter" of Powhatan, touched with pity for the unfortunate stranger, had been earnestly pleading with her father to spare his life. Failing in this, she sprang forward at the moment the executioners were about to despatch their victim, and throwing herself by his side, clasped her arms about his neck and laid her head upon his to protect him from the impending stroke. This remarkable action in a child so young moved the savages with profound astonishment They regarded it as a manifestation of the will of heaven in favor of the captive, and it was determined to spare his life and seek his friendship

Smith was released from his bonds, and was given to Pocahontas to make beads and bells for her, and to weave for her ornaments of copper The friendship which the innocent child of the forest conceived for him grew stronger every day, and ceased only with her life. Powhatan took him into his favor, and endeavored to induce him to abandon the English and cast his lot with him. He even sought to obtain his aid in an attack upon the colony. Smith declined these offers, and by his decision of character succeeded in averting the hostility of the savages from his friends at Jamestown, and in winning their good-will for the English. In a short while the Indians allowed him to return to Jamestown, upon his promise to send to King Powhatan two cannon and a grindstone. Upon arriving at Jamestown he showed the Indians who had accompanied him two of the largest cannon, and asked them to lift them. This was impossible; nor could they succeed any better with the grindstone. Smith then discharged the cannon in their presence, which so frightened them that they refused to have anything to do with them. Having evaded his promise in this manner, Smith bestowed more suitable presents upon his guides, and sent them home with gifts for Powhatan and

POCAHONTAS.

Pocahontas. The savage king was doubtless well satisfied to let the "great guns" alone after hearing the report of his messengers concerning them, and was greatly pleased with the gifts sent him.

Smith found the colony at Jamestown reduced to forty men and affairs in great confusion. His companions had believed that he had fallen a victim to the hostility of the Indians, and he was greeted with delight, as the need of his firm hand had been sadly felt. He found that a party of malcontents were preparing to run away from the colony with the pinnace, and he at once rallied his supporters and trained the guns of the fort upon the little vessel, and avowed his determination to fire upon the mutineers if they sought to depart. His firmness put an end to this danger, and the friendly relations which he had managed to establish with the Indians now enabled him to buy from the savages the food necessary to sustain the colonists through the winter. In many ways his captivity proved a great blessing to the settlement. He had not only explored the country between the James and Potomac, and gained considerable knowledge of the language and customs of the natives, but had disposed the Indian tribes subject to Powhatan to regard the colony with friendship at the most critical period of its existence. Had the savages been hostile during this winter the Jamestown colony must have perished

of starvation, but now, every few days throughout this season, Pocahontas came to the fort accompanied by a number of her countrymen,
bearing baskets of corn for the whites.

In the spring of 1608, Newport arrived from England, bringing with
him a reinforcement of one hundred and twenty emigrants. The new-
comers were joyfully welcomed by the colonists, but they proved of no
real advantage to the settlement. They were either idlers or goldsmiths,
who had come out to America in the hope of finding gold. The refiners
of the party believed they had found the precious metal in a heap of
glittering earth, of which there was an abundance near Jamestown, and
in spite of the remonstrances of Smith, would do nothing but dig gold.
Newport, who shared the delusion, loaded his ships with the worthless
earth, and sailed for England after a sojourn in the colony of fourteen
weeks.

While these fruitless labors were in progress, Smith, thoroughly
disgusted with the folly of the emigrants, undertook the exploration of
the Chesapeake bay. He spent the summer of 1608 in visiting the shores
of the bay and ascending its tributaries in an open boat, accompanied by
a few men. He explored the Chesapeake to the Susquehanna, ascended
the Potomac to the falls, and explored the Patapsco. This voyage
embraced a total distance of nearly three thousand miles, and resulted not
only in the gaining of accurate information respecting the country bordering the Chesapeake, but also in establishing friendly relations with the
tribes along its shores, and preparing the way for future friendly intercourse with them. The energetic explorer prepared a map of the
Chesapeake and its tributaries, and sent it to his employers in England,
by whom it was published. It is yet in existence, and its accuracy and
minuteness have often elicited the praise of subsequent topographers.

Smith returned to Jamestown on the 7th of September, and three days
later was made president of the council. The good effects of his administration were soon felt. In the autumn, however, another reinforcement
of idle and useless men arrived. Smith, indignant at the continual
arrival of such worthless persons, wrote to the company: "When you
send again, I entreat you rather send but thirty carpenters, husbandmen,
gardeners, fishermen, blacksmiths, masons, and diggers up of trees' roots,
well provided, than a thousand of such as we have." Upon the return
of the fleet to England the governor exerted his authority to compel the
idlers to go to work. It was ordered that six hours in each day should
be spent in useful labor by each person, and that "he who would not
work might not eat." In a short while the settlement began to assume
the appearance of a regular habitation; but still so little land had been

cultivated—only about thirty or forty acres in all—that during the winter of 1608-'9, the settlers were compelled to depend upon the Indians for food. Yet the prudent management of Smith kept the colony in good health, and during the winter not more than seven men died out of two hundred.

In the spring of 1609, great changes were made in the London

BUILDING OF JAMESTOWN.

Company, and a more earnest interest was manifested in the colony by all classes of the English people. Subscriptions were made to the stock of the company by many noblemen as well as merchants, and a new charter was obtained. By this charter the stockholders had the power to appoint the supreme council in England, and to this council were confided the powers of legislation and government, which were relinquished by the

king The council appointed the governor of the colony, who was to
rule the settlement with absolute authority according to the instructions
of the council He was made master of the lives and liberties of the
settlers by being authorized to declare martial law whenever in his
judgment the necessity for that measure should arise, and was made the
sole executive officer in its administration. Thus the emigrants were
deprived of every civil right, and were placed at the mercy of a governor
appointed by a corporation whose only object was to make money The
company, however, defeated this object by the manner in which it selected
emigrants Instead of sending out honest and industrious laborers who
were capable of building up a state, they sent only idlers and vagabonds,
men who were neither willing nor fit to work The common stock
feature was maintained, and thus the greatest obstacle to industry that
could be devised was placed in the way of the success of the colony
Still there were many who were willing to seek the new world even
under these conditions, and many others whose friends desired to get
them out of the country The company was soon able to equip a fleet of
nine vessels containing more than five hundred emigrants, and a stock of
domestic animals and fowls was included in the outfit of the expedition
Lord Delaware, a nobleman whose character commanded the confidence
of his countrymen, was made governor of the colony for life As he was
not able to sail with the expedition, he delegated his authority during his
absence to Newport, who was admiral of the fleet, Sir Thomas Gates, and
Sir George Somers, who were to govern the colony until his arrival.
The fleet sailed in the spring of 1609, but when off the American coast
was overtaken by a severe storm, and two vessels—on one of which the
admiral and the commissioners had sailed—were wrecked on one of the
Bermuda islands

Seven ships reached Virginia, and brought the worst lot of emigrants
that had yet been sent out to the colony Smith was still acting president, and as the commissioners had not arrived, was determined to hold
his position until relieved by his lawful successors. The new emigrants
at first refused to recognize his authority, but he compelled them to submit, and in order to lessen the evil of their presence, divided them into
bodies sufficiently numerous for safety, and sent them to make settlements
in other parts of Virginia These settlements proved so many failures,
and, unfortunately for the colony, Smith was so severely wounded by an
accidental explosion of gunpowder, in the autumn of 1609, that he was
obliged to relinquish the government and return to England for surgical
treatment. He delegated his authority to George Percy, and sailed for
England, never to return to Virginia again. It was to him alone that

the company owed the success of the colony, but he received in return
nothing but ingratitude.

The departure of Smith was followed by the most disastrous consequences. There was no longer an acknowledged government in Virginia,
and the settlers gave themselves up to the most reckless idleness. Their
provisions were quickly consumed, and the Indians refused to furnish
them with any more. The friendship of the savages had been due to
their personal regard for Smith, who had compelled the colonists to respect
their rights and to refrain from maltreating them. Now that Smith was
no longer at the head of affairs, the Indians regarded the settlers with
the contempt they fully merited, and hostilities soon began. Stragglers
from the town were cut off, and parties who went out to seek food among
the savages were deliberately murdered. On one occasion a plan was
laid to surprise the town and massacre the colonists. The danger was
averted by Pocahontas, who stole from her father's camp, through night
and storm, to give warning to the settlers. Failing in this effort the
Indians resolved to starve the colony, and soon the whites began to
experience the sufferings of a famine. Thirty of them seized one of the
ships, escaped to sea, and began a course of piracy. In six months the
four hundred and ninety persons left by Smith in the colony at his departure had dwindled down to sixty, and this wretched remnant would have
perished speedily had not aid reached them.

On the 24th of May, 1610, Sir Thomas Gates and the members of the
expedition who had been wrecked on the Bermudas reached Jamestown
after a stay of nine months on those islands, during which time they had
built two vessels from the wreck of their ship and the wood found on the
island. In these they managed to reach Virginia, expecting to find the
colony in a prosperous condition. They found instead the sixty men
already mentioned, so feeble and full of despair as to be helpless. In the
general despondency it was determined to abandon the colony, sail to
Newfoundland, and join the fishing vessels which came annually from
England to that island. Some of the emigrants wished to burn the town,
but this was prevented by the resolute conduct of Sir Thomas Gates. On
the 7th of June the settlers embarked, and that night dropped down the
James with the tide. The next morning they were astonished to meet a
fleet of vessels entering the river. It was Lord Delaware, who had
arrived with fresh emigrants and supplies. The fugitives hailed the
arrival of the governor with delight, and put about and ascended the
stream with him. A fair wind enabled them to reach Jamestown the
same night.

On the 10th of June, 1610, the foundations of the colony were solemnly relaid with prayer and supplication to Almighty God for success in the effort to establish a state. The authority of Lord Delaware silenced all dissensions, and his equitable but firm administration soon placed the settlement on a more successful basis than it had yet occupied. The labors of each day were opened with prayer in the little church, after which, from six in the morning till ten, and from two in the afternoon until four, all engaged in the tasks demanded of them. The good effects of the new system were soon manifest in the increased comfort and prosperity of the colony. In about a year the health of Lord Delaware gave way, and he delegated his authority to George Percy, whom Smith had chosen as his successor, and returned to England.

Fortunately for the colony, the company, before the arrival of Lord Delaware in England, had sent out Sir Thomas Dale with supplies. He reached Jamestown in May, 1611, and finding Lord Delaware gone, assumed the government. He brought with him a code of laws, prepared and sent out by Sir Thomas Smith, the treasurer of the company, without the order or sanction of the council, and which established martial law as the rule of the colony. Though he ruled with such a stern hand, Dale rendered good service to Virginia by recommending to the company to maintain the settlement at all hazards as certain of yielding them a rich reward in the end. This energetic appeal so greatly encouraged the council, which had been

WIFE OF A CHIEF

considerably disheartened by Lord Delaware's return, that in the summer of 1611 Sir Thomas Gates was sent out to Virginia with six ships and three hundred emigrants. He carried also a stock of cattle and abundant supplies. The emigrants sent out with him were of a better character and more industrious than any that had yet left England for Virginia. Gates assumed the government, and matters began to prosper again. The colony now numbered seven hundred persons, and was deemed so prosperous that Dale, with the approval of the governor, led a number of the men to the vicinity of the falls of the James, and there established another settlement, which was called Henrico in honor of the Prince of Wales. Among the changes for the better was the assignment to each settler of a few acres of land for his own cultivation. This "incipient establishment of private property" produced the happiest results, and from this time there was no scarcity of provisions in the colony, which became so powerful and prosperous as to be no longer exposed to the mercy of the savages. The Indians themselves were quick to notice this change, and some of the neighboring tribes by formal treaty acknowledged themselves subjects of King James.

The whites, however, did not always respect the rights of the Indians. Late in 1613, Pocahontas was betrayed into the hands of a foraging party under Captain Argall. Argall kept her a prisoner, and demanded of Powhatan a ransom. For three months Powhatan did not deign to reply to this demand, but prepared for war. In the meantime Pocahontas was instructed in the faith of the Christians, and at length openly embraced it, and was baptized. Her conversion was hastened by a powerful sentiment, which had taken possession of her heart. She had always regarded the English as superior to her own race, and now her affections were won by a young Englishman of good character, named John Rolfe. Rolfe, with the approval of the governor, asked her hand of her father in marriage. Powhatan consented to the union, but refused to be present at the marriage, as he was too shrewd to place his person in the hands of the English. He sent his brother Opachisco and two of his sons to witness the marriage, which was solemnized in the little church at Jamestown, in the presence of Sir Thomas Dale, the acting governor. The marriage conciliated Powhatan and his tribe, who continued their peaceful relations with the colony. King James, however, was greatly displeased at what he deemed the presumption of a subject in wedding a princess. Pocahontas was soon after taken to England by her husband, and was received there with great attention and kindness. She remained in England for a little more than a year, and then prepared to return to her own country. As she was about to sail, she died, at the age of twenty-two, A. D. 1616. She left a son, who subsequently became a man of distinction in Virginia, and the ancestor of some of the proudest families of the Old Dominion.

In the meantime the settlements of the French on the coast of Maine had attracted the attention and excited the jealousy of the English. In 1613, Captain Samuel Argall, who was cruising on the banks of Newfoundland to protect the English fishermen, discovered the French settlement of Saint Sauveur on the island of Mount Desert, and captured it. He treated the colonists with inexcusable harshness, and compelled them to leave the country. In the same year he destroyed the fortifications which Des Monts had erected on the isle of St. Croix and burned the deserted settlement of Port Royal.

At Jamestown and the other settlements that had been formed in Virginia private industry was fast placing the colony on an assured basis of success. "The condition of private property in lands, among the colonists, depended, in some measure, on the circumstances under which they had emigrated Some had been sent and maintained at the exclusive cost of the company, and were its servants One month of their time and three acres of land were set apart for them, besides a small allowance of two bushels of corn from the public store; the rest of their labor belonged to their employers. This number had gradually decreased, and in 1617 there were of them all, men, women and children, but fifty-four. Others, especially the favorite settlement near the mouth of the Appomattox, were tenants, paying two and a half bushels of corn as a yearly tribute to the store, and giving to the public service one month's labor, which was to be required neither at seed time nor harvest. He who came himself, or had sent others at his own expense, had been entitled to a hundred acres of land for each person now that the colony was well established, the bounty on emigration was fixed at fifty acres, of which the actual occupation and culture gave a further right to as many more, to be assigned at leisure. Besides this, lands were granted as rewards of merit; yet not more than two thousand acres could be so appropriated to one person. A payment to the company's treasury of twelve pounds and ten shillings likewise obtained a title to any hundred acres of land not yet granted or possessed, with a reserved claim to as much more Such were the earliest land laws of Virginia. though imperfect and unequal, they gave the cultivator the means of becoming a proprietor of the soil. These valuable changes were established by Sir Thomas Dale." *

The survivors of Raleigh's colony at Roanoke had introduced into England the use of tobacco which they had learned from the Indians, and there was now a steady demand for that article from the mother country. Encouraged by this demand, and stimulated by the acquisition of property of their own, the Virginia colonists devoted themselves with ardor to the culture of tobacco, and soon all the available land about the settlements, and even the streets and public squares of Jamestown, were planted with it. Tobacco soon became the currency of the colony, and so much attention was given to it, to the exclusion of other agricultural interests, that there was danger that not enough corn would be raised to supply the needs of the settlers

In 1616, Sir Thomas Dale, who had been governor of the colony for two years, delegated his authority to George Yeardley, and sailed for

---

* *History of the United States*   By George Bancroft, vol 1, p 150.

England   Under Yeardley's admirable administration the colony continued to increase in prosperity   A faction of the settlers, however, succeeded in removing him from his position, and replaced him with Argall, who was a selfish and brutal tyrant.   He held office for two years, and governed according to the most rigid forms of martial law   He swindled the company, and extorted their hard earnings from the settlers, who were driven to desperation by his brutalities   In their distress they appealed to the company for redress, and, as Argall had robbed the corporation also, their prayer was heard   Argall was removed from office, and the bloody code of Sir Thomas Smith was abolished   Sir George Yeardley was appointed governor, Lord Delaware having died, and reached Jamestown in April, 1619   He was greatly beloved by the Virginians, and his arrival was looked upon as the beginning of new life for the province, as indeed it was

Among the changes which Yeardley was empowered by the company to inaugurate was one which exercised the greatest influence upon the subsequent history of Virginia.   After years of blundering and arbitrary rule, the London Company had become convinced that the best way to promote the welfare of Virginia was to give the settlers a share in the management of their own affairs   "That the planters might have a hande in the governing of themselves, yt was graunted that a generall assemblie shoulde be helde yearly once, whereat were to be present the governor and consell with two burgesses from each plantation, freely to be elected by the inhabitantes thereof, this assemblie to have power to make and ordaine whatsoever lawes and orders shoulde by them be thought good and profitable for their subsistence"   In accordance with this authorization, Governor Yeardley issued his writs for the election of representatives from the various colonies, and on the 10th day of July, 1619, two delegates from each of the eleven settlements of the colony met at Jamestown, and organized the House of Burgesses of the Colony of Virginia, the first representative assembly ever convened in America. In this assembly the governor and council sat with the burgesses, and engaged in the debates and motions.   John Pory, a member of the council and the secretary of the colony, was chosen speaker, although he was not a member of the house.   Sensible of their dependence upon the Supreme Ruler of the world, the burgesses opened their deliberations with prayer, and thus established the practice.   "The assembly exercised fully the right of judging of the proper election of its members, and they would not suffer any patent, conceding manorial jurisdiction, to bar the obligation of obedience to their decisions."   Laws were enacted against idleness and vice, and for the encouragement of industry and order. He who refused to labor was to be "sold to a master for wages till he showe apparent signs of amendment." The playing of dice and cards, and drunkenness and profane swearing were prohibited under severe penalties. Inducements were held out to increase the planting of corn, mulberry trees, hemp and the vine. The price of tobacco was fixed by law at three shillings a pound for the best grade and half that price for the inferior grade. Provision was also made for "the erecting of a university and college" for the proper education of the children who should be born to the planters. It was designed to extend to the Indians the benefit of these institutions, and it was ordered that the "most towardly (Indian) boys in wit and graces of nature should be brought up in the first elements of literature, and sent from college to the work of converting the natives to Christianity."

The measures of the assembly were put in force without waiting the approval of the London Company, and the good effects of them were quickly visible in the colony. The principles of free government having been planted in the community, the settlers, who had been thereby transformed from the mere creatures of the governor into free-born Englishmen once more, began to regard Virginia as their permanent home, and set to work with a will to build houses and plant fields. One thing only was lacking to give the settlers homes in the truest sense of the word; and to supply that need Sir Edwin Sandys induced ninety young and virtuous women to emigrate to America, that the colonists might be able to marry and form domestic ties which alone could permanently attach them to America. The young women were sent over to the colony in 1619, at the expense of the company, and were married to the tenants of the corporation or to men who were well enough to do to support them. The next year sixty more were sent over, and quickly found husbands. In all cases the husbands were required to repay to the company the cost of the passage of their wives from England. This was paid in tobacco, and was regarded as a debt of honor, to be discharged at any sacrifice. In order to aid the husbands in these payments, as well as in their general matters, the company, in employing labor, gave the preference to the married men. The colony now increased in a marked degree, emigrants coming out so rapidly from England that by 1621 there were 4000 persons in Virginia. It having become understood that the colony had passed the stage at which failure was possible, and had become a permanent state, the new emigrants were largely men of family, who brought their households with them.

In July, 1621, the London Company, which was now controlled by the patriot party in England, granted to Virginia a written constitution, which gave to the colony a form of government similar to that of England herself. A governor and permanent council were to be appointed by the company. The house of burgesses was to have the power of enacting such laws as should be needed for the general good, but no law so enacted was to be valid unless approved by the company. On the other hand, no orders of the court in London were to be binding in Virginia unless ratified by the house of burgesses. Courts of justice were established and ordered to be administered according to the laws and forms of trial in use in England. Thus the common law of England was firmly established in Virginia, and under its beneficent protection the colony advanced steadily in prosperity. The colonists were to be no longer merely the subjects of a commercial corporation, and as such to hold their liberties and property at the pleasure of their masters, but were definitely accorded the right to govern themselves, and to take such measures for their safety and prosperity as in their judgment should seem best. ' On this ordinance," says Bancroft, "Virginia erected the superstructure of her liberties. Its influences were wide and enduring, and can be traced through all her history. It constituted the plantation, in its infancy, a nursery of freemen; and succeeding generations learned to cherish institutions which were as old as the first period of the prosperity of their fathers. The privileges then conceded could never be wrested from the Virginians, and as new colonies arose at the South their proprietaries could hope to win emigrants only by bestowing franchises as large as those enjoyed by their elder rival. The London Company merits the praise of having auspicated liberty in America. It may be doubted whether any public act during the reign of King James was of more permanent or pervading influence; and it reflects glory on Sir Edwin Sandys, the Earl of Southampton, and the patriot party of England, that, though they were unable to establish guarantees of a liberal administration at home, they were careful to connect popular freedom inseparably with the life, prosperity and state of society in Virginia."

CHAPTER VII

PROGRESS OF THE VIRGINIA COLONY

Introduction of Negro Slavery into Virginia—Efforts of the Assembly to Restrict Slavery—The Indians Attempt the Destruction of the Colony—Terrible Sufferings of the Whites—Aid from England—The Indian War Begun—King James Revokes the Charter of the London Company—Charles I Desires a Monopoly of the Tobacco Trade—Action of the Assembly—Sir William Berkeley's First Administration—Severe Measures against Dissenters—Close of the Indian War—Death of Opechancanough—Emigration of Royalists to Virginia—Virginia and the Commonwealth—Treaty with England—The Assembly Asserts its Independence of the Governor—The Restoration—Berkeley Chosen Governor by the Assembly—His Hypocrisy

IN August, 1619, a few months after the meeting of the first colonial legislature, there occurred an event which was destined to influence the history of Virginia and of America for remote generations, perhaps forever. A Dutch vessel of war entered the James river and offered twenty negroes for sale as slaves. These were purchased by the planters, and negro slavery was thus established in Virginia. Laborers were in demand, and the necessity for them blinded the planters to the evil they were fastening upon the colony. The first importation was followed by others, the infamous business being principally in the hands of the Dutch at this period. Still the blacks increased very slowly. The legislature from the first discouraged the traffic by a heavy tax upon female slaves.

Sir Francis Wyatt, the first governor appointed under the new constitution, reached Virginia in 1621, and the new laws were soon in successful operation. Soon after his arrival a terrible misfortune befell the colony, and almost caused its destruction. For some time there had been bad blood between the whites and the Indians. Powhatan, the friend of the English, was dead, and Opechancanough, the veteran chief, who, since the death of Powhatan, had become the leader of the nation, was bitterly hostile to the English, and not without reason. The savages originally held the best lands in the colony, but the whites, when these lands were wanted, took possession of them without regard to the rights of their dusky owners. The Indians, unable to contend with the whites in open conflict, saw themselves driven steadily away from their accus-

8

11;

tomed homes, and menaced with total destruction by the superior race. Opechancanough, though outwardly friendly to the colonists, now secretly resolved upon their destruction, and sought to accomplish this by treachery. There were about five thousand Indians, of whom fifteen hundred were warriors, within sixty miles of Jamestown, and the whites in the same region numbered in all about four thousand. These were scattered in fancied safety along both sides of the James and for some distance into the interior. A plot was organized by the Indian leader for the extermination of every settler in the colony. At noon on a designated day every settlement was to be surprised and all the inhabitants murdered. The savages in the meantime kept up their pretence of friendship. Opechancanough declared with fervor, "Sooner shall the sky fall than my friendship for the English should cease." So unsuspicious were the English that to the very last moment they received the savages amongst them without fear of harm, and in many places the latter were at the instant of the massacre in the houses of the people they meant to destroy.

On the 22d of March, 1622, a general attack was made by the savages upon all the settlements of the colony. On the previous night the plot had been revealed to a converted Indian, named Chauco, who at once hastened to Jamestown and gave warning of the danger. The alarm spread rapidly to the nearest settlements, but those at a distance could not be reached in time to avert their fate. Those settlements which had been warned were able to offer a successful resistance to their assailants, and some of those which were surprised beat off the Indians; but the number of victims, men, women, and children, who fell this day amounted to three hundred and forty-seven. All these were slain within an hour, and their fate would have been shared by the whole colony but for the warning of the friendly Indian.

The effect upon the colony was appalling. The distant plantations had been destroyed by the savages, and out of eighty settlements eight alone survived. These, and especially Jamestown, were crowded beyond their capacity with fugitives who had fled to them for shelter. Sickness soon began to prevail, the public works were discontinued, and private industry was greatly diminished. A gloom rested over the entire colony, and the population fell off. At the end of two years after the massacre, the number of inhabitants had been reduced to two thousand. Much sympathy was manifested for the suffering colonists by the people of England. The city of London sent them liberal assistance, and private individuals subscribed to their need. King James was aroused into an affectation of generous sympathy, and sent over to the colony a supply of muskets which had been condemned as worthless in England.

The whites recovered from their gloom, and on their part began to form plans for the extermination of their foes. During the next ten years expeditions were sent against the Indians at frequent intervals. The object kept sternly in view was to either destroy the savages altogether, or force them back from the seaboard into the interior. As late as 1630 it was ordered by the general assembly that no peace should be made with the Indians.

An important change now occurred in the fortunes of the colony. The London Company was bankrupt, and its stockholders having abandoned all hope of gain from the colony, held on to their shares merely as a means of exercising political power. The company was divided between two parties. One of these favored the direct rule of the colony by the sovereign, the other maintained the independent government of the province by its own legislature under the constitution granted to it. The debates between these factions greatly annoyed the king, who could never tolerate the expression of an independent opinion by any of his subjects. He endeavored in various ways to silence these disputes, and to regain the powers he had relinquished to the company, but the latter firmly refused to surrender their charter, and the colonists, who feared that the king might seek to impose his own arbitrary will upon them in the place of their constitution and the laws of England, sustained the company in its refusal. In spite of this opposition, however, James carried his point. The charter of the company was revoked, and Virginia was made a royal province. The company appealed to the courts, but these being under the influence of the crown sustained the king. Their decision was rendered in June, 1624. James did not interfere with any of the liberties or privileges of Virginia, however. Sir Francis Wyatt was retained in his office of governor, and the colony was left under the laws and in possession of the privileges secured to it in 1621. James announced his intention to prepare a code of laws for the government of Virginia, but fortunately for that province he died before he could execute his design.

Charles I succeeded his father on the English throne on the 27th of March, 1625. He was favorably disposed toward the colony, for he did not suppose the principles of civil liberty had taken so deep a root in it, and, moreover, he wished to secure for the crown the monopoly of the tobacco trade. He carried his condescension to the extent of recognizing the house of burgesses as a legislative body and requesting it to pass a bill restricting the sales of tobacco to the crown. The house answered him respectfully, but firmly, that to grant his majesty's request would be to injure the trade of the colony. Defeated in this effort to secure th s monopoly the king continued throughout his reign to seek to get the tobacco trade into his hands. He declared London to be the sole market for the sale of tobacco, and endeavored in many ways, and in vain, to regulate the trade.

In the meantime Sir Francis Wyatt retired from the government of the colony, and Sir George Yeardley was appointed his successor, in 1626. The latter died the next year, and Francis West was elected governor by the council until the pleasure of the king should be known. Upon the receipt in England of the news of Yeardley's death, Charles appointed Sir John Harvey governor of Virginia. At the same time he granted to the council in Virginia authority to fill all vacancies occurring in their body. Previous to the arrival of Harvey, West was succeeded by another governor, named Pott, elected by the council.

Harvey reached Virginia late in the autumn of 1629, and remained in office until 1639. He was greatly disliked, and his failure to enforce the claims of Virginia against the colony of Maryland, which was planted in 1634 upon territory embraced within the original grant to Virginia, made him still more unpopular. In 1635 he was removed from office by the council, and an appeal was made to the king by both Harvey and the council. Harvey returned to England to manage his case, and John West was appointed governor until the decision of the case by the king. Harvey succeeded in defeating his opponents, who were not even allowed a hearing in England, and returned to Virginia in January, 1636, and resumed his place as governor. The complaints against him we e so numerous, that in 1639 he was removed by the king, who appointed Sir Francis Wyatt his successor. In 1641 Wyatt was succeeded by Sir William Berkeley, who reached Jamestown in 1642. In the spring of this year, an effort was made to revive the London Company, but Virginia, which was now a royal province, opposed the measure, and urged the king to allow her to remain in the exercise of the self-government which had contributed in so marked a degree to her prosperity. The king, impressed with the force of the arguments by which this appeal was sustained, declared his intention to make no change in the colonial government.

Berkeley, during his first administration, proved in the main a good governor, and the colony continued to improve. The courts of justice were brought as near as possible to the English standard, and the titles to lands were arranged upon a more satisfactory basis than had hitherto been found possible. Taxes were assessed according to the wealth of the settlers, and a treaty was arranged with Maryland by which the vexed questions between the two colonies were satisfactorily adjusted. The Virginians, accustomed to freedom, were in all things, save their acknowledgment of the king's supremacy, a practically independent nation, so little were they interfered with by the sovereign. The colony was devoted to the established church of England, and even at this early day there were severe laws for the enforcement of conformity to its rules, and for the punishment of dissenters. When Puritan ministers came from New England into the colony in 1643, they were banished by the colonial government, notwithstanding they had been invited into Virginia by the Puritan settlements in that province. The majority of the Virginians, with the governor at their head, were royalists and staunch friends of the king. The Puritans living in the colony were regarded with suspicion, and when they refused to conform to the established church, it was ordered that they should be banished. Many of them passed over into Maryland and settled there. With the exception of this harmless bigotry, the colony took no share in the great quarrel which was rending the mother country in twain. It was rather a gainer by it, as the troubles which encompassed Charles I. compelled him to cease his efforts to interfere with the trade of the planters.

The chief trouble of this period was with the Indians. There had been no peace with them since the massacre of 1622, but frequent expeditions had been sent against them. In 1644, the savages, led by their veteran chieftain Opechancanough, resolved to make one more effort to exterminate the whites, forgetting that in the twenty years that elapsed their enemies had grown stronger, while they had grown weaker. On the 18th of April the frontier settlements were attacked, and three hundred of the settlers were put to death. The whites at once inaugurated vigorous measures for their defence, and a sharp warfare was waged upon the savages until October, 1646. It was brought to a close by the capture of Opechancanough, who was so decrepit that he was unable to walk, and was carried about in the arms of his people. His flesh was emaciated, the sinews so relaxed, and his eyelids so heavy that whenever he desired to see they were lifted by his attendants. Yet still the vigor of his intellect remained to him, and he was to the last both feared by his enemies and loved by his people. Berkeley, having taken him prisoner, exposed him to the rude gaze of the colonists, an indignity which stung the proud monarch of the forest to the heart. On one occasion, hearing that the governor was approaching, he caused his eyelids to be raised, and fixing upon his captor a look of stern rebuke, said to him, "If Sir William Berkeley had become my prisoner, I should not thus meanly have exposed him as a show to my people." A few days later, Opechancanough was basely assassinated by one of the colonists charged with the duty of guarding him. Thus perished one of the greatest of the native chieftains of America. In October, 1646, Necotowance, the successor of Opechancanough entered into a treaty with the colony, by which he and his people relinquished to the English the lands that had been the heritage of their fathers, and withdrew into the interior. Their power was completely broken, and submission was all that was left to them.

Virginia was now on the high road to prosperity. The population at the close of the year 1648 numbered twenty thousand, and was increasing rapidly. A fair trade had been built up with other countries, and at Christmas of this year "there were trading in Virginia ten ships from London, two from Bristol, twelve Hollanders, and seven from New England." The quarrels of the mother country had not affected the colony, though a thrill of horror and indignation ran through all Virginia when the news was received of the execution of Charles I. Upon the fall of that monarch a large number of the royalist party in England, unwilling to submit to or make any compromise with the Parliament, fled to Virginia, and were received there with sympathizing hospitality by the government and people. Many of them made the colony their permanent home, and thus began the pleasant relations between Virginia and England, which have in numerous cases remained unbroken. The Virginians regarded Charles II., then an exile at Breda, as their rightful sovereign, and it was seriously proposed to him to come over to America and be king of Virginia. Charles' interests obliged him to remain in Europe, but he continued to regard himself as king of Virginia. From this circumstance Virginia came to be called "The Old Dominion."

The Parliament, however, did not long suffer the colony to maintain this attitude. Having triumphed over all its enemies in Europe it prepared to enforce its authority in America. In 1650 an ordinance was passed forbidding all intercourse with the colonies that had adhered to the Stuarts, except by the especial permission of Parliament or the Council of State. In the spring of 1652 more energetic measures were put in force, and a fleet was despatched to America to compel the submission of the colonies. The fleet arrived off Jamestown. No resistance was attempted, for the commissioners appointed by the commonwealth were instructed to grant terms honorable to both parties. The Virginians were prepared to resist any attempt to force them into submission, but they were disarmed by the liberal spirit with which the commonwealth met them, and a treaty was concluded between England and Virginia, as equal treating with equal. It was stipulated:

"First. That this should be considered a voluntary act, not forced or constrained by a conquest upon the country, and that the colony should have and enjoy such freedoms and privileges as belong to the freeborn people of England

"Secondly That the grand assembly, as formerly, should convene and transact the affairs of Virginia, doing nothing contrary to the government of the commonwealth or laws of England

' Thirdly. That there should be a full and total remission of all acts, words, or writings against the Parliament

"Fourthly. That Virginia should have her ancient bounds and limits, granted by the charters of the former kings, and that a new charter was to be sought from Parliament to that effect, against such as had trespassed against their ancient rights.

"Fifthly. That all patents of land under the seal of the colony, granted by the governor, should remain in full force.

"Sixthly That the privilege of fifty acres of land for every person emigrating to the colony should remain in full force.

"Seventhly That the people of Virginia have free trade, as the people of England enjoy, with all places and nations, according to the laws of the commonwealth; and that Virginia should enjoy equal privileges, in every respect, with any other colony in America.

"Eighthly. That Virginia should be free from all taxes, customs, and impositions whatsoever; and that none should be imposed upon them without the consent of their grand assembly, and no forts or castles be erected, or garrison maintained, without their consent

"Ninthly That no charge should be required from the country on account of the expense incurred in the present fleet.

"Tenthly. That this agreement should be tendered to all persons, and that such as should refuse to subscribe to it should have a year's time to remove themselves and effects from Virginia, and in the meantime enjoy equal justice "

"These terms," says Bancroft, "so favorable to liberty, and almost conceding independence, were faithfully observed until the restoration Historians have, indeed, drawn gloomy pictures of the discontent which pervaded the colony, and have represented the discontent as heightened by commercial oppression. The statement is a fiction. The colony of Virginia enjoyed liberties as large as the favored New England, displayed an equal degree of fondness for popular sovereignty, and fearlessly exercised political independence."

Richard Bennett, one of the commissioners, was chosen governor in the place of Berkeley. Until now it had been customary for the governor and council to sit in the assembly, and take part in the debates. Objection was now made to their presence, and the matter was compromised by obliging them to take the oath required of the burgesses. During the protectorate Cromwell wisely let the colony alone. He appointed none of the governors, and never interfered with the management of its affairs. In 1658, Samuel Mathews being governor, the assembly, on the 1st of April, passed a law excluding the governor and council from their sessions, and thus secured to themselves a free and uninterrupted discussion of their measures. The governor and council in return declared the assembly dissolved, but that body vindicated its authority and independence by removing the governor and council, and compelled them to submit. They were then reelected to their respective positions. Thus did the spirit of popular liberty establish all its claims.

Upon the death of Cromwell, the house of burgesses met in secret session and decided to recognize Richard Cromwell as protector. "It was a more interesting question whether the change of protector in England would endanger liberty in Virginia. The letter from the council had left the government to be administered according to former usage. The assembly declared itself satisfied with the language. But that there might be no reason to question the existing usage, the governor was summoned to come to the house, where he appeared in person, deliberately acknowledged the supreme power of electing officers to be, by the present laws, resident in the assembly, and pledged himself to join in addressing the new protector for special confirmation of all existing privileges. The reason for this extraordinary proceeding is assigned, 'that what was their privilege now, might be the privilege of their posterity.' The frame of the Virginia government was deemed worthy of being transmitted to remote generations." [*]

Governor Mathews died in March, 1660, about the time of the resignation of Richard Cromwell in England. Both the mother country and the colony were thus left without a government. In this emergency the general assembly of Virginia resolved "that the supreme government of this country shall be resident in the assembly, and all writs shall issue in its name, until there shall arrive from England a commission, which the assembly itself shall adjudge to be lawful." The assembly had no thought of asserting its independence of England, but as it cherished the earnest hope that the king would be restored to his rights, it proceeded to fill the vacancy occasioned by the death of Governor Mathews by electing Sir William Berkeley, the devoted partisan of the Stuarts, governor of Virginia. Berkeley accepted the office, acknowledged the validity of the acts of the assembly, and expressed his conviction that he could in no event dissolve that body. "I am," said he, "but the servant of the assembly." We shall see in the course of this narrative how he regarded this promise in the light of subsequent events.

History of the United States. By Geo. Bancroft vol. i, p. 228

CHAPTER VIII

VIRGINIA AFTER THE RESTORATION.

Characteristics of the Virginians—Causes of the Success of the Royalists—Growth of the Aristocratic Class—Berkeley decides against the People—The Aristocratic Assembly Claims the Right to sit Perpetually—Deprives the Common People of their Liberties—Revival of the Navigation Act by Charles II.—The King bestows Virginia as a Gift upon his Favorites—Protests of the Assembly—Growing Hostility of the Virginians to the Colonial Government—The Indian War—The Governor Refuses to allow the Colonists to Defend themselves—Nathaniel Bacon—He Marches against the Indians—Rebellion of the People against Berkeley and the Assembly—The Convention—Repeal of the Obnoxious Laws—Berkeley's Duplicity—The People take up Arms—Flight of Berkeley—Destruction of Jamestown—Death of Bacon—Causes of the Failure of the Rebellion—Berkeley's Triumph—Execution of the Patriot Leaders—Berkeley's Course Condemned by the King—Death of Berkeley—The Unjust Laws Re-enacted—Lord Culpepper Governor—His Extortions—James II. and Virginia—Effects upon Virginia of the Revolution of 1688—William and Mary College Founded.

 N the 8th of May, 1660, Charles II. was proclaimed king in England, and on the 29th made his entry into London. The rebellion and the commonwealth had produced but little effect upon Virginia. The restoration was productive of the most momentous consequences in the colony. During the long period of the commonwealth Virginia had been practically independent. The people had acquired political rights, and had exercised them with prudence. The colony had prospered in a marked degree under the blessings of popular government, and the rights of the people were jealously guarded by their legislators. "No trace of established privilege appeared in its code or its government: in its forms and in its legislation Virginia was a representative democracy; so jealous of a landed aristocracy that it rested on universality of suffrage; so hostile to the influence of commercial wealth, that it would not tolerate the 'mercenary' ministers of the law, so considerate for religious freedom, that each parish was left to take care of itself. Every officer was, directly or indirectly, chosen by the people." * The restoration was to change all this.

* Bancroft's *History of the United States*, vol. 1. p. 193.

L-1

The society of Virginia was peculiar. The colony had been settled by adventurers under circumstances which compelled equality among all classes of its people. Thus there had grown up a strong population born to the enjoyment of this equality, and devoted to its maintenance. They constituted the bulk of the inhabitants. By degrees there had sprung up a colonial aristocracy composed of the large landholders. These were persons of culture, many of whom had been men of position and education in England. The laws favored the accumulation of large estates, and the possession of them awakened feelings of family pride. The large emigration of men of rank and culture at the overthrow of Charles I. greatly increased this class. The existence of an established church gave it another element of strength, since the interests of the state church and the aristocracy are always identical. Education was almost entirely confined to the landholding class, and with this never-failing weapon in their grasp they soon obtained the direction of the affairs of the colony, and retained it. Unfortunately for Virginia, the mass of the people had no means of acquiring knowledge. There were no common schools in the colony. In 1671, Sir William Berkeley wrote. "Every man instructs his children according to his ability" He added. "I thank God there are no free schools nor printing, and I hope we shall not have these hundred years, for learning has brought disobedience and heresy and sects into the world, and printing has divulged them and libels against the best government. God keep us from both!" Thus were the common people doomed to hopeless ignorance, and left helpless and at the mercy of the smaller but educated class. There was no printing press in Virginia, and the colony remained without one until nearly a century after New England had enjoyed its benefits. Bitterly did the people of Virginia atone for their neglect of their best interests. They had shown at the first the power of creating free institutions, but these institutions cannot be preserved among an ignorant people. Freedom and intelligence go hand in hand. The institution of negro slavery was another element of weakness and degradation. Labor was debased in the eyes of the whites by being made the task of a slave, when it should have been the glory of a freeman. The institution served to confirm the power of the landed aristocracy, while it sank the common people deeper into ignorance.

Thus when Sir William Berkeley entered upon his second term of office, at the period of the restoration, there were two elements, by nature hostile to each other, contending for the control of the colony—a people eager for the enjoyment of popular liberty, but sinking deeper into ignorance and helplessness, and a rising aristocracy, composed of men of wealth and education, and united by a common interest. Unhappily for the people, the governor was a natural aristocrat. In spite of his professions of loyalty to the assembly, he regarded the people with contempt, and could never tolerate the exercise of the least of their rights.

In the midst of the rejoicings in Virginia which hailed the return of Charles II. to the throne of his fathers, Berkeley took a decisive stand, and boldly declared that he was governor of Virginia, not by the election of the assembly, but by virtue of his commission from the king. At the

DESTRUCTION OF THE VIRGINIA SETTLEMENTS BY THE INDIANS.

same time he issued writs for the election of a new assembly in the name of King Charles. Popular sovereignty was struck dead in Virginia. The new assembly met in March, 1661. It was composed exclusively of landholders. Until now the assembly had been elected for but a single year, and its members were chosen by the people. This first aristocratic assembly, true to its instincts, at a blow deprived the people of the right of choosing their representatives, by assuming to itself the power to sit perpetually. Sustained by the governor, the burgesses were enabled to continue their usurpation for fourteen years, and only yielded to an insurrection The salaries of the members were paid by their respective counties, and the house, in 1662, passed a law regulating the pay and allowances of its members. The compensation was fixed at two hundred and fifty pounds of tobacco per day, or about nine dollars—a rate deemed enormous in these days of abundant wealth, and utterly unsuited to the period of poverty and struggle we are considering. In order to perpetuate its power, the assembly repealed the laws giving the right of suffrage to every citizen, and confined it to freeholders and housekeepers.

Nor did the assembly neglect to provide for the church. Conformity was required by severe laws. Every inhabitant of the colony was compelled to attend its services and to contribute a fixed sum to its support. The assessment of parish taxes was intrusted to twelve vestrymen in each parish, who had power to fill all vacancies in their number. They thus became practically a close corporation, responsible to no one for their acts Rigorous laws were directed against the Quakers. They were forbidden to hold their own religious assemblies, and their absence from church was punished by a heavy fine. In September, 1663, the house expelled one of its members "because he was well affected to the Quakers."

"The organization of the judiciary placed that department of the government almost beyond the control of the people' The governor and council were the highest ordinary tribunal, and these were all appointed, directly or indirectly, by the crown. Besides this, there were in each county eight unpaid justices of the peace, commissioned by the governor during his pleasure These justices held monthly courts in their respective counties. Thus the administration of justice in the court es was in the hands of persons holding their offices at the good will of the governor; while the governor himself and his executive council constituted the general court, and had cognizance of all sorts of causes. Was an appeal made to chancery, it was but for another hearing before the same men; and it was only for a few years longer that appeals were permitted from the general court to the assembly The place of sheriff in each county was conferred on one of the justices for that county, and so devolved to every commissioner in course . . . . But the county courts, thus independent of the people, possessed and exercised the arbitrary power of levying county taxes, which, in their amount, usually exceeded the public levy. This system proceeded so far that the commissioners, of themselves, levied taxes to meet their own expenses. In like manner, the self-perpetuating vestries made out their lists of tithables, and assessed taxes without regard to the consent of the parish.

These private levies were unequal and oppressive, were seldom—it is said, never—brought to audit, and were, in some cases at least, managed by men who combined to defraud the public." *

These were the effects upon Virginia of the restoration of Charles II. to the throne of England. The guarantee which a frequent renewal of the assembly secured to the rights of the people was removed by the perpetuation of that body. The right of suffrage—the sole protection of the liberties of a free people—was taken from a majority of the inhabitants of the province. Religious liberty, which it was fondly believed had been established, was struck down at a single blow. A system of arbitrary taxation by irresponsible magistrates was set up in the place of the carefully-scrutinized levies of the representatives of the people. Education was discouraged and the press regarded with hostility. Ignorance, with all its accompanying evils, was fastened upon the colony. Ten years sufficed to accomplish these changes; but it took more than a century for the people of Virginia to recover their lost rights.

Charles II remembered the loyalty of Virginia only in his adversity. One of his first acts was to revive in a more odious form the navigation act, which had originated in the Long Parliament as a measure for compelling the submission of the colonies to the authority of the commonwealth. In 1660, a new and enlarged navigation act was passed by Parliament. It forbade foreign vessels to trade with the colonies, and required colonists to ship certain "enumerated articles, such as sugar, tobacco, cotton, wool, ginger, or dyewoods" produced in the colony to England alone. This act bore very hard upon Virginia, as it gave to the English merchants the monopoly of her tobacco trade. The merchants were thus enabled to regulate the price of the commodity, and to supply the wants of the colonists in return upon their own terms. Efforts were made to evade this iniquitous law, but it remained fastened upon the colonies, and was the first of a long series of outrages by which Great Britain broke the ties which bound the people of America to her.

Charles was not satisfied with crippling the industry of the colony that had remained faithful to him in his adversity. In order to please his worthless favorites at home he consented to plunder the Virginians of their property. In 1649, a patent was granted to a company of cavaliers for the region lying between the Rappahannock and the Potomac, and known in Virginia as the Northern Neck. It was intended to make this region a refuge for their partisans, but the design was never carried out. Other settlers located themselves there, and in 1669 it contained a number of thriving plantations. In the latter year Lord Culpepper, one

* History of the United States By George Bancroft, vol. II., pp. 204 205.

of the most avaricious men in England, obtained from the king a patent for the Northern Neck, having previously acquired all the shares of the company to whom the grant of 1649 had been made. This patent was in direct violation of the rights of the actual settlers, and bore very hard upon them. But it was as nothing compared with the next gift of the king. In 1673, he bestowed, as a free gift, upon Lord Culpepper and the Earl of Arlington, "all the dominion of land and water, called Virginia," for a term of thirty-one years.

Even the aristocratic assembly was startled by this summary disposal of the colony and commissioners were sent to England to remonstrate with the king. "We are unwilling," the assembly declared, "and conceive that we ought not to submit to those to whom his majesty, upon misinformation, hath granted the dominion over us, who do most contentedly pay to his majesty more than we have ourselves for our labor. Whilst we labor for the advantage of the crown, and do wish we could be more advantageous to the king and nation, we humbly request not to be subjected to our fellow-subjects, but, for the future, to be secured from our fears of being enslaved." The commissioners were granted no satisfaction in England, and the efforts of the colony to obtain justice at the hands of the king failed.

Virginia at this time was a sparsely settled province. Jamestown was the only town deserving the name within the limits of the colony. The inhabitants were scattered over the country, separated from each other. They dwelt on their farms and plantations, coming together rarely except on Sundays, on court-days, and at elections. This solitary life taught them independence and self-reliance. They were proud of their personal liberty, and so long as this was not taken from them they were willing to submit to almost any form of government that might be imposed upon them. The truth is that until the restoration the Virginians were not accustomed to being governed much. The measures of the royalist governor and assembly greatly curtailed the freedom which the people had enjoyed under their former governments, and the imposition of new burdens upon them aroused a general discontent. Men began to come together to discuss their wrongs, and the hostility to the aristocratic party and the governor increased rapidly, so rapidly, indeed, that the people were ripe for insurrection in 1674, and would have risen in revolt had not some of the cooler heads induced them to try more peaceful measures of redress. Still the taxes were continued at such a rate that the colonists were driven to desperation. They complained, with justice, that they were deprived of all the fruits of their labors by the iniquitous levies made upon them, and their complaints, instead of producing a change for the better, merely brought an increase of their burdens. At length their patience was exhausted, and they only lacked an excuse for taking up arms The opportunity soon came. In the meantime the governor and the assembly, with characteristic contempt for the commons, went on extorting money from the people by unjust taxes principally for their own benefit, and put in successive operation the measures we have already described for strengthening their own power, and reducing the people to subjection to them.

The people of Maryland had become involved in a war with the Susquehannah Indians and their confederates, and the struggle was so serious that the savages extended their depredations to the Potomac, and even to the limits of Virginia. To guard against this danger the border militia were set to watch the line of the river, and in 1675 a body of them, under Colonel John Washington, crossed over into Maryland to help the people of that colony. This John Washington had emigrated from the north of England about eighteen years before, and had settled in Westmoreland county He became the great-grandfather of George Washington The war was conducted with great fury on both sides. Six of the chiefs of the Susquehannah tribe at length came into the camp of the Virginians to treat for peace, and were treacherously murdered. This barbarous act aroused the indignation of Governor Berkeley. "If they had killed my father and my mother, and all my friends," said he, "yet if they had come to treat of peace, they ought to have gone in peace " The massacre was bloodily avenged by the Indians. The Susquehannahs immediately crossed the Potomac and waged a relentless warfare along the borders of Virginia until they had slain ten whites for each one of their chiefs, a sacrifice required of them by the customs of their tribe, in order that the spirits of their braves might rest in peace. The people appealed to the governor for protection, but Berkeley refused to grant them aid. It is said that he was too deeply interested in the fur trade to be willing to offend the Indians by aiding his people. The colonists then demanded permission to defend themselves, to invade the Indian country, and drive the savages farther into the interior This was also refused, and during all this time the frontier was suffering fearfully from the outrages of Berkeley's Indian friends.

At last the patience of the people was exhausted. A leader was at hand in the person of Nathaniel Bacon. He was a young planter of the county of Henrico, a native of England, and a lawyer by profession. He was ardent in temper, eloquent and persuasive in speech, winning in manner, a true patriot, and possessed of the firmness and decision necessary in a leader of a popular movement. He had been reared in England amid the struggles which ushered in the establishment of the commonwealth, and had learned the lesson of freedom too well to forget it in a home where every incident of his daily life required the exercise of the best qualities of his nature. His love of republicanism had gained him the dislike of Governor Berkeley, who hated any man that dared to criticise his tyranny. The same principles which made him obnoxious to the governor won him the affectionate confidence of the people of Virginia, who were quick to recognize their true friend. When volunteers began to offer themselves for the war against the Indians they petitioned the governor to commission Bacon their commander-in-chief. This Berkeley refused, declaring that he would not countenance such presumption on the part of the "common people." In the meantime the murders continued, and Bacon, who shared the indignation of the people, determined that if another man was slain he would march the militia against the Indians without a commission. Almost immediately several of his own men were murdered on his own plantation near the falls of the James. He at once gave the signal. Five hundred men were soon under arms, and Bacon was made their leader. About the 20th of April, 1676, he set out on his march against the savages, whom he chastised and drove back into the interior.

The people were in arms, and they were not disposed to lay down their weapons until their grievances were redressed. The quarrel was not with the Indians, but with the government. As soon as Bacon had begun his march into the Indian country, Berkeley denounced him as a traitor, and his followers as rebels, and ordered them to disperse. He was obeyed by some who feared the loss of their property, but the populous counties bordering the bay answered him by joining the insurrection. The people of the colony with one voice demanded the dissolution of the assembly, which had unlawfully maintained its existence for fourteen years. Opposed by the entire people the governor was compelled to yield. The assembly had fairly earned the universal hatred with which it was regarded by its selfishness and its hostility to popular liberty. It was dissolved, and writs were issued for a new election. Among the new members elected was Bacon, who was returned from the county of Henrico.

The new assembly was naturally favorable to the rights of the people, and it at once proceeded to rectify many of the abuses which had produced the insurrection. Taxes were adjusted more equitably; the right of suffrage was restored to the people; the monopoly of the Indian trade, in which it was believed the governor was deeply interested, was suspended; many of the evils connected with the expenditure of the public funds were corrected; the power of the parish vestries was broken by limiting their term of office to three years, and giving the election of these officials to the freemen of the parish, a general amnesty was proclaimed for all past offences, and Bacon, amid the rejoicings of the people, was elected commander of the army destined to act against the Indians.

These measures were utterly distasteful to the haughty old governor. He refused to give them his sanction, or to sign the commission ordered for Bacon by the assembly. Fearful of treachery Bacon withdrew from the capital. The people quickly rallied to his support, and in a few days he entered Jamestown at the head of five hundred men. Berkeley, who was as courageous as he was obstinate, met him, and baring his breast said, haughtily, "A fair mark; shoot!" Bacon answered him calmly, "I will not hurt a hair of your head, or of any man's; we are come for the commission to save our lives from the Indians." The governor was at length obliged to yield. The commission was issued, the acts of the assembly were ratified, and Berkeley joined the assembly and council in sending to England an indorsement of the loyalty, patriotism, and energy of Bacon. This consent was given on the 24th of June, or, according to the new style of calculation, at present in use, on the 4th of July, 1676, just one hundred years before the Declaration of Independence.

Bacon at once marched against the Indians, and in a brilliant and successful campaign broke their power, and gave peace and security to the frontier. In the midst of these honorable labors he was again assailed by Berkeley, who had only consented to the reconciliation to gain time. The governor withdrew from Jamestown to Gloucester, which was the most populous and the most loyal county of Virginia. He summoned a convention of the inhabitants, and renewed his efforts against Bacon. The people of Gloucester, justly regarding Bacon as the defender of the colony, opposed the governor's proposals, but he persisted in spite of their advice, and again proclaimed Bacon a traitor.

This inexcusable pursuit of a man who had rendered nothing but good service to the colony aroused the indignation of the troops. "It vexes me to the heart," said Bacon, "that while I am hunting the wolves and tigers that destroy our lambs I should myself be pursued as a savage. Shall persons wholly devoted to their king and country—men hazarding their lives against the public enemy—deserve the appellation of rebels and traitors? The whole country is witness to our peaceable behavior. But those in authority, how have they obtained their estates? Have they not devoured the common treasury? What arts, what sciences, what schools of learning, have they promoted? I appeal to the king and Parliament, where the cause of the people will be heard impartially."

9

Bacon appealed to the people of Virginia to unite for the defence of their liberties against the tyranny of the governor. They responded to this call with enthusiasm, and a convention of the most eminent men in the colony assembled at Middle Plantations, now Williamsburg, on the 3d of August, 1676. It was resolved by the convention to sustain Bacon with the whole power of the colony in the campaign against the Indians. If the governor persisted in his attempt to hunt him as a traitor, the members of the convention pledged themselves to defend Bacon with arms, even against the royal troops, until an appeal could be made to the

RUINED CHURCH TOWER ON THE SITE OF JAMESTOWN.

king in person. The people of Virginia were fully resolved to protect themselves against the tyranny of Berkeley, and Bacon, strengthened by their indorsement of his course, finished his campaign against the Indians. Governor Berkeley withdrew across the bay to the eastern shore, and there collected a force of sailors belonging to some English vessels and a band of worthless Indians. With this force, "men of a base and cowardly disposition, allured by the passion for plunder," he prepared to return to Jamestown.

The people decided to regard the retreat of the governor as an abdication on his part of his office The ten years for which he had been appointed had expired, and the colonial records afforded a precedent for his removal. Bacon and four others, who had been members of the council, issued writs for the election of a representative convention to which the management of the affairs of the colony was to be committed. With the exception of a few royalists the whole people of Virginia indorsed the movement, the women were enthusiastic, and urged their husbands to risk everything, even life, in defence of their liberties

Early in September Sir William Berkeley reached Jamestown with the rabble which he called his army He took possession of the town without resistance, and was joined by a number of royalists He offered freedom to the slaves of the Virginians who were opposed to him on the condition of their joining his ranks Bacon and his party were again proclaimed traitors and rebels.

The people at once flew to arms, and Bacon soon found himself at the head of the little army that had been so successful against the Indians. Without delay they marched to Jamestown. The resistance attempted by Berkeley's cowardly followers was feeble, and the whole force, including their leader, retreated to their ships, and dropped down the river by night. The next morning the army of the people entered Jamestown. It was rumored that a party of royalists was marching from the northern counties to the support of Berkeley, and a council was held to decide upon the fate of the capital It was agreed that it should be burned to prevent it from being used as a stronghold for their enemies The torch was applied; Drummond and Lawrence, leaders of the popular party, set fire to their dwellings with their own hands, and in a few hours only a heap of smouldering ruins marked the site of the first capital of Virginia Its destruction left the colony without a single town within its limits

From the ruins of Jamestown Bacon marched promptly to meet the royalist force advancing from the Rappahannock region. The latter in a body joined the army of the people, and even the county of Gloucester, the stronghold of royalty, gave its adhesion to the patriotic movement. With the exception of the eastern shore the entire colony was united in support of the cause of popular liberty. Unhappily, at this critical juncture, Bacon was seized with a fatal fever, of which he died on the 1st of October, 1676. His followers grieved for him with passionate sorrow, and with good cause. It has been the good fortune of Virginia to give many great names to the cause of liberty, but in all the immortal roll there are none who surpassed Nathaniel Bacon in pure and disinterested patriotism. Others were permitted to accomplish more, but none cherished loftier aims or desired more earnestly the good of their fellow-citizens

The death of Bacon left the popular party without a head; and now began to be seen for the first time in Virginia the evils which the neglect of education must produce in a community. The Virginians were not lacking in courage, determination, or devotion to their liberties, and their cause was one calculated to succeed without leaders. In an educated community there would have been no lack of union or perseverance because of the death of one man, and the people would have found the means to continue their struggle until successful. In the uneducated Virginian community of 1676 the presence of a bold, capable, and resolute leader was a necessity, and his sudden removal left the popular party helpless. The grand struggle degenerated into a series of petty insurrections, the royalists took heart, and Robert Beverley, their most competent leader, was able to destroy in detail the resistance of the patriots and to restore the supremacy of Berkeley.

The governor now proceeded to take a summary vengeance upon the patriots, and more than twenty of the best men of the colony gave their lives on the scaffold for the liberties of their country. The first of these martyrs for freedom — the first American to die for the right of the people to govern themselves — was Thomas Hansford, a Virginian born, and a noble specimen of the chivalrous sons of the Old Dominion. The wife of Edmund Cheesman, upon the capture of her husband, flung herself at the governor's feet, and declaring that her exhortations had induced her husband to join Bacon, begged to be allowed to die in his place. The brutal Berkeley repelled the heroic woman with a gross insult. When Drummond was taken and brought before him the governor received him with mock courtesy. " I am more glad to see you," he said, " than any man in Virginia; you shall be hanged in half an hour." The royalist assembly, horrified at the cruelty of the governor, appealed to him to "spill no more blood." The property of the victims was confiscated, and their helpless families were turned out upon the charities of the people for whom the martyrs had died. Not content with these cruelties Berkeley attempted to silence the people, and prevent them from either censuring him or vindicating the memory of their dead heroes. Whoever should speak ill of Berkeley or his friends was to be whipped.

At last the end came, and Berkeley returned to England. His departure was celebrated with rejoicings throughout the colony; bells were rung, guns were fired, and bonfires blazed. Berkeley hoped to be able to justify his conduct in England, but upon his arrival in that country he found his course sternly condemned by the voice of public opinion. Even Charles II. censured him with all the energy that scallous monarch was master of " "The old fool," said the king, "has taken away more lives in that naked land than I for the murder of my father." His disappointment and mortification were too much for the proud man, and he died soon after his arrival in England

The failure of Bacon's rebellion brought many serious misfortunes to Virginia The insurrection was made the excuse by the king for refusing a liberal charter, and the colony was made dependent for its rights and privileges entirely upon the royal will. The assembly was composed almost exclusively of royalists, and at once proceeded to undo the work of the popular party. All the laws of Bacon's assembly were repealed, the right of suffrage was restricted to freeholders, and the iniquitous taxes were reimposed. All the abuses that had led to the rebellion were revived.

In 1677 Lord Culpepper, one of the favorites to whom Charles II. had granted Virginia, was appointed governor of the colony for life The new governor regarded his office as a sinecure, and while receiving its emoluments desired to remain in England to enjoy them In 1680, however, the king compelled him to repair to his government in person. He brought with him authority from the sovereign to settle all past grievances, but he used this power for his own profit. He extorted money from all parties, and when he had acquired a considerable sum returned to England, having spent less than a year in Virginia He left the colony in the greatest distress. The Virginians, robbed of the profits of their labors for the enrichment of their rulers, were reduced to despair Riots took place in various places, and the whole colony was on the verge of insurrection.

Rumors of these disturbances having reached England the king ordered Culpepper to return and reduce the colony to obedience He did so, and caused several influential men to be hanged as traitors, and used the power intrusted to him to wrest from the council the last remnant of its authority to control his outrages upon the people This accomplished he proceeded to force the settlers of the Northern Neck to surrender their plantations to him, or pay him the sums he demanded for the privilege of retaining them He found his residence among a people he had come to plunder very disagreeable, and in the course of a few months returned to England amid the bitter curses of the Virginians. The council reported the distress of the province to the king, and appealed to him to recall the grant to Culpepper and Arlington Arlington surrendered his rights to Culpepper, whose patent was rendered void by a process of law, and in July, 1684, Virginia became once more a royal province. Lord Howard, of Effingham, was appointed to succeed Culpepper, but he was a poorer and more grasping man than his predecessor, and the change afforded no relief to Virginia.

In 1685 James II came to the throne of England, and in the same year occurred the insurrection in England known as Monmouth's rebellion. A number of prisoners were taken in this struggle by the royal forces, and many of these were sent out to the colonies of Virginia and Maryland to be sold as servants for a term of ten years. Many of them were men of education and family. The general assembly of Virginia refused to sanction this infamous measure, and, in spite of the prohibition of King James, passed a law declaring all such persons free. Indeed at this time the practice of selling white servants in America had become so profitable that quite a thriving business was carried on between the west of England and Virginia and Maryland. Not only persons condemned for crime, but innocent people were kidnapped and sold in the colonies for a term of years for money. "At Bristol," says Bancroft, "the mayor and justices would intimidate small rogues and pilferers, who, under the terror of being hanged, prayed for transportation as the only avenue to safety, and were then divided among the members of the court. The trade was exceedingly profitable—far more so than the slave-trade—and had been conducted for years."

One of the last acts of Charles II with reference to Virginia was to forbid the setting up of a printing press within the limits of the colony. James II continued this prohibition. Effingham endeavored to take from the colony the few privileges left to it. The result was that the party of freedom increased rapidly. Many of the aristocratic party seeing that the king and the governor menaced every right and privilege they possessed went over to the popular side. The assembly began to assert the popular demand for self-government, and became so unmanageable that in November, 1686, it was dissolved by royal proclamation. A new assembly was convened, which met in April, 1688, a few months before the British revolution. The governor and council found this body more indisposed to submit to the aggressions of the crown than its predecessor had been. The people sustained their delegates, and a new insurrection was threatened. Effingham was in the midst of a hostile population, without troops to enforce his will, and was obliged to conduct himself with moderation. The royal authority was never stronger in Virginia than during this reign, but it was found impossible to establish it upon the ruins of the liberties of the colony. The result of all the long years of oppression we have been considering was simply to confirm the Virginians in their attachment to their liberties, and in their determination to maintain them at any cost. Virginia remained to the end an aristocratic colony, but it was none the less "a land of liberty."

The revolution of 1688 in England did not change affairs in Virginia materially as regarded the forms of the colonial government. The liberties of the colony were established by law too securely to be any longer at the mercy of an individual, but the power of the governor was still very great. Every department of the colonial administration, the finances, and even the management of the church, was made subject to his control. He had the power to dissolve the assembly at pleasure, and was sure to exercise it if that body manifested too great a spirit of independence. He also appointed the clerk of the assembly, who was for this reason a check upon its freedom of debate. The only means of resistance to the measures of the government which the assembly retained was to refuse to vote supplies in excess of the permanent revenue. This right was sometimes exercised, and the governor was prevented from carrying out unpopular measures by the lack of the necessary funds.

Soon after the accession of William and Mary to the throne an effort was made to establish a college in Virginia, although the printing press was still forbidden. Donations were made by a number of persons in England, and the king bestowed several liberal grants upon the proposed institution. The measure was carried through to success by the energy of the Rev. James Blair, who was sent out by the Bishop of London as commissary, " to supply the office and jurisdiction of the bishop in the outplaces of the diocese." The college was established in 1691, and was named William and Mary, in honor of the king and queen. Mr. Blair was its first president, and held that office for fifty years.

The ministry did not approve the action of the king in granting even the very moderate endowments which he bestowed upon the college. They regarded Virginia merely as a place in which to raise tobacco for the English market, and cared nothing for the interests of the people. They treated the colony with injustice and neglect in everything. The planters could sell their tobacco only to an English purchaser, who regulated the price to suit himself, and supplied the planters in return with the wares they needed at his own prices.

CHAPTER IX.

THE COLONIZATION OF MARYLAND.

THE second charter of Virginia granted to that province the country north of the Potomac as far as the headwaters of the Chesapeake bay. This grant included the territory of the present State of Maryland. The discoveries of Captain John Smith had brought the region along the head of the bay into notice, and other explorers had confirmed his statements as to its value. A very profitable trade was established with the Indians of this section, and, in order to develop its advantages, William Clayborne, a man of great resolution and of no mean abilities, a surveyor by profession, was employed by the Governor of Virginia to explore the region of the upper Chesapeake. His report was so favorable that a company was formed in England for the purpose of trading with the Indians. Under authority from this company, Clayborne obtained a license from the colonial government of Virginia, and established two trading stations on the bay, one on Kent island, opposite the present city of Annapolis, and one at the mouth of the Susquehanna. These posts were established in the spring of 1631.

In the meantime efforts were being made in England to secure the settlement of the same region. Sir George Calvert, a man of noble character, liberal education and great political experience, had become at an early day deeply interested in the question of colonizing America. Having embraced the Roman Catholic faith he relinquished his office of

Secretary of State, and made a public acknowledgment of his conversion. His noble character commanded the confidence of King James, and he was retained as a member of the Privy Council, and was made Lord Baltimore in the Irish peerage. He was anxious to found a colony in America, which might serve as a place of refuge for persons of the Catholic faith, and obtained a patent for the southern part of Newfoundland. That region was too bleak and rugged to admit of the success of the enterprise, and the attempt to settle it was soon abandoned.

Lord Baltimore next contemplated a settlement in some portion of Virginia, and in October, 1629, visited that colony with a view to making arrangements for his plantation. The laws of Virginia against Roman Catholics were very severe, and immediately upon the arrival of so distinguished a Catholic the assembly ordered the oaths of allegiance and supremacy to be tendered him. Lord Baltimore proposed a form which he was willing to subscribe, but the colonial government insisted upon that which had been ordered by the English Parliament, and which was

of such a character that no Catholic could accept it. There was nothing left for Calvert but to withdraw from Virginia, and his reception there convinced him that that province was not the place for the plantation he wished to establish.

COAT OF ARMS OF MARYLAND.

The region north of the Potomac was still uninhabited, and seemed to promise advantages equal to Virginia. Calvert applied to Charles I. for a patent for this region, and was given a territory corresponding very nearly to the present State of Maryland in extent. The king granted him a liberal charter, which, while it provided for his interests as proprietor, secured the liberties of the colonists. In this it was simply the expression of the wishes of Lord Baltimore, who desired to establish a settlement of freemen. The country embraced in the grant was given to Lord Baltimore, his heirs and assigns, in absolute possession. They were required to pay an annual tribute to the crown of two Indian arrows and one-fifth of all the gold and silver which might be found. The colonists were to have a voice in making their own laws, and they were to be entitled to all the rights and privileges of Englishmen. No taxes were to be imposed upon them without their consent, nor was the authority of the proprietor to extend to their lives or property. It was enjoined that the exercise of the faith and worship of the established Church of England should be protected in the colony, but no uniform

standard of faith or worship was imposed by the charter. The new
province was carefully separated from Virginia and made independent
of it. The colony was left free from the supervision of the crown, and
the proprietor was not obliged to obtain the royal assent to the appointments or legislation of his province. The king also renounced for
himself, his heirs and his successors, the right to tax the colony, thus
leaving it entirely free from English taxation.

These were vast powers to intrust to one man; but they were placed
in safe hands. The first Lord Baltimore was a man who hated tyranny
of all kinds, and who had carefully observed the effects of intolerance
and arbitrary rule upon the efforts that had already been made to establish successful colonies in America. He designed his colony as an
asylum in which men of all creeds could meet upon a common basis of a
faith in Jesus Christ, and his conviction that religious freedom is necessary to the success of a state confirmed in him his attachment to the

LORD BALTIMORE.

principles of civil liberty. He invited both
Protestants and Catholics to join him in his
enterprise, and adopted a form of government,
based upon popular representation, well calculated to secure them in the possession of all
their privileges. In honor of the queen of
Charles I., he named the region granted to him
Maryland. Before the patent was issued, Lord
Baltimore died, on the 15th of April, 1632,
leaving his son, Cecil, heir to his designs as
well as to his title. The charter granted to his
father was issued to him, and he proceeded at once to collect a colony for
the settlement of Maryland.

Lord Baltimore delegated the task of conducting the emigrants to
Maryland to his brother, Leonard Calvert. On Friday, November 22d,
1632, a company of 200, chiefly Roman Catholics of good birth, with
their families and servants, sailed from England in the "Ark" and the
"Dove," the former a ship of large burthen, the latter a small pinnace.
The voyage was made by way of the West Indies, and the Chesapeake
was not reached until the 24th of February, 1634. The ships anchored
off Old Point Comfort, and were visited by Sir John Harvey, Governor
of Virginia, who had been commanded by the king to welcome the new
colony with kindness.

Resting in Hampton roads for a few days, the emigrants ascended the
bay and entered the stately Potomac. Deeming it unsafe to plant his
first settlement high up the river, Calvert chose a site on a small

tributary of the Potomac, not far from its mouth. This stream, now known as the St. Mary's, he named the St. George's. An Indian village, called Yoacomoco, was selected as the site of the colony. The place was being deserted by the natives, who had suffered severely from the superior power of the Susquehannahs, and were removing farther into the interior for greater security. They readily sold their town and the surrounding lands to the English, and made with them a treaty of peace and friendship; and on the 27th of March, 1634, the colonists landed and laid the foundations of the town of St. Mary's.

A few days later, Sir John Harvey arrived from Virginia on a friendly visit. His orders from the king were to treat the settlers with friend-

MISSIONARY PREACHING TO THE INDIANS.

ship, and to aid them as far as lay in his power. About the same time the native chiefs came in to visit the colony, and were so well received that they established friendly relations with the settlers. The Indian women taught their English sisters how to make bread from the meal of the Indian corn, and the warriors instructed the Englishmen in their simple arts of the chase. The colonists obtained provisions and cattle for a while from Virginia; but, as they went to work at once and with energy to cultivate their land, the first year's harvest gave them an abundance of supplies. The proprietor sent out from England such things as were necessary to the success and comfort of the colony, treating the new settlement with a wise liberality. Thus were the foundations of Maryland laid amid peace and prosperity. The colony was successful from the first Roman Catholic settlers followed the first emigrants in considerable numbers, and even Protestants sought the shores of Maryland, which the liberality of Lord Baltimore had made a refuge to them from the persecutions of their own brethren. New settlements were formed, and within six months the colony "had advanced more than Virginia had done in as many years."

In February, 1635, the first legislative assembly of Maryland met Legislation had become necessary by this time Clayborne, who had established trading posts in the upper Chesapeake, had met the first settlers under Leonard Calvert at their anchorage at Old Point Comfort, and had endeavored to dissuade them from settling along the bay by exaggerating the dangers to be apprehended from the hostility of the Indians Failing in this effort, he became the evil genius of Maryland, as the grant to Lord Baltimore made void his license to trade with the Indians along the bay. He refused to acknowledge the authority of the proprietor of Maryland, and attempted to retain his trading posts by force of arms Within a year or two after the settlement of the colony, a bloody skirmish occurred in one of the rivers of the eastern shore, in which Clayborne's men were defeated In 1638, Leonard Calvert took forcible possession of Kent island, and hanged one or two of Clayborne's people on a charge of piracy and murder. Clayborne was in England at the time prosecuting his claims before the king Governor Harvey of Virginia had given the weight of his influence in this contest to the cause of Lord Baltimore, but the people of Virginia, who resented the grant of Maryland as an invasion of their rights, sympathized with Clayborne, and caused Harvey to be impeached and sent to England for trial. The English courts decided that Clayborne's license was not valid against the charter granted to Lord Baltimore, and Harvey was sent back to Virginia as governor, in April, 1639.

In the meantime the colony continued to grow and prosper The assembly, while acknowledging the allegiance of the people of Maryland to the king, and making ample provision for the rights of Lord Baltimore as proprietor, took care to secure the liberties of the people, and claimed for itself the exercise in the province of all the powers belonging to the British House of Commons Representative government was definitely established, and the colonists were secured in all the liberties granted to the people of England by the common law of that country Tobacco became, as in Virginia, the staple of the colony In 1642, in gratitude for the great expense which Lord Baltimore had voluntarily incurred in ... of Maryland ... law "on h a subsidy as the young and poor estate of the colony could bear." As far as the people themselves were concerned, the condition of Maryland was one of marked happiness and contentment. Harmony prevailed between all classes of the people and the government; the settlers were blessed with complete toleration in religion; emigration was rapidly increasing, and the commerce of the colony was growing in extent and value.

Maryland had its troubles, however. The Indians, alarmed by its rapid growth, began in 1642 a series of aggressions which led to a frontier war. This struggle continued for some time, but was productive of no decisive results, and in 1644 peace was restored. The Indians promised submission, and the whites, on their part, agreed to treat them with friendship and justice. Laws were enacted compelling the settlers to refrain from injustice toward the savages, and humanity to the red man was made the policy of the colony. The kidnapping of an Indian was punishable with death, and the sale of arms to the savages was constituted a felony. Efforts were also made to convert the natives to Christianity. Four missions were established among them by the priests of the Catholic Church, and the effects of

A CONVERTED INDIAN.

their devoted labors were soon manifest. A chief, named Tayac, and his wife were baptized, he taking the name of Charles and she that of Mary. About 130 other converts were afterwards added to the Christian fold among the Indians, and many of these sent their children to receive instruction at the hands of the priests. Though the effort to Christianize the savages failed, as it has ever done, the good effects of these endeavors were not lost, as the friendship for the whites aroused by them continued to influence these tribes in their policy toward the colony.

Clayborne, who had certainly cause for thinking himself wronged in being deprived of his property without just compensation, returned to

Maryland to revenge himself upon the colonists. The civil war in England furnished him with an admirable opportunity for his attempt. He was able to secure a number of followers in Maryland, and in 1644 began an insurrection. The next year the governor was driven out of the colony and obliged to take refuge in Virginia, and Clayborne was triumphant. For more than a year the rebels held possession of the government, and this whole time was a period of disorder and misrule, during which the greater part of the colonial records were lost or stolen. At the end of this time, the better classes of the people of Maryland drove out the rebels, and recalled the proprietary government. A general amnesty was proclaimed to all offenders, and peace was restored to the colony.

The year 1649 was marked in England by the execution of Charles I., and the complete establishment of the authority of the Parliament. It seemed to the people of Maryland that this triumph of the popular party was to usher in a new war upon the Roman Catholic faith, which was professed by a large majority of the colonists. Dreading a war of religion as the greatest of evils, they determined to secure the colony from it, by placing the freedom of conscience within their limits upon as secure a basis as possible. On the 21st of April, 1649, the assembly of Maryland adopted the following act: "And whereas the enforcing of conscience in matters of religion hath frequently fallen out to be of dangerous consequence in those commonwealths where it has been practised, and for the more quiet and peaceable government of this province, and the better to preserve mutual love and amity among the inhabitants, no person within this province, professing to believe in Jesus Christ, shall be anyways troubled, molested, or discountenanced for his or her religion, or in the free exercise thereof, or be compelled to the belief or practice of any other religion against their consent."

This statute, noble as it was, applied only to Christians. It was provided that "Whatsoever person shall blaspheme God, or shall deny or reproach the Holy Trinity, or any of the three persons thereof, shall be punished with death." Maryland had taken a great stride in advance in making her soil a sanctuary for Christians of all beliefs, but she had not yet accorded to her people a toleration equal to that of Rhode Island, which colony, in 1647, granted liberty to all opinions, infidel as well as Christian.

During the existence of the commonwealth, the colony was troubled with an unsettled government. It submitted to the authority of Cromwell, and the Puritans, regardless of the example of their brethren of the Catholic faith, attempted by an act of assembly, in 1654, to disfranchise the whole Roman Catholic population on the ground of their religious belief. Cromwell disapproved this action, and bluntly ordered his commissioners "not to busy themselves about religion, but to settle the civil government" In 1660, without waiting to hear the issue of matters in England, the assembly repudiated the authority of both the commonwealth and the proprietor, and asserted the sovereignty of the people as the supreme authority in Maryland.

Upon the restoration of Charles II., Lord Baltimore made his peace with the king for having yielded to the power of Cromwell, and received back all the rights he had enjoyed in Maryland He at once proceeded to re-establish his authority in the province, but being a man of humanity and of liberal views, he made a generous use of his power. A general pardon was granted to all offenders against him, his rule was once more submitted to, and for thirty years the colony was at peace.

"Like Virginia, Maryland was a colony of planters, its staple was tobacco, and its prosperity was equally checked by the pressure of the navigation acts. Like Virginia, it possessed no considerable village, its inhabitants were scattered among the woods and along the rivers, each plantation was a little world within itself, and legislation vainly attempted the creation of towns by statute. Like Virginia, its laborers were in part indentured servants, whose term of service was limited by persevering legislation; in part negro slaves, who were employed in the colony from an early period, and whose importation was favored both by English cupidity and provincial statutes. As in Virginia, the appointing power to nearly every office in the counties as well as in the province was not with the people; and the judiciary was placed beyond their control. As in Virginia, the party of the proprietary, which possessed the government, was animated by a jealous regard for prerogative, and by the royalist principles, which derive the sanction of authority from the will of heaven. As in Virginia, the taxes levied by the county officers were not conceded by the direct vote of the people, and were, therefore, burdensome alike from their excessive amount and the manner of their levy. But though the administration of Maryland did not favor the increasing spirit of popular liberty, it was marked by conciliation and humanity. To foster industry, to promote union, to cherish religious peace, . . . these were the honest purposes of Lord Baltimore during his long supremacy."*

Yet the colony continued to prosper. Emigrants came to it from almost every country of western Europe, and even from Sweden and Fin-

* *History of the United States* By George Bancroft, vol ii., p. 275

land. The only persons who had cause for complaint in Maryland were the Quakers, who were treated with considerable harshness for their refusal to perform military duty; but no effort was made to interfere with the exercise of their religion.

In 1662, Charles Calvert, the son and heir of Lord Baltimore, came to reside in the colony. Money was coined at a colonial mint, a tonnage duty was imposed upon all vessels trading with the colony, and a state house was built in 1674, at a cost of forty thousand pounds of tobacco, or about five thousand dollars. By numerous acts of compromise between Lord Baltimore and the assembly the question of taxation was adjusted upon a satisfactory basis. The people assumed the expense of the provincial government, and agreed to the imposition of an export duty of two shillings per hogshead upon all the tobacco sent out of the colony. One-half of this duty was appropriated to the support of the government, and the remainder was assigned unconditionally to the uses of Lord Baltimore, as "an act of gratitude" for his care of the colony.

On the 30th of November, 1675, Cecil Calvert, second Lord Baltimore, died. He had been for fourteen years the earnest and devoted friend, as well as the generous lord of the province, and had lived long enough to enjoy the gratitude with which the colony sought to repay his judicious care. His memory is perpetuated by the chief city of Maryland, which bears his name, and which is already the largest city on the Atlantic coast, south of the Susquehanna, and the fifth in population in the United States. Charles Calvert, who had been for fourteen years governor of Maryland, succeeded to his father's titles and possessions, and in 1676 returned to England. Previous to his departure from Maryland he gave his sanction to the colonial code of laws, which had been thoroughly revised. One of these laws prohibited the "importation of convicted persons" into the colony without regard to the will of the king or Parliament of England.

Notwithstanding the mild and equitable government of the third Lord Baltimore, the spirit of popular liberty was becoming too strong in the colony for the rule of the proprietor to be cheerfully acquiesced in much longer. The rebellion of Bacon in Virginia affected the Maryland colony profoundly, and when Lord Baltimore returned to the province in 1681, he found a large part of the people hostile to him. An attempt at insurrection was suppressed, but the seeds of trouble were too deeply sown not to spring up again.

The increase of the population had left the Roman Catholics in a small minority, so that Maryland was now to all intents and purposes a Protestant colony. During the latter part of the reign of Charles II.

the Protestants, regardless of the wise policy of toleration which had hitherto marked the history of the province, endeavored to secure the establishment by law of the Church of England in Maryland Lord Baltimore steadfastly resisted this unwise course, and maintained the freedom of conscience as the right of the people He thus added to the existing opposition to his proprietary rule the hostility of the Protestant bigots. A little later, the English ministry struck the first blow at his proprietary rights and at the religious freedom of Maryland by ordering that all the offices of the colonial government should be bestowed upon Protestants alone. " Roman Catholics were disfranchised in the province which they had planted."

Lord Baltimore hoped that the succession of James II., a Catholic sovereign, would restore him the rights of which he had been deprived in his province; but he was soon undeceived, for the king, who intended to bring all the American colonies directly under the control of the crown, would make no exception in favor of Maryland, and measures were put in force for the abolition of the proprietary government The revolution which placed William and Mary on the throne prevented the execution of these plans

The troubles of Lord Baltimore were increased by the failure of the deputy-governor, whom he had left in Maryland, to acknowledge William and Mary promptly. In August, 1689, occurred an insurrection led by "The association in arms for the defence of the Protestant religion " The deputy-governor was driven from office, the proprietary government was overturned, and William and Mary were proclaimed sovereigns of Maryland The party in power appealed to the king to annul the proprietary charter, and governed the colony by means of a convention until the royal pleasure should be known. Lord Baltimore endeavored to defend his rights, but in spite of his struggles, William III, in June, 1691, annulled the charter of Maryland, and by the exercise of his own power constituted that colony a royal province In 1692, the king appointed Sir Lionel Copley governor of Maryland. Upon his arrival in the colony he dissolved the convention and assumed the government He at once summoned an assembly, which, recognizing William and Mary as the lawful sovereigns of Maryland, established the Church of England as the religion of the colony, and imposed taxes for its support. The capital was removed from St Mary's to Annapolis, both because the old seat of government had become inconvenient and because it was desired to remove the government to the centre of Protestant influence The disfranchisement of the Catholics advanced step by step. At first the dissenters from the established church were granted toleration and pro-

10

tection, but in 1704 the triumph of bigotry was complete. All the
dissenting bodies were tolerated, but Roman Catholics were forbidden the
exercise of their faith. Mass was not allowed to be said in public, nor was
any bishop or clergyman of the Roman Catholic Church to be permitted to
seek to make converts for his faith. Other severe measures were enacted,
and in the land which Catholics had settled, the members of that communion alone were denied the rights which in the day of their power
they had offered to others. Nor did the royalist assembly manifest any
care for the true interests of the province. Education was neglected;
the establishment of printing was prohibited; and the domestic manufactures which the necessities of the colony had brought into existence
were discouraged. In 1710 the population numbered over 30,000, free
and slave.

In 1715 Benedict Charles Calvert, the fourth Lord Baltimore, succeeded in obtaining the restoration of his rights in Maryland, and the
province passed into his hands. The people had been so disgusted with
the rule of the royal governors that no opposition was made to this
change. The new Lord Baltimore, unlike the rest of his family, was a
Protestant, which was the cause of his restoration to his hereditary rights.
After his restoration the colony increased with still greater rapidity.
The establishment of a post route, in 1695, between the Potomac and
Philadelphia, had brought it into communication with the Northern
colonies. In 1729 the town of Baltimore was founded. Frederick City
was settled in 1745, and in 1751 was followed by Georgetown, now in
the District of Columbia. In 1756 the population of the colony had
increased to 154,188 souls, of whom over 40,000 were negroes. The
increase in material prosperity was equally marked. By the last-men-
tioned year the annual export of tobacco was 30,000 hogsheads, and, in
spite of the efforts of the home government to prevent it, there were
eight furnaces and nine forges for smelting copper in operation in
the province.

CHAPTER X.

THE PILGRIM FATHERS.

HE persecutions with which Queen Mary afflicted the reformers of England in her bloody effort to restore the Roman Catholic faith in that country caused many of the most eminent men of the English Church to seek safety on the continent of Europe Upon the accession of Elizabeth the Church of England became once more the religion of the state, and the reformers were free to return to their own country. They came back with broader and more liberal views than they had carried away with them, and there sprang up in the English Church a party which demanded a purer and more spiritual form of worship than that of the church These persons were called in derision *Puritans*. They adopted the name without hesitation, and soon made it an honorable distinction. The queen, however, was determined to compel her subjects to conform to the established church, and was especially resolved to make them acknowledge her supremacy over the church. To the Puritan the worship of the Church of England was only less sinful than that of Rome, and to acknowledge the queen as the head of the church was to commit blasphemy. He claimed that the queen had no control over him in matters of religion, and that it was his right to worship God in his own way, without interference. The Puritans gradually came to embrace in their number some of the best

147

men in the English Church. These sincerely deprecated a separation
from the church, and earnestly desired to carry the reformation to the
extent of remedying the abuses of which they complained, and to remain
in communion with the church. One of the reforms which they wished
to inaugurate was the abolition of Episcopacy. Failing in their efforts,
they desired to be let alone to form their own organizations and to
worship God according to their own ideas, without the pale of the Church
of England.

The queen and the bishops were not content to allow them this
freedom. England had not yet learned the lesson of toleration, and
severe measures were inaugurated to compel the dissenters to conform to
the established church. All persons in the kingdom were required to
conform to the ceremonies of the church. A refusal to do so was punished with banishment. Should any person so banished return to the
kingdom without permission he was to be put to death. Accused persons
were obliged to answer upon oath all questions concerning themselves and
their acquaintance, respecting their attendance upon public worship.
Ministers refusing to conform to the established usage were deprived of
their parishes; and if they persisted in preaching to their congregations,
or if the congregations were detected in listening to their deposed pastors,
the offenders were fined or subjected to some severer punishment.
Absence from the services of the church for a certain length of time was
also punished. The persecution thus inaugurated drove many of the
nonconformists, as they were termed, into exile from England. They
fled to Holland and Switzerland, where alone they found "freedom to
worship God." In spite of the severe measures and determined efforts
of Elizabeth, the Puritans increased steadily in numbers and importance
in England.

They were hopeful that James I. would prove a more lenient sovereign
to them than Elizabeth had been, and they had good ground for this
hope. The real character of James was unknown in England, and while
King of Scotland he had shown great favor to the Presbyterians of that
kingdom, whom it was his interest to conciliate. He had once publicly
thanked God "that he was king of such a kirk—the purest kirk in all
the world. As for the Kirk of England," he added, "its service is an
evil-said mass." This most contemptible of monarchs had scarcely
become King of England when he uttered the famous maxim, "No
bishop, no king!" which pithily states the policy of his reign. Interest
had made him the foe of episcopacy in Scotland; the same motive made
him its champion in England. Upon his entrance into his new kingdom,
the Puritans met him with an humble petition for a redress of their

grievances. James quickly saw that the majority of the English people favored a support of the church as it was, and had no sympathy with the Puritans, and he at once constituted himself the enemy of the petitioners. Still, in order to cover his desertion of the party to which he had belonged in Scotland, he appointed a conference at Hampton Court.

The conference was held in January, 1604, and the king, silencing all real debate, made the meeting merely the occasion of displaying what he regarded as his talents for theological controversy, and for announcing the decision he had resolved upon from the first. He demanded entire obedience to the church in matters of faith and worship. "I will have none of that liberty as to ceremonies," he declared. "I will have one doctrine, one discipline, one religion in substance and in ceremony. Never speak more to that point, how far you are bound to obey." The Puritans then demanded permission to hold occasional ceremonies of their own, with the right of free discussions in them, but James, who could never tolerate the expression of any opinion adverse to his own, replied: "You are aiming at a Scot's presbytery, which agrees with monarchy as well as God and the devil. Then Jack and Tom and Will and Dick shall meet, and at their pleasure censure me and my council and all our proceedings. Then Will shall stand up and say, It must be thus. Then Dick shall reply and say, Nay, marry, but we will have it thus. And therefore here I must once more reiterate my former speech, and say, The king forbids." Then turning to the bishops, he added: "I will make them conform, or I will harry them out of the land, or else worse; only hang them; that's all." The king kept his word. The severe laws against the nonconformists were enforced that year with such energy that three hundred Puritan ministers are said to have been silenced, imprisoned, or exiled. The church party proceeded in the next few years to still more rigorous measures, and were willing even to place the liberties of the nation at the mercy of the crown in order to compel the submission of the Puritans. The introduction of foreign publications into the kingdom was greatly restricted, and the press was placed under a severe censorship. The Puritans were thus forced to become the champions of popular liberty against the tyranny of the crown and the ecclesiastical party, and the issue which was to be fought out by the next generation was distinctly joined.

There was a congregation of Puritans in the north of England, composed of people of Lincolnshire and Nottinghamshire, with some from Yorkshire. The pastor was John Robinson, "a man not easily to be paralleled," who possessed in an unusual degree the love and confidence of his people. They were greatly harassed by the agents of the king and

the bishops, and were subjected to such serious annoyances that it was
with difficulty that they could hold their meetings Finding it impossible to live in peace at home without doing violence to their consciences,
they determined to leave England and seek refuge from persecution in
Holland. That country was friendly to the English, and the Dutch had
learned from their own sufferings to respect the rights of conscience in
others. It was not an easy matter to leave England, however, for it was
held by the government to be almost a crime to attempt to escape from
persecution. A vessel was hired to convey the refugees to Holland ; but
the royal officers were informed of the intended voyage, and seized the
whole company as they were about to embark. Their persons were
searched, their small possessions seized, and the whole church—men,
women, and children—thrown into prison In a short while all but seven
were released. These were brought to trial, but it was found impossible
to prove any crime against them, and they also were discharged.

This action of the government, so far from intimidating the sufferers,
but increased their resolve to leave England, and in the spring of 1608
the effort was renewed. A Dutch captain consented to convey them to
Holland, and it was agreed that the refugees should assemble upon a
lonely heath in Lincolnshire, near the mouth of the Humber, and be
taken on board by the Dutch skipper. The men of the party went to
the rendezvous by land, and got safely on board the ship ; but the boat
conveying the women and children was stranded and captured by a party
of horsemen sent in pursuit. The Dutch skipper, fearful of becoming
involved in trouble with the English authorities, at once put to sea, and
the exiles were separated from their families, who were left helpless in
the hands of their oppressors. The women and children were treated
with great harshness by their captors, and were taken before the magistrates, who found it impossible to punish them for an attempt to follow
the fortunes of their husbands and fathers. They were at a loss to know
what to do with the prisoners, who no longer had homes in England, and
at last released them unconditionally, and permitted them to rejoin their
natural protectors in Holland

The exiles reached Amsterdam in the spring of 1608. They were well
pleased to be safe in this peaceful refuge, but they did not deceive themselves with the hope that it could ever be a home to them. "They
knew they were PILGRIMS, and looked not much on those things, but
lifted up their eyes to heaven, their dearest country, and quieted their
spirits." They found it hard to earn a support in Amsterdam, and in
1609 removed to Leyden, where, by their industry and frugality, they
managed to live in comparative comfort. Their piety and exemplary

conduct won for them the respect of the Dutch, who would have openly shown them marked favor but for their fear of offending the King of England. The magistrates of Leyden bore ready witness to their purity of life. "Never," said they, "did we have any suit or accusation against any of them."

In the course of time the Pilgrims were joined by a number of their brethren from England. They were nearly all accustomed to agricultural pursuits, and in Holland they were obliged to earn their bread by mechanical labors. It was with difficulty that they could do this, and they never formed any attachment to the place of their exile. They preserved, through all their trials, their affection for their native land, and cherished the hope that they might continue Englishmen to the close of their lives. They viewed with alarm the prospect of raising their children in Holland, where they would necessarily be thrown in constant contact with, and be influenced by, the manners and customs of the country. Above all they dreaded the effect upon their children of the dissolute example of the disbanded soldiers and sailors who filled the country. These and other things made them unwilling to look upon Holland as their permanent home. But whither should they go in case of their departure from Holland? Their own country was closed against them, and the nations of continental Europe could offer them no asylum. As their conviction, that it was their duty to seek some other home, deepened, their thoughts became more irresistibly directed towards the new world. In the vast solitudes of the American continent, and there alone, they could establish a home in which they could worship God without fear or molestation, and rear their children in the ways that seemed to them good. Thither would they go.

They were anxious to make their venture under the protection of England, and declined the offers made them by the Dutch, who wished them to establish their colony as a dependency of Holland. They had heard of the excellent climate and fertile soil of Virginia, and it seemed best to them to choose that promising region as the scene of their experiment. It was necessary to obtain the consent of the London Company to their settlement, as Virginia had been granted to that body by the King of England; and in 1617 two of the leading members of the congregation—John Carver and Robert Cushman—went to England to lay their application before the company. They were kindly received by Sir Edwin Sandys, the secretary of the company. They laid before the directors the request for permission to form a settlement in Virginia, with which they had been charged by their brethren. The application was signed by the greater part of the congregation, and contained a statement of their principles, and their reasons for desiring to emigrate to America. "We verily believe that God is with us," said the petitioners, "and will prosper us in our endeavors, we are weaned from our mother country, and have learned patience in a hard and strange land. We are industrious and frugal; we are bound together by a sacred bond of the Lord, whereof we make great conscience, holding ourselves to each other's good. We do not wish ourselves home again, we have nothing to hope from England or Holland, we are men who will not be easily discouraged."

The appeal of the Pilgrims was received with such favor by the London Company that Carver and Cushman ventured to petition the king to grant them liberty to exercise their religion unmolested in the wilds of America. The most that James would consent to grant them, however, was a half promise to pay no attention to them in their new home. The London Company agreed to grant them permission to settle in Virginia, but the dissensions of that body prevented anything from being done in their behalf.

The Pilgrims were too poor to defray the cost of their emigration, and they set to work to find persons of means willing to assist them. At length they were successful, and a company was formed consisting of themselves and several merchants of London. The latter were to advance the funds necessary for the enterprise, while the former were to contribute their entire services for a period of seven years, as their share of the stock of the company. At the end of seven years the profits of the enterprise were to be divided according to the amount of each one's investment; and it was agreed that a contribution of ten pounds in money by a merchant should be entitled to as great a share of the profits as seven years of labor on the part of the emigrant. These were hard terms for the Pilgrims, but they were the best they could obtain, and they were accepted, as the exiles were willing to suffer any sacrifice in order to be able to found a community of their own in which they could bring up their children in the fear of God. The main thing with them was to reach the shores of America. Once there these men who had learned the lessons of self-denial and endurance did not doubt their ability to succeed even in the face of the heavy disadvantages they were obliged to assume.

With the funds thus obtained the Pilgrims began to prepare for their departure. A ship of sixty tons, called the "Speedwell," was purchased, and another, of one hundred and eighty tons, called the "Mayflower," was chartered. These, however, could transport but a part of the congregation, and it was resolved to send out at first only "such of the youngest and strongest as freely offered themselves." The pastor, Robinson, and the aged and infirm were to remain at Leyden until their brethren could send for them, and the colony was placed under the guidance of William Brewster, the governing elder, who was an able teacher and much respected and beloved for his noble character.

When all was in readiness, a day of fasting and prayer was held, in order that at the very beginning of their enterprise the Pilgrims might invoke the guidance and protection of God "Let us seek of God," they said, "a right way for us, and for our little ones, and for all our substance" The venerable pastor made this solemn season the occasion of delivering a tender farewell to the members of his charge who were about to depart, and of appealing to them to be true to the principles of their religion in their new home. "I charge you before God and his blessed angels," he said, in tones of deep emotion, "that you follow me no further than you have seen me follow the Lord Jesus Christ If God reveal anything to you, be ready to receive it, for I am verily persuaded that the Lord has more truth yet to break out of his holy word I beseech you, remember that it is an article of your church covenant, that you be ready to receive whatever truth shall be made known to you from the written word of God. Take heed what ye receive as truth, examine it, consider it, and compare it with other scriptures of truth before you receive it, the Christian world has not yet come to the perfection of knowledge."

From Leyden a number of the brethren accompanied the emigrants to Delft Haven, from which port they were to sail. The night before their departure, they all assembled in prayer and religious exercises, which were continued until the dawn, when they prepared to go on board the ship. Arrived at the shore, they knelt again, and the pastor, Robinson, led them in prayer—the emigrants listening to his voice for the last time on earth. "And so," says Edward Winslow, "lifting up our hands to each other, and our hearts to the Lord our God, we departed."

Southampton was soon reached, and the voyagers were transferred to the "Mayflower" and the "Speedwell." On the 5th of August, 1620, those vessels sailed from Southampton for America Soon after getting to sea, it was discovered that the "Speedwell" was in need of repairs, and that they must return to England They put about and reached the port of Dartmouth, where the smaller vessel was repaired. Eight days were consumed in this undertaking, and the voyage was resumed They were scarcely out of sight of land when the commander of the "Speedwell," alarmed by the dangers of the voyage, declared that his ship was not strong enough to cross the ocean The vessels at once put back to Plymouth, where the smaller ship was discharged. At the same

time those who had grown fainthearted were permitted to withdraw from
the expedition. The remainder of the company, to the number of one
hundred and one, sailed from Plymouth in the "Mayflower," on the 6th
of September, 1620. Some of these were women well advanced in preg-
nancy, and some were children. Their little vessel was but a frail barque
compared with the ships that now navigate the sea ; but a band of braver

THE "MAYFLOWER" IN PLYMOUTH HARBOR.

and more resolute souls never trusted themselves to the mercies of the
stormy Atlantic.

The leading man in the little band of Pilgrims was the ruling elder,
William Brewster, who was to be their preacher until the arrival of a
regularly chosen pastor. He was a man of fine education, refined and

scholarly tastes, and of pure and lofty Christian character. "He laid his hand," says Elliott, "to the daily tasks of life, as well as spent his soul in trying to benefit his fellows—so bringing himself as near as possible to the early Christian practices; he was worthy of being the first minister of New England." He was well advanced in life, and was looked up to with affectionate regard by his associates

Another was John Carver, also a man of years and ripe experience, who had sacrificed his fortune to the cause, and whose dignified and benevolent character won him the honor of being chosen the first chief magistrate of the colony

Prominent among the leaders was William Bradford. He was only thirty-two, but was a man of earnest and resolute character, firm and true, "a man of nerve and public spirit." He had begun life as a farmer's boy in England, and in Holland had supported himself by practising the art of dyeing; but, in spite of his constant labors, he had educated himself and had managed to accumulate books of his own. He systematically devoted a large part of his time to study, and thus carefully trained his natural abilities, which were very great

Edward Winslow, a man of sweet and amiable disposition, was twenty-six years old He was a gentleman by birth, and had been well educated, and had acquired considerable information and experience by travel.

Miles Standish had attained the mature age of thirty-six, and was a veteran soldier. He had seen service in the wars of the continent of Europe, and had gained an honorable distinction in them. He was not a member of the church, but was strongly attached to its institutions.

> "With the people of God he had chosen to suffer affliction,
> . In return for his zeal, they . . . made him Captain of Plymouth,
> He was a man of honor, of noble and generous nature,
> Though he was rough, he was kindly . .
> Somewhat hasty and hot   and headstrong,
> Stern as a soldier might be, but hearty and placable always,
> Not to be laughed at and scorned, because he was little of stature;
> For he was great of heart, magnanimous, courtly, courageous"

The voyage of the "Mayflower" was long and stormy. The Pilgrims had selected the country near the mouth of the Hudson as the best region for their settlement, but a severe storm drove them northward to the coast of New England Sixty-three days were consumed in the passage, during which one of their number had died, and at length land was made, and on the 9th of November, two days later, the "Mayflower" cast anchor in the harbor of Cape Cod.

The Pilgrims had come to America at their own risk and without the sanction of, or a charter from, the king or any lawful organization in England They were thrown upon their own resources, and could look to no quarter for protection or support. Appreciating the necessity of an organized government, their first acts after anchoring in Cape Cod bay were to organize themselves into a body politic and to form a government The following compact was drawn up in the cabin of the "Mayflower," and was signed by all the men of the colony, to the number of forty-one "In the name of God, amen; we whose names are underwritten, the loyal subjects of our dread sovereign King James, having undertaken, for the glory of God and advancement of the Christian faith, and honor of our king and country, a voyage to plant the first colony in the northern parts of Virginia, do, by these presents, solemnly and mutually, in the presence of God and of one another, covenant and combine ourselves together, into a civil body politic, for our better ordering and preservation, and furtherance of the ends aforesaid, and by virtue hereof, to enact, constitute and frame such just and equal laws, ordinances, acts, constitutions and offices, from time to time, as shall be thought most convenient for the general good of the colony, unto which we promise all due submission and obedience."

This was the first constitution of New England, democratic in form, and resting upon the consent of the governed It at once established the new commonwealth upon the basis of constitutional liberty, and secured to the people "just and equal laws" for the "general good." In virtue of the compact, John Carver was chosen governor of the colony for the ensuing year.

The prospect which presented itself to the Pilgrims upon their arrival at Cape Cod might well have daunted even their resolute souls. It was the opening of the winter, and they had come to a barren and rugged coast. The climate was severe, and the land was a wilderness The English colony in Virginia was five hundred miles distant, and to the north of them the nearest white settlement was the French colony at Port Royal. The "Mayflower" was only chartered to convey them to America, and must return to England as soon as they had chosen a site and established a settlement. Yet no one faltered. The new land was reached, the difficulties and dangers were such as could be overcome by patience and fortitude, and the Pilgrims without hesitation addressed themselves to the task before them.

The first thing to be done was to explore the coast and choose a site for the colony, for it was important to begin their settlement before the severity of the winter should render such an effort impossible The shallop was gotten out, but unfortunately it was found to need repairs. The ship's carpenter worked so slowly that nearly three weeks were spent in this task. This delay was a great misfortune at this advanced season of the year, and, some of the party becoming impatient, it was resolved to go ashore in the ship's boat and explore the country by land. A party of sixteen men was detailed for this purpose, and placed under the command of Captain Miles Standish. William Bradford, Stephen Hopkins and Edward Tilly were included in the party as a council of war. The explorers were given numerous instructions, and were rather permitted than ordered to go upon their journey, which was regarded as perilous, and the time of their absence was limited to two days.

Upon reaching the shore they followed it for about a mile, when they discovered several Indians watching them from a distance. The savages fled as soon as they saw they were observed, and the whites followed in pursuit. They struck the trail of the retreating Indians, and followed it until nightfall, but being encumbered by the weight of their armor and impeded by the tangled thickets through which they had to pass, they were unable to overtake the Indians. The explorers bivouacked that night by a clear spring, whose waters refreshed them after their fatiguing march. They made few discoveries, but the expedition was not entirely unprofitable. In one place they found a deer-trap, made by bending a young tree to the earth, with a noose under-ground covered with acorns. Mr. Bradford was caught by the foot in this snare, which occasioned much merriment. An Indian graveyard was discovered in another place, and in one of the graves there was an earthen pot, a mortar, a bow and some arrows, and other rude implements. These were carefully replaced by the whites, who respected the resting-place of the dead. The most important discovery was the finding of a cellar or pit carefully lined with bark, and covered over with a heap of sand, and containing about four bushels of seed corn in ears. As much of this as the men could carry was secured, and it was determined to pay the owners of the corn for it as soon as they could be found. On the third day the explorers returned to the ship, and delivered their corn, which was kept for seed.

The shallop being finished at length, a party, consisting of Carver, Bradford, Winslow, Standish and others, with eight or ten seamen, was sent out on a second expedition on the 6th of December. The weather was very cold, and their clothing, drenched with spray, froze as stiff as iron armor. They reached the bottom of Cape Cod bay that day, and landed, instructing the people in the shallop to follow them along the shore. The next day they divided, and searched the neighborhood. They found a number of Indian graves, and some deserted wigwams, but

saw no signs of the inhabitants of the country. That night they encamped near Namtasket, or Great Meadow Creek. On the morning of
the 8th of December, just as they had finished their prayers, the explorers
were startled by a war-whoop and a flight of arrows. The Indians, who
were of the tribe of the Nausites, were put to flight by the discharge of
a few guns. Some of their people had been kidnapped by the English a
few years before, and hence they regarded the new-comers as bent on the

same errand. The day
was spent in searching
for a safe harbor for the
ship, and at nightfall a
violent storm of rain and
snow drove them through
the breakers into a small
cove sheltered from the
gale by a hill. They
were so wet and chilled
that they landed at once,
and, regardless of the
danger of drawing the
savages upon them, built
a fire with great diffi-
culty, in order to keep
from perishing with the
cold. When the morn-
ing dawned, they found
that they were on an
island at the entrance to
a harbor. The day was
spent in rest and pre-
parations. The next day,
December 10th, was the
Sabbath, and notwith-
standing the need of

LANDING OF THE PILGRIMS.

prompt action, they spent it in rest and religious exercises. The next
day, December 11th, 1620, old style, or December 22d, according to our
present system, the exploring party of the Pilgrims landed at the head of
the harbor they had discovered. The rock upon which their footsteps
were first planted is still preserved by their descendants. The place was
explored, and chosen as the site of the settlement, and was named
Plymouth, in memory of the last English town from which the Pilgrims
had sailed.

The adventurers hastened back to the ship, which stood across the bay, and four days later cast anchor in Plymouth harbor. No time was to be lost; the "Mayflower" must soon return to England, and the emigrants must have some shelter over their heads before her departure. To save time each man was allowed to build his own house. This was a most arduous task. Many of the men were almost broken down by their exposure to the cold, and some had already contracted the fatal diseases which were to carry them to the grave before the close of the winter. Still they persevered, working bravely when the absence of rain and snow would permit them to do so. As the winter deepened, the sickness and mortality of the colony increased. At one time there were but seven well men in the company. More than forty of the settlers died during the winter. John Carver, the good governor of the colony, buried his son, and himself soon succumbed to the hardships from which he had never shrunk, though never able to endure them. He was followed by his heart-broken widow. The wives of Bradford and Winslow, and Rose Standish, the sweet young bride of "the Captain of Plymouth" were also among the victims. They were all buried on the shore near the rock on which they had landed, and lest their graves should tell the Indians of the sufferings and weakness of the settlement, their resting-place was levelled and sown with grass. William Bradford was chosen governor in the place of Carver, and the work went on with firmness and without repining.

At last the long winter drew to a close, and the balmy spring came to cheer the settlers with its bright skies and warm breezes. The sick began to recover, and the building of the settlement was completed. In course of time a large shed was erected for the public stores, and a small hospital for the sick. A church was also built. It was made stronger than the other buildings, as it was to serve as a fortress as well as a place of worship, and four cannon were mounted on top of it for defence against the savages. Here they assembled on the Sabbath for religious worship, and to hear the word of God from the lips of their pastor, the good Elder Brewster. In the spring the ground was prepared for cultivation, but until the harvest was grown the colonists lived by fishing and hunting.

In March, 1621, the "Mayflower" sailed for England. Not one of the Pilgrims wished to return in her. They had their trials, and these were sore and heavy, but they had also made a home and a government for themselves, where they could enjoy the benefits and protection of their own laws, and worship God in safety and in peace. They did not doubt that they would some day triumph over their difficulties and that

God would in His own good time crown their labors and their patience
with success.

In the autumn of 1621, a reinforcement of new emigrants arrived.
They brought no provisions, and were dependent upon the scanty stock
of the colony, and the increased demand upon this soon brought the
settlers face to face with the danger of famine. For six months no one
received more than half allowance, and this was frequently reduced. "I
have seen men," says Winslow, "stagger by reason of faintness for want
of food." On one occasion the whole company would have perished but
for the kindness of some fishermen, who relieved their wants. This

THE FIRST CHURCH IN NEW ENGLAND.

scarcity of provisions continued for several years, and it was not until
the end of the fourth year of the settlement that the colonists had anything like a proper supply of food. In that year neat cattle were introduced into Plymouth. None of the colonies were called upon to endure
such privations as were suffered by the Pilgrims. Yet they bore them
with unshaken fortitude, still trusting that God would give them a
pleasanter lot in the end.

The conditions of the contract with the English merchants had required
the labor of the colonists to be thrown into the common stock. This was
found to be an unprofitable arrangement, and in 1623 it was agreed that

each settler should plant for himself, and each family was assigned a parcel of land in proportion to its numbers, to cultivate, but "not for an inheritance." This arrangement gave great satisfaction and the colonists went to work with such a will that after this season there was no scarcity of food. In the spring of 1624 each colonist was given a little land in fee. The very existence of the colony demanded this departure from the hard bargain with the English merchants, and the result justified the measure. Abundant harvests rewarded the labors of the settlers, and corn soon became so plentiful that the colonists were able to supply the savages with it. These, preferring the chase to the labor of the field, brought in game and skins to Plymouth and received corn in return.

In the meantime a friendly intercourse had sprung up between the settlers and the Indians. In the first year of the settlement the red men were seen hovering upon the outskirts of the village, but they fled upon the approach of the whites. Distant columns of smoke, rising beyond the woods, told that the savages were close at hand, and it was deemed best to organize the settlers into a military company, the command of which was given to Miles Standish. One day, in March, 1621, the whole village was startled by the appearance of an Indian, who boldly entered the settlement, and greeted the whites with the friendly words, "Welcome, Englishmen! Welcome, Englishmen!" He was kindly received, and it was found that he was Samoset, and had learned a little English of the fishermen at Penobscot. He belonged to the Wampanoags, a tribe occupying the country north of Narragansett bay and between the rivers of Providence and Taunton. He told them that they might possess the lands they had taken in peace, as the tribe to which they had belonged had been swept away by a pestilence the year before the arrival of the Pilgrims. He remained one night with the settlers, who gave him a knife, a ring, and a bracelet, and then went back to his people, promising to return soon and bring other Indians to trade with them. In a few days he came back, bringing with him Squanto, the Indian who had been kidnapped by Hunt and sold in Spain. From that country Squanto had escaped to England, where he had learned the language. He had managed to return to his own country, and now appeared to act as interpreter to the English in their intercourse with his people. They announced that Massasoit, the sachem of the Wampanoags, desired to visit the colony. The chieftain was received with all the ceremony the little settlement could afford. Squanto acted as interpreter, and a treaty of friendship was arranged between Massasoit on behalf of his people and the English. The parties to the agreement promised to treat each other with kindness and justice, to deliver up offenders, and to assist each other when attacked

11

by their enemies. This treaty was faithfully observed by both parties
for fifty years. The Pilgrims expressed their willingness to pay for the
baskets of corn that had been taken by their first exploring party, and
this they did six months later, when the rightful owners presented themselves A trade with the Indians was established, and furs were brought
into Plymouth by them and sold for articles of European manufacture

Squanto was the faithful friend of the colony to the end of his life,
and was regarded by the Pilgrims as "a special instrument sent of God
for their good beyond their expectation" He taught them the Indian
method of planting corn and putting fish with it to fertilize the ground,
and where to find and how to catch fish and game. He showed them
his friendship in many ways, and was during his lifetime the interpreter
of the colony. The Pilgrims on their part were not ungrateful to him.
On one occasion it was rumored in Plymouth that Squanto had been
seized by the Narragansetts, and had been put to death. A party of ten
men at once marched into the forest, and surprised the hut where the
chief of the Narragansetts was. Although the tribe could bring five
thousand warriors into the field, the chief was overawed by the determined action of the English, whose firearms gave them a great superiority, and Squanto was released unharmed On his death-bed Squanto,
who had been carefully nursed by his white friends, asked the governor
to pray that he might go to "the Englishman's God in heaven." His
death was regarded as a serious misfortune to the colony.

Massasoit, whose tribe had been greatly reduced by pestilence, desired
the alliance of the English as a protection against the Narragansetts, who
had escaped the scourge, and whose chief, Canonicus, was hostile to him
The Narragansetts lived upon the shores of the beautiful bay to which
they have given their name, and were a powerful and warlike race
Canonicus regarded the English with hostility, and in 1622 sent them as
a defiance a bundle of arrows wrapped in the skin of a rattlesnake
Governor Bradford received the challenge from the hands of the chieftain's messenger, and stuffing the skin with powder and ball returned it
to him, and sternly bade him bear it back to his master The Indians
regarded the mysterious contents of the skin with terror and dread, and
passed it from tribe to tribe. None dared either keep or destroy it, as it
was regarded as possessed of some mysterious but powerful influence for
harm It was finally returned to the colony, and in a short while
Canonicus, who had been cowed by the spirited answer of Bradford,
offered to make a treaty of peace and alliance with the colony.

The Pilgrims endeavored to treat the Indians with justice Severe
penalties were denounced against those who should deprive the savages

of their property without paying for it, or should treat them with violence. Yet the colonists were to have trouble with the red men, and that through no fault of their own.

Among the merchants of London who had invested money in the planting of the Plymouth colony was Thomas Weston. Envious of the advance made by the colony in the fur-trade, he desired to secure all the profits of that traffic by establishing a trading-post of his own. He obtained a patent for a small tract on Boston harbor, near Weymouth, and settled there a colony of sixty men, the greater number of whom were indentured servants. These men, disregarding the warnings of the people of Plymouth, gave themselves up to a dissolute life, and drew upon themselves the wrath of the Indians by maltreating them, and stealing their corn. The Indians, unable to distinguish between the guilty and the innocent, resolved to avenge the misconduct of Weston's men by a massacre of every white settler in the country.

Before the plot could be put in execution Massasoit fell sick. Winslow visited him, and found his lodge full of medicine-men and jugglers, who were killing him with the noise they made to drive away the disease. The kind-hearted Englishman turned the Indian doctors out of the lodge, and by giving Massasoit rest, and administering such remedies as his case required, restored him to health. The grateful chief revealed the plot of his people for the extermination of the English. The Plymouth settlers were greatly alarmed, and measures were promptly taken to avert the danger. Standish, with eight armed men, was sent to the assistance of the settlement at Weymouth. They arrived in time to prevent the attack. The Indians, who had begun to collect for the massacre, were surprised and defeated in a brief engagement, and the chief, who was the leader of the conspiracy, was slain, with a number of his men. This gallant exploit established the supremacy of the English in New England, and many of the native tribes sought their friendship and alliance. The Weymouth men were unwilling to continue their colony after their narrow escape. Some went to Plymouth, where they became a source of trouble, and others returned to England. The spring of 1623 saw the last of this settlement.

In the autumn of 1623 the best harvest was gathered in that had yet blessed the labors of the Pilgrims. It was an abundant yield, and put an end to all fears of a renewal of the danger of famine. When the labors of the harvest were over Governor Bradford sent out men to collect game, in order that the people might enjoy a thanksgiving feast. On the appointed day the people "met together and thanked God with all their hearts for the good world and the good things in it." Thus was established the custom of an annual thanksgiving to God for the blessings of the year, which though at first a celebration peculiar to New England has at length become a national festival

The colonists themselves were satisfied with the progress they had made, but their merchant partners in England were greatly displeased with the smallness of the profits they had received from their investments, and in many ways made the colony feel their dissatisfaction. Robinson and his congregation at Leyden were anxious to join their friends in America, but the merchant partners refused to send them across the Atlantic, and not content with this endeavored to force upon the Plymouth people a pastor friendly to the Church of England. They soon got rid of this individual, however, whose conduct quickly enabled them to expel him from Plymouth as an evil liver. The merchants also sent a vessel to New England to oppose the colonists in the fur-trade; and demanded exorbitant prices for the goods they sold the settlers, charging them the enormous profit of seventy per cent

It was not possible, however, to destroy the results of the industry and self-denial of the Pilgrims. Seeing that their association with their English partners would continue to operate merely as a drag upon the advance of the colony, they managed in 1627, at considerable sacrifice, to purchase the entire interest of their partners. The stock and the land of the colony were then divided equitably among the settlers, and the share of each man became his own private property. Each settler was thus made the owner of a piece of land which it was to his interest to improve to the highest degree possible. Freed from the burdens under which it had labored for so long, the colony began to increase in prosperity and in population.

The government of the Pilgrims was simple, but effective. They had no charter, and were from the first driven upon their own resources. They had a governor who was chosen by the votes of all the settlers. In 1624 a council of five was given him, and in 1633 this number was increased to seven. The council assisted the governor in the exercise of his duties, and imposed a check upon his authority, as in its meetings he had merely a double vote. The whole number of male settlers for eighteen years constituted the legislative body. They met at stated times, and enacted such laws as were necessary for the welfare of the colony. The people were frequently convened by the governor, in the earlier years of the settlement, to aid him with their advice upon difficult questions brought before them. When the colony increased in population, and a number of towns were included within its limits, each town sent representatives to a general court at Plymouth.

If the colony grew slowly, it grew steadily, and at length the Pilgrims had their reward in seeing their little settlement expand into a flourishing province, in which the principles of civil freedom were cherished, religion honored, and industry and economy made the basis of the growing wealth of the little state. They had "been instruments to break the ice for others;" and "the honor shall be theirs to the world's end." Adversity could not daunt them, and prosperity had no power to move them from the sure foundation upon which they had anchored their hopes. From the first they had cherished the design of founding a state, which in the

A NEW ENGLAND HOMESTEAD.

hands of their children and their children's children would grow great, and even at this early day they began to see the realization of this hope. "Out of small beginnings," wrote Governor Bradford, the historian of the colony, almost in the spirit of prophecy, "great things have been produced by His hand that made all things out of nothing; and as one small candle will light a thousand, so the light here kindled hath shown to many, yea, to our whole nation."

CHAPTER XI.

SETTLEMENT OF MASSACHUSETTS AND RHODE ISLAND.

Settlement of New Hampshire—The English Puritans determine to form a new Colony in America—The Plymouth Council—A Colony sent out to Salem under Endicott—Colonization of Massachusetts Bay begun—A Charter obtained—Concessions of the King—Progress of the Salem Colony—The Charter and Government of the Colony removed to New England—Arrival of Governor Winthrop—Settlement of Boston—Sufferings of the Colonists—Roger Williams—His Opinions give offence to the Authorities—The Success of the Bay Colony established—Growth of Popular Liberty—The Ballot Box—Banishment of Roger Williams—He goes into the Wilderness—Founds Providence—Growth of Williams's Colony—Continued growth of Massachusetts—Arrival of Sir Henry Vane—Is elected Governor—Mrs Anne Hutchinson—The Antinomian Controversy—Mrs Hutchinson banished—Settlement of Rhode Island—Murder of Mrs Hutchinson

THE success of the Pilgrims in establishing the Plymouth colony aroused a feeling of deep interest in England, and some of those who had watched the effort were encouraged to attempt ventures of their own. Sir Ferdinand Gorges, who had taken a deep interest in the schemes to settle the new world, and John Mason, the secretary of the council of Plymouth, obtained a patent for the region called Laconia, which comprised the whole country between the sea, the St. Lawrence, the Merrimac and the Kennebec, and now embraced partly in Maine and partly in New Hampshire. A company of English merchants was formed, and in 1623 permanent colonies were established at Portsmouth, Dover and one or two other places near the mouth of the Piscataqua. These were small, feeble settlements, and were more trading-posts than towns. For many years their growth was slow, and it was not until other parts of New England were well peopled and advanced far beyond their early trials that they began to show signs of prosperity. In 1653, thirty years after its settlement, Portsmouth contained only "between fifty and sixty families" The settlers of these towns were not all Puritans, and their colonies had not the religious character of those of the rest of New England. In 1641, they were annexed at their own request to the province of Massachusetts, the general court having agreed not to require the freemen and deputies to be church members—

13

In the meantime the news of the successful planting of Plymouth was producing other and more important results in England. The persecutions of the Non-conformists, which marked the entire reign of James I., were continued through that of his son and successor, Charles I. The Puritans, sorely distressed by the tyranny to which they were subjected, listened with eagerness to the accounts of America which were sent over by the members of the Plymouth colony, and published from time to time in England. The descriptions of the Pilgrims were not exaggerated. They did not promise either fame or sudden wealth to settlers in their province, but clearly set forth the cares and labors which were to be the price of success in America. They dwelt with especial emphasis, however, upon that which was in their eyes the chief reward of all their toil and suffering—the ability to exercise their religion without restraint. Their brethren in England heard their accounts with a longing to be with them to enjoy the freedom with which they were blessed, and it was not long before a number of English Non-conformists began to concert measures for making New Eng-

land a place of refuge for the persecuted members of their faith. The leading spirit in these enterprises was the Rev. Mr. White, a minister of Dorsetshire, a Puritan, but not a Separatist. Regarding the vicinity of the present town

COAT OF ARMS OF MASSACHUSETTS.

of Salem as the most suitable place for colonization, he exerted himself with energy to secure it for his brethren.

In the meantime the Plymouth Company had ceased to exist, and its place had been taken by the council of Plymouth. That body cared for New England only as a source of profit, and sold the territory of that region to a number of purchasers, assigning the same district to different people, and thus paving the way for vexatious litigation. In 1628, it sold to a company of gentlemen of Dorchester, which White's energy had succeeded in bringing into existence, a district extending from three miles south of Massachusetts bay to three miles north of the Merrimac river. As was usual in all grants of the day, the Pacific was made the western boundary of this region. This company at once prepared to send out a colony, and in the early summer of that year one hundred persons under John Endicott, as governor, were despatched to New England. Endicott took his family with him, and in September, 1628, reached New England, and established the settlement of Salem, the site of which was already occupied by a few men whom White had placed there to hold it.

Endicott, who was a man of undaunted courage and acknowledged integrity of character, soon established his authority over the few settlements that had sprung up along the shores of the bay. At this time the site of Charlestown was occupied by an Englishman named Thomas Walford, a blacksmith, who had fortified his cabin with a palisade. The only dweller on the trimountain peninsula of Shawmut was the Rev. William Blackstone, a clergyman of the Church of England; the island now known as East Boston was occupied by Samuel Maverick. At Nantasket and a few places farther south some Englishmen had located themselves, and lived by fishing and trading in skins; and on the site

A PRIMITIVE NEW ENGLAND VILLAGE.

of Quincy was the wreck of a colony which had nearly perished in consequence of its evil ways. These, with the settlement at Salem, constituted the colony of Massachusetts Bay.

Soon after the departure of Endicott's colony from England, the company, acting upon the advice of their counsel, obtained from the king a confirmation of their grant. In March, 1629, the king granted to the colony of Massachusetts Bay a charter under which it conducted its affairs for more than fifty years. By the terms of this charter the governor was to be elected by the freemen for the term of one year, provision was made for the assembling at stated times of a general court, which was to have the power to make all the needed laws for the colony, and it was not necessary that these laws should receive the royal

signature in order to be valid This was conceding practical independence to the colony.

In the spring of 1629, a second company of emigrants sailed from
England for Massachusetts. They were, like the first, all Puritans, and
took with them, as their minister, the Rev. Francis Higginson, formerly
of Jesus College, Cambridge, a man of learning and deep piety The
colonists were instructed to do no violence to the Indians. "If any of
the salvages," so read the company's orders, "pretend right of inheritance
to all or any part of the lands granted in our patent, endeavor to purchase their tytle, that we may avoid the least scruple of intrusion " Six
shipwrights were sent over for the use of the colony, an experienced
engineer to lay out a fortified town, and a master gunner, who was to
teach the men of the colony the use of arms and military exercises.
Cattle and horses and goats were sent out also.

The voyage was prosperous, and the new settlers reached Salem about
the last of June. They found the settlement in a feeble condition, and
greatly in need of their assistance. The old and the new colonists numbered about three hundred. The majority of these remained at Salem,
and the rest were sent by Endicott to establish a colony at Charlestown,
in order to secure that place from occupation by the partisans of Sir
Ferdinaud Gorges, who claimed the region. The emigrants were
scrupulous to acquire from the Indians the right to the lands they occupied The 12th of July was observed as a day of fasting and prayer
"for the choice of a pastor and teacher at Salem " No one advanced
any claim founded on his ordination in England, personal fitness was
the only qualification recognized by the Puritans Samuel Skelton was
chosen pastor, and Francis Higginson teacher. Three or four of the
gravest members of the church laid their hands upon the heads of these
men, with prayer, and solemnly appointed them to their respective
offices "Thus the church, like that of Plymouth, was self-constituted,
on the principle of the independence of each religious community It
did not ask the assent of the king, or recognize him as its head; its
officers were set apart and ordained among themselves; it used no
liturgy, it rejected unnecessary ceremonies, and reduced the simplicity
of Calvin to a still plainer standard The motives which controlled its
decisions were so deeply seated that its practices were repeated spon-
taneously by Puritan New England." An opposition to the organization
of the church was attempted by a party led by John and Samuel Browne,
men of ability; but this was treated as a mutiny and put down, and the
Brownes were sent back to England

The charter of Massachusetts, though it made liberal concessions to the

colony, contained no provision for the rights of the people, who were left
at the mercy of the company.   For the proper government of the colony,
it was necessary to remove the charter to Massachusetts, and such a removal was advisable on another ground.   The charter contained no
guarantee for the religious freedom of the colony, and the king might at
any moment seek to interfere with this, the most precious right of the
Puritans.   The only way to escape the evils which the company had
reason to dread was for the governing council to change its place of
meeting from England to Massachusetts, which the charter gave it
authority to do.   On the 26th of August, 1629, John Winthrop, Isaac
Johnson, Thomas Dudley, Richard Saltonstall and eight others, men of
fortune and education, met at Cambridge and bound themselves by a
solemn agreement to settle in New England if the whole government of
the colony, together with the patent, should be legally transferred to that
region before the end of September   On the 29th of the month, the
court took the decisive step and ordered that "the government and
patent should be settled in New England."   This was a bold step, but
its legality was not contested by any one, and it made the government
of the colony independent of control by any power in England.

The officers of the colony were to be a governor and eighteen assistants.   On the 20th of October, a meeting of the court was held to choose
them, and John Winthrop was elected governor for one year.   It was a
fortunate selection, for Winthrop proved himself for many years the
very mainstay of the colony, sustaining his companions by his calm
courage, and setting them a noble example in his patience, his quiet
heroism and his devotion to the welfare of others.   He seemed to find
his greatest pleasure in doing good, and his liberality acted as a check
upon the bigotry of his associates and kept them in paths of greater
moderation

Efforts were made to send over new settlers to Massachusetts, and
about a thousand emigrants, with cattle, horses and goats, were transported thither in the season of 1630   Early in April, Governor Winthrop and about seven hundred emigrants sailed from England in a fleet
of eleven ships.   Many of them were "men of high endowments and
large fortune; scholars, well versed in the learning of the times; clergymen who ranked among the best educated and most pious in the realm."
They reached Salem on the 12th of June, after a voyage of sixty-one
days, and were gladly welcomed by the settlers, whom they found in
great distress from sickness and a scarcity of provisions.   About eighty
had died during the winter, and many were sick.   There was scarcely
a fortnight's supply of food in the settlement, and it was necessary

to send one of the ships back to England at once for a supply of provisions

Salem did not please the new-comers, and settlements were made at Lynn, Charlestown, Newtown, Dorchester, Roxbury, Malden, and Watertown. The governor and a large part of the emigrants settled first at Charlestown, but at length, in order to obtain better water, crossed over and occupied the little tri-mountain peninsula of Shawmut. To this settlement was given the name of Boston, in honor of the town in Lincolnshire in England, which had been the home of the Rev. John Wilson, who became the pastor of the first church of Boston. The location was central to the whole province, and Boston became the seat of government. When the year for which the first colonial officers had been chosen expired a new election was held, and Governor Winthrop and all the old officials were reelected.

The colonists now began to feel the effects of their new life. The change of climate was very trying to them, and many of them fell victims to its rigors, and to the hardships of their position A large number of them had been brought up in ease and refinement, and were unaccustomed to privation or exposure. They sank beneath the severe trials to which they were subjected. By December, 1630, at least two hundred had died Among these were the Lady Arbella Johnson and her husband, among the most liberal and devoted supporters of the colony, and a son of Governor Winthrop, who left a widow and children in England Others became disheartened, and more than a hundred returned to England, where they endeavored to excuse their desertion of their companions by grossly exaggerated accounts of the hardships of the colony. Yet among the colonists themselves there was no repining They exhibited in their deep distress a fortitude and heroism worthy of their lofty character. " Honor is due," says Bancroft, " not less to those who perished than to those who survived, to the martyrs the hour of death was the hour of triumph, such as is never witnessed in more tranquil seasons. . . Even children caught the spirit of the place; awaited the impending change in the tranquil confidence of faith, and went to the grave full of immortality. The survivors bore all things meekly, 'remembering the end of their coming hither.'" Winthrop wrote to his wife, who had been detained in England by sickness " We enjoy here God and Jesus Christ, and is not this enough ? I thank God I like so well to be here, as I do not repent my coming. I would not have altered my course though I had foreseen all these afflictions. I never had more content of mind."

Another danger which threatened the colony arose from the scarcity of provisions, but this was removed on the 5th of February, 1631, by the timely arrival of the "Lyon" from England, laden with provisions. This relief was greeted with public thanksgivings in all the settlements. The "Lyon," however, brought only twenty passengers, and in 1631 only ninety persons came out from England. The number of arrivals in 1632 was only two hundred and fifty. Thus the colony grew very slowly. By the close of the latter year the total population of Massachusetts was only a little over one thousand souls.

Among the passengers of the "Lyon" was a young minister, described in the old records as "lovely in his carriage, godly and zealous, having precious gifts," Roger Williams by name. He had been a favorite pupil of the great Sir Edward Coke, and had learned from him precious lessons of liberty and toleration. He had been carefully educated at Pembroke College, in the University of Cambridge, and had entered the ministry.

His opposition to the laws requiring conformity to the established church had drawn upon him the wrath of Archbishop Laud, and he had been driven out of England. The great doctrine which he had embraced as the result of his studies and experience was the freedom of conscience from secular control. "The civil magistrate should restrain crime, but never control opinion; should punish guilt, but never violate inward freedom." He would place all forms of religion upon an equality, and would refuse to the government the power to compel conformity to, or attendance upon, any of them

ROGER WILLIAMS.

leaving such matters to the conscience of the individual. He also favored the abolition of tithes, and the enforced contribution to the support of the church. Such views were far in advance of the age, and when Williams landed in Boston, he found himself unable to join the church in that place because of its adoption of principles the opposite of his own. Upon his arrival the church had intended engaging him to fill Mr. Wilson's place, while that minister returned to England to bring over his wife, but upon learning his views the idea was abandoned. A little later the church in Salem, which had been deprived of its teacher by the death of the Rev. Francis Higginson, called Williams to be his successor. Williams accepted the call; but Governor Winthrop and the assistants warned the people of Salem to beware how they placed in so important a position a man already at such variance with the established order of things. The warning had the desired effect upon the people of Salem, who withdrew their invitation. Williams then went to Plymouth, where he lived for two years in peace

But though unwilling to accord to Williams the liberty he desired, the colonial government was careful to take every precaution against the anticipated efforts of the Church of England to extend its authority over Massachusetts A general court held in May, 1631, ordered an oath of fidelity to be tendered to the freemen of the colony, which bound them " to be obedient and conformable to the laws and constitutions of this commonwealth, to advance its peace, and not to suffer any attempt at making any change or alteration of the government contrary to its laws " The same general court took a still more decided stand by the adoption of a law, which limited the citizenship of the colony to " such as are members of some of the churches within the limits of the same " This was practically making the state a theocracy.

Yet the people were not prepared to surrender their political rights, even when alarmed by the danger which seemed to threaten their religious establishment Until now the assistants could hold office for life, and they also possessed the power of electing the governor They were thus independent of the people The right of the freemen to choose their magistrates was now distinctly asserted, and in May, 1632, was conceded. The governor and assistants were to be elected annually, and by the votes of the freemen ; none but church-members being entitled to the privileges of freemen Another important change was brought about at the same time by the hostility of the people to levying of taxes by the board of assistants. Each town was ordered to send two of its best men to represent it at a general court " to concert a plan for a public treasury." This was the foundation of representative government in Massachusetts.

The colonists had faithfully obeyed their instructions to treat the Indians with fairness, and to seek to cultivate their friendship. Many of the native tribes sought their alliance, and the sachem of the Mohegans came from the banks of the Connecticut to make a treaty with the colony, and to urge the English to settle in his country, which he described as exceedingly fertile and inviting. In the autumn of 1632 a pleasant intercourse was opened with the Plymouth colony ; and in the same year a trade in corn was begun with Virginia, and commercial relations were established with the Dutch, who had settled along the Hudson river. The colony of Massachusetts Bay was slowly emerging from its early trials, and entering upon a more prosperous period.

Emigrants now began to come over in greater numbers, and among them were John Haynes, " the acute and subtile Cotton," and Thomas

Hooker, who has been called the "Light of the Western Churches." The freemen by the middle of the year 1634 numbered between three and four hundred, and these were bent upon establishing their political power in the state. Great advances were made in the direction of representative government, and the ballot-box was introduced in elections which had been formerly conducted by an erection of hands. As a guard against arbitrary taxation by magistrates it was enacted that none but the properly chosen representatives of the people might dispose of lands, or raise money. In the spring of 1635 the people went a step further, and demanded a written constitution for the purpose of still more perfectly securing their liberties. This demand opened a controversy which continued for ten years. The general court was composed of assistants and deputies. The first were elected by the people of the whole colony; the latter by the towns. The two bodies acted together in meetings of the assembly, but the assistants claimed the exclusive privilege of meeting and exercising a separate negative upon the proceedings of the court. This claim was energetically denied by the deputies, who were sustained by the body of the people; while the magistrates and the ministers upheld the pretensions of the assistants. In 1644 the matter was compromised by the division of the general court into two branches, each of which was given a negative upon the proceedings of the other. All parties were agreed, however, in the work of connecting the religion and the government of the colony so closely that they should mutually sustain each other against the attacks of the Church of England.

While these measures were in course of adjustment other matters were engaging the attention of the colony. After Roger Williams had been a little more than two years in Plymouth, he was called again to Salem, and accepted the invitation. This gave offence to many persons, and in January, 1634, complaints were made against Williams because of a paper he had written while at Plymouth, denying that the king had any power to grant lands in America to his subjects, since the lands were the property of the Indians. In this Williams was wrong, as the settlers in New England had been careful to obtain the consent of the natives to their occupation of the lands they had possessed. He made a proper explanation of his paper, when he understood the true state of the case, and consented that it should be burned.

Still the jealousy and dislike of the Puritans was aroused by the radical opposition of Williams to their system, although he conducted himself with a forbearance and amiableness that should have won him the love of those with whom he was thrown. Williams strongly condemned the law enforcing the attendance of the people upon religious services, declaring that a man had a right to stay away if he wished to do so. He also censured the practice of selecting the colonial officials exclusively from the members of the church, and said that a physician or a pilot might with equal propriety be chosen because of his piety, his skill in theology, or his standing in the church. These and other similar views were drawn from him in a series of controversies, held with him by a committee of ministers, for the purpose of inducing him to retract his radical sentiments. He remained firm in them, however, and his opponents declared that his principles were calculated not only to destroy religion, but also to subvert all forms of civil government. It was resolved to banish him from the colony, and as the people of Salem warmly supported Williams, they were admonished by the court, and a tract of land, which was rightfully theirs, was withheld from them as a punishment. Williams and the church at Salem appealed to the people against the injustice of the magistrates, and asked the other churches of the colony to "admonish the magistrates of their injustice." This was regarded as treason by the colonial government, and at the next general court Salem was disfranchised until the town should make ample apology for its offence. Williams was summoned before the general court in October, 1635, and maintained his opinions with firmness,

COAT OF ARMS OF RHODE ISLAND.

though with moderation. He was sentenced to banishment from the colony, not, as it was declared, because of his religious views, but because the magistrates averred his principles, if carried out, would destroy all civil government.

The season was so far advanced that it would have been barbarous to drive any one out of the colony at that time, and Williams obtained leave to remain in the province until the spring, when he intended forming a settlement on Narragansett bay. The affection of his people at Salem, which had seemed to grow cold when the town began to feel the weight of the punishment inflicted by the general court, now revived, and they thronged to his house in great numbers to hear him, and his opinions spread rapidly. The magistrates were alarmed; and it was resolved to send him at once to England in a ship that was just about to sail from Boston. He was ordered to come to Boston and embark there, but refused to obey the summons. A boat's crew was then sent to arrest him and bring him to Boston by force; but when the officers reached Salem he had disappeared.

Three days before their arrival Roger Williams had left Salem, a wan-
derer for conscience sake. It was the depth of winter, the snow lay
thickly over the country, and the weather was cold and inclement. For
fourteen weeks, he says, he "was sorely tost in .. bitter season, not knowing what bread or bed did mean." Banished from the settlements of his
own race the exile went out into the wilderness, and sought the country
of the Indians, whose friendship he had won during his stay in the
colony. He had acquired their language during his residence at Plymouth, and could speak it fluently. He went from lodge to lodge, kindly

LANDING OF ROGER WILLIAMS AT PROVIDENCE.

welcomed by the savages, and lodging sometimes in a hollow tree, until
he reached Mount Hope, the residence of Massasoit, who was his friend.
Canonicus, the great chieftain of the Narragansetts, loved him with a
strong affection, which ceased only with his life; and in the country of
these friendly chiefs Williams passed the winter in peace and safety. He
never ceased to be grateful for their aid in his distress, and during his
whole life he was the especial friend and champion of the Indians in New
England.

It was the intention of Williams to settle at Seekonk, on the Paw-
tucket river; but that place was found to be within the limits of the
Plymouth colony. Governor Winslow wrote to Williams advising him
to remove to the region of Narragansett bay, which was beyond the jurisdiction of the English, and would render any misunderstanling between

the Plymouth and Bay colonies on his account impossible. "I took his prudent motion," says Williams, "as a voice from God." Being joined by five companions, Williams embarked in a canoe in June, 1635, and passing ʌ ɪ to the west arm of Narragansett bay, landed at an attractive spot, where he found a spring of pure water He chose the place as the site of a new settlement, and in gratitude for his deliverance from the many dangers through which he had passed, named it PROVIDENCE. He sought to purchase enough land for a settlement, but Canonicus refused to sell the land, and gave it to his friend "to enjoy forever." This grant was made to Williams alone, and constituted him absolute owner of the lands included in it. He might have sold them to settlers on terms advantageous to himself; but he declined to do so In the next two years he was joined by a number of his old followers from Massachusetts, and by others who fled to his asylum. He gave a share of land to all who came to settle, and admitted them to an equality with himself in the political administration of the colony. The government was administered by the whole people. The voice of the majority decided all public measures, but in matters of conscience every man was left answerable to God alone. All forms of religious belief were tolerated and protected Even infidelity was safe here from punishment by the civil or ecclesiastical power. Williams was anxious to establish friendly relations with the Massachusetts colony; for though he felt keenly the injustice of his persecutors, he cherished no bitterness or resentment towards them. He condemned only what he considered the delusions of the magistrates of Massachusetts, but never attacked his persecutors. "I did ever from my soul," he wrote with simple magnanimity, "honor and love them, even when their judgment led them to afflict me." Winslow, touched with his true Christian forbearance, came from Plymouth to visit him, and left with his wife some money for their support, and some of the leaders of the Bay colony began to bear tardy witness to his virtues. The settlement at Providence continued to grow slowly, and was blessed with peace and an increasing prosperity.

Massachusetts in the meantime continued to receive numerous additions to her population by emigration from England. In the autumn of 1635, twelve families left Boston, and journeying into the interior, founded the town of Concord. They had a hard struggle to establish their little settlement, but persevered, and at length their labors were crowned with success. Three thousand people came over to Massachusetts this year. Among them were Hugh Peters, a man of great eloquence and ability and a devoted republican, who had been pastor to a church of exiles at Rotterdam, and Henry Vane the younger, "a man of the

12

purest mind ; a statesman of spotless integrity ; whose name the progress
of intelligence and liberty will erase from the rubric of fanatics and
traitors, and insert high among the aspirants after truth and the martyrs
for liberty." *

In the following spring (1636) Vane was elected governor of the
colony. The people were dazzled by his high birth and pleasing qualities, and committed an error in choosing him, for neither his age nor his
experience fitted him for the distinguished position conferred upon him.
The arrival of Vane seemed to promise an emigration of a number of the
English nobility, and an effort was made by several of them in England
to procure the division of the general court into two branches, and the
establishment of an hereditary nobility in the colony which should
possess a right to seats in the upper branch of the court. The magistrates of the colony were anxious to conciliate these valuable friends, but
they firmly refused to establish hereditary nobility in their new state.

Religious discussions formed a large part of the life of the colony.
Meetings were held by the men, and passages of Scripture were discussed,
and the sermons of the ministers made the subject of searching criticism
The women might attend these meetings, but were not allowed to take
part in the discussions Mrs. Anne Hutchinson, a woman of talent and
eloquence, claimed for her sex the right to participate equally with the
men in these meetings but as this was not possible, she began to hold
meetings for the benefit of the women at her own house. At these
religious doctrines were discussed and advocated which were at variance
with the principles of the magistrates Mrs. Hutchinson and her
followers held that the authority of private judgment was superior to
that of the church, and condemned the efforts of the colony to enforce
conformity to the established system as violative of the inherent rights of
Christians She was encouraged by John Wheelwright, a silenced minister,
who had married her sister, and by Governor Vane, and her opinions
were adopted by a large number of the people, and by members of the
general court and some of the magistrates.

The ministers saw their authority menaced by the new belief, and
made common cause against Mrs. Hutchinson and her protector, Governor
Vane. The colony was divided into two parties, and the religious question became a matter of great political importance. Under the established
system the ministers formed almost a distinct estate of the government,
and political privileges were entirely dependent upon theological conformity. The success of Mrs Hutchinson's views would revolutionize
the government and destroy the power of the church to control secular

* Bancroft.

affairs Such a change was not yet to be attempted. Governor Vane was too far in advance of the age, and Mrs. Hutchinson was denounced as "weakening the hands and hearts of the people towards the ministers," and as being as bad "as Roger Williams, or worse." Some went so far as to hint that she was a witch. Feeling sure that they would not receive justice at the hands of their opponents, the friends of Mrs. Hutchinson declared their intention to appeal to the king This aroused a storm of indignation in the colony, and "it was accounted perjury and treason to speak of appeals to the king " This threat changed the whole character of the question, and was fatal to the party which made it The Puritans had come to Massachusetts to escape the interference of the crown with their religious belief, and to appeal to the king in this case would be simply to place the liberties of the colony at his mercy. When the elections were held, in the spring of 1637, Governor Winthrop and the old magistrates were chosen by a large majority Vane soon after returned to England

The church party being now in power resolved to silence Mrs. Hutchinson. She was admonished to cease her teachings, and upon her refusal to obey this order, she and her followers were exiled from the colony Wheelwright and a number of his friends went to New Hampshire, and founded the town of Exeter, at the head of tide-water on the Piscataqua Mrs. Hutchinson and the majority of her followers removed, in the spring of 1638, to the southward, intending to settle on Long Island or on the Delaware Roger Williams induced them to remain near his plantation, and obtained for them from Miantonomoh, the chief of the Narragansett tribe, the gift of the beautiful island in the lower part of Narragansett bay, which they called the island of Rhodes, or Rhode Island. The number of settlers was scarcely more than twenty, but they proceeded to form a government upon a plan agreeable to the principles they professed. It was a pure democracy, founded upon the universal consent of the people, who signed a social compact pledging themselves to obey the laws made by the majority, and to respect the rights of conscience. William Coddington, who had been a magistrate in the Bay colony, was elected judge or ruler, and three elders were chosen as his assistants The settlement grew rapidly, and by 1641 the population had become so numerous as to require a written constitution.

Mrs. Hutchinson remained in Rhode Island for several years, but fearing that the hostility of the magistrates of Massachusetts would reach her even there, removed beyond New Haven into the territory of the Dutch, where, in 1643, she and all her family who were with her, except one child, who was taken prisoner, were murdered by the Indians.

CHAPTER XII.

COLONIZATION OF CONNECTICUT.

The Dutch Claim the Connecticut Valley—They build a Fort at Hartford—Governor Winslow makes a Lodgment in Connecticut for the English—Withdrawal of the Dutch —The First Efforts of the English to Settle Connecticut—Emigration of Hooker and his Congregation—They Settle at Hartford—Winthrop builds a Fort at Saybrooke—Hostility of the Indians—Visit of Roger Williams to Miantonomoh—A Brave Deed—The Pequod War—Capture of the Indian Fort—Destruction of the Pequod Tribe—Effect of this War upon the other Tribes—Connecticut Adopts a Constitution—Its Peculiar Features—Settlement of New Haven.

THE fertile region of the Connecticut had attracted the attention of the English at an early day; but before they could make any effort to occupy it the Dutch sent an exploring party from Manhattan island, in 1614, and examined the river and the country through which it flowed. They built and fortified a trading-post on the site of the present city of Hartford, but soon excited the ill-will of the Indians by their cruel treatment of them. The Dutch found themselves unable to occupy the country, and being unwilling to lose it, endeavored, but without success, to induce the Pilgrims to remove from Plymouth to the Connecticut, and settle in that region under their protection.

In 1630, the council of Plymouth granted the Connecticut region to the Earl of Warwick, who, in 1631, assigned his claim to Lords Say and Brooke, John Hampden, and others. As soon as this grant was known to the Dutch they sent a party to the site of Hartford and re-established their trading-post, and began a profitable trade with the Indians. They mounted two cannon on their fort for the purpose of preventing the English from ascending the river. Towards the latter part of the year 1633, Governor Winslow, of Plymouth, in order to secure a foothold for the English in this valuable region, sent Captain William Holmes to the Connecticut with a sloop and a number of men to make a settlement. Upon ascending the river to the site of Hartford, Holmes found his progress barred by the Dutch fort, the commander of which threatened to fire upon him if he attempted to continue his voyage. Undaunted by this threat, Holmes passed by the fort without harm, and ascended the

180

stream to Windsor, where he erected a fortified post. In 1634, the Dutch made an unsuccessful attempt to drive him away. Failing in this, and seeing that it was the deliberate purpose of the English to occupy the Connecticut valley, the Dutch relinquished all claim to that region, and a boundary line was arranged between their possessions and those of the English, corresponding very nearly to that between the States of Connecticut and New York.

In 1635, the Pilgrims determined to make settlements in this inviting region, and late in the fall of that year a company of sixty persons, men, women, and children, set out from Plymouth by land, sending a sloop laden with provisions and their household goods around by sea, with orders to join them upon the Connecticut river. They began their journey too late in the season, and their sufferings were very great in consequence. Upon reaching the river they found the ground covered with snow, and their sloop was delayed by storms and ice. Their cattle died from cold and exposure, and but for a little corn which they obtained from the Indians, and such acorns as they could gather, the whole company must have starved to death. Many of them abandoned their new home and returned by land to the settlements on the coast

COAT OF ARMS OF CONNECTICUT

The Puritans were resolved to continue the effort to settle Connecticut, and in the spring of 1636 several companies emigrated to that region. The principal party set out in June, led by the Rev Thomas Hooker It comprised about one hundred persons, and consisted principally of Hooker's congregation, who followed their pastor with enthusiasm. They drove before them a considerable number of cattle, which furnished them with milk on the march. The emigrants were largely made up of persons of refinement and culture, and comprised many of the oldest and most valued citizens of the Bay colony They were attracted to the valley of the Connecticut by the superior advantages which it offered for the prosecution of the fur trade, and by the great fertility of its soil. They had no guide but a compass, and their route lay through an unbroken wilderness The journey was long and fatiguing The emigrants accomplished scarcely more than ten miles a day, carrying their sick on litters, and making the forests ring with their holy hymns. At length the site of Hartford, where it was proposed to establish the settlement, was reached by the 1st of July. The greater number remained there; some went higher up the river and founded Springfield, and the rest went to Wethersfield, where there was already a small settlement.

In the same year the younger John Winthrop arrived from England, with orders from Lords Say and Brooke to establish a fort at the mouth of the Connecticut river. This he accomplished, naming the new settlement Saybrooke in honor of the proprietors. The settlements in Connecticut grew rapidly, the excellent soil and pleasant climate attracting many emigrants to them.

The existence of these settlements was precarious, however. The region in which they had been planted was the country of the Pequods, who inhabited it in large numbers. They were the most powerful and warlike tribe in New England, and could bring nearly two thousand warriors into the field. They occupied the southeastern part of Connecticut, and their territory extended almost to the Hudson on the west, where it joined that of the Mohegans. On the east their territory bordered that of the Narragansetts. Both of these tribes were the enemies of the Pequods and the friends of the English. This friendship was resented by the Pequods, who were already jealous of the English because of their occupation of the lands along the Connecticut. The tribe bore a bad name, and had already manifested their hostility by murdering, a few years before, a Virginia trader named Stone, together with the crew of his vessel, who were engaged in a trading expedition on the Connecticut river. Somewhat later Captain Oldham and his crew, while exploring the river, were also murdered by Indians living on Block island. The Pequods justified the murder of Stone by alleging that he had attacked them. Wishing to make a treaty with the English, they sent their chiefs to Boston for that purpose, and promised—as the magistrates understood them—to deliver up the two men who had killed Stone. Captain John Endicott was sent with a vessel, in 1636, to punish the Block Island Indians for the murder of Oldham, and was ordered to call on his return at the Pequod town, and demand the surrender of the murderers of Stone. The Pequods declined to surrender these men, but offered to ransom them. This was in accordance with their customs. But Endicott refused to accept any compensation for the crime that had been committed, and to punish the Indians destroyed their corn and burned two of their villages. This made open hostilities inevitable. The Pequods began to hang around the Connecticut settlements and cut off stragglers from them. By the close of the winter more than thirty persons had fallen victims to their vengeance.

The settlements in the Connecticut valley were now greatly alarmed. They could not muster over two hundred fighting men, and the Indians in their immediate vicinity could bring into the field at least seven hundred warriors. War was certain, and it was not known at what moment the savages would attack the settlements in overwhelming force. Connecticut called upon Massachusetts for aid, but only twenty men, under Captain Underhill, were sent to their aid. The energies and attention of the Bay colony were engrossed by the Hutchinson quarrel.

The Pequods, notwithstanding their immense numerical superiority, were unwilling to make war upon the English without the support of another tribe. They accordingly sent envoys to Miantonomoh, the chief of the Narragansetts, to endeavor to engage that tribe in the effort against the whites. Such a union would have menaced all New England, and as soon as the news of the negotiation reached Boston the government of the Bay colony prepared to prevent the alliance. Governor Vane at once wrote to Roger Williams, the friend of Miantonomoh, urging him to seek that chieftain and prevent him from joining the Pequods. It was a dangerous mission, and certainly a great service for the magistrates of Massachusetts to ask of the man whom they had driven into exile. They did not ask in vain, however. All of Williams' generous nature was aroused by the danger which threatened his brethren, and he embarked in a frail canoe, and braving the danger of a severe gale, sought the quarters of Miantonomoh. He found the Pequod chiefs already there, and the Narragansetts wavering. Knowing the errand on which he had come, the hostile chieftains were ready at any moment to despatch him, and had Miantonomoh shown the least favor to the project, Williams would have paid for his boldness with his life. He spent three days and nights in the company of the savages, and succeeded in inducing Miantonomoh not only to refuse to join the war against the English, but to promise the colonists his assistance against the Pequods. In the meantime he sent a messenger to Boston to inform the governor of the designs of the Indians.

The Pequods, left to continue the struggle alone, flattered themselves that their superiority in numbers would give them the victory, and continued their aggressions upon the Connecticut settlements to such an extent that in May, 1637, the general court of that province resolved to begin the war at once. A force of eighty men, including those sent from Massachusetts, was assembled at Hartford, and the command was conferred by Hooker upon Captain John Mason. The night previous to their departure was spent in prayer, and on the 20th of May the little force embarked in boats and descended the river to the sound, and passed around to Narragansett bay, intending to approach the Pequod town from that quarter. As the boats sailed by the mouth of the

Thames, the savages supposed the English were abandoning the Connecticut valley.

The day after the arrival of the English in Narragansett bay was the Sabbath, and was scrupulously observed. On the following day they repaired to the quarters of Canonicus, the old chief and principal ruler of the Narragansett tribe, and asked his assistance against the Pequods. Miantonomoh, the nephew and prospective successor of Canonicus, hesitated to join in the doubtful enterprise, but two hundred warriors agreed to accompany the English, who could not, however, count upon the fidelity of these reinforcements. Seventy Mohegans, under Uncas, their chief, also joined Mason. With this force the English commander marched across the country toward the Pequod towns on the Thames, and halted on the night of the 25th of May, within hearing of them.

In the meantime the Pequods, convinced that the English had fled from the Connecticut region, and never dreading an attack in their fort, which they considered impregnable, had given themselves up to rejoicing. The night, passed by the English in waiting the signal for the attack, was spent by the Pequods in revelry and songs, which could be plainly heard in the English camp. Two hours before dawn, on the morning of the 26th of May, the order was given to the little band under Mason to advance. They knew they would have to decide the battle by their own efforts, and were by no means certain that their Indian allies would not turn against them. The Pequods were posted in two strong forts made of palisades driven into the ground and strengthened with rush-work, an excellent defence against a foe of their own race, but worthless when assailed by Europeans. The principal fort stood on the summit of a considerable hill, and was regarded by Sassacus, the Pequod chief, as impregnable. The tramp of the advancing force aroused a dog, whose fierce bark awoke the Indian sentinel. The keen eye of the savage detected the enemy in the gloom of the morning, and he rushed into the fort, shouting, "The English! the English!" The next moment the English were through the palisades. On all sides they beheld the Indians pouring out of their lodges to take part in the hand-to-hand fight. The odds were too great. "We must burn them," cried Mason, and, suiting the action to the word, he applied a torch to a wigwam constructed of dry reeds. The flames sprang up instantly and spread with the rapidity of lightning. The Indians vainly endeavored to extinguish the fire, and the English, withdrawing to a greater distance, began to pick off the savages, who were doubly exposed by the light of the blazing fort. Wherever a Pequod appeared, he was shot down. The Narragansetts and Mohegans now joined in the conflict, and the victory was complete. More than six hundred Pequods, men, women and children, perished, the majority of them in the flames. The English lost only two men; and the battle was over in an hour.

As the sun rose, a body of three hundred Pequod warriors were seen advancing from their second fort. They came expecting to rejoice with their comrades in the destruction of the English. When they beheld the ruined fort and the remains of its defenders, they screamed, stamped on the ground and tore their hair with rage and despair. Mason held

YALE COLLEGE.

them in check with twenty men, while the rest of the English embarked in their boats, which had come round from Narragansett bay, and hastened home to protect the settlements against a sudden attack. Mason, with the party mentioned, marched across the country to the fort at Saybrooke, where he was received with the honors due to his successful exploit.

In a few days a body of one hundred men arrived from Massachusetts, under Captain Stoughton, and the campaign against the Pequods was

resumed. Their pride was crushed, and they made but a feeble resistance. They fled to the west, closely pursued by the English, who
destroyed their corn-fields, burned their villages and put their women
and children to death without mercy. They made a last desperate effort
at resistance in the fastnesses of a swamp, but were defeated with great
slaughter. Sassacus, their chief, with a few of his men took refuge with
the Mohawks, where he was soon after put to death by one of his own
people. The remainder of the tribe, about two hundred in number,
surrendered to the English, and were reduced to slavery. Some were
given to their enemies, the Narragansetts and Mohegans; others were
sent to the West Indies and sold as slaves. The Pequod nation was
utterly destroyed

The thoroughness and remorselessness of the work struck terror to the
neighboring tribes. If the Pequods, the most powerful of all their race,
had been exterminated by a mere handful of Englishmen, what could
they expect in a contest with them but a similar fate? For forty years
the horror of this fearful deed remained fresh in the savage mind, and
protected the young settlements more effectually than the most vigilant
watchfulness on the part of the whites could have done.

Relieved from the fear of the Indians, the people of Connecticut prepared to establish a civil government for the colony, and in January,
1639, a constitution was adopted. It was more liberal, and therefore
more lasting, than that framed by any of the other colonies. It provided for the government of the colony by a governor, a legislature and
the usual magistrates of an English province, who were to be chosen
annually by ballot. Every settler who should take the oath of allegiance
to the commonwealth was to have the right of suffrage The members
of the legislature were apportioned among the towns according to the
population. The colony was held to be supreme within its own limits,
and no recognition was made of the sovereignty of the king or Parliament. When Connecticut took her place among the States of the
American Union, at the opening of the war of the Revolution, her constitution needed no change to adapt her to her new position. It remained
in force for one hundred and fifty years.

In the year of the Pequod war (1637), John Davenport, a celebrated
clergyman of London, and Theophilus Eaton, a merchant of wealth, and
a number of their associates, who had been exiled from England for
their religious opinions, reached Boston. They were warmly welcomed,
and were urged to stay in the Bay colony, but the theological disputes
were so high there that they preferred to go into the wilderness and
found a settlement where they could be at peace. Eaton with a few men

was sent to explore the region west of the Connecticut, which had been discovered by the pursuers of the Pequods. He examined the coast of Long Island sound, and spent the winter at a place which he selected as a settlement. In April, 1638, Davenport and the rest of the company sailed from Boston and established a settlement on the spot chosen by Eaton. The settlers obtained a title to their lands from the natives, and agreed in return to protect them against the Mohawks. They named their settlement New Haven. In 1639, a form of government was adopted, and Eaton was elected governor. He was annually chosen to

VALLEY OF THE CONNECTICUT.

this position until his death, twenty years later. The colonists pledged themselves "to be governed in all things by the rules which the Scriptures held forth to them." The right of suffrage was restricted to church members. "Thus New Haven made the Bible its statute book, and the elect its freemen." In the next ten years settlements spread along the sound and extended to the opposite shores of Long island. The colony was distinct from and independent of the Connecticut colony, with which friendly relations were soon established.

CHAPTER XIII.

THE UNION OF THE NEW ENGLAND COLONIES

THE sentiments with which the people of the New England colonies regarded the mother country may be briefly stated. They were proud of the name of Englishmen, and took a deep interest in the welfare of their old home. They regarded the British constitution as the supreme law of their new states, and claimed to be true and loyal subjects of the King of England. Nevertheless, they looked upon the success of their colonies as their own work, accomplished by their own patience and heroism, and they were fully aware that they owed nothing to the mother country. They had been driven forth from her shores by persecution, and left in neglect to struggle up to the successful position they now occupied. They owed nothing to England; in their deepest distress they had never asked aid of her, and they were willing to undergo any hardship rather than do so. They had made laws and established institutions under which they had surmounted their early trials, and they regarded their paramount allegiance as due to their respective provinces. They acknowledged the right of no power beyond the Atlantic to interfere with or change their work. They would acknowledge their allegiance to the king as long as he respected the system they had built up at such great cost, and without assistance from him, but would resist any effort from him, or any one else, to interfere with it. They had made New England what she was, and they meant to retain the possession and control of their new home at any cost. They had made themselves a free people, and they meant to preserve their liberties as a precious heritage for their children.

This was the general sentiment of New England. There were some discontented persons, however, in the midst of these determined people.

They had found the stern discipline of the Massachusetts colony too oppressive, and some had been severely punished by the fiery Endicott. Upon returning to England they endeavored to induce the king to exert his power and remedy what they termed the distraction and disorder of the province of Massachusetts Their complaints were echoed by a strong party in England. Burdett wrote to Archbishop Laud that "The colonists aimed not at a new discipline, but at sovereignty, that it was accounted treason in their general court to speak of appeals to the king;" in which assertion he was right. The English archbishop began to regard the departure of so many "faithful and free-born Englishmen and good Christians" to join a new communion as a serious matter, and impediments were thrown in the way of emigration. In February, 1634, a requisition was addressed to the colony of Massachusetts ordering the colonial officials to produce the patent of the company in England. The colony took no notice of this demand A little later the king appointed the Archbishop of Canterbury and some others a special commission, with full power over the American colonies. They were authorized to make such changes in church and state as they deemed necessary; to enforce them with heavy penalties; and even to revoke all charters that contained privileges inconsistent with the royal prerogative.

The news of the appointment of this commission reached Boston in September, 1634, and it was also rumored that a governor-general for the colonies had been appointed, and had sailed from England. All Massachusetts burned with indignation, and the colony resolved to resist the attempt upon its liberties. It was very poor, but in a short space of time the large sum of six hundred pounds was raised for the public defence, and fortifications were begun and pushed forward with energy. In January, 1635, the ministers were assembled at Boston and their opinion was asked upon the question whether the colony should receive a governor-general. They answered boldly · "We ought to defend our lawful possessions if we are able; if not, to avoid and protract."

In April, 1638, the privy council demanded the surrender of the charter of Massachusetts, threatening in case of refusal that the king would take the management of the colony into his own hands. The colonial authorities were firmly resolved to give the king no pretext for interference with their affairs, and instead of complying with the order of the privy council, they addressed a remonstrance to that body against the surrender required of them, thus seeking to gain time. They were fully determined not to give up their charter, but before their remonstrance could reach England the troubles which encompassed Charles at home made it impossible for him to carry out his designs against Massachusetts.

The breaking out of the civil war in England put a stop to the emigration to New England. At the opening of the year 1640 the population of New England numbered 20,000. Some fifty towns and between thirty and forty churches had been built, and the most desponding could no longer doubt the ultimate success and prosperity of the country. The wretched cabins of the first settlers were rapidly giving way to fair and comfortable houses, and the colonists were beginning to gather about them many of the comforts and much of the refinement they had been accustomed to in England.

Nor were the Puritans mindful of material success only. Many of

HARVARD COLLEGE.

them were persons of education, and they were anxious that their children should have the opportunity of enjoying the blessings of knowledge in their new homes. In 1636 the general court made provision for the establishment at Newtown of a high school. The name of the town was changed to Cambridge as a token that the people meant that it should yet be the seat of a university. In 1637 the school was formally opened. The next year the Rev. John Harvard, of Charlestown, bequeathed to the infant institution his library and the half of his fortune, and in gratitude for this assistance the school took the name of *Harvard College.* In 1647 the general court ordered that in every town or district of fifty families there should be a common school; and that in every town or district of one hundred families there should be a grammar school, conducted by teachers competent to prepare young men for college. This system rapidly found its way into the other New England colonies, with the exception of Rhode Island.

Thus was founded the American system of common schools. Until now education had been the task of the church, or had been confided to private individuals; but now, for the first time in the history of the

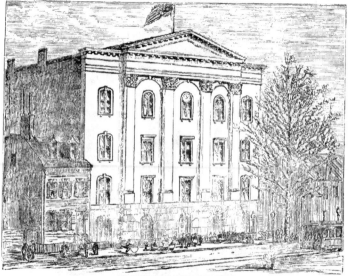

AN AMERICAN FREE SCHOOL.

world, the state took the task of educating its young citizens into its own hands, and established the schools in which it was to be conducted. Henceforth knowledge was to be restricted to no favored class; education was made free to every child, and every parent being taxed for the support of the public schools was made to feel interested in their proper conduct. From the little beginning thus made a vast and noble system has been developed, the beneficial results of which must be felt to the latest period of our national existence. Had the fathers of New England done nothing more for posterity than this, they would still deserve to be held in grateful remembrance as the founders of our public schools. Generations yet unborn shall rise up to call them blessed, and to acknowledge the truth of their conviction that ignorant men cannot make good citizens.

In 1639 a printing press, presented to the colony by some friends in Holland, was set up in Massachusetts. Stephen Daye was the printer, and in that year printed an almanac calculated for New England, and in 1640 a metrical version of the Psalms, made "by Thomas Welde and John Eliot, ministers of Roxbury, assisted by Richard Mather, minister of Dorchester." It was the first book printed in the English language in America, and continued to be used for a long time in the worship of the New England churches.

Many of the settlers went back to England at the outset of the civil war to take part in the struggle, among whom were Governor Henry Vane and Hugh Peters, and very few emigrants arrived in New England during the existence of the commonwealth. Yet the colonies continued to prosper Ship-building, which had been introduced by the first settlers of Salem, was carried on with activity, and vessels of four hundred tons were constructed. A little later the manufacture of woollen and linen cloth was begun by order of the general court in consequence of the difficulty of obtaining supplies from England.

The colonial churches were invited to send their representatives to the assembly of divines at Westminster, but they wisely neglected to do so, judging it better to remain in their obscurity than to give the English people a pretext for future interference by joining in their affairs.

The Long Parliament was friendly to New England, and granted to the colonies an exemption from all duties upon their commerce "until the House of Commons should take order to the contrary." Massachusetts took advantage of the security afforded by the friendship of the Long Parliament to establish a written constitution, or "body of liberties," which placed the rights and privileges of her people upon a more stable basis. It contained some of the severest laws of the Mosaic code, such as those against witchcraft, blasphemy, and sins against nature, but secured the freedom of the citizen, the right of representative government, and the independence of the state and the municipality. The rights of property, the freedom of inheritance, and the independence of each church from control by the others were also placed beyond dispute. "This constitution," says Bancroft, "for its liberality and comprehensiveness may vie with any similar record from the days of Magna Charta"

In April, 1642, the towns on the Piscataqua, now embraced within the limits of the State of New Hampshire, were annexed at their own request to Massachusetts. As the people of this region were not Puritans, and many of them were attached to the forms and faith of the

Church of England, the general court in September adopted a measure providing that neither the freemen nor the deputies of New Hampshire should be required to be church members. This act of justice removed all danger of political discord. In the same year Massachusetts made a less creditable and an unsuccessful effort to annex Rhode Island to her dominions

Though relieved of the interference of the mother country, the dangers of New England were not yet at an end. The Indians were still powerful upon their narrow border, the French were beginning to threaten them from the direction of Canada, and the Dutch from the Hudson. The colonies had so many interests in common that it was of vital importance that they should act in concert for their defence. After several ineffectual attempts, a league was formed in 1643 between the colonies of Massachusetts, Plymouth, Connecticut, and New Haven, under the title of *"The United Colonies of New England."* Each colony was to retain its freedom in the management of its own affairs, the authority of the union, which was intrusted to a commission of two members from each province, being limited to objects which concerned the general welfare of the colonies. Provision was made for the preservation of the purity of the gospel, the commissioners were required to be church members, and the expenses of the confederacy were to be assessed upon the colonies according to population. This union lasted for forty years.

The colony of Rhode Island desired to be admitted into the union, but its petition was refused, as it would not acknowledge the jurisdiction of Plymouth. The people of the two settlements on Narragansett bay, dreading an attempt to absorb them into some of the other colonies, now determined to apply to Parliament for an independent charter. Roger Williams was despatched to England for that purpose in 1643, and reached that country soon after the death of Hampden. The fame of his labors among the Indians had preceded him, and secured for him a cordial welcome in his native land. Assisted by Sir Henry Vane, a charter was obtained in March, 1644, organizing the settlements on Narragansett bay as an independent colony under the name of "The Providence Plantations," "with full power and authority to rule themselves." The executive council of state in England, in 1651, made some grants to Coddington which would have dismembered the little state, and Williams was obliged to make a second voyage to England to have these grants vacated. He succeeded in his efforts and the charter was confirmed. He received in this, as in his former mission, the cordial co-operation of Sir Henry Vane, whose name should be ever dear to the

13

people of Rhode Island, since but for him her territory would have been
divided among the neighboring colonies. In the interval between his
first and second voyages Roger Williams became a convert to the Baptist
faith, and founded the first church of that denomination in America.

The country between the Piscataqua and the Kennebec was assigned
to Sir Ferdinand Gorges, who, in 1639, was confirmed in his possession
by a formal charter from Charles I., who called the territory the
Province of Maine. In 1640, Gorges sent his son Thomas to Maine as
his representative. Thomas Gorges took up his residence at the settlement of Agamenticus, now the town of York, and in 1642 changed the
name of the place to Gorgeana

Since the settlement of the colony the French had claimed the region
between the St. Croix and the Penobscot, which they had settled under
the name of Acadia, as has been stated elsewhere. After the death of
Sir Ferdinand Gorges Maine was divided among his heirs. These cut it
up into four weak communities, whose helplessness laid them open to the
encroachments of the French in Canada. Apprehensive of the results of
this, Massachusetts, to whom many of the inhabitants of the province
had appealed to take such a course, in 1651 claimed the province of
Maine as a part of the territory which had been granted to the colony by
the original charter of Massachusetts. Commissioners were sent to
establish the authority of the Bay colony over the province, but the
magistrates of Maine resisted them, and appealed to the English government for protection The people of Maine were the adherents of the
king and the established church, and England was now ruled by the
Puritans, consequently Massachusetts won her cause, and Maine was
declared a part of that province. Massachusetts made a generous use of
her power, and allowed the towns of Maine very much the same government and privileges they now enjoy, and in religious matters treated
them with the same leniency she had shown to New Hampshire.

In 1646, a dispute in the Bay colony induced one of the parties to it to
appeal to Parliament to sustain his claims, and an order was sent out to
Boston in his behalf "couched in terms which involved the right of
Parliament to reverse the decisions and control the government of
Massachusetts." In plainer terms, Parliament claimed the right to
revoke the charter of the colony, as the king had done at the outset of
the civil war. The danger was great, and Massachusetts met it with
firmness. The general court met on the 4th of November, and sat with
closed doors to discuss the claim of the English government. It was
resolved "that Massachusetts owed to England the same allegiance as
the free Hanse towns had rendered to the empire; as Normandy, when

its dukes were kings of England, paid to the monarchs of France." The court also refused to accept a new charter from Parliament, as that action might imply a surrender of the original instrument, or to allow Parliament to control in any way the independence of the colony. Great as this claim was it was admitted by the English Parliament, in which the rights of the colony were stoutly maintained by Sir Henry Vane and others, and in reply to a respectful address of the general court setting forth the views of that body, a committee of Parliament declared: "We encourage no appeals from your justice. We leave you with all the freedom and latitude that may, in any respect, be duly claimed by you." Later on, upon the establishment of the commonwealth, Parliament invited the people of Massachusetts to receive a new patent from that body, but the colonial authorities wisely declined to do this, or to allow the home government any hold upon the administration of the affairs of the province.

In 1651, Cromwell, who had subdued Ireland, offered that island to the Puritans of New England as a new home, but they declined to leave America. Cromwell proved himself in many ways a judicious friend of New England, and the people of that country treasured his memory with the gratitude and respect it so richly deserved.

Though so successful in asserting her own liberties, Massachusetts had not yet learned the lesson of religious tolerance. When the Baptists began to appear in the colony severe measures were inaugurated to crush them, and one of their number—Holmes—a resident of Lynn, was whipped unmercifully. Still greater were the severities practised towards the Quakers. This sect had grown out of the Protestant Reformation, and constituted at this day the most advanced thinkers upon religious matters to be found in England. They claimed a perfect freedom in matters of faith and worship, and regarded all laws for enforcing religious systems as works of the devil. They were persons of pure lives, and even their most inveterate enemies could not charge them with wrong-doing. Previous to their appearance in Massachusetts exaggerated reports reached the colony concerning them. They were represented as making war upon all forms of religion and government.

The first of this creed who came to New England were Mary Fisher and Ann Austin, who reached Boston in July, 1656. In the absence of a special law against Quakers, they were arrested under the provisions of the general statute against heresy, their trunks were searched and their books burned by the hangman. Their persons were examined for marks of witchcraft, but nothing could be found against them, and after being kept close prisoners for five weeks, they were sent back to England.

During the year eight others were also sent back to England. Laws which were a disgrace to an enlightened community were now passed prohibiting the Quakers from entering the colony. Such as came were imprisoned, cruelly whipped, and sent away. In 1657, a woman was whipped with twenty stripes for this offence. In 1658, a law was enacted that if any Quaker should return after being banished, his or her offence should be punished with death. It was hoped that this barbarous measure would rid the colony of their presence; but they came in still greater numbers, to reprove the magistrates for their persecuting spirit, and to call them to repentance. In 1659, Marmaduke Stephenson, William Robinson, Mary Dyar, and William Leddro were hanged on Boston Common for returning to the colony after being banished.

These cruelties were regarded with great discontent by the people of the colony, whose humanity was shocked by the barbarity of the magistrates. Their opposition grew stronger every day, and at last it became evident to the magistrates themselves that their severities were of no avail. When William Leddro was being sentenced to death the magistrates were startled by the entrance into the court room of Wenlock Christison, a Quaker who had been banished and forbidden to return on pain of death. Christison was arrested, but the complaints of the people became so loud that the magistrates were obliged to pause in their bloody work. Christison and twenty-seven of his companions were released from custody, the persecution of the Quakers was discontinued, and the general court, in obedience to the will of the people, repealed the barbarous laws against that sect.

In pleasing contrast with these severities were the efforts of the Puritans to spread a knowledge of the gospel among the savages. Chief among those engaged in the good work was John Eliot, the minister of Roxbury, whose labors won him the name of "the apostle Eliot." He went among the red men in the forests, and acquired a knowledge of their language that he might preach to them in their own tongue. When he had become sufficiently proficient in it, he translated the Bible into the Indian language. This translation was printed at Cambridge, and a part of the type was set by an Indian compositor. He spent many years in the preparation of his Bible, and made a good use of it during his life, but it is now valuable only as a literary curiosity and as the evidence of the devotion of the translator to his noble work. The destruction of the race for which it was intended has made it a sealed book. Eliot gathered his savage converts into a settlement at Natick, and taught the men the art of agriculture and the women to spin and to weave cloth. He had . . . . men or priests, who resented his efforts to win their people from the worship and habits of their ancestors, but he persevered. He was greatly beloved by his disciples, and continued his labors among them far into old age, and to a limited extent to the day of his death, which took place when he had attained the ripe age of eighty-six years. "My memory, my utterance fails me," he said near the close of his life; "but I thank God my charity holds out still." When Walton, a brother minister, visited him on his death-bed, he greeted him with the words: "Brother, you are

NEWPORT, R. I.

welcome; but retire to your study and pray that I may be gone." His last words on earth were the triumphal shout with which he entered upon his reward: "Welcome joy!"

Many of the Quakers, after the persecution against them was over, joined Eliot in his labors. He had other fellow-workers. The two Mayhews, father and son, Cotton, and Brainerd thought it a privilege to labor for the souls of the poor savages. Native preachers were ordained, and at last there were thirty churches of "praying Indians" under such preachers.

CHAPTER XIV

NEW ENGLAND AFTER THE RESTORATION

THE news of the restoration of Charles II. to the English throne
was brought to Boston by Edward Whalley and William Goffe,
two of the judges of Charles I They came to seek refuge
from the vengeance of the king, having offended him beyond
forgiveness by their share in the death of his father They remained about a year in Massachusetts, protected by the people, and
preaching to them. A few months after their arrival, warrants for their
arrest and transportation to England for trial arrived from the king, and
to escape this danger they took refuge in New Haven. The royal
officers instituted a diligent search for them, and they were obliged to
change their place of concealment frequently. Great rewards were
offered for their betrayal, and even the Indians were urged to search the
woods for their hiding-places. The people whom they trusted protected
them, and aided them to escape the royal officers until the vigor of the
search was exhausted They then conducted them to a secure refuge in
the vicinity of Hadley, where they remained in seclusion and peace until
the close of their lives.

News was constantly arriving in the colonies of the execution of the
men who had been the friends of America in the Parliament, and a

general sadness was cast over the settlements by the tidings of the death of Hugh Peters and the noble Sir Henry Vane. From the first the people of New England saw plainly that they had little reason to expect justice at the hands of the royal government, and there was little rejoicing in that region at the return of the king to "his own again."

One of Charles's first acts was to revive in a more odious form the navigation act of the Long Parliament. We have spoken of the effect of this measure upon the colonies of Virginia and Maryland. This act closed the harbors of America against the vessels of every European nation save England, and forbade the exportation of certain American productions to any country but England or her possessions. This was a very serious blow to New England, and was intended as such. The colonies of that region had already built up a growing commerce, and this, together with their activity in ship-building, excited the envy and the hostility of the British merchants, who hoped, by inducing the king to place these restrictions upon the colonies, to compel the Americans to depend upon them for the supply of all their wants. Later on, America was forbidden not only to manufacture any articles which might compete with English manufactures in foreign markets, but to supply her own wants with her own manufactures. At the same time Parliament endeavored to destroy the trade that had grown up between New England and the southern colonies by imposing upon the articles exported from one colony to another a duty equal to that imposed upon the consumption of these articles in England.

Thus did Great Britain lay the foundation of that system of commercial injustice toward her colonies which eventually deprived her of them, and which her greatest writer on political economy declared to be "a manifest violation of the rights of mankind." The policy thus established in the reign of Charles II. was never departed from. Each succeeding administration remained true to the principles of the navigation act, and consistently declined to admit the claim of the colonies to just and honorable treatment at the hands of the mother country.

Charles II. was promptly proclaimed in the colonies of Plymouth, Connecticut, New Haven and Rhode Island, and those provinces were administered in his name. Massachusetts, distrusting his purposes towards her, held back, and waited until he should show his intentions more plainly

Connecticut had purchased the claims of the assigns of the Earl of Warwick to the region occupied by her, and had bought the territory of the Mohegans from Uncas, their sachem. The colony sent the younger Winthrop to England in 1661 to obtain a charter from the king. The noble character of Governor Winthrop was well known in England, and impressed even the profligate Charles. His reception was cordial and his mission entirely successful. In 1662, the king granted to the colony a charter incorporating Hartford and New Haven in one province under the name of Connecticut, and extending its limits from Long Island sound westward to the Pacific ocean, thus bestowing upon the colony those rich western lands which were subsequently made the basis of the magnificent school fund of Connecticut. The charter was substantially the same in its provisions as the constitution adopted by the Hartford colony. By it the king conferred upon the colonists the right to elect their own officers and to make and administer their own laws without interference from England in any event whatever. Connecticut was made independent in all but name, and the charter continued in force as the constitution of the State after the period of independence until 1818.

The colony of New Haven was much opposed to the union with Connecticut, and it required all Governor Winthrop's efforts to induce the people of that colony to accept it. The matter was adjusted in 1665, when the union was finally accomplished. The labors of Governor Winthrop were rewarded by his annual election as governor of Connecticut for fourteen years. Connecticut was a fortunate colony. Its government was ably and honestly administered; no persecutions marred its peace, and its course was uniformly prosperous and happy. It was always one of the most peaceful and orderly colonies of New England, and for a century its population doubled once in twenty years, notwithstanding frequent emigrations of its people to other parts of the country. The colony at an early day made a liberal provision for education, and in 1700 Yale College was founded. It was originally located at Saybrooke, but in 1718 was removed to New Haven.

Rhode Island was equally fortunate. Through its resident agent at London, John Clarke, it made application to the king for a new charter, and after some delay, caused by the difficulty of arranging satisfactorily the limits of the province, a charter was granted in 1663, formally establishing the colony of "Rhode Island and Providence Plantations." This charter continued to be the sole constitution of Rhode Island until the year 1842. By its provisions the government of the colony was to consist of a governor, deputy-governor, ten assistants, and representatives from the towns. The laws were to be agreeable to those of England, but no oath of allegiance was required of the colony, and in matters of religion the charter declared that "no person within the said colony, at any time hereafter, shall be anywise molested, punished, disquieted, or called in question for any difference in opinion in matters of religion; every person may at all times freely and fully enjoy his own judgment and conscience in matters of religious concernments." Freedom of conscience was not restricted to Christians; it was extended by the charter to infidels and pagans as well. This charter made the little colony secure against the attempts of Massachusetts to absorb her, and its reception by the people was joyful and enthusiastic.

At this period the population of Rhode Island was about twenty-five hundred It increased rapidly and steadily; the excellent harbors of the province encouraged commerce, and the little state soon began to rival her larger associates in prosperity

Massachusetts was from the first regarded with disfavor by the royal government. It delayed its acknowledgment of Charles II for over a year, and the king was not proclaimed at Boston until the 7th of August, 1661. Even then the general court forbade all manifestations of joy. These signs of the independent spirit of the people had been observed in England, and the colony had been watched by the government with anything but favor The enemies of the young state hurried their complaints before the king, and Massachusetts at length found it to her interest to send commissioners to London, as, indeed, the express orders of the king required her to do. Among the agents sent over were John Norton and Simon Bradstreet, men of ability and moderation, who commanded the confidence of all classes of the colonists. Their instructions were to assure the king of the loyalty of Massachusetts, to engage his favor for the colony, but to agree to "nothing prejudicial to their present standing according to their patent, and to endeavor the establishment of the rights and privileges then enjoyed."

The commissioners reached London in January, 1662, and were graciously received by the king, who confirmed the charter, and granted a complete amnesty for all past offences against his majesty. He required, however, that all laws derogatory to his authority should be repealed; that the colonists should take the oath of allegiance to him; that justice should be administered in his name, that the right of suffrage should be thrown open to all freeholders of competent estates, and that all who wished to do so should be free to use "the book of common prayer, and perform their devotion in the manner established in England."

These were better terms than the commissioners had reason to expect, and were not in themselves objectionable, as Massachusetts was growing beyond its early prejudices; but the acceptance of them would have implied an acknowledgment by the colony of the king's right to change its fundamental law, and to interfere with its affairs at pleasure Massa-

chusetts was at once divided into two parties, the larger of which maintained the independence of the colony of royal control, the smaller party
supported the claims of the king.   Under other circumstances no opposition would have been made to the toleration of the practices of the
Church of England in the colony; but now that it seemed that episcopacy was to be introduced as the ally of the royal power, the people of
Massachusetts resolved to prevent it from obtaining a foothold in their
midst   The general court resolved to maintain their political independence, and their religious establishment as well.   As a measure of precaution the charter was secretly intrusted for safe-keeping to a committee
of four appointed by the general court; and it was ordered that only
small bodies of officers and men should be allowed to land from ships,
and should be required to yield a strict obedience to the laws of the
province while on shore

These last measures were adopted because of the appointment by the
king of commissioners to regulate the affairs of New England   The
commissioners reached Boston in July, 1664, escorted by the fleet sent
out from England for the reduction of New Amsterdam.   They were
ordered to investigate the manner in which the charters of the New England colonies had been exercised, and had "full authority to provide for
the peace of the country, according to the royal instructions, and their
own discretion"—a power which Massachusetts was justified in regarding
as dangerous to her liberties

The commissioners cared very little for the prejudices of the people of
Massachusetts, and from the first proceeded to outrage their feelings.
They introduced the services of the Church of England into Boston to
the great disgust of the people.   The Puritans had always observed the
old Jewish custom of beginning their Sabbath at sunset   The commissioners contemptuously disregarded this custom, and spent Saturday
evening in merry-making   They soon gave cause for more serious alarm
by exercising the powers with which they had been intrusted, and proceeding to redress the grievances of the people.   All persons who had
complaints against Massachusetts were called upon to lay them before the
commissioners, and Rhode Island and the Narragansett chiefs promptly
availed themselves of the invitation   The general court now cut the
matter short by a decisive step, and sternly ordered the commissioners to
discontinue their proceedings, as contrary to the charter.   The commissioners obeyed the order, and though the firmness of the colony aroused
the indignation of the king, he was not able to shake the determination
of a free people.

Nor was this the only opposition shown by New England to the injustice of the mother country. The navigation acts were generally disregarded; they could not be enforced; and Boston and the other New England ports continued to enjoy their growing commerce as freely as before the passage of these infamous acts. Vessels from all the other colonies, and from France, Spain, Holland, and Italy, as well as from England, were to be seen at all seasons in the port of Boston. Massachusetts owned the greater number of vessels built and operated in America, and was the principal carrier for the other colonies. Its ships sailed to the most distant lands beyond the sea, and the commerce of the colony was rapidly becoming a source of great wealth. So marked indeed was the prosperity of New England, that upon the receipt of the news of the great fire in London, the colonists were able to send large sums to the assistance of the sufferers. The people of New England were industrious and frugal. Villages multiplied rapidly, and wherever a village sprang up a common school accompanied it. The villages began to assume a more tasteful and pleasing appearance, and men gave more care to the adornment and beautifying of their homes.

The population of New England in 1675 has been estimated at about 55,000 souls, divided among the colonies as follows: Plymouth, about 7000, Connecticut, about 14,000, Massachusetts, about 22,000; Maine, about 4000; New Hampshire, about 4000; Rhode Island, about 4000. The settlements lay principally along the coast, from New Haven to the northeastern border of Maine. Little progress had been made towards penetrating the interior. Haverhill, Deerfield, Northfield, and Westfield were towns on the remote frontier. This rapid growth alarmed the Indians, who had already begun to regard the whites as enemies bent on their destruction. Though there had been peace for forty years in New England, the savages saw that the policy pursued by the settlers was meant to force them back from the lands of their fathers. The whites had gradually absorbed the best lands in New England, and the red men had been as gradually crowded down upon the narrow necks and bays of the southern shores of the Plymouth and Rhode Island colonies. This had been done in pursuance of a settled policy, as the savages could be more carefully watched, and more easily managed in these localities than if left to roam at will over the country. The Indians on their part sullenly resented the course of the whites, and they had cause for complaint. They were ignorant of the art of cultivating the soil, and unwilling to practice it, and in their restricted limits it was difficult for them to obtain the means of supporting life. The game had been almost entirely driven from the forests, and the savages were forced to depend upon fish for their food; and these were obtained in scanty and uncertain quantities.

Thus the very success of New England was about to bring upon it the most serious misfortunes it had yet sustained.

Massasoit, who had been the early friend of the English, left two sons at his death, Wamsutta and Metacom, who had long been reckoned among the friends of the Plymouth colony. They were frequent visitors at Plymouth, and had received from the English the names of Alexander and Philip. At the death of Massasoit, Wamsutta or Alexander became chief of the Wampanoags. He and his brother Philip were men of more than ordinary abilities, and felt deeply the wrongs which were beginning to fall thickly upon their race. Uncas, the chief of the Mohegans, the determined enemy of Wamsutta, exerted himself, with success, to fill

KING PHILIP.

the minds of the English with suspicions of the intentions of the Wampanoag chieftain, and it was resolved to arrest him and bring him to Plymouth. Winslow was sent at the head of an armed force, and succeeded in surprising the chief in his hunting-lodge, together with eighty of his followers. The proud spirit of Wamsutta chafed with such fury at the indignity thus put upon him that he was seized with a dangerous fever, and the English were obliged to permit him to return home. "He died on his way," says Elliott. "He was carried home on the shoulders of men, and borne to his silent grave near Mount

Hope, in the evening of the day, and in the prime of his life, between lines of sad, quick-minded Indians, who well believed him the victim of injustice and ingratitude; for his father had been the ally, not the subject of England, and so was he, and the like indignity had not before been put upon any sachem."

By the death of his brother, Metacom, or Philip, became chief of the Wampanoags. He kept his own council, but the whites soon had cause to believe that he meditated a desperate vengeance upon them for the death of Wamsutta and the wrongs of his race. To make the sense of injury deeper in his mind the Plymouth authorities treated him with great harshness, and compelled him to give up his arms. A "praying Indian" who lived among his people informed the colonists that the chief meditated harm against them, and his dead body was soon after found. Three of Philip's men were suspected of the murder. They were arrested, tried at Plymouth, and found guilty by a jury composed of whites and Indians, and were put to death. This was early in 1675.

The execution of these men awoke a wild thirst for revenge among the tribe to which they belonged, and the young warriors clamored loudly for war against the English. Philip, whose vigorous mind enabled him to judge more clearly of the issue of such a struggle, entered into the contest with reluctance, for he saw that it must end in the destruction of his race. He was powerless to resist the universal sentiment of his people, and like a true hero resolved to make the best of the situation in which he was placed, and to share the fate of his nation. The Indians were tolerably well provided with fire-arms, for, in spite of the severe punishments denounced against the sale of weapons to the savages, the colonists had not been proof against the temptations of gain held out to them by this traffic. Their chief dependence, however, was upon their primitive weapons. The English, on the other hand, were well armed, and were provided with forts and towns which furnished them with secure places of refuge. They might have averted the war by conciliating the savages, but they persisted in their unjust treatment of them, regarding them as "bloody heathen," whom it was their duty to drive back into the wilderness.

Philip was able to bring seven hundred desperate warriors into the field. They had no hope of success; and they fought only for vengeance. They knew every nook and hiding-place of the forest, and in these natural defences could hope to continue the struggle as long as the leaves remained on the trees to conceal their lurking-places from the white man's search. Immediately after the execution of the three Indians at Plymouth, Philip's men had begun to rob exposed houses and carry off cattle, but the war did not actually begin until the 24th of June, 1675, the day of fasting and prayer appointed by the government as a preparation for the struggle. On that day the people of Swanzey, in Plymouth colony, while returning home from church, were attacked by the Wampanoags, and eight or nine were killed. Philip burst into tears when the news of this attack was brought to him, but he threw himself with energy into the hopeless struggle, now that it had come.

Reinforcements were sent from Massachusetts to the aid of the Plymouth colony, and on the 29th of June the united forces made an attack upon the Wampanoags, killed six or seven of their men and drove them to a swamp in which they took refuge. The English surrounded this swamp, determined to starve the Indians into submission, but Philip and his warriors escaped and took refuge among the Nipmucks, a small tribe occupying what is now Worcester county, Massachusetts. The English then marched into the territory of the Narragansetts and compelled them to agree to remain neutral, and to deliver up the fugitive Indians who should take refuge among them. This accomplished, the colonists hoped they had put an end to the war.

Philip succeeded in inducing the Nipmucks to join him in the struggle, and his warriors began to hang around the English settlements. The whites were murdered wherever they ventured to expose themselves, and a feeling of general terror spread through the colonies. No one knew the extent of the hostility of the savage tribes, or how many allies Philip had gained; nor was it certain when or where the next great blow of the savages would be struck. Some of the colonists began to give way to superstitious fears. It was asserted that an Indian bow, a sign of impending evil, had been seen clearly defined against the heavens, and that at the eclipse which occurred at this time the moon bore the figure of an Indian scalp on its face. The northern heavens glowed with auroral lights of unusual brilliancy; troops of phantom horsemen were heard to dash through the air; the sighing of the night wind was like the sound of whistling bullets, and the howling of the wolves was fiercer and more constant than usual. These things, the superstitious declared, were warnings that the colonies were about to be severely punished for their sins, among which they named profane swearing, the neglect of bringing up their children in more rigid observances, the licensing of ale houses, and the wearing of long hair by the men and of gay apparel by the women. The more extreme even declared that they were about to be "judged" for not exterminating the Quakers

In the meantime Philip, with a party of Nipmucks and his own people, carried the war into the valley of the Connecticut, and spread death along the line of settlements from Springfield to Northfield, then the most remote inland town. With the hope of withdrawing the Nipmucks, who could muster fifteen hundred warriors, from the confederacy, Captain Hutchinson, with twenty men, was sent to treat with them. His party was ambushed and murdered at Brookfield early in August. The Indians then attacked Brookfield, and burned the village with the exception of one strong house to which the colonists retreated. After a siege of two days, during which they kept up a constant fire upon the building, they attempted to burn the house, but were prevented by a shower of rain which extinguished the flames. At the same moment a reinforcement of fifty men arrived to the aid of the whites, and the savages were driven off with the loss of several of their number. Philip succeeded in drawing to his support nearly all the tribes of New England, and it was resolved by the savages to make a general effort for the destruction of the whites. A concerted attack was to be made upon a large number of settlements at the same day and hour, and the Sabbath was chosen as the day most favorable for the movement.

Deerfield in Massachusetts and Hadley in Connecticut were among the places attacked. The former was burned. Hadley was assailed while the congregation were worshipping in the church, and the whites were hard pressed by their antagonists. Suddenly in the midst of the battle

ATTACK UPON BROOKFIELD BY THE INDIANS.

there appeared a tall and venerable man with a flowing beard, and clad in a strange dress. With sword in hand he rallied the settlers, and led them to a new effort in which the savages were beaten back and put to flight. When the battle was over, the stranger could not be found, and the wondering people declared that he was an angel sent by God for their deliverance. It was Goffe, the regicide, who had suddenly left his place of concealment to aid his countrymen in their struggle with the savages. He had been lying in concealment at the house of Russell, the minister of Hadley, and returned to his place of refuge when the danger was over.

On the whole the Indians, though they succeeded in causing great suffering to the colonies, were unsuccessful in their efforts during the summer and autumn of 1675. In October, Philip returned to his old home, but, finding Mount Hope in ruins, took shelter among the Narragansetts, who protected him notwithstanding their promise to deliver up all fugitives to the English. The colonial authorities seeing that the tribe had no intention of fulfilling their promise, and being fearful that Philip would succeed in winning them over to his side, resolved to anticipate the danger and treat them as enemies.

A force was collected and sent into the Narragansett country in December, 1675. This tribe, numbering about three thousand souls, had erected a strong fort of palisades in the midst of a swamp near the present town of Kingston, Rhode Island. It was almost inaccessible, and had but a single entrance, defended by a morass, which could be passed only by means of a fallen tree. The English were led to the fort by an Indian traitor, and attacked it on the 19th of December. After a severe fight of two hours they succeeded in forcing an entrance into the fort. The wigwams were then fired, and the whole place was soon in flames. The defeat of the savages was complete, but it was purchased by the loss of six captains and two hundred and fifty men killed and wounded on the part of the English. About one thousand of the Narragansetts were slain, their provisions were destroyed and numbers were made prisoners Those who escaped wandered through the frozen woods without shelter, and for food were compelled to dig for nuts and acorns under the snow. Many died during the winter. Canonchet, the Narragansett chief, was among the survivors. "We will fight to the last man rather than become servants to the English," said the undaunted chieftain. He was taken prisoner in April, 1676, near Blackstone, and was offered his life if he would induce the Indians to make peace. He refused the offer with scorn, and, when sentenced to death, answered proudly: "I like it well I shall die before I speak anything unworthy of myself."

In the spring of 1676, Philip, who had been to the west to endeavor to induce the Mohawks to join the war against the English, returned to place himself at the head of his countrymen in New England. The work of murdering and burning was resumed with renewed fury. The Indians seemed to be everywhere and innumerable, and the whites could find safety only in their forts. The surviving Narragansetts scourged the Rhode Island and Plymouth colonies with fire and axe, and even the aged Roger Williams, was obliged to take up arms for the defence of his

home. Lancaster, Medford, Weymouth, Groton, Springfield, Sudbury
and Marlborough, in Massachusetts, and Providence and Warwick, in
Rhode Island, were destroyed either wholly or in part, and numerous
other settlements were attacked and made to suffer more or less
severely.

As the season advanced the cause of the Indians became more hopeless,
and they began to quarrel among themselves. In June the Nipmucks
submitted, and the tribes on the Connecticut refused to shelter Philip any
longer. He then appealed to the Mohawks to take up the hatchet, but
seeing that his cause was hopeless, they refused to join him. In proud
despair Philip went back to Mount Hope to die. One of his people
urged him to make peace with the whites, and was struck dead by the
hand of the chief for daring to mention such a humiliation. It became
known that Philip had returned to his old home, and Captain Church
marched against him, dispersed his followers, and took the chief's wife
and little son prisoners. Philip, who had borne the reverses and the
reproaches of his nation with the firmness of a hero, was conquered by
this misfortune. "My heart breaks," he cried, despairingly, "I am ready
to die." He was soon attacked by Church in his place of concealment,
and in attempting to escape was shot by an Indian who was serving in
the ranks of his enemies. Philip's little son was sold as a slave in Bermuda, and the grandson of Massasoit, who had welcomed and befriended
the English, was condemned to pass his days in bondage in a foreign
clime.

The death of Philip was soon followed by the close of hostilities.
The power of the Indians was completely broken. Of the Narragansetts
scarcely one hundred men were left alive, and the other tribes had
suffered severely. The Mohegans had remained faithful to the English,
and Connecticut had been happily spared the sufferings experienced by
the other colonies, which were very severe. Twelve or thirteen towns were
destroyed, and many others were seriously crippled. Six hundred houses
were burned, and the pecuniary losses amounted to the then enormous sum
of half a million of dollars. Over six hundred men, chiefly young men,
fell in the war, and there was scarcely a family which did not mourn
some loved one who had given his life for the country.

In all their distress the colonies received no aid from England. The
mother country left them to fight out their struggle of life and death
alone. The English people and government were indifferent to their fate.
One generous Non-conformist church in Dublin sent a contribution of
five hundred pounds to the sufferers. This relief was gratefully acknowledged; but to the credit of New England it should be remembered that

14

her colonies never asked assistance from England. The king was very careful, however, to exact every penny he could wring from the colonies, and towards the close of the Indian war established a royal custom-house at Boston for the collection of duties Duties were imposed upon the commerce of the colonies, and the royal government endeavored to enforce their payment by threatening to refuse the New England ships the protection which enabled them to escape the outrages of the African pirates of the Mediterranean.

The province of Maine had been restored by Charles II to the heir of Sir Ferdinand Gorges, and in 1677 Massachusetts purchased their claims for the sum of twelve hundred and fifty pounds, and thus confirmed her possession of the region between the Piscataqua and the Kennebec The region between the Kennebec and the Penobscot was held by the Duke of York, and that from the Penobscot to the St. Croix was occupied by the French.

In July, 1679, King Charles detached New Hampshire from Massachusetts, and organized it as a royal province; the first ever erected in New England. The province at once asserted its rights, and a controversy was begun with the crown, which was continued for several years. The people resisted the effort to force upon them

COAT OF ARMS OF NEW HAMPSHIRE.

the observances of the English Church, and the collection of taxes assessed by the royal officials, and Cranfield, the royal governor, finding it impossible to continue his arbitrary rule, wrote to the British government, "I shall esteem it the greatest happiness in the world to remove from these unreasonable people They cavil at the royal commission, and not at my person. No one will be accepted by them who puts the king's commands in execution "

In the last years of his reign Charles II. made a determined effort to destroy the charter of Massachusetts. Commissioners were sent by the colony to England to endeavor to defend its rights, but the royal government was resolved upon its course, and the people of Massachusetts were equally determined not to consent to the surrender of their liberties. At length, in 1684, the general court having in the name of the people distinctly refused to make a surrender of the charter to the king, the English courts declared the charter forfeited A copy of the judgment was sent to Boston, and was received there on the 2d of July, 1685 The colony was full of apprehension. The charter under which it had grown and prospered, and which secured its liberties to it without the interference of the crown, had been stricken down by the subservient courts of the mother country, and there was now no defence between the liberties of Massachusetts and the arbitrary will of the king, who had given the colony good cause to fear his hostility.

James II came to the English throne in 1685. He was even more hostile to New England than his brother Charles. He was a bigoted Roman Catholic, and was resolved to introduce that faith, not only into England, but also into the colonies. He attempted to accomplish this by proclaiming an indulgence or toleration of all creeds. As he dared not proceed openly to violate his coronation oath he hoped by this underhanded scheme to place his own religion upon such a footing in England that he would soon be in a position to compel its adoption by his subjects. He had greatly mistaken the temper of both England and America.

Joseph Dudley, who had been sent to England as one of the agents of Massachusetts in the last controversy between the colony and King Charles, now found it to his interest to become as ardent a defender, as he had formerly been an opponent, of the royal prerogative, and James finding him a willing abetter of his designs, appointed him president of Massachusetts until a royal governor should arrive, for the king was resolved to take away the charters of all the colonies and make them royal provinces. At the same time, being determined to curtail the liberty of the press, the king appointed Edward Randolph its censor. Dudley was regarded by the people as the betrayer of the liberties of his country, and both he and Randolph were cordially despised by them. The king in appointing Dudley made no provision for an assembly or general court, as he meant to govern the colonies without reference to the people. He regarded the American provinces as so many possessions of the crown, possessed of no rights, and entitled to no privileges save what he chose to allow them.

In pursuance of this plan, Sir Edmund Andros, whom the king had appointed governor of New York, was made governor-general of all New England. He reached Boston in December, 1686. Dudley was made chief justice, and Randolph, colonial secretary. The governor-general was empowered by the king to appoint his own council, impose such taxes as he should think fit, command the militia of the colonies, enforce the navigation acts, prohibit printing, and establish episcopacy in New England; and in order to enable him to enforce his will two companies of soldiers were sent over with him, and quartered in Boston. Thus were the liberties of New England placed at the mercy of a tyrant, and thus was inaugurated a despotism the most galling that was ever imposed upon men of English descent.

Andros promptly put in force a series of the most arbitrary measures. The public schools, which had been fostered with such care by the colonial governments, were allowed to fall into decay. The support which had been granted to the churches was withdrawn. The people were forbidden to assemble for the discussion of any public matter, though they were allowed the poor privilege of electing their town officers. The form of oath in use in New England was an appeal to heaven with uplifted hand. The governor now ordered the substitution of a form which required the person to place his hand on the Bible. This was particularly repugnant to the Puritans, who regarded it as "Popish practice." Probate fees were increased twenty-fold. The holders of lands were told that their titles were invalid because obtained under a charter

WADSWORTH HIDING THE CHARTER.

which had been declared forfeited. No person was allowed to leave the colony without a pass signed by the governor. The Puritan magistrates and ministers were refused authority to unite persons in marriage. The clergyman of the Church of England stationed at Boston was the only person in New England who could perform a legal marriage. Episcopacy was formally established, and the people were required to build a church for its uses. At the command of the king a tax of a penny in the pound, and a poll-tax of twenty pence, was imposed upon every person in the colony without regard to his means, rich and poor being taxed alike. Some of the towns had the boldness to refuse to pay this tax, and John Wise, the minister of Ipswich, advised his fellow-townsmen to resist it. He and a number of others were arrested and fined. When they pleaded their privileges under the laws of England, they were told by one of the council: "You have no privilege left you but not to be sold as slaves." "Do you think," asked one of the judges, "that the laws of England follow you to the ends of the earth?" The iniquitous exactions of Andros and his associates threatened the country with ruin. When the magistrates mentioned this, they were told, "It is not for his majesty's interest you should thrive." "The governor invaded liberty and property after such a manner," wrote Increase Mather, "as no man could say anything was his own."

The other colonies came in for their share of bad treatment. Soon after he reached Boston, Andros demanded of the authorities of Rhode Island the surrender of their charter. Governor Clarke declined to comply with this demand, and Andros went to Providence, broke the seal of the colony, and declared its government dissolved. He appointed a commission irresponsible to the people for the government of Rhode Island, and then had the effrontery to declare that the people of that colony were satisfied with what he had done.

In October Andros went to Connecticut with an armed guard to take possession of the government of that colony. He reached Hartford on the 31st of the month, and found the legislature in session, and demanded of that body the surrender of the charter. The discussion was prolonged until evening, and then candles were brought, and the charter was placed on the table. Suddenly the lights were extinguished, and when they were re-lighted the charter could not

THE CHARTER OAK.

be found. It had been secured by Joseph Wadsworth of Hartford, and carried to the southern part of the city, where it was concealed in a hollow oak tree, which was afterwards known as the "Charter Oak." Andros, furious at the disappearance of the charter, was not to be balked in his purpose of seizing the colonial government, and taking the record book of the assembly, he wrote the word "*Finis*" at the end of the last day's proceedings. He then declared the colonial government at an end, and proceeded to administer the affairs of the province in the spirit in which he had governed Massachusetts and Rhode Island.

The people of New England had borne these outrages with a patience which no one had expected of them. They were a law-abiding people, and wished to exhaust all legal means of redress before proceeding to extreme measures for their protection; but the party in favor of driving Andros and his fellow-plunderers out of the country was rapidly growing stronger, and it was not certain how much longer the policy of forbearance would be continued. Increase Mather was appointed to go to England and endeavor to procure a redress of the grievances of the colonies. It was a dangerous mission, for the king was in full sympathy with the men whom he had placed over the liberties of New England. It was also difficult to leave America without the knowledge of Andros and his colleagues, but Mather succeeded in escaping their vigilance, and was on his way to the old world when relief arrived from a most unexpected quarter.

The efforts of James to bring about the re-establishment of the Roman Catholic religion in England roused the whole English nation against him, and in 1689 the nation invited William, Prince of Orange, the husband of James' eldest daughter, Mary, to come over to England and assume the throne. James, left without any adherents, fled to France, and William and Mary were securely seated upon the throne.

The news of the landing of William in England and the flight of King James reached Boston on the 4th of April, 1689. The messenger was at once imprisoned by Andros, but his tidings soon became known to the citizens. On the morning of the 18th the people of Boston took up arms, and having secured the person of the commander of the royal frigate in the harbor, seized the royalist sheriff. The militia were assembled, and Andros and his companions were obliged to take refuge in the fort. Simon Bradstreet, the governor who had held office at the time of the abrogation of the charter, was called upon by the people to resume his post, and the old magistrates were reinstated and organized as a council of safety. Andros and his creatures attempted to escape to the frigate, but were prevented and were compelled to surrender. The next day reinforcements came pouring into Boston from the other settlements, and the fort was taken and the frigate mastered. Town meetings were now held throughout the colony, and it was voted to resume the former charter. The people were almost unanimous in favor of this course, but the counsels of a more timid minority prevailed, and the council, which had appointed itself to the control of affairs, decided to solicit a new charter from William and Mary. A general court was convened on the 22d of May. The people of the colony were anxious that Andros, Dudley, and Randolph should receive prompt punishment for their offences, but the authorities wisely determined to send them to England for trial.

Plymouth, upon the receipt of the news from Boston, seized the agent of Andros, imprisoned him, and re-established the government which Andros had overthrown, under the constitution signed on board the "Mayflower." There were none of the old Pilgrim fathers living to witness this event, but their children were none the less determined to maintain unimpaired the liberties they had inherited from them

Rhode Island promptly resumed her charter and reinstated the officers whom Andros had displaced. Connecticut, upon hearing of the downfall of the governor-general, brought out her charter from its hiding-place, and restored the old officers to their positions.

Thus the work of James II. was overthrown, and the destinies of New England were once more in the hands of her own people. The generation that had settled New England had nearly all been gathered to their rest, and their children were in some respects different from the fathers. They had learned lessons of toleration, and had acquired many of the refining graces that the elder Puritans regarded as mere vanity. They retained, however, the earnest and lofty virtues which had made the first generation superior to hardships and trials of all kinds, and which had enabled them in the face of every discouragement to lay the foundations of the great commonwealths which to-day cherish their memories as their most precious legacies. The fathers of New England richly merited the honor which succeeding generations have delighted to bestow upon their memories. However they may have erred, they were men who earnestly sought to do right in all things, and who did their duty fearlessly according to the light before them.

In the first generation we have noticed an extraordinary degree of influence exerted by the ministers. This was due to no desire of the Puritans to connect church and state, but was owing to the fact that the ministers represented the best educated and most intellectual class of that day, and the people regarded them as the best qualified guides in the community. As New England advanced in prosperity her schools and colleges were able to turn out numbers of educated men, who embraced the other learned professions, and divided the influence with the ministers. New England always chose its leaders from among its most intelligent men, and its people always yielded a willing homage to the claims of intellect.

At the downfall of Andros there were about two hundred thousand white inhabitants in the English colonies of North America. Of these, Massachusetts, including Plymouth and Maine, had about forty-four thousand; New Hampshire and Rhode Island about six thousand each; Connecticut about twenty thousand; making the total population of New England about seventy-six thousand.

CHAPTER XV.

WITCHCRAFT IN MASSACHUSETTS.

Results of the Failure of Massachusetts to Resume her Charter—The New Charter—Loss
of the Liberties of the Colony—Union of Plymouth with Massachusetts Bay—Belief in
Witchcraft—The History of Witchcraft in Massachusetts—The Case of the Goodwin
Children—Cotton Mather espouses the Cause of the Witches—Samuel Parris—He
Originates the Salem Delusion—A Strange History—A Special Court Appointed for the
Trial of the Witches—The Victims—Execution of the Rev George Burroughs—Cotton
Mather's Part in the Tragedies—The General Court takes Action in behalf of the
People—End of the Persecution—Failure of Cotton Mather's Attempt to Save his Credit.

THE decision of the magistrates of Massachusetts to disregard the
wishes of a majority of the people of the colony, who desired an
immediate restoration of the government under the old charter,
and to wait for a new charter from William and Mary, gave
great offence to the popular party. Had the wish of this party
been promptly complied with, Massachusetts might have recovered every
liberty and privilege of which she had been deprived by King James.
Increase Mather distinctly declares that "had they at that time entered
upon the full exercise of their charter government, as their undoubted
right, wise men in England were of opinion that they might have gone
on without disturbance." The self-constituted government hesitated,
however, and the opportunity was lost.

When the convention of the people met, in May, 1689, they refused to
acknowledge the council that had taken charge of affairs upon the downfall of Andros, and demanded that the governor, deputy governor, and
assistants elected in 1686 should be restored to office. The council
refused to comply with this demand, and the matter was referred to the
people, who sustained their representatives. A compromise was effected,
and the council agreed to permit the officers of 1686 to resume their
places until instructions could be received from England. Agents were
sent to England to solicit a restoration of the charter, and their appeal
was supported by the English Presbyterians with great unanimity.
Even the Archbishop of Canterbury urged the king "not to take away
from the people of New England any of the privileges which Charles I.
had granted them."

In spite of the pressure exerted upon him in behalf of the colony, King William granted to Massachusetts a charter which placed the liberties of the province so entirely at the mercy of the crown that the colonial agent refused to accept it. There was no help for it, however, and the charter became the fundamental law of Massachusetts Under the old charter the governor of Massachusetts had been elected annually by the votes of the freemen, he was now to be appointed by the king and to serve during the royal pleasure He was given power to summon the general court, and to adjourn or dissolve that body. The election of magistrates of all kinds, which had been confided to the people by the old charter, was taken from them, and henceforth these officials were to be appointed by the governor with the consent of the council. The old charter had made the decision of the colonial courts final, the new permitted appeals from these tribunals to the privy council in England. The old charter had given to the general court full powers of legislation, the new conferred upon the governor the right to veto any of its measures, and reserved to the crown the power of cancelling any act of colonial legislation within three years after its passage. The council was at first appointed by the king, but was subsequently elected by the joint ballot of the two branches of the general court

To compensate the people for the loss of their political power the king greatly enlarged the limits of the colony. Massachusetts and Plymouth were united in one province, the name of the former being given to the whole. The Elizabeth islands were also added to the province, and its northern boundary was extended to the St Lawrence. Toleration was granted to every religious sect except the Roman Catholics. New Hampshire was separated from the jurisdiction of Massachusetts and made a separate province; but Maine and the vast wilderness beyond it were confirmed to the Bay colony. The charter bore the date of October 7th, 1691. Upon the nomination of Increase Mather, one of the colonial agents, Sir William Phipps, a native of New England, a well-meaning but incompetent man, who was in religious matters strongly inclined to superstition, was appointed governor of Massachusetts. William Stoughton, "a man of cold affections, proud, self-willed, and covetous of distinction"—a man universally hated by the people—was appointed deputy governor to please Cotton Mather. The members of the council were chosen entirely for their devotion "to the interests of the churches"

While these matters were in progress of settlement, there occurred in Massachusetts one of the most singular delusions recorded in history, and which was in some respects the last expiring effort of ecclesiastical ambition to control the political affairs of the colony The clergy had always sought in New England, as in other lands, to fight their political enemies with spiritual weapons   They now carried this to an extreme which taught the people of New England a lesson that was not soon forgotten.

The belief in witchcraft has not been confined to any single nation, and at this time was common to America and Europe. "The people did not rally to the error; they accepted the superstition only because it had not yet been disengaged from religion." It was believed that as Christians were united with God by a solemn covenant, so were witches leagued with the devil by a tie which, once formed, they could not dissolve. Those, who thus placed themselves in the archfiend's power were used by him as instruments to torment their fellow-men   They were given power to annoy them by pinching them, thrusting invisible pins into them, pulling their hair, afflicting them with disease, killing their cattle and chickens with mysterious ailments, upsetting their wagons and carts, and by practising upon them many other puerile and ludicrous tricks.   The witches generally excited their arts upon those whom they hated, but it was a matter of doubt how many persons were included in their dislikes.   One of the most popular superstitions was that of the " Witches' sacrament," a gathering at which the devil, in the form of " a small black man," presided, and required his followers to renounce their Christian baptism and to sign their names in his book   They were then re-baptized by the devil, and the meeting was closed with horrid rites which varied in different narratives according to the imagination of the relators.

The belief in the existence of witchcraft was held by some of the leading minds of this period   Sir Matthew Hale, Lord Chief Justice of England, was firmly convinced of the truth of the doctrine, and it was advocated by many of the clergy in England. In New England the clergy held it to be heresy to deny the existence of witches, which they claimed was clearly taught in the Scriptures   It was evidently to their interest to maintain this belief, as it made them the chief authorities in such cases, and furnished them with a powerful weapon against their adversaries

By the early settlers of New England the Indians were supposed to be worshippers of the devil, and their medicine-men to be wizards. Governor Hutchinson, in his " History of Massachusetts," thus sums up the cases of supposed witchcraft that had occurred in the colony previous to the time of which we are now writing

" The first suspicion of witchcraft among the English was about the year 1645, at Springfield, upon Connecticut river; several persons were supposed to be under an evil hand, and among the rest two of the minister's children. Great pains were taken to prove the facts upon several of the persons charged with the crime, but either the nature of the evidence was not satisfactory, or the fraud was suspected, and so no person was convicted until the year 1650, when a poor wretch, Mary Oliver, probably weary of her life from the general reputation of being a witch, after long examination, was brought to confession of her guilt, but I do not find that she was executed. Whilst this inquiry was making, Margaret Jones was executed at Charlestown, and Mr. Hale mentions a woman at Dorchester, and another at Cambridge about the same time, who all at their death asserted their innocence. Soon after, Hugh Parsons was tried at Springfield, and escaped death. In 1655 Mrs Hibbins, the assistant's widow, was hanged at Boston. In 1662, at Hartford in Connecticut, one Ann Cole, a young woman who lived next door to a Dutch family, and no doubt had learned something of the language, was supposed to be possessed with demons, who sometimes spoke Dutch and sometimes English, and sometimes a language which nobody understood, and who held a conference with one another. Several ministers who were present took down the conference in writing and the names of several persons, mentioned in the course of the conference, as actors or bearing parts in it; particularly a woman, then in prison upon suspicion of witchcraft, one Greensmith, who upon examination confessed and appeared to be surprised at the discovery. She owned that she and the others named had been familiar with a demon, who had carnal knowledge of her, and although she had not made a formal covenant, yet she had promised to be ready at his call, and was to have had a high frolic at Christmas, when the agreement was to have been signed. Upon this confession she was executed, and two more of the company were condemned at the same time. In 1669 Susanna Martin, of Salisbury, was bound over to the court upon suspicion of witchcraft, but escaped at that time.

"In 1671 Elizabeth Knap, another *ventriloqua*, alarmed the people of Groton in much the same manner as Ann Cole had done those of Hartford; but her demon was not so cunning, for, instead of confining himself to old women, he railed at the good minister of the town and other people of good character, and the people could not then be prevailed on to believe him, but believed the girl when she confessed that she had been deluded, and that the devil had tormented her in the shape of good persons; so she escaped the punishment due to her fraud and imposture.

"In 1673 Eunice Cole of Hampton was tried, and the jury found her not legally guilty, but that there were strong grounds to suspect her of familiarity with the devil.

"In 1679 William Morse's house, at Newbury, was troubled with the throwing of bricks, stones, etc , and a boy of the family was supposed to be bewitched, who accused one of the neighbors, and in 1682 the house of George Walton, a Quaker, at Portsmouth, and another house at Salmon Falls (both in New Hampshire), were attacked after the same manner

"In 1683 the demons removed to Connecticut river again, where one Desborough's house was molested 'by an invisible hand, and a fire kindled, nobody knew how, which burnt up a great part of his estate, and in 1684 Philip Smith, a judge of the court, a military officer and a representative of the town of Hadley, upon the same river (a hypochondriac person), fancied himself under an evil hand, and suspected a woman, one of his neighbors, and languished and pined away, and was generally supposed to be bewitched to death. While he lay ill, a number of brisk lads tried an experiment upon the old woman Having dragged her out of her house, they hung her up until she was near dead, let her down, rolled her some time in the snow, and at last buried her in it and left her there, but it happened that she survived and the melancholy man died."

These cases, which were not generally regarded in the enlightened spirit of the writer we have quoted, served to confirm the common belief in witchcraft. Increase Mather published a work in 1684 containing an account of the cases which had already occurred in the colony, and giving detailed descriptions of the manner in which the afflicted persons had exhibited their "deviltry." The publication of this work seemed to revive the trouble and in a more aggravated form, for it is a singular fact that the general discussion of delusions of this kind rarely fails to produce an increase of the evil

In 1688 a case occurred which excited general interest, and was the beginning of one of the saddest periods in the history of New England. The daughter of John Goodwin, a child of thirteen years, accused the daughter of an Irish laundress of stealing some linen The mother of the laundress, a friendless emigrant, succeeded in disproving the charge, and abused the girl soundly for making a false accusation Soon after this, the accuser was seized with a fit, and pretended to be bewitched in order to be revenged upon the poor Irish woman. Her younger sister and two of her brothers followed her example. They pretended to be dumb, then deaf, then blind, and then all three at once.

"They were struck dead at the sight of the 'Assembly's Catechism,'" says Governor Hutchinson, dryly, "'Cotton's Milk for Babes' and some other good books, but could read in Oxford jests, popish and Quaker books, and the common prayer without any difficulty." Nevertheless their appetite was good, and they slept soundly at night. The youngest of these little impostors was less than five years old. It was at once given out that the Goodwin children were bewitched, and no one suspected or hinted at the fraud. They would bark like dogs and mew like cats, and a physician who was called in to treat them solemnly declared that they were possessed by devils, as he discovered many of the symptoms laid down in Increase Mather's book. A conference of the four ministers of Boston, and one from Charlestown, was held at Goodwin's house, where they observed a day of fasting and prayer. As a result of their efforts, the youngest child, a boy of less than five years, was delivered of his evil spirit. The ministers now had no doubt that the children had been bewitched, and as the little ones accused the Irish woman of their misfortune, she was arrested, tried for witchcraft, convicted and hanged, notwithstanding that many persons thought the poor creature a lunatic.

Among the ministers who had investigated this case and had procured the execution of the woman was Cotton Mather, the son of Increase Mather, then president of Harvard college. He was a young man who had but recently entered the ministry, and was regarded as one of the most learned and gifted preachers in the colony. He was withal a man of overweening vanity, and full of ambition. He could not bear contradiction, and was devoted to the maintenance of the political power of the clergy. He was superstitious by nature, and was firmly convinced of the reality of witchcraft. He had become deeply interested in the case of the Goodwin children, and in order to study it more deeply took the eldest girl to his house, where he could observe and experiment upon her devil at his leisure. She was a cunning creature, and soon found that it was to her interest to humor the young pastor in his views, and she played upon his weakness with a shrewdness and skill which were remarkable in one so young, and exhibit the credulity of the investigator in a most pitiable light.

Mather carried on his experiments with a diligence which would have seemed ludicrous had its object been less baneful to the community. He read the Bible, and prayed aloud in the presence of the girl, who would pretend to be thrown into a fit by the pious exercise. At the same time she read the Book of Common Prayer, or Quaker or Popish treatises, without any interruption from her familiar spirits. The minister then tested the proficiency of the devil in languages, by reading aloud passages of the Bible in Hebrew, Greek, and Latin, which the girl professed to understand. When he tried her with an Indian dialect, however, she could not comprehend him   By other experiments, designed to ascertain if the spirits could read the thoughts of others, Mather came to the sage conclusion that "all devils are not alike sagacious " The girl flattered his vanity, and lulled his suspicion of fraud by telling him that his own person was especially protected against the evil spirits by the power of God, and that the devils did not dare to enter his study.

The vanity of Cotton Mather was elated to the highest pitch by what he deemed his successful experiments, and he wrote a book upon witchcraft, in which he endeavored to prove the truth of his theories, and declared that he should esteem it a personal insult if any one should hereafter venture to deny the existence of witchcraft.   His book was reprinted in London, with a preface by Richard Baxter, the well-known author of "The Saints' Rest," warmly indorsing it.   It was very generally read in New England, and had a most pernicious effect upon the people by inducing them to give credit to the stories of the writer rather than to listen to the promptings of their own good sense.   Still there were some in Boston who had the boldness to differ with Mather, and these the indignant divine denounced as "sadducees " Mather supported his views by his sermons.   "There are multitudes of sadducees in our day," he declared.   "A devil in the apprehension of these mighty acute philosophers is no more than a quality or a distemper   . . Men counted it wisdom to credit nothing but what they say and feel.   They never saw any witches; therefore there are none."   The ministers of Boston and Charlestown gave their young colleague their hearty support, and declared that those who doubted the existence of witchcraft were guilty of atheism, and indorsed Mather's book as proving clearly that "there is both a God and a devil, and witchcraft."   Thus did the clergy of Massachusetts set themselves to the task of forcing their own narrow views upon the people.   It was a needed lesson.   New England had passed the time when clerical rule in political affairs could be productive of good, and was now to be taught the danger of permitting it to extend beyond this period.

At this juncture Mather's power was greatly strengthened by the appointment of his friend and parishioner, Sir William Phipps, as governor of the province, and the nomination of his father-in-law and many of his intimate friends to the council   The ambitious Stoughton, the deputy governor, was also subject to his influence.   Here was a fine opportunity to endeavor to establish the power of the clergy upon the old foundations which were being destroyed by the growing intelligence and independence of the people. Many of the ministers, under the lead of Cotton Mather, had committed themselves to the doctrine of witchcraft, and the people must accept it upon their simple assertion. No inquiry must be allowed into the matter, the opinions of the ministers must be adopted by the laity. And so Mather and his followers resorted to the usual weapons of superstition to accomplish the success of their plans.

In 1692 a new case of witchcraft occurred in Salem village, now the town of Danvers. The minister of this place was Samuel Parris, between whom and a number of his people there had for some time existed dissensions of such a bitter nature that the attention of the general court had been directed to them. In February, 1692, the daughter and niece of Parris, the former a child of nine years, and the latter of less than twelve, gave signs of being bewitched. Parris at once recognized the opportunity which was thus offered him for vengeance upon his enemies, and deliberately availed himself of it. He demanded of the children the names of the persons who had bewitched them, and then proceeded to accuse those whom he succeeded in inducing the girls to denounce. The first victim was Rebecca Nurse. She was known in the community as a woman of exemplary Christian character, but she was one of the most resolute opponents of Parris. Upon his accusation she was arrested and imprisoned. The next Sunday Parris preached a sermon from the text, "Have I not chosen you twelve, and one of you is a devil." As it was evident that his remarks were to be directed against Mistress Nurse, Sarah Cloyce, a sister of the accused, at once left the church. This in itself was a serious offence in those days, and Parris took advantage of it to accuse the offender of witchcraft, and she was sent to join her sister in prison. Mather, who deemed his credit at stake, lent his active aid to the persecution of these unfortunate people, and had the vanity to declare that he regarded the efforts of "the evil angels upon the country as a particular defiance unto himself." Parris scattered his accusations right and left, becoming both informer and witness against those whom he meant to destroy for their opposition to him. In a few weeks nearly one hundred persons were in prison upon the charge of witchcraft. Abigail Williams, Parris's niece, aided her uncle with her tales, which the least examination would have shown to be absurd. George Burroughs, one of the ministers of Salem, had long been regarded by Parris as a rival, and he now openly expressed his disbelief in witchcraft, and his disapproval of the measures against those charged with that offence. This boldness sealed his doom. He was accused by Parris, and committed to prison "with the rest of the witches." "The gallows was to be set up, not for those who professed themselves witches, but for those who rebuked the delusion."

Governor Bradstreet, who had been chosen by the people, was unwilling to proceed to extreme measures against the accused, as he had no faith in the evidence against them. The arrival of the royal governor and the new charter in Boston in May, 1692, placed Cotton Mather and his fellow-persecutors in a position to carry out their bloody designs. The general court alone had authority to appoint special courts, but Governor Phipps did not hesitate to appoint one himself for the trial of the accused persons at Salem, and this illegal tribunal, with Stoughton as its chief judge, met at Salem on the 2d of June. In this court Parris acted as prosecutor, keeping back some witnesses, and pushing others forward as best suited his plans.

The first victim of the court was Bridget Bishop, "a poor, friendless old woman." Parris, who had examined her at the time of her commitment, was the principal witness against her. Deliverance Hobbs being also accused, a natural infirmity of her body was taken as a proof of her guilt, and she was hanged, protesting her innocence. Rebecca Nurse was at first acquitted of the charges against her, but the court refused to receive the verdict of the jury, and Parris was determined that the woman against whom he had preached and prayed should not escape him, and the jury were induced to convict her, and she was hanged. John Willard, who had been compelled by his duty as a constable to arrest the accused, now refused to serve in this capacity any longer, as he had become convinced of the hypocrisy of the instigators of the persecution. He was immediately denounced, tried, and hanged.

When George Burroughs, the minister, was placed on trial the witnesses produced against him pretended to be dumb. "Who hinders these witnesses from giving their testimonies?" asked Stoughton, the chief judge. "I suppose the devil," replied Burroughs, contemptuously. ' How comes the devil," cried Stoughton, exultingly, "so loath to have any testimony borne against you?" The words of the prisoner were regarded as a confession, and his remarkable bodily strength was made an evidence of his guilt. He was convicted, and sentenced to be hanged. He was executed on the 19th of August with four others. As he ascended the scaffold Burroughs made an appeal to the people assembled to witness the execution, and effectually vindicated himself from the absurd charges against him, and repeated the Lord's prayer, which was regarded as a test of innocence. The spectators were powerfully affected, and seemed about to interfere in favor of the victim. Cotton Mather, who was present on horseback, now excited himself to complete the judicial murder

He harangued the people, insisted on the guilt of Burroughs, reminding them that the devil could sometimes assume the form of an angel of light, and even descended to the falsehood of declaring that Burroughs was no true minister, as his ordination was not valid. His appeal was successful, and the execution was completed

Giles Cory, an old man over eighty years of age, seeing that no denial of guilt availed anything, refused to plead, and was *pressed to death*, in accordance with an old English law, long obsolete, which was revived to meet his case. Samuel Wardwell confessed his guilt, and escaped the gallows. Overcome with shame for his cowardice, he retracted his confession, and was hanged for denying witchcraft. A reign of terror prevailed in Salem; the prisons were full, and no one could feel sure how long he would escape accusation and arrest Many persons confessed their guilt to save their lives Children accused their parents, parents their children, and husbands and wives each other of the most impossible offences, in the hope of escaping the persecution themselves. Hale, the minister of Beverley, was a zealous advocate of the persecution until the bitter cup was presented to his own lips by the accusation of his wife Many persons were obliged to fly the colony, and the magistrates, conscious that they were already exceeding their powers, were careful not to demand their surrender

We have mentioned only some of the principal cases to show the character of the persecution, as our limits forbid the relation of all. The total number hanged was twenty; fifty-five were tortured or terrified into confessions of guilt The accusations were at first lodged against persons of humble station, but at length reached the higher classes. Governor Phipps' wife and two sons of Governor Bradford are said to have been among the accused "Insanity," says Judge Story, "could hardly devise more refinements in barbarity, or profligacy execute them with more malignant coolness" Every principle of English justice was violated to secure the condemnation of the accused, and people were encouraged by the magistrates to accuse others as a means of securing the favor of the authorities.

These terrible deeds were not the work of the people of Massachusetts, and under a popular government would have been impossible; for though the belief in witchcraft was general, the sentiment of the people was against the barbarity of the court The Salem tragedies were the work of a few men, not one of whom was responsible in any way to the people "Of the magistrates at that time, not one held office by the suffrage of the people; the tribunal, essentially despotic in its origin, as in its character, had no sanction but an extraordinary and an illegal commission; and Stoughton, the chief judge, a partisan of Andros, had been

15

rejected by the people of Massachusetts. The responsibility of the tragedy, far from attaching to the people of the colony, rests with the very few, hardly five or six, in whose hands the transition state of the government left for a season unlimited influence. Into the interior of the colony the delusion did not spread at all " *

Stoughton's court, having hanged twenty of its victims, adjourned about the last of September, 1692, until November, and on the 18th of October the general court met. The indignation of the people had been gathering force, and men were determined to put a stop to the judicial murders and tortures which had disgraced them so long. Remonstrances were at once presented to the assembly against "the doings of the witch tribunals," the people of Andover leading the way in this effort. The assembly abolished the special court, and established a tribunal by public law. It was ordered that this court should not meet until the following January The governor attempted to undo the work of the assembly by appointing Stoughton chief judge of the new court. When that tribunal met at Salem in January, 1693, it was evident that the public mind had undergone a marked change. The influence of the leaders of the delusion was at an end The grand jury rejected the majority of the presentments offered to it, and when those who were indicted were put on trial, the jury brought in verdicts of acquittal in all but three cases. The governor, now alive to the force of public sentiment, reprieved all who were under sentence to the great disgust of Stoughton, who left the bench in a rage when informed of this action. The persecutors, anxious to cover their defeat by the execution of one more victim, employed all their arts to procure the conviction of a woman of Charlestown, who was commonly believed to be a witch. They supported their charge by more important evidence than had been presented in any case at Salem, but the jury at once returned a verdict of " not guilty."

Cotton Mather was intensely mortified by the failure of his efforts to force the people into a general acceptance of his views. He got up a case of witchcraft in Boston, but was careful to caution his possessed people to refrain from accusing any one of bewitching them ' Robert Calef, an unlettered man, but one whose common sense could not be led astray by Mather, promptly exposed the imposture in a pamphlet, which effectually destroyed Mather's influence for harm. Mather, unable to reply to him, denounced him as an enemy of religion, and complained that Calef's book was "a libel upon the whole government and ministry of the land," forgetting that only seven or eight ministers, and no magistrate commanding the confidence of the people, had any share in the tragedies. Calef continued his writings, however, undismayed by the indignation of his adversary, and his book was finally published in England, where it attracted considerable attention.

The danger was now over. It was no longer possible to procure a conviction for witchcraft. The indignant people of Salem village at once drove the wretched Parris and his family from the place. Noyes, the minister of Salem, who had been active in the persecutions, was compelled to ask the forgiveness of the people, after a public confession of his error. The devotion of the rest of his life to works of charity won him the pardon he sought. Sewall, one of the judges, struck with horror at the part he had played in the persecution, made an open and frank confession of his error, and implored the forgiveness of his fellow-citizens His sincerity was so evident that he soon regained the favor he had lost. Stoughton passed the remainder of his life in proud and haughty disregard of the opinion of his fellow-men, scorning to make any acknowledgment of error, and evincing no remorse for his cruelties

As for the prime mover of the delusion, the Rev Cotton Mather, nothing could induce him to admit that he could by any possibility have been in error, not even the recollection of the sorrow he had brought upon some of the best people in the colony could shake his impenetrable self-conceit, or humble him. When it was plain to him that he was the object of the indignation of all good men in New England, he had the hardihood to endeavor to persuade them that after all he had not been specially active in the sad affair "Was Cotton Mather honestly credulous?" asks Bancroft. "Ever ready to dupe himself, he limited his credulity only by the probable credulity of others. He changes, or omits to repeat, his statements, without acknowledging error, and with a clear intention of conveying false impressions He is an example how far selfishness, under the form of vanity and ambition, can blind the higher faculties, stupefy the judgment, and dupe consciousness itself. His self-righteousness was complete till he was resisted."

And yet this man was not to die without rendering to the country a genuine service. In 1721, having become satisfied that inoculation was a sure preventive of small-pox, he advocated the introduction of it into the colony. He was opposed by the whole body of the clergy, who declared that it was an attempt to defeat the plans of the Almighty, who "sent the small-pox as a punishment for sins, and whose vengeance would thus be only provoked the more." The people of the colony were also bitterly opposed to inoculation, and threatened to hang Mather if he did not cease his advocacy of it His life was at one time in serious danger, but he persevered, and at length had the satisfaction of seeing the practice of inoculation generally adopted by the people who had so hotly opposed it.

CHAPTER XVI.

THE SETTLEMENT OF NEW YORK.

WHEN the hope of finding a northwest passage to India began to die out, a company of "certain worshipful merchants" of London employed Henry Hudson, an Englishman and an experienced navigator, to go in search of a northeast passage to India, around the Arctic shores of Europe, between Lapland and Nova Zembla and frozen Spitzbergen. These worthy gentlemen were convinced that since the effort to find a northwest passage had failed, nothing remained but to search for a northeast passage, and they were sure that if human skill or energy could find it, Hudson would succeed in his mission. They were not mistaken in their man, for in two successive voyages he did all that mortal could do to penetrate the ice-fields beyond the North Cape, but without success. An impassable barrier of ice held him back, and he was forced to return to London to confess his failure. With unconquerable hope, he suggested new means of overcoming the difficulties; but while his employers praised his zeal and skill, they declined to go to further expense in an undertaking which promised so little, and the "bold Englishman, the expert pilot, and the famous navigator" found himself out of employment. Every effort to secure aid in England failed him, and, thoroughly disheartened, he passed over to Holland, whither his fame had preceded him.

The Dutch, who were more enterprising and more hopeful than his own countrymen, lent a ready ear to his statement of his plans, and the Dutch East India Company at once employed him, and placed him in command of a yacht of ninety tons, called the "Half Moon," manned by a picked crew. On the 25th of March, 1609, Hudson set sail in this vessel from Amsterdam, and steered directly for the coast of Nova Zembla. He succeeded in reaching the meridian of Spitzbergen; but here the ice, the fogs, and the fierce tempests of the north drove him back, and turning to the westward, he sailed past the capes of Greenland, and on the 2d of July was on the banks of Newfoundland. He passed down the coast as far as Charleston harbor, vainly hoping to find the north*west* passage, and then in despair turned to the northward, discovering Delaware bay on his voyage. On the 3d of September he arrived off a large bay to the north of the Delaware, and passing into it, dropped

anchor "at two cables' length from the shore," within Sandy Hook. Devoting some days to rest, and to the exploration of the bay, he passed through The Narrows on the 11th of September, and then the broad and beautiful "inner bay" burst upon him in

COAT OF ARMS OF NEW YORK.

all its splendor, and from the deck of his ship he watched the swift current of the mighty river rolling from the north to the sea. He was full of hope now, and the next day continued his progress up the river, and at nightfall cast anchor at Yonkers. During the night the current of the river turned his ship around, placing her head down stream; and this fact, coupled with the assurances of the natives who came out to the "Half Moon" in their canoes, that the river came from far beyond the mountains, convinced him that the stream flowed from ocean to ocean, and that by sailing on he would at length reach India—the golden land of his dreams.

Thus encouraged, he pursued his way up the river, gazing with wondering delight upon its glorious scenery, and listening with gradually fading hope to the stories of the natives who flocked to the water to greet him. The stream narrowed, and the water grew fresh, and long before he anchored below Albany, Hudson had abandoned the belief that he was in the northwest passage. From the anchorage a boat's crew continued the voyage to the mouth of the Mohawk. Hudson was satisfied that he

had made a great discovery—one that was worth fully as much as finding
the new route to India. He was in a region upon which the white man's
eye had never rested before, and which offered the richest returns to
commercial ventures. He hastened back to New York bay, took possession of the country in the name of Holland, and then set sail for
Europe. He put into Dartmouth, in England, on his way back, where
he told the story of his discovery. King James I. prevented his continuing his voyage, hoping to deprive the Dutch of its fruits; but Hudson
took care to send his log-book and all the ship's papers over to Holland,
and thus placed his employers in full possession of the knowledge he had
gained   The English at length released the "Half Moon," and she
continued her voyage to the Texel, but without her commander.

The discovery of Hudson was particularly acceptable to the Dutch, for
the new country was rich in fur-bearing animals, and Russia offered a
ready market for all the furs that could be sent there. The East India
Company, therefore, refitted the "Half Moon" after her return to
Holland, and despatched her to the region discovered by Hudson on a
fur trading expedition, which was highly successful. Private persons
also embarked in similar enterprises, and within two years a prosperous
and important fur trade was established between Holland and the country
along the Mauritius, as the great river discovered by Hudson had been
named, in honor of the Stadtholder of Holland. No government took
any notice of the trade for a while, and all persons were free to engage
in it

Among the adventurers employed in this trade was one Adrian Block,
noted as one of the boldest navigators of his time. He made a voyage to
Manhattan island in 1611, then the site of a Dutch trading-post, and
secured a cargo of skins, with which he was about to return to Holland,
when a fire consumed both his vessel and her cargo, and obliged him to
pass the winter with his crew on the island   They built them log huts
on the site of the present Beaver street—the first houses erected on the
island—and during the winter constructed a yacht of sixteen tons, which
Block called the "Onrust"—the "Restless" In this yacht Block made
several voyages of discovery, and explored the coasts of Long Island
sound, and gave his name to the small island near the eastern end of the
sound. He soon after went back to Europe.

In the meantime Hudson had not been permitted by the English king
to take service again with the Dutch, and after apprising his employers
in Holland of his discoveries, he was engaged by an English company to
make further explorations in their behalf He sailed to the north of his
former route, reached the coast of Labrador, and passing through the

straits, entered the bay which bears his name. He spent the remainder of the season in exploring its coasts, and resolved to winter there, hoping to push his discoveries still farther northward in the spring. In the spring of 1611 he found it impossible to continue his voyage, as his provisions had begun to run low, and with tears turned his vessel's prow homeward. His men now broke out into mutiny, and seizing Hudson and his son and four others, who were sick, they placed them in the shallop and set them adrift. And so the great navigator, whose memory is perpetuated by one of the noblest of the rivers of America, and whose genius gave the region through which it flows to civilization, perished amid the northern seas. "The gloomy waste of waters which bears his name is his tomb and his monument."

In 1614 the Dutch built a fort on the lower end of Manhattan island, and in the next few years established forts or trading houses along the river as far as Fort Orange, on the site of Albany. These were merely trading-posts, no effort being yet made to occupy the country with a permanent colony. In 1621 the Dutch West India Company was organized for the purpose of trading with America, and took possession of the country along the Hudson, intending to hold it merely as temporary occupants. The States General of Holland granted them the monopoly of trade from Cape May to Nova Scotia, and named the whole region New Netherland. The Dutch thus extended their claims into regions already claimed by the English and French, and prepared the way for future quarrels and complications.

The English, now awake to the importance of Hudson's discoveries, warned the Dutch government to refrain from making further settlements on "Hudson's river," as they called the Mauritius, but the latter, relying upon the justice of their claim, paid no attention to these warnings, and in the spring of 1623 the Dutch West India Company sent over thirty families of Walloons, or one hundred and ten persons in all, to found a permanent colony. These Walloons were Protestants from the frontier between France and Flanders, and had fled to Amsterdam to escape religious persecution in their own country. They were sound, healthy, vigorous, and pious people, and could be relied upon to make homes in the new world. The majority of them settled around the fort on the lower end of Manhattan island, and the colony was named New Amsterdam. The remainder established themselves on Long island, about where the Brooklyn navy yard now stands, and there Sarah de Rapelje, the first white child born in the province of New Netherlands, saw the light. Eighteen families ascended the river and settled around Fort Orange.

In the same year (1623) a party under command of Cornelis Jacobsen
May, who gave his name to the southern cape of New Jersey, ascended
the Delaware, then called the South river, and built Fort Nassau, on the
east side of the river a few miles below the present city of Camden.
This was done in order to establish the claim of the Dutch to this region.

In 1626 the West India Company sent out to New Amsterdam the

FIRST SETTLEMENT OF NEW YORK.

first regular governor of the province, Peter Minuits by name. He
brought with him a koopman, or general commissary, who was also the
secretary of the province, and a schout, or sheriff, to assist him in his
government. The only laws prescribed for the colony were the instructions of the West India Company. The colonists, on their part, were to

regard the orders of the governor as their law. He was authorized to punish minor offences at his discretion; but cases requiring severe or capital punishment were to be sent to Holland for trial. Minuits set to work with great vigor to lay the foundations of the colony. He called a council of the Indian chiefs, and purchased the island of Manhattan from them for presents valued at about twenty-four dollars in American money. He thus secured an equitable title to the island and won the friendship of the Indians. To encourage emigration the company granted to each emigrant as much land as he could properly cultivate, and it was ordered that any member of the company who in four years should induce fifty persons to settle anywhere within the limits of New Netherland, the island of Manhattan alone excepted, should be termed "Patroon," or "Lord of the Manor," and should be entitled to purchase a tract of land sixteen miles in length by eight in width for the support of this dignity. A number of persons availed themselves of this privilege, and secured from the Indians by purchase the best lands and the most valuable trading places in the province. Those who were inferior to them in wealth were of necessity compelled to become the ten-
ants of the patroons, and thus a
check was placed upon the improvement of the colony. In
order to compel the colonists to
purchase their supplies from Holland, the company forbade them

COAT OF ARMS OF DELAWARE.

to manufacture even the simplest fabrics for clothing, on pain of banishment. The patroons were enjoined to provide a minister and a schoolmaster for their tenants, but no provision was made for them by the company, which was careful, however, to offer to furnish the patroons with African slaves if their use should be found desirable.

In 1629 Samuel Godyn and Samuel Blommaert purchased from the Indians the region between Cape Henlopen and the mouth of the Delaware river, and in 1631 a colony of thirty souls was planted on Lewes creek, in the present State of Delaware. "That Delaware exists as a separate commonwealth is due to this colony. According to English rule, occupancy was necessary to complete a title to the wilderness, and the Dutch now occupied Delaware." Less than a year later De Vries came over from Holland with a reinforcement, and found only the ruins of the settlement, the people of which had been massacred by the Indians.

Under the vigorous administration of Minuits New Netherland prospered; houses were built, farms laid off; the population was largely increased by new arrivals from Europe. During this period New Amsterdam fairly entered upon its career as one of the most important places in America. It was a happy settlement as well; the rights of the people were respected, and they were practically as free as they had been in Holland. Troubles with the Indians marked the close of Minuit's administration. The latter were provoked by the murder of some of their number by the whites, and by the aid rendered by the commander at Fort Orange to the Mohegans in one of their forays upon the Mohawks. Alarmed by the hostility of the savages, many of the families at Fort Orange, and from the region between the Hudson and the Delaware, abandoned their settlements and came to New Amsterdam for safety, thus adding to the population of that town. Minuits was recalled in 1632, and left the province in a prosperous condition. During the last year of his government New Amsterdam sent over $60,000 worth of furs to Holland.

Minuits was succeeded by Wouter Van Twiller, a clerk in the company's warehouse at Amsterdam, who owed his appointment to his being the husband of the niece of Killian Van Rensselaer, the patroon of Albany. Irving has thus sketched this redoubtable governor. "He was exactly five feet six inches in height, and six feet five inches in circumference. His head was a perfect sphere, and of such stupendous dimensions that dame Nature, with all her sex's ingenuity, would have been puzzled to construct a neck capable of supporting it; wherefore she wisely declined the attempt, and settled it firmly on the top of his back bone just between the shoulders. His body was oblong and particularly capacious at bottom, which was wisely ordered by Providence, seeing that he was a man of sedentary habits and very averse to the idle labor of walking. His legs were very short, but sturdy in proportion to the weight they had to sustain; so that, when erect, he had not a little the appearance of a beer barrel on skids. His face—that infallible index of the mind—presented a vast expanse, unfurrowed by any of those lines and angles which disfigure the human countenance with what is termed expression. Two small gray eyes twinkled feebly in the midst, like two stars of lesser magnitude in a hazy firmament; and his full-fed cheeks, which seemed to have taken toll of everything that went into his mouth, were curiously mottled and streaked with dusky red, like a Spitzenberg apple. His habits were as regular as his person. He daily took his four stated meals, appropriating exactly an hour to each; he smoked and doubted eight hours, and he slept the remaining twelve of the four-and-twenty."

Van Twiller ruled the province seven years, and, in spite of his stupidity, it prospered. In 1633 Adam Roelantsen, the first school-master, arrived—for the fruitful Walloons had opened the way by this time for his labors—and in the same year a wooden church was built in the present Bridge street, and placed in charge of the famous Dominie Everardus Bogardus. In 1635 the fort, which marked the site of the present Bowling Green, and which had been begun in 1614, was finished, and in the same year the first English settlers at New Amsterdam came into the town. The English in New England also began to give the Dutch trouble during this administration, and even sent a ship into "Hudson's river" to trade with the Indians. Influenced by De Vries, the commander of the fort, the governor sent an expedition up the river after the audacious English vessel, seized her, brought her back to New York, and sent her to sea with a warning not to repeat her attempt. The disputes between the English and the Dutch about the Connecticut settlements also began to make trouble for New Amsterdam. Van Twiller possessed no influence in the colony, was laughed at and snubbed on every side, and was at length recalled by the company in 1638. The only memorial of Van Twiller left to us is the Isle of Nuts, which lies in the bay between New York and Brooklyn, and which he purchased as his private domain. It is still called the "Governor's Island."

Van Twiller was succeeded by William Kieft, a man of greater abili-ties, but unscrupulous and avaricious. He had become a bankrupt in Holland, and hoped to find in America the means of restoring his for-tunes. His administration of the province was full of troubles, the greater part of which were due to his recklessness and rapacity.

The colonists were forbidden to sell fire-arms to the Indians, but some of the traders along the Hudson had violated this order, and it was esti-mated that the Mohawks had at least four hundred warriors armed with muskets. They were willing to pay large prices for the guns, as these weapons enabled them to meet on equal terms their enemies, the Canada Indians, who had been armed by the French. During Van Twiller's administration the colony had been on good terms with the Mohegans and other tribes of the Algonquin race, who were generally known as the river Indians. Kieft, soon after his arrival, demanded of them the payment of a tribute, which he pretended he had been ordered by the company to levy upon them. They refused his demand with contempt, and from this time the friendship which they had entertained for the Dutch began to disappear.

A year or two later the Raritans, a tribe living on the river of that name, were accused of stealing some hogs from the colony. The animals had been taken by some Dutch traders; but Kieft, instead of investigating the matter, sent a party of soldiers among the Raritans and destroyed their corn and killed several of their number. The savages determined upon revenge, and with their usual unreasoning fury attacked the settlement which De Vries—who was always a friend of the Indians —had founded on Staten island, and killed four men. The people of the colony now urged the governor to conciliate the savages by kind treatment, but he refused to do so Another cause of trouble soon arose. Twenty years before a Dutch trader had killed an Indian chief in the presence of a little nephew of the warrior. That child, now grown to manhood, came into the colony in 1641, and avenged his uncle by killing an innocent settler. Kieft ordered the Indians to surrender the young man that he might be punished for his crime; but the savages refused to give him up, but offered to ransom him. Kieft refused their proposition, and the matter remained an open source of trouble.

With the hope of finding a remedy for the Indian difficulty, the people obtained from the governor, in 1642, permission to hold a meeting of the heads of families at New Amsterdam. These appointed twelve of their number to investigate the affairs of the colony. This was the first representative assembly of New Netherland, and its career was short. Venturing to pass beyond the Indian question, and to criticise the administration of the governor in other matters, it was dissolved.

Near the end of the year 1642 the Mohawks sent a band of warriors armed with muskets to demand tribute of the river tribes. These, too weak to contend with their enemies, fled to the Dutch for protection Kieft was at this time angry with the Indians for refusing to surrender to him one of their number who had killed a Dutchman who had made him drunk and then ill-treated him, and he resolved to take a signal vengeance upon them, and exterminate them. De Vries, to whom he communicated his plan, remonstrated with him in the hope of inducing him to abandon it. "If you murder these poor creatures who have put themselves under your protection, you will involve the whole colony in ruin, and their blood, and the blood of your own people, will be required at your hands," said De Vries Nothing, however, could move the governor from his purpose.

The Indians who had sought the protection of the Dutch were encamped with the Hackensack tribe just above Hoboken. On the night of the 25th of February the garrison of the fort at New Amsterdam, reinforced by the crews of some Dutch privateers in the river, crossed the Hudson and attacked the unsuspecting savages. Nearly a hundred were killed, and when the morning came many of the poor wretches were seen crowding along the shore of the river in the vain attempt to cross

over to their supposed friends at New Amsterdam They were forced
into the stream and drowned. A company of Indians, trusting to the
friendship of the Dutch, had encamped on Manhattan island, near the
fort. They were put to death almost to a man

The massacre was regarded by the colonists with horror and detesta-
tion, and they took no part in the joy with which the governor greeted
the troops on their return from their bloody work. He was not allowed
to rejoice long, however When it became known among the Algonquins that their brethren had been murdered, not by the Mohawks, but
by the Dutch, every tribe took up the hatchet to avenge them, and a
general warfare began along the entire line of the Dutch settlements.
Several villages were destroyed, and a number of settlers were murdered
or carried into captivity. The colony was threatened with ruin, and
Kieft was obliged to open negotiations for peace It was in this war
that Mrs. Anne Hutchinson and her family, who had taken refuge in the
territory of the Dutch, were murdered by the savages.

On the 5th of March, 1643, a conference was held at Rockaway
between sixteen Indian chiefs and De Vries and two other envoys from
the colony. One of the principal sachems arose, holding in his hands a
bundle of small sticks "When you first arrived on our shores," said
the Indian, addressing the whites, "you were destitute of food We
gave you our beans and our corn; we fed you with oysters and fish: and
now, for our recompense, you murder our people." He then laid down
one of the little sticks and proceeded· "The traders whom your first
ships left on our shores to traffic till their return, were cherished by us
as the apple of our eye. We gave them our daughters for their wives.
Among those whom you have murdered were children of your own
blood." "I know all," said De Vries, interrupting his recital of wrongs.
He then invited the chiefs to go with him to the fort. They accompanied him to New Amsterdam, where presents were exchanged and a
treaty of peace negotiated. The younger warriors were not satisfied.
Kieft's presents were niggardly. They were not regarded by the
savages as a sufficient compensation for the wrongs they had suffered,
and the war was renewed.

The leader of the Dutch in this campaign was Captain John Underhill, who had served in the Pequod war in New England, and had
removed to New Amsterdam in consequence of having been made to do
penance in public at Boston in 1640. The war continued for two years,
and though the colony suffered severely, the Dutch were able to inflict
such heavy losses upon the savages that the latter were at length as
anxious for peace as the whites. Sixteen hundred of the Indians had

fallen, but the colony had been brought to the verge of ruin, and the population of New Amsterdam was reduced to one hundred souls. On the 30th of August, 1645, the chiefs of the Algonquins and a deputation from their old enemies, the Mohawks, who came as mediators, met the whites on the spot now known as the Battery, and concluded a peace

The close of the war was hailed with rejoicings throughout the colony. Kieft was regarded with universal hatred as the author of the terrible sufferings of the struggle, and his barbarous conduct was censured and disavowed by the company, and he was recalled   Hated throughout the colony he at length determined to return to Europe. Freighting a vessel with his ill-gotten gains he sailed from Manhattan in 1647. As he neared the shores of the old world his ship was wrecked on the coast of Wales, and all on board perished

Kieft, in the vain hope of conciliating the people, appointed, immediately after the close of the war, a new municipal council of eight members. The first act of this council was to demand of the States General of Holland the removal of Kieft. Their demand was complied with, as we have seen, and in 1647 Peter Stuyvesant was made governor of New Netherlands, and reached New Amsterdam in the same year.

Stuyvesant was essentially a strong man. A soldier by education and of long experience, he was accustomed to regard rigid discipline as the one thing needful in every relation of life, and he was not slow to introduce that system into his government of New Amsterdam. He had served gallantly in the wars against the Portuguese, and had lost a leg in one of his numerous encounters with them. He was as vain as a peacock, as fond of display as a child, and thoroughly imbued with the most aristocratic ideas—qualities not exactly the best for a governor of New Amsterdam. Yet he was, with all his faults, an honest man, he had deeply at heart the interests of the colony, and his administration was mainly a prosperous one.

He energetically opposed from the first all manifestations in favor of popular government. His will was to be the law of the province. "If any one," said he, "during my administration shall appeal, I will make him a foot shorter, and send the pieces to Holland, and let him appeal in that way " He went to work with vigor to reform matters in the colony, extending his efforts to even the morals and domestic affairs of the people He soon brought about a reign of material prosperity greater than had ever been known before, and exerted himself to check the encroachments of the English on the east, and the Swedes on the south. He inaugurated a policy of kindness and justice toward the Indians, and soon changed their enmity to sincere friendship. One thing, however, he dared not do—he could not levy taxes upon the people without their consent, for fear of offending the States General of Holland. This forced him to appoint a council of nine prominent citizens, and, although he endeavored to hedge round their powers by numerous conditions, the nine ever afterwards served as a salutary check upon the action of the governor.

The English in Connecticut made great efforts to extend their territories westward at the expense of New Netherland, and gave Stuyvesant no little annoyance by their aggressions. During his administration the colony received large accessions of English emigrants from New England, who came to New Netherland "to enjoy that liberty denied to them by their own countrymen." They settled in New Amsterdam, on Long island, and in Westchester county Being admitted to an equality with the Dutch settlers they exercised considerable influence in the affairs of the colony, and towards the close of his administration gave the governor considerable trouble by their opposition to his despotic acts. Stuyvesant entered into an arrangement with Connecticut for the proper adjustment of the boundaries of the two colonies, and left the English in possession of half of Long island.

Upon his removal from his place as governor of New Amsterdam Peter Minuits offered his services to Gustavus Adolphus, king of Sweden, who was anxious to found in America a colony which might prove a place of refuge for the persecuted Protestants of Europe. The offer was accepted by the king, and the shores of the Delaware were chosen as the site of the new settlement. Near the close of 1637 a little company of Swedes and Fins embarked in two vessels under the direction of Minuits, and sailed for America. The Delaware was reached early in 1638, and the new-comers purchased from the natives the country on the west side of the river from Cape Henlopen to Trenton. A fort was built within the limits of the present State of Delaware, on the site of the present city of Wilmington, and named Fort Christiana, in honor of the youthful queen of Sweden, the daughter of Gustavus.

Kieft, the Dutch governor of New Netherland, protested against this occupation of the country by the Swedes, as Holland claimed the region along the Delaware. Sweden was too formidable a power for her colony to be attacked, however, and Kieft contented himself with his protest. Fresh emigrants came out from Scandinavia, and New Sweden grew rapidly. The Dutch fort Nassau was renewed, but the Swedes succeeded in maintaining their ascendency along the Delaware in spite of it. Their plantations were extended along the river, and the smallest of the American commonwealths was permanently settled by Europeans.

When Stuyvesant was made governor of New Netherland the Dutch West India Company resolved to enforce their claim to Delaware, and in 1651 built Fort Casimir on the site of Newcastle The Swedes regarded this as an encroachment upon their domain, and in 1654 captured the fort. Upon the receipt of this news the Dutch Company indignantly ordered Stuyvesant "to drive the Swedes from the river, or compel their submission " In September, 1655, Stuyvesant, with a force of six hundred men, sailed from Manhattan into the Delaware. The Swedish forts were compelled to surrender one after another, and the colonists were forced to submit to the establishment of the rule of the Dutch. They were allowed to retain their possessions, and on the whole were treated well Many of them, however, were dissatisfied with their new rulers, and in the next few years emigrated to Maryland and Virginia.

The territory now included in the State of New Jersey was also claimed by the Dutch. They built Fort Nassau on the Delaware to establish this claim, but the Swedes were the first to settle the country. Soon after, establishing themselves in Delaware, they crossed over to the eastern side of the river, and built a line of trading-posts extending from Cape May to Burlington

New Amsterdam continued to prosper, and was even at this early day rapidly becoming an important commercial town. Stuyvesant's arbitrary temper was held in check to a considerable extent by the more liberal policy of the company, who sincerely desired the prosperity of the colony. "Let every peaceful citizen," wrote the directors, "enjoy freedom of conscience, this maxim has made our city the asylum for fugitives from every land; tread in its steps, and you shall be blessed " The infant metropolis from the first acquired a cosmopolitan character It contained settlers from every nation of Europe, and even from Africa; for the Dutch at an early day introduced negro slavery into the colony.

The people of New Netherland had no political rights, and the West India Company, with every disposition to treat the colony with fairness, did not mean to allow the settlers to have any voice in governing themselves. Town meetings were positively forbidden, and every care was taken to discourage any manifestation of public spirit Nevertheless the colonists were beginning to feel the promptings of the spirit of democracy, and the English settlers who had come into the province were by no means content to remain without the privileges of freemen A series of disputes at once arose with the fiery old governor, who entertained the most profound contempt for the people, and laughed in scorn at the assertion of their ability to govern themselves.

The discontents went on increasing, however, and at length the people appointed a convention of two delegates from each settlement for the purpose of deliberating on the affairs of the colony. Stuyvesant was bitterly opposed to this assembly, but deemed it best not to seek to prevent its meeting, as such a step would have brought about a collision with the people. The convention addressed the governor as follows: "The States General of the United Provinces are our liege lords, we submit to the laws of the United Provinces; and our rights and privileges ought to be in harmony with those of the fatherland, for we are a member of the state, and not a subjugated people. We, who have come together from various parts of the world, and are a blended community of various lineage, we, who have, at our own expense, exchanged our native lands for the protection of the United Provinces, we, who have transformed the wilderness into fruitful farms, demand that no new laws shall be enacted but with the consent of the people; that none shall be appointed to office but with the approbation of the people; that obscure and obsolete laws shall never be revived." This was too much for the governor. He attempted to reason with the deputies, who had the temerity to demand the right of self-government, and finding them firm dissolved the convention with the haughty declaration "We derive our authority from God and the West India Company, not from the pleasure of a few ignorant subjects." The West India Company entirely approved the course of the governor. "We approve the taxes you propose," they wrote to Stuyvesant; "have no regard to the consent of the people. Let them indulge no longer the visionary dream that taxes can be imposed only with their consent."

Neither the company nor the governor could understand that this persistent disregard of the rights of the people was alienating all classes of the colonists, and making them long for the conquest of New Netherland by the English as the only means of obtaining the privileges of the freemen of the English colonies.

Nor was this an idle hope. For a long time past the English government had seriously entertained the idea of driving out the Dutch, and adding New Netherland to its American possessions. The English claim extended to the entire Atlantic coast as far south as Florida, and the Dutch were regarded as intruders. Cromwell and his son had each contemplated making such an effort, and at the return of Charles II. to the throne the plan was more seriously discussed, and at length put in operation. Charles, although at peace with Holland, and in spite of the charter which he had granted to Connecticut, bestowed upon his brother, the Duke of York, afterwards James II., the entire region between the

16

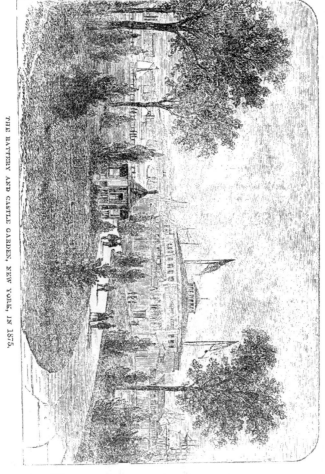

THE BATTERY AND CASTLE GARDEN, NEW YORK, IN 1875.

Connecticut and Delaware rivers. This was in February, 1664. A squadron was at once fitted out for the purpose of seizing the Dutch colony, and was placed in command of Richard Nicolls, an officer of the Duke of York's household. The fleet touched at Boston to land the commissioners sent out by Charles to the New England colonies, and to receive reinforcements. Governor Winthrop, of Connecticut, also embarked on board of it.

The first intimation Stuyvesant had of the intended robbery was the appearance of the fleet within the Narrows on the 28th of August, 1664.

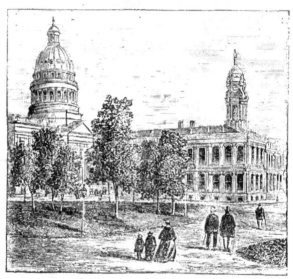

THE CITY HALL PARK, NEW YORK, IN 1675.

The next day Nicolls demanded the surrender of the town and fort of New Amsterdam. Stuyvesant, who had made preparations for defending the place, endeavored to resist the demand, but the citizens refused to sustain him, and he was obliged to submit. On the 8th of September he embarked his troops for Holland, and put to sea. The English at once took possession of the fort and town, and their vessels ascending the Hudson, received the submission of the other Dutch forts and settlements along the river. A few weeks later the Dutch and the Swedes along the Delaware submitted to the English, and the entire province was in their hands. The name of New Amsterdam was changed to New York, which name was also bestowed upon the province, and Fort Orange was called Albany, all in honor of the new proprietor. Nicolls was appointed governor

The English set themselves to work to conciliate the Dutch residents, a task not very difficult, as the English settlers in the province had already prepared the way for the change, and the treatment the colony had received from the West India Company had prevented the formation of any decided attachment to the rule of Holland The English system of government was introduced, the towns were allowed to elect their own magistrates, and the desires of the people for representative government seemed about to be gratified.

The Mohawks had been the friends of the Dutch, and they now readily entered into an alliance with the English as their successors. This alliance remained unbroken all through the colonial period, and during the war of the Revolution, and in the first-named period proved of the

CUAT OF ARMS OF NEW JERSEY

greatest advantage to the colonies, as the Mohawks, whose hatred of the French was deep and unrelenting, proved a formidable obstacle in the way of invading parties from Canada

Immediately upon becoming master of the province the Duke of York proceeded to divide it. He sold to Lord Berkeley and Sir George Cartaret, both of whom were already proprietaries of Carolina, the country between the Hudson and the Delaware This purchase was named New Jersey, in honor of the island of Jersey, of which Cartaret was governor, and corresponded in size very nearly to the present State of that name The new proprietors made liberal offers to induce emigrants to settle in their territory, and among other things offered them lands free of rent for five years. They granted to the province a political establishment consisting of a governor, a council, and assembly of representatives of the people, who were given the power to make the laws necessary for their government The proprietors reserved the right to appoint the governor and judicial officers, and to veto the proceedings of the assembly Negro slavery was also introduced. These offers drew a large number of settlers to New Jersey, and many families came over from Long island to the new province The principal settlement was named Elizabethtown, in honor of Cartaret's wife The colony prospered, no trouble was experienced from the neighboring Indians, whose power had been thoroughly broken by the Dutch, and everything went on happily until the year 1670, when the proprietaries demanded the rents due for the lands held by the settlers. The demand was refused. Many of the colonists had lived in the province under the rule of the Dutch, and had bought their lands from the Indians, and they claimed that the grant of the province to Cartaret could not invalidate these purchases, as the king had no claim to the lands which he so lavishly bestowed upon his favorites. Others refused to pay rent because they had made their plantations without any assistance from the proprietaries, and did not acknowledge any debt to them. The representative of the proprietaries was obliged to fly from New Jersey for safety, and went to England to obtain assistance in enforcing his demands.

The Duke of York heard the complaints of the proprietaries, but the only attention he paid to them was to appoint Sir Edmund Andros, who subsequently became infamous for his tyranny in New England, governor of New Jersey. This was a flagrant violation of the rights of Cartaret and Berkeley, and an act thoroughly characteristic of the last of the Stuarts. Berkeley in disgust sold his half of the province, known as West Jersey, to an English Quaker named Edward Byllinge, who subsequently made over his claim to William Penn, who made an arrangement with Cartaret to divide the Jerseys. Cartaret retained East Jersey, and the line of division was drawn from the northwest corner of the province to the sea at Little Egg harbor. This purchase became the cause of considerable litigation in after years, and West Jersey was claimed by Pennsylvania until the next century, when, as we shall see, the dispute was settled.

New Jersey received a considerable accession to her population in consequence of the re-establishment of episcopacy in Scotland. The Cameronians or Covenanters refused to submit to the authority of the church, and thus became the objects of a cruel persecution. As so many of their faith had done before them, they sought refuge from their persecutors in America, and in 1683 and the following years large numbers of them came over and settled in East Jersey. This portion of the State was the cradle, as it is now one of the strongholds, of Presbyterianism in America.

In the meantime matters in New York had not been conducted to the satisfaction of the people. The promises made to the colonists by the English authorities were not kept. The province was treated as the absolute property of the Duke of York, and the governor and his council were constituted the highest authority for both the making and execution of the laws. Representative government was denied them, arbitrary taxes were imposed by Governor Nicolls, and the titles to the lands held by the settlers, not even excepting the Dutch patents, were declared invalid, in order that by issuing new title-deeds Nicolls might gain enormous fees. Lovelace, the successor of Nicolls, carried his tyranny to

BROADWAY, NEW YORK, IN 1875.

a still greater extent. His system of government is thus summed up: "The method for keeping the people in order is severity, and laying such taxes as may give them liberty for no thought but how to discharge them." When the people of a number of the towns ventured to remonstrate with the governor, he ordered their petition for the redress of their grievances to be publicly burned before the town house in New York. The settlements in Delaware were treated with equal injustice

In 1673, war having broken out between Holland and England, a Dutch squadron entered the harbor of New York. The people, thoroughly cured of their partiality for English rule by the injustice they had suffered, made no resistance and surrendered the town. Its name was changed to New Orange, and the authority of the Dutch was again extended over the province, and also over Long island, New Jersey and Delaware. The Mohawks sent a deputation of their chiefs to congratulate the Dutch upon the recovery of their colony. The next year, however, peace was made between England and Holland, and the Dutch surrendered their conquests in America. New York passed once more into the hands of the Duke of York, and East Jersey into those of Cartaret.

In the same year the Duke of York appointed Sir Edmund Andros governor of New York. The eastern settlements of Long island were anxious to adhere to Connecticut, but the governor compelled them on pain of being declared rebels to acknowledge themselves a part of New York. The claim of the duke extended within the limits of Connecticut as far as the river of that name, and in the summer of 1675 Andros sailed with several armed sloops for that colony to establish his authority as far as the river. The government of Connecticut, warned of his purpose, determined to resist him, and Captain Bull, the commander of the fort at Saybrooke, was ordered to pay no attention to his claim. Andros, arriving off Saybrooke, hoisted the royal standard and demanded the surrender of the fort. Bull instantly ran up the English colors, and refused to comply with the demand. Andros, who was a coward at heart, quailed before the firmness of the Connecticut captain, and abandoned his undertaking and sailed for Long island. Thus ended the attempt of the Duke of York to dismember Connecticut. Andros returned to New York to disgust the people of that province with his tyranny.

When James II became king he compelled the proprietaries of New Jersey to surrender their claim to the jurisdiction of that province to him, and annexed it to New York. In 1683 the grievances of the people of New York had become so unendurable that James, then Duke of York, deemed it best to conciliate them, and allowed the freeholders to send representatives to an assembly. This assembly met in October, 1683, and its first act was to demand the rights of Englishmen. "Supreme legislative power," they declared, "shall forever be and reside in the governor, council, and people, met in general assembly. Every freeholder and freeman shall vote for representation without restraint. No freeman shall suffer but by the judgment of his peers, and all trials shall be by a jury of twelve men. No tax shall be assessed, on any pretence whatever, but by the consent of the assembly No seaman or soldier shall be quartered on the inhabitants against their will No martial law shall exist. No person professing faith in God by Jesus Christ shall at any time be any ways disquieted or questioned for any difference of opinion." These privileges were conceded by the Duke of York, who solemnly promised not to change them except for the advantage of the colony, but he had scarcely become king when he overturned the liberties he had conceded and made New York a royal province, dependent entirely upon his unrestrained will for its privileges.

The people of New York were Protestants, many of whom had had cause to dread the restoration of the Roman Catholic religion in England. When James gave evidence of his intention to compel the acceptance of that faith by all his subjects, the colonies included, they were greatly discontented. Their fears were increased by the appointment by the king of a Roman Catholic as collector of customs at New York. Nicholson, the royal governor, was also exceedingly unpopular. As soon as the news of the overthrow of James II. in England reached New York, Jacob Leisler, the senior captain of the military companies, was requested by his men to take possession of the fort and assume the management of affairs until the government should be settled by the orders of King William. Leisler was a prominent merchant and was very popular with the common people, but he was opposed by the great land-holders, who were principally Dutch, and by the party devoted to the Church of England. He found himself at the head of about five hundred armed men, and taking possession of the fort avowed his intention to hold it until the will of King William should be known. He was sustained by a large majority of the people of New York, but the aristocratic party, and the church-men, who hated him, as he was a Presbyterian, denounced him as a rebel, and sustained the council of Nicholson, the last governor appointed by King James, which withdrew to Albany in August, 1689.

Leisler appointed his son-in-law, Milbourne, his secretary. Later in the year the people of Albany, being in danger of an attack from the French from Canada, asked aid from New York. Leisler sent Milbourne with a body of troops to their assistance, but the old council refused to acknowledge his authority, or to allow him to assume the command of the fort, and he went back with his men to New York, leaving the people of Albany to depend upon their own exertions for the defeat of the French. In their necessity they asked for and received aid from (. . .   .

In December letters from the English government were received, addressed to Nicholson, or, in his absence, to "such as, for the time being, take care for preserving the peace and administering the law" in New York. A commission for Nicholson accompanied these documents, but he was on his way to England, and Leisler, who was temporarily in authority in New York, regarded his position as confirmed by the letters from England, and caused himself to be proclaimed governor. He ordered the members of the old council at Albany to be arrested, and summoned an assembly to provide for the wants of the colony.

Upon first taking charge of affairs Leisler had addressed a letter to King William setting forth his reasons for his action, and asking the king to make known his royal pleasure concerning the colony. No answer was sent by the king to this communication, but on the 30th of January, 1691, a ship suddenly arrived in the harbor having on board a company of English soldiers, commanded by a Captain Ingoldsby, who had been sent by Colonel Henry Sloughter, whom King William had appointed governor of New York. The aristocratic party at once rallied around Ingoldsby as their leader, and that officer demanded of Leisler the surrender of the fort. Leisler insisted that he should produce his authority for such a demand, and, as none could be shown, refused to give up the fort, but offered Ingoldsby every assistance for himself and his men, and avowed his intention to submit to Sloughter upon his arrival. In the time which elapsed between the arrivals of Ingoldsby and the new governor party spirit ran so high that a collision occurred between the soldiers and the people, in which one man was wounded.

Sloughter reached New York on the 19th of March, 1691. Leisler at once sent messengers to receive his orders, but the messengers were detained. The next morning Leisler addressed a letter to Sloughter, asking to whom he should deliver up the fort. Sloughter returned no answer to this letter, but ordered Ingoldsby to "arrest Leisler and the persons called his council."

Leisler, Milbourne, and six others were arrested and immediately arraigned before a tribunal composed of their inveterate enemies, on a charge of treason. This was a frivolous pretence, for it was well known that Leisler, who was an enthusiastic admirer of King William, had never dreamed of denying his authority; but it was as good a charge as any other, as the fate of the prisoners was decided from the first. The prisoners denied the authority of the court, and refusing to plead before it, appealed to the king. The presiding officer of the court was the chief justice of New York, the infamous Joseph Dudley, who had been driven out of New England by the people whose liberties he had outraged. The prisoners, in spite of their appeal, were condemned to death.

Sloughter was unwilling to disregard their appeal as entirely as the court had done, and wished to leave the matter to the king; but the enemies of Leisler were resolved upon his death. Taking advantage of the known weakness of the governor, they made him drunk at a dinner party, and in this state induced him to sign the death warrant of the prisoners. The next morning at daybreak (May 16th) Leisler and Milbourne were hurried from their weeping families to the gallows. In spite of a pouring rain, the people who had gotten news of the tragedy crowded around the place of execution to cheer their martyrs in their last moments. "Weep not for us, who are departing to our God," said Leisler to the multitude. Milbourne saw standing among the crowd one of the men who had been prominent in their condemnation, and cried out to him : "Robert Livingston, I will implead thee for this at the bar of God." Then turning to the people, he said : "I die for the king and queen, and for the Protestant religion, in which I was born and bred. Father, into thy hands I commend my spirit." The judicial murder was then completed, and New York's first martyrs laid down their lives in behalf of the rights of the people.

The popular party was now more than ever embittered against the aristocratic class, and the principles which Leisler and Milbourne upheld were more than ever insisted upon Their friends, "who were distinguished always by their zeal for popular power, for toleration, for opposition to the doctrine of legitimacy," continued the struggle, and at length succeeded in making their principles the law of the colony.

The royalist assembly, while denying to the people an equality with themselves in political matters, were yet indisposed to surrender to the crown the independence of the colony, and, with their successors, insisted upon the right of self-government, and the regulation of taxation by the assembly, with such firmness that in 1705 Queen Anne yielded so far as to permit the assembly to appoint "its own treasurer to take charge of extraordinary supplies."

The memory of Leisler and Milbourne was vindicated after their death. The son of the former made the appeal to the king which had been denied his father, and Parliament at length reversed the attainder under the charge of treason, and restored their estates to their families. Dudley exerted all his arts to prevent this act of justice. As for Governor Sloughter, who was at the best but a poor weak adventurer, he died of the effects of his dissipation six months after the execution of his victims.

In 1692 Benjamin Fletcher was appointed to succeed Sloughter. He

was an officer of the royal army, and was as passionate and avaricious as
he was incompetent in other respects. He was a firm ally of the aristocratic party, and a bitter foe to popular liberty. In 1693, in order to
assist New York against the attacks of the French in Canada, all the
colonies were required to contribute their quota of troops to her defence.
An effort was also made to place the militia of New Jersey and Connecticut under the orders of the governor of New York. The authorities of

NASSAU STREET, NEW YORK, IN 1875.

Connecticut, however, were resolved not to relinquish the control of their
militia, which would have been to sacrifice the rights secured to the
people by the charter. In order to enforce his authority, Governor
Fletcher repaired to Hartford, where the assembly of Connecticut was in
session. At the time of his arrival a company of militia was engaged in
training in the town. Governor Fletcher rode up to this force; but its

commander, Captain Wadsworth, paid no attention to him, and did not even acknowledge his presence. Fletcher, who had boasted that he would not stir from the colony until he was obeyed, ordered his secretary to read his commission in the hearing of the troops. As the secretary commenced to read, Wadsworth ordered the drums to be beaten, and the secretary's voice was drowned. "Silence!" cried Fletcher; "begin again with the commission." "Music! music!" ordered Wadsworth, the same man who had hid the charter from Governor Andros. The drummers began again, and the governor, in a rage, ordered them to cease their music. Wadsworth sharply commanded the bewildered musicians to go on with their drumming, and then turning upon Fletcher, said to him fiercely. "If I am interrupted again I will make daylight shine through you." The voice and manner of the man convinced the governor that he was in earnest, and he went back to New York, satisfied of the impossibility of bringing the Connecticut militia under his orders.

New York was the most northern colony in which the authority of the Church of England was established. A number of its people were members of that communion, and in the colonial government the influence of that church was predominant. The vast majority of the people, however, were hostile to it, and it was not until 1695 that Governor Fletcher was able to obtain for it anything like favor from the assembly. The representatives of the people were fearful that if it obtained a firm footing among them, the British government might bestow upon it a power which would be dangerous to the other denominations. Naturally it enjoyed the favor of the home government, and engrossed all the provision made by England for religious matters in the colony. Lord Cornbury, the royal governor, attempted in 1705 to silence a Presbyterian minister for preaching without a license from the governor; but a jury, composed of Episcopalians, acquitted the prisoner. The same governor connived at the seizure by the Episcopalians of a church in Jamaica, which had been built by the whole town, but the colonial court restored it to its rightful owners. The spirit of popular liberty and toleration was growing rapidly in New York, and its colonial history is the story of a constant struggle between the people and the royal governors for the assertion and maintenance of their rights. Nearly all the governors regarded their position as but a means of enriching themselves, and systematically defrauded both the king and the colony.

By 1732 the population of New York city numbered a little less than nine thousand souls. In that year a case of the deepest interest occurred in that city. John Peter Zenger had established a newspaper called the *Weekly Journal* which ventured to censure the arbitrary action of the

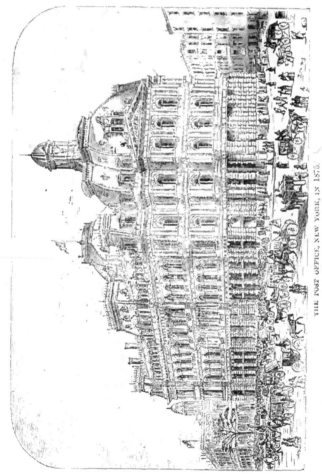

THE POST OFFICE, NEW YORK, IN 1875.

253

governor and assembly in levying illegal taxes upon the colony This
was a bold step, for until now no newspaper had dared to criticise the
action of the government Cosby, the governor of New York, resolving
to make an example of the offender, arrested Zenger on the charge of
libel, and caused his paper to be publicly burned. Zenger employed
two lawyers to defend him, and these increased the anger of the government by denying the competency of the court, inasmuch as the appointment of the chief justice, Delancy, had been made by Cosby without the
consent of the council, and was therefore illegal. The court at once
struck their names from its list of attorneys, and this arbitrary action so
intimidated the remaining members of the bar that Zenger found it impossible to procure counsel

In this helpless condition he was put on trial, and the court had
actually begun its proceedings when a stranger, a venerable and noble-
looking man, entered the room and took his seat at the bar. He
announced his name to the court, and stated that he had come to act as
counsel for the prisoner. A murmur of admiration greeted the announcement of his name He was Andrew Hamilton, speaker of the assembly
of Pennsylvania, the famous "Quaker lawyer" of Philadelphia. In the
trial which ensued, Hamilton offered to prove the truth of the alleged
libel, but was not allowed to do so ; the chief justice quoting English
precedents in support of his decision. Hamilton then made an eloquent
appeal to the jury, declaring that they of their own knowledge knew the
statements of Zenger's paper to be true, and urged them to maintain the
great principles of the freedom of the press and liberty of speech throughout the colonies, which principles, and not John Peter Zenger, he
solemnly declared were on trial before them. In spite of the unfavorable
charge of the judge, the jury brought in a unanimous verdict of
acquittal, which was announced amid the cheers of the people Thus
while the freedom of the press was still in doubt in England, and thirty-
seven years before the famous trial for libel of the publisher of the
Letters Junius established it in the mother country, the people of New
York declared themselves its guardians, and struck down the effort
of the royal power to impose shackles upon their most vigilant defender

In 1702 the proprietaries of New Jersey surrendered their rights
of jurisdiction to the crown, and Queen Anne united the two Jerseys in
one province, and placed it under the governor of New York It was
given a separate assembly, but this concession of partial independence of
its neighbor did not suit the province, and after many protests it was
given its own governor in the person of Lewis Morris, in 1708. During
the rest of the colonial period it remained a royal province.

CHAPTER XVII.

COLONIZATION OF PENNSYLVANIA

ONE of the most remarkable results of the English Reformation was the rise and growth of the Society of Friends, or Quakers, as they came to be called. Discarding what seemed to them superfluous and unnecessary forms in religion, they confined themselves to a simpler and more primitive expression of their faith. Believing that the only evil a Christian should resist is the evil of his own heart, they opposed no resistance to persecution or to ill-treatment from their fellow-men; and as servants of the Prince of Peace were unchangeably opposed to war and bloodshed. They held the doctrine of the Trinity, that we obtain salvation by the atoning blood of Christ; that man was created a free and responsible agent, that he forfeited his right to the blessings of the Creator by his fall, and will owe his restoration to his lost estate to the mercy of God and the blood of Christ; that the Holy Scriptures are the work of inspiration, and a good rule of life and faith. With them the test of Christianity was not a man's standing in the church, but the answer of a good conscience, the sense of true inward communion between the soul of the individual and God. They conducted their worship in silence, and regarded all their members as sent by God to preach His gospel, therefore, any one, even women, was free to speak in their meetings the message which came to him from the Holy Spirit. They denied that the right to preach was restricted to any particular class, and refused to acknowledge the authority of the regular clergy. Oaths were regarded as unlawful for Christian men, and temper-

255

anee and the utmost simplicity in all things were enjoined upon their people. They refused to recognize the social distinctions which prevailed in the world, though they admitted the power of the magistrates to enforce the laws, and regarded all men as equals. Their dress was simple, and in proportion to the means of the wearer, and their lives were blameless. They admitted the right of all men to worship God in their own way, and thus extended to all others the perfect toleration they claimed for themselves.

The founder of this sect was the good George Fox, the son of a weaver of Leicestershire, and "by his mother descended from the stock of the martyrs." He began to teach his doctrines about the middle of the seventeenth century, and at first his converts were people of the humbler classes of England. He was met with a determined opposition from both the established church and the Presbyterians, and was imprisoned, set in the stocks, cruelly beaten, and otherwise persecuted, and driven from place to place. Yet he persevered, and his doctrines began to

COAT OF ARMS OF PENNSYLVANIA

spread. Distressed by the persecutions to which his followers were subjected, he visited America after the restoration of Charles II, in the hope of finding there a place of refuge for his people, but could find none. Puritan New England was hostile to his doctrines, and the power of the Church of England was strong enough in the southern colonies to defeat his object.

Among Fox's converts were a few from the higher classes of English society. One of these was destined to be, next to its founder, the greatest benefactor of his faith, and one of the choice instruments of the Almighty in the settlement and Christianization of America. This was William Penn. He was the son and heir of Admiral Sir William Penn, one of the most distinguished naval commanders of England. The admiral desired for his son the advantages which his high position would readily secure to him, but the young man at an early day, happening to converse with a simple-minded Quaker, became so deeply impressed with his principles that he adopted them as his own. This greatly annoyed the father, but supposing that it was a mere boyish notion which his son would outgrow, William was sent to study at the University of Oxford, and after leaving that institution was made to travel through Europe to improve his mind and to remove his tendency to Quakerism.

William returned to England after an absence of two years, greatly improved in mind, but still true to his religious convictions. In 1666, while travelling in Ireland, Penn met his old friend Thomas Loe, and heard him speak of the glorious triumph of the faith of a Christian over the adversities of the world. His enthusiasm was once more awakened to such an extent that he from that moment began to seek to draw others into the communion which had given him so much happiness. His course gave offence to the authorities, and he was imprisoned. He addressed a remonstrance to the viceroy of Ireland, in which he declared: "Religion is my crime and my innocence; it makes me a prisoner to malice, but my own freeman."

Being liberated, he went back home, but only to meet with mockery and persecution. He was ridiculed by his companions of his own rank in life, and it was a common jest in society, says Pepys, that "William Penn was a Quaker again, or some very melancholy thing." His father, disappointed and indignant at the failure of his hopes, turned him out of his house without a penny; but his mother, truer to her nature, supplied him with sufficient funds to relieve his most pressing wants.

Penn now began to defend his doctrines through the press, and thus brought them into greater prominence. This soon made him the victim of the ecclesiastical authorities, and the Bishop of London threatened him with imprisonment for life if he did not recant his doctrines. He answered firmly: "Then my prison shall be my grave." He was committed to the Tower on a charge of heresy, and kept in close confinement. Charles II., naturally kind-hearted, was touched by his firmness, and sent the learned Stillingfleet, himself a man of humanity, to reason with him. "The Tower," said Penn, "is to me the worst argument in the world." At the end of a year his father's friend, the Duke of York, procured his release, for the consistency of the young man had won back for him the affection and sympathy of the stern old admiral.

Every effort was now made to draw William Penn away from his faith. A high rank in the royal navy, the favor of the king, and many other inducements were held out to him; but he refused them all, and remained true to his principles. In less than a year after his release from the Tower he was arrested for having spoken at a Quaker meeting. He protested his right to do this, and declared that no power on earth should prevent him from worshipping the God who made him. He was placed on trial for his offence, and boldly demanded to know on what law the indictment against him was founded. "On the common law," replied the recorder. "Where is that law?" asked Penn. "The law which is not in being, far from being common, is no law at all." He conducted his own defence, and as he was pleading earnestly for his

17

rights as an Englishman, was hurried out of court. He appealed to the
jury to remember that they were his judges. The jury, in spite of an
unfavorable charge from the judge, brought in a verdict of acquittal.
The court ordered them back to their room, with the angry declaration :
"We will have a verdict, by the help of God, or you shall starve for it."
"You are Englishmen," cried Penn to the jurors, as they were retiring :
"Mind your privilege ; give not away your right." At last, after being
kept two days and nights without food, the jury repeated their verdict of
"not guilty," and were fined by the court for daring to assert their
independence. Penn was fined for contempt of court, and sent back to
prison. His fine was soon discharged by his father, who died shortly
afterwards. "Son William," said the dying admiral, to whom earthly
honors now appeared in their true light, "if you and your friends keep
to your plain way of preaching and living, you will make an end of the
priests."

Penn was now nearly twenty-six years old, and had inherited from

WILLIAM PENN.

his father a handsome estate. He continued to
explain and defend his doctrines through the
press, and in 1671 was arrested and sentenced
to six months' imprisonment in Newgate. From
his prison he addressed a noble plea to Parliament and to the nation for toleration. Upon
his release from prison, Penn travelled in Holland and Germany, and upon his return to England, in 1673, married a woman of great beauty,
whose noble character rendered her a fitting companion to him. He took no part in public affairs
until the imprisonment of George Fox, upon his
return to England from America, called him once more to the defence of
his brethren. Fox being released, he and Penn and several others
travelled through Holland and a part of Germany, seeking to make
converts to their faith—an effort in which they were very successful
among the Dutch and German peasantry. Returning to England, he
once more appealed to Parliament, but without success, to do justice to
the Quakers, and grant them the toleration to which they were entitled.

Despairing of success in England, Penn now directed the whole of his
energies to securing a home for his persecuted brethren in the new world.
A number of Quakers were already settled along the banks of the Delaware and in New Jersey, and in 1675 the embarrassments of Lord
Byllinge, who had purchased Lord Berkeley's interest in New Jersey,
obliged him to sell his share of that province. It was purchased by

William Penn, Gawen Lourie, and Nicholas Lucas for the benefit of the Quakers This placed the Friends in possession of an asylum, but it left them more at the mercy of the English government and church than they desired to be, and New Jersey was divided into two equal parts, Cartaret, Berkeley's former partner, retaining East Jersey, and West Jersey becoming the property of the Quakers. This was accomplished in 1676, and in March of the following year a government resting upon the will of the people, and seeming to the inhabitants protection and equality in all their political and religious rights and privileges, was set up in West Jersey The English Quakers came over to the new province in great numbers, with the good wishes of Charles II, and peaceful relations were established with the Indians Byllinge, who had retained some interest in the province, now began to be troublesome, and claimed the right to nominate the deputy governor. The people denied his claim, and, at the instigation of William Penn, amended their constitution so as to place the choice of all their officers in their own hands, and then elected a governor

Penn had now become deeply interested in the colonization of America, and wished to secure for his faith a wider domain than West Jersey. He had inherited from his father a claim against the English government amounting to £16,000. He now proposed to exchange this claim for a grant of territory in America Charles II, who was always in want of money, and who never set much value upon the lands of the new world, readily accepted his offer, as it was urged by Lords North, Halifax, and Sunderland, and the Duke of York, who were firm friends of William Penn. The king, in 1681, granted to Penn a district lying west of the Delaware river, and corresponding very nearly to territory embraced in the present State of Pennsylvania, which name the king bestowed upon it in honor of the proprietor. The Duke of York claimed Delaware as his own property, and Penn, who wished to have free access to the sea, purchased it of him the next year The territory was granted to Penn as absolute proprietor, the people were secured in the right of self-government, religious equality was guaranteed to all, the acts of the colonial legislature were to be submitted to the king and council, who had the power to annul them if contrary to the law of England; the power of levying customs was reserved to Parliament; and no taxes were to be imposed upon the people save by the colonial legislature or by Parliament.

Penn then invited all persons who desired to do so to settle in Pennsylvania, and in a proclamation declared his intention to leave the settlers free to make their own laws "I propose," he said, "to leave myself and successors no power of doing mischief, that the will of no one man may hinder the good of a whole country." "God," he declared, "has furnished me with a better resolution, and has given me his grace to keep it."

His resolution was soon tested. Soon after he obtained his patent a company of traders offered him six thousand pounds and an annual payment of a stipulated sum for the monopoly of the Indian traffic between the Delaware and the Susquehanna. He had already straitened himself very much by his expenditures for his colony, and his family had been obliged to endure some deprivations in consequence. The offer was tempting, but he declined it firmly. What was free to him should be free to every inhabitant of Pennsylvania, and he would derive no advantage at the expense of his people.

A company was collected and sent out to Pennsylvania, under William Markham, Penn's nephew, and the personal character of the proprietor of the colony was deemed by all a sufficient guarantee for the protection of their liberties. Penn intended following this company as soon as he could, and in the meantime enjoined Markham to continue the establishment already existing along the Delaware, and to govern in accordance with the laws of England. In 1682 he prepared to go out to America to superintend the formal establishment of his colony. As he was about to sail, he wrote to his wife, to whom he was devoted with all the ardor of his youth. "Live low and sparingly till my debts be paid; I desire not riches, but to owe nothing, be liberal to the poor, and kind to all." With regard to their children, he wrote "Let their learning be liberal; spare no cost, for by such parsimony all is lost that is saved."

Penn took out with him one hundred emigrants, and reached Newcastle on the 27th of October, 1682, after a long and trying voyage. In the presence of the Swedish, Dutch and English settlers, who welcomed him with joy, he took formal possession of the province, which was surrendered to him by the agents of the Duke of York. He pledged himself to the people to grant them liberty of conscience and all their civil privileges. From Newcastle Penn went up the river to Chester, where a settlement had been formed by emigrants from the north of England, who had preceded him.

Early in November, accompanied by a few friends, Penn ascended the Delaware in an open boat to the mouth of the Schuylkill, and passing a little distance beyond this landed on the beautiful site now occupied by the city of Philadelphia. The place at which he landed was long known as the "Blue Anchor Landing," from a tavern of that name which stood there. A little later, under a spreading elm, Penn met the chiefs of the neighboring Indian tribes, and entered into a treaty of peace and friendship with them. This treaty was confirmed by no oath, but it remained unbroken for fifty years, and as neither side sought to evade its obligations, which were simply of peace and good will, the colony of Pennsylvania escaped in its earlier years the horrors of a savage warfare from which the other settlers suffered. "We will live," said the Indian sachems, "in love with William Penn and his children as long as the moon and the sun shall endure." They kept their word. "Penn came without arms; he declared his purpose to abstain from violence; he had no message but peace; and not a drop of Quaker blood was ever shed by an Indian." The scene of the treaty was at Shackamaxon, now Kensington, in the city of Philadelphia.

PENN'S TREATY WITH THE INDIANS.

On the pleasant tract lying between the Delaware and the Schuylkill, which was purchased from the Swedes, who had on their part purchased it from the Indians, Penn in 1683 laid out the capital of his province, which he named PHILADELPHIA, the city of Brotherly Love, in token of the principles which he meant should constitute the common law of his possessions. It was abundantly supplied with streams of pure water, and was admirably situated for purposes of trade. He did not wish it to be built after the manner of European cities, but designed it to be a "greene country town, gardens round each house, that it might never be burned, and always be wholesome." The streets were laid off by marking their course through the primitive forest by blazing the trees, and the

building of dwellings was begun. In the first year of Penn's arrival in
the colony, twenty-three ships with emigrants arrived in Pennsylvania.
In three years after its foundation Philadelphia contained upwards of
six hundred houses, and the colony had a population of ten thousand.
The Indians proved the firm friends of the colonists, and supplied
them with wild fowl and venison in return for articles of European
manufacture.

Penn from the first refused to retain in his hands the exercise of the
vast powers with which the charter granted him by the king invested
him. As early as December, 1682, he convened a general convention of
the people, and gave them a charter of liberties which Bancroft thus
sums up: "God was declared the only Lord of conscience; the first day
of the week was reserved as a day of leisure, for the ease of the creation.
The rule of equality was introduced into families by abrogating the
privileges of primogeniture. The word of an honest man was evidence
without an oath.
The mad spirit of
speculation was
checked by a system
of strict accounta-
bility, applied to
factors and agents.
Every man liable to
civil burdens pos-
sessed the right of
suffrage; and, with-
out regard to sect,

PENN LAYING OUT THE PLAN OF PHILADELPHIA.

every Christian was eligible to office. No tax or custom could be levied
but by law. The Quaker is a spiritualist; the pleasures of the senses,
masks, revels and stage plays, not less than bull-baits and cock-fights,
were prohibited. Murder was the only crime punishable by death.
Marriage was esteemed a civil contract; adultery a felony. The Quakers
had suffered wrong from imprisonment; the false accuser was liable to
double damages. Every prison for convicts was made a workhouse.
There were neither poor-rates nor tithes. The Swedes, and Finns, and
Dutch were invested with the liberties of Englishmen."* In March,
1683, the first general assembly of Pennsylvania met at Philadelphia.
"I am ready," said Penn to this body, "to settle such foundations as
may be for your happiness." Under the guidance of the founder of the

---

* Bancroft's History of the United States, vol. ii., p. 385.

colony, the assembly established a constitution which made Pennsylvania emphatically a free state. A government was established, consisting of a governor, a legislative council and an assembly composed of representatives of the people. As the charter made the proprietor responsible to the king for the legislation of the colony, no act of legislation was to be valid until it had passed the great seal of the province. With this exception the entire power of the province was left in the hands of the people. "But for the hereditary office of proprietary, Pennsylvania had been a representative democracy. In Maryland, the council was named by Lord Baltimore; in Pennsylvania, by the people. In Maryland, the power of appointing magistrates, and all, even the subordinate executive officers, rested solely with the proprietary; in Pennsylvania, William Penn could not appoint a justice or a constable; every executive officer, except the highest,

SETTLEMENT OF PHILADELPHIA.

was elected by the people or their representatives; and the governor could perform no public act, but with the consent of the council. Lord Baltimore had a revenue derived from the export of tobacco, the staple of Maryland; and his colony was burdened with taxes: a similar revenue was offered to William Penn, and declined, and tax-gatherers were unknown in his province."

Thus did the "Quaker king" complete one of the sublimest surrenders of political power in all the annals of history. "I desired," he said, in his grand simplicity, "to show men as free and happy as they can be."

The colony improved rapidly. Men were attracted from all parts of Great Britain, from Ireland, the Low countries, from Germany and Sweden, to Pennsylvania. The personal character of William Penn, not less than the advantages afforded them, induced them to settle in the happy colony. Philadelphia especially grew with rapidity, and already gave promise of becoming the principal city of colonial America. Schools were opened, and liberally encouraged, for ignorance had no advocates in this thrifty community. The printing press was also set up, and put to work.

In August, 1684, Penn, having successfully established his colony, took an affectionate leave of his people, and returned to England to look after his family. He reached England in October.

Lord Baltimore claimed Delaware as a part of the country granted to him. Penn sustained his claim to that region by pleading the actual settlement of the Dutch previous to the grant to Lord Baltimore, and his purchase of the rights which the Duke of York had derived from the Dutch. The English courts decided, in 1685, that Delaware did not constitute a part of Maryland, and sustained Penn's claim to the former colony. The boundaries of the two colonies were settled by a compromise.

During Penn's absence in England the people of Delaware, who had little sympathy with the Quakers, began to be restless. They presented to

PENN'S TREATY MONUMENT.

the proprietary a list of grievances, and were granted by Penn a separate government.

The fall of James II., who continued the friend of William Penn, though

so widely opposed to him in religion, was the beginning of trouble for the proprietor of Pennsylvania. Penn did not relinquish his friendship for the dethroned king, and his enemies made this constancy, which in no way interfered with his loyalty to William and Mary, the means of injuring him in the estimation of the new king. William was induced to believe the charges of disloyalty which were brought against Penn, and deprived him of his patent and proprietorship of Pennsylvania. Penn was also imprisoned several times for disloyalty.

During this period the colony was much annoyed by a disturbance led by one George Keith, who pushed the Quaker doctrine of non-resistance to the verge of absurdity. He argued that no Quaker could with consistency take part in public affairs as a magistrate or legislator. As the liberties of the colony were the work of Quakers the inference was plain. If Keith was right, then Pennsylvania had no lawful government, and must apply to the king for one. Keith produced such trouble in the colony that even the tolerant Quakers were at length obliged to lay hands on him. He was tried and fined for using seditious language; but lest their action should seem to be a punishment of opinion the Quaker magistrates remitted the fine. He subsequently became a clergyman of the English Church.

This disturbance gave the king a pretext for declaring Pennsylvania a royal province, and in April, 1693, Benjamin Fletcher was appointed by William and Mary governor of Pennsylvania, to which province Delaware was reunited. The people, indignant at this invasion of their rights, attempted no resistance, but refused to recognize the royalist gov-

CHESTNUT STREET, PHILADELPHIA, IN 1875.

ernor. Some of the magistrates resigned their offices upon his arrival. Upon the meeting of the assembly the hostility to Fletcher increased. The members of the assembly declared the laws they had made under the charter granted to Penn to be valid, and refused to have new ones, or recognize any other authority. A charter granted by King Charles was, they maintained, as valid as one granted by King William, and they refused to re-enact their old laws, as such a course would be to brand them as illegal. Fletcher demanded that the assembly should appropriate a sum for the defence of New York against the Indians. His demand was flatly refused. The assembly was willing, however, to make an appropriation for the relief of the people of New York who had suffered by this war, but only upon condition that this sum should be disbursed by officers of its own appointment. Fletcher refused to consent to this condition, as he regarded it as an infringement of the king's prerogative, and the assembly was dissolved, A. D. 1694.

In the meantime Penn had been restored to his proprietary rights. The king expressed himself satisfied of his innocence, which was estab-

UNIVERSITY OF PENNSYLVANIA.

lished before the council, and in August, 1694, the patent for his restoration was formally issued. Penn was anxious to return to Pennsylvania, but was detained in England by his inability to raise the funds necessary for the voyage. He had spent a large part of his fortune in planting the colony, and the persecutions and annoyances to which he had been subjected in England had caused him great loss. Nor was this his only trouble. His wife and eldest son had died during his trials, and some whom he had imagined his friends in his prosperity had in his adversity shown themselves his enemies. He retained his serenity of mind, however, and persevered in the good work to which he had devoted his life. Being unable to go to Pennsylvania he sent his nephew, Markham, as his deputy Markham summoned an assembly, and this body, alarmed at the recent changes in their charter, which had threatened to deprive them of their political rights, endeavored to provide against a recurrence of the danger by assuming the power of framing a constitution for themselves. The assembly of 1696 made still further changes, and placed the control of the colonial government entirely in the hands of the people by giving them the election of all the officials of the province

Penn returned to Pennsylvania in November, 1699, and sanctioned the action of the people. One of the members of the council proposed that they should make a constitution that should be "firm and lasting" to them and to their descendants "Keep what . good in the charter and frame of government," said Penn, "and lay aside what is burdensome, and add what may best suit the common good." It was agreed by all parties that it would be best to surrender the old charter and frame a new constitution This was attended with considerable difficulty, as Delaware dreaded the loss of its independence. It was conciliated by being given its own legislature, but was under the administration of the governor of Pennsylvania. The two colonies were never again united The constitution secured to the people all the political privileges they claimed Penn, whose sole desire was for the welfare of the colony, held back nothing for himself.

Among the earliest emigrants to Pennsylvania were many Germans, who had been converted to the Quaker doctrines by William Penn during his missionary labors on the continent of Europe. They settled at Germantown, to which they gave its name. Towards the close of the seventeenth century the severe wars in Europe drove out large numbers of Germans from the Rhine valley They sought refuge in England at first, and from that country passed over to Pennsylvania. They were chiefly Lutherans, and members of the German Reformed Church They settled chiefly in the southern part of Pennsylvania, and clung together instead of separating, thus giving to this part of the State the peculiar characteristics which distinguish it to the present day. They held aloof from the English, and allowed the German language alone to be taught to their children They attracted other settlers from their native country, and the region occupied by them was soon thickly settled, and was noted as one of the best cultivated sections of the province

About the beginning of the eighteenth century a large emigration from the north of Ireland and from Scotland began to set in, and continued for some years. These people were nearly all Presbyterians, and located themselves chiefly in the eastern and central sections of the province They were an energetic, industrious, and intelligent community, and set

to work with a will to improve their new home. They advanced the
frontier of Pennsylvania steadily westward by their new plantations, and
proved themselves among the most desirable settlers that had yet come
into the province.

William Penn had come to Pennsylvania with the intention of passing
the remainder of his life there; but rumors now began to reach the
colony that it was the intention of the crown to deprive Pennsylvania of

its charter and make
it a royal province.
These reports made
it necessary for Penn
to return to Eng-
land, a step to which
nothing but the im-
portance of being
near the home gov-
ernment to defend
the liberties of his
people could have
forced him. He had
done his work in
America well, and
could go back to his
native land with the
satisfaction that he
had successfully laid
the foundations of a
great and rapidly-
growing state, and
had placed the liber-
ties of its people
upon such a secure
basis that they would
endure for all time.

MASONIC TEMPLE, PHILADELPHIA, IN 1875.

He had founded a democracy, and had proved by the most generous surrender of his truly regal powers that his chief aim in life was the good
of his fellow-men. After making such arrangements as he deemed best
for the welfare of his "young countrie," he went back to England in 1701.

There were not wanting efforts after his arrival in England to deprive
him of his proprietary rights and to convert Pennsylvania into a royal
province; but the deep reverence with which the English people had now

come to regard the virtues of William Penn prevented the consummation of these designs, and saved the people of Pennsylvania from the rule of royal governors, such as plundered the sister province of New York. The crown could never be persuaded to rob the man whose pure life was an honor to the nation. In his last years Penn was so poor that he was for a while an inmate of a debtors' prison. He had bought the province of Pennsylvania from Charles II., and had confirmed his claim by purchasing the lands from the Indians, so that he was absolute owner of the unoccupied lands of the colony. He thus had it in his power to relieve his distress by selling his claims, but in his deepest poverty he refused to part with Pennsylvania, except upon terms which would secure to his people the full and perfect enjoyment of the liberties he had guaranteed them. He died in 1718, peacefully, and amid the sympathy of his countrymen in England, and the sorrow of those whom he had befriended in his beloved Pennsylvania. By his pure life he won for the people of his faith the respect of all candid men, and by his fidelity to the principles he professed he became the benefactor of millions who will ever count it a privilege to honor his name.

Penn left three sons, who were all minors at the time of his death. They succeeded to his rights as proprietary of Pennsylvania, and the government of the colony was administered for them by deputies until the Revolution, when their claims were purchased by the State.

CHAPTER XVIII.

SETTLEMENT OF THE CAROLINAS.

E have related the efforts of the French to colonize the shores of the beautiful region which they named Carolina, and the failure of Raleigh's attempt to found a city upon Roanoke island. We have now to consider the successful planting of this same region with English settlements.

After the settlement of Virginia the attention of the English was frequently drawn to the fertile region south of the James, and as their plantations spread in that direction adventurous explorers went into this region, and returned with reports of its great beauty and fertility. When the severe measures of the Virginia colony for enforcing conformity to the established church were put in operation, many dissenters withdrew from the limits of the colony and settled in what are now the northeastern counties of North Carolina Among these were a company of Presbyterians, who settled upon the Chowan. Others followed them, and by the year 1663 these counties contained a prosperous and growing community of English-speaking people

In 1663 Charles II , who always displayed the most remarkable liberality in his gifts of American lands, granted to eight of his favorites the vast region extending from the present southern boundary of Virginia to the St John's river in Florida and from the Atlantic to the Pacific.

270

Those upon whom this rich gift was bestowed were the Earl of Clarendon, the prime minister, Lord Ashley Cooper, who was afterwards Earl of Shaftesbury, the Duke of Albemarle, Lord Craven, Sir John Colleton, Lord John Berkeley, his brother, Sir William Berkeley, the governor of Virginia, and Sir George Carteret. They were given absolute power over their territory, the king reserving only a claim upon their allegiance. The country had been called Carolina by the first French settlers in honor of Charles IX. of France; the old name was retained in honor of Charles II. of England.

The proprietors had but one object in view: to enrich themselves; but they claimed to be influenced by a "pious zeal for the propagation of the gospel." They at once set to work to prepare a code of laws for the government of their province. This task was committed to Ashley Cooper, Earl of Shaftesbury, and the great philosopher, John Locke, then an almost unknown man. These produced a code known as "The Grand Model," or "Fundamental Constitutions." This was a system which might have been successful if the people for whom it was intended had been some European community of the Middle Ages, but it was utterly unsuited to a colony in the woods of America, composed of men whose personal independence and sturdy love of freedom were the indispensable conditions of the success of their enterprise.

COAT OF ARMS OF SOUTH CAROLINA.

By the terms of the "Grand Model" an order of nobility was created, into whose hands the sole right to rule was committed. Earls, barons, and squires were made the natural heads of the various classes of society, and the common people were attached to the soil as tenants. A simple tenant could never rise above his humble position, and was denied the right of suffrage; only those who possessed fifty acres of land were allowed this right, or were entitled to the name of freemen. The freemen were allowed an assembly, but that body was placed entirely under the control of the nobility. Religious freedom was promised to all persons, but the constitution expressly declared that the only orthodox establishment was the Church of England. Trial by jury was guaranteed, but with the destructive provision that a majority should decide the verdict of the jury.

It was very clear that this magnificent constitution would not suit the settlers in the log cabins of North Carolina, but the proprietors, ignorant of the people they had to deal with, proceeded to organize their government in England by electing the Duke of Albemarle to the rank of

Palatine, as the head of their system was termed. Sir William Berkeley, then governor of Virginia, was ordered to establish the authority of the proprietors over the settlers on Albemarle sound. This he did, and appointed William Drummond, a Scotchman and one of the settlers, governor. This was the same Drummond who afterwards took part in Bacon's rebellion in Virginia, and was hanged by Berkeley, as has been related. A simple form of government was established, and the people of North Carolina were left in peace until it should be time to collect the quit-rents which the proprietors claimed as due for their occupation of their lands

In 1661, a few years previous to this action of Berkeley, a company from New England had made a settlement on the Cape Fear river. The colony did not prosper, however, though liberal inducements were held out to it, and many of the emigrants returned home. In 1664 a colony from the Barbadoes joined the settlers on the Cape Fear. The new-comers had been sent out by a company at the Barbadoes, who purchased from the Indians a tract of land thirty-two miles square on the Cape Fear, and asked of the proprietors of Carolina a confirmation of their purchase and a separate charter of government. A liberal charter was granted them, the country was named Clarendon, and Sir John Yeamans, a resident of Barbadoes, was appointed governor. He was instructed to "make things easy to the people of New England; from thence the greatest supplies are expected." In 1665 he led a company of emigrants from Barbadoes, and formed a settlement on the Cape Fear. The effort to found a town was unsuccessful, and the emigrants found great diffi-culty in contending against the natural barrenness and poverty of the region in which they had located. They devoted themselves to the cutting and export of lumber, and established a trade in boards, staves and shingles to the West Indies, which is still carried on by their de-scendants. This trade was found to be profitable, and emigration increased. In 1666 the colony is said to have had a population of eight hundred souls.

In the meantime the settlements on Albemarle sound and the Chowan had prospered, and had increased steadily in population, under the simple government established over them. This government consisted of a council of six persons named by the proprietaries and six chosen by the assembly, and an assembly consisting of the governor, the council and twelve representatives chosen by the freeholders of the colony. The proprietaries had confirmed the colonists in the possession of their lands, and had solemnly promised them religious toleration and exemption from taxation except by the colonial legislature. In 1669 the assembly, feeling secure in these guarantees, enacted a series of laws for the government of the colony, which remained in force in North Carolina until near the close of the next century. It was enacted that no emigrant should be sued for a debt contracted before his settlement in the colony until he had been a resident of the province for five years. Marriage was made a civil contract, and for its validity required simply the consent of the contracting parties before a magistrate in the presence of witnesses. No emigrant could be taxed during his first year's residence in the colony. New settlers were invited by the offer of large bounties in lands, but no title to these lands could be obtained until after a two years' residence in the colony. The governor's salary and the other expenses of the province were secured by the imposition of a fee of thirty pounds of tobacco in every law suit. The members of the assembly served without compensation.

In 1670 the constitution of Shaftesbury and Locke was sent over by the proprietaries, and the governor was ordered to establish it in the colony. It met with a determined resistance from both legislature and people, who could never be induced to submit to it.

The people upon whom the proprietaries endeavored to force their "Grand Model" were in many respects the most singular community in America. Many of them had fled from injustice and persecution in other colonies, and in the solitude of the forests of North Carolina had become possessed of an independence which scorned any control but that of the government established by their own consent. The plantations were chiefly along the rivers and the shores of Albemarle sound, there were no roads but the paths marked through the forests by the blazing of the trees; the inhabitants visited each other and travelled through the country in their boats, scarcely any, even among the women and children, being unacquainted with the use of the oar. The people were attached to their beautiful "summer land," and to the freedom which they enjoyed in it. They had little use for laws, for they were mainly a simple-hearted and virtuous race, who, by pursuing the paths of right, gave no cause for restraint. They had no court-house until 1722. Their first church was not built until 1705, and the freedom of conscience which they enjoyed was perfect. Yet they were a God-fearing people, and George Fox, who visited them in 1672, testifies to their readiness to hear the word of God and to their homely virtues. They were cut off from the world, careless of the struggles which rocked Europe to its foundations, and anxious only to live in the peaceful enjoyment of the good things God had given them, and to rear their children in the ways which they deemed conformable to his will. There were no towns in the colony,

18

and in power and importance North Carolina could not compare with any of her more northern sisters; but there were no communities in which the people were happier or more contented than in this one   When the cruelties of Berkeley drove many of the Virginians from their province, they fled to North Carolina, and were kindly received by the people, who treated Berkeley's demands to surrender the refugees for punishment with contempt   "Are there any who doubt man's capacity for self-government, let them study the early history of North Carolina; its inhabitants were restless and turbulent in their imperfect submission to a government imposed on them from abroad, the administration of the colony was firm, humane and tranquil, when they were left to take care of themselves. Any government but one of their own institution was oppressive." *

These were the people for whom the "Grand Model" was designed, and who successfully resisted its imposition   The proprietaries had withdrawn the government they had first established, at the time when the constitutions of Shaftesbury and Locke were offered to the colony, and the refusal of these constitutions by the colonists left North Carolina without any regularly established system of government   In this state of affairs Stevens, the governor, continued to administer the old system until a settlement of the matter in dispute could be had   He died in 1674, and the assembly elected Cartwright, their speaker, as his successor, by whom the government was administered for two years.   Eastchurch, the new speaker, was sent to England to explain the grievances of the colony to the proprietaries, and to endeavor to secure the withdrawal of the obnoxious constitution.   Without withdrawing their favorite system, the proprietaries, who were disposed to conciliate the colony, thought best to leave matters in their present condition, and appointed Eastchurch governor   They did away with much of the good effect of this measure by coupling this appointment with that of Miller as collector of customs   He had been driven out of the colony by the people some time before, and he was now sent to compel the payment of the revenues claimed by the proprietaries, and to enforce the navigation acts in North Carolina.

The enforcement of the navigation acts meant simply the certain crippling and the probable ruin of the industry of North Carolina.   The commerce of the colony was small, and was already struggling against natural difficulties.   The whole province contained a little less than four thousand inhabitants, and its exports consisted of about eight hundred hogsheads of tobacco, a small quantity of Indian corn, and a few cattle   These were shipped in a few small vessels which came for them from

Bancroft's History of the United States vol ii p 173

New England, and brought in return the few articles of foreign manufacture which the planters could afford to purchase. Yet this humble trade was made the object of the envy of the English merchants, and it was resolved by a rigorous enforcement of the navigation acts to cut the North Carolinians off from the use of the New England markets, and to compel them to send their products to England for sale. Never was the iniquitous policy of England toward her colonies more strikingly and perfectly illustrated than in her treatment of North Carolina at this period.

The effort to enforce the navigation act was met by a deliberately planned and executed insur-rection of the people, who published to the world a de-claration of the causes which had impelled them to this action, and which were chiefly the loss of their liberties by the changes in the govern-ment, the imposition of exces-sive taxes, and the interrup-tion of their commerce by the burdens laid upon it by the navigation acts. The leader of the movement was John Culpepper. One of the mem-bers of the council joined the insurrection; but the rest, with Miller, who, in addition to his office of collector, had been acting as governor in the absence of Eastchurch, were arrested and imprisoned. When Eastchurch arrived, the colonists refused either to

A SETTLER'S CABIN.

acknowledge his authority or to allow him to enter the colony. In the meantime they arranged matters upon the old popular system, and sent Culpepper and another of their number to England to negotiate a settle-ment with the proprietaries.

Miller escaped from confinement and repaired to England to oppose the efforts of Culpepper. By cunningly making himself the champion of the navigation acts, Miller succeeded in arousing a strong sentiment against Culpepper, who was arrested on a charge of resisting the collection of the revenue and embezzling the public funds. In support of this arbitrary act, the government pleaded an old statute of Henry VIII., by which a colonist could be arraigned in England for an offence committed in a colony. Culpepper demanded to be tried in North Carolina, upon the scene of his alleged crime; but this was refused him, and he was put on trial in England. The Earl of Shaftesbury, shrewdly perceiving that such a course was repugnant to the real sentiment of the English people, and that it offered him an opportunity to increase his popularity, undertook the defence of Culpepper, and procured his acquittal.

The proprietaries now appointed as governor one of their number, Seth Slothel, who had purchased the rights of Lord Clarendon. Slethel on his voyage out was captured by the Algerine pirates, and during his absence the government of North Carolina was administered by governors appointed by the insurgents, who seem to have acted with the

COAT OF ARMS OF SOUTH CAROLINA.

consent, or at least without the opposition of the proprietaries, who were much at a loss to know how to enforce their authority in the province. They instructed the colonists to "settle order among themselves," and appear to have left them very much to their own devices. The government was well and fairly administered and order was maintained; an act of amnesty was published; and when Slothel reached the colony, in 1683, after his release from his captivity, he found it peaceful and orderly.

The administration of Slothel was unfortunate for the province. He could enforce neither the constitutions of the proprietaries nor the navigation acts, as he was expected to do; so he devoted his energies to the task of enriching himself, which he accomplished by robbing the colonists and defrauding his proprietary associates in England. In 1688 the colonists, greatly exasperated by his exactions, to which they had submitted for about five years, drove him out of the province by condemning him to an exile of a year, and forever disqualifying him from holding the office of governor. This was their boldest act yet, and was an open defiance of the proprietaries.

In the meantime the southern portion of Carolina had been brought under English rule. In 1670 a company of emigrants was sent out by the proprietaries, under the direction of William Sayle and Joseph West, the latter of whom was the commercial agent of the proprietaries. They went by way of Barbadoes, and landed at Port Royal, where the ruins of Fort Carolina, which had been erected by the French, were still to be seen. After a short delay here, they removed to a more favorable location farther northward, between two rivers, which they named the Ashley and Cooper, in honor of the Earl of Shaftesbury, one of the proprietaries. In 1680 this settlement was abandoned for a better situation nearer the harbor. This last settlement was the foundation of the city of Charleston. The first plantation on the Ashley river was afterwards known as Old Charleston. At present not even a log cabin remains to mark the site.

The emigrants to South Carolina had been furnished with a copy of the constitutions of Shaftesbury and Locke, but they were as averse to the acceptance of them as were the people of North Carolina, for they perceived that such a system as that devised by the proprietaries could not be put in operation in America. Immediately upon their arrival they proceeded to establish a form of government suited to their needs. It consisted of a governor, a council composed of five members appointed by the proprietaries and five by the assembly, and an assembly of twenty delegates chosen by the people. Thus was representative government established as the basis of the political life of the province, and throughout all her subsequent history it was cherished by South Carolina as her most precious possession.

The colony grew rapidly in population, the delightful climate, the rich soil, and the liberal offers of lands by the proprietaries attracting settlers in considerable numbers. In 1671 Sir John Yeamans brought over African slaves from Barbadoes, thus introducing negro slavery into the colony at the very outset of its existence. This species of labor being found well suited to the necessities of the province was generally adopted in the remaining years of the century, and became the basis of the industry of South Carolina, which was from the first a purely agricultural State. The negroes multiplied rapidly by natural increase and by fresh importations; "so rapidly," says Bancroft, "that in a few years, we are told, the blacks were to the whites in the proportion of twenty-two to twelve; a proportion that had no parallel north of the West Indies."

The white population also increased rapidly. The dissenters, as all the Protestant sects who differed from the Church of England were called, came over to the colony in large numbers, hoping to find there the toleration they were denied at home. They consisted of Dutch and German Protestants, and Presbyterians from the north of Ireland and from Scotland. The last were generally people of culture, and gave to

the colony many clergymen, physicians, lawyers, and schoolmasters
Churchmen from England also emigrated in considerable numbers, as the
" Grand Model" established their church as the orthodox faith of the
province. Dutch emigrants came also from New York to escape the
outrages of the English governors of that province. Last of all were the
Huguenots, who were induced to settle in South Carolina by Charles II.,
who was sincerely anxious to give them a refuge from their persecutions
in Europe, and who wished them to establish in Carolina the culture of
the vine, the olive, and the silk-worm The revocation of the Edict of
Nantes drove thousands of the Huguenots from France Large numbers
of them joined their brethren in South Carolina They were almost
invariably persons of education and refinement. In France they had
constituted the most useful and intelligent part of the population. They
had almost monopolized the mechanical skill and mercantile enterprise
of their native land, and their loss was severely felt by it for many generations. In South Carolina they soon became sufficiently numerous to
constitute an important part of the population, and their influence was
felt in a marked degree, and for the good of the colony They brought
with them the virtues which had won them the respect and confidence
of the people of Europe, and the industry which could not fail to place
them among the most prosperous citizens of the new state They mingled
freely and intermarried with the other classes of the people of the
province, and thus became the ancestors of a splendid race who did honor
to their country and upheld her cause with their valor in her hour of
trial in the next century

The early years of South Carolina were marked by a constant struggle
between the colonists and the proprietaries The latter vainly attempted
to introduce the "Grand Model" as the law of the province, and the
former steadily resisted it A little later the proprietaries offered to make
some modifications in their constitutions, but these concessions were rejected also The governor, Sir John Yeamans, regarded his office solely
as a means of repairing his fortunes at the expense of both proprietaries
and colonists, and was dismissed by his employers. West, who was a
man of ability and liberality, was appointed his successor, and under him
the colony prospered, but, as he was too friendly to the people, he was
removed also.

In 1684 a small colony under Lord Cardross, a Presbyterian, settled
at Port Royal These settlers had fled to America to escape persecution
in England, but their effort to find an abiding place in the new world
was not destined to be successful Lord Cardross returned to Europe in
a year or two and in 1686 the Spaniards from St. Augustine, who

claimed the region as a dependency of their own, invaded the little settlement and laid it waste. Of the ten families which had constituted the colony, some returned to Scotland, while the remainder disappeared among the colonists in the vicinity of the Cooper and Ashley rivers.

In 1685 the proprietaries ordered the colonial authorities to enforce the navigation acts in the ports of the province. A rigid execution of this order would have been as fatal to the feeble commerce of South Carolina as to that of the settlements in the northern part of the province, and it was resisted by the colonists as a violation of their natural rights and of the promises made to them at the time of their emigration. In order to establish their authority more firmly the proprietaries appointed James Colleton governor, with the rank of landgrave. He was the brother of one of the proprietaries, and it was supposed that this fact and his aristocratic rank would give him a moral power which his predecessors had not possessed. The new governor attempted to enforce the constitutions, but was met with a determined resistance, and when he undertook to collect the rents claimed by the proprietaries, and the taxes he had been ordered to levy, the assembly seized the records of the province, imprisoned the colonial secretary, and defied the governor to execute his orders. In 1690 they went still further, and having proclaimed William and Mary, disfranchised Colleton, and banished him from South Carolina.

Disputes now ran high in the colony, chiefly in regard to rents and land tenures. The "cavaliers and ill-livers," as the party devoted to the interests of the proprietaries was termed, endeavored to compel the remainder of the settlers—the Presbyterians, Quakers, and Huguenots, the last of whom had recently been admitted to all the privileges of citizenship—to submit to their high-handed measures. They hoped among other things to secure the supremacy of the Church of England in the colony, notwithstanding the fact that a majority of the people were dissenters. The troubles went on increasing, and at length the proprietors, in the hope of putting an end to them, consented to abandon their effort to force upon the Carolinas the legislation of Shaftesbury and Locke. In April, 1693, they abolished the fundamental constitutions by a formal vote, and decided to allow the government of the province to be conducted according to the terms of the charter.

Thomas Smith was appointed governor, but in spite of his many virtues he was unacceptable to the people, and the proprietaries determined to send out to Carolina one of their own number with full powers to investigate and remedy the grievances of the colony. John Archdale, "an honest member of the Society of Friends," was chosen, and at once repaired to Carolina   He was a man of great moderation, and was well suited to the task before him   He succeeded in harmonizing the hostile factions which divided the province, and in the formation of the council selected two men of the moderate party to one high churchman, an arrangement which fairly represented the actual state of parties, and gave satisfaction to the mass of the people.   He remitted the quit-rents for three and four years, and arranged the price of lands and the system of conveyances upon an equitable basis, and gave the colonists the privilege of paying their dues to the proprietaries either in money or in produce. He established peaceful relations with the Indians, and put an end to the infamous practice of kidnapping them, which had prevailed since the establishment of the colony.   The savages in the Cape Fear region had suffered especially from this, and now showed their gratitude by treating with kindness the sailors who were cast away on their coast.   Friendly relations were also begun with the Spaniards at St. Augustine.   Several Yemmassee Indians, who had been converted by the missionaries, having been captured and exposed for sale in Carolina, were ransomed by Archdale, who sent them to the governor of St Augustine.   The Spaniard gratefully acknowledged this kindness, and returned it by forwarding to South Carolina the crew of an English vessel which had gone ashore on the coast of Florida.   The colonial government was organized by Archdale on a plan similar to that of Maryland   The council was appointed by the proprietaries, and the assembly elected by the people, and the militia were charged with the defence of the colony.   Archdale's administration was so satisfactory to all parties that upon his withdrawal from the province the assembly declared that he had, "by his wisdom, patience, and labor, laid a firm foundation for a most glorious superstructure'

Archdale went back to England in 1697, and the proprietaries, failing to profit by the lesson of his success, attempted to introduce a measure which would give the political power of the colony exclusively into the hands of the landowners   This measure was resolutely rejected by the colonial assembly   The majority of the people of the colony were, as has been stated, dissenters, Presbyterians, Quakers, and Huguenots. They had consented, in order to pacify the high church party, that one minister of the Church of England should be maintained at the public expense, but the churchmen were resolved to force their system upon them.   In 1704 the churchmen had a majority of one in the assembly; the governor was favorable to them, and the council was no longer arranged upon the just plan of Archdale   The assembly, in violation of the plainest principles of justice, disfranchised the dissenters, and established the Church of England as the religion of the colony.   This action was approved by the council and governor, and was sustained by the proprietaries in spite of the earnest opposition of Archdale. The disfranchised people appealed for justice to the queen and the House of Lords. The committee of the lords declared that the proprietaries had forfeited their charter, and advised its recall, and the house pronounced the intolerant acts null and void, which decision was proclaimed by the queen in June, 1706. In November of the same year the colonial legislature repealed its acts, and restored to the dissenters their political rights, but the laws establishing the Church of England as the religion of the province remained unrepealed until the Revolution.

The disputes in the colony went on, but in spite of them South Carolina continued to prosper, and its population increased rapidly. During Archdale's residence in the colony the captain of a ship from Madagascar gave him some rice, which he distributed among the planters for the purpose of ascertaining whether it could be cultivated in the maritime regions of the province, which were unsuited to the culture of wheat. The experiment was entirely successful, and the colony at once embarked in the culture of rice, which has ever since been one of its principal industries. Carolina rice soon took rank as the best grown in any country. The fur trade was also carried on with great activity, and the manufacture of tar and the export of lumber also became prominent sources of wealth. It was believed that the colony could successfully manufacture a large part of the woollen fabrics necessary to the supply of its wants, and the attempt was made. It was struck down by the British government in pursuance of its plan to compel the colonies to depend upon England for all their supplies. Parliament forbade the several colonies to export woollen goods to any other province or to any foreign port. They were to ship their products to England alone, and to receive their supplies from her only. English merchants were to be privileged to set a price to suit their own interests upon the products of the colonies, and also upon the articles of European manufacture sold them in return. The effect of this iniquitous law upon Carolina was to drive her back into agricultural pursuits, and thus to increase the demand for slaves, which was promptly supplied by British traders.

In 1702 England was at war with France and Spain, and James Moore was governor of Carolina. He was a needy adventurer, who endeavored to fill his purse by kidnapping Indians and selling them as slaves. This being too slow a process, he determined to plunder the Spanish settlement of St. Augustine. He attacked that place with a force of whites and Indians. The town was readily taken, but he could make no impression upon the citadel, and despatched a vessel to Jamaica for cannon to reduce the fort. The garrison in the meantime sent an Indian runner to Mobile with news of their situation, and word was sent from Mobile to Havana. In a short while two Spanish ships of war arrived at St. Augustine to the relief of the garrison, and Moore was obliged to raise the siege. He abandoned his stores and retreated overland to Charleston. The only result of his expedition was the accumulation of a debt which the colony was obliged to carry for many years.

Moore's next effort was directed against the Appalachee Indians of Florida. These had been converted to the Roman Catholic faith by the Spanish missionaries, and had begun to adopt habits of civilization; they lived in villages, and supported themselves by cultivating the soil. They were also very friendly to the French, who had settled Louisiana. Moore professed to be very apprehensive of the effects of the Spanish and French influence upon the Appalachees, and declared his intention to cripple them before they could do any harm to the English settlements.

His real motive was the hope of plunder. The only crime of the poor savages was their adoption of the Roman faith. In 1705, with a force of about fifty white men and one thousand Seminole warriors, Moore invaded the

ATTACK OF THE SPANIARDS ON CHARLESTON IN 1706.

settlements of the Appalachees, destroyed them, killed many of the natives, and made prisoners of large numbers, who were removed to the region of the Altamaha. The churches were plundered and destroyed, and the country of the Appalachees was given to the Seminoles as a reward for their services. They at once occupied it, and thus became a barrier between their English friends and the Spanish settlements.

In 1706 the Spaniards and French sent a combined fleet to Charleston to avenge the attacks upon St. Augustine and the Appalachees. The attack of the fleet was repulsed by the people, who were led by William Rhet and Sir Nathaniel Johnson, and the assailants were forced to withdraw with the loss of one ship belonging to the French and upwards of three hundred men.

North Carolina continued to prosper. Her people were happy and contented under their simple system of government, which was described by Spotswood as "scarce any government at all." In 1704 the proprie-

TORTURE OF LAWSON BY THE TUSCARORAS.

310

taries attempted to establish the Church of England in this part of their province, the people of which were nearly all Presbyterians, Quakers, and Lutherans. It was ordered that all who refused to submit to the laws for the establishment and support of the English church should be disfranchised. The people opposed a general and determined resistance to this measure, and at the end of a year there was but one clergyman of the English church within the limits of the colony. The resistance finally culminated in open rebellion. The colony was divided into two parties, one of which sustained the authority of the proprietors, the other the rights of the people. Each party had its governor and assembly, and for six years the colony remained in a state of anarchy. The Quakers were the leading spirits of the popular party, and maintained their rights with a steadfastness characteristic of their race.

Thus far North Carolina had escaped a war with the Indians. The Tuscaroras, who occupied the central and northwestern portions of the present State, had emigrated at some remote period from the north, and they now viewed with jealousy and distrust the encroachments of the whites upon their lands. About 1711 the proprietaries assigned large tracts in the country of this tribe to a company of Germans from the region of the Neckar and the Rhine, who had fled to America to escape religious persecution. A company of these exiles had come out under the direction of De Graffenreid, and in September, 1711, De Graffenreid accompanied Lawson, the surveyor-general of the province, in an expedition up the Neuse, for the purpose of locating these lands and of ascertaining how far the river was navigable. They were captured by a party of sixty Indians and hurried to a distant village of the Tuscaroras. Lawson was regarded with bitter hostility by the Indians, who looked upon him as responsible above all others for the loss of their lands, as he had been compelled by his duties to locate the grants of the proprietaries, and he was put to death with cruel torments. De Graffenreid was also condemned to die; but he told the savages that he had been but a short time in the country, and that he was the "chief of a different tribe from the English," and promised that he would take no more of their land. The Indians kept him a prisoner for five weeks, and then permitted him to return to his friends. During this time the Tuscaroras and Corees, whom they had drawn into an alliance with them, attacked the settlements of the whites on the Roanoke and Pamlico sound, and for three days spread death and devastation all along the frontier of the colony. A large number of the unoffending settlers were slain and many homesteads were destroyed.

The people of North Carolina appealed to Virginia and South Carolina for assistance. South Carolina sent a small body of troops and a force of friendly Indians, and Governor Spotswood of Virginia, unable to send assistance, engaged one tribe of the Tuscaroras in a treaty of peace. The people of North Carolina, divided by their internal dissensions, took scarcely any part in the struggle. The South Carolina forces attacked the Tuscaroras in their fort and compelled them to make peace. The troops, however, on their return home, violated the treaty by seizing some of the Indians for the purpose of selling them as slaves. The war broke out again, and was prosecuted with vigor for about a year, and resulted in the expulsion of the Tuscaroras from North Carolina.

The Yemmassees had for some time been hostile to the Spaniards, as they resented the efforts of the priests to convert them to Christianity. They had acted as the allies of the English in the war with the Tuscaroras, but after the close of that struggle the unscrupulous traders, who regarded them as "a tame and peaceable people," had treated them so badly, and plundered them so systematically, that they were driven into hostility to the English. They thereupon renewed their friendship with the Spaniards, and induced the Catawbas, the Creeks, and Cherokees, who had also been friendly to the English, to join them against their former allies. In 1715 the savages, suddenly, and without warning, attacked the settlements on the frontier. The alarm was sent to Port Royal and Charleston, and the assailed people fled towards the settlements along the coast. The Indians continued their depredations, and the colony prepared as rapidly as possible to resist them. Aid was sent from North Carolina, whose government had now been placed on a more stable footing. Governor Craven took the field without delay, with such troops as he could raise, and a long and bloody struggle ensued. The power of the savages was broken, however. The Yemmassees were compelled to take refuge in Florida, where they were provided for by the Spaniards, and the other tribes were driven farther westward.

The contests between the proprietaries and the colonists now came to an end. The proprietaries had made no effort to help the colonists during their struggle with the Indians, and the latter determined to have no more to do with their former lords. The dispute was carried before Parliament, which body declared that the proprietaries had forfeited their charter. In 1720 the king appointed Francis Nicholson provisional governor of Carolina. In 1729 the controversy was ended by the purchase of the proprietaries' interests by the crown for the sum of $110,000. Carolina thus became a royal province, and was divided by the king into two separate states, known respectively as North and South Carolina, to each of which a royal governor was appointed.

CHAPTER XIX.

SETTLEMENT OF GEORGIA

General James Edward Oglethorpe—His Efforts to Reform Prison Discipline of England
—Proposes to Found a Colony in America for the Poor and for Prisoners for Debt—A
Charter Obtained from the King—Colonization of Georgia—Savannah Settled—First
Years of the Colony—Labors of Oglethorpe—Arrival of New Emigrants—Augusta
Founded—The Moravian Settlements—The Wesleys in America—George Whitefield—
War between England and Spain—Oglethorpe Invades Florida—Failure of the Attack
upon St Augustine—The Spaniards Invade Georgia—Oglethorpe's Stratagem—Its Suc-
cess—Battle of "Bloody Marsh"—Close of the War—Charges against Oglethorpe—His
Vindication—His Return to Europe—Changes in the Colonial Government—Introduc-
tion of Slavery into Georgia—Prosperity of the Colony

THE severe laws in force in England in the last century against
debtors aroused the opposition of many philanthropists, who
strove to procure their abolition or amelioration Among these
was General James Edward Oglethorpe, an officer of the English
army and a member of Parliament   He was a man of fortune,
and of generous nature, and devoted himself with energy to reform not
only the laws against debtors but the entire prison discipline of England
There were at this time upwards of four thousand men in prison for
debt. Their condition was most pitiful   They had no hope of relief
save through the mercy of the creditors who had consigned them to their
prisons, and were treated with a severity due only to criminals.   It
seemed an outrage to the generous Oglethorpe to visit such heavy punishments upon persons whose only crimes were their misfortunes, and he
endeavored to have the laws authorizing imprisonment for debt repealed,
and failing in this conceived the plan of establishing in America a place
of refuge to which the poor and unfortunate might resort, and earn a
support by their own industry   He succeeded in interesting others in his
benevolent scheme, and in 1732 a petition, signed by a number of men
of rank and influence, was presented to George II., praying him to grant
to the petitioners a tract of unoccupied land in America for the purpose
of founding such an asylum as that proposed by Oglethorpe.   The king
responded favorably to this appeal, and granted to Oglethorpe and
twenty other persons the region between the Savannah and the Altamaha

286

rivers. This region was to be held "in trust for the poor," for a period of twenty-one years, by the trustees named in the charter, and was to constitute a home for unfortunate debtors and Protestants from the continent of Europe, who might wish to seek safety there from persecution. The territory thus assigned formed a part of South Carolina, but was formally separated from it and named Georgia in honor of the king. The "free exercise of religion" was secured to all sects "except Papists." No grant of land to any single settler was to exceed five hundred acres, a condition which it was hoped would prevent the rich from securing the best lands, and give to the poor an opportunity to become landowners. It was believed that the climate and soil of the new province were specially adapted to the raising of silk-worms and the cultivation of the vine.

The scheme of Oglethorpe enlisted the sympathies of all classes of the English people. Liberal donations were made in its behalf, and its benevolent projecter exerted himself with energy to secure a colony with which to lay the foundations of the new state. It was determined to take none but the poorest and most helpless, and Oglethorpe himself decided to accompany them, and give his personal care to the planting of the colony. One hundred and fifty persons, comprising thirty-five families, were embarked, and they sailed from England in November, 1732. They reached Charleston in fifty-seven days, and were formally welcomed by the assembly of South Carolina and presented with a supply of cattle and rice. From Charleston the company sailed to Port Royal, while Oglethorpe hastened to explore the Savannah and select a site for the settlement. He chose a location at Yamacraw Bluff, on the right bank of the river, about twenty miles from its mouth. He purchased the land from the Yamacraw Indians, and the foundations of a town were laid. The place was named Savannah from the river on which it stood. Oglethorpe hastened forward the clearing of the land and the building of houses, but for nearly a year contented himself with a tent which was erected under four wide-spreading pines. "The streets were laid out with the greatest regularity; in each quarter a public square was reserved; the houses were planned and constructed on one model—each a frame of sawed timber, twenty-four feet by sixteen, floored with rough deals, the sides with feather-edged boards, unplaned, and the roof shingled." A garden was laid off by the river-side, to be the nursery of European fruits and other productions.

COAT OF ARMS OF GEORGIA.

Friendly relations were cultivated with the Indians. The chief of the Yamacraws came in bringing a buffalo skin, on the inner side of which was painted the head and feathers of an eagle. " Here is a little present," said Tomo-chichi, as the chief was named. " The feathers of the eagle are soft, and signify love ; the buffalo skin is warm, and is the emblem of protection ; therefore love and protect our little families." The Muscogees, Creeks, Cherokees, and Oconees also sent their chiefs to Savannah to make an alliance with the English. The savages were well pleased with the noble and commanding appearance of Oglethorpe and his frank and kind manner of dealing with them, and trusted implicitly in the promises he made them. The distant Choctaws also sent messengers to open friendly relations with the new settlers, and a profitable trade was established with the tribes as far west as the Mississippi.

Thus far the colony of Georgia was a success, and the friends of the

OGLETHORPE.

movement in England were not slow to make public the accounts which came to them of its delightful climate and fertile soil, and all who were oppressed or in need were invited to seek the protection and advantages which the new land offered. The fame of the colony attracted the attention of a number of German Protestants in and around Salzburg, who were undergoing a severe persecution for the sake of their religion. Their sufferings enlisted the sympathy of the people of England, and the " Society for the Propagation of the Gospel" invited them to emigrate to Georgia, and secured for them the means of doing so. The Germans readily accepted the offer, and rejoiced greatly that they were thus afforded an opportunity of spreading the gospel among the Indians. Nearly one hundred persons set out from Salzburg, taking with them their wives and little ones in wagons, and journeyed across the country to Frankfort-on-the-Main. They carried with them their Bibles and books of devotion, and as they journeyed lightened their fatigues with those grand old German hymns, which they were to make as precious in the new world as they were to the people of God in the old. From Frankfort they proceeded to the Rhine and floated down that stream to Rotterdam, where being joined by two clergymen—Bolzius and Gronau—they sailed to England. They were warmly received by a committee of the trustees of the colony and forwarded to Georgia.

A stormy passage of fifty-seven days brought them to Charleston, in

A SOUTHERN PLANTATION.

March, 1734, where they were met by Oglethorpe, who led them to their destination. They were assigned a location on the Savannah, a short distance above the town of Savannah, where they began without delay to lay off a town which they named *Ebenezer*, in gratitude to God for his guidance of them into a land of plenty and of rest from persecution. Others of their countrymen joined them from time to time, and their settlement grew rapidly, and became noted as one of the most orderly, thrifty, and moral communities in the new world

In 1734 the town of Augusta was laid out at the head of boat navigation on the Savannah, and soon became an important trading-post. Emigrants came over from England in large numbers, and Oglethorpe had the satisfaction of seeing his colony fairly started upon the road to prosperity. He was justly proud of the success of the colony, for it was mainly due to his disinterested efforts. Governor Johnson of South Carolina, who had watched the labors of Oglethorpe with the deepest interest, wrote: "His undertaking will succeed, for he nobly devotes all his powers to serve the poor and rescue them from their wretchedness." The pastor of Ebenezer bore equally emphatic testimony to his devotion. "He has taken care of us to the best of his ability," said the pastor. ' God has so blessed his presence and his regulations in the land, that others would not in many years have accomplished what he has brought about in one "

In April, 1734, Oglethorpe, whose presence was required in Europe, sailed from Savannah, taking with him several Indians, and enough of the raw silk which had been produced in the colony to make a dress for the queen. Georgia was left to manage its own affairs during the absence of the founder. As the colonists regarded the use of ardent spirits as the sure cause of the debt and misery from which they had fled, they prohibited their introduction into the colony; but it was found impossible to enforce this law The importation of negro slaves was also forbidden. The colony was a refuge for the distressed and oppressed of all nations, and it seemed a violation of the spirit in which it was founded to hold men in bondage. "Slavery," said Oglethorpe, "is against the gospel as well as the fundamental law of England We refused, as trustees, to make a law permitting such a horrid crime "

The visit of Oglethorpe to England was productive of great benefit to Georgia Parliament was induced to grant it assistance, and the king became deeply interested in the province which had been called by his name. Emigrants from England continued to seek its hospitable shores, and the trustees induced a band of Moravians, or United Brethren, to emigrate to the colony They came in 1735, with the intention of becoming missionaries of the gospel among the savage tribes, and under their leader Spangenberg, formed a new settlement on the Ogeechee, south of the Savannah They claimed and received a grant of fifty acres of land for each of their number, in accordance with a law which had been passed for the encouragement of emigration In the same year a company of Scotch Highlanders, under their minister, John McLeod, arrived, and founded the town of Darien, on the Altamaha In 1736 Oglethorpe himself returned, bringing with him three hundred emigrants.

Among the new-comers were two brothers, men of eminent piety, who were destined to exercise a powerful influence upon the world. They were John and Charles Wesley, sons of a clergyman of the Church of England, and themselves ministers of that communion Charles Wesley had been selected by Oglethorpe as his secretary, and John Wesley came with the hope of becoming the means of converting the Indians to Christianity. He did not succeed in realizing his noble ambition, but we cannot doubt that his experience in America formed a very important part of the training by which God was preparing him for the great work he meant to intrust to him at a later day. The preaching of Wesley had a marked effect upon the colony. Crowds flocked to hear him, neglecting their usual amusements in their eagerness to listen to him. His austerity of life, however, involved him in troubles with the people, and his popularity at length disappeared. His brother Charles was too tenderly moulded for so rough a life as that of the infant colony, and his health sank under it The brothers remained in Georgia only two years, and then went back to Europe, never to return to America.

Soon after the departure of the Wesleys came to the colony George Whitefield, their friend and associate, the "golden-mouthed" preacher of the century. In his own land he had begun to preach the message of his Master when but a mere youth, and had proclaimed it to the inmates of the prisons and to the poor in the fields, and now he had come to bring the gospel to the people of the new world He visited the Lutherans at Ebenezer, and was deeply impressed with the care with which they protected the orphan and helpless children of their community. He determined to establish an institution similar to the orphan house at Halle in Germany, and by his personal exertions succeeded in raising in England and America the funds necessary for the success of his enterprise. He thereupon established near Savannah the first orphan asylum in America. He watched it with unceasing care during his life, but after his death it languished and was at length discontinued. Whitefield did not confine his labors to Georgia. He visited every colony in America, and finally died and was buried in New England. The memory of his wonderful eloquence is still retained in this country by the children of those who listened to him.

Immediately upon his return to Georgia, Oglethorpe proceeded to visit the Lutheran settlement at Ebenezer, to encourage the people and lay out their town. The Germans repaid his care by their industry, and in a few years their total annual product of raw silk amounted to ten thousand pounds. The culture of indigo was also carried on by them with marked success.

Oglethorpe, having visited the Scotch settlement at Darien, now resolved to come to a definite understanding with the Spaniards at St. Augustine respecting the southern border of Georgia, and to sustain the pretensions of Great Britain to the country as far south as the St. John's. Proceeding with a detachment of Highlanders to Cumberland island, he marked out the location for a fort, to be called St. Andrew's, and on the southern end of Amelia island, at the mouth of the St John's, built Fort St. George. The Spaniards on their part claimed the whole coast as far north as St. Helena's sound, and Oglethorpe, a little later, decided to abandon Fort St. George, but strengthened Fort St. Andrew, as it defended the entrance to the St. Mary's, which stream was finally settled upon as the boundary between Georgia and Florida. Oglethorpe was commissioned a brigadier-general by the king, and was charged with the defence of Georgia and South Carolina. He repaired to England and raised a regiment of troops, with which he returned to Georgia in 1738.

Spain and England were rapidly drifting into war. The system of restrictions by which the European governments sought to retain the exclusive possession of the commerce of their respective colonies was always a fruitful source of trouble. It now operated to bring England and Spain to open hostilities. The Spanish colonies were forbidden by law to trade with any port but that of Cadiz. The merchants of this place, being given a monopoly of the colonial commerce, were enabled to fix their prices without fear of competition, and thus earned large fortunes. The trade of the Spanish-American colonies, however, was too tempting not to produce rivals to the merchants of Cadiz. The English, who had watched its growth with eager eyes, determined to gain a share of it. By the terms of a treaty between the two nations, an English vessel was allowed to visit Portobello, in the West Indies, once a year, and dispose of its cargo. This vessel was followed by smaller ones, which in the night replaced with their cargoes the bales of goods that had been discharged during the day. An active smuggling trade sprang up between the English and Spanish-American ports, and English vessels repeatedly sought these ports, under the pretence of distress, and sold their goods. These enterprises were carried to such an extent that the Spanish merchants were unable to compete with the English smugglers in the colonial markets, and the tonnage of the port of Cadiz fell from fifteen thousand to two thousand tons. The Spaniards visited with severe punishments all who were detected in engaging in this illicit traffic. Some of the offenders were imprisoned, and others were deprived of their

GATHERING SUGAR-CANE.

ears. The English people resented the punishment of these traders as an infringement of the freedom of trade, and regarded the smugglers who had suffered at the hands of Spanish justice as martyrs. The popular sentiment was therefore in favor of a war with Spain, and the English government, which had all along connived at this illicit trade, which was rapidly crippling a rival power, shared the national feeling.

The English colonists, who had watched the growth of the trouble between the two European countries, had grievances of their own. South Carolina was a sufferer by the loss of numerous runaway negro slaves, who escaped to the Spaniards at St. Augustine. The return of these fugitives was demanded, and was refused, not because the Spaniards were opposed to slavery, but because they were always ready to injure the English colonies by any means in their power. Moreover, the Spanish authorities of Florida had ordered the English to withdraw from Georgia, and it was not certain that they would refrain from seeking to enforce this order. Oglethorpe had become convinced that war was inevitable, and in order to be prepared for it had visited Europe and raised a regiment of six hundred men, as has been related.

War was declared against Spain by England in October, 1739. Admiral Vernon was sent against Portobello with his fleet, and captured that town and its fortifications, and gained some other successes over the Spaniards in Central America. In 1740 the American colonies were ordered by the British government to contribute each its quota to a grand expedition against the Spanish possessions in the West Indies. Each colony made its contribution promptly, and Pennsylvania, in the place of troops, voted a sum of money. The expedition reached Jamaica in January, 1741, but instead of proceeding at once to attack Havana, which was only three days distant, and the conquest of which would have made England supreme in the West Indies, the fleet was detained for over a month at Jamaica by the dissensions between Wentworth, the incompetent commander of the land forces, and Vernon, the admiral of the fleet. The expedition numbered over one hundred vessels, of which twenty-nine were ships of the line, and was manned with fifteen thousand sailors and twelve thousand troops, and supplied with every requisite for a successful siege. Havana might have been taken, and England have gained a hold upon the southern waters of America which could never have been wrested from her. Instead of undertaking this important measure, the expedition attacked Carthagena, the strongest fortress in Spanish America. The Spaniards defended it with obstinacy and held the English in check until the besieging force, decimated by the ravages of the climate, was compelled to withdraw. The war continued through the next year, but England gained no advantage in the West Indies which could at all compensate her for her losses in the struggle.

In the autumn of 1739, upon the breaking out of the war, Oglethorpe was ordered to invade Florida and attack St Augustine. He hastened to Charleston and urged upon the authorities of South Carolina, which formed a part of his military command, the necessity of acting with promptness and decision. He was granted supplies and a force of four hundred men, which, added to his own regiment, gave him a force of one thousand white troops He was also furnished with a body of Indian warriors by the friendly tribes, and with his little army invaded Florida in the spring of 1741, and laid siege to St. Augustine. He found the garrison more numerous and the fortifications stronger than he had been led to believe. The Indians soon became disheartened and began to desert, and the troops from South Carolina, "enfeebled by the heat, dispirited by sickness and fatigued by fruitless efforts, marched away in large bodies." The small naval force also became dissatisfied, and Oglethorpe, left with only his own regiment, was obliged to withdraw into Georgia after a siege of five weeks. During this campaign Oglethorpe made a few prisoners, whom he treated with kindness. He prevented the Indians from maltreating the Spanish settlers, and, throughout the invasion, "endured more fatigues than any of his soldiers, and in spite of ill health, consequent on exposure to perpetual damps, he was always at the head in every important action."

The invasion of Florida was a misfortune for Georgia in every way. Not only were some of the inhabitants lost to the colony by death, and the industry of the province greatly interfered with by the calling off of the troops from their ordinary avocations, but a serious misfortune was sustained in the withdrawal of the Moravians from the province. Uncompromisingly opposed to war they withdrew from Georgia in a body, and settled in Pennsylvania, where they founded the towns of Bethlehem and Nazareth

In the last year of the war, 1742, the Spaniards resolved to avenge the attack upon Florida by driving the English out of Georgia. A strong fleet with a considerable land force was sent from Cuba to St. Augustine, from which it proceeded to the mouth of the St. Mary's. Oglethorpe had constructed a strong work called Fort William, on the southern end of Cumberland island, for the defence of this river. With no aid from Carolina, and with less than a thousand men, Oglethorpe was left to defend this position as well as he could He posted his main force at Frederica, a small village on St. Simon's island. The Spanish fleet attacked Fort William in June, and succeeded in passing it and entering the harbor of St. Simon's. The troops were landed, and arrangements were made for a combined attack upon Frederica

Oglethorpe now resolved to anticipate the attack of the enemy by a night assault upon their position, but as his forces were approaching the Spanish camp, under cover of darkness, one of his soldiers, a Frenchman, betrayed the movement by firing his gun, and escaping into the enemy's lines, where he gave the alarm. Oglethorpe by a happy strata-

gem now induced the enemy to withdraw, and drew upon the deserter the
punishment he merited   He bribed a Spanish prisoner to carry a letter
to the deserter, in which he addressed the Frenchman as a spy of the
English, and urged him to use every effort to detain the Spaniards before
Frederica for several days longer, until a fleet of six English ships of
war, which had sailed from Charleston, could reach and destroy St.
Augustine. The letter was delivered by the released prisoner to the
Spanish commander, as Oglethorpe had known would be the case, and
the deserter was placed in confinement. Fortunately, at this moment,
some vessels from South Carolina, laden with supplies for Oglethorpe,
appeared in the offing   These the Spanish commander was confident
were the ships on their way to attack St Augustine. He determined to
strike a vigorous blow at Frederica before sailing to the relief of his
countrymen in Florida. On his march towards the English position he
was ambuscaded and defeated, with great loss, at a place since called
"Bloody Marsh." The next night he embarked his forces, and sailed
for St Augustine to defend it from the attack which had no existence
save in the fertile brain of Oglethorpe, whose stratagem was thus entirely
successful.   On their withdrawal the Spaniards renewed their attempt to
capture Fort William, but without success.   The firmness and vigor of
Oglethorpe had saved Georgia and Carolina from the ruin which the
Spaniards, who had no intention of occupying the country, had designed
for them.

Yet the founder and brave defender of Georgia was not to escape the
experience of those who seek with disinterested zeal to serve their fellow-
men   The disaffected settlers sent an agent to England to lodge complaints against him with the government. In July, 1743, having made
sure of the tranquillity and safety of the colony, Oglethorpe sailed for
England to meet his accuser, and upon arriving in his native country demanded an investigation of his conduct in the land for which he had
sacrificed so much. The result of the inquiry was the triumphant
acquittal of Oglethorpe, and the punishment of his accuser for making
false charges.   Oglethorpe was promoted to the grade of major-general
in the English army   He did not return to Georgia again, but he had
the satisfaction of knowing that during his ten years of sacrifice and toil
in America he had successfully laid the foundations of a vigorous state,
and had placed it far beyond the possibility of failure, and that his name
was honored and loved by the people for whom he had given his best
efforts without any personal reward. He died at the age of ninety years.
After the departure of Oglethorpe many improvements were made in the
government of Georgia which was changed from a military rule to a

civil establishment The forms and customs of the English law were introduced, and the usual magistrates appointed.

Slavery had been forbidden by the trustees, but the majority of the people were dissatisfied with this prohibition The Germans and the Scotch were opposed to the introduction of slave labor, but the greater number of the English, many of whom had been reduced to poverty by their idleness and wastefulness, were of the opinion that the agricultural wealth of the colony could not be properly developed by white labor alone. "They were unwilling to labor, but were clamorous for privileges to which they had no right" They declared that the use of strong liquors was rendered absolutely necessary by the climate, and demanded the repeal of the laws against their introduction. Negro slaves were hired from the Carolina planters at first for a few years, and finally for a term of one hundred years, which was a practical establishment of slavery in the colony Within seven years after Oglethorpe's departure slave-ships from Africa brought their cargoes direct to Savannah, and sold them there. The scruples of the Germans were at length overcome, and they were induced to believe that negroes might be led into the Christian fold by their proper treatment by Christian masters, and that in this way their change of country might result in benefit to them "If you take slaves in faith," wrote their friends from Germany, "and with the intent of conducting them to Christ, the action will not be a sin, but may prove a benediction." Even the pious Whitefield took this view of the subject, and urged the trustees to grant permission to the colonists to hold slaves, as indispensable to the prosperity of Georgia

The trustees were so strongly urged to this step by all classes of the colony, and so overrun with complaints, that the twenty-one years of their guardianship having expired, they were glad to surrender their trust, which they did in 1752, and Georgia became a royal province. Privileges similar to those granted the other colonies were allowed it. The king appointed the governor and some of the other higher officials, and the assembly discharged the duties, and enjoyed the rights appertaining to similar bodies in the other provinces. Georgia was always a favored colony Among the most important privileges bestowed upon it was the right to import and hold negro slaves, which was conferred upon it by Parliament after a careful examination into the matter. After this the colony grew rapidly, and cotton and rice were largely cultivated. In 1752, at the time of the relinquishment of the colony to the crown, Georgia contained a population less than 2500 whites, and about 400 negroes. In 1775, at the outbreak of the Revolution, the population numbered about 75,000 souls, and its exports were valued at over half a million of dollars.

CHAPTER XX.

THE FRENCH IN THE VALLEY OF THE MISSISSIPPI.

Origin of the Hostility of the Iroquois to the French—Settlement of Canada—Plans of
the French respecting the Indians—The Jesuits—Their Work in America—Success of
their Missions—The Early Missionaries—Foundation of a College at Quebec—Efforts
of the Jesuits to Convert the Iroquois—Father Jogues—Death of Ahasistari—Father
Allouez—The Missions on the Upper Lakes—Father Marquette—His Exploration of
the Upper Mississippi—Death of Marquette—La Salle—Efforts of France to secure the
Valley of the Mississippi—La Salle Descends the Mississippi to its Mouth—His Effort
to Colonize the Lower Mississippi—The First Colony in Texas—Its Failure—Death of
La Salle—Lemoine d'Ibberville—Settlement of Louisiana—Colony of Biloxi—Settle-
ment of Mobile—Crozat's Monopoly—Founding of New Orleans—Detroit Founded—
Slow Growth of the French Colonies—Occupation of the Ohio Valley by the French—
Wars with the Indians—Extermination of the Natchez Tribe—War with the Chickasaws.

E have already spoken of the explorations of Samuel Champlain
in Canada and in the northern part of New York. It is necessary now, in order to obtain a proper comprehension of the
period at which we have arrived, to go back to the time of his
discoveries and trace the efforts of France to extend her dominion over the great valley of the Mississippi. We have seen Champlain
in one of his last expeditions accompanying a war party of the Hurons
and Algonquins against their inveterate enemies, the Iroquois, or Five
Nations. By his aid the former were enabled to defeat the Iroquois, and
that great confederacy thus became the bitter and uncompromising
enemies of the French nation. They cherished this hostility to the latest
period of the dominion of France in Canada, and no effort of the French
governors was ever able to overcome it.

The efforts of Champlain established the settlement of Canada upon a
sure basis of success, and after his death settlers came over to Canada
from France in considerable numbers. Quebec became an important
place, and other settlements were founded. It was apparent from the
first that the French colonies must occupy a very different footing from
those of England. The soil and the climate were both unfavorable to
agriculture, and the French settlements were of necessity organized
chiefly as trading-posts. The trade in furs was immensely valuable, and
the French sought to secure the exclusive possession of it. To this end

THE GREAT CAÑON AND LOWER FALLS OF THE YELLOWSTONE.

it was indispensable to secure the friendship of the Indians, especially of those tribes inhabiting the country to the north and west of the great lakes.

In 1634, three years before the death of Champlain, Louis XIII. granted a charter to a company of French nobles and merchants, bestowing upon them the entire region embraced in the valley of the St. Lawrence, then known as New France. Richelieu and Champlain, who were members of this company, were wise enough to understand that their countrymen were not suited to the task of colonization, and that if France was to found an empire in the new world, it must be by civilizing and Christianizing the Indians, and bringing them under the rule of her king, and not by seeking to people Canada with Frenchmen. From this time it became the policy of France to bring the savages under her sway The efforts of the settlers in Canada were mainly devoted to trading with the Indians, and no attempt was made to found an agricultural state.

Champlain had conceived a sincere desire for the conversion of the savages to Christianity, and had employed several priests of the order of St Francis as his companions, and these had gained sufficient success among the savages to give ground for the hope that the red men might yet be brought into the fold of Christ. Father Le Caron, one of this order, had penetrated far up the St. Lawrence, had explored the southern coast of Lake Ontario, and had even entered Lake Huron. He brought back tidings of thousands of the sons of the forest living in darkness and superstition, ignorant of the gospel, and dying " in the bondage of their sins " In France a sudden enthusiasm was awakened in behalf of the savages, and at court zeal for the conversion of the Indians became the sure road to distinction. Much of this was the result of genuine disinterested regard for the welfare of the red men, but much also was due to the conviction that by such a course the power of France would be most surely established in Canada.

The missions were placed entirely in the hands of the Jesuits, an order well suited to the task demanded of it. It had been established by its founder for the express design of defeating the influences and the work of the Reformation, and its members were chosen with especial regard to their fitness for the duties required of them. They were to meet and refute the arguments by which the Reformers justified their withdrawal from the Roman Church, to beat back the advancing wave of Protestantism, and bring all Christendom once more in humble submission to the feet of the Roman pontiff The Reformers had made a most successful use of education in winning men from Rome, the Jesuits would take their own weapons against the Protestants. They would no longer command absolute and unquestioning submission to their church; but would educate the people to accept the faith of Rome as the result of study and investigation, and in order that study and investigation should lead to this desired result, the control of these processes should be placed exclusively in the hands of the members of the Jesuit order, who should direct them as they deemed best. Such a task required a band of devoted men, carefully trained for their special work, and such an order the Jesuits became. Surrendering his conscience and will to the direction of his superiors, and sinking his personality in that of his order, the Jesuit became a mere intellectual machine in the hands of his superior. Bound by a most solemn oath to obey without inquiry or hesitation the commands of the Pope, or the superiors of the order, the Jesuit holds himself in readiness to execute instantly, and to the best of his ability, any task imposed upon him. Neither fatigue, danger, hunger, nor suffering, was to stand in his way of perfect and unhesitating obedience. No distance was to be considered an obstacle, and no lack of ordinary facilities of travel was to prevent him from attempting to reach the fields in which he was ordered to labor. The merit of obedience in his eyes atoned for every other short-coming; devotion to the church, the glory of making proselytes, made even suffering pleasure and death a triumph, if met in the discharge of duty. Such an order was in every way qualified for the work of Christianizing the savages, and America offered the noblest field to which its energies had yet been invited. There, cut off from the ambitious schemes and corrupt influences which had enlisted their powers in Europe, the Jesuits could achieve, and did achieve their noblest and most useful triumphs. There, their influence was for good alone, and their labors stand in striking contrast with those which won for the order the universal execration of Europe. Not only did they win the honor of gaining many converts to the Christian faith, but they were the means of extending the dominion of their country far beyond the boundaries of Canada, and of bringing the great valley of the Mississippi under the authority of France.

By the year 1536 there were thirteen Jesuit missionaries in Canada laboring among the Indians. Not content with remaining around the posts, they pushed out beyond the frontier settlements into the boundless forest, making new converts and important discoveries. Each convert was regarded as a subject of France and the equal of the whites, and the kindliest relations were established between the French and the natives. Many of the traders took them Indian wives, and from these marriages sprang the class of half-breeds afterwards so numerous in Canada.

The limits of Canada were too narrow for the ambition of the Jesuits;

they burned to carry Christianity to the tribes in the more distant regions beyond the lakes. In the autumn of 1634 Fathers Brabeuf and Daniel accompanied a party of Hurons, who had come to Quebec on a trading expedition, to their home on the shores of the lake which bears their name. It was a long and difficult journey of nine hundred miles, and it taxed the endurance of the missionaries to the utmost, but they persevered, and finally gained a resting-place at the Huron villages on Georgian bay and Lake Simcoe. There they erected a rude chapel in a little grove, and celebrated the mysteries of their religion in the midst of the wondering red men, who looked on with awe and not without interest. Six missions were soon established among the Indian villages in this part of the lake, and converts began to reward the labors of the

DULUTH, AT THE HEAD OF LAKE SUPERIOR.

devoted priests. Father Brabeuf had not an idle moment. The first four hours of the day were passed in prayer and in the flagellation of his body; he wore a shirt of hair, and his fasts were frequent and severe. The remainder of the day was given to catechizing and teaching the Indians. As he passed along the streets of the village he would ring his little bell, and in this way summon the warriors to converse with him upon the mysteries of the Christian faith. He spent fifteen years in his labors among the Indians, and hundreds of converts were by means of him gained to Christ among the dusky children of the forest.

The great Huron chief, Ahasistari, was among the converts of Father Brabeuf. "Before you came to this country," he said to the missionary, "when I have incurred the greatest perils and have alone escaped, I have said to myself, 'Some powerful Spirit has the guardianship of my days.'" That Spirit he now declared was Jesus Christ, and as he had before adored him in ignorance, he now became his acknowledged servant. Being satisfied of his sincerity, Father Brabeuf baptized him, and the chief, in the enthusiasm of his new belief, exclaimed, "Let us strive to make the whole world embrace the faith in Jesus."

The report of the successful efforts of the missionaries gave great satisfaction in France, and the king and queen and the nobles made liberal donations in support of the missions and for the assistance of the converts. A college for the education of missionaries was founded at Quebec in 1635. This was the first institution of learning established in America, and preceded the founding of Harvard College by two years. Madame de la Peltrie, a wealthy young widow of Alençon, with the aid of three nuns, established in 1639 the Ursuline Convent for the education of Indian girls. The three nuns came out from France to take charge of it, and were received with enthusiasm, especially by the Indians. Montreal being regarded as a more suitable place, the institution was removed to that island and permanently established there.

The labors of the missionaries had thus far been confined to the Huron and Algonquin tribes, whom they found very willing to listen to them, and among whom they counted their converts by thousands. They had encountered but little hostility from them, and the dangers of the enterprise were merely those inseparable from the unsettled condition of the country. They were anxious to extend their efforts to the fiercer and more powerful Iroquois, as the conversion of the tribes of this confederacy would not only swell the number of their converts, but would extend the influence of France to the very borders of the English settlements on the Atlantic coast.

The Iroquois, or Five Nations, consisted, as has been said, of the Seneca, Cayuga, Onondaga, Oneida and Mohawk tribes. They occupied almost all that part of Canada south of the Ottawa, and between Lakes Ontario, Erie and Huron, the greater part of New York and the country lying along the south shore of Lake Erie, now included in the States of Ohio and Pennsylvania. They were generally called by the English the Mohawks. They were the most intelligent, as well as the most powerful, of the tribes with whom the French missionaries came in contact. Their traditions related that their confederacy had been formed in accordance with the instructions of Hiawatha, the greatest and wisest of their chiefs, who had been blessed by the Great Spirit with more than human beauty and wisdom and courage. He had made his people great, united and prosperous, had then taken a solemn leave of them, and had

sailed out into the distant sunset in a snow-white canoe amid the sweetest
music from the spirit land. They were regarded with dread by the surrounding tribes, many of which were tributary to them. Their influence
extended eastward as far as New England, and westward as far as the
countries of the Illinois and the Miamis. They regarded the Hurons as
their hereditary enemies, and the French, as the allies of the Hurons,
now shared this hostility. The savages long remembered, and never
forgave, the alliance of Champlain with the Hurons and Algonquins, to
which reference has been made.

The Jesuit missionaries vainly endeavored to add the tribes of the
Five Nations to their converts. The latter, regarding the French as
enemies, could never be made to look upon the missionaries of that race
as friends, and considered the efforts of the good fathers in their behalf

DUBUQUE, IOWA.

as a species of incantation designed for their destruction. They closed
the region south of Lake Ontario to the French traders and priests, and
kept a vigilant watch over the passes of the St. Lawrence for the purpose
of breaking up the trade of the French at Montreal with the tribes on
the lakes. The only route by which the lakes could be reached in safety
was by the Ottawa and through the wilderness beyond. Yet occasionally
a trading party would slip through the blockade established by the
Iroquois, and, descending the lakes and the St. Lawrence, reach Montreal
and Quebec in safety. These expeditions constituted the only means by
which the Jesuit missionaries in the remote regions could communicate
with their principal establishment at Montreal.

In the summer of 1642 Father Jogues, who had labored with great success in the country now embraced in the State of Michigan, left the Sault Sainte Marie under the escort of the great Huron war chief Ahasistari and a number of his braves, and, descending the Ottawa and the St. Lawrence, reached Montreal and Quebec in safety. On the 1st of August he set out on his return, accompanied by a larger fleet of Huron canoes. Before the mouth of the Ottawa was reached the party was attacked by a band of Mohawks, and the canoes were so much damaged that the occupants were forced to make for the opposite shore. The greater number escaped, but a few, among whom were Father Jogues and Father Goupil, a fellow-priest, were taken prisoners. Ahasistari had succeeded in reaching a place of safety, and from his concealment saw the missionaries prisoners in the hands of their enemies. He knew the fate that awaited them, and resolved to share it with them. Father Jogues might have escaped, but as there were among the prisoners several converts who had not yet received baptism, he decided to remain with them in the hope of being able to administer the sacred rite to them before their execution. Ahasistari strode through the midst of the astonished Mohawks to the side of the priest. "My brother," said the chief, "I made oath to thee that I would share thy fortune, whether death or life; here am I to keep my vow." He received absolution from the hands of his teacher, and died at the stake with the firmness of a Christian and a hero. Jogues and Goupil were carried to the Mohawk, and in each village through which they were led were compelled to run the gauntlet. On an ear of corn which was thrown to them for food a few drops of the dew had remained, and with these Father Jogues baptized two of his converts. Goupil was not so fortunate. He was seen in the act of making the sign of the cross over an Indian child, and was struck dead by a blow from the tomahawk of the child's father, who supposed he was working a spell for the little one's harm. Father Jogues had expected the same fate, but he was spared, and even allowed to erect a large cross near the village at which he was detained, and to worship before it at pleasure. He escaped at length and reached Albany, where he was kindly received by the Dutch, who enabled him to return to France, from which country he sailed again for Canada. He went boldly into the Mohawk country and began again the efforts which he had made during his captivity to convert his enemies to the true faith, but his labors were soon cut short by his murder by a Mohawk warrior. Other missionaries sought the country of these tribes, but only to meet torture and death at their hands.

In 1645 the French, who desired to secure their possessions, made a
20

treaty of peace with the Five Nations The latter professed to forget
and bury the wrongs of the past, and agreed to be the true friends of the
French. The Algonquins joined in the peace, but neither tribe was
sincere in its professions of friendship.

The Abenakis of Maine, who had heard of the good deeds of the
Jesuit fathers, sent messengers to Montreal asking that missionaries might
be sent to dwell among them. Their appeal was favorably considered,
and Father Dreuilettes made his way across the wilderness to the head
of the Kennebec, and descended that stream to a point within a few miles
of its mouth, where he established his mission. Large numbers of the
savages came to him for religious instruction, and he found them ready
to embrace the truths he taught them. He entered heartily into all the
modes of Indian life, hunting and fishing with them, and winning their
confidence and affection. After remaining with them about a year he
returned to Quebec, escorted by a band of his converts. He gave such
favorable accounts of the disposition of the Maine Indians that a permanent mission was established among them.

By the close of the year 1646 the French had established a line of
missions extending across the continent from Lake Superior to Nova
Scotia, and between sixty and seventy missionaries were actively engaged,
in instructing and preaching to the savages. How far the labors of these
devoted men were actually successful will never be known, as their work
was of a character which cannot be submitted to any human test They
did not succeed, however, in changing either the character or the habits
of their converts. They were still wild men, who scorned to engage in
the labor of cultivating their lands, and lived by hunting and fishing.
They learned to engage in the religious services of the missionaries, to
chant matins and vespers, but they made no approach to civilization.
When in after years the zeal of the whites for their conversion became
less active, and the missionaries less numerous, they fell back into their
old ways

In 1648 the peace between the Mohawks and the Hurons was broken,
and the war blazed up again fiercer than ever Bands of Mohawk warriors invaded the territory of the Hurons, and both the savage and the
missionary fell victims to their fury. On the morning of the 4th of July
the village of St Joseph, on Lake Simcoe, was attacked by a war party
of the Mohawks The Huron braves were absent on a hunting expedition, and only the old men and the women and children of the tribe
were left in the village. This was the village founded by the missionaries Brabeuf and Daniel, the latter of whom, now an old man, was
still dwelling with his converts. At the opening of the attack the good

priest hastened to baptize such as he could, and to give absolution to all whom he could reach   Then, as the Mohawks forced the stockade which protected the village, and swarmed in among the wigwams, he advanced calmly from the chapel to meet them, and fell pierced with numerous arrows

During the next year the Jesuit missions in Upper Canada were broken up   At the capture of the village Father Brabeuf and his companion Gabriel Lallemand were made prisoners, and were subsequently put to death with the cruellest tortures   They bore their sufferings with a firmness which astonished their persecutors. The Hurons were scattered, and their country was added to the dominion of the Five Nations. Many of the captive Hurons were adopted into the conquering tribes   A large number of these had embraced Christianity—so many, indeed, that the Jesuits, who had been in nowise discouraged by the terrible scenes which had marked the war, began to cherish the hope that the presence of these converts would induce the Iroquois to receive a missionary among them   It was decided to make the attempt among the Onondagas, and Oswego, which was then principal village, was chosen as the site of the mission   The Iroquois made no effort to disturb the missionaries, and priests were sent among the other tribes of the confederacy. Encouraged by this reception the French undertook to secure a firm footing in this inviting region by establishing a colony at the mouth of the Oswego, and fifty persons were despatched to that point to begin a settlement there   This aroused the alarm of the Indians, who compelled the colonists to withdraw, and forced the missionaries to depart with them. This was the last effort of the French to obtain possession of New York. The Five Nations were not to be reconciled with them on any terms, and their hostility made it useless to attempt the colonization of that fertile region.

Defeated in their hope of obtaining a footing in the country of the Five Nations, the Jesuit fathers turned their attention more energetically to the vast region beyond the lakes. In 1654 two young fur-traders had penetrated into the country beyond Lake Superior, and after an absence of two years had returned to Quebec, bringing with them accounts of the powerful and numerous tribes occupying that region   They brought with them a number of Indians, who urged the French to open commercial relations with and send missionaries among these tribes   Their request was promptly granted, and missionaries were soon on the ground. One of these, the aged Father Mesnard, while journeying through the forests, wandered off from his attendants, and was never seen again. His cassock and breviary were found by the Sioux and were long retained by them as a protection against evil.

In 1665 Father Claude Allouez ascended the Ottawa, and crossed the wilderness to the Sault Ste-Marie, on a mission to the tribes of the far west. In October he reached the principal town of the Chippewas at the head of Lake Superior. He found the tribe in great excitement; the young warriors were eager to engage in a war against the formidable Sioux, and the old men were seeking to restrain them. A grand council was in progress, which was attended by the chiefs of ten or twelve of the neighboring tribes for the purpose of preserving peace if possible. Father Allouez was admitted to this assembly, and exhorted the warriors to abandon their hostile intentions, and urged them to join the French in an alliance against the Five Nations. His appeal was successful, the war against the Sioux was abandoned, and the savages came in from all parts of the surrounding country to listen to the words of the missionary. A chapel was built on the shore of the lake, and the mission of the Holy Spirit was founded. The fame of the missionary spread far to the west and north, and the tribes dwelling north of Lake Superior, the Pottawatomies from Lake Michigan, who worshipped the sun, and the Sioux and the Illinois from the distant prairies of the west, came to the mission to hear the teachings of the missionary. They told him of their country, an unbroken expanse of level land, without trees, but covered with long, rich grass, upon which grazed innumerable herds of buffalo and deer; of the rice which grew wild in their distant homes; of the rich yield of maize which their fields produced, of the copper mines of which they but dimly comprehended the value, and of the great river which flowed through their country from the far north to the unknown regions of the south, and which Allouez understood them to call the "Messipi." After remaining at his mission for two years Allouez returned to Quebec to ask for other laborers in the great field around him, and to urge the French to establish permanent settlements of emigrants or traders in the Lake Superior country. He remained at Quebec two days, was given an assistant, and at once returned to his post, where he continued his labors for many years. "During his long sojourn he lighted the torch of faith for more than twenty different nations."

In 1668 the French West India Company, under whose auspices the settlement of Canada had been conducted, relinquished their monopoly of the fur-trade, and a great improvement in the condition and prospects of Canada ensued. In the same year Fathers Claude Dablon and James Marquette established the mission of Ste-Marie at the rapids through which the waters of Lake Superior rush into those of Huron. "For the succeeding years," says Bancroft, "the illustrious triumvirate, Allouez, Dablon, and Marquette, were employed in confirming the influence of

France in the vast regions that extend from Green bay to the head of Lake Superior, mingling happiness with suffering, and winning enduring glory by their fearless perseverance."

In 1669 Father Allouez went to establish a mission at Green bay, and Father Marquette took his place at the mission of the Holy Spirit. Marquette had heard so much of the Mississippi that he resolved to undertake the discovery of the upper waters of that stream. He employed a young Illinois warrior as his companion, and from him learned the dialect of that tribe. In 1673, accompanied by a fellow-priest named Joliet, five French boatmen, and some Indian guides and interpreters, bearing their canoes on their backs, Marquette set out from his mission, and crossing the narrow portage which divides the Fox river from the Wisconsin, reached the headwaters of the latter stream. There the guides left them, wondering at their rashness in seeking to venture into a region which the simple imagination of the savages filled with vague terrors. The adventurers floated down the Wisconsin, and in seven days entered the Mississippi, "with a joy that could not be expressed." Raising the sails of their canoes they glided down the mighty father of waters, gazing with wonder upon the magnificent forests which lined its shores, and which swarmed with game, and admiring the boundless prairies which stretched away from either bank to the horizon.

One hundred and eighty miles below the mouth of the Wisconsin the voyagers for the first time discovered signs of human beings. They landed, and found an Indian village a few miles distant from the river. They were kindly received by the inhabitants, who spoke the language of the Indians who had come with Marquette, and a week was passed at this hospitable village. The villagers told the travellers that the lower river extended far to the south, where the heat was deadly, and that in those latitudes the stream abounded with monsters which destroyed both men and canoes. At the departure of the whites the chief of the tribe hung around Marquette's neck the peace-pipe, and explained to him that it would prove a safeguard to him among the tribes into whose territory his journey would lead him.

Continuing their voyage the explorers reached the mouth of the Missouri, and noticed the strong, muddy stream which it poured into the Mississippi. "When I return," said Marquette, "I will ascend that river and pass beyond its headwaters, and proclaim the gospel." One hundred and twenty miles farther south they passed the mouth of the Ohio, of which river they had heard from the Illinois at the village they had visited. As they proceeded further south the heat became more intense, for it was the month of July. They met with Indians, whose hostility was disarmed by the peace-pipe which Marquette bore. Some of these Indians were armed with axes of European manufacture, which they had obtained either from the Spaniards in the far south, or from the English in Virginia. The voyage was continued to the mouth of the Arkansas. Marquette was now satisfied that the great river flowed into the Gulf of Mexico, and as he was fearful of falling into the hands of the Spaniards in that region he decided to bring his voyage to an end, and return to the lakes. The task of ascending the river was accomplished with great difficulty, and at length the mouth of the Illinois was reached. As they supposed this stream would lead them to the lakes the voyagers

ALTON, ILL.

ascended it to its headwaters, and then crossed the country to the site of Chicago, from which they continued the voyage by way of Lake Michigan to Green bay.

Marquette despatched Joliet to Quebec to report the results of the voyage, but himself remained at Green bay. It was his purpose to preach the gospel among the Illinois, who had begged him during his voyage to come back to them. He was detained at Green bay for some time by feeble health, but in 1675 went back to the Illinois, and began his labors among them. Feeling that his end was near he undertook to return to the mission of St. Mary's, but fell ill on the way. He gave absolution to all his companions, and retired to pray. An hour afterwards, uneasy at his absence, his people went to seek him, and found him kneeling, but praying no longer, for his spirit had gone to receive its reward. He was buried on the banks of the river that bears his name, and his memory was long cherished with affection by the Indians.

The work of exploration which Marquette had begun was taken up by a bolder and firmer hand. Robert Cavalier de la Salle, a man of good family, had been educated for the service of the Jesuits, but had abandoned his design of entering that order after completing his education. In 1667 he had emigrated to Canada to seek his fortune, and had established himself as a fur-trader on Lake Ontario. Encouraged by the governor of Canada he had explored Lake Ontario, and had ascended to Lake Erie. When the French governor a few years later built Fort Frontenac to guard the outlet of Lake Ontario, La Salle was granted an extensive domain, including Fort Frontenac, now the town of Kingston, on condition that he would maintain the fort. He thus obtained the monopoly of the fur-trade with the Five Nations. Here he was residing at the time of the death of Marquette.

The news of Marquette's discoveries filled him with the deepest interest, and he was eager to continue the exploration of the river at the point at which Marquette had discontinued it, and to trace it to its mouth. He was already on the road to fortune, but the prospect of winning greater fame was too tempting to be resisted, and leaving his possessions on Lake Ontario, he sailed for France and laid before Colbert, the minister, the schemes he had formed for the exploration and colonization of the valley of the Mississippi. He obtained a grant of valuable privileges and received permission to attempt the task of adding that vast region to the dominions of France. He returned to Fort Frontenac in the autumn of 1678, bringing with him as his lieutenant an Italian veteran named Tonti and a number of mechanics and seamen, together with the materials for rigging a ship. Before the winter had set in he ascended Lake Ontario to the Niagara river, where he built a trading-post. Then passing around the falls, he constructed a vessel of sixty tons at the foot of Lake Erie. Tonti and Father Hennepin, a Franciscan, went among the Senecas during the construction of the ship and established friendly relations with them, and La Salle exerted himself to procure furs with which to freight his vessel. The vessel completed, he ascended Lake Erie, passed through the straits into Lakes Huron and Michigan, and entered Green bay. Then loading his vessel with a cargo of valuable furs, he sent her to the Niagara, with orders to return with supplies as soon as possible. During her absence La Salle and his companions ascended Lake Michigan in canoes as far as the mouth of the St Joseph's, where they built a fort. Then crossing over to the valley of the Illinois, he built a fort on a bluff near the site of Peoria, and awaited the return of the "Griffin." The vessel had been wrecked on the voyage to Niagara, and when it became evident that she would not return, La Salle named his fort Crèvecœur ("Heartbreak").

Supplies were necessary to the exploration of the Mississippi, and La Salle being determined to obtain them, took with him three companions and crossed the wilderness to Fort Frontenac, which he reached in the spring of 1680. During his absence Father Hennepin, by his orders,

FALLS OF ST. ANTHONY.

explored the upper Mississippi as far as the falls, which he named in honor of St. Anthony, the patron saint of the expedition. In the summer of 1680 La Salle returned to the Illinois, but various causes intervening to delay him, he was not able to undertake his exploration of the Mississippi until 1682. In that year he built a barge on the upper Illinois, and embarking with his companions, floated down that stream to the Mississippi, which he descended to the Gulf of Mexico. He named the country along the banks of the river LOUISIANA, in honor of Louis XIV., King of France. Then ascending the Mississippi, he returned by the lakes to Quebec, and in 1683 sailed for France to enlist the government and people in his project for colonizing the country along the lower Mississippi

His design was encouraged by the king, and emigrants were readily found. In 1684 he sailed from France with four ships and two hundred and eighty persons to plant a colony at the mouth of the Mississippi Unhappily the commander of the fleet was not in sympathy with La Salle, and being jealous of his authority, manifested a degree of stubbornness which was fatal to the expedition One hundred of the colonists were soldiers, of the rest, some were volunteers, some mechanics, some women, and some priests. After a long voyage they entered the Gulf of Mexico in January, 1685. They sailed past the mouth of the Mississippi, and when La Salle perceived his error, Beaujeu, the commander of the fleet, refused to return, but continued his western course until the bay of Matagorda was reached There La Salle, weary of his disputes with Beaujeu, resolved to land, hoping that he might yet find the mouth of the Mississippi A careless pilot, in attempting to get the store-ship into the harbor, wrecked her, and all the supplies which Louis XIV had provided with a lavish hand were lost

The colony, which was named Fort St. Louis, was from the first doomed to misfortune, and in a little more than two years was reduced by disease and suffering to thirty-six persons In January, 1687, La Salle, leaving twenty men at Fort St. Louis, set out with sixteen men to march across the continent to Canada to obtain aid for the settlement. His remarkable courage and determination would doubtless have accomplished this feat, but on the way he was murdered by two of his men, who regarded him as the author of their sufferings. Of the rest of his companions, five who kept together reached a small French post near the mouth of the Arkansas, after a journey of six months The twenty men left at Fort St. Louis were never heard of again The effort to colonize Texas completely failed, and all that was accomplished by La Salle's enterprise was the establishment of the claim of France to this region

To La Salle is due the credit of having been the first to comprehend the importance of securing to France the great region watered by the Mississippi and its tributaries, and it was through his efforts that the attention of France was seriously directed to its colonization. His remarkable qualities must always command the admiration and his sad fate elicit the sympathy of all generous hearts.

While La Salle was vainly striving to accomplish some good result with the Texas colony, his friend and lieutenant Tonti, in obedience to his instructions, started from the Illinois and descended the Mississippi almost to its mouth, hoping to meet him. At length, despairing of seeing him, Tonti engraved a cross and the arms of France upon a tree on the banks of the river, and returned to the Illinois.

In 1699, twelve years after the death of La Salle, another and this time a successful effort was made to secure Louisiana to France Lemoine d'Ibberville, a native of Canada and a man of ability and courage, resolved to plant a colony near the mouth of the Mississippi. With four vessels and two hundred emigrants, some of whom were women and children, he sailed from Canada for the mouth of the Mississippi. He landed at the mouth of the river Pascagoula, and with two barges manned by forty-eight men searched the coast for the mouth of the Mississippi He found it and ascended as high as the mouth of the Red river. Here he was met by the Indians, who, to his astonishment, gave him a letter which had been placed in their charge fourteen years before It was from Tonti, and was addressed to La Salle. He had given it to the Indians, and had charged them to deliver it to the first Frenchman they met. D'Ibberville returned to the gulf by way of Lakes Maurepas and Pontchartrain, which he named after two of the ministers of Louis XIV Deeming the shores of the Mississippi too marshy for colonization, D'Ibberville formed a settlement at Biloxi, at the mouth of the Pascagoula, within the limits of the present State of Mississippi, and soon afterwards sailed for France to obtain reinforcements and supplies, leaving one of his brothers, Sauville by name, as governor, and the other, Bienville, to explore the Mississippi and the country along its banks.

Early in 1700 D'Ibberville returned from France, and about the same time Tonti, La Salle's former lieutenant, now an aged man, arrived from the country of the Illinois Acting upon Tonti's advice, D'Ibberville ascended the Mississippi for four hundred miles, and on the site of the present city of Natchez built a fort which he named Rosalie, in honor of the Duchess of Pontchartrain Neither the settlement at Biloxi nor Rosalie prospered, however. The colonists were a shiftless set, and instead of seeking to cultivate the soil and establish homes for themselves, went farther west to seek for gold In 1702 D'Ibberville removed the colony from Biloxi to Mobile, which was founded in that year, and became the capital of Louisiana and the centre of the French influence in the south This settlement languished, however, and in ten years only two hundred emigrants were added to its population It was forced to depend upon the French colonies in the West Indies for subsistence.

In 1714 the French government, becoming convinced that it was necessary to make a more vigorous effort to colonize Louisiana if it meant to hold that country granted a monopoly of trade to Arthur

Crozat, who agreed to send over every year two ships laden with emigrants and supplies, and also a cargo of African slaves. The king, on his part, agreed to furnish the sum of ten thousand dollars annually for the protection of the colony. In the same year a trading-house was established at Natchitoches on the Red river, and another on the Alabama, near the present site of Montgomery. Fort Rosalie was made the centre of an important trade, and matters began to wear a new aspect in Louisiana. In 1718 Bienville, who had become satisfied of the propriety of removing the seat of government from Mobile to the more productive region of the lower Mississippi, put the convicts to work to clear up the thicket of cane which covered the site on which he meant to locate his

HUMBOLDT PALISADES, PACIFIC RAILWAY.

new city, and upon the ground thus prepared erected a few huts, the germ of the great city of *New Orleans.* It grew more rapidly than any of the settlements in Louisiana. In 1722 it contained about one hundred log huts, and a population of seven hundred. In 1723 the seat of government was removed from Mobile to New Orleans; and in 1727 the construction of the levee was begun.

While these efforts were in progress on the lower Mississippi the French were even more active in the west. Detroit was founded in 1701, and the villages of Kaskaskia and Cahokia were formed around the stations of the missionaries on the east bank of the Mississippi, above the mouth of the Ohio. The French population in America grew very slowly, however. In 1690 the population of Canada was only twelve hundred; that of Acadia, or Nova Scotia, less than one thousand; and that of Louisiana less than five hundred

France had formed a deliberate and magnificent plan with respect to her American possessions. She meant to build up a mighty empire in the valley of the Mississippi, extending from the great lakes to the Gulf of Mexico, and touching Canada Her efforts to accomplish this were lavish and persistent, but the unhealthiness of the climate and the almost constant wars with the Natchez and Chickasaw Indians disheartened the settlers, and the French population grew so slowly that it could not accomplish the destiny demanded of it by the government at home As late as 1740 Louisiana contained only about five thousand whites and less than two thousand five hundred negroes. The slow increase of the population made it necessary to hold the country by a series of military posts By the year 1750 more than sixty of these posts had been built between Lake Ontario and the Gulf of Mexico, by way of Green bay, the Illinois, the Wabash, and the Maumee rivers, and along the Mississippi to New Orleans. The most important of these forts were held by garrisons of regular troops, who were relieved once in six years. They accomplished this in the face of the constant hostility of their old enemies, the tribes of the Five Nations, and the Natchez and Chickasaws. In 1718 the French extended their claim to the country south of Lake Erie, as far east as the mountains, which they explored, and took formal possession of by burying at the most important points leaden plates engraved with the arms of France According to the ideas of the times their claim was a valid one.

In the meantime the settlements of Louisiana had been obliged to struggle against the constant hostility of the Natchez Indians, who occupied the country around the present city which bears their name. They were not very numerous, but were more intelligent and civilized than the tribes among whom they dwelt They worshipped the sun, from which deity their principal chief claimed to be descended They watched the growing power of the French with alarm, and at length resolved to put a stop to the progress of the whites by a general massacre. On the 28th of November, 1729, they fell upon the settlement at Fort Rosalie and massacred the garrison and settlers, seven hundred in number They were not long permitted to exult over their success When the news of the massacre reached New Orleans Bienville resolved to retaliate severely upon the aggressors He applied to the Choctaws, the hereditary enemies of the Natchez, for assistance, and was furnished by them with sixteen hundred warriors. With these and his own troops Bienville besieged the

Natchez in their fort; but they escaped under the cover of the night and fled west of the Mississippi. They were followed by the French and forced to surrender; after which they were taken to New Orleans and sent to St. Domingo, where they were sold as slaves. The Great Sun was among the captives, and the tribe of the Natchez was completely destroyed.

It was well known to the French that the Chickasaws, a powerful tribe dwelling between the territory of the Natchez and the Ohio on the north, and as far as the country of the Cherokees on the east, had incited the Natchez against them. Bienville therefore resolved to turn his arms against them. They had also given great trouble to the French by attacking and plundering their trading-boats descending the Mississippi from the posts on the Illinois. Bienville concerted measures for a combined attack upon the Chickasaws with D'Artaguette, governor of the Illinois country, and two expeditions were despatched against the Indians. Bienville, with a strong force of French troops and twelve hundred Choctaw warriors, sailed in boats from New Orleans to Mobile and ascended the Tombigbee five hundred miles, to the place now known as Cotton Gin Point. He landed here and marched twenty-five miles overland to the principal fort of the Chickasaws, which he at once attacked. He was repulsed with the loss of one hundred men, and was so discouraged that he returned to New Orleans. D'Artaguette entered the Chickasaw country with fifty Frenchmen and one thousand Indians. He was defeated and taken prisoner, and was burned at the stake in May, 1735. In 1740 another effort was made by the French to crush the Chickasaws, but was equally unsuccessful.

CHAPTER XXI.

THE ENGLISH AND FRENCH COME IN CONFLICT.

THE territory of the Five Nations lay between the English and French colonies. The friendship which these tribes had borne to the Dutch was transferred to the English upon the conquest of New Netherlands by the latter, and they remained the faithful and devoted allies of Great Britain until after the Revolution. Though they remained at peace with the French for some years after the treaty which has been mentioned in the preceding chapter, they regarded a renewal of hostilities with them as certain, and were on the whole anxious to resume the struggle at the earliest moment. James II., eager to establish the Roman Catholic religion in America, instructed the governor of New York to cultivate friendly relations with the French, and to exert all his influence to induce the Five Nations to receive Jesuit missionaries. The governor, however, saw that the French were rapidly monopolizing the fur-trade, and he encouraged the Five Nations to regard them with suspicion and dislike. The French by their own bad treatment of the Mohawks put an end to the hope of a lasting peace with them.

Upon the escape of James II. to France, Louis XIV. warmly espoused the cause of the dethroned king, which he declared was the cause of legitimate monarchy as opposed to the right of the people to self-government, and the war which was thus begun in Europe spread to the possessions of the rival powers in America. The objects of the two parties in America were very different. That of the people of New England, who were principally interested in the struggle, was to secure their northern frontier against invasion from Canada, and to get possession of the

319

fisheries. The French, on the other hand, wished to obtain entire control of the valley of the Mississippi, which would make them sole masters of the fur-trade, and to extend their power over the valley of the St. Lawrence, and thus obtain control of the fisheries also. To accomplish their first object the friendship of the Indian tribes in the valley of the Mississippi was indispensable, and they exerted every means of which they were possessed to gain it. They renewed their efforts to win over the Five Nations, but without success. The war between these tribes and the French was soon renewed, as has been related, and on the 25th of August, 1689, a band of fifteen hundred Mohawk warriors surprised and captured Montreal, and put two hundred of the inhabitants to death with horrible cruelty. An equal number of whites were made prisoners.

BURNING OF DOVER.

In the same year Count Frontenac was appointed governor of Canada for the second time. He came resolved to break the power of the English, and reached Canada just in time to hear of the capture of Montreal. He at once set to work to incite the Indians to a series of incursions against the English settlements which should thoroughly establish his influence over the savage warriors, who would obey none but a successful chief, and at the same time strike terror to the enemies of France. The first blow was struck at Dover, in New Hampshire. The commander of the garrison at this place was Major Richard Waldron. Thirteen years before, during King Philip's war, two hundred Eastern Indians came to Dover to treat of peace. Waldron treacherously seized them and sent them to Boston, where some of them were hanged and the remainder sold into slavery The savages had neither forgotten nor forgiven the wrongs of their brothers, and now they resolved to meet the whites with their own weapons of deceit and treachery.

On the evening of the 27th of June, 1689, two Indian squaws came to Dover and asked for a night's lodging Waldron, now an old man of eighty, was unsuspicious of harm. Their request was granted, and the squaws were lodged in his house. In the dead of the night the women arose, unbarred the gates, and admitted the warriors who had lain in ambush near the town Waldron's house was first entered, the first duty of the savages being to discharge their debt of vengeance. The brave old man seized his sword and defended himself until he was felled to the floor by a blow which stunned him. He was then seated in a chair and placed on a table, and the savages saluted him with jeers "Who will judge Indians now?" they asked. "Who will hang our brothers? Will the pale face Waldron give us life for life?" As they spoke they gashed him across the breast with their knives, inflicting wounds equal in number to their friends whom he had betrayed. The old man bore his tortures firmly until he died, the Indians then set fire to the house and burned the rest of the settlement. Nearly half the inhabitants were murdered, and the remainder were carried into captivity.

The other frontier towns suffered severely from Maine to New York. A band of French and Indians, in February, 1690, toiled across the wilderness from Montreal to central New York on snow-shoes, and surprised Schenectady. The place was burned, the majority of the settlers were killed, and many women and children were carried into captivity. A few escaped through the snow to Albany. Deerfield and Haverhill in Massachusetts, Salmon Falls in New Hampshire, and Casco in Maine met a similar fate. The French had resolved to make the war one of extermination, and neither they nor their savage allies showed any mercy to the English in their hour of triumph.

The savages were incited to their bloody task by the Jesuit missionaries. The first race of missionaries, whose good deeds we have chronicled in the last chapter, had died out, and their successors could conceive of no higher standard of duty than the extermination of the English heretics. They roused the fury of their dusky converts against the English as the enemies of the Roman religion, and then, confessing and absolving the savage warriors, sent them forth to murder and destroy, with the solemn assurance that such acts on their part would win them the favor of their Father in heaven When peace was made two Jesuit priests, Thury and Bigot, induced the Eastern Indians to break the treaty and renew the war, and even took pride in acknowledging themselves the instigators of the atrocities of the savages These things were well understood among the English, and they came to regard the Jesuit missionaries as the enemies of mankind Menaced by the French and Indians on the frontiers, the English Protestants may be excused for regarding with suspicion the Roman Catholics of Maryland So deep was the horror which the work of the Jesuits aroused, that even in Rhode Island, the home of perfect toleration, it was enacted that a Roman Catholic should not become a freeman of the province

In May, 1690, a congress of delegates from Massachusetts, Connecticut, and New York was held at New York for the purpose of concerting a plan for an invasion of Canada. It was resolved to send an army against Montreal by way of Lake Champlain, while Massachusetts should despatch a fleet to attack Quebec The first expedition, composed of the troops of New York and Connecticut, advanced to Lake Champlain, attended by a strong force of Mohawk allies Frontenac promptly assembled his French and Indians for the defence of Montreal, and succeeded in inflicting a sharp defeat upon the Mohawks, under Colonel Philip Schuyler, who led the advance of the English army. The Mohawks were unable to regain their lost ground, and the provincial troops were delayed by the dissensions of their leaders until the provisions ran short and the small-pox broke out among the men. It then became necessary to abandon the attempt.

In the meantime Massachusetts equipped a fleet of thirty-two vessels and two thousand men, and despatched it to the St Lawrence under the command of the governor, Sir William Phipps, whose incompetency produced the failure of the expedition. Frontenac was promptly informed of the departure of the fleet by an Indian runner from the Piscataqua, who reached Montreal in twelve days. Frontenac at once set out for Quebec, and arrived there three days in advance of the English fleet, which was obliged to feel its way cautiously up the St. Lawrence. When the hostile vessels arrived off the city, Quebec was prepared to offer a determined resistance. After a few harmless demonstrations, Sir William Phipps withdrew and returned to Boston, to the great disappointment of the colony A large debt had been incurred in this enterprise and a number of valuable lives had been lost, but nothing had been gained.

The Eastern Indians continued their aggressions, but were severely punished by Captain Samuel Church, who had served with distinction in King Philip's war. On one occasion he was so exasperated by the cruelties of the savages that he put a number of his prisoners, including some women and children, to death. The savages mercilessly avenged the murder of their friends, and carried death and desolation along the bor-

21

ders of New England   Nearly every settlement in Maine was destroyed
by them or abandoned by the inhabitants, who fled to the other colonies
for protection. The Indians prowled around the frontier posts They
had been well armed by the French, and shot down the men without
mercy. The women and children were generally spared and carried to
Canada, where they were sold to the French as slaves In 1693 peace
was made with the Abenakis, or Eastern Indians, but within a year the
Jesuits had succeeded in inducing the savages to resume hostilities.

A party of Indians attacked the house of a farmer named Dustin,
residing near Haverhill. He was at work in the field when the shouts
of the savages warned him of the danger of his wife and children
Throwing himself on his horse, he hastened to their rescue, and on the
way met his children flying for safety pursued by the savages. He threw
himself in front of the little ones, and by a few well-aimed shots kept the
pursuers back until the children reached a place of safety. Hannah
Dustin, her youngest child—only a few days old—her nurse, and a boy
from Worcester, unable to fly, were made prisoners by the Indians The
little one was killed, and the two women and the boy were carried away
by the savages to their village situated on an island in the Merrimac,
just above Concord. Hannah Dustin resolved to escape, and communicated her plan to her companions Each secured a tomahawk, and at
night began the destruction of their captors, twelve in number Ten
Indians were killed and one squaw was wounded. The twelfth, a child,
was purposely spared. Then collecting the gun and tomahawk of the
murderer of her infant, and a bag-full of scalps, the heroic woman
secured a canoe, and embarking in it with her companions, floated down
the Merrimac and soon reached Haverhill, where they were received with
astonishment and delight by their friends.

This struggle, which is known in American history as *King William's
War*, was brought to a close in September, 1697, by the Peace of Ryswick. It had lasted seven years, and had caused severe suffering to the
northern colonies, without yielding them any compensating advantages.

The Five Nations were also severe sufferers Failing to win them
from their alliance with the English, Frontenac several times invaded
their country with an army of French troops and Indians, and ravaged
it with great cruelty. Frontenac led these expeditions in person, though
he was seventy-four years old.

The people of New York, regarding the Jesuits as the true authors of
the miseries endured by the English and their allies, enacted a law in
1700, that every Romish priest who voluntarily came into the province
should be hanged.

Five years after the Peace of Ryswick, the War of the Spanish Succession, or, as it is known in American history, *Queen Anne's War*, began in Europe. It soon extended to America, and embroiled the English and French in this country. The English settlements on the western frontier of New England were almost annihilated by the Indians, and the French were unusually active.

The people of Deerfield were warned by the friendly Mohawks that

BURNING OF DEERFIELD, MASS.

the French and Indians were meditating an attack upon their settlement, and through the winter of 1703–4 a vigilant watch was kept by night and day. The winter was very severe; the snow lay four feet deep, and the clear, cold atmosphere made it almost as hard as ice. Profiting by this, a war party of about two hundred French and one hundred and forty-two Indians, under the command of Hertel de Rouville, set out from Canada, and by the aid of snow-shoes crossed the country on the snow and reached the vicinity of Deerfield on the last night of February, 1701. Towards daybreak on the 1st of March the sentinels, supposing that all was safe, left their posts at Deerfield, and the enemy at once silently mounted on the snow-drifts to the top of the palisades and entered the enclosure, which had an area of twenty acres   A general massacre followed   The town was destroyed, forty persons were killed, and one hundred and twelve were carried away into Canada.

Among the captives were the minister Williams, his wife Eunice, and their five children   The sufferings of the prisoners on the march to Canada were fearful   Two men starved to death   The infant whose cries disturbed the captors was tossed out into the snow to die; and the mother who faltered from fatigue or anguish was despatched by a blow from the tomahawk   Eunice Williams had brought her Bible along with her, and in the brief intervals afforded by the halts of the savages for rest, drew from its sacred pages the consolations she so sorely needed. Her strength soon failed, as she had but recently recovered from her confinement   Her husband sought to cheer her by pointing her to "the house not made with hands," and she assured him that she was satisfied to endure any suffering, counting it gain for Christ's sake.   Perceiving that her end was near, she commended her children to God and to their father's care, and was immediately killed by the savages, as she could go no farther.   The Williams family were taken to Canada, and a few years later were ransomed, with the exception of the youngest daughter, with whom the savages refused to part.   She was adopted into a village of Christian Indians near Montreal, and became a convert to the Roman Catholic faith, and subsequently married a Mohawk chief   Years afterwards she appeared at Deerfield clad in the dress of her tribe.   She had come to visit her relatives, but no entreaties could induce her to remain with them, and she went back to her adopted people and to her children.

The war was conducted with brutal ferocity by the French   Hertel de Rouville gained eternal infamy by his butcheries of helpless women and children.   Vaudreuil, the governor of Canada, urged on his forces to deeds of fresh atrocity, but at length the savages became disgusted with their bloody work and refused to murder any more English.   The French succeeded, however, in inducing some of them to continue their assistance, and in 1708 Haverhill was surprised by the French and Indians under Rouville, and its inhabitants massacred with the most fiendish cruelty.   None of them escaped death or captivity.   Filled with horror and indignation, Colonel Peter Schuyler, of New York, wrote to the Marquis de Vaudreuil: "I hold it my duty towards God and my neighbor, to prevent, if possible, these barbarous and heathen cruelties. My heart swells with indignation when I think that a war between Christian princes, bound to the exactest laws of honor and generosity, which their noble ancestors have illustrated by brilliant examples, is degenerating into a savage and boundless butchery. These are not the methods for terminating the war."

"Such fruitless cruelties," says Bancroft, "inspired our fathers with a deep hatred of the French missionaries; they compelled the employment of a large part of the inhabitants as soldiers, so that there was one year

RETURN OF THE DAUGHTER OF EUNICE WILLIAMS TO THE INDIANS.

during this war when even a fifth part of all who were capable of bearing arms were in active service. They gave birth also to a willingness to exterminate the natives. The Indians vanished when their homes were invaded; they could not be reduced by usual methods of warfare; hence a bounty was offered for every Indian scalp; to regular forces under pay the grant was ten pounds—to volunteers in actual service, twice that sum; but if men would, of themselves, without pay make up parties and patrol the forests in search of Indians, as of old the woods were scoured for wild beasts, the chase was invigorated by the promised 'encouragement of fifty pounds per scalp.'"

In 1707 Massachusetts, New Hampshire, and Rhode Island made a combined attempt to conquer Acadia. A fleet was despatched against Port Royal, but without success. In 1710 a second expedition was sent from Boston against Port Royal, aided this time by an English fleet. Port Royal was taken, the French were driven out of the greater part of Acadia, and that province was annexed to the English dominions and called Nova Scotia. The name of Port Royal was changed to Annapolis, in honor of the Queen of England.

Encouraged by this success, the English government the next year attempted the conquest of Canada by two expeditions, one by land and the other by sea. A powerful fleet and a strong army was despatched from England to cooperate with the colonists. The effort was unsuccessful. The fleet, which was badly handled by the admiral in attempting to ascend the St Lawrence, was wrecked with the loss of eight vessels and eight hundred and eighty-four men, and was obliged to return to Boston. The failure of the fleet to accomplish anything compelled the abandonment of the land expedition against Montreal. In 1713 the war was brought to an end by the treaty of Utrecht, by which Acadia was ceded permanently to Great Britain, and became a province of the English crown.

After the close of Queen Anne's war the colonies remained at peace for nearly thirty years, during which time they were molested by neither French nor Indians. In 1744 the disputes in Europe concerning the succession to the Austrian throne culminated in a war, which is known in European history as the war of the Austrian succession, and in America as King George's war. As usual, England and France were arrayed on opposite sides, and their colonies in America soon became involved in hostilities. The French were the first to receive information from Europe of the existence of war, and began the struggle by attacking and capturing the English fort at Canso and carrying the garrison prisoners to Louisburg.

Louisburg, the principal port of the island of Cape Breton, was at this time the strongest fortress in America, and from its secure harbor the French were constantly despatching privateers against the merchant vessels and fishermen of New England. These depredations caused such serious loss to the eastern colonies that at length Governor Shirley proposed to the general court of Massachusetts to undertake the capture of Louisburg as the only means of putting a stop to them, and this measure was laid by the general court before the other colonies. It was understood that no aid was to be expected from the mother country, which was too busy   colonies would be obliged to depend entirely upon their own resources for their success. Nevertheless, the measure was popular, and the enthusiasm of the colonists was aroused to the highest point. Nearly all the northern colonies had suffered severely at the hands of the French and Indians, and in every shipping port were to be found scores of men who had been robbed and otherwise maltreated by the French privateers. Pennsylvania and New Jersey, under the influence of the Quaker dislike of war, declined to send troops, but furnished a fair supply of money to defray their share of the expenses of the expedition; New York made a contribution of money and of a number of pieces of artillery, Connecticut gave five hundred men, and New Hampshire and Rhode Island each contributed a regiment. Massachusetts, being the most interested in the success of the expedition by reason of being the largest owner of shipping, undertook the principal part of the expense and agreed to furnish a majority of the troops and the vessels. There was no difficulty in procuring volunteers, but those who offered themselves were civilians, ignorant of military discipline, and utterly unprepared to attempt the reduction of such a fortress as that against which the expedition was directed. These disadvantages, however, were lost sight of in the enthusiasm aroused by the hope of destroying the ability of the French to prey upon the commerce of the colonies. Sir William Pepperell, a wealthy merchant of Maine, was elected commander of the expedition, which rendezvoused at Boston in the early spring of 1745. One hundred vessels and a force of over three thousand men were assembled, and about the 1st of April sailed for Canso, which was reached on the 7th. The ice was drifting in such quantities that the fleet could not enter the harbor of Louisburg, and was obliged to remain at Canso for more than two weeks. Admiral Warren, commanding the West India squadron, had been invited to join the expedition, but in the absence of instructions from England had declined to do so. Almost immediately afterwards he received orders from home to render Massachusetts every aid in his power, and at once joined the New England fleet at Canso with four ships of war and a detachment of regular troops.

At length, the ice having moved southward, the New England fleet entered the harbor of Louisburg on the 30th of April. The fortress was built on a neck of land on the south side of the harbor, and its walls were from twenty to thirty feet high and forty feet thick at the base, and were surrounded with a ditch eighty feet in width. Outlying forts protected the main work, and there was not a foot of the walls that was not swept by the fire of the artillery. Nearly two hundred and fifty cannon of all sizes constituted the armament of the fortress, and the principal

outwork, the "royal battery," was deemed capable of withstanding an
attack of five thousand men. The garrison numbered sixteen hundred
men. To attack this fortress the New England troops brought with
them eighteen cannon and three mortars.

As the fleet drew near the town the French marched down to the beach
to oppose the landing of the troops. Immediately the whale-boats of
the ships were lowered and manned, and at a signal from the flagship
darted for the shore with a speed which astonished and struck terror to
the French, who were quickly driven to the woods. The landing was
secured, and the next day a detachment of four hundred men marched
by the town, giving it three cheers as they passed, and took position near
the northeast harbor, completely cutting off the fortress from communication with the country in its rear. This completed the investment, as
the fleet closed the harbor, and prevented the approach of relief by sea.
That night the troops in the royal battery spiked the guns of that work,
abandoned it, and retreated into the town. It was immediately occupied
by the New Englanders, who drilled the spikes out of the vent-holes of
the guns, and turned them against the town. Batteries were erected by
the colonial troops, and their fire opened upon Louisburg. The volunteers proved admirable soldiers, exciting the surprise of the English
naval officers by the readiness and facility with which they discharged the
various duties required of them. Numbers of them were mechanics by
profession, and their skill was of the greatest service in this emergency.
A New Hampshire colonel, who was a carpenter, constructed sledges with
which to drag the artillery across a morass to the positions assigned the
batteries. The weather was mild and singularly dry, and the men were
healthy. "All day long the men, if not on duty, were busy with amusements—firing at marks, fishing, fowling, wrestling, racing, or running
after balls shot from the enemy's guns."

In the meantime the ships of Admiral Warren blockaded the harbor,
and not only prevented French vessels from entering the port, but succeeded in decoying into the midst of the English fleet the French frigate
"Vigilante" of sixty guns, which was captured after a sharp engagement
of several hours. She was loaded with stores for the fortress, and these
fell into the hands of the victors.

The French commander, who had shown but little energy during the
siege, was now so thoroughly disheartened that on the 17th of June, just
seven weeks after the commencement of the investment, he surrendered
the town and fortifications. As the colonial troops entered the place to
take possession of it they were astonished at the strength of the works.
"God has gone out of the way of his common providence in a remark-

able and miraculous manner," they said, " to incline the hearts of the French to give up, and deliver this strong city into our hands " The capture of Louisburg by the undisciplined volunteers of America was the greatest success achieved by England during the war The colonists were justly proud of it. Bells were rung and bonfires lighted in all the colonies, and the people rejoiced greatly at the success of their brethren and friends. England with characteristic selfishness claimed the glory exclusively for the squadron of Admiral Warren

France was greatly alarmed at the capture of Louisburg, which seriously threatened her dominion in America, and measures were at once begun for its recovery, and for the destruction of the English colonies. In 1746 a large fleet was despatched to America under the Duke d'Anville, but many of the vessels were lost at sea, and the fleet was greatly weakened by pestilence. In the midst of these misfortunes the Duke d'Anville suddenly died, and his successor lost his mind, and committed suicide. The expedition made no serious demonstration against the English, and resulted in total failure. In 1747 another fleet was sent out from France for the same purpose, but was captured after a severe fight by an English fleet under Admirals Anson and Warren

In spite of these successes, however, the frontiers of the northern colonies suffered considerably, and the English government resolved to attempt once more the conquest of Canada. All the colonies were required to furnish men or money to this enterprise, and eight thousand men were enlisted The British government delayed, however, and finally abandoned the enterprise. On the 18th of October, 1748, the treaty of Aix-la-Chapelle closed the war The treaty required that all places taken by either party during the war should be restored, and Louisburg was delivered up to the French, to the great disgust of the New England colonies, who saw all the results of their sacrifices thrown away, and their commerce and fisheries once more placed at the mercy of the French England had never regarded the interests of her colonies as worth considering, however, and it was not to be expected that she should manifest any concern for them now.

It was commonly believed in America, and with good reason, that the king did not desire that New England should enjoy the security necessary to her prosperity His majesty was beginning to be jealous of his American subjects, who had, as Admiral Warren expressed it, " the highest notion of the rights and liberties of an Englishman," and he was resolved to keep them so weak that they should not forget their dependence upon him. Peter Kalm, a Swedish traveller, who visited New York in 1748, thus records the prevailing sentiment in America at this period " The

English colonies in this part of the world have increased so much in wealth and population that they will vie with European England   But to maintain the commerce and the power of the metropolis they are forbid to establish new manufactures, which might compete with the English; they may dig for gold and silver only on condition of shipping them immediately to England; they have, with the exception of a few fixed places, no liberty to trade to any ports not belonging to the English dominions, and foreigners are not allowed the least commerce with these American colonies. And there are many similar restrictions   These oppressions have made the inhabitants of the English colonies less tender to their mother land   This coldness is increased by the many foreigners who are settled among them; for Dutch, Germans, and French are here blended with English, and have no special love for old England. Besides, some people are always discontented, and love change, and exceeding freedom and prosperity nurse an untamable spirit. I have been told not only by native Americans, but by English emigrants, publicly, that within thirty or fifty years the English colonies in North America may constitute a separate state entirely independent of England. But as this whole country is towards the sea unguarded, and on the frontier is kept uneasy by the French, these dangerous neighbors are the reason why the love of these colonies for their metropolis does not utterly decline   The English government has, therefore, reason to regard the French in North America as the chief power that urges their colonies to submission."

The war not only served to confirm the hostility of the Americans to France, but it also aided in opening the eyes of some of the most sceptical of the colonists as to the deliberate intention of the mother country to persist in the injustice with which she had for so long treated her colonies. Great Britain was slowly but surely alienating her American subjects, and was preparing them in the most certain manner for the great effort they were shortly to make to rid themselves of her tyranny.

During the last year of the war an incident occurred at Boston which might have opened the eyes of the ministry to the growing determination of the Americans to resist any interference with their liberties. Desertions from the English ships-of-war in Boston harbor had become so frequent that Sir Charles Knowles, the commanding officer, sent his boats up to Boston one morning and seized a number of seamen in the vessels at the wharves, and a number of mechanics and laborers engaged in work on shore. The people of Boston indignantly demanded of the governor the release of the impressed men   As his excellency declined to interfere in the matter the people seized the commanders and officers of the s.... prisoners until the ....

CHAPTER XXII.

THE FRENCH AND INDIAN WAR

THE three wars between the English and French in America which we have just considered were but a prelude to the great struggle which was to decide which of these powers should control the destinies of the new world. The English, as we have seen, were growing stronger and more numerous along the Atlantic coast, and were directing their new settlements farther into the interior with each succeeding year. The French held Canada and the valley of the Mississippi, but their tenure was that of a military occupation rather than a colonization.

Between the possessions of these hostile nations lay the valley of the Ohio, a beautiful and fertile region, claimed by both, but occupied as yet by neither. The French had explored the country, and had caused leaden plates engraved with the arms of France to be deposited at its principal points to attest their claim; and had opened friendly relations with the Indians. The region had been frequently visited by the traders, who brought back reports of its remarkable beauty and fertility and of its excellent climate. The British government regarded this region as a portion of Virginia, and one of the chief desires of the Earl of Halifax, the prime minister of England, was to secure the Ohio valley by planting an English colony in it. A company was organized in Virginia and

I

Maryland for this purpose and for the purpose of trading with the Indians, and was warmly supported by the Earl of Halifax. It was named the Ohio Company, and at length succeeded in obtaining a favorable charter from the king, who, in March, 1749, ordered the governor of Virginia to assign to the Ohio Company five hundred thousand acres of land lying between the Monongahela and Kanawha rivers, and along the Ohio. The company were required to despatch within seven years at least one hundred families to the territory granted them, to locate without delay at least two-fifths of the lands they desired to occupy, and to build and garrison a fort at their own cost They were granted an exemption from quit rents and other dues for ten years, and this freedom from taxation was extended by the company to all who would settle in their domain.

A number of Indian traders had located themselves west of the Alleghanies, and in order to supply these with the articles needed for their traffic with the Indians, the Ohio Company built a trading-post at Wills' creek, within the limits of Maryland, on the site of the present city of Cumberland Here one of the easiest of the passes over the Alleghanies began, and by means of it the traders could easily transport their goods to the Indian country west of the mountains and return with the furs then traffic enabled them to collect

Being anxious to explore the country west of the mountains, the company employed Christopher Gist, one of the most experienced Indian traders, and instructed him " to examine the western country as far as the falls of the Ohio, to look for a large tract of good level land, to mark the passes in the mountains, to trace the courses of the rivers, to count the falls, to observe the strength and numbers of the Indian nations "

Gist set out on his perilous mission on the last day of October, 1750, and crossing the mountains reached the Delaware towns on the Alleghany river, from which he passed down to Log-town, a short distance below the head of the Ohio. " You are come to settle the Indians' lands ; you shall never go home safe," said the jealous people, but in spite of their threats they suffered him to proceed without molestation. He traversed the country to the Muskingum and the Scioto, and then crossing the Ohio explored the Kentucky to its source, and returned to Wills' creek in safety. He reported that the region he had traversed merited all the praise that had been bestowed upon it, that it possessed a pleasant and healthy climate, and was a land of great beauty The soil was fertile and the streams abundant and excellent. The land was covered with a rich growth of the most valuable and beautiful trees, and abounded in small level districts and meadows covered with long grass and white clover, c   '   ' l. '' ' l.   ,nd l ' k. " l . ., . l , l . ds Wild turkeys and other game abounded, and the country offered every attraction to settlers who were willing to improve it Gist also reported that the agents of the French were actively engaged in seeking to induce the western tribes to make war upon the English and prevent them from obtaining a footing west of the mountains. The purposes of the English were well known to the French, who viewed them with alarm, as the successful occupation of the Ohio valley by the English would cut off the communication established by the French between Canada and the Mississippi. This the French were resolved to prevent at any cost. The Indians regarded both of the white nations as intruders in their country. They were willing to trade with both, but were averse to giving up their lands to either "If the French," said they, "take possession of the north side of the Ohio, and the English of the south, where is the Indian's land?"

The possession of the Ohio valley was thus of the highest importance to the French. Their fortified post of Fort Frontenac gave them the command of Lake Ontario, which they further secured by constructing armed vessels for the navigation of the lake. They retained their hold upon Lake Erie by strengthening Fort Niagara, which La Salle had built at the foot of that lake. They entered into treaties with the Shawnees, the Delawares, and other powerful tribes between the lake and the Ohio, and steadily pushed their way eastward towards the mountains. They began their advance into the valley of the Ohio by building a fort at Presque Isle, now the city of Erie, in Pennsylvania, another on French creek, on the site of the present town of Waterford, and a third on the site of the present town of Franklin, at the confluence of French creek with the Alleghany.

These rapid advances eastward alarmed the English government, which instructed the governor of Virginia to address a remonstrance to the French authorities and to warn them of the consequences which must result from their intrusion into the territory of the English. To do this it was necessary for the governor to despatch his communication to the nearest French post by the hands of some messenger of sufficient resolution to overcome the natural dangers of such an undertaking, and of sufficient intelligence to gain information respecting the designs and strength of the French ; and Governor Dinwiddie was somewhat at a loss to find such a person. Fortunately the man needed was at hand, and the attention of the governor being called to him, his excellency decided to intrust him with the delicate and dangerous mission.

The person selected for this task was a young man in the twenty-second year of his age, George Washington by name. He was a native of West-

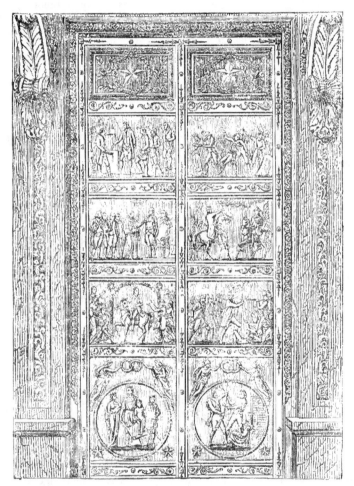

THE BRONZE DOOR IN THE NATIONAL CAPITOL COMMEMORATING THE EVENTS OF THE
LIFE OF GEORGE WASHINGTON.

moreland county, Virginia, where he was born on the 22d of February, 1732. He was a great-grandson of the Colonel John Washington whom we have noticed is the leader of an expedition against the Indians in the time of Sir William Berkeley. His father, Augustine Washington, was a wealthy planter, but his death, when George was eleven years old, deprived his son of his care and also of the means of acquiring an education. He soon acquired all the learning that it was possible to gain at a country school, from which he passed to an academy of somewhat higher grade, where he devoted himself principally to the study of mathematics. His half brother, Lawrence, who was fourteen years older than himself, had received a careful education and directed the studies of his younger brother, to whom he was devotedly attached.

Though deprived of the care of his father at such an early age it was the good fortune of George Washington to possess in his mother a guide well qualified to fill the place of both parents to her fatherless children. She was a woman of rare good sense, of great decision of character, and one whose life was guided by the most earnest Christian principle. Her tenderness and sweet womanly qualities won the devoted love of her children, and her firmness enforced their obedience. From her George inherited a quick and ardent temper, and from her he learned the lesson of self-control which enabled him to govern it.

As a boy, Washington was noted for his truthfulness, his courage, and his generosity. He was both liked and respected by his schoolmates, and such was their confidence in his fairness and good judgment that he was usually chosen the arbiter of their boyish disputes. He joined heartily in their sports, and was noted for his skill in athletic exercises. He was a fearless rider, and a good hunter, and by his fondness for manly sports developed his naturally vigorous body to a high degree of strength. He was cheerful and genial in temper, though reserved and grave in manner. He early acquired habits of industry and order, and there are still existing many evidences of the careful and systematic manner in which he discharged every duty assigned him at this early age.

At the age of fourteen it was decided that he should enter the navy, and his brother Lawrence, who had served with credit in that branch of the royal service, had no difficulty in obtaining for him a midshipman's warrant. The ship he was to join lay in the Potomac, and his trunk was sent on board; but at the last moment his mother, dreading the effect of the temptations of a seaman's life upon a boy so young, appealed to him by his affection for her to remain with her. Washington was sorely disappointed, but he yielded cheerfully to his mother's wish.

The marriage of his brother Lawrence gave to the young man a second home at Mount Vernon, where he passed a large part of his time. Here he was brought into constant contact with the most cultivated and refined society of Virginia, an association which had a happy influence upon the formation of his character. There also he formed the acquaintance and won the friendship of Lord Fairfax, the grandson of Lord Culpepper, and the inheritor of Culpepper's vast estates in Virginia, which comprised about one-seventh of the area of the State of Virginia as it existed prior to the separation of West Virginia in 1861. Lord Fairfax conceived a great fondness for the young man, and took a deep interest in his future welfare. Washington, upon leaving school, had chosen the profession of a surveyor as his future avocation, and soon after his first meeting with Lord Fairfax was employed by that nobleman to survey the lands belonging to him, many of which had been occupied by settlers without right or title. It was an arduous and responsible task, and Washington, who was just entering his seventeenth year, seemed almost too young for it; but "Lord Thomas" had satisfied himself of his young friend's capability for it, and the result justified the opinion he had formed. His work was done with care and accuracy, and his measurements were so exact that they are still relied upon.

His life as a surveyor was in many respects a hard one, but he enjoyed it. It gave new vigor to his naturally robust constitution and his splendid figure, and while yet a youth he acquired the appearance and habits of mature manhood. He also learned forest life in all its various phases, and by his constant intercourse with the hunters and Indians, gained a knowledge of the character and habits of these wild men which in after years was of infinite value to him.

During his surveying expeditions Washington was a frequent visitor at Greenway Court, the seat of Lord Fairfax, where, in addition to the other attractions, there was a well-selected library, of which the young man regularly availed himself. His reading was of a serious and useful nature; "Addison's Spectator" and the "History of England" were among his favorite works.

Though the heir to a considerable estate, Washington supported himself during this period by his earnings as a surveyor. "His father had bequeathed to the eldest son, Lawrence, the estate afterwards called Mount Vernon. To Augustine, the second son, he had given the old homestead in Westmoreland county. And George, at the age of twenty-one years, was to inherit the house and lands in Suffolk county. As yet, however, he derived no benefit from this landed property. But his industry and diligence in his laborious occupation supplied him with abundant pecuniary means. His habits of life were simple and economical; he indulged in no ... and expensive pleasures."

In 1751, in order to prepare for any emergency to which the hostility of the French and Indians might give rise, the colony of Virginia was divided into military districts, each of which was placed in charge of an adjutant and inspector, with the rank of Major, whose duty it was to keep the militia in readiness for instant service. Washington had at an early day evinced a great fondness for military exercises, and as a boy had often drilled his school-fellows in the simplest manœuvres of the troops. As he advanced towards manhood, his brother Lawrence,

THE WASHINGTON STATUE IN UNION SQUARE, NEW YORK.

Adjutant Muse, of Westmoreland, and Jacob Vanbraam, a fencing-master, and others, had given him numerous lessons in the art of war. Though but nineteen years old, he was regarded by his acquaintance as one of the best-informed persons upon military matters in the colony, and at the general desire of those who knew him he was commissioned a major in the colonial forces, and placed in command of one of the military districts. He discharged his duties with ability and zeal, and gave such satisfaction that when Governor Dinwiddie, in 1752, divided the province into four military districts, Major Washington was placed in command

22

of the northern district. "The counties comprehended in this division
he promptly and statedly traversed, and he soon effected the thorough
discipline of their militia for warlike operations." He was discharging
the duties of this position when selected by the governor of Virginia to
bear his message to the commander of the French forces on the O io.

Governor Dinwiddie intrusted to his young envoy a letter addre. sed to
the commander of the French forces on the Ohio, in which he demanded
of him his reasons for invading the territory of England while Great
Britain and France were at peace with each other. Washington was
instructed to observe carefully the numbers and positions of the French,
the strength of their forts, the nature of their communications with
Canada and with their various posts, and to endeavor to ascertain the
real designs of the French in occupying the Ohio valley, and the proba-

bilities of their
being vigorously
supported from
Canada. "Ye're
a braw lad," said
the governor, as
he delivered his
instructions to the
young major, "and
gin you play your
cards weel, my
boy, ye shall hae
nae cause to rue
your bargain."

Washington re-
ceived his instruc-

WASHINGTON'S JOURNEY TO THE OHIO.

tions on the 30th of October, 1753, and on the same day set out for
Winchester, then a frontier post, from which he proceeded to Wills'
creek, where he was to cross the mountains. Having secured the services of Christopher Gist as guide, and of two interpreters, and four others,
Washington set out on his journey about the middle of November.
They crossed the mountains, and journeyed through an unbroken country,
with no paths save the Indian trails to serve as guides, across rugged
ravines, over steep hills, and across streams swollen with the recent rains,
until in nine days they reached the point where the Alleghany and
Monongahela unite and form the Ohio. Washington carefully examined
the place, and was greatly impressed with the advantages offered for the
location of a fort by the point of land at the junction of the two rivers.

The judgment expressed by him at the time was subsequently confirmed by the choice of this spot by the French for one of their most important posts—Fort Duquesne.

Washington had been ordered by the governor to proceed direct to Logstown, where he was to hold an interview with the Delaware chief known as the Half King, to acquaint the Indians with the nature of his mission, and ascertain their disposition towards the English. While he was at this place he met several French deserters from the posts on the lower Ohio, who told him the location, number, and strength of the French posts between Quebec and New Orleans by way of the Wabash and the Maumee, and informed him of the intention of the French to occupy the Ohio from its head to its mouth with a similar chain of forts. The Half King confirmed the story of the deserters. He had heard that the French were coming with a strong force to drive the English out of the land. A "grand talk" was held with the chiefs in council by Washington, and they answered him, by the Half King, that what he had said was true; they were brothers, and would guard him on his way to the nearest French post. They wished neither the English nor the French to settle in their country, but as the French were the first intruders they were willing to aid the English in their efforts to expel them. They agreed to break off friendly relations with the French; but Washington, who knew the Indian character well, was not altogether satisfied with their promises.

On the 30th of November he set out from Logstown with his companions, attended by the Half King and three other Indians, and on the 4th arrived at the French post at Venango. The officer in command of this fort had no authority to receive his letter, and referred him to the Chevalier St. Pierre, the commander of the next post. They treated the English with courtesy, and invited Washington to sup with them. When the wine was passed around they drank deeply and soon lost their discretion. The sober and vigilant Washington noted their words with great attention, and recorded them in his diary. "They told me," he writes, " that it was their absolute design to take possession of the Ohio, and, by G—d, they would do it; for, that although they were sensible the English could raise two men for their one, they knew their motions were too slow and dilatory to prevent any undertaking of theirs. They pretend to have an undoubted right to the river, from a discovery made by one La Salle sixty years ago; and the rise of this expedition is to prevent our settling on the river or waters of it, as they heard of some families moving out in order thereto." The French officers then informed Washington of their strength south of the lakes, and of the number and location of their posts between Montreal and Venango.

The French exerted every stratagem to detach the Indians from Washington's party, and they met with enough success to justify Washington's distrust of them. All had come to deliver up the French speech-belts, or, in other words, to break off friendly relations with the French. The Delaware chiefs wavered and failed to fulfil their promise; "but the Half King clung to Washington like a brother, and delivered up his belt as he had promised."

The party left Venango on the 7th of December, and reached Fort Le Bœuf, the next post, on the 11th. It was a strong work, defended by cannon, and near by Washington saw a number of canoes and boats, and the materials for building others, sure indications that an expedition down the river was about to be attempted. He obtained an interview with St. Pierre, the commander, an officer of experience and integrity,

THE HALF KING.

greatly beloved as well as feared by the Indians. He received the young envoy with courtesy, but refused to discuss questions of right with him. "I am here," he said, "by the orders of my general, to which I shall conform with exactness and resolution." On the 14th St. Pierre delivered to Washington his answer to the letter of Governor Dinwiddie, and next day the party set out on its return. They descended French creek in canoes, at no little risk, as the stream was full of ice. At Venango, which was reached on the 22d, they found their horses, which were so feeble that it was doubtful whether they would be able to make the journey home. "I put myself in an Indian walking-dress," says Washington, "and continued with them three days, until I found there was no possibility of their getting home in any reasonable time. The horses became less able to travel every day; the cold increased very fast, and the roads were becoming much worse by a deep snow continually freezing; therefore, as I was uneasy to get back to make report of my proceedings to his honor the governor, I determined to prosecute my journey the nearest way through the woods on foot."

Taking Gist as his only companion, and directing their way by the compass, Washington set out on the 26th, by the nearest way across the country, for the head of the Ohio. The next day an Indian who had lain in wait for them fired at Washington at a distance of only fifteen steps, but missed him, and was made a prisoner by him. Gist was anxious to kill the savage on the spot, but Washington would not allow this, and they kept the fellow until dark, and then released him. They travelled all night and all the next day in order to make sure of escaping from the enemies they felt certain their freed captive would set upon their trail.

At dark on the 28th they reached the Alleghany, and spent the night on the banks of that stream. The next morning they set to work with one poor hatchet to construct a raft, on which to pass the river, which was full of floating ice. They completed their raft about sunset,

WASHINGTON AND GIST CROSSING THE ALLEGHANY.

and launched it upon the stream. It was caught in the floating ice, and Washington was hurled off into the water and nearly drowned. Unable to reach the opposite shore, they made for an island in mid-stream, and passed the night there. The cold was intense, and Gist had all his fingers and several of his toes frozen. The next morning the river was a solid mass of ice, hard enough to bear their weight. They at once crossed to the opposite bank and continued their journey, and on the 16th of January, 1754, were at Williamsburg, where Washington delivered to the governor of Virginia the reply of the French commander, and reported the results of his journey.

The French commander returned a courteous but evasive answer to Governor Dinwiddie's communication, and referred him for a definite

settlement of the matter to the Marquis Duquesne, the governor of
Canada. It was clear from the tone of his letter that he meant to hold
on to the territory he had occupied, and the governor of Virginia was
satisfied from Major Washington's report of his observations that St.
Pierre was about to extend the line of French posts down the Ohio.
The authorities of Virginia resolved to anticipate him, and in the spring
of 1754 the Ohio Company sent a force of about forty men to build a
fort at the head of the Ohio, on the site to which Washington had called
attention

In the meantime, measures were set on foot in Virginia for the protection of the frontiers   A regiment of troops was ordered to be raised,
and it was the general wish that Major Washington should be appointed
to the command.   He declined the commission when tendered him, on
the ground of his youth and inexperience, and was made lieutenant-
colonel, the command of the regiment being conferred upon Colonel Joshua
Fry.   Washington was ordered to repair to the west to take charge of
the defence of the frontiers, and in April, 1754, reached Wills' creek
with three companies of his regiment.

Just at this moment news arrived that the party sent to build a fort at
the head of the Ohio had been driven away by the French.   A force of
one thousand men, with artillery, under Captain Coutrecoeur, had
descended the Alleghany and had surrounded the English.   One hour was
given them to surrender, and being utterly unable to offer any resistance,
they capitulated upon condition of being allowed to retire to Virginia.
Immediately upon the withdrawal of the English the French forces occupied the unfinished work, completed it, and named it Fort Duquesne.
This was a more important act than either party believed it at the time
It was the beginning of the final struggle by which the power of France
in America was broken   In the history of Europe this struggle is known
as the *Seven Years' War;* in our own history as the *French and Indian
War.*

Hostilities were now inevitable, and Washington, who was on his
march to the Ohio when the news of the aggression of the French was
received, resolved to push forward without delay   Colonel Fry had
fallen sick, and the direction of affairs on the border had passed entirely
into the hands of the young lieutenant-colonel.   He intended to proceed
to the junction of Red Stone creek and the Monongahela, the site occupied by the present town of Brownsville, to erect a fort there, and hold
it until he could be reinforced.   His force was poorly provided with
clothing and tents, and was deficient in military supplies of all kinds.
The country to be traversed was a wild, unbroken region, without roads

or bridges, and through it the artillery and wagons were to be transported. The little force moved slowly and with difficulty, and Washington pushed on in advance with a small detachment, intending to secure the position on the Monongahela and await the arrival of the main body, when the whole force could descend the river in flat-boats to Fort Duquesne.

On the 20th of May he reached the Youghiogheny and there received a message from his ally, the Half King, telling him that the French were in heavy force at Fort Duquesne. This report was confirmed at the Little Meadows by the traders, and by another message from the Half King on the 25th of May, warning Washington that a force of French and Indians had left Fort Duquesne on a secret expedition. Washington was sure that this expedition was destined to attack him, and advanced to the Great Meadows and took position there. On the morning of the 27th Gist arrived and reported that he had seen the trail of the French within five miles of the Great Meadows. In the evening of the same day a runner came in from the Half King, and with a message that the French were close at hand. Taking with him forty men, Washington set off for the Half King's camp, and by a difficult night-march through a tangled forest in the midst of a driving rain, reached it about daylight. The runners of the Half King found the French encamped in a deep glen not far distant, and it was decided to attack them at once. The Half King and his warriors placed themselves under Washington's orders, and the march was resumed towards the French camp. The French were surprised, and an action of about a quarter of an hour ensued. The French lost ten men killed, among whom was their commander, Jumonville, and twenty-one prisoners. This was the first blood shed on the American continent in the long struggle which won America for the free institutions of the Anglo-Saxon race.

Washington was very anxious to follow up the advantage he had gained, and had already appealed to the governors of Maryland and Pennsylvania for assistance, but no aid reached him. Unable to advance in the face of the rapidly increasing forces of the French, he threw up a stockade fort at Great Meadows, which he named Fort Necessity, from the fact that the provisions of the troops were so nearly exhausted that the danger of a famine was imminent. On the 3d of July six hundred French and one hundred Indians suddenly appeared before the fort and occupied the hills surrounding it. The attacking party were able to shelter themselves behind trees and could command the fort from their safe position, while the English were greatly exposed, and it was evident to the most inexperienced that the fort was untenable. Nevertheless, the

work was held for nine hours under a heavy fire, and amid the discom-
forts of a severe rain-storm. At length De Villiers, the French commander, fearing that his ammunition would be exhausted, proposed a
parley and offered terms to Washington. The English had lost thirty
killed and the French but three. The terms of capitulation proposed by
De Villiers were interpreted to Washington, who did not understand
French, and in consequence of the interpretation, which was made by "a
Dutchman little acquainted with the English tongue," Washington and
his officers "were betrayed into a pledge which they would never have
consented to give, and an act of moral suicide which they could never
have deliberately committed. They understood from Vanbraam's interpretation, that no fort was to be built beyond the mountains *on lands belonging to the King of France;* but the terms of the articles are, ' neither
in this place nor beyond the mountains.'" The Virginians were allowed
to march out of the fort with the honors of war, retaining their arms and
all their stores, but leaving their artillery. This they did on the next
morning, July 4th, 1754. The march across the mountains was rendered
painful by the lack of provisions, and after much suffering the troops
arrived at Fort Cumberland in Maryland. Although the expedition had
been unsuccessful, the conduct of Washington had been marked by so
much prudence and good judgment that he received the thanks of the
general assembly of Virginia.

Governor Dinwiddie had already thrown many obstacles in the way of
the defence of the colony, and he now refused to reward the provincial
officers with the promotions they had so well earned. In order to avoid
this he dissolved the Virginia regiment, and reorganized it into independent companies, no officer of which was to have a higher rank than
that of captain. It was also ordered that officers holding commissions
from the king should take precedence of those holding commissions from
the colonial government. Washington, feeling that he could no longer
remain in the service with self-respect, resigned his commission and withdrew to Mount Vernon. Soon afterwards Governor Sharpe, of Maryland, having been appointed by the king commander-in-chief of the forces
of the southern colonies, proposed to Washington, through a friend, to
return to the army and accept the rank of colonel, but with the actual
authority of a captain. Washington declined the offer with characteristic
dignity. "If you think me," he wrote, "capable of holding a commission that has neither rank nor emolument annexed to it, you must maintain a very contemptible opinion of my weakness, and believe me more
empty than the commission itself."

In the meantime, although peace still remained nominally unbroken between England and France, each nation was perfectly convinced of the certainty of a conflict in America, and each began to prepare for it. France sent large reinforcements to Canada, and the English went on rapidly with their plans for the conquest of that country. The British government was very anxious that the colonies should bear the brunt of the struggle, though it was fully determined to send a royal army to their assistance, and urged upon them to unite in some plan for their common defence.

For the purpose of carrying out the wishes of the home government a convention of delegates from seven of the colonies assembled at Albany, New York, on the 19th of June, 1754. "The Virginia government was represented by the presiding officer, Delancey, the lieutenant-governor of New York;" but New Hampshire, Massachusetts, Rhode Island, Connecticut, New York, and Maryland were represented by their own delegates. The first object of this convention was to secure the friendship of the powerful confederacy of the Six Nations, on the northern border, and this was successfully accomplished.

BENJAMIN FRANKLIN.

The leading man of this convention was Benjamin Franklin. He was a native of Boston, and the son of a tallow chandler. While still a youth he had removed to Philadelphia, and by the force of his own genius had risen from poverty and obscurity to great prominence among the public men of Pennsylvania, and the literary and scientific men of his day. He had chosen the avocation of a printer; and by his industry, energy, and integrity had accumulated property enough to make him independent. He was among the most active men in America in promoting the advancement of literary, scientific, and benevolent institutions, and had already won a world-wide reputation by his discoveries in science, and especially by his investigations in electricity and lightning. He was not inexperienced in public affairs. He had served as clerk to the general assembly of Pennsylvania, as postmaster of Philadelphia, as a member of the provincial assembly of Pennsylvania, and in 1753 had been appointed by the king postmaster-general of the American colonies. In each of these positions he had served with distinction, and now, at the ripe age of forty-eight, he had come to take part in the most important convention ever held in America.

Franklin had long been of the opinion that the true interests of the colonies required their union in all measures relating to their common welfare. Believing that the force of circumstances would soon drive them into such a union, he sought to accomplish that end through the medium of this convention. Accordingly he presented to the convention a plan for the union of all the American colonies, which union he intended should be perpetual. He proposed that while each colony should retain the separate and independent control of its own affairs, all should unite in a perpetual union for the management of their general affairs. This confederacy was to be controlled by a general government to consist of a governor-general and a council. The seat of the federal government was to be Philadelphia, which city he regarded as central to all the colonies. The governor-general was to be appointed and paid by the king, and was to have the power of vetoing all laws which should seem to him objectionable. The members of the council were to be elected triennially by the colonial legislatures, and were to be apportioned among the colonies according to their respective population. "The governor-general was to nominate military officers, subject to the advice of the council, which, in turn, was to nominate all civil officers. No money was to be issued but by their joint order. Each colony was to retain its domestic constitution; the federal government was to regulate all relations of peace or war with the Indians, affairs of trade, and purchases of lands not within the bounds of particular colonies; to establish, organize, and temporarily to govern new settlements, to raise soldiers, and equip vessels of force on the seas, rivers, or lakes, to make laws, and levy just and equal taxes. The grand council were to meet once a year to chose their own speaker, and neither to be dissolved nor prorogued, nor continue sitting longer than six weeks at any one time, but by their own consent."

This plan met with considerable opposition, was thoroughly discussed, and was finally adopted by the convention. It was not altogether acceptable to the colonies, each of which dreaded that the establishment of a central government would result in the destruction of the liberties of the individual provinces. Connecticut promptly rejected it, New York received it with coldness, and Massachusetts showed a more active opposition to it. Upon its reception in England it was at once thrown aside by the royal government. The union proposed by the plan was too perfect, and would make America practically independent of Great Britain, and so the board of trade did not even bring it before the notice of the king.

Franklin regarded the failure of his plan of union with great regret. In after years he wrote "The colonies so united would have been sufficiently strong to defend themselves. There would then have been no need of troops from England, of course the subsequent pretext for taxing America, and the bloody contest it occasioned, would have been avoided. But such mistakes are not new, history is full of the errors of states and princes"

The plan for the union of the colonies having failed, the British government resolved to take into its own hands the task of carrying on the war, with such assistance as the colonies might be willing to afford. A million of pounds was voted for the defence of the British possessions in America, and four strong fleets were sent to sea, together with numerous privateers, which nearly destroyed the French West Indian trade. In 1755 Major-General Edward Braddock was appointed commander-in-chief of the English forces in America. He had served under the Duke of Cumberland, in his expedition into Scotland against the Pretender Charles Edward, in 1746, and was regarded as one of the most promising officers in his majesty's service. Braddock sailed from Cork, in Ireland, early in January, 1755, and on the 20th of February arrived at Alexandria, in Virginia. He was soon followed by two regiments of infantry, consisting of five hundred men each, the largest force of regulars Great Britain had ever assembled in America.

A conference of the colonial governors with the new commander-in-chief was held at Alexandria, and a plan of campaign was decided upon. Four expeditions were to be despatched against the French. The first, under Braddock in person, was to advance upon Fort Duquesne; the second, under Governor Shirley of Massachusetts, was to attempt the capture of Fort Niagara, the third, under William John, the Indian agent among the Mohawks, and a man of great influence over them, was to be directed against Crown Point; and the fourth was to capture the French posts near the head of the Bay of Fundy, and expel the French from Acadia

It was now evident that the war was about to commence in good earnest, and the colonies exerted themselves to support the efforts of the mother country to the extent of their ability.

General Braddock was thoroughly proficient in the theory of his profession, but his experience of actual warfare had been limited to a single campaign, and that a brief one. He possessed the entire confidence of his superiors in England, and his faith in himself was boundless. He believed that the regulars of the British army were capable of accomplishing any task assigned them, and entertained a thorough contempt for the provincial troops that were to form a part of his command. Soon after his arrival in Virginia he offered Washington a position on his staff as aid-de-camp, with the rank of colonel, which was promptly accepted.

Had General Braddock been a different man the presence of Washington in his military family might have been of the greatest service to him, for the experience of the young colonel would have made him an invaluable counsellor. Braddock was in a strange country, and was charged with

WILLS' CREEK NARROWS, MD.

the conduct of a campaign in which the ordinary rules of warfare as practised in Europe could not be adhered to. He knew nothing of the difficulties of marching his army through a tangled wilderness and over a mountain range of the first magnitude. Unfortunately for him he was not aware of his ignorance, and would neither ask for nor listen to advice or information upon the subject. "He was, I think, a brave man," says Franklin, "and might probably have made a figure as a good officer in some European war. But he had too much self-confidence, too high an opinion of the validity of regular troops, and too mean a one of both

Americans and Indians." During one of his interviews with him Franklin undertook to impress upon him the necessity of guarding against the danger of Indian ambuscades. "He smiled at my ignorance," says Franklin, and replied. 'These savages may indeed be a formidable enemy to your raw American militia, but upon the king's regular and disciplined troops, sir, it is impossible they should make any impression.'"

The army assembled at Wills' creek, to which place General Braddock repaired in his coach. The bad roads had put him in a passion, and had broken his coach, and he was in no mood upon his arrival to pursue a sensible course. He was advised to employ Indians as scouts on the march, or to use them to protect a force of Pennsylvanians who were making a road over the mountains for the passage of the army, but he refused to do either. Washington urged him to abandon his wagon-train, to use pack-horses in place of these vehicles, and to move with as little baggage as possible. Braddock ridiculed this suggestion. Neither he nor any of his officers would consent to be separated from their cumbrous baggage, or to dispense with any of the luxuries they had been used to.

A month was lost at Wills' creek, and in June the army began its march. It was greatly impeded by the difficulty of dragging the wagons and artillery over roads filled with the stumps of trees and with rocks. Such little progress was made that Braddock, greatly disheartened, privately asked Washington to advise him what to do. As it was known that the garrison at Fort Duquesne was small, Washington advised him to hasten forward with a division of the army in light marching order, and seize the fort before reinforcements could arrive from Canada. Braddock accordingly detached a division of twelve hundred men and ten pieces of cannon, with a train of pack-horses to carry the baggage, and pushed on in advance with them, leaving Colonel Dunbar to bring up the main division as promptly as possible. A famous hunter and Indian-fighter named Captain Jack, who was regarded as the most experienced man in savage warfare in the colonies, now offered his services and those of his men to Braddock to act as scouts. Braddock received him with frigid courtesy, and refused his offer, saying that he "had experienced troops upon whom he could rely for all purposes."

Instead of pushing on with energy with his advance division, Braddock moved very slowly, gaining but a little more than three miles a day. "They halt," wrote Washington, "to level every mole hill and to erect a bridge over every brook." On the 8th of July the army reached the east bank of the Monongahela, about fifteen miles above Fort Duquesne, having taken about double the necessary time in the march from Wills' creek. On the same day, Washington, who had been ill for some days, and was still unwell, rejoined Braddock.

Early on the morning of the 9th of July the march was resumed. The Monongahela was forded a short distance below the mouth of the Youghiogheny, and the advance continued along the southern bank of that river. About noon the Monongahela was forded again, and the army was planted upon the strip of land between the rivers which form the Ohio. Washington was well convinced that the French and Indians were informed of the movements of the army, and would seek to interfere with it before its arrival before the fort, which was only ten miles distant, and urged Braddock to throw in advance the Virginia Rangers, three hundred strong, as they were experienced Indian fighters. Braddock angrily rebuked his aide, and as if to make the rebuke more pointed, ordered the Virginia troops and other provincials to take position in the rear of the regulars. The general was fully convinced of the ability of his trained troops to take care of themselves. They made a gallant show as they marched along with their gay uniforms, their burnished arms and flying colors, and their drums beating a lively march. Washington could not repress his admiration at the brilliant sight, nor his anxiety for the result.

In the meantime the French at Fort Duquesne had been informed by their scouts of Braddock's movements, and had resolved to ambuscade him on his march. Early on the morning of the 9th a force of about two hundred and thirty French and Canadians and six hundred and thirty-seven Indians, under De Beaujeu, the commandant at Fort Duquesne, was despatched with orders to occupy a designated spot and attack the enemy upon their approach. Before reaching it, about two o'clock in the afternoon, they encountered the advanced force of the English army, under Lieutenant-Colonel Thomas Gage, and at once attacked them with spirit.

The English army at this moment was moving along a narrow road about twelve feet in width, with scarcely a scout thrown out in advance or upon the flanks. The engineer who was locating the road was the first to discover the enemy, and called out "French and Indians!" Instantly a heavy fire was opened upon Gage's force, and his indecision allowed the French and Indians to seize a commanding ridge, from which they maintained their attack with spirit. There, concealed among the trees, they were almost invisible to the English, who were fully exposed to their fire, as they occupied a broad ravine, covered with low shrubs, immediately below the eminence held by the French.

The regulars were quickly thrown into confusion by the heavy fire and the fierce yells of the Indians, who could nowhere be seen, and their losses were so severe and sudden that they became panic-stricken. They were ordered to charge up the hill and drive the French from their cover, but refused to move, and in their terror fired at random into the woods. In the meantime the Indians were rapidly spreading along the sides of the ravine and continuing their fire from their cover among the trees with fearful accuracy. The advance of the English was driven back, and it crowded upon the second division in utter disorder. A reinforcement of eight hundred men under Colonel Burton arrived at this moment, but only to add to the confusion. The French pushed their lines forward now and increased the disorder of the English, who had by this time lost nearly all their officers. Braddock now came up, and gallantly exerted himself to restore order, but "the king's regulars and disciplined troops" were so utterly demoralized that not one of his commands was obeyed.

The only semblance of resistance maintained by the English was by the Virginia Rangers, whom Braddock had insulted at the beginning of the day's march. Immediately upon the commencement of the battle they had adopted the tactics of the Indians, and had thrown themselves behind trees, from which shelter they were rapidly picking off the Indians.

BRADDOCK'S DEFEAT.

Washington entreated Braddock to allow the regulars to follow the example of the Virginians, but he refused, and stubbornly endeavored to form them in platoons under the fatal fire that was being poured upon them by their hidden assailants. Thus through his obstinacy many useful lives were needlessly thrown away. The officers did not share the panic of the men, but behaved with the greatest gallantry. They were the especial marks of the Indian sharpshooters, and many of them were killed or wounded. Two of Braddock's aides were seriously wounded, and their duties devolved upon Washington in addition to his own. He passed repeatedly over the field carrying the orders of the commander and encouraging the men. When sent to bring up the artillery, he found it surrounded by Indians, its commander, Sir Peter Halket, killed, and the men standing helpless from fear. Springing from his horse he appealed to the men to save the guns, pointed a field piece and discharged it at the savages, and entreated the gunners to rally. He could accomplish nothing by either his words or example. The men deserted the guns and fled. In a letter to his brother, Washington wrote: "I had four bullets through my coat, two horses shot under me, yet escaped unhurt, though death was levelling my companions on every side around me." *

Braddock had five horses shot under him, and at length himself

received a mortal wound. As he fell, Captain Stewart, of the Virginia troops, caught him in his arms. He was borne from the field, though he begged to be left to die on the scene of his defeat. His fall was fortunate for the army, which it saved from destruction. The order was given to fall back, and the "regulars fled like sheep before the hounds." The French and Indians pressed forward in pursuit, and all would have been lost had not the Virginia Rangers themselves been in the rear, and covered the flight of the regulars with a

RETREAT OF BRADDOCK'S ARMY.

determination which checked the pursuers. The artillery, wagons, and all the camp train were abandoned, and the savages, stopping to plunder these, allowed the fugitives to recross the river in safety.

---

* Washington attributed his wonderful escape from even a wound to the overruling providence of God. The Indians regarded the matter in the same light. About fifteen years after the battle, while examining some lands near the mouth of the Great Kanawha

Having seen the general as comfortable as circumstances would permit, Washington rode all that night and the next day to Dunbar's camp to procure wagons for the wounded and soldiers to guard them. With these he hastened back to the fugitives.

Braddock, unable to ride or to endure the jolting of a wagon, was carried in a litter as far as the Great Meadows. He seemed to be heart-broken and rarely spoke. Occasionally he would say, as if speaking to himself, with a deep sigh, "Who would have thought it?" It is said that he warmly thanked Captain Stewart for his care and kindness, and apologized to Washington for the manner in which he had received his advice. He had no wish to live, and he died at Fort Necessity on the night of the 13th of July. He was buried the next morning before daybreak as secretly as possible for fear that the savages might find and violate his grave. Close by the national road, about a mile west of Fort Necessity, a pile of stones still marks his resting-place.

The losses of the English in the battle were terrible. Out of eighty-six officers, twenty-six were killed and thirty-six wounded. Upward of seven hundred of the regulars were killed or wounded. The Virginia Rangers had suffered terrible losses, for they had not only borne the brunt of the battle, but had lost many of their number by the random fire of the frightened regulars. Dunbar, who succeeded Braddock in the command, still had fifteen hundred effective men left to him; but he was too badly frightened to attempt to retrieve the disaster, which a competent officer might have done with such a force. He broke up his camp, destroyed his stores, and retreated beyond the mountains. Disregarding the entreaties of the colonists not to leave the frontiers exposed to the savages, he continued his retreat to Philadelphia, and went into winter quarters there.

The effect of these reverses upon the colonists was most marked. When they understood that Braddock's splendid force of disciplined regulars had been routed by a mere handful of French and Indians, their respect for the invincibility of British troops was destroyed, and their confidence in their own prowess was greatly increased by the proud reflection that the only thing that had been done to save the army of Braddock from total destruction had been accomplished by the provin-

river, Washington was visited by an old chief. The chief told him "he was present at the battle, and among the Indian allies of the French, that he singled him out, and repeatedly fired his rifle at him, that he also ordered his young warriors to make him their only mark, but that on finding all their bullets turned aside by some invisible and inscrutable interposition, he was convinced that the hero at whom he had so often and so truly aimed must be, for some wise purpose, specially protected by the Great Spirit. He now came, therefore, to testify his veneration."

23

cials. Washington's conduct was a subject of praise in all the colonies, and brought his name conspicuously before the whole people of America. In a sermon preached a few months after Braddock's defeat, the Rev. Samuel Davies, a learned clergyman, spoke of him as "that heroic youth, Colonel Washington, whom I cannot but hope Providence has hitherto preserved in so signal a manner for some important service to his country."

The retreat of Dunbar left the frontiers of Virginia and Pennsylvania at the mercy of the savages, who maintained a desultory but destructive warfare along the entire border. The defence of this exposed region was

BURNING OF KITTANNING BY GENERAL ARMSTRONG.

intrusted to Colonel Washington; but he had so few men as to make his undertaking a hopeless one. The frontier settlements of Virginia were destroyed; the beautiful valley of the Shenandoah was ravaged with merciless fury, and the more protected regions were kept in a state of constant uneasiness and alarm. Governor Dinwiddie was repeatedly appealed to to furnish more men, but refused, and endeavored to excuse his delinquency by saying: "We dare not part with any of our white men to any distance, as we must have a watchful eye over our negro slaves."

Pennsylvania met her troubles with greater vigor and resolution.

About thirty miles above Fort Duquesne, on the Alleghany river, was the Indian village of Kittanning, the home of a noted chief named Captain Jacobs. Together with the Delaware chief Shingis, he had, at the instigation of the French, kept up a continual warfare upon the frontier settlements. A military force for the defence of the frontier was raised by the colony and placed under the command of Benjamin Franklin as colonel. He soon resigned, and was succeeded by Colonel John Armstrong, a man better suited to the position, and who subsequently became a major-general in the war of the Revolution. Armstrong resolved to destroy Kittanning and the tribe inhabiting it as the best means of putting a stop to their outrages, and called for volunteers for the enterprise. Three hundred men responded. Towards the last of September, 1756, they crossed the mountains on horseback, and in a few days reached the vicinity of Kittanning. Dismounting and leaving their horses in charge of a guard, they silently surrounded the village. The Indians spent the night in carousing within hearing of the whites, and retired to rest at a very late hour. Just before daybreak the whites attacked the village and set it on fire. It was completely destroyed, and Jacobs and all but a handful of his men were slain. The few survivors fled farther west, and the Pennsylvania frontier was relieved of the sufferings it had so long endured.

CHAPTER XXIII.

THE FRENCH AND INDIAN WAR—CONTINUED.

WHILE the events we have related were transpiring in the Ohio valley other expeditions were despatched against the French. One of these was directed against that part of Acadia, or Nova Scotia, which still remained in the hands of the French. It lay at the head of the Bay of Fundy, and was defended by two French forts. This region was the oldest French colony in North America, having been settled sixteen years before the landing of the Pilgrims, but was regarded by the English as within their jurisdiction In May, 1755, an expedition of three thousand New England troops was despatched from Boston, under Colonel John Winslow, to attack these forts and establish the English authority over the French settlements. Upon reaching the Bay of Fundy Winslow was joined by three hundred English regulars under Colonel Monckton, who assumed the command. The forts were taken with comparatively little effort, and the authority of England was extended over the whole of Nova Scotia. The Acadians agreed to acknowledge the authority of their new masters, and to observe a strict neutrality between France and England in the war; and the English on their part promised not to require of them the usual oaths of allegiance, to excuse them from bearing arms against France, and to protect them in the exercise of the Catholic religion.

The Acadians numbered about seventeen thousand souls. They were a simple and harmless people, and were enjoying in a marked degree the blessings of industry and thrift. They had begun their settlements by depending upon the fur-trade and the fisheries for their support, but had abandoned these pursuits for that of agriculture, which was already

yielding them rich rewards for their skill and labor. They were proud
of their farms and took but little interest in public affairs, scarcely knowing what was transpiring in the world around them. It is hard to
imagine a more peaceful or a happier community than this one at the
time they passed under the baleful rule of England. Crime was unknown
among them, and they seldom carried their disputes before the English
magistrates, but settled them by the arbitration of their old men. They
encouraged early marriages as the best means of preserving the morality
of their people, and when a young man married, his neighbors turned
out in force and built him a house, and for the first year of his marriage
aided him to establish himself firmly, while the bride's relatives helped
her to furnish the home thus prepared. Thus the people were taught to
regard and practise neighborly kindness as one of the cardinal Christian
virtues. They were devoted Catholics, and practised their religion without bigotry. They were attached to the rule of France by language and
religion, and would have been glad to see her authority re-established
over them; but they submitted peacefully to the rule of the English and
faithfully observed the terms of their surrender.

Unfortunately for the Acadians their possessions soon began to excite
the envy of the English. Lawrence, the governor of Nova Scotia, expressed this feeling in his letter to Lord Halifax, the English premier.
"They possess the best and largest tract of land in this province," he
wrote, "if they refuse the oaths, it would be much better that they were
away." The English authorities had prepared a cunningly devised
scheme for dispossessing these simple people of their homes, and they
now proceeded to put it in execution. The usual oaths of allegiance had
not been tendered to the Acadians upon their surrender, as it was known
that as Frenchmen and Catholics they could not take them, as they
required them to bear arms against their own brethren in Canada, and to
make war upon their religion. It was resolved now to offer the oaths to
them, and thus either drive them into rebellion or force them to abandon
their homes. When this intention was known, the priests urged them to
refuse the oaths. "Better surrender your meadows to the sea," they declared, "and your houses to the flames, than, at the peril of your souls,
take the oath of allegiance to the British government." As for the
Acadians themselves, "they, from their very simplicity and anxious sincerity, were uncertain in their resolves, now gathering courage to flee
beyond the isthmus, for other homes in New France, and now yearning
for their own houses and fields, their herds and pastures."

The officers sent by the English authorities to enforce their demands
conducted themselves with a haughtiness and cruelty which added greatly

to the sorrows of the Acadians. Their titles to their lands were declared
null and void, and all their papers and title-deeds were taken from them.
Their property was taken for the public service without compensation,
and if they failed to furnish wood at the times required, the English
soldiers "might take their houses for fuel." Their guns were seized, and
they were deprived of their boats on the pretext that they might be used
to communicate with the French in Canada. At last, wearied out with
these oppressions, the Acadians offered to swear allegiance to Great
Britain This, however, formed no part of the plan of their persecutors,
and they were answered, that by a British statute persons who had been
once offered the oaths, and who had refused them, could not be permitted
to take them, but must be treated as Popish recusants

This brought matters to a crisis, and the English now resolved to strike
the decisive blow A proclamation was issued, requiring "the old men,
and young men, as well as all lads over ten years of age," to assemble on
the 5th of September, 1755, at a certain hour, at designated places in
their respective districts, to hear the "wishes of the king." In the
greater number of places the order was obeyed. What happened at the
village of Grand Pré, the principal settlement, will show the course pursued by the English in all the districts Four hundred and eighteen of
the men of the place assembled. They were unarmed, and were marched
into the church, which was securely guarded Winslow, the New England
commander, then addressed them as follows : " You are convened together
to manifest to you his majesty's final resolution to the French inhabitants
of this his province. Your lands and tenements, cattle of all kinds, and
live stock of all sorts, are forfeited to the crown, and you yourselves are
to be removed from this his province I am, through his majesty's
goodness, directed to allow you liberty to carry off your money and household goods, as many as you can, without discommoding the vessels you
go in." He then declared them, together with their wives and children,
a total of nineteen hundred and twenty-three souls, the king's prisoners.
The announcement took the unfortunate men by surprise, and filled them
with the deepest indignation , but they were unarmed, and unable to resist They were held close prisoners in the church, and their homes,
which they had left in the morning full of hope, were to see them no
more They were kept without food for themselves or their children
that day, and were poorly fed during the remainder of their captivity.
They were held in confinement until the 10th of September, when it was
announced that the vessels were in readiness to carry them away. They
were not to be allowed to join their brethren in Canada lest they should
serve as a reinforcement to the French in that province, but were to be

scattered as paupers through the English colonies, among people of another race and a different faith

On the morning of the 10th, the captives were drawn up six deep The English, intending to make their trial as bitter and as painful as possible, had resolved upon the barbarous measure of separating the families of their victims The young men and boys were driven at the point of the bayonet from the church to the ship and compelled to embark They passed amid the rows of their mothers and sisters, who, kneeling, prayed heaven to bless and keep them Then the fathers and husbands were forced by the bayonet on board of another ship, and as the vessels were now full, the women and children were left behind until more ships could come for them They were kept for weeks near the sea, suffering greatly from lack of proper shelter and food, and it was December before the last of them were removed. Those who tried to escape were ruthlessly shot down by the sentinels. "Our soldiers hate them," wrote an English officer, ' and if they can but find a pretext to kill them they will."

In some of the settlements the designs of the English were suspected and the proclamation was not heeded Some of the people fled to Canada; others sought shelter with the Indians, who received them with kindness; others still fled to the woods, hoping to hide there till the storm was over The English at once proceeded to lay waste their homes, the country was made desolate in order that the fugitives might be compelled through starvation to surrender themselves.

Seven thousand Acadians were torn from their homes and scattered among the English colonies on the Atlantic coast, from New Hampshire to Georgia. Families were utterly broken up, never to be re-united. The colonial newspapers for many years were filled with mournful advertisements, inquiring for a lost husband or wife, parents sought their missing children, and children their parents in this way. But of all these inquiries few were answered. The exiles were doomed to a parting worse than death, and their captors had done their work so well that human ingenuity could not undo it. Some of those who had been carried to Georgia attempted to return to their homes. They escaped to sea in boats, and coasted from point to point northward, until they reached New England, when they were sternly ordered back. Their homes were their own no longer.

More than three thousand Acadians fled to Canada, and of these about fifteen hundred settled south of the Ristigouche. Upon the surrender of Canada they were again subjected to the persecutions of the English. "Once those who dwelt in Pennsylvania presented a humble petition to

the Earl of Loudon, then the British commander-in-chief in America;
and the cold-hearted peer, offended that the prayer was made in French,
seized their five principal men, who in their own land had been persons
of dignity and substance, and shipped them to England, with the request
that they might be kept from ever again becoming troublesome by being
consigned to service as common sailors on board ships of war. No doubt
existed of the king's approbation. The lords of trade, more merciless
than the savages and than the wilderness in winter, wished very much
that every one of the Acadians should be driven out; and when it seemed

SCENE ON THE COLORADO.

that the work was done, congratulated the king that 'the zealous endeavors
of Lawrence had been crowned with an entire success.' I know not if
the annals of the human race keep the record of sorrows so wantonly inflicted, so bitter and so perennial, as fell upon the French inhabitants of
Acadia. 'We have been true,' they said of themselves, 'to our religion,
and true to ourselves; yet nature appears to consider us only as the objects of public vengeance.' The hand of the English official seemed
under a spell with regard to them; and was never uplifted but to curse
them." *

While these sorrows were being heaped upon the helpless Acadians by England the provincial forces were serving the cause elsewhere with more credit to their manhood. As has been stated the expedition against the French fort at Crown Point, on Lake Champlain, had been intrusted to General William Johnson. His army consisted principally of troops from Massachusetts and Connecticut. They were joined at Albany by a regiment from New Hampshire. The troops rendezvoused at the head of boat navigation, on the Hudson, in July, 1755, under the command of General Lyman. They numbered about six thousand men. A fort was built and named by the troops, in honor of their commander, Fort Lyman. In August Johnson arrived with the stores and artillery, and assumed the command of the expedition. He ungenerously changed the name of the fort to Fort Edward. Leaving a strong force to garrison it he moved with five thousand men to the head of Lake George, from which he intended to descend the lake in boats.

The French had been informed of Johnson's movements by their scouts. Baron Dieskau, the governor of Canada, placed the entire arms-bearing population of the Montreal district in the field, and resolved to prevent Johnson from reaching Crown Point by attacking him in his own country. With a force of two hundred French regulars, and about one thousand two hundred Indians, he set out across the country to attack Fort Edward. Upon arriving in the vicinity of the fort the Indians learned that it was defended by artillery, of which they were greatly afraid, and refused to attack it. Dieskau was, therefore, compelled to change his plan, and resolved to strike a blow at Johnson's camp, which he was informed was without cannon.

In the meantime the scouts of the English had detected the movement against Fort Edward. Ignorant of the change in Dieskau's plans Johnson sent a force of one thousand men, under Colonel Ephraim Williams of Massachusetts, and two hundred Mohawks, under their famous chief Hendrick, to the relief of the fort. Their march was reported to the French, who placed themselves in ambush along the road they were pursuing, and attacked them as soon as they had fairly entered the defile. The English were at once thrown into confusion. Hendrick was shot down at the first fire, and Williams fell a few moments later. The English and Mohawks then began a rapid retreat to their camp, closely pursued by their assailants.

The sound of the firing was soon heard in Johnson's camp, and as it drew nearer it became apparent that the detachment was retreating. The troops were gotten under arms, and the trees in front of the camp were hurriedly felled to form a rude breastwork. A few cannon had just

arrived from the Hudson, and these were placed to command the road
by which the French were approaching. These arrangements were just
completed when the fugitives of Williams' command appeared in full
retreat, with the French and Indians but a few hundred yards behind
them. Dieskau urged his men forward with the greatest energy, intending to force his way into the English camp along with the fugitives
The artillery was carefully trained upon the road by which he was
advancing, and the moment the fugitives were past the guns they opened
with a terrific fire of grape, which caused the Canadians and Indians to
break in confusion, and take to the woods for shelter   The regulars held
their ground, and maintained a determined contest of five hours, in which
they were nearly all slain   The Indians and Canadians did little execution, as they stood in dread of the artillery   At length Dieskau, seeing
that his effort had failed, drew off his men, and retreated. He was pursued for some distance by the English.   Towards evening he was suddenly attacked by the New Hampshire regiment, which was marching
from Fort Edward to Johnson's assistance. The French were seized
with a panic at this new attack, and abandoning their brave commander,
fled for their lives. Dieskau, who had been severely wounded several
times, was taken prisoner. He was kindly treated, and was subsequently
sent to England, where he died.

General Johnson was slightly wounded at the commencement of the
battle, and withdrew from the field, leaving the command to General
Lyman, to whom the victory was really due. Notwithstanding this Johnson did not even mention Lyman's name in his report of the battle, but
claimed all the honor for himself. He was rewarded by the king with a
baronetcy, and the gift of twenty-five thousand dollars General Lyman
was not even thanked for his services.

Johnson made no effort to improve his victory. The expedition
against Crown Point, which might now have been undertaken with a
better prospect of success, was abandoned, and Johnson contented himself with building a useless log fort at the head of Lake George, which
he named Fort William Henry.   Late in the fall he placed a garrison in
this fort, and then returned to Albany, where he disbanded his army.

The expedition under Governor Shirley, against Fort Niagara, was
equally unsuccessful. By the month of August Shirley had advanced
no farther than Oswego. Here he received the news of Braddock's
defeat, which so disheartened him that, after building and garrisoning two
forts at Oswego, he returned to Albany   By the death of Braddock
Shirley succeeded to the chief command of all the royal forces in
America.

In December, 1755, Shirley held a conference with the colonial governors, at New York, to decide upon the campaign for the next year. It was agreed that three expeditions should be undertaken in 1756: one against Niagara, a second against Fort Duquesne, and a third against Crown Point. In the meantime Lord Loudon was appointed by the king commander-in-chief of the forces in America. He sent over General Abercrombie as his lieutenant. Abercrombie arrived in June with several regiments of British regulars. He relieved General Shirley from command, but nothing was to be done until the arrival of the commander-in-chief, who did not reach America until July.

Lord Loudon was a more pompous and a slower man than Braddock, and more incompetent. A force of seven thousand men was assembled at Albany for the expedition against Ticonderoga and Crown Point, and Loudon at once repaired thither, and assumed the command. The colonists were confident that something of importance would now be accomplished, but they were destined to disappointment. The commander-in-chief and his subordinates spent their time in settling the relative rank of the royal and provincial officers. Notwithstanding the fact that all that had been accomplished during the war had been gained by the colonial forces, there was an iniquitous regulation which gave the precedence to the lowest officer holding a royal commission over one holding a higher rank from any of the colonies. This led to many disputes, and the colonists saw themselves robbed of the honors they had so fairly won. This was only one of the many wrongs by which Great Britain succeeded in alienating the people of America from their attachment to her.

In the meantime Dieskau had been succeeded as governor of Canada by the Marquis de Montcalm, the ablest of the rulers of New France. He was a man of genuine ability and of indomitable energy. He reached Quebec in 1756, and at once set out for Ticonderoga, which he placed in a state of defence. Perceiving the exposed condition of the English forts at Oswego he resolved to capture them. Collecting a force of five thousand Frenchmen, Canadians, and Indians, he crossed the lake from Frontenac, and reached Oswego on the 5th of August. He soon drove the English out of Fort Oswego; but Fort Ontario, the second work, opposed a more vigorous resistance to him. The garrison held out until their commander, Colonel Mercer, was killed, and they had lost all hope of receiving aid from Albany, when they capitulated. An immense amount of military stores, one hundred and thirty-five pieces of cannon, and all the boats and vessels Shirley had prepared for the expedition against Niagara fell into the hands of Montcalm. The Iroquois had viewed the erection of the forts at Oswego by the English with great jealousy, and in order to conciliate them Montcalm wisely destroyed the works, and withdrew into Canada

Loudon had detached a force under Colonel Webb to the assistance of the Oswego forts, but it was sent so late that it was met on the way by the news of the capture of the forts. Colonel Webb, in dismay, fell back rapidly, and obstructed the road to Albany.

Having failed to accomplish anything against the enemy Lord Loudon now undertook to subjugate the colonies of New York and Pennsylvania. He was firmly convinced that the colonists needed to be taught submission to the will of the royal commander, and as he had been made a sort of viceroy of all the colonies, he thought the present a fitting occasion to teach them this lesson He demanded of the cities of Albany, New York, and Philadelphia free quarters for his troops during the winter The mayor of New York refused the demand "as contrary to the laws of England and the liberties of America" "G—d d—n my blood," said the viceroy to the mayor; "if you do not billet my officers upon free quarters this day, I'll order here all the troops in North America under my command, and billet them myself upon the city." There was no reasoning with "the master of twenty legions," and the magistrates were obliged to get up a subscription for the free support, during the winter, of an army that had passed a whole campaign without coming in sight of the enemy. In Philadelphia the matter was settled very much in the same way. Albany was also obliged to submit, but the magistrates took occasion to tell the royal officers that they did not want their services, as they could defend their frontiers themselves "The frontier was left open to the French; this quartering troops in the principal towns, at the expense of the inhabitants, by the illegal authority of a military chief, was the great result of the campaign." It was becoming clear to the colonists that their safety from the depredations of the French and savages was not to be gained by the royal troops, but by their own efforts.

A congress of governors was held at Boston in January, 1757, and it was resolved that there should be but one expedition this year, and that this should be sent under the Earl of Loudon against Louisburg. The frontier posts, especially Forts Edward and William Henry, were to be defended, and Washington, with the Virginia troops, was to guard the border of that colony against the expeditions of the French from Fort Duquesne. The last was a difficult and almost impossible duty, for the French from Fort Duquesne could choose their point of attack anywhere on the long and exposed frontier, while the force under Washington was utterly inadequate to the task of watching the entire line.

Leaving Bouquet to guard the frontier of Carolina against the Cherokees, and Webb to hold the country between Lake George and the Hudson, Lord Loudon, on the 20th of June, 1757, sailed from New York with six thousand regulars to attack Louisburg. He proceeded to Halifax, where he was joined by a fleet of eleven ships of war and four thousand troops, bringing his whole force to ten thousand regulars and sixteen ships of the line and a number of frigates. The campaign of this redoubtable warrior is thus described by Bancroft: "He landed (at Halifax), levelled the uneven ground for a parade, planted a vegetable

SITE OF FORT WILLIAM HENRY ON LAKE GEORGE.

garden as a precaution against the scurvy, exercised the men in mock battles and sieges and stormings of fortresses, and when August came, and the spirit of the army was broken, and Hay, a major-general, expressed contempt so loudly as to be arrested, the troops were embarked, as if for Louisburg. But ere the ships sailed, the reconnoitring vessels came with the news that the French at Cape Breton had one more ship than the English, and the plan of campaign was changed. Part of the soldiers landed again at Halifax, and the Earl of Loudon, leaving his garden to the weeds, and his place of arms to briars, sailed for New York

The Marquis of Montcalm was a very different man from the Earl of Loudon. As a man he was superior to him in every way; as a commander he was active, quick, and resolute; while Loudon was incompetent, slow, and pompous. Montcalm had stationed himself at Ticonderoga in order to be able to watch the English, and he resolved to take advantage of Lord Loudon's absence to attack Fort William Henry at the head of Lake George On the 2d of August he appeared before the fort with a force of about six thousand French and Canadians and seventeen hundred Indians, and laid siege to it. The garrison consisted of about three thousand men, under Colonel Monroe, a gallant officer Montcalm summoned him to surrender the fort, but Monroe returned an indignant refusal to this demand, and sent to General Webbe, at Fort Edward, fifteen miles distant, to ask for assistance. Webbe might easily have saved the fort, as he had four thousand men under his command, but he made no effort to do so Colonel Putnam, afterwards famous in the Revolution, eagerly sought and at last received permission to march with his regiment to Monroe's assistance, but he had proceeded only a few miles when Webbe commanded him to return to Fort Edward. In the place of assistance, the timid Webbe then sent to Monroe a letter greatly exaggerating the force of the French, and advising him to surrender This letter was intercepted by Montcalm, who was on the point of raising the siege, and he forwarded it to Monroe, with a renewed demand for his surrender. The brave veteran held out, however, until nearly all his guns were disabled and his ammunition nearly exhausted. He then hung out a flag of truce, and Montcalm, who was too true a hero not to appreciate valor in a foe, granted him liberal terms The garrison were allowed to march out with the honors of war upon giving their parole not to serve against France for eighteen months. They were to retain their private property, and were to liberate all their prisoners. On the 9th of August the fort was surrendered to the French.

Montcalm had kept the savages from liquor in order to be able to restrain them in the hour of victory. They now sought and obtained rum from the English, and spent the night in dancing and singing The next morning, as the English marched out of their camp, the Indians fell upon them and began to plunder them From robbery, the excited savages soon passed to murder, and many of the English were killed and others made prisoners. The French officers threw themselves into the melee and exerted themselves gallantly to control the Indians. Many of them were wounded in these efforts. Montcalm in an agony implored the Indians to respect the treaty "Kill me," he cried, as he struggled to restrain the savages, "but spare the English, who are under my protection" He called to the English soldiers to defend themselves The retreat to Fort Edward became a disorderly flight Only about six hundred men reached there in a body More than four hundred had sought shelter in the French camp, and were sent by Montcalm to their friends under the protection of a strong escort. He also sent one of his officers to ransom those who had been taken prisoners by the Indians. The vast stores accumulated at Fort William Henry were carried away by the French, and the work itself demolished.

The loss of Fort William Henry greatly frightened General Webbe at Fort Edward In spite of his force of six thousand men, and the withdrawal of the French to Lake Champlain, he seriously contemplated a retreat to beyond Albany. Lord Loudon, who had arrived at New York, was equally impressed with the danger, and proposed to take position with his army on Long Island for the defence of the continent.

The campaign was over, and the French were everywhere triumphant. With the exception of Acadia, they held all the country they had occupied at the beginning of the war The English had lost the forts at Oswego and William Henry, and immense quantities of supplies. They had been entirely expelled from the valleys of the Ohio and the St. Lawrence, and the hostile parties of the Indians were enabled to extend their ravages far into the interior of the colonies

America was thoroughly disgusted with the incompetency and cowardice of the royal commanders. The old spell of British invincibility was broken, and the colonists were rapidly losing their respect for the troops sent over from England to protect them Men were coming to the conclusion that their connection with Great Britain was simply a curse to the colonies. They regarded the conduct of the war thus far by the royal officials as simply "a mixture of ignorance and cowardice," and were satisfied that they were amply able to defend themselves against the French and Indians without any assistance whatever from England.

The royal officials sought to cover their failures by complaints against the Americans. The hearty disgust and contempt with which the colonists regarded their pusillanimous conduct was reported by them to the home government as evidence of a mutinous spirit on the part of the Americans. Throughout the colonies they pursued one uniform system of seeking to force the provinces into submission to their own illegal acts, and to compel them to an acknowledgment of the arbitrary power of the crown "Everywhere," says Bancroft, "the royal officers actively asserted the authority of the king and the British nation over America.

Did the increase of population lead the legislatures to enlarge the representative body? The right to do so was denied, and representation was held to be a privilege conceded by the king as a boon, and limited by his will.   Did the British commander believe that the French colonies through the neutral islands derived provisions from the continent? By his own authority he proclaimed an embargo in every American port. Did South Carolina, by its assembly, institute an artillery company? Lyttleton interposed his veto, for there should be no company formed but by the regal commission.   By another act, the same assembly made provision for quartering soldiers, introducing into the law the declaratory clause, that 'no soldier should ever be billeted among them.' This also Lyttleton negatived; and but for the conciliatory good temper of Bouquet, who commanded at Charleston, the province would have been inflamed by the peremptory order which came from Loudon to grant billets under the act of Parliament " *

In the eyes of Great Britain America was merely an out-of-the-way corner of the world which existed by the bounty of England, and which was entitled to no rights, no privileges save what the king in his goodness should see fit to allow its people; and in theory and practice every royal official, from the viceroy down to the most insignificant government clerk, arrogated to himself the power of oppression which he claimed for the sovereign.

* Bancroft's *History of the United States*, vol iv, p. 270.

CHAPTER XXIV.

THE FRENCH AND INDIAN WAR—CONCLUDED.

THE gross mismanagement of affairs in America aroused a storm of indignation in England, and the king was obliged to yield to the popular sentiment, and change his ministers. At the head of the new ministry he placed William Pitt, the leader of the popular party, who was destined to become one of the greatest of English statesmen. His great talents had raised him from the insignificant position of ensign in the guards to the leadership of the government of Great Britain, and were now to be the means of retrieving the disasters of his country, and regaining for her her lost power and prestige.

A truly great man, Pitt knew how to admire and sympathize with merit in others, and was not blinded by the glitter of rank, nor hampered by an aristocratic faith in the divinity of royalty. He appreciated and sympathized with the Americans more perfectly than any of his predecessors in office, and began his career with the wise determination to encourage and develop their patriotism by a generous and systematic assistance of their efforts. He caused the government of Great Britain to assume the expenses of the war, and announced that the sums expended by the colonies for the public defence, since the commencement of hostilities, would be refunded, and that henceforth the British govern-

24

ment would provide the funds for the pro-ecution of the war The colonies were each required to furnish troops, but Pitt "stipulated that the colonial troops raised for this purpose should be supplied with arms, ammunition, tents, and provisions, in the same manner as the regular troops, and at the king's expense, so that the only charge to the colonies would be that of levying, clothing, and paying the men. The governors were also authorized to issue commissions to provincial officers, from colonels downwards, and these officers were to hold rank in the united army according to their commissions Had this liberal and just system been adopted at the outset, it would have put a very different face upon the affairs of the colonies " * These energetic and just measures were promptly responded to by the colonies, which placed a force of twenty-eight thousand men in the field To these Pitt added twenty-two thousand British regulars, making a total of fifty thousand men, the largest army that had ever been assembled in America, and exceeding in number the entire male population of Canada.

The Earl of Loudon was recalled, and instead of a single supreme command three separate expeditions were organized under different officers. An expedition against Louisburg was placed under the orders of Lord Jeffrey Amherst, an able and upright soldier, assisted by Brigadier-General James Wolfe, who, though only thirty-one years old, had spent eighteen years in the army, and had served at Dettingen, Fontenoy, and Laffeldt. He was considered one of the ablest commanders in the English service, and was universally beloved. To General Forbes the task of conquering the Ohio valley was assigned, and the expedition against Ticonderoga and Crown Point was intrusted to General Abercrombie. Pitt had little faith in Abercrombie, who had been Lord Loudon's most trusted lieutenant; but retained him to please Lord Bute, and associated with him, as his second in command, the young and gifted Lord George Howe, in the hope that Howe's genius would redeem Abercrombie's faults, and lead him to victory.

The expedition against Louisburg consisted of a fleet of twenty ships of the line and eighteen frigates, under Admiral Boscawen, and an army of fourteen thousand men, under General Amherst. The fleet reached Cabarus bay on the 2d of June, 1758. The fortifications of Louisburg were somewhat dilapidated, but were held by a garrison of thirty-two hundred men, commanded by Chevalier Drucour, an officer of experience and determination. These frigates were sunk across the mouth of the harbor to close it against the English, and within the basin lay five

* Sparks' Writings of Washington, vol ii, p 289—Note.

ships of the line, one fifty-gun ship, and two frigates, which took part in the defence of the place.

The surf was so heavy that Amherst was unable to land his troops until the 8th. The first division was led by Wolfe, under the cover of the fire of the fleet. He forbade a gun to be fired from his command, and, upon nearing the shore, leaped into the water, followed by his men, and in the face of a sharp resistance, drove the French from their outposts into the town. The place was now regularly invested, and, after a bombardment of fifty days, during which the shipping in the harbor was destroyed, the town and fortifications were surrendered to the English on the 27th of July. With Louisburg the French gave up the islands of Cape Breton and Prince Edward. Five thousand prisoners and an immense quantity of military supplies were secured by the English. Halifax being already the chief naval station of the English in these waters, Louisburg was abandoned. Amherst, Wolfe, and Boscawen were honored by the English government for their victory. The season was too far advanced after the capture of Louisburg to admit of the commencement of

WOLFE'S ATTACK ON LOUISBURG.

operations against Quebec, and Amherst was suddenly called away from the coast to take charge of the army on Lake George.

Abercrombie had assembled a force of seven thousand English regulars and nine thousand Americans at the head of Lake George. Among the American troops were Stark and Putnam, afterwards famous in the war for independence, the former serving as a captain in the New Hampshire regiment, the latter as a major of Connecticut troops. Abercrombie was commander-in-chief, but the troops had little confidence in him. They were devoted to Lord Howe, who was the real leader of the expedition. On the 5th of July the army broke up its camp, and embarking in ten hundred and thirty-five boats, with the artillery on rafts, descended the lake to its lower end, from which they were to advance overland upon Fort Carillon, which the French had erected on the promontory of Ticonderoga. The next morning Lord Howe pushed forward with the advanced guard, and encountered a scouting party of the French. A sharp conflict ensued. The French were easily driven back, but Lord Howe was killed almost at the first fire. His death cast a gloom over the army, which promised ill for the success of the undertaking.

Abercrombie continued to advance, and on the morning of the 9th sent Clerk, his chief engineer, to reconnoitre the French position at Ticonderoga. Clerk reported that the French works were feeble, and imperfectly armed. Stark, of New Hampshire, and some of the English officers saw that they were both strong and well provided with artillery. They so reported to Abercrombie, but he accepted the statement of his engineer, and, without waiting for his artillery, ordered an assault upon the French lines that very day.

The Marquis of Montcalm was commanding in person at Ticonderoga,

ABERCROMBIE'S EXPEDITION ON LAKE GEORGE.

and had disposed his small force of thirty-six hundred and fifty men in a line of breastworks thrown up about half a mile beyond the fort, and extending across the promontory on which that work stood. The death of Lord Howe had deprived the English of their only leader capable of contending against this accomplished commander, and the incompetency of Abercrombie was to render easy what might have been, under other circumstances, a most difficult undertaking.

Abercrombie could have brought up his artillery by the next day, but he was unwilling to wait for it, as he anticipated an easy victory. He stationed himself in a place of safety about two miles from the field, and ordered his troops to assail the French intrenchments with the bayonet.

The attack was made in gallant style, and was continued with energy during the afternoon. The English performed prodigies of valor, but were not able to overcome the strength of the French works, or the activity with which the defenders maintained their position. Unlike the English commander, Montcalm was everywhere along his line, cheering his men with his presence and example, and distributing refreshments to them with his own hands. Without a commander who dared place himself under fire, with no one on the spot to direct their movements, the valor of the English was thrown away. A volley from an advanced party of their own men completed their confusion, and they broke helplessly, and fell back in disorder towards Lake George. Abercrombie made no effort to rally them; he was too badly frightened for that; and

ATTACK ON TICONDEROGA.

led the army towards the landing-place, on Lake George, with such haste that but for the energetic action of Colonel Bradstreet the troops would have rushed pell-mell into the boats, without any semblance of order, and with a still greater loss of life.

The English lost nearly two thousand men in the attack upon the French works; but they still had left a force of more than four times the strength of the French, and their artillery had not been engaged. With this force they might have taken Ticonderoga, but Abercrombie was too much terrified to attempt anything of the kind. On the morning of the 9th he embarked his troops and hastened to the head of Lake George. Montcalm was astounded at his retreat, but as he had too small a force, and his men were exhausted, he made no effort at pursuit. Arrived at the head of Lake George, the frightened Abercrombie sent the artillery

and ammunition back to Albany for safety, and occupied his army with
the erection of Fort George, near the ruins of Fort William Henry.
The news of this disaster caused General Amherst to hasten with four
regiments and a battalion from Louisburg to Lake George. He reached
the camp of Abercrombie on the 5th of October. In November orders
arrived from England appointing Amherst commander-in-chief of the
royal forces in America, and recalling Abercrombie, who returned to
England to attempt to excuse his cowardice by villifying America and
the Americans. He could not deceive Pitt, however, whose indignation
at his pusillanimous conduct was only restrained by the influence of Lord
Bute in the royal councils.

After Abercrombie's retreat, Colonel Bradstreet, of New York, at his
earnest solicitation, obtained leave from the council of war to undertake
an expedition against Fort Frontenac, which being situated at the foot of
Lake Ontario, commanded both the lake and the St. Lawrence. Its possession was of the highest importance to the French, as it was their main

depot for the supply
of the posts on the
upper lakes and the
Ohio with military
stores. Collecting a
force of 2700 men,
all Americans, con-
sisting chiefly of
troops from New
York and Massachu-
setts, Bradstreet
hastened to Oswego

INVESTMENT OF FORT FRONTENAC.

before his movements were known to the enemy. From Oswego he
crossed the lake in open boats, and landed on the Canada side within a
mile of Fort Frontenac. His sudden arrival struck terror to the garrison, and the greater part secured their safety by an instantaneous flight.
The next day the fort surrendered. The victors captured with it a vast
quantity of military stores destined for the forts in the interior, and a
fleet of nine armed vessels, with which the French controlled the lake.
Two of the vessels were laden with a part of the stores and sent to Oswego, and the remainder of the vessels and stores, together with the fort,
were destroyed. The English then recrossed the lake to Oswego. The
capture of Fort Frontenac was an event of great importance, as it led, as
we shall see further on, to the abandonment by the French of their posts
in the valley of the Ohio.

For the reduction of Fort Duquesne a force of seven thousand men was assembled under General Forbes. Of these, five thousand were from Pennsylvania and Virginia, the troops from the latter colony being under the command of Colonel Washington. The Pennsylvania troops assembled at Raystown, on the Juniata, and the Virginians at Fort Cumberland. Washington urged upon Forbes the advantages of adopting the old road cut by Braddock's army in his advance to the Ohio, but Forbes, at the suggestion of some land-speculators, decided to construct a new and a better road farther to the north. As regarded the future settlement of the west this was an excellent plan, but as far as it concerned the immediate object of the campaign it was a mistake, as it involved a large expenditure of labor and a great waste of time.

While this road was being constructed General Bouquet, with the advanced guard, crossed Laurel Hill and established a post at Loyal Hanna. The new road progressed very slowly, only forty-five miles being constructed in six weeks. Bouquet had with him a force of about two thousand men, chiefly Highlanders and Virginians. Learning from his scouts that Fort Duquesne was held by a garrison of only eight hundred men, of whom three hundred were Indians, Bouquet, without orders from General Forbes, resolved to attempt the capture of the fort by a sudden blow. He detached a force of eight hundred Highlanders, and a company of Virginians, under Major Grant, to reconnoitre Fort Duquesne. The French were fully informed of all of Grant's movements, but they allowed him to approach unmolested, intending to disarm his vigilance and then attack him. Grant affected the usual contempt for the provincial troops, and upon arriving before the fort, placed Major Lewis with the Virginians to guard the baggage, and sent his regulars forward to reconnoitre and make a sketch of the work. He was greatly encouraged by the fact that the French allowed him to approach without firing a gun at him, and in his self-complacency marched right into an ambuscade which the enemy had prepared for him. The French commander had posted the Indians along the sides of the defile by which Grant was advancing, and at a given signal the garrison made a sudden sally from the fort against the Highlanders, while the Indians opened a heavy fire upon them from their place of concealment. The regulars were quickly thrown into confusion, and their officers were found incapable of conducting such a mode of warfare. Attracted by the firing, Major Lewis, with a company of Virginians, hastened to the scene of the encounter, and by engaging the enemy hand-to-hand enabled the regulars to save themselves from a general massacre. The detachment was routed with heavy loss, and both Grant and Lewis were taken prisoners. The fugitives retreated to the point where the baggage had been left. It was guarded by Captain Bullit, whom Lewis had left there with one company of Virginians By the gallant and skilful resistance of this little force the French and Indians were checked, and finally driven back in confusion. The English then continued their retreat with all speed to Loyal Hanna. Again the provincials had saved the regulars from total destruction. General Forbes had the magnanimity to acknowledge and compliment the Virginians for their services, and Captain Bullit was promoted to the rank of major.

General Forbes was greatly disheartened by the news of Grant's disaster. A council of war was called to deliberate upon the future operations of the army, and decided that as it was now November, and they were still fifty miles from Fort Duquesne, with an unbroken forest between them and the fort, nothing more could be accomplished until the spring. The enterprise was on the point of being abandoned when fortunately three prisoners were brought in, from whom Washington drew the information that the garrison of Fort Duquesne was reduced to a very small force, that the Indians had all deserted the French, and that the expected reinforcements and supplies from Canada had not arrived. It was evident that a well-executed effort would result in the capture of the fort.

This information decided General Forbes to continue the expedition. A force of twenty-five hundred picked troops was placed under Washington's command, and he was ordered to push forward as rapidly as possible, and prepare the road for the advance of the main army. Washington was ably seconded in his movements by the energetic Armstrong, and the march was pressed with such vigor that in ten days the army arrived in the vicinity of Fort Duquesne. The French now saw that the fall of the fort was inevitable. They had but five hundred men, and Bradstreet's capture of Fort Frontenac had cut them off from the reinforcements and supplies they had expected from Canada Unwilling to stand a siege, the result of which was certain, they abandoned the fort on the night of the 24th of November, and embarking in flat boats, floated down the Ohio to join their countrymen in the valley of the Mississippi On the 25th the English army arrived before the fort, and, finding it deserted and in ruins, occupied it At the universal desire of the army Forbes named the place Fort Pitt, which has since been changed to Pittsburgh. The splendid city which occupies the site is the proudest monument that has been built to the memory of the "Great Commoner."

Two regiments, composed of Pennsylvanians, Virginians, and Marylanders, under Mercer, were left in garrison Fort Pitt, which was restored

SOUTHERN VIEW OF PITTSBURGH.

to its former strength   General Forbes then returned east of the mountains, and Washington resigned his commission and retired to private life.   The object of the campaign was accomplished, and he could now enjoy the rest to which five years of constant service had entitled him.

The capture of Fort Duquesne was the most important event of the war.   It put an end to the French occupation of the valley of the Ohio, and settled the claim of Great Britain to that valuable region.   The Indians, having no longer the support and encouragement which they had derived from the French at this post, ceased their hostile efforts, and during the remainder of the war the frontiers of Virginia and Pennsylvania were at peace.   The capture of the fort was followed by a large emigration west of the mountains, which, beginning the next spring, soon placed a large and energetic population of Englishmen and their families in the valley of the Ohio.   The Indians, disheartened by the defeat of the French, began to form treaties of peace or neutrality with the English

Washington's services in this campaign were acknowledged with pride throughout the colonies, but the British government took no notice of them.   Not even Pitt, with all his appreciation of America, thought it worth while to offer him any promotion or reward, as had been done in the case of other meritorious provincial commanders   Soon after his withdrawal from the army he took his seat in the house of burgesses, to which he had been elected   That body ordered its speaker to publicly thank Colonel Washington in the name of the house and of the people of Virginia for his services to his country.   The speaker discharged this duty with ease and dignity, but when Washington attempted to reply he blushed and stammered, and was unable to speak a word.   The speaker relieved his confusion by coming to his assistance with the kind remark, "Sit down, Mr Washington; your modesty equals your valor, and that surpasses the power of any language I possess."

The English cause was now more successful than it had ever been, and Canada was exhausted by the efforts she had put forth for her defence.   This was clear to Montcalm, who had no hope of holding New France against the attacks of Great Britain, and it was also clear to the far-seeing mind of Pitt   The British minister, therefore, resolved that the next campaign should be decisive of the war   He promptly reimbursed the colonies for the expenses incurred by them during the past year, and found no difficulty in enlisting them heartily in his schemes.   Three expeditions were ordered for the year 1759.   Amherst was to advance by way of Lake Champlain, and after capturing Ticonderoga and Crown Point, was to lay siege to Montreal   Wolfe was to ascend the St Lawrence and attack Quebec, and was to be joined by Amherst if the latter should be successful in his efforts against Montreal; and General Prideaux was to proceed by way of Oswego to capture Fort Niagara, and then descend Lake Ontario and join Amherst at Montreal.

Amherst moved promptly against Ticonderoga, which post was abandoned by the French upon his approach. Crown Point fell into his hands in the same manner, but here the advance of the English was stayed. No boats had been provided to transport the army down Lake Champlain, and Amherst was forced to halt until these could be procured.

RUINS OF FORT TICONDEROGA.

He was thus unable to invest Montreal, or to coöperate with Wolfe in the movement against Quebec.

General Prideaux began his march to Oswego about the same time, and proceeding from Oswego laid siege to Fort Niagara. He was killed by the bursting of a gun soon after the commencement of the siege, and the command devolved upon Sir William Johnson, who pressed the attack with vigor. On the 23d of July, 1758, the fort capitulated; but Johnson was obliged to abandon the attempt to descend the St. Lawrence to Wolfe's assistance from a lack of boats and provisions.

The expedition against Quebec assembled in June, 1758, at Louisburg, under the command of General Wolfe. It consisted of eight thousand troops and a fleet of twenty-two ships of the line, besides frigates and some smaller vessels. On the 26th of June the Isle of Orleans was reached, and the troops were immediately landed. A short distance up the river Quebec rose defiantly, its seemingly impregnable citadel of St Louis crowning the lofty cliffs that rose from the river's brink. For the defence of the place Montcalm had six greatly reduced battalions of regulars and a force of Canadian militia. A few Indians remained faithful to him, but the majority of the tribes, doubtful of the issue of the contest, preferred to remain neutral The French commander, seeing the inferiority of his force to that of the English, put his trust chiefly in the natural strength of his position, which he believed would enable him to hold it even with his small force.

The situation of Quebec was peculiar. It lay on a peninsula, between the river St. Charles on the north and the St. Lawrence on the south and east. On these sides it was perfectly protected by the river, leaving the west side alone exposed. The lower town was situated on the beach, while the upper stood on the cliffs two hundred feet above the water, and above this still rose the castle of St Louis Above the city the high promontory on which the upper town was built stretched away for several miles in an elevated plain, and from the river to this plain the rocks rose almost perpendicularly. Every landing-place was carefully guarded, and the whole range of cliffs seemed bristling with cannon. The French commander did not believe it possible for an army to scale these cliffs. Montcalm located his camp below the city, between the St Charles and the Montmorenci rivers, and covered the river front of his position with many floating batteries and ships of war.

The naval superiority of the English at once gave them the command of the river. The French were driven from Point Levi, opposite the city, and upon it Wolfe erected batteries, from which he bombarded the lower town and soon laid it in ashes. The upper town and the citadel were beyond the range of his guns, and could not be injured by this fire.

Wolfe now decided to storm the French camp on the opposite side of the St Lawrence, and in the month of July attacked them from the direction of the Montmorenci, but owing to the haste of the first division, which advanced to the assault before it could be properly supported by the second, the attack was repulsed with a loss of five hundred men. This repulse greatly disheartened the English commander, whose sensitive spirit suffered keenly under the dread that his enterprise was doomed to failure The learned news of the capture of Fort Niagara and the occu-

pation of Ticonderoga and Crown Point, and eagerly watched for the
approach of the promised assistance from Amherst. It never came, and
Wolfe saw that he must take Quebec by his own efforts or not at all.
He attempted several diversions above the city in the hope of drawing
Montcalm from his intrenchments into the open field, but the latter
merely sent De Bougainville with fifteen hundred men to watch the
shore above Quebec and prevent a landing. Wolfe fell into a fever,
caused by his
anxiety, and his
despatches to his
government cre-
ated the gravest
uneasiness in
England for the
success of his
enterprise.

Though ill,
Wolfe examined
the river with
eagle eyes to de-
tect some place
at which a land-
ing could be at-
tempted. His
energy was re-
warded by his
discovery of the
cove which now
bears his name.
From the shore
at the head of
this cove a steep
and difficult

GENERAL JAMES WOLFE.

pathway, along which two men could scarcely march abreast, wound up to
the summit of the heights, and was guarded by a small force of
Canadians. Wolfe at once resolved to effect a landing here and ascend
the heights by this path. The greatest secrecy was necessary to the success of the undertaking, and in order to deceive the French as to his real
design, Captain Cook, afterwards famous as a great navigator, was sent
to take soundings and place buoys opposite Montcalm's camp, as if
that were to be the real point of attack. The morning of the 13th of

September was chosen for the movement, and the day and night of the 12th were spent in preparation for it.

At one o'clock on the morning of the 13th, a force of about five thousand men under Wolfe, with Monckton and Murray, set off in boats from the fleet, which had ascended the river several days before, and dropped down to the point designated for the landing. Each officer was thoroughly informed of the duties required of him, and each shared the resolution of the gallant young commander, to conquer or die. As the boats floated down the stream, in the clear, cool starlight, Wolfe spoke to his officers of the poet Gray, and of his "Elegy in a Country Church-yard." "I would prefer," said he, "being the author of that poem to the glory of beating the French to-morrow." Then in a musing voice he repeated the lines :

> "The boast of heraldry, the pomp of power,
>   And all that beauty, all that wealth e'er gave,
> Await alike the inexorable hour ,
>   The paths of glory lead but to the grave"

In a short while the landing-place was reached, and the fleet, follow-ing silently, took position to cover the landing if necessary. Wolfe and his immediate command leaped ashore, and secured the pathway. The light infantry, who were carried by the tide a little below the path, clambered up the side of the heights, sustaining themselves by clinging to the roots and shrubs which lined the precipitous face of the hill. They reached the summit and drove off the picket-guard after a slight skirmish. The rest of the troops ascended in safety by the pathway, and a battery of two guns was abandoned on the left to Colonel Howe. Having gained the heights, Wolfe moved forward rapidly to clear the forest, and by daybreak his army was drawn up on the Heights of Abraham, in the rear of the city.

Montcalm was speedily informed of the presence of the English. "It can be but a small party come to burn a few houses and retire," he answered incredulously. A brief examination satisfied him of his danger, and he exclaimed in amazement "Then they have at last got to the weak side of this miserable garrison. We must give battle and crush them before mid-day." He at once despatched a messenger for De Bougain-ville, who was fifteen miles up the river, and marched from his camp opposite the city to the Heights of Abraham, to drive the English from them. The opposing forces were about equal in numbers, though the English troops were superior to their adversaries in steadiness and deter-mination. The battle began about ten o'clock, and was stubbornly con-tested. It was at length decided in favor of the English. Wolfe, though wounded several times, continued to direct his army until, as he was leading them to the final charge, he received a musket ball in the breast. He tottered, and called to an officer near him: "Support me; let not my brave fellows see me drop." He was borne tenderly to the rear, and water was brought him to quench his thirst. At this moment the officer upon whom he was leaning cried out: "They run! they run!" "Who run?" asked the dying hero, eagerly. "The French," said the officer, "give way everywhere." "What?" said Wolfe, summoning up his

DEATH OF GENERAL WOLFE BEFORE QUEBEC.

remaining strength, "do they run already? Go, one of you, to Colonel Burton; bid him march Webb's regiment with all speed to Charles river to cut off the fugitives." Then, a smile of contentment overspreading his pale features, he murmured: "Now, God be praised, I die happy," and expired. He had done his whole duty, and with his life had purchased an empire for his country.

Monckton, the second in rank, having been wounded, the command devolved upon General Townshend, a brave officer, but incapable of following up such a success with vigor. He recalled the troops from the

pursuit, and contented himself with the possession of the battle-field
At this moment De Bougainville arrived with his division, but Townshend declined to renew the engagement.

Montcalm had borne himself heroically during the battle, and had
done all that a brave and skilful commander could do to win the victory.
As he was endeavoring to rally his troops at their final repulse, he was
wounded for the second time, and was carried into the city The surgeon
informed him that his wound was mortal. "So much the better," he
answered cheerfully , "I shall not live to see the surrender of Quebec."
De Ramsay, the commandant of the post, asked his advice about the
defence of the city   "To your keeping," answered Montcalm, "I commend the honor of France I will neither give orders nor interfere any
further. I have business of greater moment to attend to My time is
short. I shall pass the night with God, and prepare myself for death "
He then wrote a letter to the English commander, commending the
French prisoners to his generosity, and at five o'clock on the morning of
the 14th his spirit passed away Succeeding generations have paid to
his memory the honors it deserves, and on the spot where the fate of
Quebec was decided the people of Canada have erected, to commemorate
the heroism of the conqueror and the conquered, a noble monument
inscribed with the names of WOLFE and MONTCALM.

The French lost five hundred killed and one thousand prisoners, while
the loss of the English was six hundred in killed and wounded   Five
days afterward, on the 18th of September, the city and garrison of Quebec
surrendered to General Townshend. The capture of this great stronghold was hailed with rejoicings in both America and England. Congratulations were showered upon Pitt, who modestly put them aside with
the reverent remark "I will aim to serve my country , but the more a
man is versed in business, the more he finds the hand of Providence
everywhere "

In April, 1760, De Levi, the French commander at Montreal, attacked
Quebec with a force of ten thousand men, hoping to reduce it before the
arrival of reinforcements from England.   Murray, the English commander, marched out with three thousand men to attack him, and in a
severe battle on the 26th of April was defeated and driven back to the
city with a loss of one thousand men. The French then laid siege to
Quebec, but on the 9th of May an English fleet arrived to its relief, and
De Levi was obliged to withdraw to Montreal In September Montreal
itself was invested by a powerful force under General Amherst. Seeing
that there was no hope of resistance, the French commander surrendered
the town on the 8th of September, 1760. With this capture Canada

passed entirely into the hands of the English. Detroit and the other posts on the lakes were soon given up by the French, and the dominion of France in America was confined to the valley of the Mississippi. There were no further hostilities between the English and French, but, as we shall see, the war was kept up by the Indians for some years later.

The French and Indian war was closed by the treaty of Paris, on the 10th of February, 1763. By this treaty Great Britain obtained all the French territory east of the Mississippi, with the exception of the island of New Orleans, the northern boundary of which was the rivers Iberville and Amité, and Lakes Maurepas and Pontchartrain. Florida was ceded to England by Spain in exchange for Havana. France ceded to Spain the island of New Orleans and all Louisiana west of the Mississippi. Thus Great Britain was mistress of the whole of the vast region east of the Mississippi, with the exception of the island of New Orleans, from the Arctic Ocean to the Gulf of Mexico. The region west of the Mississippi was claimed by Spain. In all the vast continent of America France retained not one foot of ground.

In the meantime the Indians of the southwest had become involved in war with the whites. The Cherokees, who had always been friendly to the English, had done good service during the early part of the war by protecting the frontiers of Virginia, and had served also in Forbes' expedition against Fort Duquesne. They received for their services no reward or pay from any source, and as they were setting out for their homes neither General Forbes nor the colonial authorities supplied them with either food or money. To avoid starvation on their march they were compelled to plunder the barns of some of the settlers, and this led to a conflict which rapidly spread into a border war. Lyttleton, the governor of South Carolina, exerted himself to prevent the restoration of peace, and with success, as he desired the credit of exterminating the Cherokees. He was opposed by the legislature and people of the colony, but in 1759 he sent a force into their country, which committed such ravages that the Cherokees, driven to despair, resolved upon a war of extermination. They made a league with the Muscogees, and sent to the French in Louisiana for military stores. The Carolinians asked aid of General Amherst, who sent them a force of twelve hundred men, principally Highlanders, under General Montgomery. Reinforced by a body of Carolinians, Montgomery invaded the Cherokee country in 1760, and laid it waste. This tribe had made great advances in civilization, and had settled in villages, and engaged in the cultivation of their lands. Their homes were made desolate, and they were driven to the mountains. Montgomery then rejoined Amherst, in the north, in obedience to orders;

25

but the Indians for many years maintained a desultory warfare along the southwestern border

The surrender of Canada to the English was viewed with the greatest disfavor by the Indians of the north and west, who were attached to the French, and were unwilling to submit to the rule of the English   Immediately after the surrender the English occupied all the French posts along the lakes, and in the Ohio valley, with small garrisons.   The contrast between these and the French, who had formerly held these forts, soon impressed itself forcibly upon the minds of the savages.   The French had been friendly and kind to the Indians, and had sought to convert them to Christianity, the English were haughty and domineering, and insulted their priests, and denounced their religion.   The French had prohibited the sale of rum to the Indians; the English introduced it, and finding it profitable continued it, with a recklessness of consequences which did not escape the keen observation of the savages.   The demoralization of the red men was rapid, and drunkenness and its attendant vices wrought sad changes in them   The tribes were bitterly hostile to the men who were ruining their people, and all were alarmed by the rapidity with which emigration had been pouring over the mountains since the capture of Fort Duquesne.   They saw that they were about to be driven from their homes, and forced westward, before the advancing tide of the whites   .

The most determined opponent of the English rule was Pontiac, a chief of the Ottawas.   He was a Catawba by birth, had been brought from his native country as a prisoner, and had been adopted into the Ottawa tribe, whose chief he had become by his bravery and skill.   He was the idol of his own people, and his influence over the neighboring tribes was boundless   He was styled "the king and lord of all the country of the northwest," and bitterly resented the English occupation of his dominions   The first English officer who came to take possession of the French forts was received by him with the stern demand, "How dare you come to visit my country without my leave?"   This "forest hero" now resolved to unite all the tribes of the northwest in a last determined effort to drive out the English, and regain the independence of the red man.   The plan of operations which he adopted was most comprehensive, and was the most remarkable exhibition of genuine leadership ever given by an Indian.   He began negotiations with the neighboring tribes, and induced the Delawares, Shawnees, the Senecas, Miamis, and many of the smaller tribes, occupying the great region of the upper lakes, the valley of the Ohio, and a portion of the Mississippi valley, to join his people in their effort against the English.   He sent a prophet to all the tribes to declare to them that the Great Spirit had revealed to him "that if the English were permitted to dwell in their midst, then the white man's diseases and poisons would utterly destroy them." The conspiracy was pressed forward with energy, and though it was more than a year in forming, it was kept a profound secret.

The principal post on the upper lakes was Detroit. It was surrounded by a numerous French population engaged in agriculture and trading. It was the centre of the trade of this region, and its possession was of the highest importance to the English. Pontiac was anxious to obtain

possession of this fort, and sent word to Major Gladwin, the commandant, that he was coming on a certain day, with his warriors, to have a talk with him. The chief was resolved to make this visit the occasion of seizing the fort, and massacring the garrison; and he and his warriors selected for the attempt cut down their rifles to a length which enabled them to conceal them under their blankets, in order to enter the fort with their arms. The plot was revealed to Gladwin by an Indian girl, whose affections had been won by one of the English officers, and when Pontiac and his warriors repaired to the fort for their "talk" Gladwin made him

PONTIAC.

aware that his conspiracy was discovered, and very unwisely permitted him to leave the fort in safety. Pontiac now threw off the mask of friendship and boldly attacked Detroit. This was the signal for a general war. In about three weeks' time the savages surprised and captured every fort west of Niagara, with the exception of Detroit and Pittsburgh. The garrisons were, with a few exceptions, put to death. Over one hundred traders were killed and scalped in the woods, and more than five hundred families were driven, with the loss of many of their numbers, from their settlements on the frontier. Pontiac endeavored,

without success, to capture Detroit, and a large force of the warriors of
several of the tribes laid siege to Pittsburgh, the most important post in
the valley of the Ohio. The ravages of the Indians were extended over
the wide territory between the Ohio and the Mississippi, and the settlements in that region were for the time completely broken up.

General Bouquet, with a force of five hundred men, consisting chiefly
of Scotch Highlanders, was sent from eastern Pennsylvania to the relief
of Fort Ligonier, which was located at the western base of the mountains, and of Pittsburgh. Their march lay through a region which had
been desolated by the Indians, and they were obliged to depend upon the
stores they carried with them   Upon reaching Fort Ligonier Bouquet
found the communication with Pittsburgh cut off, and could learn nothing
of the fate of the fort or garrison. Leaving his cattle and wagons at
Ligonier, he pushed forward with his men in light marching order, determined to ascertain if Pittsburgh still held out. He had to fight his way
through the Indians, who turned aside from the siege of the fort, and
ambushed the Highlanders at nearly every step   They were overwhelmingly defeated by the gallant Highlanders, for Bouquet was now a veteran
Indian fighter, and had learned to fight the savages with their own tactics.
Their rout was complete, and Bouquet reached Pittsburgh in safety, to the
great joy of the garrison

Bouquet's victory was decisive. The Indians were utterly disheartened, and fled westward, and from that day the Ohio valley was freed
from their violence. The tide of emigration once more began to flow
over the mountains, and this time it was to know no cessation. The
tribes concerned in Pontiac's conspiracy lost hope, and were overawed by
the preparations of the English for their destruction, and began to withdraw from the confederacy, and make peace with the whites. Pontiac
soon found himself deserted by all his followers, even by his own people;
but his proud spirit would not brook the thought of submission. He
would make no treaty, he was the mortal foe of the English, and would
never acknowledge their rule   Leaving his home and his people, he set
out for the country of the Illinois, for the purpose of stirring up the
more distant tribes to war. A proclamation from Lord Amherst offered
a reward for his murder, and he soon fell, the victim of the hired
assassin.

The long war was over. It had brought both loss and gain to the
colonies. It had involved them in an expenditure of $16,000,000, of
which sum but $5,000,000 had been refunded by the English govern-
ment. Thus the debts of the colonies were greatly increased. Thirty
thousand men had been killed, or had died from wounds or disease dur-

ing the war, and the sufferings of the settlers along the extended and exposed frontiers had been almost incalculable.

On the other hand, the war had greatly increased the business of the colonies, especially in those of the north. Large sums had been spent in America by Great Britain for the support of her armies and fleets, and many fortunes were built up by enterprising men during this period Above all the Americans had been taught their own strength, and the value of united action They had often proved their superiority to the regular troops of the English army, and had learned valuable lessons in the art of war In the long struggle Washington, Gates, Morgan, Montgomery, Stark, Putnam, and others were trained for the great work which was to be required of them in future years. The colonies were bound together by a common grievance, arising out of the haughty contempt with which the royal commanders treated the provincial troops, and sacrificed their interests to those of the regulars. The lesson that the colonies could do without the assistance of England, and that their true interests demanded a separation from her, was deeply implanted in the minds of many of the leading men. Another gain for the colonies was a positive increase in their liberties, resulting from the war The necessity of securing the cordial cooperation of the Americans during the struggle caused the royal governors to cease their efforts to enforce arbitrary laws, during the existence of hostilities, as the enforcement of such measures would have alienated the colonists, and have prevented them from raising the needed supplies of men and money. The colonial assemblies were careful to take advantage of this state of affairs They made their grants of supplies with great caution, and retained in their own hands all the disbursements of the public funds. They thus accustomed the people to the practices of free government, and taught them their rights in the matter, so that when the war closed the royal governors found that they were no longer able to practise their accustomed tyranny.

CHAPTER XXV.

CAUSES OF THE AMERICAN REVOLUTION.

HE treaty of Paris placed England in control of the North American continent east of the Mississippi, and the English government was of the opinion that this possession brought with it the right to treat America as it pleased, without regard to the rights or liberties of her people. We have already considered some of the many acts of injustice by which Great Britain drove the colonies into rebellion against her We have now to relate those bearing more immediately on the separation

The navigation acts of 1660 and 1663 were passed, as we have seen, for the purpose of crippling the commerce of the colonies, and confirming their dependence upon England They were severely felt throughout all the colonies, and especially in New England, which was largely dependent upon its commerce These acts were the beginning of a policy deliberately adopted by England, and persisted in by her for more than a century, for the purpose of enriching her mercantile class by depriving the colonists of the just rewards of their labors. The Americans were regarded by the mother country as inferiors, and as dependents, who had been planted by her in "settlements established in distant parts of the world for the benefit of trade." The natural right of all men to acquire property and wealth by the exercise of their industry was denied to them; they were to labor only that the British merchant might grow rich at their expense. Every species of industry in America, save the mere cultivation of the soil, was to be heavily taxed that it might be crushed out of existence. The Americans were to be obliged to ship their products to England for sale, and to be compelled to purchase in her markets the supplies they needed. No foreign country might trade directly with the colonies. Such articles of foreign production as were needed must be shipped to England, and then transferred to British vessels for transportation to the colonies, in order that they might yield a profit to the English ship-owner. The only direct trade which was allowed, and was not taxed, was the infamous traffic in negro slaves, against which every colony protested, and which Great Britain compelled them to accept. Even the trees in the "free woods," suitable for masts, were claimed by the king, and marked by his "surveyor-general of woods." It was a criminal offence to cut one of them after being so marked.

In spite of these outrages the colonies persisted in their efforts to establish manufactures and a commerce of their own. As early as 1643 iron works were established in Massachusetts, and in 1721 the New England colonies contained six furnaces, and nineteen forges. Pennsylvania was still more largely engaged in the manufacture of this metal, and exported large quantities of it to other colonies. By the year 1756 there were eight furnaces and nine forges, for smelting copper, in operation in Maryland. In 1721 the British ironmasters endeavored to induce Parliament to put a stop to the production of iron in America, but without success. In 1750 they were more successful. In that year an act of Parliament forbade, under heavy penalties, the exportation of pig-iron from America to England, and the manufacture by the Americans of bar-iron or steel for their own use. All the iron works in the colonies were ordered to be closed, and any that might afterwards be erected were to be destroyed as "nuisances."

Some of the colonies had engaged in the manufacture of woollen goods, and the making of hats had become a very large and profitable business. In 1732 Parliament forbade the transportation of woollen goods of American manufacture from one colony to another, and the same restriction was placed upon the trade in hats. As an excuse for this outrage it was argued that as the Americans had an unlimited supply of beaver and other furs open to them, they would soon be able to supply all Europe, as well as themselves, with hats. England was unwilling that America should manufacture a single article which she could supply, and in order to cripple the industry of the colonies still further it was enacted by Parliament that no manufacturer should employ more than two apprentices. In 1733 the famous "Molasses Act" was passed, imposing a duty on sugar, molasses, or rum imported into any of the British possessions from any foreign colony. The object of this act was to benefit the British West India possessions by compelling the North American colonies to trade with them

In order to enforce the various restrictions upon the trade of the colonies Great Britain established in America a large force of customs officers, who were given unlawful powers for this purpose. Parliament enacted that any sheriff or officer of the customs, who *suspected* that merchandise imported into the colony in which he was stationed had not paid the duty required by law, might apply to the colonial courts for a search warrant, or "writ of assistance," and enter a store or private dwelling and search for the goods he *suspected* of being unlawfully imported   These writs were first used in Massachusetts in 1761, and aroused a storm of indignation from the people, who felt that their most sacred rights were being violated by them   They were resisted, and the case was carried before the courts in order to test their validity. James Otis, the attorney for the crown, resigned his office rather than argue in behalf of them, and with great eloquence pleaded the cause of the people. His speech created a profound impression throughout the colonies, and aroused a determination in the hearts of his fellow-citizens to oppose the other enactments of Parliament which they felt to be unjust. This trial was fatal to the writs, which were scarcely ever used afterwards. "Then and there," says John Adams, "was the first opposition to arbitrary acts of Great Britain. Then and there American Independence was born."

The spirit of opposition soon manifested itself in the New England colonies. The manufactures, trade, and fisheries of that section were almost ruined, and the people had no choice but to defend themselves. Associations were formed in all the colonies pledging themselves not to purchase of English manufacturers anything but the absolute necessities of life   Families began to make their own linen and woollen-cloths, and to preserve sheep for their wool   Homespun garments became the dress of the patriot party, and foreign cloths were almost driven out of use. It was resolved to encourage home manufactures in every possible way, and associations were formed for this purpose   These measures became very popular, and were adopted by the other colonies in rapid succession.

England was blind to these signs of alienation and danger, and such of her public men as saw them regarded them as of no importance. It was resolved to go still further, and levy direct taxes upon the colonies. In 1763 such a proposition was brought forward by the ministers. It was claimed by them that as the debt of England had been largely increased by the French war, which had been fought in their defence, it was but right that they should help to defray the expense by paying a tax to the English government.

In the meantime the colonies had warmly discussed the intentions of Great Britain respecting them, and all strenuously denied the right of the mother country to tax them without granting them some form of representation in her government. They claimed the right to have a voice in the disposal of their property, and they regarded the design of Parliament as but a new proof of the indisposition of the mother country to treat them with justice. The feeling of the Americans towards England at this period has been aptly described as "distrust and suspicion, strangely mixed up with filial reverence—an instinctive sense of injury, instantly met by the instinctive suggestion that there must be some constitutional reason for doing it, or it would not be done." In spite of the injuries they had received at her hands the Americans were warmly attached to England. They gloried in her triumphs, were proud to trace their descent from her, and claimed a share in her great history and grand achievements. Had England been wise she might have strengthened this attachment to such an extent that the ties which bound the two countries could never have been sundered. But England was not only careless of the rights of Americans, she was grossly ignorant of their country and of their character. "Few Englishmen had accurate ideas of the nature, the extent, or even the position of the colonies. And when the Duke of Newcastle hurried to the king with the information that Cape Breton was an island, he did what perhaps half his colleagues in the ministry, and more than half his colleagues in Parliament, would have done in his place. They knew that the colonies were of vast extent; that they lay far away beyond the sea; that they produced many things which Englishmen wanted to buy, and consumed many things which Englishmen wanted to sell; that English soldiers had met England's hereditary enemies, the French, in their forests; that English sailors had beaten French sailors on their coasts. But they did not know that the most flourishing of these colonies had been planted by men who, prizing freedom above all other blessings, had planted them in order to secure for themselves and their children a home in which they could worship God according to their own idea of worship, and put forth the strength of their minds and of their bodies, according to their own conception of what was best for them here and hereafter."* The few Americans who visited Great Britain found themselves looked upon as aliens and inferiors; their affection for the land of their fathers was met with contempt, and they were ridiculed as barbarians. The English colonial officials made this feeling apparent to those Americans who remained at home. Everywhere the colonists saw themselves treated with injustice. The hard-earned glories of their troops in the colonial wars were denied them and claimed for the English regulars, and there was scarcely a provincial who had borne arms but had some petty insult or injury, at the hands of the royal authorities, to complain of. Looking back over their history the Americans could not remember a time when they had not been treated with injustice by Great Britain. They owed that country nothing for the planting of the colonies; that was the work of their ancestors, who had been forced to fly from England to escape wrong and injury. They had been left to conquer their early difficulties without aid, and with scanty sympathy from England, who had taken no notice of them until they were sufficiently prosperous to be

SAMUEL ADAMS.

profitable to her. Then she had rarely laid her hand upon them but to wrong them. She had pursued such a uniformly unjust policy towards them that their affection for her was rapidly giving way to a general desire to separate from her. They owed her nothing; they were resolved to maintain their liberties against her. Some of the leading men of the colony had already begun to dream of the future greatness of America, and had become convinced that the true interests of their country required a separation from England.

In spite of this feeling England persisted in her course of folly. In March, 1764, the House of Commons resolved, "that Parliament had a

---

* Historical View of the American Revolution. By G. W. Greene, p. 15.

right to tax America." The next month (April) witnessed the enforcement of this claim in the passage of an act of Parliament levying duties upon certain articles imported into America By the same act iron and lumber were added to the "enumerated articles" which could be exported only to England The preamble to this measure declared that its purpose was to raise "a revenue for the expenses of defending, protecting, and securing his majesty's dominions in America"

The colonists protested against this act as a violation of their liberties, and declared that they had borne their full share of the expense of the wars for their defence, that they were now able to protect themselves without assistance from the king, and added the significant warning that "taxation without representation was tyranny" No one yet thought of armed resistance; the colonists were resolved to exhaust every peaceful means of redress before proceeding to extreme measures. As yet the desire for separation was confined to a few far-seeing men.

Prominent among these was Samuel Adams, of Boston, a man in whom the loftiest virtues of the old Puritans were mingled with the graces of more modern times. Modest and unassuming in manner, a man of incorruptible integrity and sincere piety, he was insensible to fear in the discharge of his duty He was a deep student of constitutional law, and was gifted with an eloquence which could move multitudes. His clear vision had already discerned the dangers which threatened his country, and had discovered the only path by which she could emerge from them in safety. His plan was simple: resistance, peaceable at first; forcible if necessary. Under his guidance the people of Boston met and protested against the new plan of taxation, and instructed their representatives in the general court to oppose it. "We claim British rights, not by charter only," said the Boston resolves; "we are born to them If we are taxed without our consent, our property is taken without our consent, and then we are no more freemen, but slaves." The general court of Massachusetts declared "that the imposition of duties and taxes by the Parliament of Great Britain upon a people not represented in the House of Commons is absolutely irreconcilable with their rights" A committee was appointed to correspond with the other colonies, with a view to bringing about a concerted action for the redress of grievances. In Virginia, New York, Connecticut, and the Carolinas equally vigorous measures were taken.

In Virginia the first indication of the intention of the people to resist the arbitrary measures of the crown was given in a matter insignificant in itself, but clearly involving the great principle at issue. In that colony tobacco was the lawful currency, and the failure of a crop, or a rise in the price of tobacco, made such payments often very burdensome. In the winter of 1763 the legislature passed a law authorizing the people of the colony to pay their taxes and other public dues in money, at the rate of twopence a pound for the tobacco due. The clergymen of the established church had each a salary fixed by law at a certain number of pounds of tobacco, and as this measure involved them in a loss they refused to acquiesce in it, and induced Sherlock, the bishop of London, to persuade the king to refuse the law his signature. "The rights of the clergy and the authority of the king must stand or fall together", was the sound argu-

PATRICK HENRY.

ment of the bishop. Failing of the royal signature the law was inoperative.

The matter was soon brought to an issue in Virginia. The Rev. Mr. Maury, one of the clergymen affected by the law, brought a suit to recover damages, or the difference between twopence per pound and the current market price of tobacco, which was much higher. This was popularly known as the "Parsons' Cause." It was a clearly joined issue between the right of the people to make their own laws on the one side, and the king's prerogative on the other. The "parsons" secured the best talent in the colony for the prosecution of their claims; the cause of the "people" was confided to a young man of twenty-seven, whose youth was supplemented by the additional disadvantages of being poor and unknown. He was Patrick Henry, the son of a plain farmer, and a native of the county of Hanover. He had received but little education, as his father's straitened circumstances had compelled him to put his son to the task of earning his bread at the early age of fifteen years. He entered a country store, and the next year went into business with his elder brother, William, who being too indolent to attend to business left the store to the management, or rather the mismanagement of Patrick. The young man was brimming over with good nature, and could never find it in his heart to refuse any one credit, and was too kind-hearted to press unwilling debtors to payment   He let the store "manage itself," and amused himself by studying the character of his customers, and with his flute and violin   He was also a great reader, and read every work he could buy or borrow   The store survived about a year, and the next two or three years were passed by Patrick in settling its affairs.   At the age of eighteen he married, and began life as a farmer.   He soon grew tired of this pursuit, and selling his farm once more engaged in mercantile life.   It was not suited to him, nor he to it.   He passed his days in reading, this time giving his attention to works of history and philosophy. Livy was his favorite, and he read it through at least once a year for many years   His second mercantile enterprise ended in bankruptcy in a few years, and in extreme want he determined to try the law.   He obtained a license to practice after a six weeks' course of study, and entered upon his new career utterly ignorant of its duties   It is said that he could not then draw up the simplest legal paper without assistance   He was then twenty-four years old, but it was not until he had reached the age of twenty-seven that he obtained a case worthy of his powers, for he had genius, and it only required the proper circumstances to draw it out   He had passed days in communion with nature in his frequent hunting and fishing excursions, and had drunk deeply of the wisdom she imparts to her votaries.   He had studied men with the eye of a master, and he had at last fallen into the position from which he could rise to his true place among the leading spirits of the age.   In the case with which he was now intrusted, a decision of the court on a demurrer, in favor of the claims of the clergy, had left nothing undetermined but the amount of damages in the cause which was pending.

"The array before Mr Henry's eyes," says his biographer, William Wirt, "was now most fearful.   On the bench sat more than twenty clergymen, the most learned men in the colony, and the most capable, as well as the severest critics before whom it was possible for him to have made his debut.   The court-house was crowded with an overwhelming multitude, and surrounded with an immense and anxious throng, who, not finding room to enter, were endeavoring to listen without, in the deepest attention.   But there was something still more awfully disconcerting than all this; for in the chair of the presiding magistrate sat no other person than his own father.   Mr. Lyons opened the cause very briefly : in the way of argument he did nothing more than explain to the jury that the decision upon the demurrer had put the act of 1750 entirely out of the way, and left the law of 1748 as the only standard of their damages; he then concluded with a highly wrought eulogium on the benevolence of the clergy."

When it came Patrick Henry's turn to speak, he rose awkwardly, amid a profound silence. No one had ever heard him speak, and all were anxious to see how he would acquit himself. He clutched nervously at his papers, and faltered out his opening sentences with a degree of confusion which threatened every moment to put an end to his effort. The people watched their champion in sorrow and indignation; the clergy exchanged glances of triumph, and eyed the speaker with contempt, while his father, overcome with shame, seemed ready to drop from his chair. But suddenly there came a change over the young advocate. Warming with his subject, he threw off his embarrassment and awkwardness, and stood erect and confident. His look of timidity gave place to one of command; his countenance glowed with the fire of genius, and startled the gazers by the aspect of majesty which it assumed for the first time. His tones grew clear and bold, his action graceful and commanding, and the astounded jury and audience were given a display of eloquence such as was without a parallel in the history of the colony. Henry knew that the case was against him, but he pleaded the natural right of Virginia to make her own laws independently of the king and Parliament. He proved the justness of the law; he drew a striking picture of the character of a good king, who should be the father of his people, but who becomes their tyrant and oppressor, and forfeits his claim to obedience when he annuls just and good laws. The opposing counsel cried out at this bold declaration, "He has spoken treason," but was silenced by the excited throng.

"They say," says Mr. Wirt, "that the people, whose countenances had fallen as he arose, had heard but a very few sentences before they began to look up; then to look at each other in surprise, as if doubting the evidence of their own senses; then, attracted by some gesture, struck by some majestic attitude, fascinated by the spell of his eye, the charm of his emphasis, and the varied and commanding expression of his countenance, they could look away no more. In less than twenty minutes they might be seen in every part of the house, on every bench, in every window, stooping forward from their stands, in death-like silence; their features fixed in amazement and awe, all their senses listening and riveted upon the speaker, as if to catch the last strain of some heavenly visitant. The mockery of the clergy was soon turned into alarm, their triumph into confusion and despair, and at one burst of his rapid and overwhelming invective, they fled from the bench in precipitation and terror. As for the father, such was his surprise, such his amazement, such his rapture, that, forgetting where he was, and the character which he was filling, tears of ecstasy streamed down his cheeks without the power or inclination to repress them."

The jury brought in a verdict of one penny damages for the "parsons," and the court overruled the motion of their counsel for a new trial. Henry from that moment took his place among the leaders of the patriot party in Virginia. He had struck a chord which responded in every American heart; he had denied the right of the king to make laws for the colonies.

The remonstrance of Massachusetts was followed by similar appeals from Connecticut, New York, Rhode Island, and Virginia. The petition of New York was couched in such strong terms that no member of Parliament could be found bold enough to present it. These remonstrances were unheeded by Parliament, which pronounced them "absurd" and "insolent." That body persisted in its determination to tax the colonies, and Grenville, the prime minister, warned the Americans that in a contest with Great Britain they could expect nothing but defeat. He announced the intention of the English government to levy the taxes, and graciously added that if the colonies preferred any special form of taxation, their wishes would be met as far as possible. In March, 1765, the measure known as the "Stamp Act" passed the House of Commons by a vote of five to one, and was adopted almost unanimously by the House of Lords. It met with a warm opposition in the Commons from the friends of America, prominent among whom was Colonel Barré, who had served with Wolfe in America, and had learned to appreciate the American character. The measure received the royal signature at once. The poor king would have signed any thing he was bidden—*he was insane.* The act imposed a duty on all paper, vellum, and parchment used in the colonies, and required that all writings of a legal or business nature should be made on "stamped paper;" otherwise they were declared null and void.

GEORGE THE THIRD.

In order to enforce the "Stamp Act," Parliament, two months later, passed "the Quartering Act." It authorized the ministers to send as many troops as they should see fit to America, to enforce submission to the acts of Parliament. Wherever these troops should be stationed, it should be the duty of the people, at their own expense, to furnish them with quarters, fuel, bedding, cider or rum, candles, soap, "and other necessaries."

The news of the passage of these acts produced the most intense excitement in America. The general assembly of Virginia was in session when the news was received in May. The royalist leaders were amazed at the folly of the ministry, but deemed it best to take no action in the matter. Patrick Henry, now a member of the assembly, rose in his place and offered a series of resolutions, declaring that the people of Virginia were bound to pay only such taxes as should be levied by their own assembly, and that all who maintained the contrary should be regarded as enemies of the liberties of the colony. These resolutions provoked an exciting debate, in which Henry in a magnificent oration exposed the tyranny of the British government, and stirred the hearts of the burgesses with a determination to resist. "Cæsar had his Brutus," exclaimed the orator in one of his loftiest flights, "Charles the First his Cromwell, and George the Third —." The assembly was in an uproar. "Treason! treason!" shouted the speaker. A few joined in the cry, but the majority waited in breathless suspense the completion of the sentence of Henry, who, fixing his eye upon the speaker, added in a tone which was peculiar to himself, "may profit by their example. If that be treason, make the most of it." The resolutions were adopted by a large majority. The next day, during Henry's absence, the timid assembly rescinded some of the resolves, and modified the others. The assembly, for thus daring to exercise its right of expressing its opinion, was at once dissolved by the governor; but too late to prevent its action from producing its effect. Copies of the resolutions of Henry were forwarded to Philadelphia, where they were printed and circulated through the colonies. They aroused the drooping spirits of the people, and it was resolved everywhere that the stamps should not be used in America

The general court of Massachusetts ordered that the courts should not require the use of stamps in conducting their business, and in June, before the Virginia resolutions reached Boston, issued a circular inviting all the colonies to send delegates to a Congress to be held at New York in October. In the meantime associations were organized in all the colonies as far south as Maryland, called "Sons of Liberty," for the purpose of stopping the use of stamps. The people were resolved to take the matter in their own hands. In Boston the mob attacked the house of Oliver, the secretary of the colony, who had been appointed to distribute the stamps, and compelled him to resign. They also attacked the houses of some of the most prominent supporters of the ministry, but the patriots sincerely deplored and condemned these violent proceedings At Wethersfield, Connecticut, five hundred farmers seized Jared Ingersol, the stamp officer for that colony, compelled him to resign, and then to remove his hat and give "three cheers for liberty, property, and no stamps."

Similar scenes were enacted in the other colonies, expressive of the determination of the people to resist the measures of the crown.

On the 7th of October, 1765, the *First Colonial Congress* met at New York. It was composed of delegates from the colonies of Massachusetts, Rhode Island, Connecticut, Pennsylvania, Maryland, South Carolina, New York, and New Jersey. New Hampshire, though not represented by a delegate, gave her support to its measures, and Georgia formally signified her acceptance of the work of this body. Timothy Ruggles, of Massachusetts, was chosen president. The session extended over three weeks, and resulted in the adoption of a "Declaration of the Rights and Grievances of the Colonies," a petition to the king, and a memorial to both Houses of Parliament. In the Declaration of Rights the Congress took the ground that it was a violation of their rights to tax them without granting them a representation in the Parliament of Great Britain, and that as such representation was impossible because of the distance between the two countries, no taxes could be legally imposed upon the colonies but by their own assemblies. The measures of the Congress were, as soon as possible, indorsed by all the colonial assemblies, and thus the colonies were drawn into that union which, in their own language, became "a bundle of sticks, which could neither be bent nor broken."

At length the 1st of November arrived, the day on which the Stamp Act was to go into operation. Not a man could be found to execute the law, all the stamp officers having resigned through fear of popular violence. Governor Colden, of New York, declared he was resolved to have the stamps distributed, but the people of the city warned him that he would do so at his peril, and burned him in effigy. Colden became alarmed at these demonstrations, and on the 5th of November delivered the stamps to the mayor and council of New York. In all the colonies the 1st of November was observed as a day of mourning. Bells were tolled, flags hung at half-mast, and business suspended. The merchants of New York, Boston, and Philadelphia united in an agreement to import no more goods from England, to countermand the orders already sent out, and to receive no goods on commission until the Stamp Act should be repealed. Their action was promptly sustained by the people, who pledged themselves to buy no articles of English manufacture, and to encourage home productions. Circulars were sent throughout the colonies urging the people to unite in such action, and were heartily responded to. Business went on without the use of stamps, and the courts ignored them in their proceedings.

The news of these proceedings should have warned the English ministers of their folly: it only made them more determined to persist in it.

26

They resolved not to repeal the Stamp Act. To comply with the request of the colonists now that they had resisted the law, would, they declared, be simply a surrender to rebellion. "Sooner than make our colonies our allies," said one of their number, "I would wish to see them returned to their primitive deserts." The friends of America, led by the aged and infirm William Pitt, made a determined effort to procure the repeal of the Stamp Act, and they were now supported by all the influence of the English merchants, who found their trade rapidly falling off in consequence of the non-intercourse resolves adopted by the Americans.

STAMP ACT OFFICIAL BEATEN BY THE PEOPLE.

Swathed in flannels, Pitt proceeded to the House of Commons, and in a speech of great vigor urged the House to repeal the obnoxious and unconstitutional measure. In reply to Grenville, the prime minister, who accused him of exciting sedition in America, he said, "Sir, I have been charged with giving birth to sedition in America. Sorry I am to have the liberty of speech in this House imputed as a crime. But the imputation will not deter me: it is a liberty I mean to exercise. The gentleman tells us that America is obstinate, that America is almost in rebellion I rejoice that America has resisted." The House started at these words, but Pitt continued firmly, "If they had submitted, they would have voluntarily become slaves. They have been driven to madness by injustice. My opinion is that the Stamp Act should be repealed, absolutely, totally, immediately." Edmund Burke, then a rising young man, eloquently sustained the appeal of the great commoner

The Commons had already begun to waver, but before yielding entirely, they wished to ascertain from competent witnesses the exact temper and disposition of the Americans. For this purpose, Benjamin Franklin, who was residing in London at the time as the agent of several of the colonies, was summoned before the bar of the House to give the desired information. He appeared, in answer to the summons, on the 13th of February, 1766. He was questioned by Lord Grenville and Charles Townshend, and by several friends of the ministry, and delivered his answers with firmness and clearness He told them that the colonists could not pay for the stamps, as there was not enough gold and silver in the colonies for that purpose, that they had incurred more than their share of the expense of the last war, for which Great Britain had in no way reimbursed them; that they were still burdened with heavy debts contracted in consequence of this war, that they were well disposed towards Great Britain before 1763, and considered Parliament as "the great bulwark and security of their liberties and privileges; but that now their temper was much altered, and their respect for it lessened; and if the act is not repealed, the consequence would be a total loss of the respect and affection they bore to this country, and of all the commerce that depended on that respect and affection." He startled the House by declaring that in a few years America would be amply able to supply herself with all the necessities of life then furnished her by Great Britain. "I do not know," said he, "a single article imported into the northern colonies but what they can either do without or make themselves. The people will spin and work for themselves, in their own houses. In three years there may be wool and manufactures enough." "If the legislature," he was asked, "should think fit to ascertain its right to lay taxes, by any act laying a small tax, contrary to their opinion, would they submit to pay the tax?" "An internal tax," he replied, "how small soever, laid by the legislature here, on the people there, will never be submitted to They will oppose it to the last The people will pay no internal tax by Parliament." "May they not," asked a friend of Grenville, "by the same interpretation of their common rights, as Englishmen, as declared by Magna Charta and the Petition of Right, object to the Parliament's right of external taxation?"* "They never have hitherto," answered Franklin, promptly. "Many arguments have been lately used here to show them that there is no difference, and that if you have no right to tax them internally, you have none to tax them externally, or make any other law to bind them. At present they do not reason so, but in time they may be convinced by these arguments."

Franklin's testimony was conclusive. The Stamp Act was repealed on the 18th of March, 1766, not because it was acknowledged by England as a measure of injustice, but because it could not be enforced without a collision with the colonies, which the ministry were not as yet prepared for. The people of London greeted the repeal with great joy. Bonfires were lighted, bells were rung, the city was illuminated, and the shipping in the Thames was decorated with flags. The news was sent by special messengers to the nearest ports, in order that it might reach America with as little delay as possible.

In America the news of the repeal of the Stamp Act was received with the greatest joy. The bells were rung in the principal cities, the imprisoned debtors were released from captivity, the associations for non-intercourse with England were dissolved, and everywhere Pitt was hailed as the champion of the liberties of America. New York, Virginia, and Maryland each voted a statue to him.

The rejoicings of the Americans were premature. Parliament in repealing the Stamp Act solemnly asserted, by a bill for that purpose, its right and power to "bind the colonies in all cases whatsoever." England was only baffled for the moment, she had not relinquished her designs upon the liberties of America.

The repeal of the Stamp Act brought with it the fall of Grenville's ministry. Another was appointed under the leadership of the Marquis of Rockingham, but it was short-lived, and soon gave way. The king then summoned William Pitt, who had in the meantime been created Earl of Chatham, to form an independent ministry, late in 1766. This act was regarded with great hope in America, as Pitt was universally considered the colonists' best friend. These hopes were doomed to disappointment. In January, 1767, Charles Townshend, the chancellor of the exchequer in Pitt's cabinet, taking advantage of the absence of the prime minister, declared in the House of Commons that it was his intention, at all risks, to derive a revenue from America by laying taxes upon her, and that he knew how to raise this revenue from her. Having thus thrown down the gauntlet to his official chief it became evident that either the Earl of Chatham must relinquish the premiership, or Townshend must leave the

* The carrying of duties by Parliam on articles imported into the **colonies.**

cabinet. Chatham was anxious to dismiss him from the chancellorship, but as it was known that Townshend was acting in accordance with the sympathies and wishes of the king, no one was willing to risk his prospects by accepting the chancellorship in Townshend's place, and Chatham, unable to fill his place, was obliged to retain him. In utter disgust Chatham withdrew from active participation in the affairs of the cabinet, and Townshend remained supreme director of the colonial policy of England. In May Townshend revealed his plan for raising a revenue in America. It was to levy a duty, to be collected in the colonies, on certain articles of commerce, such as wine, oil, paints, glass, paper, and lead colors, and especially upon tea, which last commodity he declared the Americans obtained cheaper from the Dutch smugglers than the English themselves. He was told that if he would withdraw the army from America there would be no necessity for taxing the colonies. He replied, "I will hear nothing on the subject; it is absolutely necessary to keep an army there." In June, 1767, an act was passed by Parliament levying upon the colonies the duties proposed by Townshend; and a board of commissioners of the customs for America was established, with its head-quarters at Boston. Soon after their appointment the "Romney" frigate entered Boston harbor, and the new commissioners, confident in her protection, treated the people of Boston with unbearable haughtiness. Her officers frequently stopped the New England vessels as they entered the harbor, and impressed seamen from their decks.

The colonies were moved with the profoundest indignation upon the receipt of the news of the imposition of the new taxes. The colonial newspapers, which now numbered twenty-five, were filled with appeals to the people to stand up for their liberties. The old associations for non-importation of English goods were revived, and on every hand the declaration was unanimous that the Americans would neither eat, drink, nor wear anything imported from England. The general court of Massachusetts issued a circular letter to the other colonial assemblies inviting them to unite with her in measures for obtaining redress.

The English ministers were greatly incensed at the new resistance of the colonists, and in June, 1768, ordered the general court of Massachusetts to rescind its circular letter. Their demand was refused, and the general court, led by James Otis and Samuel Adams, expressed its conviction that Parliament would better serve the cause of peace by repealing its obnoxious laws. The circular had been favorably received by the other colonies, and Massachusetts was constantly receiving from them encouragement to persist in her resistance to the tyranny of the ministry. As a punishment for the refusal of the general court to rescind its circu-

lar, that body was dissolved by the royal governor of Massachusetts.
Some of the other colonial assemblies that had shown sympathy with
Massachusetts were also dissolved by their respective governors.

A very bitter feeling existed between the people and the royal officials,
and, to make matters worse, at this crisis the revenue officers at Boston
seized a schooner belonging to John Hancock, one of the patriot leaders,
on the pretext that her owner had made a false entry of her cargo, which
consisted of wine. The schooner was towed under the guns of the
"Romney" frigate, and a crowd collected in Boston and attacked the

FANEUIL HALL IN 1775.

houses of the commissioners of customs, who were forced to fly to the fort
on Castle island for safety.

The report of this outbreak was transmitted to England as proof that
Massachusetts was almost in a state of insurrection, and it was resolved
by the ministry to send troops to overawe "the insolent town of Boston,"
and to hold Massachusetts as a conquered country. A regiment of regulars under General Gage reached Boston in September, 1768, but the
assembly refused to provide quarters or food, or the other necessaries
which were demanded by their commander in accordance with the
"Quartering Act." General Gage was obliged to encamp a part of his
men on Boston Common, while he lodged the rest temporarily in Faneuil

Hall. With considerable difficulty he hired several houses in Boston and quartered his troops in them. The assembly of New York also refused to provide food or quarters for the royal troops, and was dissolved by the governor of the province.

The wrath of the English officials was concentrated upon Boston, which was held as though it were a conquered city. Sentinels were placed at the street corners, and the citizens were challenged by them as they went about their daily duties. The ill-feeling between the citizens and the troops gave rise to several encounters between them. On the evening of the 2d of March, 1770, a sentinel was attacked by the mob. A detachment of troops was sent to his aid, and was stoned by the mob. At length a soldier fired his musket at the crowd and his comrades poured in a volley, killing three and wounding five citizens. The city was thrown

THE BOSTON MASSACRE.

into an uproar, the alarm bells were rung, and crowds poured into the streets. The danger of a general collision was very great, but the people were persuaded to disperse upon the promise of Hutchinson, the governor, that justice should be done. This outbreak was known at the time as "the Boston Massacre." The next morning a meeting of the citizens was held at Faneuil Hall. Resolutions were passed, demanding the removal of the troops from the city to the fort on Castle island, and the arraignment before the civil courts of Captain Preston, the officer who ordered the troops to fire. The soldiers were removed from the town as the only means of preserving the peace, and Captain Preston and six of his men were arraigned for murder. John Adams and Josiah Quincy, two leaders of the patriot party, undertook the defence of the accused officer and his men in order to make sure that they should have a fair trial. They were acquitted of murder, but two of the soldiers were convicted of manslaughter. The calmness and deliberation with which the trial was conducted had a happy effect in England, and exhibited the fairness and moderation of the colonists in the most favorable light

The British merchants now began to feel the effect of the non-importation associations of the Americans, and their trade suffered even more than it had done in the times of the Stamp Act, in consequence of the cessation of orders for goods from the colonies They now began to sustain the demand of the colonists for the repeal of the unjust taxes. Lord North, who was now prime minister, was willing to grant their demand, and to remove all the taxes except the duty on tea, which he retained at the express command of the king, who had now recovered his reason, and was the real director of the policy of his government. George III. held on with the most stubborn tenacity to the assertion of his right to tax the colonies, and insisted "that there should be always one tax, at least, to keep up the right of taxing." This concession was made in May, 1770, and for nearly a year there was a lull in the excitement. The matter was not settled, however, for the Americans had not resisted the amount of the tax, but the imposition of any tax at all. They were contending for a principle, not for the saving of a few dollars.

The bad feeling which was rapidly growing up between the colonists and the mother country was greatly increased by the injustice and annoyance heaped upon the colonists by the royal officials. Almost every colony had to complain of these outrages, and the king's officers seemed to think they could not do their cause better service than by exasperating the Americans. In New York the people had erected a liberty pole in the fields, now the City Hall Park One night in January, 1770, a party of soldiers from the fort cut down the pole. This act was bitterly resented by the citizens, and frequent quarrels occurred between them and the troops, though there was no actual bloodshed.

Early in 1772 the armed schooner "Gaspé" was stationed in Narragansett bay to enforce the revenue laws. Her commander, Lieutenant Dudingston, undertook to execute his orders in the most insulting and arbitrary manner Market boats and other vessels passing the "Gaspé" were compelled to lower their colors to her, and armed parties from the schooner were sent ashore on the neighboring islands, and carried off such provisions as they desired. Complaint was made by the citizens of Providence to the governor of Rhode Island, who referred the matter to the chief justice, Hopkins, for his opinion The chief justice declared "that any person who should come into the colony and exercise any authority by force of arms without showing his commission to the governor, and, if a custom-house officer, without being sworn into his office, was guilty of a trespass, if not piracy." It was clear from the opinion of the chief justice that Dudingston was exceeding his authority, and the governor sent a sheriff on board the "Gaspé" to ascertain by what orders the lieutenant acted. Dudingston referred the matter to the admiral at Boston, who replied "The lieutenant, sir, has done his duty. I shall give the king's officers directions that they send every man taken in molesting them to me. As sure as the people of Newport attempt to rescue any vessel and any of them are taken I will hang them as pirates."

The insolence of the admiral caused even more indignation than the outrages of Dudingston, and the citizens of Rhode Island resolved to take the matter into their own hands at the earliest opportunity. On the 9th of June, 1772, the Providence packet, a swift sailer, was passing up the bay when she was hailed by the "Gaspé." She paid no attention to the hail, and being of light draught stood in near the shore. The "Gaspé" gave chase, and, attempting to follow her, ran aground on Namquit, a short distance below Pautuxet. The tide falling soon, left her fast. The news of her disaster was conveyed to Providence by the packet, and a plan was at once matured for her destruction. On the following night a party of men in six or seven boats, led by John Brown, a leading merchant of Providence, Captain Abraham Whipple of Providence, Simeon Potter of Bristol, and others, left Providence and dropped down towards the position of the "Gaspé." They were discovered as they approached, and were hailed by Dudingston. One of the party in the boats fired and Dudingston fell wounded. The schooner was then boarded without opposition, her crew were set ashore, and the "Gaspé" was set on fire and burned to the water's edge. A large reward was offered for the perpetrators of this bold act. All were known in Providence; but in spite of this, the royal officials were not able to secure the apprehension of any of them. The secret was faithfully kept.

The non-importation associations had, upon the repeal of the duties we have mentioned, limited their opposition to the use of tea, and the East India Company in England found itself burdened with an enormous stock of tea which it could not dispose of as usual in consequence of the cessation of sales in America. The company therefore proposed to pay *all* the duties on the tea in England, and ship it to America at its own risk, hoping that the fact of there being no duty to pay *in America* would induce the colonists to purchase it. This plan met the determined opposition of the king, who would not consent to relinquish the assertion of his right to tax the Americans. Lord North could not understand that it was not the amount of the tax but the principle involved in it, that was opposed by the Americans, and he proposed, that the East India Company should pay *three-fourths* of the duty in England, leaving the other fourth—about three pence on a pound—to be collected in America. His lordship was told plainly that the Americans would not purchase the tea on these conditions, but he answered: "It is to no purpose the making objections, for the king will have it so   The king means to try the question with the Americans."

There were men in America who fully understood that the king meant "to try the question with the Americans," and were willing the trial should come. Samuel Adams was satisfied as to what would be the result, and was diligently working to prepare the people for it. He had the satisfaction of seeing public opinion in America daily assume a more enlightened and determined condition. A convention of all the colonies for taking action for a common resistance seemed to him a necessity, and he sent forth circulars to the various provinces urging them to assert their rights upon every possible occasion, and to combine for mutual support and protection.

The news of the agreement between the East India Company and the government for the exportation of tea increased the determination of the colonists to resist the tax. It was also resolved that the tea should neither be landed nor sold. A meeting was held in Philadelphia and resolutions were passed requesting those to whom the tea was consigned "to resign their appointments." It was also resolved that whosoever should "aid or abet in unloading, receiving, or vending the tea" should be regarded "as an enemy to his country." Meetings of a similar nature were held in New York and Charleston, and similar resolutions were adopted   A fast-sailing vessel reached Boston about the 1st of November, 1773, with the news that several ships laden with tea had sailed from England for America. On the 3d of November a meeting was held at Faneuil Hall, and on motion of Samuel Adams, it was unanimously resolved to send the tea back upon its arrival   A man in the crowd cried out· "The only way to get rid of it is to throw it overboard"   The meeting invited the consignees of the tea to resign their appointments. Two of these men were sons of Governor Hutchinson, who was intensely hated by the people of Massachusetts because of his double-faced policy, which had been detected and exposed by Dr. Franklin. Until this discovery Hutchinson had induced the people of Massachusetts to believe that he was their best friend, when in reality he had suggested to the British government nearly all the unjust measures that had been directed against that colony.

The first of the tea-ships reached Boston on the 25th of November,

1773. A meeting of the citizens was held at Faneuil Hall, and it was ordered that the vessel should be moored to the wharf, and a guard of twenty-five citizens was placed over her to see that no tea was removed. The owner of the vessel agreed to send the cargo back if the governor would give his permit for the vessel to leave Boston. This the governor withheld, and in the meantime two other ships arrived with cargoes of tea and were ordered to anchor beside the first. The committee appointed by the meeting of citizens waited on the consignees, but obtained no satisfaction from them. The law required that the tea must be landed within twenty days after its arrival, or be seized for non-payment of duties. The consignees and the governor had determined to wait until the expiration of this time, when the royal authorities would seize the tea and remove it beyond the reach of the citizens. The duties could then be paid and the tea landed and sold. Their intentions were fully understood by the patriots. When the committee made its report to the meeting of citizens, it was received in a dead silence, and the meeting adjourned without taking any action upon it. This ominous silence alarmed the consignees. Hutchinson's two sons fled to the fort and placed themselves under the protection of the troops, while the governor quietly left the city.

On the 16th of December another meeting was held. The next day the time allowed by law would expire and the tea would be placed under the protection of the fort and the armed ships in the harbor. The owner had gone to see the governor, at Milton, to obtain a pass for his vessels, without which they could not leave the harbor. This the governor refused on the ground that he had not a proper clearance. He returned to Boston late in the evening and reported the result of his mission to the meeting. Then Samuel Adams arose and gave the signal for the action that had been determined upon by saying, "This meeting can do nothing more to save the country."

Instantly a shout rang through the room, and a band of forty or fifty men "dressed like Mohawk Indians," with their faces blackened to prevent recognition, hastened from the meeting to the wharf where the ships were moored. A guard was posted to prevent the intrusion of spies, and the ships were at once seized. Three hundred and forty-two chests of tea were broken open and their contents poured into the water. The affair was witnessed in silence by a large crowd on the shore. When the destruction of the tea was completed, the "Indians" and the crowd dispersed to their homes. Paul Revere was despatched by the patriot leaders to carry the news to New York and Philadelphia.

At New York and Philadelphia the people would not allow the tea to be landed, and at Charleston it was stored in damp cellars, where the whole cargo was soon ruined. At Annapolis a ship and its cargo were burned; the owner of the vessel himself setting fire to the ship.

The British government was greatly incensed at the refusal of the colonists to allow the tea to be landed, and determined to compel the Americans to submit to the authority of Great Britain. Boston, in particular, was to be made a terrible example to the rest of the colonies. A bill was introduced into Parliament, and passed by a majority of four to one, closing the port of Boston to all commerce, and transferring the seat of government to Salem. The British ministry boasted that with ten

DESTRUCTION OF TEA IN BOSTON HARBOR.

thousand regulars they could "march through the continent," and they were resolved to bring America to her knees and make her confess her fault in dust and humiliation. In addition to the Boston Port Bill, Parliament passed other measures of equal severity. By one of these the royal officers were ordered to quarter the troops sent out from England on all the colonies at the people's expense; another provided that if any officer, in the execution of the Quartering Act, should commit an act of violence, he should be sent to England for trial. The deliberate purpose of this last act was to encourage the military and other officials to acts of violence and oppression by shielding them from punishment in America. The lives of the American people were thus placed at the mercy of every petty official bearing a royal commission. Another law, known as the "Quebec Act," granted unusual concessions to the Roman Catholics of Canada, in order to attach them to the royal cause in the event of a collision between England and the colonies.

Boston was largely dependent upon her commerce, and the closing of her harbor entirely destroyed her trade and brought great loss and suffering to her people. The outrage to which she was thus subjected was resented by the whole country, and evidences of sympathy poured in upon her from every quarter. Salem refused to allow the establishment of the seat of government within her limits, and offered the use of her port to the merchants of Boston free of charge. Marblehead made a similar offer. Large numbers of the people of Boston were thrown out of employment by the closing of Boston harbor, and their families, left helpless, suffered considerably. The various colonies came forward promptly to their relief. The neighboring towns sent in provisions and other necessaries of life, and money was subscribed in other parts of the country. South Carolina sent to Boston two hundred barrels of rice, and promised eight hundred more when they were wanted. North Carolina sent a contribution of £2000 in money, and money and provisions were sent from Virginia and Maryland. In the former colony, the farmers beyond the Blue Ridge raised a contribution of one hundred and thirty-seven barrels of flour and sent it to Boston. Even the city of London sent $150,000 to the relief of Boston. Cheered by these evidences of sympathy, Boston resolved to hold out to the end.

One of the first and most determined of the colonies in expressing her sympathy for Massachusetts was Virginia. Upon the receipt of the news of the closing of the port of Boston, the assembly of this colony passed resolutions of sympathy with Massachusetts, and appointed the 1st of June, the day designated for the enforcement of the Port Bill, as a day of fasting and prayer. For this bold action the governor dissolved the assembly. It met the next day—May 25th—in spite of Governor Dunmore's prohibition, in the coffee room of the Raleigh Tavern, and declared that an attack on Massachusetts was an attack on every other colony and ought to be opposed by the united wisdom of all. The assembly urged that a general congress of all the colonies should be held to take united action for the redress of grievances, and a committee was appointed to correspond with the other colonies for the purpose of bringing about this congress. The 1st of June was rigidly observed in Virginia as a fast day. George Mason charged his family to be careful to attend church on that day clad in mourning.

In the meantime Hutchinson had been replaced as governor of Massachusetts by General Gage, the commander-in-chief of the British army in North America. He landed in Boston on the 17th of May, 1774, and was well received by the people. He was a man of mild character and great good-nature, and utterly unfit for the task of coercing a free people. The determined attitude of the patriots bewildered him. He brought with him instructions for "the seizure and condign punishment of Samuel Adams, John Hancock, Joseph Warren, and other leading patriots; but he stood in such dread of them that he never so much as attempted their arrest." He was greatly perplexed to know how to manage the people of Boston. It was clear to him that they intended to resist the injustice of the mother country, but they kept so carefully within the law that he could not take hold of their acts. They held meetings and discussed

their grievances, but violated no law, and discountenanced violence of all kinds. He was authorized by the British government to fire upon the colonists whenever he should see fit; but their prudent and peaceful course gave him no opportunity for so doing. The government at length undertook to put a stop to the town meetings of the Americans by forbidding them to hold such meetings after a certain day. They evaded this law by convoking the meetings before the designated day, and "keeping them alive" by adjourning them from time to time. Faneuil Hall and

JOHN HANCOCK.

the Old South Church were the favorite places of meeting; but many of these assemblies were held under the Liberty Tree.

In the meantime the recommendation of Virginia for a general congress was accepted by the other colonies, and measures were set on foot to bring it about. The need of such an assembly, which should represent the whole country, was becoming more and more apparent every day. In the various colonies delegates were chosen, and it was agreed, at the instance of the legislature of Massachusetts, that the congress should meet in Philadelphia on the 5th of September, 1774. Martin, the royalist governor of Georgia, prevented that colony from choosing delegates to the congress, and General Gage attempted a similar interference with the general court of Massachusetts. Samuel Adams, as usual, had anticipated him, however. On the 17th of June, having privately ascertained the sentiments of the members, he locked the door of the room in which the meeting of the assembly was held, and so kept out the governor's secretary, who came to dissolve the session, and who knocked in vain for admission. Thus safe from executive interference, the general court proceeded to appoint its delegates to the congress, and to make provision for their support. This accomplished, the doors were opened and the members submitted to the dissolution pronounced by Governor Gage.

The act of Parliament by which the British government undertook to prohibit the town meetings of Massachusetts was known as the "Regulating Act." It was introduced into Parliament by Lord North in April, and received the royal assent in May, 1754. It was an infamous measure. It annulled the charter of the colony, and "without previous notice to Massachusetts, and without a hearing, it arbitrarily took away rights and liberties which the people had enjoyed from the foundation of the colony, except in the evil days of James II." All the power of the colony was concentrated in the hands of the royal governor by conferring upon him the appointment of all the courts of justice and every official connected with them. The courts were all to be remodelled in the interest of the king, and Gage at once set to work to appoint the new judges. The whole colony united in a determined resistance to them. In many of the towns the citizens would not allow the new courts to be opened, and in Boston no man could be found to serve as a juror in the courts appointed for that city. A meeting of the citizens of Boston was held at Faneuil Hall on the 26th of August, 1774, and was attended by delegates from the counties of Worcester, Middlesex, and Essex. It adopted a series of resolutions denying the authority of Parliament to change any of the laws of the province, and declared that the new government set up by Gage under the Regulating Act was unconstitutional, and that the new officers, should they attempt to act, would become the enemies of the province although they bore the commission of the king. In order to provide for the safety of the colony a provincial congress with large executive powers was advised by the convention. Gage found himself unable to enforce the new laws. "The chief justice and his colleagues, repairing in a body to the governor, represented the impossibility of exercising their office in Boston or in any other part of the province; the army was too small for their protection; and besides, none would act as jurors. Thus the authority of the new government, as established by act of Parliament, perished in the presence of the governor, the judges, and the army." Thus defeated Gage began to increase the number of troops at Boston.

On the 1st of September Gage sent a detachment to Quarry Hill, near Charlestown, and seized the public magazine in which the province of Massachusetts kept its powder for its militia, and brought it to Boston. The news of this seizure roused the people of the surrounding counties to a high state of indignation. A body of several thousand of the best citizens of Middlesex, "leaving their guns in the rear," marched to Cambridge to protest against the outrage. They compelled Danforth, a county judge and a member of Gage's council, Phipps, the high sheriff, and Oliver, the lieutenant-governor, to resign their places. They attempted no violence, and inasmuch as Gage had acted within the letter of the law in removing the powder, dispersed quietly, satisfied for the time with their protest. Their demonstration thoroughly alarmed Gage, who kept the troops in Boston under arms all night, posted cannon to command the approaches to the town, and doubled all the guards. At the same time he wrote to England for reinforcements.

The news of the seizure of the Massachusetts powder spread rapidly through the province and into the adjoining colonie The seizure was made on Thursday morning, and by Saturday morning twenty thousand men were under arms and advancing upon Boston. They were stopped by expresses from the patriots at Boston, but their prompt action showed the spirit of the province. When 'the news reached Israel Putnam, in his home in Connecticut, the old hero at once called on the militia to go with him to the aid of Boston, where the report said the people had been fired on by the royal troops and shipping. His call was answered by thousands, but later advices from Boston put a stop to the march. "But for counter intelligence," wrote Putnam to the patriots at Boston, "we should have had forty thousand men, well equipped and ready to march this morning. Send a written express to the foreman of this committee when you have occasion of our martial assistance; we shall attend your summons, and shall glory in having a share in the honor of ridding our country of the yoke of tyranny which our forefathers have not borne, neither will we. And we much desire you to keep a strict guard over the remainder of your powder, for that must be the great means, under God, of the salvation of our country."

The excitement was not without its good results, however. It led every man to examine the condition of his means of resistance, and to supply his deficiencies in arms and equipments. The royal authority

---

* Bancroft.

was at an end outside of Boston, and active royalists found it best to seek safety within that city.

The general congress, or, as it is better known, the Old Continental Congress, met in Carpenter's Hall, in Philadelphia, on the 5th of September, 1774. It numbered fifty-five members, consisting of delegates from every colony save Georgia, whose governor had prevented the election of delegates. Among the members were many of the most eminent men in the land. From Virginia came George Washington, Patrick Henry, and Richard Henry Lee; from Massachusetts Samuel Adams and John Adams; from New York Philip Livingston, John Jay, and William Livingston; from Rhode Island the venerable Stephen Hopkins; from Connecticut Roger Sherman; from South Carolina Edward

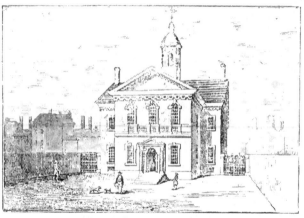

CARPENTER'S HALL, PHILADELPHIA.

and John Rutledge and Christopher Gadsden; and from New Jersey the Rev. John Witherspoon, the President of Princeton College. The members of this illustrious body were not strangers to each other, though the majority of them met now for the first time. They had corresponded with each other, and had discussed their wrongs so thoroughly that each was well acquainted with the sentiments of his colleagues, and all were bound together by a common sympathy.

The congress was organized by the election of Peyton Randolph, of Virginia, as speaker. Charles Thomson, of Pennsylvania, an Irishman by birth, and the principal of the Quaker High School in Philadelphia, was then chosen secretary. It was proposed to open the sessions with

27

prayer Some of the members thought this might be inexpedient, as all the delegates might not be able to join in the same form of worship. Up rose Samuel Adams, in whose great soul there was not a grain of sham. He was a strict Congregationalist. "I am no bigot," he said "I can hear a prayer from a man of piety and virtue, whatever may be his cloth, provided he is at the same time a friend to his country." On his motion the Rev Mr. Duché, an Episcopal clergyman of Philadelphia, was invited to act as chaplain. Mr Duché accepted the invitation

When the congress assembled the next morning all was anxiety and apprehension, for the rumor of the attack upon Boston, which had reached Putnam and aroused Connecticut, had gotten as far as Philadelphia The chaplain opened the session by reading the thirty-fifth Psalm, which seemed, as John Adams said, ordained by Heaven to be read that morning, and then broke forth into an extempore prayer of great fervor and eloquence At the close of the prayer a deep silence prevailed in the hall It was broken by Patrick Henry, who rose to open the day's proceedings He began slowly and hesitatingly at first, "as if borne down by the weight of his subject," but as he proceeded he rose grandly to the duty of the occasion, and in a speech of masterly eloquence he recited the wrongs of the American colonies at the hands of Great Britain, and declared that all government in America was dissolved, and urged upon the congress the necessity of forming a new government for the colonies. Towards the close of his speech he struck a chord which answered in every heart. "British oppression," he exclaimed, "has effaced the boundaries of the several colonies; the distinctions between Virginians, Pennsylvanians, New Yorkers, and New Englanders are no more. I am not a Virginian, but an American." The deputies were astonished at his eloquence, as well as at the magnitude of the interests with which they were intrusted.

The congress continued its sessions for seven weeks It had no authority to bind the colonies to any course; its powers were merely advisory, and it did not transcend its authority It drew up a Declaration of Rights, in which it defined the natural rights of man to be the enjoyment of life, liberty, and property It claimed for the Americans, as British subjects, the right to participate in the making of their laws, and the levying of taxes upon their own people The right of trial by jury in the immediate vicinity of the scene of the alleged offence, and the right of holding public meetings and petitioning for the redress of grievances, were solemnly asserted A protest was entered against the maintaining of standing armies in America without the consent of the colonies, and against eleven specified acts passed since the opening of the reign of

George III., as violative of the rights of the colonies. The declaration concluded with the solemn warning, "To these grievous acts and measures Americans cannot submit."

Congress then addressed itself to a plan for obtaining redress. It was agreed to form an "American Association," whose members were to pledge themselves not to trade with Great Britain or the West Indies, or with persons engaged in the slave trade; not to use tea or any British goods; and not to trade with any colony which should refuse to join the

HARBOR OF NEW YORK IN 1875.

association. For the purpose of enforcing the objects of this association committees were to be appointed in the various parts of the country to see that its provisions were carried into effect.

Other papers were adopted by the congress, setting forth its views more clearly. A petition to the king was prepared by John Dickinson, of Pennsylvania, who also drafted an address to the people of Canada. A memorial to the people of the colonies was written by Richard Henry Lee, of Virginia, and an address to the people of Great Britain by John Jay, of New York. These papers were forwarded to England to be laid before the British government, and on the 26th of October the congress adjourned to meet on the 10th of May, 1775.

In January, 1775, Lord North presented the papers adopted by congress to the House of Commons, and at the same time they were laid before the House of Lords by Lord Dartmouth. The venerable Earl of Chatham made this the occasion of a powerful appeal to the majority in Parliament to reverse their arbitrary course towards the Americans before it should be too late. Referring to the papers laid before the House, he said: "When your lordships look at the papers transmitted us from America, when you consider their decency, firmness and wisdom, you cannot but respect their cause and wish to make it your own. For myself, I must avow, that in all my reading—and I have read Thucydides, and have studied and admired the master states of the world—for solidity of reason, force of sagacity, and wisdom of conclusion under a complication of difficult circumstances, no nation or body of men can stand in preference to the general congress at Philadelphia. The histories of Greece and Rome give us nothing equal to it, and all attempts to impose servitude upon such a mighty continental nation must be in vain. We shall be forced ultimately to retract; let us retract while we can, not when we must. These violent acts must be repealed; you will repeal them; I pledge myself for it, I stake my reputation on it, that you will in the end repeal them. Avoid, then, this humiliating necessity."

The king was furious when the words of the greatest statesman of his kingdom were repeated to him. Neither the wisdom nor the eloquence of Chatham could turn the king or the ministers from their mad course. They had but one plan for America now. She must submit humbly to their will; if she should resist, she must be crushed into submission. The king meant to try the question with the Americans.

CHAPTER XXVI

THE AMERICAN REVOLUTION

WHILE the Continental Congress was in session, matters were in a most serious state in Massachusetts. General Gage, alarmed by the threatening aspect of the Americans, began to fortify Boston Neck, the narrow peninsula which united the city with the main land. A regiment was stationed at these works to prevent communication between the citizens and the people in the country. The news of this action spread rapidly. At Portsmouth, New Hampshire, a company of volunteers seized the fort and carried off one hundred and fifty barrels of powder and several cannon. At Newport forty-four cannon were seized by the people and sent to Providence for safe-keeping.

In the midst of this excitement, Gage, thinking such a step might conciliate the people, summoned the general court to meet at Salem; but alarmed at the growing spirit of liberty, countermanded the order. The

121

members of the general court met, however, at Salem, on the 5th of
October, 1774, but finding no one to organize them adjourned to Concord,
where they resolved themselves into a provincial congress, of which John
Hancock was elected president. This congress existed as the government
of the people, and was independent of the authority of the king. They
protested their loyalty to King George, and their desire for peace, and
endeavored to induce Gage to desist from fortifying Boston Neck. Gage

THE MINUTE MAN.

refused to comply with their demand, and warned them to desist
from their unlawful course. The
provincial congress paid no attention to his warning, but proceeded
to call out the militia to the number of twelve thousand. They
were allowed to remain at their
homes, but were required to be
ready for service at a minute's
warning. Hence they were known
as "Minute Men." Two com-
mittees of safety were appointed:
one to call out the minute men
when their services were needed;
the other to supply them with
provisions and ammunition. Two
general officers, Artemas Ward
and Seth Pomeroy, were appointed. The other New England colonies were invited to increase the number of minute men
to twenty thousand. The sum
of £20,000 was voted for the
military service, and Massachusetts prepared for the worst. In
every colony military prepara-

tions were set on foot, and the whole of America began to prepare for the
coming storm which all thinking men now saw was close at hand.

The papers drawn up by the Continental Congress had been widely
circulated in England, and had aroused a great deal of sympathy for
America, and it was hoped by many that the new Parliament, which met
in January, 1775, would see the necessity of doing justice to the colonies.
The cause of America was eloquently pleaded by the Earl of Chatham

and others, but the king and the ministers were resolved to compel the submission of the Americans, and the majority in Parliament sustained them. A measure known as the "New England Restraining Bill" was introduced by Lord North, which deprived the people of New England of the privilege of fishing on the banks of Newfoundland. In March news arrived that all the colonies had endorsed the action of the Continental Congress, and had pledged themselves to support it. To punish them the provisions of the Restraining Bill were extended to every colony save New York, Delaware, and North Carolina. These colonies were exempted in the hope of inducing them to desert the American cause. The measure failed of its object, and the three favored colonies remained firm in their support of the congress.

General Gage now resolved to take a decisive step. He learned that the patriots had established a depot of provisions and military stores at Concord, eighteen miles from Boston, and resolved to seize these supplies at once. The military force under his command at Boston numbered three thousand men, and he felt himself strong enough, not only to seize these stores, but also to arrest John Hancock and Samuel Adams, who were lodging at Lexington. Accordingly, on the night of the 18th of April, 1775, he detached a force of eight hundred men under Lieutenant-Colonel Smith, and shortly before midnight had them conveyed across Charles river to Cambridge, from which place they began their march to Concord. Gage had conducted the whole movement with the greatest secrecy, but his preparations had been detected by the patriot leaders in Boston, and Hancock and Adams had been warned of their danger. The British had hardly embarked in their boats when two lanterns were displayed from the tower of the Old North Church. Paul Revere, the chosen messenger, who had been awaiting this signal, at once set off from Charlestown and rode in haste to Lexington to warn the patriots of the approach of the British troops. At the same time William Dawes left Boston by the road over the Neck, and rode at full speed towards Lexington, arousing the country as he went along with his stirring tidings. Other messengers were sent forward by these men, and the alarm spread rapidly through the country.

From Cambridge the British pushed forward rapidly towards Lexington. They had not gone far when they heard in advance of them the firing of alarm guns, and the tolling of bells. The British officers were astonished at the rapidity with which their movement had been discovered; but they could not doubt the meaning of these signals. The country was being aroused, and their situation was becoming serious. Lieutenant-Colonel Smith sent a messenger to General Gage for reinforce-

THE BATTLE OF LEXINGTON, APRIL 19, 1775.

451

ments, and ordered Major Pitcairn to push forward with a part of the force and seize the two bridges at Concord. Pitcairn obeyed his orders promptly, and arrested every one whom he met or overtook save a countryman, who escaped and reached Lexington in time to give the alarm.

Pitcairn's division reached Lexington at daybreak on the 19th of April. They found seventy or eighty minute men, and several other persons, assembled on the common. They were ignorant of the intentions of the British, and supposed they merely wished to arrest Adams and Hancock, who had left the village upon the first alarm. As he saw the group Pitcairn ordered his men to halt and load their muskets, and

BRITISH TROOPS ON CONCORD COMMON.

called out to the Americans, "Disperse, ye villains, ye rebels, disperse; lay down your arms; why don't you lay down your arms and disperse?" The Americans stood motionless and silent, "witnesses against aggression; too few to resist; too brave to fly." Pitcairn, seeing that his order was not obeyed, discharged his pistol, and ordered his men to fire. A few straggling shots followed this order, and then the regulars poured a close heavy volley into the Americans, killing seven, and wounding nine of them. Parker, the commander of the minute men, seeing that the affair was to be a massacre instead of a battle, ordered his men to disperse. The British then gave three cheers for their victory. In a little while Colonel Smith arrived with the remainder of his command, and the whole party then pushed on towards Concord.

The alarm had already reached Concord, and in a little while news was received of the massacre at Lexington. The minute men promptly assembled on the common, near the church, and awaited the approach of the enemy. The minute men from Lincoln came in at an early hour, and a few from Acton. About seven o'clock the British were seen advancing in two divisions, and as it was evident that they were about four times as numerous as the Americans, the latter retreated to the summit of a hill on the opposite side of the Concord river, and there awaited the arrival of reinforcements, which were coming in from the surrounding country. The British occupied the town, and posting a force of one hundred men to hold the North bridge, began their search for arms and stores. The greater part of these had been secreted, but the soldiers found a few that could not be removed, and gave the rest of their time to plundering the houses of the town. "This slight waste of stores," says Bancroft, "was all the advantage for which Gage precipitated a civil war."

Between nine and ten o'clock the American force had increased by the arrival of the minute men from Acton, Bedford, Westford, Carlisle, Littleton, and Chelmsford, to about four hundred and fifty. Below them, in full view, were the regulars plundering their homes, and from the town rose the smoke of the fires the soldiers had kindled for the destruction of the few stores they had managed to secure. Not knowing whether they meant to burn the town or not, the officers of the minute men resolved to advance and enter Concord. Barret, the commanding officer, cautioned the men not to fire unless attacked. As their approach was discovered the British began to take up the planks of the North bridge, and to prevent this the Americans quickened their pace. The regulars then fired a volley which killed two of the minute men. The fire was returned, and two of the soldiers were killed and several wounded. These volleys were followed by some desultory skirmishing, and about noon Colonel Smith drew off his men and began to retreat by the way he had come.

With the retreat of the British from Concord the real work of the day began. The country was thoroughly aroused, and men came pouring in from every direction eager to get a shot at the regulars. The road by which the royal forces were retreating was narrow and crooked, and led through forests and thickets, and was bordered by the stone walls which enclosed the farms. At every step the militia and minute men hung upon the enemy, and kept up an irregular but fatal fire upon them from behind trees, fences, and houses. Flanking parties were thrown out to clear the way, but without success. The number of the Americans increased at every step. Each town took up the strife as the regulars entered its limits. Far and wide the alarm was spreading through the country, and the people were getting under arms. By noon a messenger rode furiously into the distant town of Worcester and shouted the alarm. Instantly the minute men of the town got under arms, and after joining their minister in prayer, on the common, took up the march for Cambridge. The whole province was rising, and the enemies of the fugitive regulars were increasing every moment.

Smith hurried his command through Lexington at a rapid rate, and a short distance beyond the town met Lord Percy advancing to his assistance with twelve hundred infantry and two pieces of artillery. Percy

THE FIGHT AT CONCORD BRIDGE.

formed his men into a square, enclosing the fugitives, who dropped helplessly on the ground, "their tongues hanging out of their mouths like those of dogs after a chase," and with his cannon kept the Americans at bay. He could not think of holding his position, however, and after a halt of half an hour resumed the retreat, first setting fire to some houses in Lexington. The fighting now became more energetic than ever. From either side, from in front and the rear, the Americans kept up a constant fire upon the British, who revenged themselves by murdering some helpless people along the road, and burning houses. Below West Cambridge the British broke into a run, and at length, about sunset, succeeded in escaping across Charlestown Neck, where they were safe under the fire of their shipping. Had the militia from Marblehead and Salem, who were on the march, been more alert, the entire British force would have been captured, as they were in no condition to resist a determined attack in front.

The loss of the Americans during the day was forty-nine killed, thirty-four wounded, and five missing. The British lost in killed, wounded, and missing two hundred and seventy-three men, or more than fell in Wolfe's

army in the battle of the Heights of Abraham. Many of the officers, including Colonel Smith, were wounded.

The news of the conflicts at Lexington and Concord spread rapidly through New England, and was sent by express messengers to New York and the colonies farther south. In New England it produced a general uprising of the people, and in ten days Boston was blockaded by an irregular army of twenty thousand provincial troops, whose encampments extended from Roxbury to the Mystic river, above Charles-

RETREAT OF THE BRITISH FROM LEXINGTON.

town, a distance of ten miles. John Stark, who had served with gallantry in the old French war, was on his way to Boston in ten minutes after he was informed of the fighting. Israel Putnam, a veteran soldier, and as true a hero as ever lived, was ploughing in his field when the courier rode by with the tidings of the battle. He left his plough, sprang on his horse, and after rousing his neighbors rode from his home, in Connecticut, to Cambridge, without even stopping to change his clothes. The Massachusetts Congress took energetic measures for the support of the army before Boston, and in a few days this force began to assume a more regular character.

Matters had also reached a crisis in Virginia. On the night of the 20th of April Lord Dunmore seized the powder in the magazine at Williamsburg, and sent it, under guard of a party of marines, on board an armed schooner in the James river. The inhabitants on the morning of the 21st took arms to compel the restoration of the powder, but were persuaded to refrain from violence. In a few days the news from Lexington and Concord was received, and it was the general belief that Dunmore's course was only a part of a general plan to disarm the colonies. On the 2d of May Patrick Henry summoned the independent companies of

CAPTURE OF TICONDEROGA BY ALLEN.

Hanover to meet him at a certain place, and led them towards Williamsburg, determined to compel the governor to restore the powder, or pay its full value in money. On the march they were met by a messenger from Dunmore, who paid them the full value of the powder in money. This money was soon after forwarded to Congress. The companies then disbanded, and returned home. Dunmore, thoroughly frightened, fled with his family on board a man-of-war, and declared " Patrick Henry and his associates to be in rebellion." Afraid to meet the Virginians in an open fight, he threatened to arm their slaves against them, and inaugurate a general massacre.

The middle and southern colonies were prompt to follow the example

of New England. The people of New York seized the provisions intended for the king's troops at Boston, shut up the custom-house, and
forbade any vessels to leave the harbor for ports or colonies acknowledging the authority of Great Britain. The arms and ammunition belonging
to the city were seized by the volunteers, and measures were set on foot
for a general resistance to the authority of the king. New Jersey was
equally determined, and in Pennsylvania enthusiastic meetings of citizens
resolved "to associate for the purpose of defending, with arms, their
lives, their property, and liberty." Military companies were formed, and
trained in the exercise of arms. The people of Maryland compelled
their royalist governor to surrender to them all the arms and ammunition
of the province. The militia officers of South Carolina at once resigned
their commissions from the governor, and regiments of militia for the defence of the colony were raised and drilled. At Charleston the royal
arsenal was seized, and its contents distributed among the people. Georgia also placed herself in the ranks of her patriot sisters, and seizing the
ammunition and arms within her limits prepared for resistance. North
Carolina took a more decisive stand than any of the colonies. The
spirit of resistance ran high within her borders. A convention of the
people of Mecklenburg county was held at Charlotte on the 29th of May,
and adopted a series of resolutions declaring themselves independent of
the control of Great Britain, and renouncing all allegiance to her. This
was the famous "Mecklenburg Declaration of Independence." The
whole country, from New Hampshire to Georgia, was united in its determination to resist the injustice of Great Britain with arms. Massachusetts had struck the first blow, but every colony was now prepared and
determined to bear its part in the great struggle for freedom.

The Massachusetts Committee of Safety were anxious to secure the
important posts of Ticonderoga and Crown Point on Lake Champlain.
The possession of these posts would not only enable the Americans to
command the entrance to Canada, but would give them the large quantities of military supplies stored in these forts. The project was entered
into with great energy by Benedict Arnold, then commanding a company
before Boston, and by Ethan Allen of Vermont. Allen was the leader
of the Green Mountain Boys, a military organization in Vermont, which
had been formed to resist the authority of New York, which claimed
Vermont as a part of its territory. The people of Vermont, however,
preferred the authority of New Hampshire to that of New York. The
dispute had become quite animated when the outbreak of the Revolution
drew the attention of all parties to more stirring events. Arnold, upon
hearing that Allen was preparing to seize the forts, set out at once for

Vermont, and overtook the Green Mountain Boys near the head of Lake Champlain. Producing a colonel's commission he ordered Allen to surrender the command to him, but the latter refused, and was sustained by his men, and Arnold at length agreed to serve as a volunteer. Securing a few boats Allen crossed the lake with his little force, about two hundred and seventy in number, and at daybreak, on the morning of May 10th, surprised Fort Ticonderoga, and made prisoners of the garrison before they were fairly awake. Not a blow was struck. The astounded commander of the fort asked Allen by whose authority he acted. "In the

INDEPENDENCE HALL IN 1776.

name of the Great Jehovah and the Continental Congress," was the instant reply, delivered in stentorian tones. The commandant instantly submitted. On the 12th of May Seth Warner, Allen's lieutenant, surprised Crown Point, and secured the fort. Arnold secured a number of boats and, descending the lake, captured St. John's, in the "Sorel." Sixty prisoners were taken in this expedition, and besides two of the most important military posts in America the patriots secured two hundred cannon, and a large supply of ammunition.

On the 10th of May, the day of the capture of Ticonderoga, the second Continental Congress met at Philadelphia. This time they assembled in the State-house, a place more suited to the dignity of such a body; and calculated to give more publicity to their proceedings. No change was at first made in the officers of the preceding session, but in a few days Peyton Randolph resigned his position to return home to attend the Virginia legislature, which had been summoned by the governor Thomas Jefferson was appointed to fill his place as a delegate. John Hancock of Massachusetts, who had been specially exempted by the king from all offers of amnesty, was chosen president of the Congress. Three new members of note now entered the Congress. They were Benjamin Franklin, a delegate from Pennsylvania, and George Clinton and Robert R Livingston, delegates from New York. Franklin had just returned from England, where he had resided for several years as the agent for some of the colonies. He had been in constant official contact with the leading men of Great Britain, and was thoroughly informed as to the policy of the British government respecting America. He was, therefore, a most valuable acquisition to the Congress.

The circumstances under which this Congress assembled were very different from those which had attended the meeting of its predecessor. Then there was hope that the remonstrances of the colonies would open the eyes of the British government to the folly of its course; but those remonstrances had been received with fresh outrages, their petitions had "been spurned with contempt from the foot of the throne," and the British army had begun the war at Lexington and Concord. Massachusetts, driven beyond the point of forbearance, had taken up arms, and had besieged the royal troops in Boston. A state of war actually existed, and Congress must either sustain Massachusetts, and so involve every colony in the struggle, or leave her to meet the power of Great Britain unaided. The whole country was in favor of standing by Massachusetts, and the delegates in Congress reflected this feeling. It was therefore resolved by Congress to place all the colonies in a state of defence, and to prepare for a vigorous prosecution of the war should it be found impossible to avert it. At the same time, as a last means of preserving peace, a new petition was addressed to the king stating the grievances of the colonies, and asking for justice at his majesty's hands. Addresses were also issued to the people of Great Britain, Ireland, and Jamaica. To the people of Great Britain they declared, after relating their wrongs, and their failure to obtain redress· "We are reduced to the alternative of choosing an unconditional submission to the tyranny of irritated ministers, or resistance by force. The latter is our choice. We have counted the cost of this contest, and we find nothing so dreadful as voluntary slavery." In the petition to the king Congress denied that it was the intention of the colonies to cast off their allegiance, but asserted their intention to maintain their rights. When this petition was presented to the king, in September, he refused to take any notice of it.

In view of the altered position of affairs Massachusetts consulted the Congress as to the propriety of establishing a regular system of government, and was advised to make such regulations for that purpose as were necessary, and to continue them as a temporary expedient until it should be known whether the king would allow the colony to resume the government guaranteed to it by its charter. In order to avoid the trouble which would ensue from an interruption of the regular postal communication between the colonies, Congress assumed the power of organizing a general system of mails for the whole country, and appointed Dr. Franklin postmaster-general.

From these acts Congress advanced to others still more important. A "Federal Union" of the colonies was organized, in which each colony retained the exclusive control of its internal affairs, but delegated to Congress authority to direct all matters pertaining to the general welfare of the colonies, such as the power to declare war, make peace, and negotiate treaties of alliance and friendship with foreign countries. In the exercise of these powers Congress assumed the general government of America. A day of fasting and prayer to God, for his assistance in the struggle for freedom, was enjoined upon all the colonies. All persons were forbidden to furnish provisions under any circumstances. Measures were adopted for the organization and enlistment of an army, and for the purpose of erecting fortifications at suitable points, and procuring arms and ammunition. In order to raise the funds needed for carrying out these objects "Bills of Credit," to the amount of two millions of dollars, were issued, and for their redemption Congress pledged the faith of the "United Colonies." The provincial congress of Massachusetts requested the Congress at Philadelphia to adopt the New England forces before Boston as the "Continental Army," and this request was at once complied with. As General Ward, the commander of these troops, held his commission from Massachusetts, it was necessary for Congress to appoint a commander-in-chief commissioned by itself.

With respect to this appointment the members were divided. Some thought that as the troops were all New England men, the commander should be chosen from the same section. Others favored the appointment of a commander who would inspire the confidence of, and be acceptable to, the entire country. The name of General Ward was suggested by the first party; but a majority of the delegates favored the appointment

28

of Colonel Washington, who was a member of Congress, and chairman of the committee on military affairs, in which capacity he had proposed the plan for the organization of the army, and had suggested the most important measures for defence. He had profoundly impressed the delegates with his great and commanding character, his military ability, and his wisdom as a statesman. Patrick Henry, on his return home from the first Congress, had been asked who was the greatest man in that body. His reply expressed the views of his colleagues respecting Washington. "If you speak of eloquence," he said, "Mr. Rutledge, of South Carolina, is, by far, the greatest orator; but if you speak of solid information and sound judgment Colonel Washington is unquestionably the greatest man on that floor." Dr. Warren wrote from Massachusetts to Samuel Adams, in Congress, about this time, that the appointment of Colonel Washington as commander-in-chief would give great satisfaction to many leading men in Massachusetts. John Adams was anxious for the appointment, and having satisfied himself of the wishes of the greater part of the delegates, ventured openly to allude to Washington as the proper person for the position, and spoke of him

WASHINGTON.

as a gentleman whose "skill and experience as an officer, whose independent fortune, great talents, and excellent universal character, would command the approbation of all America, and unite the cordial exertions of the colonies better than any other person in the Union." On the 14th of June Mr. Johnson, of Maryland, formally nominated Washington to the office of commander-in-chief, and he was unanimously chosen by ballot. The next day his election was communicated to him by the President of Congress. Washington rose in his place, and thanked the House for the unexpected honor conferred upon him, assured them of his devotion to the cause, and announced his acceptance of the great trust confided to him. He declared his intention to refuse the pay affixed to the office, which had been placed at five hundred dollars a month, and added: " I will keep an exact account of my expenses. These, I doubt not, they will discharge, and that is all I desire." Congress, on its part, pledged its hearty support to the new commander, and resolved " to maintain and assist, and adhere to him with their lives and fortunes in the defence of American liberty."

Washington lost no time in proceeding to assume the command conferred upon him. After a few days spent in preparation, in Philadelphia, he left that city on the 21st of June, for the head-quarters of the army, accompanied by Generals Lee and Schuyler.

A few days after the election of the commander-in-chief Congress appointed four major-generals, one adjutant-general, with the rank of brigadier, and eight brigadier-generals for the subordinate commands in the American army. The major-generals were, Artemas Ward, Charles Lee, Philip Schuyler, and Israel Putnam. The adjutant-general was

GENERAL ISRAEL PUTNAM.

Horatio Gates. The brigadiers were Seth Pomeroy, Richard Montgomery, David Wooster, William Heath, Joseph Spencer, John Thomas, John Sullivan, and Nathaniel Greene.

In the meantime the blockade of Boston had been continued by the provincial army, under General Ward. These forces numbered about fifteen thousand men, and had come from their respective towns in independent companies, and were without any regular organization. They had no uniform, but the majority wore their ordinary homespun working-clothes; they were deficient in arms, a few had muskets, but the majority had rifles and fowling-pieces The artillery consisted of nine pieces of cannon, and was commanded by Colonel Gridley, who had directed the artillery at the siege of Louisburg The Massachusetts troops were commanded by General Ward; those from New Hampshire by Colonel Stark; the Connecticut troops by Putnam, and the regiment from Rhode Island by Nathaniel Greene, a young blacksmith Save for the solemnity of the cause, and the earnestness and determination which animated the whole force, there was little to save this quaint assemblage from the ridicule which the royal officers heaped upon it It did to ordinary view seem the height of folly to oppose such an ill-provided and unorganized mass to the splendidly equipped veterans who served King George.

Yet this force, "with calico frocks and fowling-pieces," hemmed in within the narrow limits of Boston, the splendid army of ten thousand men, commanded by such generals as Howe, Burgoyne, and Sir Henry Clinton, which Gage had concentrated in Boston Burgoyne could not repress his astonishment upon reaching Boston. "What!" he exclaimed, "ten thousand peasants keep five thousand king's troops shut up! Well, let us get in, and we'll soon find elbow-room" In spite of his immense superiority, however, Gage did not venture to attack the American lines. He contented himself with issuing a proclamation declaring the province under martial law, and offering a free pardon to all rebels who should return to their allegiance, with the exception of Samuel Adams and John Hancock. These rebels were cut off from all hope of the king's mercy, and were given to understand that they could expect nothing but the most summary punishment.

General Gage now determined to extend his lines and to occupy Dorchester Heights, overlooking South Boston, and Bunker Hill, an eminence rising beyond Charlestown, on the north of Boston. The execution of this design was fixed for the 18th of June, and in the meantime Gage's intention became known in the American camp. To prevent it, it was resolved, at the instance of the Massachusetts Committee of Safety, to seize and fortify these eminences, beginning with Bunker Hill The more prudent opposed this undertaking as too rash; it was certain to bring on a general engagement of the opposing forces, and the Americans were too poorly provided with arms and ammunition to hope for success. Others insisted that no time should be lost in securing the heights. Putnam was confident they could be held with proper intrenchments, and that thus protected the troops could be relied upon to hold their position. The great scarcity of ammunition rendered the undertaking one of peculiar daring, and it was necessary to select for the command an officer whose firmness and discretion could be depended upon. The choice fell upon Colonel William Prescott of Massachusetts, and a brigade was placed under his orders.

Soon after sunset on the 16th of June a force of about eleven hundred men, armed principally with fowling-pieces, and carrying their scanty stock of powder and ball in their old-fashioned powder horns and pouches, assembled on Cambridge Common. Langdon, the President of Harvard College, one of the chaplains of the army, offered up an impressive prayer, and then the order was given to march and the column

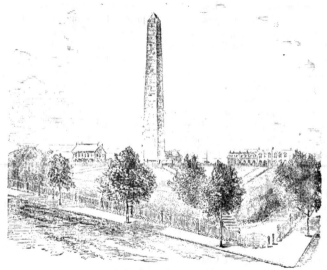

BUNKER HILL MONUMENT.

moved off in the darkness. No one knew the object of the expedition, but the presence of several wagons loaded with intrenching tools made it evident that the movement was one of importance. Charlestown Neck was strongly guarded, but the detachment passed it in safety and reached the summit of Bunker Hill without being observed. The Committee of Safety had suggested that Bunker Hill should be secured, but Prescott's orders from General Ward were to fortify Breed's Hill, a lower eminence but nearer to Boston, and commanding the harbor more perfectly. It was a more exposed position than the other, but Prescott decided to obey his orders. Colonel Gridley, who was an experienced engineer, marked

out a redoubt about eight rods square, and in the clear June starlight
the men set to work with a will to construct the fortification before the
morning should reveal them to the British. It was midnight when the
men began their labors. A strong guard was thrown out along the shore
of the harbor to prevent a surprise, and the men could distinctly hear the
call of the sentinels on the men-of-war in the harbor. During the night
Putnam came over to the hill to encourage the Connecticut troops by his
presence, but assumed no command.

The early morning light revealed to the astonished royalists the half-
finished redoubt on Breed's Hill and the Americans still busily at work
upon it. The sloop-of-war "Lively," lying off the present navy yard,
without waiting for orders, opened a steady fire upon the redoubt, and
her example was soon followed by the other war vessels and the floating
batteries in the harbor. A battery of heavy guns was posted on Copp's
Hill in Boston, about twelve hundred yards distant, and opened on the
redoubt. This fire was well calculated to demoralize a raw force such as
that within the redoubt, but it produced no effect upon the Americans,
who went on with their task quietly and with energy. Gridley soon
withdrew from the hill, and Prescott, thus deserted, and without an
engineer, prepared to extend his line to the best of his ability. He prolonged it from the east side of the redoubt northward for about twenty
rods towards the bottom of the hill; but the men were prevented from
completing it by the heavy fire of the British artillery. One man ventured beyond the redoubt early in the day, and was killed by a shell.
Prescott ordered him to be instantly buried, lest the sight of his body
might dishearten the men. To inspire the troops with confidence, Prescott sprang upon the parapet and walked slowly up and down the work
examining it and issuing his orders.

In the meantime the firing had aroused the people of Boston, who
crowded the house-tops and every available point from which a view of
the action could be obtained. General Gage reconnoitred the American
position from Boston, through his glass, and observed Prescott, who was
standing on the redoubt inspecting the work. "Who is that officer in
command?" he asked of Councillor Willard, who was by his side.
"Will he fight?" Willard had recognized Prescott, who was his
brother-in-law, and replied "He is an old soldier, and will fight to the
last drop of his blood." Gage thereupon determined to dislodge the
Americans from their position without loss of time, and summoned a
council of his officers at his head-quarters, in which it was decided to
cross Charles river, effect a landing at Moulton's Point, and attack the
works in front. Clinton and Grant decided an attack from

the direction of Charlestown Neck, which would have resulted in the capture of the whole American force, but Gage refused to place his attacking column between the American army at Cambridge and the detachment on the hill.

The bustle in Boston as the British prepared for the attack could be distinctly seen by the Americans, and urgent messages were sent to General Ward for reinforcements and provisions. Putnam hurried to Ward's head-quarters to urge this demand; but Ward, who was greatly oppressed by the scarcity of powder in the camp, hesitated to weaken the main body, and it was not until eleven o'clock on the morning of the 17th of June that he gave orders for the regiments of Stark and Reed to advance to Prescott's assistance. The arrival of these troops greatly cheered the little band under Prescott, who had been working all night, and were greatly in need of food. In the meantime Prescott had posted the Connecticut troops behind a rustic breastwork which he had constructed on the north of the redoubt. A stone fence ran down the side of the hill towards a swamp in this direction. Behind this the Americans placed a post and rail fence which they had torn up, and filled the interval between them with new-mown hay, thus forming a rude shelter. A part of the reinforcements joined Knowlton at this breastwork, and the remainder halted on Bunker Hill to enable Putnam to hold that point, the possession of which he considered essential to the safety of the force on Breed's Hill. About two o'clock General Warren arrived. He held the commission of a major-general, and both Prescott and Putnam offered to relinquish the command to him, but he refused it, saying he had come to serve as a volunteer, and took his place in the ranks at the redoubt.

At noon twenty-eight barges filled with regulars, under the command of Generals Howe and Pigott, left Boston, and crossing the harbor, landed at Moulton's Point, under the cover of a heavy fire from the shipping. General Howe now discovered that the American position was stronger than he had supposed, and sent over to General Gage for reinforcements. While awaiting their arrival he refreshed his men with provisions and grog. His reinforcements having arrived, General Howe found himself at the head of over two thousand veteran troops, splendidly equipped in every respect. Opposed to him were about fifteen hundred imperfectly armed Americans. Gage had threatened that if Charlestown Heights were occupied by the provincials he would burn the town of Charlestown. He now proceeded to execute his barbarous threat, and fired the town by means of shells from the battery on Copp's Hill, hoping that the flames and smoke would screen the approach of his attacking party under General Howe. A change of wind prevented this, however, and carried the smoke in the opposite direction.

About half-past two o'clock on the afternoon of the 17th of June General Howe gave the order to advance   One division, under General Pigott, was ordered to storm the redoubt, while the other was led by General Howe in person against the rail fence, for the purpose of turning the American left flank and cutting off the retreat of the force in the redoubt. Prescott passed along his line as he saw the advance of the enemy, and encouraged his men with his cheering words. "The red coats," he said, "will never reach the redoubt if you will but withhold your fire till I give the order, and be careful not to shoot over their heads." Putnam had come down to the rail fence to encourage the men posted there, and as he saw the advance of the enemy called out to the troops. "Wait till you see the whites of their eyes, aim at their waist-bands; pick off the handsome coats"

The British advanced in splendid style up the side of the hill, firing rapidly as they moved on   The Americans awaited their advance in a deep silence   As Pigott's division came within forty yards of the redoubt, the defenders levelled their guns and took a steady aim. A minute or two later Prescott gave the command, "Fire!" A sheet of flame broke from the rampart and tore great gaps in the English line, which reeled and staggered back down the hill. The officers exerted themselves gallantly to rally the men, and once more the line advanced. This time the Americans suffered them to come nearer, and again drove them back with a fatal fire before which whole ranks went down. They broke in such confusion that Pigott himself ordered a retreat. The division under General Howe was equally unfortunate. It was suffered to advance within thirty yards of the rail fence, and was then driven back by a fire which broke it in confusion. The British retired to the shore from which they had started   Greatly astonished, but not disheartened by his repulse, General Howe reformed his line, and after an interval of fifteen minutes moved off again against the works, his plan being the same as that of the first assault. This time the Americans reserved their fire as before, and once more sent the whole British line reeling and broken down the hill. Officers of experience on the English side subsequently declared that they had never seen such firing in any battle in which they had been engaged. A deafening cheer from the patriot line greeted the repulse of the enemy. "If we can drive them back once more," cried Prescott, "they cannot rally again." A shout from the redoubt answered him   "We are ready for the red coats again!"

General Clinton had witnessed the repulse of the regulars from his

BATTLE OF BUNKER HILL.

441

position on Copp's Hill, and was filled with astonishment and indignation at the sight Without waiting for orders, he crossed over to Charlestown with reinforcements, and offered his services to General Howe as a volunteer. Many of the English officers were opposed to another attack , but as it was learned that the ammunition of the Americans was very low, Howe resolved to storm the works with the bayonet, and this time to break through the open space between the redoubt and the rail fence breastwork. His men were ordered to lay aside their knapsacks, and many of them threw off their coats also. A raking fire of artillery drove the Americans from the breastwork extending from the redoubt into that work for shelter, and the order was given to the regulars to advance with fixed bayonets. The Americans were nearly out of ammunition, and in the whole command there were not fifty men with bayonets to their guns They met the advance of the enemy with a sharp fire, but their powder having given out, were not able to check them Pressing on the British assailed the redoubt on three sides with the bayonet. A desperate hand-to-hand struggle followed ; the Americans fighting with clubbed guns and with stones It was impossible to hold the work, however, and Prescott gave the order to retreat. The men fell back in good order The aged General Pomeroy, who was serving as a volunteer in the ranks, clubbed his gun and retreated with his face to the regulars, keeping them at bay by his determined action The detachment at the rail fence, under Knowlton, Stark, and Reed, held their position until their comrades had withdrawn from the redoubt, and then retreated in good order down the hill, thus preventing the enemy from cutting off the retreat of Prescott's party One of the last to leave the redoubt was General Warren, who had borne himself with great gallantry in the engagement. He had scarcely left the trenches when he fell shot through the head, thus consecrating the spot with his blood, and leaving to his country a noble memory which she has ever held in grateful honor.

Putnam had gone to the rear before the final attack of the enemy to collect men for a reinforcement On his return he met the retreating provincials passing over Bunker Hill Without orders from any one, he rallied such as would obey him, and for the first time during the day assumed the command. With these forces, and a detachment which arrived too late to take part in the battle, he withdrew to Prospect Hill, where he began to fortify his position The British made no effort to pursue him, but contented themselves with occupying Breed's and Bunker Hills.

In this battle the Americans lost four hundred and fifty men, killed, wound   ...   The British out of   ... of less than three thousand, lost one thousand and fifty-four, including eighty-three officers, thirteen of whom were killed. Among the killed was Major Pitcairn, who had ordered his men to fire on the patriots at Lexington. The victory was dearly bought by the British.

In its moral effects the battle was worth as much to the Americans as a success. It taught them that undisciplined provincials could hold their ground against the king's regulars, and inspired them with a confidence in their own ability to maintain the struggle. They had held their ground against twice their number, and were driven from it only when their ammunition failed. General Gage was deeply impressed with this lesson, and made no attempt to assume the offensive. When the news of the battle reached England the ministers were greatly dissatisfied with their victory. Gage was recalled, and General Howe was appointed his successor.

Washington, who had started on his journey to New England before the arrival of the news of the battle, was met on the way by the courier who bore the tidings to Congress. He hastened his journey and reached Cambridge on the 2d of July. The next day he formally assumed the command of the army. He was received with an enthusiasm which was most gratifying to him, and at once set to work to place the army in a proper condition for the service required of it. He was fully aware of the magnitude of the task he had undertaken, and his letters written at the time indicate a deep reliance upon God for assistance in discharging it. The army numbered about fourteen thousand men, and was without organization, without uniforms, poorly armed, and imperfectly clothed. It must be disciplined, supplied with arms and clothing, and with ammunition. At the same time the enemy in Boston must be watched and kept in check. To make the army effective its force must be raised to twenty or twenty-five thousand men, and the petty jealousies which divided it must be removed.

It was resolved to maintain the present position of the army before Boston, and to capture or drive out the British force in that city. Washington established his head-quarters at Cambridge, which was his centre, and was under the immediate command of General Putnam. The right wing, under General Ward, held Roxbury, and the left, under General Charles Lee, was at Prospect Hill. About this time the army was joined by a force of riflemen from Virginia, Maryland, and Pennsylvania, under Daniel Morgan, who was destined to achieve distinction during the war. He was rough and uneducated, but was one of the truest sons of America. He was never found wanting in any position in which he was placed, and was a man upon whose devotion and integrity absolute reliance could be placed by his commanders.

The winter was passed in the organization of the army. The want of ammunition prevented Washington from assuming the offensive, though he greatly desired to do so. It was necessary to observe the greatest care to prevent this state of affairs from becoming known to the British, and at the same time every effort was made to supply the deficiency. These efforts were partially successful.

It was proposed to attack Canada soon after the capture of the forts at Ticonderoga and Crown Point. This proposal met with little favor in Congress until it was known that the British were assembling a force of regulars, and enlisting the Indians in Canada, for the invasion of New York. Then, as a measure of self-defence, the proposed invasion of that country was sanctioned, and preparations for it were actively begun Two expeditions were determined upon; one by way of Lake Champlain, the other across the wilderness, by way of the Kennebec and Chaudiere rivers The first was intrusted to General Philip Schuyler, who had been appointed by Washington to the command in New York, and the latter to Colonel Arnold, who was in the camp at Cambridge, eager for some opportunity to distinguish himself.

A force of New York and New England troops was assembled on Lake Champlain under Schuyler, who was ably seconded by Brigadier-General Richard Montgomery, who had served under Wolfe in the old French war. Schuyler moved down the lake to the Isle aux Noix in the Sorel river, and occupied that island. In September he made an attempt to capture St. John's, but finding it much stronger than he had supposed, resumed his former position. Falling seriously ill soon after, he was obliged to withdraw to Albany, and relinquished the command to Montgomery. Reaching Albany he succeeded in securing supplies, ammunition, and reinforcements, and sent them to Montgomery. That energetic officer at once assumed the offensive, and captured St. John's, on the Sorel river, on the 3d of November, after a spirited resistance, and in spite of the efforts of Sir Guy Carleton to relieve it. On the 13th of November Montgomery arrived before Montreal, which surrendered upon his first summons This capture enabled the American commander to supply his men with woollen clothes, of which they were very much in need Although it was the beginning of the winter, and his force was reduced to three hundred men, poorly clad, and lacking almost every kind of supplies, Montgomery set out without delay to join Arnold before Quebec.

Arnold had left the camp at Cambridge in September with a force of eleven hundred men, including three companies of riflemen under Morgan. He was to ascend the Kennebec, and march across the wilderness to Quebec, where he was to unite his force with the army from New York. The march across the unbroken wilderness of Maine and Canada is one of the most memorable in history. It consumed two months of time, and was marked by intense suffering and unceasing and severe labor. The troops had to cut their way through an unbroken wilderness, ford icy streams, climb mountains, and brave the rigors of the Canadian winter. Their provisions gave out, and they were reduced to the necessity of eating their dogs and chewing their moccasins. At length, on the 9th of November, Arnold with about six hundred and fifty effective men reached the St. Lawrence, at Point Levi. Could he have crossed over to Quebec at once, that city must have fallen into his hands; but he was unable to do so, as he had no boats; and in a few days Sir Guy Carleton arrived from Montreal, which he had abandoned to Montgomery, and put the city in a state of defence. Eluding the two armed vessels which held the river, Arnold crossed his command to the opposite side of the St. Lawrence, and

ARNOLD'S MARCH TO QUEBEC.

climbing the cliffs by the path which Wolfe had ascended, occupied the Heights of Abraham, and endeavored to draw the garrison out of their works to meet him. They declined his challenge, and finding it impossible to besiege the city without artillery, he moved to a point twenty miles up the river, where he met Montgomery, from whom he obtained clothing for his men, who had lost nearly all their clothes in their march through the wilderness.

Montgomery now assumed the command of the united forces, which numbered less than a thousand men, and on the 5th of December laid siege to Quebec. Having no materials for the proper construction of a battery, a novel expedient was adopted. Gabions were filled with ice and snow, over which water was poured. The cold soon froze this to a solid mass; but, as the ice was brittle, it afforded no protection against the fire of the enemy's guns. The Americans soon found their artillery too light to make any impression upon the walls of the city, and as a last resort it was determined to attempt the capture of the place by an assault, which was ordered for the 31st of December. The attack was made with

GENERAL RICHARD MONTGOMERY.

spirit, but was unsuccessful. Montgomery was shot down while leading the attack on the lower town, and his column was driven back. Arnold was severely wounded in the assault upon the upper town, and the command passed to Morgan, the next in rank. Morgan succeeded in carrying the two batteries which defended the entrance to Quebec, and in forcing his way into the town; but being overpowered by numbers was compelled to surrender. He and his men were treated with especial kindness by Sir Guy Carleton in recognition of their bravery. The attack having proved a failure, Arnold, whose force had been reduced to five hundred men, fell back to a position about three miles above Quebec, and held it all winter, hoping to receive such reinforcements as would enable him to take Quebec.

In April, 1776, General Wooster joined Arnold with reinforcements, and assuming the command, made another unsuccessful effort to capture Quebec. Wooster was soon recalled, and was succeeded by General Thomas. Sir Guy Carleton, governor of Canada, was heavily reinforced, and Thomas was obliged to abandon the attempt on Quebec and retreat. His movement was so hasty that he left his baggage, artillery, and sick in Carleton's hands. The British commander, with a humanity rare among his countrymen during this struggle, treated the sick prisoners with great kindness. Thomas fell back as far as the Sorel, where he died of the small-pox, which was making great ravages among the troops. Sir Guy Carleton continued to advance, and defeated a portion of the army under General Thompson at Three Rivers. Thompson and a number of his officers and men were made prisoners. The remainder secured their retreat and joined General Sullivan on the Sorel. The wreck of the army now fell back from Canada to Crown Point in a most miserable and disheartened condition. Thus ended the invasion of Canada, the most disastrous expedition attempted by the Americans during the war, yet still one the failures of which were greatly offset by the heroic daring of the troops engaged. Carleton was able to occupy the entrances to Canada with a strong force, and to make any future attempt at invasion impossible.

While these events were transpiring in Canada, Virginia was also the scene of war. Towards the close of the year 1775 Lord Dunmore, the royalist governor of Virginia, who had taken refuge on board a man-of-war, issued a proclamation offering freedom to the negro slaves and indentured white servants of the patriots who would join him in the servile war he meant to inaugurate. With a force collected in this manner, he landed at Norfolk and took possession of the town. Fugitive slaves joined him in considerable numbers, and it seemed likely that he would be able to carry out his threat and scourge Virginia and North Carolina with a warfare of massacre and servile violence. Several regiments were raised in Virginia to drive him out of the province. The second of these, under Colonel Woodford, seized the narrow peninsula which connects Norfolk with the mainland, and on the 9th of December was attacked by Dunmore's forces, which were summarily defeated. In revenge, Dunmore returned in January, 1776, and bombarded and burned Norfolk, then the largest and richest town and the principal shipping port of Virginia.

On the 5th of September, 1775, the Continental Congress resumed its
sessions. Delegates from Georgia appeared and were admitted to seats in
the Congress, and the colonies assumed the style of the *Thirteen United
Colonies*. Matters were not very encouraging when Congress met. The
army was in need of everything that could contribute to its efficiency,
and the New England coast was harassed with the armed vessels of
Great Britain, which laid its towns under exaction, or subjected them to
bombardment, and committed other gross outrages upon the inhabitants.
On the 18th of October the town of Falmouth, now Portland, in Maine,
was burned by Lieutenant Mowatt of the British navy. The other
towns, warned by the fate of Falmouth, proceeded to fortify themselves,
and escaped with nothing worse than an occasional engagement with some
royal cruiser.

Naval matters very largely occupied the attention of the whole country
at this period. The only way in which the needed supplies could be
obtained was by purchase abroad or the capture of the enemy's ships.
Maryland, Virginia, and South Carolina promptly established naval
boards for the purpose of fitting out cruisers for this service; and among
the first acts of Washington, after assuming the command of the army,
was to send out armed vessels to the St. Lawrence and the New England
waters to seize the supply ships of the English on their way to Canada
and Boston. A number of vessels were captured by these cruisers, and a
considerable quantity of arms, ammunition, and other stores thus accumulated. Congress appointed a secret committee to import powder from the
West Indies, and to erect mills in the interior for its manufacture, and
foundries for casting cannon. Licenses were issued to privateers, and a
naval committee was appointed to superintend the formation of a marine
force for the defence of the harbors, and was charged with the building
of thirteen frigates. In December a secret committee was appointed to
open and conduct a correspondence with foreign nations, or with friends
of the cause in Europe.

Parliament, in the meantime, had not been idle, but had enacted
stringent measures for the prosecution of the war and the punishment of
the colonists. The measures adopted by the British government were
cruel and barbarous. The Americans were to be treated as criminals and
as deserving of death. They were made subject to the pains and penalties of treason if captured, and could in no case expect the treatment of
prisoners of war. The crews of all vessels captured in trading to the
colonies were condemned beforehand to serve in the marine corps of the
royal navy. It was decided to increase the British army in America to
forty thousand men. Twenty-five thousand of these troops were to be

raised, and the effort to enlist men was begun in England, but without success   Recruits could not be found in sufficient numbers to repay the effort   The ministry could not hope for better success in Ireland, as they had been warned by General Howe that the Irish were strong sympathizers with the Americans and could not be relied upon to fight against them.   In this emergency the government resolved to employ German troops for the subjugation of America, and negotiations were opened with Brunswick and Hesse Cassel, two petty German States.   The result was that Great Britain hired seventeen thousand troops from these states for the conquest of the English-speaking people of America.   These mercenaries were generally known as Hessians, and became the objects of the bitter hatred of the Americans—a hatred which they fully earned by their subsequent cruelties towards the colonists.

These measures were not adopted by the British government without opposition.   There was a determined minority in England, consisting of such men as Burke, Barré, and the Duke of Grafton, who manfully sought to obtain justice for the colonies up to the last moment at which a settlement was possible.   The corporation of London and the mercantile interests of the country generally were opposed to the measures of the government, and sought to procure a just and peaceful settlement; but all efforts were in vain.   The king and the ministry were resolved upon the subjugation of America; nothing else would satisfy them.

29

CHAPTER XXVII.

THE DECLARATION OF INDEPENDENCE.

The Siege of Boston—Difficulties of the American Army—Activity of the Privateers—Clinton's Expedition—Colonel Knox arrives from Ticonderoga with Cannon—Seizure of Dorchester Heights by Washington—The British Evacuate Boston—Royalist Plots in New York—Paper Money Issued by Congress—Gates sent to the North—The British Attack Charleston—Battle of Fort Moultrie—The Howes in New York Bay—Change in the Character of the War—Growing Sentiment in Favor of Independence—Virginia Proposes that the Colonies Assert their Independence—Action of Congress—The Declaration of Independence—Articles of Confederation Adopted by Congress—Lord Howe's Efforts at Conciliation—Addresses a Letter to Washington—Battle of Long Island—Defeat of the Americans—Retreat from Long Island—Evacuation of New York by the Americans—Loss of Fort Washington—Washington Retreats through New Jersey—He Crosses the Delaware—Darkest Period of the War—Washington's Determination to Continue the War—Lord Howe's Proclamation—Its Effect—Congress at Baltimore—Carleton Invades New York—Defeats Arnold on Lake Champlain—Carleton Retires into Canada—Battle of Trenton—Happy Effects of the Victory—Congress confers Dictatorial Powers upon Washington—Commissioners sent to France

THE winter of 1775-76 was passed by the army before Boston in inaction. There was not ammunition enough in the camp to enable Washington to attack Boston, and the British were well content to remain within their lines without seeking to raise the siege   Washington exerted himself to the utmost to obtain artillery and powder. Henry Knox, a bookseller of Boston, who had entered the military service of the colonies, had attracted the attention of the commander-in-chief by his skill in the use of artillery, and in planning the works erected for the defence of the camp   Knox now proposed to go to Ticonderoga and bring away from that place and from Crown Point all the artillery and powder that could be spared, and his plan was at once approved by Washington, who urged Congress to commission him a colonel of artillery   At the same time he wrote to Schuyler, the commander in New York, to give Knox every assistance in his power in his effort to bring the artillery from Lake Champlain to Boston. Great difficulties were experienced during the winter in inducing the troops to renew their enlistments. It required all the ingenuity and tact of which Washington was master to remove the prejudices and jealousies which had grown up   the commencement of the blockade of

Boston, and which threatened to disband the army. He succeeded in a greater degree than he had expected. At the opening of the year 1776 he had about ten thousand men in camp, many of whom were raw troops newly enlisted, and without arms. Still they were a more harmonious and contented force than the first army. Towards the close of 1775 the privateers made extensive captures from the British. Captain Manly, of the schooner "Lee," captured a British brig, off Cape Ann, laden with arms, artillery, and military stores for the British army at Boston. These were sent at once to Washington, and proved of the greatest service. Among the captures was an immense mortar, which Putnam named the "Congress," and placed in position at Lechmere Point, on the north of Boston.

GENERAL HENRY KNOX.

Matters were gloomy indeed. The people were anxious that Boston should be attacked, but such a course was impossible. As late as the 10th of February, 1776, Washington wrote: "Without men, without arms, without ammunition, little is to be done." To increase the discouragement of the patriots news came of the defeat of the attempt to conquer Canada. The British were collecting a fleet for a demonstration against some point on the Atlantic coast, and as it was not certain where the blow would fall, a feeling of general uneasiness prevailed along the entire seaboard.

This expedition sailed from Boston, under Sir Henry Clinton, about the 1st of February. Washington, who had for some time suspected that it was designed to capture New York, had already sent General Charles Lee to raise troops to occupy that important city, and hold it against the British. Lee executed his task with energy, and on the 4th of February entered New York, and encamped in the suburbs, in what is now the City Hall Park. Governor Tryon, who had taken refuge on board a man-of-war, threatened to bombard the city if the American forces should enter it; but Lee informed him that the first shot fired at

New York would be the signal for the execution of the leading friends of the royal cause in that city. This decisive answer induced Tryon to delay his barbarous purpose. That afternoon Sir Henry Clinton, with his fleet, entered the harbor. Finding that he had come too late to secure the city, Clinton declared that he had merely called at the harbor to pay a visit to his friend Tryon, and in a few days he sailed away for North Carolina, where the royalist Governor Martin, who, like Tryon, had taken refuge on board a man-of-war, had been endeavoring to stir up an insurrection of the Tories, as the royalists were called. The command of this movement was to be assumed by Clinton. Martin also expected

SIEGE OF BOSTON.

to be reinforced by seven regiments and a fleet under Sir Peter Parker, which were on their way from Ireland. To gain time, and stir up the Tories to prompt action, he commissioned two retired officers of the British army, Scotchmen, named McDonald and McLeod, who had recently settled in North Carolina, to raise troops among the friends of the king in the interior. They succeeded in raising about fifteen hundred men, and set off for the coast to join Martin. The patriots at once rallied in considerable force to oppose their march, and intercepted them at Moore's Creek Bridge, near Wilmington. On the 25th of February, a sharp engagement was fought here, which resulted in the defeat of the Tories. McLeod was killed, and McDonald was taken prisoner. Eighteen hundred stand of arms, one hundred and fifty swords, two medicine-chests, and the sum of fifteen thousand pounds sterling, in gold, fell into the hands of the victors, and went far toward supplying their deficiencies. The contemplated rising of the Tories was put down in the interior counties, and Martin, finding his hopes of raising troops in North Carolina destroyed, withdrew with Clinton to the Cape Fear to await the arrival of the fleet of Sir Peter Parker.

In the meantime a Union flag had been provided for the army before Boston, and was formally displayed for the first time in the American camp on the 1st of January, 1776. It retained the English cross in the upper left hand corner, in token of the relations still existing between the colonies and England; and bore on its broad field thirteen stripes of alternate red and white, representing the thirteen colonies united for the defence of their liberties. Towards the close of February the stock of powder was considerably increased,
and a little later
Colonel Knox ar-
rived from Ticon-
deroga with the can-
non and ammuni-
tion from that post.
He had transported
them on sledges
across the long
stretch of country

WASHINGTON WATCHING THE BRITISH EVACUATE BOSTON.

between Lake Champlain and Boston, and had overcome difficulties in the accomplishment of this task which seemed at first insurmountable. The arrival of these guns gave Washington a fair supply of heavy ordnance, and put an end to the long delay which had prevailed in the American camp. The regular army had been increased to fourteen thousand men, and had been reinforced by six thousand militia from Massachusetts.

All now was bustle and activity. The newly arrived cannon were mounted to command the city, and Washington was at length able to attempt the long-desired demonstration against the enemy in Boston. As early as December, 1775, Congress had urged him to undertake the capture of Boston, and had authorized him to destroy the city if he could expel the British in no other way, and John Hancock, who was a large property-owner, regardless of the fate of his possessions, had written to him: "Do it, and may God crown your attempt with success." All

through the winter Washington had been held back from such an attempt
by the advice of his council of war, which hesitated to assume the offensive with an insufficient supply of ammunition and artillery   Putnam
had succeeded in fortifying the neighboring heights on the mainland, but
had been obliged to do much of this work at night to avoid the fire of
the enemy's shipping   The last obstacle to decisive action was now
removed. Washington resolved to seize the eminence on the south of
Boston, known as Dorchester Heights. It commanded the town from
that quarter, and also the shipping in the harbor   Its possession by the
Americans would force Sir William Howe either to evacuate the city or
risk a general engagement for its recovery

On the evening of the 2d of March a heavy fire was opened upon the
British lines by the American batteries, and also upon Boston. A number of houses were set on fire, and the attention of the British was fully
occupied in extinguishing the flames. The bombardment was renewed
the next night. At dark, on the evening of the 4th of March, the
Americans renewed their fire with redoubled vigor, and were replied to
with spirit by the British, and during the whole night the roar of cannon
went on, covering the movements of the Americans from observation by
the enemy   The force assigned for the seizure of Dorchester Heights
was placed under the command of General Thomas, and in case the movement should be discovered, and the enemy should seek to dislodge this
detachment from the heights, General Putnam was ordered to cross
Charles river, with a column of four thousand picked troops, and attack
the city from that quarter. Under the cover of the heavy cannonade
the column of General Thomas passed the narrow isthmus in safety, and
reached the heights by eight o'clock, undiscovered by the enemy. They
at once set to work, though the ground was frozen to a depth of more
than eighteen inches, and by morning had thrown up a series of earthworks which entirely commanded both the city and the harbor   General
Howe was greatly astonished as he examined these works through his
glass when the mists of the morning cleared away   "The rebels," he
said, "have done more work in a night than my whole army would have
done in a month " The British admiral declared that his ships could not
remain in the harbor, as the possession of the heights by the Americans
placed the fleet entirely at their mercy   It was evident to all the British
commanders that the heights must be recovered, or the city abandoned,
and General Howe determined to storm the American works that night,
and made preparations for an attack. This movement was prevented by
a severe storm, which put a stop to the cooperation of the fleet, and when
the storm had died away the works had been so greatly strengthened as

to render an assault hopeless. A council of war was held, and it was resolved to abandon the town. As such a step required some time, Howe secured the safety of his army by declaring that he would burn the town if his troops were fired on during their embarkation. A deputation of the citizens proceeded to the American camp and informed General Washington of Howe's determination, and in order to save the city from further suffering the British were allowed to depart in peace. They consumed eleven days in their embarkation. They embarked about fifteen hundred Tories with them, and after plundering a number of stores and private houses, and robbing the inhabitants of a considerable supply of provisions, they embarked on the 17th of March, and dropping down the

MEDAL STRUCK BY CONGRESS IN HONOR OF THE RECAPTURE OF BOSTON.

bay anchored in Nantasket roads. They had scarcely left the city when the American army, under Washington, marched in and occupied the place. The long siege of ten months was at an end, and Boston was again free. The patriot army was received with enthusiasm, and matters soon began to resume their accustomed condition.

By the capture of Boston the Americans obtained possession of two hundred and fifty pieces of artillery, four mortars, and a considerable quantity of ammunition, provisions, and clothing, which the British could not carry away. After the departure of the British fleet from Nantasket roads several transports with troops, not aware of the evacuation, entered the harbor, and were captured. Several storeships, laden with military supplies of all kinds, also arrived from England, and were captured in the same way. These captures were of the highest importance to the patriots. Their supply of ammunition was in this way increased more than sevenfold.

The capture of Boston was justly esteemed the most important success of the war. It freed New England from the presence of the English, and enabled her to contribute men and money to the defence of the middle colonies. On motion of John Adams, Congress adopted a unanimous vote of thanks to Washington and the army, and ordered a gold medal to be struck in commemoration of the deliverance of Boston.

The British fleet remained in Nantasket roads for several days after the evacuation of Boston, and then bore away for Halifax. Washington was fearful that its destination was New York, and leaving General Ward with five regiments to hold Boston, hastened southward with the main body of the army. He reached New York on the 13th of April, and set to work with vigor to put the city and its approaches in a state of defence. He soon discovered that the Tories in the city were in constant communication with Governor Tryon and the British ships in the harbor. Severe measures were at once adopted to stop this intercourse. A conspiracy for the recovery of the city by Tryon was discovered, and his agents were found tampering with the American soldiers. One Thomas Hickey, a deserter from the British army, was hanged "for mutiny, sedition, and treachery," and this vigorous measure at once put a stop to the plots of the Tories.

Congress, in February, 1776, found itself obliged to issue four millions of dollars of additional paper money in order to meet the expenses of the war, which were heavier than had been supposed. For the proper management of the finances, an auditor-general and assistants were appointed to act under the financial committee of Congress, and it was not long before this branch of the public service assumed the form of a treasury department. In April a war office was established by Congress under the supervision of a committee of its members. John Adams was made chairman of this committee, and resigned his post of chief-justice of Massachusetts to accept it.

The retreat of Sullivan from Canada now became known, and the conduct of that officer was approved by Congress, which passed a vote of thanks to him. At the same time it appointed Major-General Horatio Gates to the command of the army in his place. Gates was an Englishman by birth, and had joined the colonial movement in the hope of winning honors and fame by his services. He had served in the British army during the colonial period, but had failed to receive the rewards he deemed himself entitled to, and had resigned his commission in disgust,

and had come to America to reside a few years before the rupture with
England. His experience and skill made him a valuable acquisition to
the American army, but his ambition and jealousy were destined to
cause it considerable trouble. Gates at once claimed that his command
embraced not only the troops on Lake Champlain, but also the whole
northern army under Schuyler. The matter was referred to Congress,
and it was decided that Gates was independent of the control of Schuyler
only while in Canada. Elsewhere he was subject to Schuyler's command.

In the meantime Congress had sent General Charles Lee to the south
to take command of the troops assembling to oppose Sir Henry Clinton,
who was waiting off the mouth of the Cape Fear river for the arrival of
the fleet of Sir Peter Parker from Ireland. This fleet joined Clinton in
May, and a little later Congress learned by means of intercepted letters
that Charleston, in South Carolina, was the object of attack. The command of the strong
military force which
the fleet brought was
to be held by Sir
Henry Clinton, to
whom the general
direction of the ex-
pedition was intrust-
ed. Lee hastened at
once to Charleston.
He found there a
force of about six

ATTACK ON FORT MOULTRIE.

thousand men, from the Carolinas and Virginia; but the city was not
defended by a single fortification. Had Clinton assailed it at once, it must
have fallen into his hands, as he arrived in the harbor on the 4th of June,
the very day that Lee reached the city; but he delayed his attack until
he could fortify his own position, and so gave Lee time to erect works
for the defence of the city.

The key to the American position was Fort Moultrie, a small
work built of palmetto logs, and situated on the southwest point of Sullivan's island. It was commanded by Colonel William Moultrie, whose
name it bore. In front of it lay the British fleet under Sir Peter Parker.
Sir Henry Clinton had taken position with two thousand men on Long
island, which was separated from Sullivan's island by only a narrow
creek, and was building batteries to cover his passage of the creek. His
plan was to allow the fleet to breach the walls of Fort Moultrie, and then
to cross his troops to Sullivan's island under the cover of his batteries,

and carry the fort by storm. Lee, who was ignorant of the capacity of
the soft, spongy palmetto wood for resisting the force of cannon shot, regarded the effort to hold Fort Moultrie as madness. He stationed a force
under Colonel Thompson on Sullivan's island opposite Clinton to dispute
his passage of the creek, and took position on the mainland with the rest
of his force where he could support either Moultrie or Thompson, as
might be necessary.

On the 28th of June, the enemy's fleet opened fire on Fort Moultrie,
which replied with spirit, and for ten hours the cannonade was maintained with great vigor by both sides. The enemy's balls buried themselves in the soft, spongy wood of the palmetto logs, and thus did little

SERGEANT JASPER AT FORT MOULTRIE.

injury to the fort; but the well-directed fire of the American guns inflicted
great damage upon the fleet. The British were finally compelled to
withdraw with heavy loss, and abandoned and set fire to one of their
ships. During the engagement the flag of the fort was shot away, and
fell outside of the walls. Sergeant Jasper, of the South Carolina forces,
at once sprang over the wall, and amidst a heavy fire secured the flag,
tied it to a pole, and set it up again on the ramparts. This done, he rejoined his comrades at the guns. A few days later, Governor Rutledge
presented Jasper with his own sword, and offered him a lieutenant's commission. Jasper accepted the sword, but declined the commission on the
ground that he could neither read nor write.

Clinton made repeated efforts to cross the creek and storm the fort during the battle, but was as often driven back by the batteries under Thompson At length, the fleet having withdrawn, he embarked his men, and soon after sailed for New York to join the troops assembling near that city

Washington was correct in supposing that New York was the true destination of Sir William Howe after leaving Nantasket roads. That commander sailed first to Halifax, where he landed the civilians and other useless incumbrances he had been obliged to carry away from Boston. Then, refitting his command, he awaited the arrival of his brother, Admiral Lord Howe, who was on his way from England with reinforcements In the latter part of June he sailed from Halifax for New York, and arrived within Sandy Hook on the 28th of June, the very day of the attack on Fort Moultrie He landed his forces on Staten island, where he was received with enthusiasm by the Tories A little later he was joined by Sir Henry Clinton from Charleston, and about the middle of July Lord Howe arrived with reinforcements, a large part of whom were Hessians, hired as we have stated by the king of England from the duke of Hesse Cassel, in Germany. Their arrival raised the strength of the British army in New York bay to 30,000 men Their attack upon the city was merely a question of time, and under the most favorable circumstances it was scarcely to be hoped that Washington would succeed in maintaining his hold upon New York In the meantime an event of the highest importance had changed the whole character of the war as regarded the Americans

The colonists had taken up arms to resist the aggressions of the king and government of Great Britain upon their liberties, and to compel the mother country to respect the rights guaranteed to them by their charters and by the British constitution Thus far the war had been waged for these ends At the outset of the struggle a few far-seeing persons, such as Samuel Adams and Patrick Henry, had been convinced that an appeal to arms would render the final separation of the colonies from England inevitable, and that such an issue was but the fulfilment of the destiny of their country, and as such to be desired. The great majority of the people, however, neither thought of nor wished for independence They would have been satisfied to secure their liberties and privileges as English subjects, and would gladly have continued loyal to the king. The events of the war had made it plain to the most skeptical that England did not intend to do justice to her colonies Neither the king, the ministry, nor Parliament were disposed to swerve from their purpose of reducing America to absolute submission to their will They were determined that the colonists should bear every burden of British citizenship,

and enjoy none of its privileges save what they should see fit to allow
them. Americans were not to enjoy either liberty or property as lawful
rights, but both these possessions were to be held by them at the pleasure

INDEPENDENCE HALL, PHILADELPHIA, IN 1875.

of Great Britain. This determination was so clear that none could mistake it. Since the commencement of the struggle public opinion in
America had undergone a great change, and the party in favor of a total
and final separation from the mother country had increased so rapidly

that it now embraced the great majority of the American people. Now that they had become convinced that they could maintain their liberties only by a total and unqualified separation from Great Britain, they did not hesitate to choose that course. Their choice was made without regret. At the commencement of the war a very genuine attachment bound the people of the colonies to England; but the course of the royal government and the severities of the British commanders in the northern colonies, and the outrages of the royal governors in the south, had entirely alienated the people from their love for England.

Still there were many Tories, or friends of the king, in America, and they were active and bitter in their opposition to the patriots. From the

INTERIOR OF INDEPENDENCE HALL.

first the Americans regarded the Tories with a feeling of hatred which increased as the struggle went on, and this feeling was soon extended to all who fought under the royal flag or sought to uphold its cause.

Not only had the people been gradually coming to view independence as desirable and indispensable; the exercise by Congress of the functions of a supreme government had accustomed them to it, and had shown them their capacity for conducting a general government for the whole country. Early in March, 1776, Congress granted letters of marque and reprisal against British commerce, and somewhat later sent Silas Deane as its commissioner to France to seek assistance from that country. In May it had formally recommended the colonies to disregard the royal governments and adopt systems suited to their needs, and in harmony with the changed state of affairs   To all men it was evident that a formal renunciation of allegiance to Great Britain and the assertion of their independence by the colonies was merely a question of time.

It was, therefore, a surprise to no one when the first definite action looking towards independence was taken.   On the 15th of May, 1776, the general assembly of Virginia instructed the delegates of that colony in Congress to offer a resolution in favor of the separation of the colonies from England, and the formal declaration of their independence.   On the 30th of May Massachusetts instructed her delegates to support this resolution.   On the 7th of June Richard Henry Lee, of Virginia, offered a resolution in Congress, "that the united colonies are, and ought to be, free and independent states, and that their political connection with Great Britain is, and ought to be, dissolved "   The resolution was seconded by John Adams, of Massachusetts, and was debated with great earnestness. It was adopted by a bare majority of one—seven colonies voting for it, and six against it   In accordance with the resolution, a committee was appointed to draw up a declaration of independence, and, in order that the delegates might have an opportunity to ascertain the wishes of their constituents, the consideration of the subject was postponed until the 1st of July   Two other committees were also appointed.   One of these was charged with the preparation of a plan for uniting the colonies in a single government ; the other was to report a plan for securing alliances with foreign nations.   The committee charged with the preparation of a declaration of independence consisted of Benjamin Franklin, John Adams, Thomas Jefferson, Roger Sherman, and Robert R. Livingston.

On the 28th of June the committee reported the declaration to Congress   It was written by Thomas Jefferson, and with a few verbal alterations was adopted by the committee as it came from his hand   It reviewed in a clear and comprehensive manner the causes which had impelled the colonies to take up arms for the defence of their liberties, and which now induced them to sever the ties that bound them to Great Britain   The declaration concluded in these memorable words   " We, therefore, the representatives of the United States of America, in general Congress assembled, appealing to the Supreme Judge of all the world for the rectitude of our intentions, do, in the name and by the authority of the good people of these colonies, solemnly publish and declare that these united colonies are, and of right ought to be, free and independent states, that they are absolved from all allegiance to the British crown, and that all political connection between them and the state of Great Britain is, and ought to be, dissolved : and that, as free and independent states, they have full power to levy war, conclude peace contract alli-

VIEW IN THE GRAND CAÑON OF THE COLORADO RIVER.

463

ances, establish commerce, and to do all other acts and things which independent states may of right do. And for the support of this declaration, with a firm reliance on the protection of a Divine Providence, we mutually pledge to each other our lives, our fortunes, and our sacred honor."

The declaration was debated in Congress, and a few passages, which it was feared might offend the friends of the colonies in Great Britain, were stricken out. The vote was then taken by colonies, and though some of the delegates voted against it, the declaration received the votes of all the colonies with the exception of New York, which accepted it a few days later. On the 4th day of July 1776, the Declaration of Independence was

formally adopted by Congress, and was ordered to be published to the world, and to be read at the head of the regiments of the army.

Congress was in session in the hall of the state house in Philadelphia. In the spire of this venerable building hung a bell, inscribed with the words of Scripture: "Proclaim liberty throughout all the land unto all the inhabitants thereof." On the morning of the 4th of July vast crowds assembled around the building, as it was known that Congress would on that day take definite action upon the declaration. The bell-ringer stationed himself in the tower ready to proclaim the good news the moment it should be announced to him, and had posted his

OLD BELL OF INDEPENDENCE HALL.

little son at the door of the hall to await the signal of the door-keeper. When the announcement of the vote was made, the door-keeper gave the signal and the boy ran quickly to the tower. The old man heard him coming, and clutched the bell-rope with a firm grasp. The next instant the glad cry of the boy's voice was heard. "Ring! ring!" he cried; and then the deep, sonorous tones of the bell went rolling out of the tower, and were answered with a mighty shout from the assembled throng without. The declaration was received by all the states and by the army with enthusiasm. Thus the thirteen united colonies became the thirteen United states. It should not be forgotten that the declaration did not make the colonies independent states, or states in any sense. It was simply their announcement to the world that they had, each for itself, by the exercise of its own sovereign power, assumed the independence which rightfully belonged to it.

The Declaration of Independence put an end to all the hopes that had been cherished of an accommodation with Great Britain, and caused those who were still wavering to embrace the cause of their country. It relieved Congress of the disadvantage under which it had hitherto acted, and enabled it to pursue a more vigorous and decisive policy in the prosecution of the war. There was no retreat now; nothing remained but to continue the struggle until Great Britain should be compelled to acknowledge the independence of the states, or they should be reduced to the condition of conquered provinces.

On the 12th of July the committee appointed to prepare a plan for the union of the States reported one, which is thus summed up:

DECLARATION OF INDEPENDENCE PROCLAIMED IN PHILADELPHIA.

"1st. The style of the confederacy was to be 'The United States of America.'

"2d. Each State retained its sovereignty, freedom, and independence and every power and right which is not expressly delegated to the United States.

"3d. The object of the confederation was for their mutual defence, the security of their liberties, and their mutual and general welfare, binding themselves to assist each other against all force offered to or attacks made upon them, or any of them, on account of religion, sovereignty, trade, or any other pretence whatever.

"4th. In determining all questions in Congress each State was to have one vote.

"5th. Each State was to maintain its own delegates.

"6th. The free inhabitants of each State, paupers, vagabonds, and fugitives from justice excepted, were to be entitled to all privileges and immunities of free citizens in the several States.

"7th. All fugitives from justice from one State into another were to be delivered up on demand.

" 8th. Full faith and credit were to be given to the records of each State in all the others.

" 9th. Congress was to grant no title of nobility.

" 10th No person holding any office was to receive a present from a foreign power.

" 11th. No State was to form any agreement or alliance with a foreign power without the consent of the States in Congress assembled

" 12th. No two or more States were to form any alliance between themselves without the like consent of the States in Congress assembled.

" 13th No State, without the like consent of Congress, was to keep war ships or an army in time of peace, but each was to keep a well-organized and disciplined militia, with munitions of war.

" 14th No State was to lay any duty upon foreign imports which would interfere with any treaty made by Congress.

" 15th No State was to issue letters of marque, or to engage in war, without the consent of the Congress, unless actually invaded or menaced with invasion.

" 16th. When Federal land forces were raised, each State was to raise the quota required by Congress, arm and equip them at the expense of all the States, and to appoint all officers of and under the rank of colonel.

" 17th Each State was to levy and raise the quota of tax required by Congress for Federal purposes.

" 18th The faith of all the States was pledged to pay all the bills of credit emitted, or money borrowed on their joint account, by the Congress

" 19th. It was agreed and covenanted that Canada might accede to the union so formed if she chose to do so.

" 20th (and lastly) Each State was to abide by the determination of all the States in Congress assembled, on all questions which, by the confederation, were submitted to them. The Articles of Confederation were to be inviolably observed by every State, and the Union was to be perpetual No article of the confederation was to be altered without the consent of every State.

" The delegations of power by each of the States to all the States, in general Congress assembled, upon a like analysis, may be stated as follows.

" 1st. The sole and exclusive power to determine on war and peace, except in case a State should be invaded or menaced with invasion.

" 2d. To send and receive ambassadors.

" 3d. To make treaties, with a proviso, etc.

"4th. To establish rules for captures

"5th. To grant letters of marque and reprisal

"6th. To appoint courts for trial of piracies and other crimes specified.

"7th. To decide questions of dispute between two or more States, in a prescribed manner.

"8th. The sole and exclusive power to coin money and regulate the value.

"9th. To fix a standard of weights and measures.

"10th. To regulate trade with the Indian tribes.

"11th. To establish post-offices.

"12th. To appoint all officers of the militia land forces, when called out by Congress, except regimental.

"13th. To appoint all officers of the Federal naval forces.

"14th. To make rules and regulations for the government of land and naval forces.

"15th. To appropriate and apply public money for public expenses, the common defence, and general welfare

"16th To borrow money and emit bills of credit.

"17th. To build and equip a navy.

"18th. To agree upon the number of land forces, and make requisitions upon the States for their quotas, in proportion to the value of all land within each State.

"The foregoing powers were delegated with this limitation. The war power, the treaty power, the power to coin money, the power to regulate the value thereof, the power of fixing the quotas of money to be raised by the States, the power to emit bills of credit, the power to borrow money, the power to appropriate money, the power to regulate the number of land and naval forces, and the power to appoint a commander-in-chief of the army as well as the navy, were never to be exercised unless nine of the States were assenting to the same.

"These articles form the original basis and first Constitution of the existing Federal Union of the United States of America." *

These Articles of Confederation were adopted, after discussion, by Congress, voting by States, and were then submitted to the several States for ratification by them. In the meantime Congress continued to exercise the powers conferred by them. By the early part of 1777 all the States save Maryland had ratified and adopted the articles. That State did not give her full assent to them until 1781.

---

* Hon Alexander H Stephens

Lord Howe arrived in New York bay about the middle of July, as has been stated. He was vested with full powers by the king to settle the quarrel between America and England if the Americans would agree to submit unconditionally to the king   Failing to accomplish a settlement, he and his brother, Sir William Howe, were charged with the supreme conduct of the war.   Lord Howe was a man of amiable disposition, and really desired peace; but as he was fully convinced of the justice of the royal pretensions, he could not understand or appreciate the claims or grievances of the Americans.   Moreover, he had come too late   The American people meant that their separation from Great Britain should be final.   Lord Howe was greatly deceived upon his arrival as to the actual state of feeling in America.   He was received with loyal addresses by the Tories of Long and Staten islands and the New Jersey shore, and was assured by Governor Tryon that the country was full of friends of the king who might be induced to join him if properly supported

Lord Howe, therefore, resolved to attempt a peaceful settlement before proceeding to hostilities; and issued a circular addressed to the people of America, offering them the royal pardon if they would cease their rebellion, lay down their arms, and trust to the clemency of the king. Congress gave to this circular the widest publicity, by causing it to be published in every newspaper in the Union, in order that the people might see that the only settlement that would be accepted by England was their voluntary and absolute submission to her arbitrary will. " They must fight or be slaves "

About the same time Lord Howe addressed a letter to the American commander-in-chief, styling him George Washington, Esquire   No notice of this communication was taken by Washington, and Howe sent him another letter addressed to George Washington, etc , etc   Washington, rightly considering that the omission of his official title was an insult to his country, refused to receive the letter.   Adjutant-General Patterson, of Lord Howe's staff, who bore the communication, expressed his regret that the letter could not be opened.   Lord Howe, he said, came vested with great powers, and was sincerely anxious for peace.   Washington, who had received him with kindly courtesy, replied that he was aware that Lord Howe was intrusted with the power to grant pardons, but that as the Americans were engaged in the defence of their rights, and had committed no crime, they had no need of pardon, and his lordship's good intentions could not be of service to them.

It was now plain to Lord Howe that he had been deceived by Tryon and his friends, and that nothing could be accomplished save by force of arms. His circular had produced no effect, and he could detect no sign of wavering on the part of the Americans.

It had been evident for some time that the next effort of the British would be to get possession of the city of New York. Their fleet already held the harbor, and should they succeed in securing the Hudson they would be able to establish a direct communication with Canada, and to isolate New England and New York from the Middle States and the South. Reinforcements were sent to Washington from Pennsylvania, Maryland, Virginia, and Delaware. These gave the American commander a force of about twenty-five thousand men; but scarcely seventeen thousand were fit for duty; the remainder being disabled by sickness. Washington erected two forts on Manhattan island, one just above Kingsbridge, named Fort Washington, and the other just below it, named Fort Independence. Kingsbridge furnished the only communication between the island of Manhattan and the mainland, and these forts were erected for its defence, as well as to hold the enemy's vessels in check should they attempt to ascend the Hudson. On the New Jersey side of the river, opposite Fort Washington, a third work was erected, and named Fort Lee. Other forts were built higher up the Hudson to hold the river against the enemy and maintain the communication between the Northern and Southern States. One of these, called Fort Montgomery, was located at the entrance to the Highlands, opposite the promontory of Anthony's Nose; another was built six miles higher up the river, and was known as Fort Constitution.

For the defence of the heights of Brooklyn, which commanded the city of New York, Washington caused a line of works to be erected on a range of hills a short distance south of Brooklyn, and established there an intrenched camp. General Nathaniel Greene was placed in command of this position, and exerted himself with vigor to strengthen it. When he had matured his plans he was suddenly taken ill, and was obliged to relinquish the command to General Sullivan.

The British fleet lay in Gravesend bay, just without the Narrows, and Washington was for a while uncertain whether they would make their first attempt against the force on Long island, or attack the city of New York. It soon became evident that the capture of the lines on Long island would be their first care, and Sullivan was reinforced with six battalions, all that could be spared from New York, and on the 24th of August General Putnam was placed in command of the forces on Long island.

On the night of the 26th of August the British crossed over from

Staten island to Long island, and prepared to give battle. Their plan was to engage the attention of the Americans by a direct attack with two divisions, while Sir Henry Clinton, with a third division, was to turn the left flank of the Americans and gain their rear. They hoped, if these movements were successful, to surround and capture the entire force under Putnam. Clinton began his march about nine o'clock on the night of the 26th, guided by a Long island Tory. About daylight, on the morning of the 27th of August, the enemy made their attack upon the front of

the American position, and engaged their attention in this direction, while Clinton, by a rapid march, gained their rear. For a while the Americans fought well, but finding themselves almost surrounded, and in danger of being captured, they abandoned the field and retreated within the intrenchments at Brooklyn. The Hessian troops behaved with great barbarity during the engagement, and a number of the Americans were cruelly and wan-

GENERAL JOHN SULLIVAN.

tonly bayoneted by them. A part of the engagement was fought in the beautiful region now occupied by Greenwood cemetery.

Washington hastened to Brooklyn as soon as informed of the battle, and arrived just in time to witness the defeat of his troops. He was powerless to repair the disaster, and could only look on in helpless agony. "My God!" he exclaimed, with tears: "What brave fellows I must lose this day!"

The American loss was very severe in this battle. Out of a force of five thousand men engaged they lost two thousand men, a large num-

ber of whom were prisoners. The British had sixteen thousand men
engaged, and lost four hundred. Had they followed up their victory
by an immediate assault upon the American intrenchments they must
have carried them; but General Howe believed that Washington had a
much stronger force for their defence than was the case, and encamped
in front of the intrenchments, intending to begin operations against them
the next day. The 28th, however, was a day of drenching rain, and the
enemy were unable to do more than break ground for a battery. On
the 29th a dense fog hung over the island; but it lifted for a moment,
and enabled the Americans to detect an unusual commotion among the

THE RETREAT FROM LONG ISLAND.

British shipping. It seemed plain that the enemy were preparing to
enter the East river with their fleet, and so separate the force on Long
island from that in New York. Washington at once summoned a
council of war, and it was decided to retreat from Long island without
delay. It was a hazardous attempt, for the army under General Howe
was so close to the American lines that the conversations of the men
could be heard, and the British fleet might at any moment seize the East
river. To withdraw a force of nine thousand men across a wide, deep
river, in the face of such an army and fleet, was a task which required
the greatest skill. It was successfully accomplished, however. Every

boat in and around New York and Brooklyn was impressed, and though the orders for the retreat were not issued until noon on the 29th, everything was in readiness for the retreat by eight o'clock that evening. At midnight the troops took up their silent march from the intrenched line to the ferry, where the boats, manned by Glover's regiment, which was composed of fishermen from Marblehead, awaited them. By eight o'clock the next morning the entire army, with all its cattle, horses, and wagons, was safe upon the New York side of the river.

Howe was greatly mortified at the escape of the American army, for he had regarded it as a sure prize, and prepared, with the aid of his ships, to seize the upper part of Manhattan island, and confine the Americans to the city of New York, where their surrender would be inevitable. Before proceeding to the execution of this plan he resolved to make another effort to induce the Americans to abandon their cause, as he rightly believed their defeat on Long island would be followed by a season of great depression. A few days after the retreat he released General Sullivan, who had been taken prisoner in the battle, on parole, and sent a letter by him to Congress, asking that body to send an informal committee, whom he would receive as private gentlemen, to confer with him on some measure of reconciliation. Congress, willing to hear what he had to propose, sent Dr. Franklin, John Adams, and Edward Rutledge to confer with him. They met Lord Howe at a house on Staten island, opposite Amboy. The only terms his lordship had to propose were the unconditional submission of the Americans to the royal mercy. He was informed that the Americans would consent to treat with Great Britain only as "a free and independent nation," and that it was useless to propose any other basis for a settlement. Lord Howe thereupon expressed his regret that he should be obliged to distress the Americans. Dr. Franklin thanked him for his good feeling, and remarked: "The Americans will endeavor to lessen the pain you may feel by taking good care of themselves." The report of the interview was made public by Congress, and had a happy effect. It convinced all classes that England had no terms to offer them but such as embraced a shameful surrender of their liberties.

Fearful that Howe would seek to shut him up in New York, Washington left a force within the city to hold it, and encamped with the main body of his army on Harlem Heights, at the northern end of the island, from which he could secure his retreat into Westchester county. The army was reduced to less than twenty thousand men, and was disheartened by the defeat on Long island. It was seriously debated whether New York should be defended or not, and it was proposed to burn the city to the ground, in order to prevent the enemy from securing comfortable winter-quarters in it. Congress ordered that the city should not be destroyed, but it was evident that it could not be held

Washington was anxious to learn the intentions of the enemy, who still remained on Long island, and Captain Nathan Hale, a talented young officer of the Connecticut line, volunteered to enter their lines and procure the desired information He proceeded to the British camp, obtained the information wanted, and was returning in safety when he was arrested by a party of the enemy, among whom was a Tory relative, who recognized him He was taken to Howe's head-quarters, and the next morning, September 22d, without any form of trial, was hanged as a spy. He met his death with firmness, saying "I only regret that I have but one life to lose for my country "

In the meantime the British had seized the islands at the mouth of the Harlem river, and had erected a battery on one of them On the 15th of September they crossed in force to Manhattan island, at Kipp's bay, about three miles above the city. They easily drove back the force stationed there to resist their landing, and secured their position. Washington at once sent General Heath to hold the enemy in check, and ordered Putnam to evacuate the city of New York, and retire to Harlem Heights, without the loss of a moment Putnam obeyed his orders promptly, and retreated from the city along the line of the Bloomingdale road, now the upper part of Broadway. His march was retarded by a crowd of women and children fleeing from the city, and was exposed to the fire of the enemy's ships in the Hudson. By great exertions he managed to save his command, but was obliged to leave his heavy artillery and three hundred men in the hands of the enemy The British at once took possession of New York, and threw up a line of intrenchments above the city, from the Hudson, at Bloomingdale, to the East river, at Kipp's bay The Americans now held the upper part of the island, and erected a double line of earthworks from river to river, about four miles below Kingsbridge.

On the 16th of September the enemy made an attack upon the American advanced posts, but were handsomely repulsed by the Virginia and Connecticut troops. Major Leitch, the commander of the Virginians, and Colonel Knowlton, the commander of the Connecticut regiment, and one of the captains at Bunker Hill, were killed. In spite of these losses the spirits of the troops, which had been much depressed by the recent disasters, were greatly cheered.

A lull of several weeks followed, during which the Americans suffered greatly from sickness. They were without proper hospital accommodations, "and they lay about in almost every barn, stable, shed, and even under the fences and bushes."

Howe now began to move his army towards Long island sound, for the purpose of marching across the mainland to the Hudson, and cutting off the retreat of Washington from Manhattan island, and at the same time sent his fleet up the Hudson. His intention was understood by Washington, who left three thousand men to defend Fort Washington, and with the main body of his army fell back to the line of the Bronx, near the village of White Plains. Here he was attacked, on the 28th of October, by General Howe, who was advancing from the direction of New Rochelle, and who was still hopeful of gaining the American rear. A spirited encounter ensued, in which each party lost about four hundred men, and the British intrenched themselves in front of the American position.

Apprehensive of an effort on the part of the enemy to storm his line, Washington caused the troops to spend the night in strengthening the rude works which covered it. They labored with such diligence that the next morning the British commander decided that the line was too strong to be attacked, and determined to wait for reinforcements. That night Washington silently abandoned his lines at White Plains, and withdrew to the heights of North Castle, five miles distant. Howe, unwilling to follow him further, marched to Dobb's ferry, on the Hudson, and encamped.

This movement of the British commander caused Washington to fear that he meant to cross over into New Jersey. He accordingly made a new disposition of his forces to meet any emergency. General Charles Lee, who had recently returned from the South, was left at North Castle with a portion of the army to watch Howe; Heath, with another portion, was ordered to occupy Peekskill to defend the passes of the Highlands; and Putnam was stationed, with a third detachment, on the west side of the Hudson to hold that region. With the remainder of his troops Washington crossed the Hudson and joined General Greene at Fort Lee, arriving there on the 13th of November. A force of three thousand Pennsylvania troops had been left to hold Fort Washington, on Manhattan island. Washington was in favor of withdrawing them at once, but left the matter to the decision of General Greene and Colonel Magaw, the commander of the fort, who determined to hold it. The result proved their error. Fort Washington was attacked on the 16th of November by a force of five thousand Hessians and some English troops, under General Knyphausen, and was taken by storm. The enemy lost nearly one thousand men, and took over two thousand prisoners. Washington witnessed the capture from Fort Lee without the ability to aid the garrison.

Fort Washington having fallen, Fort Lee was no longer of service, and the commander-in-chief resolved to abandon it before it was too late. The removal of the stores was at once begun, but before it could be completed Lord Cornwallis, with a force of six thousand men, crossed the Hudson below Dobb's ferry, and by a rapid march across the country endeavored to confine the Americans to the strip of land between the Hudson and the Hackensack. An immediate retreat from Fort Lee became necessary, in order to secure the bridge over the Hackensack. All the heavy cannon at Fort Lee, a considerable quantity of provisions and military stores, and three hundred tents were abandoned, and fell into the hands of the British. The passage of the Hackensack was

secured, and the army began its memorable retreat across New Jersey, closely followed by the enemy, under Cornwallis.

RETREAT OF WASHINGTON ACROSS NEW JERSEY.

From the Hackensack Washington fell back behind the Passaic, at Newark. As his rear-guard passed out of the town the advance of Cornwallis entered Newark. The Raritan was crossed at New Brunswick, and Washington left a force of twelve hundred men at Princeton, under Lord Stirling, and pushed on to Trenton to secure the passage of the Delaware. The British hung closely upon him during the whole retreat, the opposing forces being often within cannon-shot of each other. On the 8th of December, with scarcely three thousand men, Washington crossed the Delaware at Trenton, and went into camp in Pennsylvania. The enemy reached the river soon after, but, as all the boats had been secured by the Americans, were unable to cross over. Lord Cornwallis was very anxious to procure boats, cross the river, and push on to Philadelphia, but Howe decided to wait until the river should be frozen, and to pass it on the ice. In the meantime, the Hessians were stationed in Trenton, and guarded the river for some distance above and below the town.

The American war had now entered its darkest period for the Americans. New York was lost to them, they had been driven from New Jersey, and their army seemed melting away. During the painful retreat across New Jersey, Washington had exerted himself to the utmost to call in the other detachments of his army. General Schuyler was directed to send him the Pennsylvania and New Jersey troops in his command; but the enlistments of these troops were rapidly expiring, and they could not be induced to renew them. General Charles Lee was ordered to cross the Hudson and join the commander-in-chief with all speed, but he

moved with a slowness and carelessness that were criminal. He remained about a fortnight on the east side of the Hudson, and then began his march with such slowness that he did not reach Morristown until the 8th of December. On the 13th, while lying carelessly apart from his troops, at a small inn at Baskingridge, he was captured by a troop of British cavalry. The command

GENERAL CHARLES LEE.

passed to General Sullivan, and in a few days he had united his forces with those of the commander-in-chief. General Lee had an abiding confidence in his own ability, and was reluctant to lose his independent command by joining Washington. His natural self-conceit had been greatly increased by his success at the South, and he was firmly convinced that he alone was capable of guiding the American cause through the difficulties which encompassed it. Influenced by this feeling he disregarded the authority of the commander-in-chief, and subjected him to great inconvenience. He was not untrue to the cause he had embraced, but his patriotism was of a different type from that which animated Washington

The enlistments of a large part of the troops expired on the 1st of December, and nothing could induce them to remain in the army. Whole regiments abandoned the service, and the handful of reinforcements which was obtained from Philadelphia fell far short of supplying their place The people were disheartened, and it seemed that the cause was hopeless A force of six thousand militia was raised in Massachusetts and Connecticut, and was on the point of marching to Washington's assistance, when the fleet of Sir Peter Parker entered Newport harbor, and landed a force on the island of Rhode Island, which took possession of Newport In view of this invasion it was deemed best to retain the New England militia at home.

Washington was fully alive to the danger which threatened the cause; but he was calm and cheerful. During the retreat through New Jersey he said to Colonel Reed. "Should we retreat to the back parts of Pennsylvania, will the Pennsylvanians support us?" "If the lower counties are subdued, and give up," said the colonel, "the back counties will do the same." Washington passed his hand over his throat, and said, with a smile: "My neck does not feel as though it was made for a halter We must retire to Augusta county, in Virginia Numbers will be obliged to repair to us for safety, and we must try what we can do in carrying on a predatory war, and if overpowered we must cross the Allegheny mountains."

At this juncture of affairs Lord and General Howe issued a proclamation, by virtue of their authority as commissioners appointed by the crown for the settlement of the war, in which all persons in America in arms against his majesty's government were ordered to disperse and return to their homes, and all civil officers were commanded to discontinue their treasonable practices, and relinquish their usurped authority. A full and free pardon was offered to every one who would, within sixty days, appear before certain designated officials, claim the pardon offered, and take an oath pledging him to obey the laws, and submit to the authority of the king. Large numbers of persons, most of whom were possessed of property which they desired to save, at once came forward, made their submission, and took the required oath. Some of these were men who had borne a prominent part in the patriot movement ; among them were two delegates from Pennsylvania to the Continental Congress, and the president of the New Jersey convention, which had ratified the Declaration of Independence. Within ten days after the proclamation was issued between two and three thousand persons submitted, and swore allegiance to the king. In Philadelphia great excitement prevailed, and General Putnam, who was in command there, feeling that there was danger that the royalists in the city might succeed in obtaining control of it, advised that, until matters were placed on a more certain footing, Congress should hold its sessions at some safer place. Accordingly it adjourned on the 12th of December to meet in Baltimore.

The only quarter in which the Americans had been able to oppose anything of a successful resistance to the British was the region of Lake Champlain. We have related the retreat of Sullivan and Arnold from Canada, and the appointment of Gates to the command of their forces. The army halted at Forts Ticonderoga and Crown Point, which it strengthened, and awaited the development of the plans of Sir Guy Carleton, the British commander in Canada.

That officer had determined to secure the control of Lakes Champlain and George, and then to push on to the Hudson, open communication with the Howes at New York, and spend the winter at Albany. He would thus entirely sever the communication between New England and New York, and the Middle and Southern States. Sullivan had wisely destroyed all the boats on Lake Champlain which he did not need for his own purposes, and as there was no road along the shore by which he could advance, Carleton was obliged to construct a fleet before he could attempt to ascend the lake. He exerted himself with such energy that in three months he had a fleet of five large and twenty small vessels, and a number of armed boats assembled at the foot of the lake.

Gates was informed of Carleton's design, and ordered Arnold, who was possessed of some nautical knowledge, to construct a flotilla and take command of it for the purpose of contesting Carleton's effort to ascend the lake. Arnold set to work with enthusiasm, and soon had a force of vessels afloat about half as strong as that of the enemy. He chose a favorable position, and awaited Carleton's approach. A sharp encounter occurred between the opposing forces early in October near Valcour island, but was indecisive, and at nightfall Carleton took position to cut off Arnold's retreat. The night was dark and cloudy, and taking advantage of it, Arnold passed the enemy, and sailed for Crown Point. His vessels were in bad condition, however, and two were sunk on the voyage. Only six succeeded in coming within sight of Crown Point, near which they were overtaken by Carleton on the 6th of October. Arnold made a gallant fight with his remaining vessels. One was taken with her crew, and Arnold's flag-ship, the " Congress," was cut to pieces, and half of her crew were slain. Resolved not to surrender, Arnold ordered the vessels to be run aground, and set them on fire. He and his men then waded ashore, and by a sharp fire from their rifles kept the enemy from the burning galleys until they were entirely consumed. The Americans then hastened to Crown Point, where they set fire to the fort and the stores, and continued their retreat to Ticonderoga Gates greatly strengthened the defences of this post, and when Carleton arrived before it, he found it too strong to be attacked He therefore abandoned his attempt to reach the Hudson, and returned to Canada

A few weeks later, feeling that the lake country was safe for the winter, Gates, in obedience to orders from Washington, sent him part of his force, and shortly afterwards marched with the remainder of his troops to the assistance of the commander-in-chief.

Including these troops, Washington's force now numbered about six thousand men fit for duty. The enlistments of many of them would expire on the last day of December, and it was of the highest importance that something should be done to revive the confidence of the country before these men should be lost to the army. The circumstances in which Washington was placed required a blow to be struck in some quarter. A victory would be productive of the most important moral results; a defeat could do no more than ruin the cause, and a policy of inaction was sure to accomplish that.

An opportunity at once presented itself The British had ceased their pursuit, and though they held New Jersey in strong force, had scattered their detachments through the State. General Howe was in New York, and Lord Cornwallis was at the same place, and was about to sail for England Both commanders believed the American army to be too seriously crippled to assume the offensive during the winter. The Hessians, who constituted the advance-guard of the royal forces, were stationed along the Delaware Colonel Donop had his head-quarters at Burlington, and Colonel Rahl was at Trenton with a force of fifteen hundred men. Rahl was a brave and competent officer, but he entertained such a thorough contempt for the Americans that he neglected to protect his position by earthworks or other defences. The Hessians kept the country in terror; they were inveterate thieves, and plundered both patriot and royalist without mercy. They had earned the deep and abiding hatred of the American soldiers by bayoneting the wounded in the battles in which they had been engaged.

Washington now determined to recross the Delaware and attack the Hessians at different points. A force of twenty-four hundred picked troops under his own command was to cross the river a few miles above Trenton and attack the enemy at that place, and at the same time another detachment under Reed and Cadwallader were to cross over from Bristol and drive the Hessians under Colonel Donop out of Burlington. These attacks were to be simultaneous, and were ordered to be made at five o'clock on the morning of the 26th of December.

The division of Washington was accompanied by a train of twenty-four field-pieces under Colonel Knox. The river was high and full of floating ice, and the weather was cold and stormy. A detachment of boats had been collected for the service, and was manned by Colonel Glover's regiment of Marblehead fishermen, who had ferried the army over the East river in the retreat from Long island. The march was begun just after dark on Christmas night, and Washington hoped to reach the New Jersey shore by midnight; but the passage of the river

WASHINGTON CROSSING THE DELAWARE.

was difficult and tedious by reason of the floating ice and the high wind which repeatedly swept the boats out of their course; and it was four o'clock before the artillery was landed. The march was at once resumed. Washington, with the main body, moved by a wide circuit to gain the north of the town, while a detachment under Sullivan was ordered to advance by the river road and attack the enemy from the west and south sides.

A blinding storm of hail and snow delayed the advance of the troops, but also concealed their movements from the enemy; and it was eight o'clock before Trenton was reached. The attack was at once begun, and was pressed with vigor. The Hessians were completely taken by surprise; they flew to arms promptly, but by this time the Americans had gained the main street, and were sweeping it with a battery of six pieces. Colonel Rahl was mortally wounded while leading his grenadiers to the charge, and his men, seized with a panic, endeavored to retreat. Finding that they were surrounded, about one thousand of them threw down their arms and surrendered. The remainder succeeded in escaping and joining Colonel Donop at Burlington.

The Americans lost two men killed, and two were frozen to death on the march. Several were wounded. They took one thousand prisoners with their arms. Thirty-two of the captives were officers.

Washington now learned that the ice was so thick in front of Bristol that Reed and Cadwallader had not been able to get their cannon over the river, and had not attacked the enemy at Burlington. He therefore deemed it best to withdraw into Pennsylvania, as Donop's force was still intact at Burlington, and the enemy had another column at Princeton, a few miles distant. On the evening of the 26th he returned to his camp beyond the Delaware. The next day he learned from Reed and Cadwallader, who had crossed

BATTLE OF TRENTON.

the Delaware on the 27th, that Donop had called in all his detachments along the river, and had retreated in haste to New Brunswick and Princeton.

The news of the victory at Trenton was received with delight in all parts of the country, and men began to take hope. Several regiments, whose terms of enlistment expired on the last day of December, were induced to remain six weeks longer. Washington resolved to make an effort to recover New Jersey, and men of influence were sent to rouse the militia of that State to take up arms for the defence of their homes. Altogether matters assumed a more promising aspect than they had worn at any period of the war. On the 30th of December Washington recrossed the Delaware and took position at Trenton.

About the same time Congress bestowed upon Washington the highest proof of their confidence in his wisdom and integrity that a free people can ever confer upon a leader. On the 27th of December Congress con-

31

ferred upon General Washington, by a formal resolution, unlimited military power for six months The committee, in their letter informing him of this act, wrote " Happy is it for this country that the general of their forces can safely be intrusted with the most unlimited power, and neither personal security, liberty, nor property be in the least endangered thereby." The confidence of the country was not misplaced. Never was dictatorial power used more wisely or unselfishly, and never did its exercise produce more beneficial results.

It was resolved by Congress to secure assistance from abroad, and on the 30th of December Benjamin Franklin, Silas Deane, and Arthur Lee—the last of whom was appointed in place of Mr. Jefferson, who could not go—were sent as commissioners to France to secure the assistance of the government of that country France was not yet prepared to go to war with England, and the commissioners could do no more than secure aid in money, which was expended in the purchase of supplies and military stores, which were shipped to the United States It was arranged that this money should be repaid by Congress in the produce of the country, especially in tobacco, which was to be shipped to France through a mercantile house. The assistance thus obtained was of the greatest service to the Americans.

CHAPTER XXVIII.

THE YEAR 1777

Howe attempts to Crush Washington—Battle of Princeton—The British Confined to the Seaboard—Recovery of New Jersey—The American Army in Winter Quarters at Morristown—Effects of the American Successes—Difficulty of Procuring Troops—Washington Refuses to Exchange Prisoners—His Course Approved by Congress—Measures of Congress—Naval Affairs—Tryon Burns Danbury—Gallantry of Arnold—Troubles in the Northern Department—Congress Adopts a National Flag—"The Stars and Stripes"—Course of France towards the United States—France decides to Assist the Americans—Lafayette—His arrival in America—Capture of the British General Prescott—Howe threatens Philadelphia—Washington moves Southward—Battle of the Brandywine—Washington Retreats to the Schuylkill—Wayne's Defeat at Paoli—Philadelphia Evacuated by the Americans—It is Occupied by the British—Battle of Germantown—The British Attack the Forts on the Delaware—They are Abandoned by the Americans—Burgoyne's Army in Canada—Advance of Burgoyne into New York—Investment of Ticonderoga—It is Abandoned by the Americans—The Retreat to Fort Edward—Burgoyne reaches the Hudson—Murder of Miss McCrea—Siege of Fort Schuyler—Battle of Bennington—Critical Situation of Burgoyne—Gates in Command of the American Army—Battles of Behmus' Heights and Stillwater—Surrender of Burgoyne's Army—Clinton in the Highlands

REAT was the astonishment of General Howe when he learned of the battle at Trenton. He could scarcely believe that a handful of militia had captured a strong force of veteran troops led by such a commander as Colonel Rahl. He at once took prompt measures to repair the disaster. Lord Cornwallis, who was on the eve of sailing for England, was ordered to resume his command in New Jersey, and a force of seven thousand men was rapidly collected and placed under his orders. These troops rendezvoused at Princeton.

Washington was informed of these movements, and ordered Generals Mifflin and Cadwallader to join him without delay. They reached Trenton the 1st of January, with thirty-five hundred men. This increased the American force to about five thousand men fit for duty. Upon the approach of Cornwallis' army, Washington took position behind the Assunpink, and prepared to dispute the passage of that stream. The fords and bridge over the creek were carefully guarded, and were swept by the fire of the artillery placed to command them. A force under General Greene and Colonel Hand was thrown forward to hold the enemy

483

in check, and so retarded their movements that the British army did not arrive before Trenton until four o'clock in the afternoon of January 2d, 1777. Cornwallis made several determined efforts to force a passage of the creek, but was each time driven back by the well-directed fire of the provincials. Thinking that he could accomplish more the next day, the British commander drew off his men, resolving to renew the attack in the morning, when, he boasted, he would "bag the fox." Both armies encamped for the night in sight of each other, reddening the sky with the glow of their camp-fires.

The situation of the American army was now critical in the extreme. A retreat into Pennsylvania was impossible, as the Delaware was full of

COLLEGE OF NEW JERSEY, AT PRINCETON.

floating ice, and could not be passed in the face of such an army as that of Cornwallis. The issue of the next day's conflict was, to say the least, doubtful, for the army of Cornwallis was composed mainly of veteran troops, and he was himself a leader of genuine ability. In this emergency Washington determined upon one of the most brilliant and well-conceived operations of the war. It was known to him that the British had their main depot of supplies at New Brunswick, and he supposed from the presence of so many troops with Cornwallis that this depot had been left unguarded. He therefore resolved to break up his camp, and march by an unfrequented road around the left flank of the enemy to Princeton, capture the force stationed there, and then hasten to New Brunswick and secure the stores at that place. Sending his heavy baggage and stores down the river to Burlington, Washington silently withdrew his army from its position at midnight, leaving the camp-fires burning to deceive the enemy, and a small force to watch the British and destroy the bridges after the army had passed on.

A forced march brought the Americans within three miles of Princeton by daybreak on the morning of the 3d of January. The army was divided into two divisions, one under Washington, and the other under General Mercer, which approached the town by different routes. Three British regiments on their way to Trenton had passed the previous night

BATTLE OF PRINCETON.

at Princeton, and had resumed their march at dawn. The first of these, under Colonel Mawhood, was encountered by the division of General Mercer, about two miles from Princeton. As Mawhood supposed Mercer's force to be a party retreating from Trenton, he at once resolved to attack it. His attack was successful. The Americans were driven back, and General Mercer was wounded, bayoneted, and left on the field apparently dead. Mercer's troops fell back in confusion, and a body of Pennsylvania militia, which had been sent by Washington to their assistance, was held in check by the fire of the British artillery.

At this moment, Washington, who had been rendered anxious by the obstinate and continued firing, arrived on the field   A glance showed him the broken and shattered regiments of Mercer falling back in confusion, and the Pennsylvania militia wavering under the heavy cannonade directed against them. Not a moment was to be lost, and putting spurs to his horse, he dashed forward in the face of the fire of Mawhood's artillery, and waving his hat, called upon the troops to rally and follow him   The effect was electrical, the fugitives rallied with a loud cheer and reformed their line, and at the same moment a Virginia regiment, which had just arrived, dashed out of a neighboring wood and opened a heavy fire upon the enemy   A little later the American artillery came up, and opened a shower of grape upon the British   Mawhood was driven back, and with great difficulty succeeded in regaining the main road, along which he retreated with all speed to Trenton

The second British regiment, advancing from Princeton to Mawhood's assistance, was attacked by St Clair's brigade, and was speedily driven across the country towards New Brunswick   The third regiment, seeing the fate of their comrades, became panic-stricken. A portion fled towards New Brunswick, and the remainder took refuge in the college building at Princeton   They surrendered after a few shots from the American artillery.

The Americans lost but a few men in this battle; but General Mercer, a brave and efficient commander, was mortally wounded, and died a few days after the engagement. The British lost about one hundred killed and three hundred prisoners.

Eager to secure the stores at New Brunswick, Washington pushed on with speed in that direction, but after passing a few miles beyond Princeton decided to abandon the attempt   He was sure that Cornwallis would pursue him as soon as his retreat from Trenton was discovered, and his men were too much exhausted to reach New Brunswick before the arrival of the enemy   They had been without rest for a night and a day, and some of them were barefooted   His generals sustained him in the opinion that it was injudicious to continue the movement against New Brunswick, and he reluctantly abandoned it, and withdrew in the direction of Morristown.

When Cornwallis discovered the withdrawal of the Americans on the morning of the 3d of January, he was greatly perplexed to know in what direction they had gone. In a little while the sound of the cannonade at Princeton revealed to him the route taken by them, and he at once understood the design of Washington   He must save his stores at any risk, and he broke up his camp and set out for Princeton and New Brunswick. The Americans had obstructed the Princeton road, and had

broken down the bridge over Stony creek, a few miles from the town
Without waiting to rebuild the bridge, the British commander forced his
men through the icy waters, which were breast high, and hastened through
Princeton with all speed. Believing that Washington had hurried on to
New Brunswick, Cornwallis marched direct to that place, and did not
notice the deflection of the American army from the main route. Reaching New Brunswick, he made arrangements to defend the town, which he
supposed would be attacked.

In the meantime the American army retreated to a strong position at
Morristown, where the troops erected huts in which to pass the winter.
Finding that the enemy did not attack him, Washington ventured to
extend his line. His right was at Princeton, under General Putnam,
and his left, under General Heath, was in the Highlands. His own
head-quarters were at Morristown. For six months neither party
attempted any movement of importance. Washington was not idle,
however. Though he had but the skeleton of an army at Morristown,
he displayed such activity in cutting off the foraging parties of the
British that they were unable to draw any supplies from the country
beyond their lines, and rarely ventured without their camps. By the
beginning of spring Cornwallis had abandoned every post in New Jersey
save New Brunswick and Perth Amboy. From these points he could
communicate with and draw his supplies from New York by water.
Thus was New Jersey almost entirely redeemed from the enemy. The
militia of the State recovered from their former despondency, and warmly
seconded the efforts of Washington against the British.

Confidence was returning to the country, and though men felt that the
struggle might yet be long and arduous, it was not as hopeless as they
had feared.

Washington passed the winter in endeavoring to reorganize the army,
and fit it for the work required of it in the spring. The policy of short
enlistments adopted by Congress was the source of very great trouble,
and the expiration of the enlistments of a large part of the army during
this winter caused the commander-in-chief the greatest anxiety. He
repeatedly condemned this policy, and endeavored to procure the substitution of a longer term. Great efforts were made to procure recruits,
but they came in very slowly. In order to check the ravages of the
small-pox in the camp, the recruits were inoculated immediately upon
their arrival.

Efforts were now made to bring about an exchange of prisoners. The
British objected to an exchange of man for man, on the ground that the
Americans were rebels, and such an exchange would be an acknowledg-

ment of their belligerent rights. Somewhat later General Howe, who
had about five thousand prisoners in New York, renewed the negotiation.
The British had treated the captured Americans with great severity, and
had confined them in warehouses in New York, and in foul hulks
anchored in the bay. They were improperly fed, and were allowed to
remain almost naked. Their sufferings were fearful, and they were
reduced and emaciated in strength and body, until they were truly said
to resemble " walking corpses." British cruelty never exhibited itself in
a more inhuman form than in the treatment of these unfortunate captives

UNITED STATES NAVY YARD, BROOKLYN.

by the royal officials. More than ten thousand of them died in New
York, during the war, from the effects of this treatment. When General Howe's proposal to exchange these men for the Hessians taken by
the Americans was received, it was declined by Washington. The Hessians had been well fed and well treated by the Americans, and were hale
and hearty, and Washington was unwilling to liberate them for service
in the British army, and to receive in exchange for them half-starved
men, who were so weak that they could scarcely reach their homes. It

was a stern necessity, but it was recognized by Congress, and Washington's view of the matter was sustained

During the winter five more major-generals were commissioned by Congress. They were Stirling, St. Clair, Mifflin, Stephen, and Lincoln. Arnold, who was the senior brigadier in the service, justly conceived that his rank and services in battle entitled him to promotion, and was indignant at having been passed over in the new appointments, and complained bitterly of the injustice done him Eighteen brigadier-generals were also appointed. Among them were George Clinton, of New York, Glover, the commander of the Marblehead regiment, Woodford and Muhlenberg, of Virginia; and Hand and Anthony Wayne, of Pennsylvania.

Congress gave great attention to the reorganization of the army during this session A quartermaster's department was organized, with General Mifflin at its head. Four regiments of cavalry were ordered to be enlisted. The hospital service was reorganized, and placed under the control of Dr Shippen, of Philadelphia; and Dr Rush, of Philadelphia, one of the signers of the Declaration of Independence, was appointed surgeon-general of the army

Efforts were also made to place the navy upon a better footing. Several of the frigates ordered by Congress to be built had been completed and equipped; but the work on the rest was delayed by the want of funds. Efforts were made to complete them, as they were greatly needed : all the vessels constituting the American fleet being at this time blockaded in the harbor of Providence, Rhode Island, by the enemy

Since the beginning of the struggle a destructive warfare had been carried on by the privateers of New England against the commerce of Great Britain, especially against the vessels of that country trading to the West Indies During the first years of the war nearly three hundred of these were captured by the privateers. The cargoes of the captured vessels were valued at the immense sum of five millions of dollars. The American merchantmen also maintained a regular communication with France, Spain, and Holland, and a profitable trade was carried on between the United States and those countries. It was attended with great risk, however, and many of the American vessels were captured by the British men-of-war.

Washington remained at Morristown some time after the spring opened, and exerted himself to the utmost to take the field as soon as the enemy should develop their plans. The first months of the season were employed by the British commander in a series of plundering expeditions. One of these was directed against Peekskill, where the Americans had collected a large quantity of stores. General McDougall, commanding the American force at that point, found it impossible to defend the stores, and set fire to them and retreated to the heights overlooking the town. The enemy made no attempt to follow him, and returned down the river. General Heath had been transferred to the command of the forces in Massachusetts, and was succeeded in the command of the Highlands by General Putnam.

In the latter part of April General Tryon, the last royalist governor of New York, was sent by General Howe, with a force of two thousand men, to destroy a large quantity of stores collected by the Americans at Danbury, in the western part of Connecticut, about twenty-three miles from the sound On the 26th of April, Tryon landed near Norwalk, and marched to Danbury, where he burned the stores and set fire to the town Thus far he had met with no opposition, but the alarm had spread immediately after his landing, and the Connecticut militia, to the number of six hundred men, assembled under Generals Silliman and Wooster. Arnold chanced to be at New Haven, and collecting a small force of volunteers, hurried to join Silliman and Wooster, and the whole command hastened after the marauders

Tryon began his retreat from Danbury before daylight on the morning of the 27th, and was soon after attacked by the militia. During the 27th and 28th, the British were harassed at every step by the little band of Americans, who, though too weak to defeat them in any single encounter, hung upon their march and inflicted upon them a loss of nearly three hundred men: The enemy at last came under the protection of the guns of their ships, and the Americans were forced to withdraw. Tryon then re-embarked his exhausted troops and returned to New York The American loss was slight. The brave old General Wooster, a veteran of sixty-eight years, was mortally wounded at the head of his men, and died a few days later. Arnold behaved with such distinguished gallantry in this affair that Congress rewarded him with the rank of major-general, and presented him with a horse handsomely equipped. Even this acknowledgment of his merit was mingled with injustice, for the date of his commission still left him below the rank he was entitled to, and he felt the second slight as another undeserved injury

The Connecticut militia were very indignant at the burning of Danbury, and resolved to avenge it. In the latter part of May, a party of one hundred and seventy men, under Colonel Meigs, crossed the sound in whale-boats to the east end of Long Island They carried their boats during the night fifteen miles across the neck, and launching them again, proceeded to Sag Harbor, where they destroyed twelve vessels and a large quantity of stores collected there by the British and made ninety prisoners. They then returned to Connecticut without the loss of a man.

Recruits came in to the American camp very slowly, and various expedients were adopted by Washington to hasten the enlistments. At his instance, Congress declared that all indented servants who enlisted in the army should receive their freedom at once. Bounties in land were offered to such Hessians as should desert the British service. This last measure did not accomplish much towards crippling the enemy.

In the northern department, Schuyler was left with a mere skeleton of an army. He had but seven hundred men, at the most, at Ticonderoga, and he was fearful that Carleton would learn his weakness, pass Lake Champlain on the ice, capture Ticonderoga, and push on to Albany. He repeatedly urged the commander-in-chief to send him reinforcements and supplies, but his request could not be granted, as there were none to be spared from Washington's army. During the winter a persistent effort was made to drive Schuyler from his command, in order that Gates might succeed to it. Charges were brought against him with such recklessness that he offered his resignation to Congress. That body refused to accept it; but as the efforts of his enemies were not discontinued, Schuyler went to Philadelphia, in April, 1777, and demanded an investigation into his conduct. Gates succeeded him in his command. Schuyler was fully vindicated by the report of the investigating committee of Congress, and was ordered to resume his command. Gates was greatly surprised by the result, and reluctantly relinquished the command of the northern department to his rival, and repaired to Philadelphia to seek redress at the hands of Congress for what he termed his wrongs.

GENERAL PHILIP SCHUYLER.

Until now the Americans had been without a national flag. Congress, in June, 1777, remedied this very serious want by adopting the old "Union Flag," with its thirteen stripes; but substituted, in place of St. George's Cross, a group of thirteen stars, one for each State. Thus the "Stars and Stripes" became the national ensign of the republic—a star having been added for each additional State that has since joined the original thirteen

The war in America had been watched with the deepest interest in Europe, and especially by France The French government had been convinced long before the outbreak of the revolution that the treatment which the colonies were receiving from Great Britain would ultimately cause their separation from her, and ten years before the war began, the Duke de Choiseul, the prime minister of Louis XV., had sent Baron De Kalb to examine and report the state of the feelings of the colonists towards Great Britain. De Kalb was a shrewd observer, and furnished his government with ample proofs that England was alienating the Americans by her treatment of them. Choiseul conceived the hope that, by offering the Americans free trade with France, they would be made to resent the course of England even more decidedly. When the revolution began, the French government was fully prepared for it, and was ready to avenge the loss of Canada by aiding the new republic in its efforts to throw off the authority of Great Britain. It was merely waiting to see whether the Americans were able to maintain the stand they had taken The news of the defeat on Long island, the loss of New York, and the retreat through New Jersey, filled the friends of America with serious alarm, and it was generally believed in Europe that the Americans would not be able to withstand the superior force of the mother country

In the early spring of 1777 it was known in Europe that the American army, which it was supposed had been driven in hopeless disorder over the Delaware without the means of continuing the war, had suddenly rallied and beaten a force of veteran troops at Trenton, and again at Princeton, and had recovered New Jersey from the enemy. This intelligence produced the most profound astonishment in Europe, and was received in France with genuine satisfaction. The Americans were extolled as a race of heroes, and the prudence and good generalship of Washington were spoken of with the highest praise.

The French government now felt justified in aiding the patriots ; but it proceeded with caution American privateers were secretly fitted out, with the connivance of the government, and were permitted to sell their prizes in French ports, and the protests of the British ambassador against such acts were unheeded The government made secret grants of arms and military stores to the Americans, and three ship-loads were sent out in the spring of 1777. Two of these vessels were captured by the English, but the third reached America in safety, and its cargo went to supply the deficiencies of the army at Morristown.

In the spring of this year the commissioners sent to France by Congress reached that country. They had full powers to enter into an alliance with the French king. They were granted several private interviews by the Count de Vergennes, the French prime minister, and were secretly encouraged to hope for the success of their mission. As yet, however, France was not prepared to declare war against Great Britain.

Though the government delayed its action, there were generous hearts in France who were determined to give all the aid and comfort in their power to the struggling patriots. One of these was the youthful Marquis de Lafayette, the heir of a noble name, the possessor of wealth and a high social position, and the husband of a beautiful and accomplished wife. He had heard at a dinner party given by the French officials at Mayence to the Duke of Gloucester, a brother of the king of England, the story of the war then going on in America, and its causes, related by the lips of the royal guest. His generous heart at once went out in sympathy to the patriots, and he resolved to leave his family and all his advantages at home, and go to the aid of the Americans. He revealed his intention to the Count de Broglie, a Marshal of France, who regarded his enterprise as Quixotic, and refused to aid him. Finding him determined, the count introduced his young friend to the Baron de Kalb, an officer of experience and merit, who had visited America as Choiseur's agent in the last reign. De Kalb introduced Lafayette to Silas Deane, then the only American commissioner in France. The news of the loss of New York and of New Jersey arrived about this time, but did not lessen the ardor of Lafayette; and though the newly-arrived commissioners, Franklin and Lee, candidly told him that they could not encourage him to hope for a successful issue of their cause, he avowed his determination to proceed. He purchased a vessel, which was loaded with arms and supplies by the commissioners. The French government attempted to prevent him from sailing, but he succeeded in getting

LAFAYETTE.

off, accompanied by De Kalb and several others. He reached Philadelphia, offered his services to Congress without pay, and was commissioned a major-general in the American army, though not yet
twenty years old.

Lafayette was not the only foreigner whose services were accepted by
Congress. De Kalb; Count Pulaski and Thaddeus Kosciusko, natives
of Poland; and Conway, an Irishman who had seen thirty years' service
in the French army, and who, in an evil hour for this country, came to
America; and, later still, Baron Steuben, one of Frederick the Great's
veterans, and who did good service to the cause by introducing into the
American ranks the drill and discipline of the Prussian army, were commissioned and assigned to duty by Congress.

About the middle of May, Washington broke up his camp at Morristown, and occupied the heights of Middlebrook in order to watch the
British to better advantage. Howe made repeated efforts to draw him
from this strong position into the open field, where the superior

discipline of the royal
troops would give him
an advantage, but
Washington out-
generalled him com-
pletely, and Howe
finding it impossible
to bring on an engage-
ment, withdrew his
army to Staten island.

LAFAYETTE OFFERING HIS SERVICES TO DR. FRANKLIN.

While these move-
ments were in progress, the British sustained a serious loss in the
capture of General Prescott, one of their principal officers, who had
earned the dislike of the Americans by his arbitrary and contemptu-
ous treatment of them. He was commanding the British forces at
Newport, and had his head-quarters on the outskirts of the town.
On a dark night in July, a company of picked men, under Colonel
Barton, crossed Narragansett bay in whale boats, and passing silently
through the British fleet, landed near Prescott's quarters. The sentinel at the door was secured, and the astounded general was roused
from his bed, and hurried away without being allowed time to dress.
He was conveyed within the American lines, and was afterwards exchanged for General Charles Lee.

Washington now learned of the invasion of New York by the army
of General Burgoyne, to which we shall refer further on. It was evident

that Burgoyne was trying to reach the Hudson. Washington's spies in
New York informed him that Howe was preparing to send off the larger
part of his force by water, and the commander-in-chief was perplexed
to know whether Howe intended ascending the Hudson to coöperate with
Burgoyne, or to transport his army to Philadelphia by water. Towards
the last of July Howe sailed with his fleet from New York, and stood
out to sea. Ten days later his ships were reported off the mouth of the
Delaware. Washington now felt confident that his design was to attack
Philadelphia, and crossed the Delaware with his army, and marched to
Germantown to await the development of the enemy's plans. About the
same time the British fleet stood out to sea again. Its destination was

SCENE ON THE WISSAHICKON.

uncertain, and Washington held his army in readiness to march at a
minute's notice to the threatened point.

While awaiting the movements of Sir William Howe, Washington
visited Philadelphia, where Arnold was in command and was engaged
in fortifying the city, to consult with Congress, and push forward the
measures for the defence of the place. While there he met the newly-
arrived Lafayette. Washington was an acute judge of men, and at his
first interview with Lafayette was deeply impressed with the noble and
earnest character of the young soldier, and conceived for him a warm
regard which ended only with his life.

In the midst of the uncertainty attending Howe's movements, Washington received urgent appeals from Schuyler for assistance. He sent
him two brigades from the Highlands, and ordered Colonel Morgan to

join him with his riflemen, who were regarded as more than a match for
the Indians of Burgoyne's army. Arnold was also sent to assume command of a division in the northern army, as he was familiar with the
country. Putnam was ordered to prevent Sir Henry Clinton, who had
been left at New York, from ascending the Hudson and forming a junction with Burgoyne; and General Lincoln, commanding the militia of
Massachusetts, was directed to march with a portion of his force to
Schuyler's assistance.

As nothing had been heard of the British fleet, Washington was about
to move from Germantown into New Jersey once more, when news was
received that the enemy had ascended the Chesapeake to its head, and
had landed their forces at Elkton, in Maryland, about sixty miles from
Philadelphia. The Delaware had been obstructed and fortified a short distance below Philadelphia, and Howe had ascended the Chesapeake in order

to secure an undis-
puted landing. He
intended to march
his army across the
country towards
Philadelphia, while
the fleet should re-
turn to the Dela-
ware, and aid the
army in reducing
the forts on that
river. He had

BATTLE OF THE BRANDYWINE.

eighteen thousand men with him, and effected his landing at Elkton,
without opposition, on the 25th of August, and at once began his advance
towards Philadelphia.

Washington had but eleven thousand effective men with him, and was
in no way prepared to undertake a campaign in the open country.
Nevertheless, he advanced at once to dispute the progress of the enemy,
and by forced marches succeeded in reaching the vicinity of Wilmington
before the arrival of the British. Upon examining the country he decided to contest the passage of the Brandywine creek, and stationed his
army along its left bank. The British were advancing by the main
road to Philadelphia, which crossed the Brandywine at Chadd's ford,
and as Washington supposed their main effort would be made at this
point, he stationed the greater part of his army to cover it. On the 11th
of September the British army reached the creek. Howe ordered General Knyphausen to make a feint at Chadd's ford, as if he were about to

force a passage, while he sent Cornwallis with a strong column to pass the creek higher up and turn the American right flank. This plan was successfully carried out. Washington was deceived by the officer sent to ascertain if the enemy were threatening his right, and was left in ignorance of Cornwallis' movement until it was too late to prevent it. Being outflanked, the American army was compelled to fall back, with a loss of twelve hundred men. The troops did not know they had suffered a reverse, but supposing they had merely experienced a check were in high spirits. Lafayette was wounded in this battle; and Pulaski so greatly distinguished himself that he was subsequently rewarded by Congress with the rank of brigadier-general and the command of the cavalry.

THE SCHUYLKILL, AT PHILADELPHIA.

Sir William Howe did not push his advantage, but remained for two days near the battle-field. Washington, in the meantime, retreated to Chester, and then to the Schuylkill, which he crossed on the 12th of September, and proceeded to Germantown, where the army went into camp. The men were in excellent spirits, and a day or two later Washington recrossed the river, and moved towards the enemy, whom he encountered about twenty-five miles from Philadelphia, on the 16th. A violent rain-storm prevented the two armies from engaging, and injured the arms and ammunition of the men so much that Washington deemed it best to withdraw to Pott's Grove, on the Schuylkill, about thirty miles

32

from Philadelphia. At the same time he detached General Wayne, with a force of fifteen hundred men, to gain the enemy's rear and cut off their wagon train. A Tory carried information of this movement to the British commander, and Wayne was himself surprised at Paoli tavern, on the 20th of September, and defeated with a loss of three hundred men.

It being impossible to save the city of Philadelphia from capture the military stores were removed, and a contribution was levied upon the people to supply the army with clothing, shoes, and other necessaries during the winter. Congress in view of the great danger which threatened the country conferred dictatorial powers upon Washington for sixty days, and then extended this time to a period of four months Congress then adjourned to meet at Lancaster, from which, a few days later, it transferred its sessions to York beyond the Susquehanna.

Howe crossed the Schuylkill by a night march, and on the 26th of September entered Philadelphia The bulk of his army was stationed at Germantown, and a small detachment was left to hold the city.

The Americans, though they had lost Philadelphia, still held the forts on the Delaware, a short distance below the mouth of the Schuylkill. The work on the Pennsylvania side was called Fort Mifflin, and was built on a low mud island. Immediately opposite, at Red Bank, on the New Jersey shore, was Fort Mercer. Both works were armed with heavy guns, and commanded the river perfectly. The channel was obstructed with heavy logs fastened together and sunk in the stream so securely as to render their removal difficult Above these obstructions were several floating batteries.

After landing the British army at Elkton, Lord Howe carried his fleet down the Chesapeake, and entering the Delaware took position below the forts to await the coöperation of the army in the attack upon them.

Washington having learned that Howe had withdrawn a part of his force from Germantown to aid in the operations against the fort, resolved to surprise the remainder. A night march of fourteen miles brought the American army to Germantown at sunrise on the morning of the 4th of October. A heavy fog hung over the country and prevented the commander-in-chief from seeing either the position of the enemy or that of his own troops The British were taken by surprise, and were driven in disorder The victory seemed within the grasp of Washington, when the Americans abandoned the pursuit to attack a stone house in which a few of the enemy had taken refuge. While thus engaged they were seized with an unaccountable panic, which threw them into confusion. The British rallied, and assailing the Americans in their turn, drove them from the field with a loss of one thousand men. Washington was greatly mortified by this failure. He wrote to Congress: "Every account confirms the opinion I at first entertained, that our troops retreated at the instant when victory was declaring herself in our favor."

Howe now drew in his army nearer to Philadelphia, and prepared for an immediate attack on the forts on the Delaware. These held that river so securely that the British fleet was not able to bring supplies up to the city. The provisions of the army were nearly exhausted, and if the forts could not be reduced it would be necessary to evacuate Philadelphia in order to obtain food. On the 22d of October, Count Donop was sent with a force of twelve hundred picked Hessians to storm Fort Mercer, at Red Bank, while the fleet reduced Fort Mifflin. Donop's attack was

THE BATTLE OF GERMANTOWN—CHEW'S HOUSE.

repulsed with a loss of four hundred men, the Hessian commander himself being among the slain. In the attack on Fort Mifflin the British lost two ships, and the remainder were more or less injured by the fire of the American guns.

Shortly after this repulse, the British erected batteries on a small island in the Delaware, which commanded Fort Mifflin, and on the 10th of November opened a heavy bombardment of the fort from these works and from their fleet. The bombardment was continued until the night of the 15th. The works being nearly destroyed, Fort Mifflin was abandoned on the night of the 16th, and on the 18th the garrison was withdrawn from the fort at Red Bank. The British now removed the obstructions from the river, and their fleet ascended to Philadelphia.

General Howe constructed a strongly fortified line from the Schuylkill to the Delaware, above Philadelphia, and went into winter quarters with his army behind these defences.

The season being too late for active operations, Washington withdrew his army to Valley Forge on the Schuylkill, about twenty miles from Philadelphia, and went into winter quarters. From this position he could protect Congress, which was sitting at York, and insure the safety of his principal depot of supplies at Reading.

In the northern department the year had been marked by the most important events. Sir Guy Carleton was succeeded in the command of the British forces in Canada by General Burgoyne, an officer of ability and

ATTACK ON RED BANK.

integrity. He was strongly reinforced, and soon had under his command a finely equipped army of ten thousand men. About eight thousand of these were British and Hessian regulars, the remainder Canadians and Indians. The army was plentifully supplied with artillery of the most improved pattern, which was under the immediate command of General Philips, a veteran who had served with great distinction in the seven years war. The second in command of the army was General Frazer, an officer of acknowledged skill, who was greatly beloved by the troops. Baron Reidesel, the commander of the Hessians, was also an old soldier. Altogether, the force under Burgoyne was the most splendid body of troops Great Britain had yet assembled in America. With this army Burgoyne was to advance by way of Lake Champlain to the Hudson, while a detachment under General St. Leger was to move eastward by way of Oswego and descend the Mohawk to the Hudson. Having secured the Hudson, Burgoyne was to open communication with Sir Henry Clinton in New York, capture the forts in the Highlands, and so cut off New England from the Middle and Southern States.

To oppose his advance General Schuyler had a weak army between Albany and Lake Champlain. General St. Clair with a detachment of three thousand men held Ticonderoga, and though he seriously feared that his force was too weak to offer much resistance, trusted to the natural strength of his position, and hoped to be able to hold Ticonderoga until aid could reach him.

ALBANY, NEW YORK, IN 1875.

On the 2d of July Burgoyne's army appeared before Ticonderoga, and invested that post. Opposite Fort Ticonderoga, on the right hand side of the outlet of Lake George, is a lofty hill known as Mount Defiance. The Americans had neglected to fortify this hill, thinking it inaccessible to artillery. General Philips was of a different opinion, and in three days of hard labor succeeded in dragging his guns to the summit of Mount Defiance, from which they commanded the forts on both sides of the lake. St. Clair now saw that the forts were untenable, and that he must evacuate them at once in order to save his army. Sending his baggage and stores in boats up the lake to Skenesborough, now Whitehall, he evacuated Fort Ticonderoga and crossed over to Fort Independence, on the opposite side of the lake. His withdrawal was discovered before it was completed, and the British at once followed in pursuit Burgoyne ordered General Frazer to follow St Clair's command, while he himself passed up the lake and destroyed the stores at Skenesborough. Upon his approach, on the afternoon of the 7th, the American force at Skenesborough set fire to the stores, and retreated rapidly to Fort Anne, which was reached the next morning. The British appeared before this fort the same day, but were held in check, and that night the Americans set fire to Fort Anne and retreated to Fort Edward, sixteen miles farther.

On the afternoon of the 7th, General Frazer came up with St. Clair's rear guard at Hubbardton, and defeated it with severe loss. St. Clair continued his retreat through the woods, and a week later reached Fort Edward with his exhausted troops.

General Schuyler had advanced to Fort Edward with a force of five thousand men, nearly all of whom were militia; many were without arms, and there was a woful scarcity of ammunition and provisions in his camp Schuyler was joined here by the remnant of St. Clair's command, and as Burgoyne had halted for a few days at the head of Lake Champlain, which was twenty-four miles distant from Fort Edward, Schuyler set his men to work to obstruct the road between those two points by felling trees across it and destroying bridges So thoroughly was this work done that Burgoyne's army consumed a fortnight in its advance from Skenesborough to the Hudson. It reached the neighborhood of Fort Edward on the 29th of July Schuyler at once abandoned the fort, and fell back to Saratoga, from which he moved to Stillwater, near the mouth of the Mohawk.

The loss of Ticonderoga and the northern forts was regarded by Congress as an evidence of the incapacity of Schuyler and his subordinates, and so little allowance was made for the serious disadvantages under which those officers labored, that Congress ordered all the northern generals to be recalled and their conduct investigated It was not until Washington called the attention of Congress to the fact that a compliance with this order would leave the northern army without officers, that that body consented to suspend its unwise decree The prejudice against Schuyler, though unjust, was deep, and his removal from his command was resolved upon Washington declined to deprive him of his command, as his confidence in Schuyler was unshaken, and Congress took the matter in its own hands. "The eastern influence prevailed," says Irving, "and Gates received the appointment so long the object of his aspirations, if not intrigues "

Upon reaching Fort Edward, Burgoyne, confident that the game was in his own hands, issued a proclamation calling upon the people to send representatives to a convention to meet at Castleton to provide for the re-establishment of the royal authority. This was met by a proclamation from Schuyler, who declared that he would punish as traitors all who should comply with Burgoyne's call, or in any way give aid and comfort to the enemy. There was not much need for this threat, for the militia of the northern district were rapidly rallying to Schuyler's aid; the people of the whole region were profoundly excited, and they were determined that the British army should never leave their country.

Much of this feeling was caused by the outrages of the Indians in Burgoyne's army, who prowled about the country, murdering and plundering the people who were exposed to their fury. One of their crimes roused the whole northern region to action. A beautiful young girl, Jenny McCrea by name, was visiting a friend near Fort Edward. She was betrothed to a young Tory who had fled to Canada some time since, and was now serving as a lieutenant in Burgoyne's army. When her friends removed

SIEGE OF FORT SCHUYLER.

from Fort Edward to Albany, to avoid the danger which threatened them, she lingered behind in spite of their invitation to accompany them, hoping to meet her lover upon the advance of Burgoyne's forces. The house in which she was staying was attacked by a party of Indians, and she was taken prisoner. Anxious for her safety she promised her captors a liberal reward if they would conduct her to her lover in the British camp. On the way they quarrelled over the promised reward, and in their rage murdered the poor girl and carried her scalp into the British camp. Burgoyne was horror-struck at the atrocious deed, and promptly disavowed it; but the news of the murder roused a stern desire for vengeance throughout the northern department. The terrible scenes of the old French war were not forgotten, and the people were fearful they would now be revived under British influence unless Burgoyne's army were destroyed. Thousands flocked to the American camp, with such arms as they could procure, eager to crush the enemy.

In the meantime St. Leger had moved from Oswego into the valley of the Mohawk, and had laid siege to Fort Schuyler or Stanwix, on the site of the present city of Rome. The fort was commanded by Colonel Gansevoort. The siege was begun on the 3d of August, and a few days later news was received by the little garrison that General Herkimer with eight hundred militia was advancing to their assistance. On the 6th of August Herkimer reached a place called Oriskany, where, owing to the impatience of his men, he fell into an ambush of Tories and Indians. The fight which ensued was one of the most desperate of the war; quarter

BURGOYNE'S ENCAMPMENT ON THE HUDSON.

was neither asked nor given by either party. Herkimer was mortally wounded, but continued to cheer on his men, until a successful sally from the fort compelled St. Leger to recall the force engaged with Herkimer to defend his own camp. The American militia then retreated, carrying with them their commander, who died a few days later. Fort Schuyler was left in a critical condition, and Arnold was sent at his own request to its relief. He caused the strength of his force to be greatly exaggerated, and spread a report that Burgoyne had been defeated. The Indians deserted St. Leger rapidly upon hearing these reports, and that commander hastily abandoned his camp, and retreated into Canada with the remainder of his force.

Burgoyne had now reached the Hudson, and had full command of Lakes George and Champlain; but the people of the country were hostile to him, and he found it hard to procure either cattle or horses. Though his camp on the Hudson was but eighteen miles from Lake George, this lack of animals made it almost impossible to transport his supplies across the intervening country, and his army was beginning to run short of provisions.

To obtain horses and provisions, Burgoyne, early in August, sent a force of five hundred Germans and a detachment of Indians and Tories, under Lieutenant-Colonel Baum, to seize the stores collected by the Americans at Bennington, Vermont, and to collect such horses and cattle as they could on the march. He was told that the people of the neighborhood were largely devoted to the king, and that the stores were unguarded.

GENERAL JOHN STARK.

The news of the approach of this force spread rapidly through the country, and the Green Mountain Boys, as the Vermont militia were termed, flew to arms. Colonel Stark, who had retired from the Continental army on account of having been neglected in the recent promotions, was in the neighborhood, and was offered the command of the gathering forces. He accepted it promptly, and issued a warning to the people along the route of the British to drive off their horses and cattle,

and to conceal their grain and wagons to prevent their capture by the
enemy.   A messenger was sent with all speed to Manchester to Colonel
Seth Warner, urging him to march at once with his regiment to Bennington, where he was needed.

Baum had advanced to within six miles of Bennington when he heard
of the approach of the militia under Stark.   He halted, intrenched his
position, and sent to Burgoyne for reinforcements.   Colonel Breyman

BATTLE OF BENNINGTON.

with five hundred Hessians and two pieces of artillery was despatched to
his assistance.

Stark was prevented from making an immediate attack upon Baum by
a furious rain-storm, which also delayed the march of Breyman and
Warner.   During the night of the 15th of August, Stark was joined by
the militia from Berkshire, Massachusetts.   They were anxious to engage
the enemy at once, and were impatient at the delay caused by the storm.
One of their number, Parson Allen, approached Stark.   "General," said
he, "the people of Berkshire have often been called out to no purpose;
if you don't give them a chance to fight now, they will never turn out

again." Stark remarked his earnestness, and said with a smile, "You would not turn out now, while it is dark and raining, would you?" "Not just now," answered the parson. "Well," said Stark, "if the Lord should once more give us sunshine, and I don't give you fighting enough, I'll never ask you to turn out again."

The morning of the 16th came bright and clear, and Stark at once began his advance upon the enemy. Arriving in sight of the British works, he pointed them out to his men. "There are the red coats! We must beat them to-day, or Molly Stark sleeps a widow to-night." A spirited attack was made upon the British lines, both in front and in the rear, and after two hours' hard fighting they were carried by storm. Baum fell mortally wounded, and his men laid down their arms. The Indians and Tories had escaped to the woods at the opening of the battle.

The fighting had scarcely ended when the force under Colonel Breyman appeared, and at once engaged the Americans. At the same moment Warner's regiment, which had pushed forward all night in the rain, reached the field. The battle was continued until nightfall, when Breyman abandoned his artillery and made a hurried retreat to Burgoyne's camp on the Hudson. The Americans had fourteen killed and forty wounded. They took six hundred prisoners, one thousand stand of arms, and four pieces of cannon.

Burgoyne now found himself in a most critical condition. He had reached the Hudson, but his troops were short of provisions, his efforts against Fort Schuyler and Bennington had failed, and his force was being reduced by the desertions of the Indians. Burgoyne, who was a man of humanity and true soldierly spirit, had no sympathy with the barbarous policy of his government in employing the savages against the Americans, and had sternly cut short their cruelties. The Indians had taken offence at his course, and were leaving his army in great numbers. He made no effort to detain them, preferring to lose their services rather than allow them to continue their atrocities. On the other hand the American army was daily growing stronger. The militia were flocking to it in great numbers, and reinforcements were received from the Highlands. The militia of New Hampshire and Massachusetts were threatening Ticonderoga, the capture of which post would cut off his communications with Canada. The contrast between the present condition of the British army and that of a few weeks before was marked indeed.

Matters were in this state when General Gates arrived, late in August, and assumed the command of the army, which was now six thousand strong, and receiving reinforcements every day. Schuyler, superior to all sense of personal wrong, cheerfully rendered him all the assistance in his power in mastering the question before him; but Gates repaid this generosity with characteristic jealousy. He did not even invite Schuyler to his first council of war held a few days later. He at once left the position at the mouth of the Mohawk, and on the 12th of September advanced to Behmus' Heights, a spur of hills bordering the Hudson. The army now numbered nine thousand effective men, indifferently armed, but resolved to conquer. "Gates had no fitness for command," says Bancroft, "and wanted personal courage." He intrenched his position, and for the defence of his right and left flanks erected strong batteries.

GENERAL HORATIO GATES.

Burgoyne by great exertions succeeded in bringing up a month's provisions from Lake George for his army, which was now reduced to about six thousand men. He resolved to adhere to his original plan, and endeavor to force his way to Albany, and on the 13th of September crossed the Hudson at Schuylerville, and encamped on the plains of Saratoga, intending to decide the campaign by a general engagement. On the morning of the 19th of September he advanced against the American position. Gates wished to await the attack of the enemy in his intrenched position, but Arnold urged him to throw forward a force to hold them in check, and not permit them to turn the American left, as they evidently intended. After considerable solicitation he obtained the desired permission from Gates, and moved forward to check the advance of the British. A determined conflict immediately ensued and continued until nightfall. It was one of the most stubbornly contested engagements of the war, and its result was mainly due to the skill and courage of Arnold, who held the enemy in check during the day, and prevented the success of their plan for turning Gates' left flank The British remained in possession of the field at night, and the Americans rejoined their main body. The latter regarded the battle as a victory, as they had accomplished all they had expected

Burgoyne's difficulties thickened rapidly On the 17th a detachment of Massachusetts militia seized the posts at the outlet of Lake George and captured a fleet of three hundred boats loaded with supplies for Burgoyne's army, and took three hundred prisoners ' This force then united with another and laid siege to Ticonderoga. These successes completely destroyed Burgoyne's communication with Canada, and with it his means of supplying his army In this emergency he was greatly encouraged by the receipt of a letter from Sir Henry Clinton at New York, informing him that he (Clinton) would in a few days make an effort to ascend the Hudson and open communication with him Burgoyne thereupon resolved to endeavor to hold his position until the arrival of Clinton Three weeks passed away in inaction, and though skirmishes between the advanced parties were frequent, neither commander cared to attack the other; Burgoyne because he was anxious to defer a decisive engagement, Gates because he was scantily supplied with ammunition

The success of the battle of Behmus' Heights was generally attributed by the troops to Arnold, who was very popular with them. Gates' jealousy was most probably aroused by this belief, and he unceremoniously deprived Arnold of his command During this delay the American army was increased by the arrival of the Massachusetts militia and other reinforcements, to about eleven thousand men.

Burgoyne's situation was now more critical than ever. His best officers favored a retreat to Fort Edward; but the British commander decided before undertaking that movement to reconnoitre the American position in strong force. If it was found that it could not be attacked, he was willing to retreat to Fort Edward. A force of fifteen hundred picked men and ten pieces of cannon, commanded by the most experienced officers in the army, was sent on the 7th of October to reconnoitre the American position Gates, by the advice of Morgan, attacked this force on both flanks, and sent Morgan with his riflemen to cut the enemy off from their camp.

The sound of the firing roused Arnold, who was brooding over his wrongs. He mounted his horse and rode at full speed to the battle-field in spite of the efforts of Gates to stop him. He reached the scene of action, and was recognized by the troops, who received him with cheers

Without orders or any definite command, he placed himself at the head
of the troops and led them against the enemy. The British, led by General Frazer, held their ground manfully, but at length Frazer was mortally wounded by one of Morgan's riflemen, and his line gave way.
Burgoyne fearlessly exposed himself in the effort to rally the men, but
was at length obliged to order a retreat to the camp. This was accomplished with extreme difficulty, and the Americans, following in close
pursuit, made a determined attack upon the British intrenchments, which
were stubbornly defended. In this attack Arnold displayed great hero-

BURGOYNE'S RETREAT.

ism, and was wounded within the enemy's works. Though they failed
to capture the whole line, the Americans carried the camp of Colonel
Breyman's regiment of Hessians, the key to Burgoyne's position, and took
a number of prisoners.

The Americans bivouacked on the field, intending to renew the battle
the next day, but during the night Burgoyne abandoned his sick and
wounded, and silently withdrew from his intrenchments. The roads
being rendered bad by the rains, he halted and took position about two
miles from the town of Saratoga. On the night of the 9th, finding that

the Americans held the Hudson in such heavy force as to render its passage impracticable, he retreated to Saratoga. He then sent out a detachment to rebuild the bridges on the road to Fort Edward, but found the road in the possession of the Americans, who also held Fort Edward, and had captured all the boats laden with provisions for his army. He was thus left with but three days' rations for his men. On the 12th the American army, which had followed the British closely, invested their position, and opened a heavy fire upon their camp. On the 13th Burgoyne called a council of his officers, and it was resolved to open negotiations with Gates. He proposed to Gates to surrender his army on condition that they should be allowed to sail for England from the port of Boston, first pledging themselves not to serve again in North America during the war. Gates had heard of the successes of Clinton on the Hudson, and was fearful that he would reach Albany. He therefore weakly agreed to Burgoyne's proposal, and consented that

SURRENDER OF BURGOYNE.

the British army should march out of its camp with the honors of war; that the troops should be taken to Boston and sent to England, and that they should pledge themselves not to serve again in America during the war. These matters being arranged the British army surrendered on the 17th of October, and was fed by the Americans, for its provisions were exhausted. About six thousand prisoners were surrendered, together with nearly five thousand muskets, forty-two brass field-pieces, and a large quantity of military stores   Upon the surrender of Burgoyne, the British garrison at Ticonderoga evacuated that place, and retreated into Canada.

Congress refused to ratify the terms granted to Burgoyne by Gates. It was plain that if they were sent to England they could release an equal number of troops there, who could be sent to the aid of Sir Henry Clinton in New York. This would deprive the United States of one of the most important results of the surrender. Burgoyne and two attendants were permitted to return to England, but the captive troops were held as prisoners of war, and the next year were marched to Charlottesville, Virginia, and quartered in log huts, where the greater part of them remained until near the close of the war.

Some time before Burgoyne's surrender, Sir Henry Clinton, having received reinforcements from England, resolved to undertake the capture of the forts in the Highlands of the Hudson, the garrisons of which had been greatly weakened by the detachments sent from them to Washington and Gates   On the 6th of October he attacked and captured Forts Montgomery and Clinton. General George Clinton, who commanded at these forts, finding he could not hold them, sent to General Putnam for assistance, but his messenger deserted to the enemy, and the forts were abandoned   General Tryon was sent to occupy Kingston, which he ordered to be burned. When the enemy heard of Burgoyne's surrender, they retreated, setting fire to the house of every patriot along the river. Clinton then dismantled the captured forts, and returned to New York, taking with him all the heavy cannon and stores.

The capture of Burgoyne's army was hailed with delight throughout the country. It was the most important success of the war, and put an end to the danger of invasion from Canada. Gates was greatly puffed up by his triumph, and imagined himself the hero of the war. He sent his official report of the surrender to Congress direct, and not through the commander-in-chief, as his duty required, thus offering a grave insult to Washington.

General Schuyler now demanded an investigation of his conduct previous to his relinquishment of his command to Gates. He was thoroughly acquitted of the charges of mismanagement brought against him by his enemies, and was strongly urged by Congress to remain in the army. He declined to do so, and resigned his commission; but was soon afterwards returned to Congress from the State of New York.

THE sufferings of the American army during the long winter at Valley Forge were very great Many were barefooted, and their marches through the frost and snow could be traced by the blood from their feet. They were without clothing, without food, and were utterly unable to keep the field. Yet in spite of these sufferings many persons severely censured the commander-in-chief for going into winter quarters without attacking Philadelphia In reply to one of these remonstrances from the legislature of Pennsylvania, Washington wrote to Congress on the 23d of December, 1777 "Men are confined to hospitals or in farmers' houses for want of shoes. We have this day no less than two thousand eight hundred and ninety-eight men in camp unfit for duty, because they are barefoot and otherwise naked. Our whole strength in continental troops amounts to no more than eight thousand two hundred in camp fit for duty. Since the fourth instant our numbers fit for duty from hardships and exposures have decreased nearly two thousand men. Numbers still are obliged to sit all night by fires. Gentlemen reprobate the going into winter quarters as much as if they thought the soldiers were made of stocks and stones. I can assure those gentlemen that it is a much easier and less distressing thing to draw remonstrances in a comfortable room by a good fireside than to occupy a

33   513

cold, bleak hill, and sleep under frost and snow without clothes or blankets. However, although they seem to have little feeling for the naked and distressed soldiers, I feel superabundantly for them, and from my soul I pity those miseries which it is neither in my power to relieve nor prevent."

Congress did little or nothing to relieve the sufferings of the army. It promised the troops one month's extra pay, but made no effort to provide food or clothing for them. It authorized Washington to impress whatever articles were needed, but he remonstrated against this arbitrary use of power, as he was convinced that it would not supply the wants of the army, but would certainly anger the people of the country. Congress towards the close of the winter manifested so much hostility to the army

SUFFERINGS OF THE TROOPS AT VALLEY FORGE.

because of its appeals for food and clothes, that Washington earnestly remonstrated against this feeling and reminded that body that the troops were "citizens, having all the ties and interests of citizens." It is not too much to say that the personal influence of Washington went further than anything else in keeping the army together during this trying winter. Under any other commander the troops would have dispersed. Encouraged by the calm and lofty patience of Washington, the troops remained faithful to their cause and bore their sufferings with a heroic fortitude which their descendants will ever bear in grateful honor.

All this while the British army was comfortably quartered in Philadelphia, and the officers were billeted upon the inhabitants. They were amply supplied with every comfort, and their leisure time was given up to pleasure and dissipation on a scale the Quaker City had never dreamed of. "By a proportionate tax on the pay and allowances of each officer a house was opened for daily resort, and for weekly balls, with a gaming table which had assiduous votaries, and a room devoted to the game of chess. Thrice a week plays were enacted by amateur performers. . .

The officers, among whom all ranks of the British aristocracy were represented, lived in open licentiousness." The contrast between the pleasures and ease of these well-fed troops and the sufferings and privations of the ragged patriots at Valley Forge was marked indeed; and when it is remembered that the comforts of the British could have been purchased by the patriots at the price of desertion their heroic constancy becomes more striking.

The patriotism of Washington was not appreciated by all parties. A number of discontented members of Congress and officers of the army were anxious that he should be removed or forced to resign in order that their favorite General Gates might be promoted to the chief command of the army. One of the prime movers of the intrigue was an Irish adventurer named Conway, who had been promoted to the rank of brigadier-general, from which circumstance the plot is known as the "Conway Cabal." The entire truth concerning this plot will never be known, for after its failure the actors in it were only too glad to disavow their connection with it. The conspirators did not dare to make an open attack upon the commander-in-chief, but undertook by means of anonymous letters, underhanded appeals to the officers and men of the army, and comparisons between Gates' success and what they termed Washington's failure, to destroy the confidence of the troops in their leader, and to disgust him with his command and so drive him to resign it. Generals Mifflin and Gates were very active in this conspiracy, and even Sullivan and Wayne were in favor of the scheme of making Gates commander-in-chief. Dr. Benjamin Rush wrote a letter, to which he did not dare sign his name, to Patrick Henry, then governor of Virginia, representing the army of Washington as without a head, and disparaging Washington as no general. "A Gates, a Lee, or a Conway," he added, "would in a few weeks render them an irresistible body of men. Some of the contents of this letter ought to be made public in order to awaken, enlighten, and alarm our country." Patrick Henry took no notice of this paper save to forward it to Washington. A similar anonymous document was forwarded to Henry Laurens, the president of Congress, who also sent it to Washington. Great efforts were made to win over Lafayette to the plot, but without the least success.

Washington was to a great extent aware of the plot against him but took no public notice of it. He was deeply pained by the unjust censure to which he was subjected, but he never for a moment harbored the thought of laying down the great work he had assumed. He knew his course would bear the most rigid inspection. He knew that the capture of Burgoyne's army, which had made Gates the hero of the hour, was due to no skill on the part of that officer, but was the result of the plan of defence Washington had long before arranged with General Schuyler. In his efforts to contend against General Howe he was under many disadvantages, not the least of which was the fact that his army was encamped in a region abounding in Tories who refused him any support and constantly aided the British. His army was unperfectly disciplined; it was inferior in numbers and equipment to the enemy; and was in no condition to meet Howe in the open field, still less to undertake the difficult task of driving him from his intrenchments at Philadelphia. "Had the same spirit pervaded the people of this and the neighboring States, as the States of New York and New England," said Washington, "we might have had General Howe nearly in the same situation of General Burgoyne." Washington knew that the salvation of the country demanded his presence at the head of the army. He trusted to time for his vindication, and was chiefly anxious that the enemy should not learn of the dissensions in the councils and camp of the Americans. He firmly opposed the appointment of Conway to the post of "inspector of the armies of the United States," but Congress, under the influence of the cabal, appointed Conway to that place with the rank of major-general.

In a little while the action of the conspirators became known and aroused such a storm of indignation from the officers and men of the army, from the legislatures of the States, and from the great mass of the people that Gates and Conway and their associates cowered before it, and Congress became heartily ashamed of having given the plot any encouragement. The only effect of the conspiracy was to raise Washington higher in the confidence and affection of his countrymen. The members of the conspiracy were ever afterwards anxious to deny their share in it, and exerted themselves to prevent the truth concerning it from becoming known

The punishment of Gates came as soon as he was intrusted with an independent command, as we shall see. As for Conway, he was despised by the better part of the officers of the army, and found his position so unenviable that he addressed a note to Congress complaining that he had been badly treated, and intimated his intention to resign because he was not ordered to the northern department   Congress was by this time ashamed of having bestowed upon him such undeserved honors, and gladly interpreted his letter as an actual resignation of his rank, and at once ended the difficulty by accepting it. Conway was profoundly astonished. He was confident that Congress would become terrified by his threat to resign, and urge him to remain in the service, and was utterly unprepared for the action of that body. He hastened to explain his letter, but was not listened to. Some time after this he ventured to denounce the commander-in-chief, and was challenged to a duel by General Cadwallader, who had already charged him with cowardice at the battle of Germantown. Conway was wounded; and believing himself near death wrote to Washington, apologizing for his conduct towards him "You are," he said, "in my eyes the great and good man. May you long enjoy the love, veneration, and esteem of these States whose liberties you have asserted by your virtues." His wound was not mortal as he had supposed, and he recovered, and soon left the country.

The winter was passed by Washington in an effort to increase the army, and render it more efficient. Baron Steuben, a Prussian officer, who had served under Frederick the Great, was appointed inspector, with the rank of major-general. He introduced into the army the drill and discipline of the Prussian service, and greatly increased its efficiency. The various States, save Georgia and South Carolina, were called upon by Congress to contribute their quota of troops to the army In consideration of their large slave population, and the necessity of retaining their troops for their own defence, those States were excused from compliance with this demand. Count Pulaski succeeded in raising an independent body of cavalry, and Major Henry Lee organized a regiment of light horse, which under his command subsequently became noted as one of the most efficient corps of the army Congress proposed to increase the force of the army to sixty thousand men, but was never able to bring it to more than half that number.

The inability of Congress to pay the troops compelled many of the officers to leave the army, in order to provide for their families, who were suffering. Congress called upon the States to raise money for the public expenses by taxing their people, but some of them neglected to respond to this appeal, and the remainder were too poor to render much assistance. Congress issued new bills of credit, but the value of the "Continental Currency," as this money was called, had depreciated so greatly that a pair of shoes could not be bought for less than from five to six hundred dollars in these bills. The Tories and the British depreciated them still further by flooding the country with counterfeits.

A great improvement was made in the supply of provisions furnished the army by the appointment of General Greene, at the request of Washington, to the post of quartermaster-general, which had been held by General Mifflin, who had neglected its duties on all occasions. At the urgent solicitation of the commander-in-chief, Greene assumed the distasteful position for one year, and discharged its duties with a skill and precision which kept the army so well supplied with provisions and ammunition that it was never, during his administration, obliged to abandon a movement because of a lack of these necessities.

In April, 1778, General Prescott was exchanged for General Charles Lee, who at once returned to duty in the army   During his captivity Lee, who was willing to ruin the cause if he could benefit himself, proposed a plan to the British ministry by which they could, in his opinion, bring the war to a successful close.   The ministers did not see fit to adopt Lee's plan, but filed it away among the British archives, and the traitor was exchanged and permitted to resume his command in the American army, to become again a source of trouble and loss to it. *

In the meantime the American cause had assumed a new phase abroad. The English government had confidently expected that Burgoyne's expedition would be successful, and the result of his operations was watched by France with the deepest anxiety.   When news arrived of the defeat of Burgoyne the astonishment of King George and his ministers was equalled only by their mortification.   It was resolved to wipe out the humiliation by a more vigorous prosecution of the war   It was rumored that France was about to aid the Americans, and that Holland was on the point of loaning them money.   These rumors aroused the English people to a heartier support of the government than they had yet given it, and many of the principal cities offered to raise troops to supply the places of those who had been surrendered by Burgoyne.   At the same time the friends of America were greatly encouraged, and resolved to make a new effort to put a stop to the war by offering America such terms as would either induce her to renew her former connection with Great Britain, or to become the ally and friend of that country.   A considerable sum of money was subscribed by these for the relief of the American prisoners, who were left by the government without even the necessaries of life.

When Parliament assembled a strong attack was made upon the policy of the king by the friends of America   The employment of the Hessians, and, above all, of the barbarous Indians of North America, whose cruelties shocked the English people, was severely denounced   The mercantile class was seriously discontented.   Its trade with America was destroyed, and the activity of the American cruisers was so great that six hundred English vessels had already been captured , and it was necessary to convoy merchantmen, by vessels of war, from one port of the kingdom to another   Thus far the war had caused an expenditure of twenty thousand lives and one hundred millions of dollars, and the conquest of America was as far off as at the commencement of hostilities.

---

* The reader is referred to the work of Mr George H Moore, " The Treason of General Charles Lee, for the details of this plan

Under this pressure the king was constrained to yield, and, in January, 1788, Lord North presented to Parliament two bills by which his majesty hoped to maintain his authority in America, and conciliate his revolted subjects. The first of these renounced all intention on the part of Great Britain to levy taxes in America; the other appointed five commissioners to negotiate with the Americans for the restoration of the authority of England and the close of the war. The consent of the king to these measures was wrung from him by the complaints of a large part of the English people, and by his fear that France would openly aid the United States. These bills involved a direct surrender of the whole ground of the war; but indicated no change of opinion on the part of the king.

This action on the part of Great Britain aroused the French government to a more energetic course. Louis XVI was opposed to treating with the United States; but the French ministers were aware that a prompt recognition on their part of the independence of the republic would effectually neutralize the measures of Great Britain, and prevent a reconciliation. France was perfectly willing that America and England should weaken each other by their contest, but she was resolved that Great Britain should never recover her colonies. The capture of Burgoyne's army had demonstrated the ability of America to continue the war, and the French ministers resolved to lose no time in concluding an alliance with her. On the 17th of December, 1777, the Count de Vergennes caused Franklin and Deane to be informed of the king's intention not only to acknowledge but to support the independence of America, and on the 6th of February a treaty of friendship and commerce, and a second treaty of defensive alliance, were concluded between the United States and France. The latter bound the United States to support France in case Great Britain should declare war against her. The king of France acknowledged the independence of the United States of America, and agreed to assist them with his fleet and army. No peace was to be made without mutual consent, and not until the independence of the United States should be acknowledged by Great Britain. These treaties were ratified by Congress, and were hailed with joy by the Americans, whose confidence was revived by the assurance of the assistance of one of the most powerful states of Europe.

When the news of the treaties was received in England, the friends of America urged the government to abandon the war, and acknowledge the independence of the United States, as the only means of retaining the good feeling and trade of that country. The government would not even entertain the proposition. The most it would do was to pass the conciliatory bills of Lord North. If they failed to accomplish the desired end the war must go on. In March France formally communicated to England her treaties with America. This was regarded by England as equivalent to a declaration of war, and the British ambassador was at once recalled from Paris.

In June the British commissioners, appointed to treat under Lord North's conciliatory measures, arrived in America and opened negotiations. Congress demanded, as a prelude to any negotiations, that the independence of the United States should be recognized by England, and her fleets and armies withdrawn from America. The commissioners having no authority to treat upon any such basis returned to England,

SIR HENRY CLINTON.

having first made several ineffectual efforts to detach prominent Americans from the cause by bribery.

The course of Sir William Howe had not pleased the British government, and he was removed from his command on the 11th of May, 1788, and was replaced by Sir Henry Clinton. About the same time Clinton was informed by his government that a large French fleet might be expected at any moment on the American coast, and was ordered to evacuate Philadelphia and concentrate all his forces at New York. He accordingly sent his sick and wounded, and most of his stores, with his fleet around to New York by sea; while, with his army, twelve thousand strong, he left Philadelphia on the 18th of June, and, crossing the Delaware, began his march through New Jersey to New York. As soon as Washington learned of his movement he broke up his camp, on the 24th of June, and crossed the Delaware in pursuit of the British army. The intense heat of the weather, and the heavy train which the British carried with them, caused them to move very slowly, and Washington soon overtook them. A council of war was called, at which General Charles Lee, who held the second rank in the American army, urged that Washington should confine his efforts to harassing the British on the march. It was resolved, however, to attack the enemy and force them to a general engagement. Lee at first declined to take any part in the battle, but at the last moment changed his mind, and solicited a command

Upon the adjournment of the council of war, on the 27th of June, Washington sent Lafayette, with two thousand men, to occupy the hills near Monmouth Court-house, and confine the enemy to the plains. On the morning of the 28th of June Lee, who had asked for a command, was sent forward by Washington, with two brigades, to attack the enemy. Upon coming up with Lafayette, who was his junior, Lee assumed the command of the whole advanced force, and marched in the direction of the enemy, who had encamped on the previous night near Monmouth Court-house, and had resumed their march, early on the morning of the 28th. As soon as Clinton heard of Lee's advance, he determined to drive him back, and for this purpose wheeled about with his whole rear division, and made a sharp attack upon Lee, who fell back to higher ground. A misunderstanding of his order caused one of his subordinate officers to abandon his position, and Lee's whole force fell back in some confusion In the excitement of the moment Lee forgot to send word to Washington of his movement, and the first the commander-in-chief, who was advancing with the main body, knew of it was the right of Lee's command falling back rapidly, and in disorder. Riding up to the fugitives he asked them why they were retreating, and was answered that they did not know, but had been ordered to do so. Suspecting that the retreat had been ordered for the purpose of ruining the plan of battle, Washington hastened forward until he met General Lee, and sternly demanded of him: "What is the meaning of all this, sir?" Lee was disconcerted for a moment, and then answered that the retreat was contrary to his orders; and moreover that he did not wish to encounter the whole British army. "I am sorry," said Washington, "that you undertook the command unless you meant to fight the enemy." Lee answered that he did not think it prudent to bring on a general engagement. Washington replied, sternly, "Whatever your opinion may have been, I expect my orders to be obeyed"

Washington at once reformed the men on a commanding eminence, and hurried the main body of the Americans forward to their support. The British soon appeared in force, and endeavored to dislodge the Americans from their position, and failing in this, attempted, but without success, to turn their left flank. The battle lasted until nightfall, and the American army bivouacked on the field, expecting to renew the engagement the next morning, but during the night Clinton skilfully withdrew from his lines and continued his retreat. The weather was so warm that Washington did not deem it prudent to continue the pursuit, and Clinton was allowed to regain New York without further molestation   The Americans lost about two hundred men in this engagement, a number of whom died from the effects of the extreme heat. The British lost three hundred men. During the retreat, two thousand Hessians deserted from the British ranks.

As General Lee possessed a large share of the confidence of the commander-in-chief, he might have saved himself from the consequences of his fault, had he sought to explain his conduct in a proper manner. On the day after the battle he addressed an insulting letter to Washington, and met the reply of the commander-in-chief with another letter still more disrespectful in tone, demanding a court of inquiry. The court found him guilty of disobedience of orders, and of disrespect to the commander-in-chief, and sentenced him to be suspended from his rank for one year. Towards the close of his term of punishment he addressed an insolent letter to Congress, in consequence of some fancied neglect, and was dismissed from the army. A few years later he died in Philadelphia.

After the battle of Monmouth, Washington halted for a short time to refresh his men, and then marching to the Hudson crossed that stream, and took position at White Plains, in New York, to be ready to coöperate with the French fleet, which was daily expected, in an attack upon the city of New York. The French fleet under Count D'Estaing, with four thousand troops on board, had arrived in the Delaware just after Lord Howe had sailed for New York. Failing to find the enemy in the Delaware, D'Estaing sailed for New York, but Lord Howe withdrew his vessels into Raritan bay, and as the larger French ships could not cross the bar, the contemplated attack upon New York was abandoned, to the great regret of Washington.

The French fleet brought the American commissioners who had negotiated the treaty with France, and also Monsieur Gerard, the first ambassador from the French king to the United States.

In place of the combined attack upon New York, it was resolved by Washington, in concert with the French admiral, to attack Newport and drive the British out of Rhode Island   The British had established one of their principal depots of supplies at this point, and had there a force of six thousand men under General Pigot   It was arranged that a force of American troops under General Sullivan should attack the enemy by land, while the French fleet and army should coöperate with Sullivan from the sea. On the 29th of July D'Estaing reached Narragansett bay with his fleet, and on the 8th of August entered Newport harbor, in spite of the fire of the British batteries. A whole week had been lost, however, by the failure of the American troops to reach the positions assigned them as promptly as the French fleet The delay was unavoidable, but it ruined the enterprise On the 9th Lord Howe arrived off Newport harbor with his fleet to the assistance of General Pigot. On the 10th D'Estaing sailed out to engage the British fleet, but before this could be effected a sudden and terrible storm scattered both fleets. Howe returned to New York, and D'Estaing made his way back to Narragansett bay in a crippled condition. Instead of landing the four thousand French troops he had brought with him, the French admiral sailed to Boston with his whole force to refit.

Sullivan in the meantime had crossed from the mainland to the island of Rhode Island, and had taken position before the British intrenchments in front of Newport Here he awaited the return of the French fleet, and in the meanwhile kept up a steady fire upon the British works. Upon D'Estaing's return he informed Sullivan of his intention to sail to Boston to refit his ships Sullivan earnestly begged him to remain two or three days, as the British must certainly surrender by the end of that time D'Estaing refused to do so. Sullivan then asked that the French troops might be left to coöperate with him, and this also was refused. Left alone, Sullivan was obliged to retreat to the mainland, as he learned that aid was on its way from New York to Pigot He effected this movement with skill and success, on the night of the 30th of August. The next day Sir Henry Clinton reached Newport with a squadron of several ships and a reinforcement of four thousand men.

As he had arrived too late to attack the force under Sullivan, Clinton sent the troops he had brought with him, under Major-General Grey, to ravage the coasts to the eastward. Grey destroyed a large number of vessels along the coasts, and stripped Fair Haven, New Bedford, and the island of Martha's Vineyard of everything that could be carried off, and returned to New York laden with plunder.

Late in October a British fleet which had been despatched from England under Admiral Byron in pursuit of D'Estaing, arrived off Boston harbor. Byron was unwilling to venture within the harbor, and the French would not leave their place of security, and the English remained off Boston until a storm arose and scattered their fleet. On the 1st of November the French, taking advantage of the enforced withdrawal of their enemy, stood out to sea and sailed for the West Indies, and on the same day Clinton despatched a force of five thousand British troops from New York to the West Indies.

Brutal as was the conduct of General Grey, it had been already surpassed by the British and their Indian allies in Pennsylvania. The inhabitants of Wyoming valley, a beautiful region on the Susquehanna, had driven away the Tories from that region, and these had resolved upon revenge. Early in July a force of about eleven hundred Tories and Indians, under Colonel John Butler and the Indian chief Brandt, entered the Wyoming valley. Nearly all the able-bodied settlers were absent with the American army, and upon hearing of the approach of the enemy a small force had been despatched by Washington under Colonel Zebulon Butler, to the assistance of the settlers. This force was defeated by the Tories and Indians, who then proceeded to lay waste the valley and murder the inhabitants. They performed their bloody work in the most barbarous manner, and the beautiful valley was made a desolation. In the following month Cherry valley in New York was ravaged with equal cruelty by a force of Tories and Indians, and the inhabitants were either murdered or carried into captivity. The entire region of the upper Susquehanna and Delaware and the valley of the Mohawk were at the mercy of the savage allies of Great Britain.

SURRENDER OF SAVANNAH.

In the latter part of November, Sir Henry Clinton sent a force of two thousand men from New York under Colonel Campbell to attack Savannah, Georgia, which was held by a garrison of one thousand men under General Robert Howe. The British carried the American position after a sharp engagement, and on the 29th of December, Savannah surrendered to them. General Prevost, the English commander in Florida, now repaired to Savannah, and assumed the command. On his march across the country he captured Sunbury, a fort of considerable importance. Upon reaching Savannah he sent Colonel Campbell to seize Augusta, which was quickly secured and fortified. Georgia was thus entirely subdued by the British by the middle of January, 1779.

After the failure of the attack upon Newport the American army went into winter quarters, occupying a series of cantonments extending from the eastern end of Long Island sound to the Delaware. This disposition enabled them to oppose a force to the British at every important point. Washington established his head-quarters at Middlebrook, New Jersey, near the centre of his line. The winter passed away without any event of importance. The British held New York and Newport with too strong a force to make an attack upon either post successful, and the withdrawal of the French fleet to the West Indies left Washington without any means of encountering the naval force of the enemy.

The season was not without its trials, however. Washington wrote at the beginning of the year 1779, "Our affairs are in a more distressed, ruinous, and deplorable condition than they have been since the commencement of the war." The currency of the country grew more worthless every day. During the year 1779 the enormous sum of one hundred and thirty-one million of dollars was issued in continental bills. The magnitude of the volume of the currency only served to depreciate it more and more, and though supplies and articles of trade were plentiful, their owners refused to accept the depreciated bills of Congress, and would sell for gold and silver only. "A wagon-load of money," Washington wrote to the president of Congress, "will not purchase a wagon-load of provisions." During the year the currency depreciated from $8 for one dollar to $41 50 for one dollar. Congress had so little specie that everything must have gone to ruin but for the exertions of Robert Morris, a member of Congress from Pennsylvania, and a leading merchant of Philadelphia, who borrowed large sums of money on his own credit, and loaned them to the government. This he continued to do throughout the war.

Congress had long before this been deprived of many of its ablest members, who had resigned their seats in order to accept appointments in their own States, or to enter the army. Their places were filled with weaker men, and many dissensions mark the deliberations of the Congress of this period. Many members of Congress and a large part of the people seemed to regard the alliance with France as decisive of the war, and were disposed to relax their efforts. During the winter it was proposed to join the French in an expedition for the recovery of Canada for France, and the scheme found favor with a majority of the delegates in Congress. Washington opposed it with firmness. He pointed out to Congress the difficulties of the undertaking, and declared his conviction that it was not to the interest of the United States that a power different in race, language and religion from the people of this republic should have a footing upon this continent. In addition to this he did not desire the people of the United States to increase their obligations to a foreign, even though a friendly, power.

The American forces in the Southern States were commanded by General Benjamin Lincoln. The Tories were very numerous and very active in this region, and the feeling between them and the patriots was one of the bitterest hostility, and often manifested itself in bloody and relentless conflicts. Seven hundred Tories under Colonel Boyd set out in February, 1779, to join Colonel Campbell at Augusta. On the 14th they were attacked at Kettle creek, by a force of patriots under Colonel Pickens, and were defeated with heavy loss. Pickens hung five of his prisoners as traitors.

General Lincoln now sent General Ashe with two thousand men to drive the British out of Augusta. Upon hearing of his approach Colonel

Campbell evacuated Augusta and fell back to Brier creek, a small stream about halfway to Savannah. Ashe followed him, but without observing proper caution, and on the 3d of March was surprised and routed by Campbell, with the loss of nearly his entire force. This defeat encouraged General Prevost to attempt the capture of Charleston. He marched rapidly across the country

GENERAL BENJAMIN LINCOLN.

to Charleston, and demanded its surrender. Lincoln, who had been reinforced, no sooner heard of this movement than he hastened by forced marches to the relief of Charleston, and compelled Prevost to retire to St. John's island, opposite the mainland. The British threw up a redoubt at Stone ferry to protect the crossing to this island. It was attacked on the 20th of June by the forces of General Lincoln, who were repulsed with heavy loss. A little later Prevost withdrew to Savannah. The intense heat of the weather suspended military operations in the south during the remainder of the summer.

In September, 1779, the French fleet under Count D'Estaing arrived off the coast of Georgia from the West Indies, and the admiral agreed to join Lincoln in an effort to recapture Savannah. The American army began its investment of the city on the 23d of September, and everything promised favorably for success; but D'Estaing became impatient of the delay of a regular siege, and declared that he must return to the West Indies to watch the British fleet in those waters. Savannah must either be taken by assault, or he would withdraw from the siege. To please him Lincoln consented to storm the British works, and the assault was made on the 9th of October, but was repulsed with severe loss. D'Estaing himself was wounded, and the chivalrous Count Pulaski was killed. Lincoln now retreated to Charleston, and the French fleet sailed to the West Indies, having a second time failed to render any real assistance to the Americans. This disaster closed the campaign for the year in the south.

In the meantime Sir Henry Clinton had been ordered by his government to harass the American coast, and in accordance with these instructions despatched a number of plundering expeditions from New York against exposed points. One of these was sent in May, under General Mathews, into the Chesapeake. Mathews entered the Elizabeth river, plundered the towns of Norfolk and Portsmouth, and burned one hundred and thirty merchant vessels and several ships of war on the stocks at Gosport, near Portsmouth. He then ascended the James for some distance and ravaged its shores. He destroyed in this expedition two millions of dollars worth of property, and carried off about three thousand hogsheads of tobacco.

Upon the return of this expedition, Clinton ascended the Hudson for the purpose of destroying two forts which the Americans were constructing a short distance below West Point, for the protection of King's ferry, an important crossing-place between the Eastern and Middle States. One of these, which was being built at Stony Point, was abandoned. The work on Verplanck's Point, on the east side of the Hudson, immediately opposite, was compelled to surrender early in June.

Returning to New York, Clinton sent General Tryon with twenty-five hundred men to plunder the coast of Long Island sound. He plundered New Haven, burned Fairfield and Norwalk, and committed other outrages at Sag Harbor, on Long island. In the course of a few days this inhuman wretch burned two hundred and fifty dwelling-houses, five churches, and one hundred and twenty-five barns and stores. Many of the inhabitants were cruelly murdered, and a number of women were outraged by the British troops. Tryon would have carried his outrages further had he not been recalled to New York by Clinton, who feared that Washington was about to attack him.

The loss of Stony Point was a serious blow to Washington, as it compelled him to establish a new line of communication between the opposite sides of the Hudson by a longer and more tedious route through the Highlands. He resolved, therefore, the recapture of the post from the British at all hazards. The British had greatly strengthened the fort, which the Americans had left unfinished, and the only way in which it could be captured was by a surprise. It was a desperate undertaking, and Washington proposed to General Anthony Wayne to attempt it. Wayne readily consented, and the two generals made a careful reconnoissance of

GENERAL ANTHONY WAYNE.

the position. It was agreed to make the attempt at midnight, and in order to guard against a betrayal of the movement every dog in the vicinity was put to death. A negro who visited the fort regularly to sell fruit, and who had been for some time acting as a spy for the Americans, agreed to guide them to the work.

At midnight on the 15th of July, the storming party, guided by the negro, approached the fort in two divisions. Not a man was permitted to load his musket lest the accidental discharge of a gun should ruin the movement. The negro, accompanied by two soldiers who were disguised as farmers, approached the first sentinel and gave the countersign. The sentinel was at once seized and gagged, and the same was done with the second sentinel. The third, however, gave the alarm, and the garrison flew to arms and opened a sharp fire upon the Americans. The latter now dashed forward at a run, scaled the parapet, and in a few moments the two opposite divisions met in the centre of the fort. The Americans took more than five hundred prisoners, and all the supplies and artillery of the fort fell into their hands. Though they were justly exasperated by the brutal outrages of the British, which we have related, they conducted themselves towards their prisoners with a noble humanity. The British historian Stedman declares, "They (the Americans) would have been fully justified in putting the garrison to the sword; not one man of which was put to death but in fair combat." It was one of the most brilliant expeditions of the war. Wayne now proceeded to prepare for the reduction of the fort at Verplanck's Point, but while he was thus engaged a heavy British force ascended the river to its relief, and he was obliged to forego his attack, and also to abandon Stony Point.

On the night of the 18th of June, Major Henry Lee made a bold dash

STORMING OF STONY POINT.

at the British fort at Paulus Hook, now Jersey City, and captured it, taking one hundred and fifty-nine prisoners. The British made great efforts to intercept him, but he effected his retreat in safety, bringing off his prisoners, and losing only two men. For these gallant exploits Wayne and Lee were each voted a gold medal by Congress.

Towards the close of the summer of 1779, Washington resolved to inflict upon the Indians a severe punishment for their outrages upon the whites, and especially for the massacres of Wyoming and Cherry valley in the previous year. Early in August General Sullivan was sent into western New York with three thousand men, with orders to ravage the country of the Six Nations. He was joined by General James Clinton

34

with two thousand men, and on the 29th of August attacked and defeated a force of seventeen hundred Indians and Tories at Newtown, now Elmira. Sullivan followed up this victory by pushing forward into the Indian country, and laying it waste with fire and sword. In the course of a few weeks he destroyed more than forty Indian villages, and burned all the cornfields and orchards. The beautiful valley of the Genesee was made a desert, and to avoid starvation the Indians and their Tory allies were obliged to emigrate to Canada. They were quieted but for a time by the terrible vengeance of the Americans, and soon renewed their depredations, and continued them to the end of the war.

Congress had made great efforts to increase the force of the navy,

and the number of American men-of-war had been materially enlarged. Many of them had been captured, however, by the enemy, and the navy was still weak and unable to render much service to the cause. The privateers were unusually active, and were hunted with unremitting vigilance by the English war vessels. They managed to inflict great losses upon the commerce of Great Britain, however. A number of American cruisers were fitted out in France, and kept the English coast in terror.

John Paul Jones, a native of Scotland, who had been brought to

LIEUTENANT-COLONEL HENRY LEE.

Virginia at an early age, was one of the first naval officers commissioned by Congress. He was given the command of the "Ranger," a vessel of eighteen guns, and by his brilliant and daring exploits kept the English coast in a state of terror, and even ventured to attack exposed points on the coast of Scotland. In 1779 he was given command of a small squadron of three ships of war fitted out in France, and sailing from L'Orient, proceeded on a cruise along the coast of Great Britain. On the 23d of September, he fell in with a fleet of merchantmen convoyed by two English frigates, and at once attacked them. The battle began at seven in the evening, and was continued for three hours with great fury. Jones lashed his flagship, the "Bon Homme Richard," to the English frigate "Serapis," and the two vessels fought muzzle to muzzle until the

"Serapis" surrendered. The other English vessel was also captured. The battle was one of the most desperate in the annals of naval warfare, and Jones' flagship was so badly injured that it sunk in a few hours after the fighting was over.

In October, Sir Henry Clinton, in obedience to orders from home, evacuated Newport, and concentrated his forces at New York, which place he believed was in danger of an attack by the Americans and French. Until the close of the season Washington cherished the hope that the French fleet would return and assist him in an effort to regain New York, and had called out the militia for this purpose. When he learned that D'Estaing had sailed to the West Indies after the failure of the

JOHN PAUL JONES.

attack upon Savannah, he dismissed the militia to their homes, and went into winter quarters in New Jersey, with his head-quarters at Morristown.

While these events had been transpiring upon the Atlantic seaboard, the United States had been steadily pushing their way westward beyond

COAT OF ARMS OF KENTUCKY.

the mountains. In 1769, before the commencement of the Revolution, the beautiful region now known as Kentucky had been visited and explored by Daniel Boone, a famous Indian hunter. He was charmed with the beauty of the country and the excellence of the climate, and resolved to make it his home. The reports of Boone and his companions aroused a great interest in the new country among the inhabitants of the older settlements in Virginia and North Carolina, more especially as it was in this region that the lands given to the Virginia troops for their services in the French war were located. Surveyors were soon after sent out to lay off these lands, and in 1773 a party under Captain Bullit reached the falls of the Ohio, and built a fortified camp there for the purpose of surveying the region. This was the commencement of the city of Louisville, but the actual settlement of the place was not begun until 1778. In 1774 Harrodsburg was founded by James Harrod, one of Boone's companions ; and in 1775 Daniel Boone built a fort on the site of the present town of Boonesborough. The savages made repeated attacks upon his party, but failed to drive them away. The fort was finished by the middle of April, and soon after Boone was joined by his wife and daughters, the first white women in Kentucky.

The region of Kentucky was claimed by Virginia, but the settlers submitted to the authority of that province with impatience. They sent a

delegate to the Continental Congress in October, 1775, and claimed representation in that body as an independent colony under the name of Transylvania ; but the delegate of the fourteenth colony was not admitted by Congress, as Virginia claimed the territory as her own. In the spring of 1777 the general assembly of Virginia organized the Kentucky region as a county, and established a court of quarter sessions at Harrodsburg. In this condition Kentucky remained during the

DANIEL BOONE.

Revolution. The population increased rapidly in spite of the war and of the unremitting hostility of the Indians.

During the Revolution the Kentucky settlements suffered very much from the hostility of the Indians, who were urged on by the emissaries of Great Britain to a war of extermination. The principal agent of the mother country in this barbarous warfare was Hamilton, the British commander at Detroit. In order to put a stop to his intrigues and deprive the Indians of his aid, Congress resolved to despatch a force to attack Detroit.

While this plan was in contemplation the State of Virginia, in 1778, sent Colonel George Rogers Clarke with a force of two hundred men to conquer the territory northwest of the Ohio, which Virginia claimed as a part of her possessions. Clarke was a backwoodsman, but one of nature's heroes. He assembled his men at Pittsburg, and descended the Ohio to the falls in flat-boats. There he established a settlement of thirteen families, the germ of the present city of Louisville. Being joined by some Kentuckians he continued his descent of the river to a short distance below the mouth of the Tennessee. Landing and concealing his boats, he struck across the country and surprised and captured the town of Kas-kaskia, within the limits of the present State of Indiana. A detachment was sent to Kahokia, and received its submission. The people of these towns were of French origin, and were greatly averse to the English rule under which they had lived since the conquest of Canada. The alliance between the United States and France made them very willing to acknowledge the authority of the Union, to which they readily swore allegiance. The fort at Vincennes

GENERAL GEORGE ROGERS CLARKE.

was in a weak condition and was held by a small garrison, and readily submitted to Clarke.

Hamilton no sooner heard of the successes of Clarke than he set out from Detroit on the 7th of October, 1778, with a force of three hundred and fifty warriors, and on the 17th of December reoccupied Vincennes. He now prepared to drive the Americans out of the Illinois country, and spent the winter in trying to arouse the savages against them. He offered a significant reward for every American scalp brought in to him, but offered nothing for prisoners. At the same time he proposed to invade Virginia in the spring with an overwhelming force of Indians.

Clarke and his party were in very great danger. They were entirely cut off from Virginia and without hope of reinforcements. In this emergency, Clarke, who had learned that Hamilton had greatly weakened the garrison at Vincennes, resolved to stake the fate of the west on a single issue, and attempt the capture of that post. On the 7th of February, 1779, he left Kaskaskia with one hundred and thirty men, and marched across the country towards Vincennes. On the 18th they were within nine miles of Vincennes. The Wabash had overflowed the country along its banks, and in order to reach the object of their march,

FRANKFORT, KENTUCKY.

Clarke and his men were obliged to cross the submerged lands, up to their armpits in water. They were five days in crossing these " drowned lands," and had the weather been less mild, must have perished. On the 23d Vincennes was reached, and the town was at once carried. Clarke then laid siege to the fort, assisted in this task by the inhabitants of the town, and in twenty-four hours compelled Hamilton and his men to surrender themselves prisoners of war.

Clarke was unable to advance against Detroit because of the insufficiency of his force. His successes, however, were among the most important of the war. They not only put an end to the British scheme of a general Indian war along the western frontier of the United States, but established the authority of the Union over the country east of the Mississippi, and prevented Great Britain from asserting a claim to that region at the conclusion of peace, a few years later. Returning to the Ohio, Clarke built a blockhouse at the falls. The conquered territory was claimed by Virginia, and was erected by the legislature of that State into the county of Illinois. By order of Governor Jefferson of Virginia, Clarke established a fort on the Mississippi, about five miles below the mouth of the Ohio, which he named Fort Jefferson, and entered into friendly relations with the Spaniards at St. Louis.

The Tennessee region, which formed a part of the province of North Carolina, had been settled previous to the outbreak of hostilities. Fort London, about 30 miles southwest of Knoxville, was built in 1756, and in 1770 the Cumberland valley was settled, and Nashville was founded. By the commencement of the revolution the Tennessee country was quite thickly settled, and the population was increasing at an encouraging

COAT OF ARMS OF TENNESSEE.

rate. In 1776 the Cherokees, incited by the British, waged a formidable war upon the settlers, but were defeated by the forces of Virginia and North Carolina. A little later the legislature of North Carolina organized the Tennessee settlements as the "District of Washington."

CHAPTER XXX.

THE CLOSE OF THE WAR

THE winter of 1779–80 was passed by the American army in huts near Morristown. It was one of the severest seasons ever experienced in America. The harbor of New York was frozen over as far as the Narrows, and the ice was strong enough to bear the heaviest artillery. Communication between New York and the sea was entirely cut off, and the British garrison and the citizens suffered from a scarcity of provisions. Knyphausen was afraid the Americans would seek to pass the Hudson on the ice and attack the city, and landed the crews of the shipping in the harbor, and added them to the garrison. His precautions were useless, as the American army was too weak and too poorly supplied to undertake the capture of New York.

The troops at Morristown suffered very greatly during the winter. They had scarcely clothing enough to protect them from the cold, and provisions were so scarce that in order to keep his men from starvation, Washington was compelled to impress supplies from the people of the surrounding country. The heavy snows made the army entirely dependent upon New Jersey for its subsistence, as transportation from a long distance could not be effected. The people of New Jersey bore the sacrifices imposed upon them with a noble cheerfulness, and though their State was drained almost to exhaustion, were untiring in their efforts to provide food and clothing for the troops The Continental currency had fallen so low that one dollar in silver was worth thirty dollars in paper by the beginning of the year 1780, but neither officers nor men could obtain their pay in this depreciated currency It was almost impossible for the government to purchase anything with its notes

About the last of December, 1789, Sir Henry Clinton, leaving a strong garrison under General Knyphausen to hold New York, sailed south, with the greater part of his army, in the fleet of Admiral Arbuthnot He

CHARLESTON SOUTH CAROLINA, IN 1875

proceeded first to Savannah, and then moved northward for the purpose of besieging Charleston. General Lincoln exerted himself with energy to fortify that city. Four thousand citizens enrolled themselves to assist the regular garrison in the defence, but only two hundred militia from the interior responded to Lincoln's call for aid. Reinforcements were received from Virginia and North Carolina, and Lincoln was able to muster seven thousand men, of whom but two thousand were regular troops In February, 1780, the British landed at St John's island, about thirty miles below Charleston. Clinton advanced towards the city along the banks of the Ashley, while the fleet sailed around to force an entrance into the harbor The advance of Clinton was very gradual, and Lincoln was enabled to strengthen his works, and prepare for a siege. It was not until early in April that Clinton's army appeared before the American works and began preparations to reduce them. A day or two later the British fleet passed Fort Moultrie with but little loss, and took position off the city.

Clinton had lost nearly all his horses on the voyage from New York, and was anxious to replace them from the country north of Charleston. The Americans had stationed bodies of militia at different points north of the city to keep open the communications with Charleston, and to prevent the foraging parties of the British from reaching the interior Clinton intrusted the task of breaking up these posts and obtaining fresh horses to Lieutenant-Colonel Banastre Tarleton, a young and energetic officer. Tarleton was short of stature, of a dark, swarthy complexion, and broad shouldered and muscular. He was insensible to fatigue, unscrupulous as to the means by which he accomplished his objects, merciless in battle, and unflagging in pursuit. He was one of the most efficient officers in the English army, and one of the most cruel. By purchase from friends and seizures from foes, he soon supplied Clinton with all the horses he needed. He then began his attempt to break up the American posts north of Charleston On the night of the 14th of April, he surprised a body of fourteen hundred cavalry under General Huger and Colonel William Washington, at Monk's Corner, about thirty miles north of Charleston. The Americans were defeated with a loss of one hundred prisoners and four hundred wagons laden with stores A little later Fort Moultrie surrendered, and soon after Tarleton cut to pieces another detachment of American cavalry

Charleston was now completely invested, and the siege was pressed with vigor by Clinton Lincoln's situation became every day more hopeless The fire of the British artillery destroyed his defences and dismounted his cannon, and as he was entirely cut off from the country he had no hope of relief from without On the 9th of May, a terrible fire was opened upon the defences and the city of Charleston. The city was set on fire in five places, and the American works were reduced to a mass of ruins On the 12th, Lincoln surrendered the town and his army to Sir Henry Clinton. The prisoners, including every male adult in the city, numbered about six thousand men The regulars were held as prisoners of war, but the militia were dismissed to their homes on their promise not to serve again during the war.

Clinton followed up his capture of the city by a series of vigorous measures. Tarleton was despatched into the interior to attack a Virginia regiment under Colonel Beaufort, which was advancing to the relief of

Charleston Beaufort began his retreat as soon as he heard of the surrender of Charleston, but was overtaken and surprised by Tarleton at Waxhaw's, on the boundary of North Carolina. The British had made a forced march of one hundred and five miles in fifty-four hours. They gave no quarter to the Americans, and put to the sword all who were unable to escape. Their barbarous conduct on this occasion was termed by the American's "Tarleton's quarters." A second column was sent by Clinton towards Augusta, and a third towards Camden to reduce the country between Charleston and those points. They encountered but little resistance. Clinton issued a proclamation threatening to visit the severest punishments upon those who refused to submit to the royal authority, and this was followed a little later by another, offering pardon to all who would return to their allegiance and assist in restoring the authority of the king. The measures of the British commander were entirely successful, and South Carolina was so completely subjugated that early in June, Sir Henry Clinton sailed for New York, leaving Lord Cornwallis to complete the conquest of the State The country abounded in Tories, who exerted themselves actively to assist the British commander in his efforts to hold the Carolinas in subjection. Large numbers of them joined the British army, and "loyal legions" were formed in various parts of the country The only resistance kept up by the Americans was maintained by the partisan corps of patriots led by Marion, Sumter, and Pickens. The exploits of these daring bands caused the British commander to feel that he could not hold the Carolinas except by the aid of a strong force, and kept him in a state of constant uneasiness On the 16th of August, Sumter defeated a large body of British and Tories at Hanging Rock, east of the Wateree river. Large numbers of negroes deserted their masters and fled to the British

In order to offer a definite resistance to the British, and to collect a regular army to oppose them, the Baron De Kalb was sent to take command of the troops in the south, and all the regulars south of Pennsylvania were ordered to join him De Kalb managed to collect about two regiments, and with these moved slowly southward. A lack of provisions forced him to halt three weeks on Deep river, one of the upper tributaries of the Cape Fear.

Matters were so bad in the south that Congress resolved to send General Gates, the conqueror of Burgoyne, to take command of the army in that quarter. General Charles Lee, who knew that Gates was not the man to retrieve such losses, predicted that "his northern laurels would soon be changed into southern willows." Gates hastened southward, and overtook De Kalb at Deep river, and assumed the command De Kalb advised him to move into South Carolina by a circuitous route through the county of Mecklenburg, which was true to the patriot cause, and where provisions could be easily obtained. Gates declined to take his advice, and marched towards Camden by the direct route, which led through a barren and almost uninhabited region. He was sure that his wagons from the north laden with provisions would overtake the troops in two days; but he was mistaken the wagons never made their appearance, and the troops suffered greatly from hunger and disease. His army increased every day by reinforcements from Virginia and North Carolina. On the 13th of August, he reached Clermont, about twelve miles from Camden. His force now amounted to nearly four thousand men, nearly two-thirds of whom were Continentals

Upon the approach of Gates, Lord Rawdon, the British commander in this part of the State, fell back to Camden, where he was joined by Cornwallis, who had just arrived from Charleston, and who assumed the command. On the night of the 15th, Gates moved nearer to Camden, and at the same time Cornwallis advanced to attack Gates, whom he hoped to surprise. The advanced guards encountered each other in the woods, and the two armies halted until morning. The battle began with dawn, on the 16th of August. The militia fled at the first charge of the British, but the Continentals, under the brave De Kalb, stood firm, though attacked in front and flank At length De Kalb fell mortally wounded, and the Continentals gave way. The American army was completely routed, and was broken up into small parties and scattered through the country. These continued a disorderly retreat, closely followed for about thirty miles by Tarleton's cavalry, who cut them down without mercy.

The battle of Camden was the most disastrous defeat incurred by the Americans during the whole war. They lost nearly eighteen hundred men in killed and prisoners, and all their artillery and stores A few days after the battle, Gates reached Charlotte, North Carolina, with about two hundred men, the remains of the army which his incapacity had ruined.

A few days previous to the battle, Sumter surprised a detachment convoying stores to the British army at Camden, and took two hundred prisoners. As soon as Cornwallis heard of this, he sent Tarleton in pursuit of the "Game Cock," as he styled Sumter. Tarleton pushed forward with such vigor that half of his men and horses were broken down. He overtook Sumter at Fishing Creek, on the west bank of the Catawba, and routed him with the loss of the greater part of his partisan corps, and rescued the prisoners

All united the Protest in th Carolinas now

ceased for a time. The true policy of Cornwallis was to conciliate the people by acts of clemency, but instead of this he exasperated them by his unnecessary severity. Among the prisoners taken at the defeat of Sumter were a number who had given their parol not to serve during the war. Some of these were hanged on the spot; the remainder were subjected to a severe imprisonment. These severities aroused a desire for vengeance among the people, and gave many recruits to Marion, who from the swamps of the lower Pedee maintained a constant and severe partisan warfare against the British. At the same time, Sumter by great exertions recruit-
ed his command, and resumed his operations in the upper country. These bands were deficient in arms at first, but supplied themselves from the enemy. They made their own gunpowder, cast their own bullets, and provided food for themselves and their horses. By their rapid and secret movements they kept the British in a state of constant alarm. They would make

GENERAL FRANCIS MARION.

a sudden and unexpected attack upon the enemy at some exposed point, and before pursuit could be attempted would be miles away, or safe in the labyrinths of the swamps.

Gates continued to retreat slowly to the northward after his defeat. He had now about a thousand men with him. Virginia and Maryland made great exertions to reinforce him, but without success.

In September, Cornwallis advanced northward with the main body of his army. Upon reaching Charlotte he despatched Colonel Ferguson, one of his most trusted officers, to rally the Tories among the mountains

in the interior. Cornwallis intended to advance from Charlotte by way
of Salisbury and Hillsborough into Virginia, and form a junction with a
force to be sent to the lower Chesapeake by Sir Henry Clinton. The
success of this movement would complete the subjugation of the south.
The patriots in the country through which his army passed were very
active. His expresses were captured or shot, and his plans made known
to the Americans. While Ferguson was on the march, Cornwallis
advanced to Salisbury.

The movement of Ferguson roused the patriots of the interior counties
to arms, and they assembled rapidly, with the intention of cutting him
off from the army under Cornwallis. They came from all directions,

BATTLE OF KING'S MOUNTAIN.

from as far as Kentucky and Tennessee. Their weapons were their rifles,
to the use of which they had been trained from childhood; they had no
baggage; and they moved forward as rapidly as their horses could carry
them. These forces had been gathering for several days before the rumors
of their march reached Colonel Ferguson. He regarded the reports with
distrust at first, but upon receiving more accurate information began a
rapid retreat. About the same time the various parties of the Americans
effected a junction. They numbered three thousand men. A council of
war was held, and it was resolved to send forward a detachment to bring
Ferguson to a stand, and to follow with the main body as quickly as
possible.

Nine hundred men, mounted on swift horses, were sent forward, under

Colonel Campbell. They rode for thirty-six hours, a large part of the time through a drenching rain, and dismounted but once during this period. Ferguson, alarmed and astounded at this determination to crush him, fell back to a strong position on King's mountain, near the Catawba. He was attacked there on the 7th of October by the Americans, and defeated after a hotly contested fight. Ferguson and about one hundred and fifty of his men were killed, the remainder were compelled to surrender. The prisoners numbered about nine hundred and fifty, of whom about one hundred and fifty were wounded. The Americans lost twenty killed and a somewhat larger number wounded. The North Carolinians selected ten of the Tories who had earned their fate by their cruelties to the Americans, and hanged them on the spot. The Americans then separated and returned home, after seeing their prisoners safe in the hands of the proper authorities. Their victory raised the drooping spirits of their countrymen, and encouraged them to fresh exertions to resist the British. As soon as Cornwallis heard of it, he abandoned his forward movement, and, falling back into South Carolina, took position between the Broad and Saluda rivers. He remained there until the close of the year.

Marion took advantage of the change of feeling caused by the victory of King's mountain to renew his operations on the Pedee, but Tarleton compelled him to withdraw to his fastness in the swamps. Sumter was more successful in the northern part of the State, and defeated a detachment sent in pursuit of him. Tarleton then went after him in person, but was defeated and forced to retreat. Sumter was wounded in this engagement, and was compelled to withdraw from the field for several months. During this period his command, deprived of their leader, disbanded. The contest in the Carolinas degenerated into a savage civil war. The patriots and Tories fought each other wherever they met, and destroyed each other's property throughout the State. The country was thus kept in constant terror.

Upon the retreat of Cornwallis from Salisbury, Gates advanced southward as far as Charlotte. Here he was relieved of his command by General Nathaniel Greene, who had been appointed by Congress, at the urgent solicitation of Washington, to take charge of the southern department. Gates had given great dissatisfaction by his failure in the south, and Congress ordered a court of inquiry to examine into his conduct. Greene was placed in charge of the entire south from Delaware to Georgia, "subject to the control of the commander-in-chief." Thus Washington was given the supreme direction of the war. Greene possessed his entire confidence, and the most cordial and affectionate relations existed between them. Greene found the remnants of Gates' army in a half mutinous condition. The men were without pay, without clothing, and suffering for the necessaries of life. Reinforcements were sent him from the north, among which were Morgan's regiment of riflemen, Lee's legion of light-horse, and several batteries of artillery.

We must now return to the army under Washington. As the spring opened the sufferings of the troops at Morristown increased. Food was so scarce that the troops were driven to desperation. Two regiments of

Connecticut troops declared their intention to abandon the army and march home, or wrest provisions from the people of the surrounding country by force. Washington was compelled to exert all his influence and authority to restore order. It was with great difficulty that provisions were procured, and the wants of the troops supplied. The danger caused by this state of affairs was so great that Congress authorized Washington to declare martial law.

The news of these troubles in the

GENERAL NATHANIEL GREENE.

American camp induced Knyphausen to undertake an expedition into New Jersey. He landed at Elizabethtown, with five thousand men, on the 6th of June, and marched towards Springfield. His advance was warmly contested by the militia of the region, but he penetrated as far as the village of Connecticut Farms. Being unable to advance farther he caused the village to be sacked and burned; and Mrs. Caldwell, the wife of the minister of the village, was murdered by some of the British troops. The militia of the region gathered in force, and Knyphausen was obliged to make a hasty retreat to Elizabethtown.

The murder of Mrs. Caldwell aroused the most intense excitement throughout New Jersey It was denounced as one of the most infamous deeds of the war, and gave rise to a fierce and general spirit of vengeance. Her husband, an eloquent and highly esteemed minister, animated his countrymen by his stirring sermons, and he soon had the satisfaction of seeing that his labors were not in vain.

After the return of Sir Henry Clinton to New York, Washington moved a part of his troops towards the Highlands. Knyphausen again advanced from Elizabethtown towards Springfield, hoping to gain the passes beyond Morristown before his march should be discovered. His advance was detected, however, and General Greene, who was in command of the American forces, prepared to resist him A sharp fight ensued, in which Greene succeeded in checking the British advance The New Jersey regiment, of which Caldwell was chaplain, was engaged in the battle. The wadding of the men gave out, and Caldwell, mounting his horse, galloped to the Presbyterian church, and returned with an armful of Dr. Watts' hymn books, which he distributed among the troops, with the pious injunction, "Now put Watts into them, boys!" The militia came flocking in to the support of General Greene, and Knyphausen finding it impossible to advance farther, burned Springfield and fell back to Elizabethtown.

The Americans were greatly encouraged in the spring by the return of Lafayette, who had spent the winter in France. He had been successful in his endeavors to induce the French court to send another fleet and army to the assistance of the patriots, and he now brought the good news that a new expedition was on its way to America. In July a fleet under Count de Tiernay, with an army of seven thousand men, under Count de Rochambeau, reached Newport The Count de Rochambeau was directed by his government to place himself under the orders of General Washington in order to avoid disputes that might arise from military etiquette. This expedition was the first division of the army to be sent to America by France. The second division was to sail from Brest, but was unable to do so, as it was blockaded in that harbor by a British squadron. Thus the supplies of arms and clothing which were to have been sent to the American army were delayed, and the troops under Washington were unable to cooperate with the French in an attack upon New York An English fleet had followed the French across the Atlantic, and Clinton was anxious to secure its cooperation in an attack upon the French at Newport. He could not agree with Admiral Arbuthnot upon a plan of attack, and the English admiral contented himself with blockading the French in Newport harbor Washington called out the militia of New

35

England to assist in the defence of Newport in case of an attack. The French fleet was shut up in this port, and to the great disappointment of Washington, was unable to take part in any combined operation.

Some weeks later Washington, anxious to strike a decisive blow at the enemy, invited the French commanders, De Tiernay and Rochambeau, to meet him at Hartford, to arrange a plan for an attack upon New York. The meeting was held, but it was decided to ask the coöperation of the French admiral in the West Indies, as the fleet at Newport was not strong enough to cope with the British fleet at New York. Until the answer of the admiral was received nothing could be done.

While absent at Hartford a plot was discovered which involved the fair fame of one of the most brilliant officers of the American army. General Benedict Arnold had been disabled by the wounds he had

received at Quebec and Saratoga from undertaking active service, and through the influence of Washington had been placed in command of Philadelphia after its evacuation by Clinton in 1778. There he lived in a style far beyond his means, and became involved in debts, which he was unable to pay. To raise the funds to discharge them he engaged in privateering and mercantile speculations. These were generally unsuccessful, and merely increased his difficulties. His haughty and overbearing manner involved him in a quarrel with the authorities of Pennsylvania, who accused him before Congress of abusing his official position and misusing the public funds. He was tried by a court-martial and was sentenced to be reprimanded by the commander-in-chief. Washington performed this disagreeable task as delicately as possible, but did not lose his confidence in Arnold. He knew him as an able officer, but, as his acquaintance with him was limited, was most likely ignorant of the faults of Arnold's character, which were well known to the members of Congress from Connecticut, who had no confidence in him. To them he was known to be naturally dishonest, regardless of the rights of others, and cruel and tyrannical in his dealings with those under his authority. Arnold never forgave the disgrace inflicted upon him by the sentence of the court-martial, and cherished the determination to be revenged upon Washington for the reprimand received from him.

While in Philadelphia, Arnold had married a member of a Tory family, and was thus enabled to communicate readily with the British officers. He opened a correspondence with Sir Henry Clinton, signing himself Gustavus. He kept up this correspondence for several months, and then made himself known to the British commander. In the meantime, at his earnest solicitation, he was appointed by Washington, in August, 1780, to the command of West Point, the strongest and most important fortress in America. He did this with the deliberate intention of betraying the post into the hands of the enemy.

The correspondence had been conducted on the part of Sir Henry Clinton by Major John André of the British army, a young man of amiable character and more than ordinary accomplishments. He wrote under the assumed name of John Anderson. He was an especial favorite of Sir Henry Clinton, and was beloved by the whole army in which he served. Soon after the appointment of Arnold to the command of West Point, André volunteered to go up the Hudson and have an interview with him for the purpose of completing the arrangements for the betrayal of that fortress. His offer was accepted by Clinton, and he ascended the Hudson as far as Haverstraw in the sloop of war "Vulture." He was set ashore and was met near Haverstraw on the west bank of the Hudson by General Arnold, on the 22d of
September. The meeting took place about dark, and the night had passed before the arrangements were completed. Much against his will, André was compelled to pass the next day within the American lines. During the 23d the "Vulture," having attracted the attention of the Americans, was fired upon and forced to drop down the river. André found the man who had set him ashore unwilling to row him back to the sloop, and he was compelled to return to New York by land. He changed his uniform for a citizen's dress, and, provided with a pass from Arnold, under the name of John Anderson, set out for New York along the east bank of the river, which he deemed safer than the opposite shore.

All went well until André reached the vicinity of Tarrytown. There he was stopped by three young men, John Paulding, David Williams, and Isaac Van Wart. They asked him his name and destination, and he, supposing them to be Tories, did not use the pass given him by Arnold,

but frankly avowed himself a British officer travelling on important business. To his dismay he then learned that his captors were of the patriot
party, and he offered them his watch, purse, and any reward they might
name if they would suffer him to proceed. They refused to allow him
to stir a step, and searched his person. They found concealed in his
boots papers giving the plan of West Point, and an account of its garrison. André was taken by his captors before Colonel Jamison, the commander of the nearest American post. Jamison recognized the hand-
writing as that of Arnold, but, unwilling to believe that his commander
could be guilty of treason, he detained the prisoner, and wrote to Arnold
informing him of the arrest of André and of the papers found upon his
person. The papers themselves he forwarded by a special messenger to
Washington, who was on his return from Hartford.

Arnold received Colonel Jamison's letter as he sat at breakfast with
some of his officers. He concealed his emotion, and excusing himself
to his guests, called his
wife from the room,
told her he must flee
for his life, and hast-
ening to his barge,
escaped down the river
to the "Vulture,"
and was received on
board by the com-
mander of that vessel.
From his place of
safety he wrote to

CAPTURE OF MAJOR ANDRÉ.

Washington asking him to protect his wife, who, he declared, was innocent of any share in his plot.

When he learned that Arnold was safe, André wrote to Washington,
and confessed the whole plot. He was at once brought to trial upon the
charge of being within the American lines as a spy. The court-martial
was presided over by General Greene, and Lafayette and Steuben were
among its members. André asserted that he had been induced to enter
the American lines by the misrepresentations of Arnold. He denied that
he was a spy, and though cautioned not to say anything that might crim-
inate himself, he frankly confessed the whole plot. He was sentenced
upon his own confession to be hanged. Clinton made great exertions
to save him, and Washington, whose sympathy was won by the amiable
character of André, was anxious to spare him. The circumstances of the
case demanded that the law should be executed, and André was hanged

at Tappan, near the Hudson, on the 2d of October, 1780. Congress voted to each of his three captors a pension of two hundred dollars for life and a silver medal.

The plot of Arnold had been discovered by the merest chance, and the American cause had narrowly escaped a crushing disaster. The loss of West Point would have given the British the entire control of the Hudson, and have enabled them to separate New England from the Middle and Southern States. It might have proved fatal to the cause, and certainly would have reduced Washington to great extremities. Arnold

WEST POINT IN 1875.

received for his treachery the sum of ten thousand pounds sterling and a commission as brigadier-general in the English service. He was regarded with general contempt by the English officers, who refused to associate with him, and were greatly averse to serving under him.

In the summer of 1780 it seemed likely that England would be involved in war with the whole civilized world. The claim of Great Britain to the right to search the vessels of neutral nations for articles contraband of war was productive of great annoyance to the northern powers, whose commerce was subjected to serious loss by these arbitrary measures. Cathaiine II. of Russia determined to resist it, and oiganized with Denmaik and Sweden a league known as the "Armed Neutiality," foi the purpose of enforcing the principle that neutral ships in time of war aie entitled to carry merchandise without being liable to search or seizure by the belligeient powers.

Holland joined this league, and concluded a secret commercial treaty with the United States. This treaty was discovered by Great Britain almost immediately, and in the following manner The American min- ister to Holland, Heniy Laurens, was captured at sea by a British frigate. He threw his papeis, the tieaty among them, into the sea, but they weie recoveied by an English sailor, who sprang oveiboard and secuied them. They were laid before the British goveinment, which demanded that Holland should disavow the treaty and the correspondence with the United States. The Dutch government returned an evasive answer, and England immediately declared war against Holland The English fleet at once proceeded to attack the Dutch possessions and commerce in all paits of the world. Holland declared war against Great Britain, and her fleet was added to that of France against England. Spain now made an alliance with France against England, and sent her fleet to coöpeiate with the French in the West Indies, and also laid siege to Gibraltar. The Irish about the same time demanded a reform of the many abuses from which that island had been suffering since the battle of the Boyne, and this demand was sustained by a foice of eighty thousand armed Protestant volunteers which had been raised for the defence of Ireland against a threatened attack of the French. They demanded an independent parlia- ment, and even thieatened a total sepaiation fiom Great Britain. In the face of these difficulties the spiiit of England rose higher than ever, and that country, with a vigor worthy of her ancient renown, put forth all her energies to find a way out of her difficulties. The whole world was arrayed against her, but in the face of it she held her own. The heroism manifested by England at this trying period is worthy of the highest admiiation.

The American army passed the winter of 1780–81 in cantonments east and west of the Hudson The Pennsylvania troops were stationed near Morristown, and the New Jersey regiments at Pompton Though the troops were better piovided with food than duiing the previous winter, their sufferings were still very severe. They were neglected by Congiess, which was too much occupied with its dissensions to make any serious effoit to ielieve the wants of the soldiers The Pennsylvania troops had an especial cause of complaint Their enlistments were for three yeais or the war The three yeais had expired, but the goveinment refused to discharge them on the ground that the enlistments were for the period of the war, no matter how long it should last. The troops on the other hand contended that the words "for the war" meant that the enlistments should expire if the war closed in less than three years

On the 1st of January, 1781, thirteen hundred Pennsylvania troops left the camp at Morristown under arms, and set off for Philadelphia, to obtain redress from Congress General Wayne, their commander, placed himself in front of them, and, pistol in hand, attempted to stop their march. In an instant their bayonets were at his breast. " We love, we respect you," they exclaimed, " but you are a dead man if you fire Do not mistake us; we are not going to the enemy , were they now to come out you would see us fight under your orders, with as much resolution and alacrity as ever " They halted at Princeton, where they were met by the agents of Sir Henry Clinton, who endeavored to induce them to join the British service. They promptly seized these men and delivered them up to General Wayne as spies At a later period it was proposed to reward them for this action, but they refused to accept anything, saying " We ask no reward for doing our duty to our country ."

Congress was greatly alarmed by the approach of these troops, and a committee, accompanied by Reed, the president of Pennsylvania, was sent to meet them. The committee met the leaders of the mutineers, and agreed to relieve their immediate wants, and to secure them their back pay by means of certificates Permission was given to all who had served three years to withdraw from the army Upon these conditions the troops returned to duty. The disaffection in the army was increased by the yielding of Congress. On the 20th of January the New Jersey troops at Pompton mutinied, but this outbreak was quelled by a detachment sent from West Point by Washington

The mutiny opened the eyes of the country to the sufferings of the army, and aroused all parties to the necessity of providing for the troops. It was clearly understood that a failure to sustain the army would result in the defeat of the cause Urgent appeals were made by Congress to all the States, and especially to those of New England, to supply the wants of the army, and Congress endeavored to negotiate a loan abroad. Direct taxation was resorted to to provide money at once.

The year 1781 opened with a military expedition under the command of the traitor Arnold, now a brigadier-general in the British service Early in January he was sent by Sir Henry Clinton, with sixteen hundred British and Tories, from New York to the Chesapeake, to ravage the shores of Virginia After plundering the plantations along the lower bay and the James, Arnold ascended that river, and landing his troops marched to Richmond. Thomas Jefferson, then governor of Virginia, called out the militia, but only a handful responded. Arnold occupied Richmond, burned the public buildings and some private dwellings, and then re-embarked and dropped down the river to Portsmouth. Washington was anxious to capture him, and sent Lafayette, with a force of twelve hundred men, southward, by land, to prevent Arnold from escaping overland to join Cornwallis in the Carolinas, and at the same time the French fleet sailed from Newport for the Chesapeake to prevent the escape of the traitor by water. The British Admiral Arbuthnot followed the French fleet, and brought it to an engagement off the mouth of the Chesapeake. The French were worsted and obliged to return to Newport, and Admiral Arbuthnot entered the bay, and reinforced Arnold with two thousand British troops, under General Philips, who assumed

BATTLE OF THE COWPENS.

the command at Portsmouth, and fortified his position there. From his camp he sent out detachments to ravage the country in all directions. Lafayette, in the meantime, upon hearing of the failure of the plan, halted at Annapolis, in Maryland. Arnold, upon being superseded by Philips, returned to New York.

Early in January Cornwallis, who was at Winnsborough, South Carolina, sent Colonel Tarleton, with a force of one thousand cavalry and light infantry, to cut off Morgan's division from the column under General Greene. Morgan was between the Broad and Catawba rivers at the time, and upon hearing of Tarleton's approach began to retreat towards the Catawba. Tarleton pushed on with such speed that Morgan saw he must be overtaken. He accordingly halted, and took position at the "Cowpens," about thirty miles west of King's mountain, and rested his men. Tarleton arrived in front of this position on the 17th of January, and made an impetuous attack upon the Americans. At first he drove the militia before him, but Morgan keeping his Continentals well in hand, suddenly wheeled upon him, and drove him from the field. The two forces were about equal. Morgan lost but eighty men, while the loss of the British was over six hundred. Tarleton escaped from the field with only a few of his cavalry.

Cornwallis moved forward as soon as he learned of Tarleton's defeat. He supposed that Morgan would be encumbered with his wounded and prisoners, and would be slow in leaving the scene of his victory, and he hoped by a rapid march to come up with him, crush him, and rescue the prisoners before he could join General Greene. Morgan was much too wary to be caught in such a trap. He felt sure Cornwallis would seek to avenge Tarleton's defeat, and leaving his wounded under a flag of truce, he resumed his retreat with all speed immediately after the battle, and hurrying towards the Catawba, crossed that river. Two hours after he had passed it the advance of Cornwallis' army reached the bank of the river, but, owing to a sudden rise in the stream, were unable to cross it. The British were detained in this manner for two days, during which Morgan rested his men, and sent off his prisoners to a place of safety.

GENERAL DANIEL MORGAN.

Two days after the passage of the Catawba Morgan was joined by the troops under General Greene, who had heard of the victory of the Cowpens, and was advancing to the assistance of his lieutenant. Greene was not yet strong enough to meet the British, and he continued the retreat towards the Yadkin. He moved slowly, and his rear-guard was still engaged in the passage of the Yadkin, when the advanced guard of Cornwallis reached that stream, on the 3d of February. Cornwallis had burned all his heavy baggage, and had reduced his army to the strictest light marching order, in the hope of being able to intercept Greene. A skirmish ensued on the banks of the Yadkin, and night coming on the British commander deferred the passage of the stream until the next day. During the night a heavy rain swelled the river so high that it could not

be forded, and the Americans had secured all the boats on the other side.
Greene, profiting by this delay, hurried on to cross the Dan into Virginia, where he could receive reinforcements and supplies. Morgan was left to cover the retreat of the army, but falling ill was obliged to relinquish the command of the rear-guard to Colonel Otho H Williams.

Cornwallis passed the Yadkin as soon as possible, and strained every nerve to prevent Greene from crossing the Dan. He supposed the Americans would not be able to cross at the lower ferries, but would be obliged to pass the river higher up, where it could be forded He therefore urged his army to its utmost exertions to secure these fords before the arrival of the Americans. Perceiving Cornwallis' error, Colonel Williams retreated towards the upper fords, and so confirmed the British commander in his delusion. Having led the British sufficiently out of the way, Williams wheeled about, and by a rapid march of forty miles in twenty-four hours, down the river, rejoined Greene, who had moved with all speed to the lower ferries, where, in anticipation of his retreat, he had collected a supply of boats. The Dan was passed on the 15th of February, and the American army was safe from its pursuers. An hour or two later Cornwallis, who had discovered his mistake, and had marched with speed from the upper fords, appeared on the opposite bank of the river, only to see his adversary safely beyond his reach The river was too deep to be forded, and Greene had all the boats in his possession. Cornwallis was deeply mortified at his failure to intercept Greene. He had pursued him for over two hundred miles, and had made great sacrifices to come up with him, but the American commander had managed to elude him, and had successfully carried out one of the most brilliant retreats in history. The Americans regarded their escape as providential; and not without cause. Their way across the Carolinas might be tracked by the blood from their feet, and twice, when the enemy had come within gunshot of them, the rising of the waters of the Catawba and the Yadkin, which they had passed in safety, had held back the British and enabled them to escape. After resting his men for a few days on the banks of the Dan, Cornwallis fell back to Hillsborough.

Having received reinforcements, General Greene recrossed the Dan, about the last of February, and advanced into the Carolinas to watch Cornwallis and encourage the patriots of that region. Cornwallis, being short of supplies, moved slowly southward Greene followed him cautiously, too weak to risk a battle, but ready to take advantage of the first error on the part of his adversary. His movements were conducted with the utmost circumspection, and in order to guard against a surprise he never remained in the same place more than one day, and kept secret until the last moment the places he selected for his encampments   In the meantime he was gradually receiving reinforcements, from Virginia and Maryland, until his army numbered four thousand men

Feeling himself strong enough to attack the enemy, Greene left his baggage at a point of safety, and advanced to Guilford Court-house, seventeen miles distant, with the intention of bringing Cornwallis to a decisive engagement.   Here he was attacked by Cornwallis, on the 15th of March, and after one of the hardest-fought battles of the war, was compelled to retreat.   Greene withdrew in good order, and Cornwallis, though victorious on the field, was so sorely crippled that he was unable to make any pursuit, and was obliged to fall back to Wilmington, near the mouth of the Cape Fear river.   By the time he reached that place, his army had been so much weakened by desertions, and losses in battle, that it amounted to but fourteen hundred men.

Greene lost a thousand militia by desertion during his retreat, but was soon enabled to supply their places.   He then moved into South Carolina for the purpose of attacking the British force under Lord Rawdon, which was posted at Camden.   He advanced to Hobkirk's Hill, about two miles from Camden, where he was attacked, on the 25th of April, by Lord Rawdon.   After a sharp engagement Greene was defeated, and obliged to retreat   He withdrew his army in good order, having inflicted upon his adversary a loss about equal to his own.   Rawdon was unable to derive any advantage from his victory, as he could not bring Greene to another general engagement.   The activity of the American partisan corps in his rear alarmed him for the safety of his communications with Charleston, and he abandoned Camden and fell back to Monk's Corner

In the meantime Lee, Marion, Pickens, and the other partisan leaders had broken up the fortified posts of the British with such success, that by the month of June, 1781, only three positions of importance remained to the British in South Carolina—Charleston, Nelson's Ferry, and Fort Ninety-six, near the Saluda   The last-named position was of the greatest importance, and was held by a force of Carolina Tories   Lee and Pickens were sent against Augusta, Georgia, and captured it after a close investment of seven days..   General Greene himself marched against Ninety-six, and laid siege to it.   Being informed that Lord Rawdon was marching to relieve it, he determined to carry the fort by assault before Rawdon could arrive.   The assault was made on the 18th of June, but was repulsed with severe loss.   Greene then raised the siege and retreated across the Saluda.

Early in July the excessive heat put an end to active operations on the part of the two armies. Greene withdrew to the high hills of the Santee, and the British went into camp on the Congaree. A bitter partisan warfare now sprung up between the patriots and the Tories, and continued through the summer. Houses were pillaged and burned, farms were laid waste, and no quarter was given by either party. Even women and children were included in these dreadful massacres.

Lord Rawdon now resolved to add to the horrors of this warfare by executing as traitors those who had given their parole not to engage in the war, or had received a protection, if they should be taken in arms. Among the prisoners taken by the British, at the capture of Charleston, was Colonel Isaac Hayne, a distinguished citizen of that place. His wife was dying and his children were helpless, and he gave his parole to remain

BATTLE OF EUTAW SPRINGS.

neutral, in order to be able to take care of them, and was promised protection. At a later period, the British commander being in need of reinforcements, Hayne was ordered to take up arms against his country in behalf of the king. He regarded himself as relieved from his parole by this command, and soon after escaped from Charleston, and raised a partisan corps, at the head of which he was captured. He was condemned to die as a traitor; and though the inhabitants of Charleston, both patriot and royalist, petitioned for his pardon, it was refused, and he was hanged, by order of Lord Rawdon, on the 5th of August. His execution was regarded by the Americans as cruel and unjust, and as contrary to military law. General Greene felt himself obliged to retaliate by executing as deserters all those prisoners who had formerly served in his own army, and so bitter was the feeling of the American troops that they could scarcely be prevented from shooting the British officers who fell into their hands.

Lord Rawdon now sailed for England, and left the command of his army to Colonel Stewart, an officer of ability and experience At the close of the summer General Greene, whose army had been increased by the commands of Marion and Pickens to twenty-five hundred men, resumed the offensive. He attacked the British at Eutaw Springs, on the 8th of September, and after a severely contested battle the left wing of the British was routed In the moment of victory the American army stopped to plunder the enemy's camp, and the British taking advantage of the delay, rallied and made a stand in a large stone house, from which they could not be driven. Greene was forced to draw off his troops and leave the field to the British, who lost seven hundred men in the engagement The American loss was five hundred men. Both sides claimed the victory, but the advantage certainly was not with the British, who lost more than a third of their men. Colonel Stewart, in view of this loss, fell back to the vicinity of Charleston Greene followed him as far as Monk's Corner, and then returned to the hills of the Santee. The American commander had abundant reason to be satisfied with the result of his operations in South Carolina. He had rescued the greater part of the State from the British, and had confined them to the region between the Santee and the lower Savannah. He had repeatedly engaged the enemy with the most inadequate means, and under the most unfavorable circumstances, and had never failed, even though defeated, to accomplish the object for which he fought. He had baffled the British commanders over again, and, like William of Orange, had managed to derive greater advantages from his reverses than his adversaries were able to draw from their victories.

Washington was well pleased with the achievements, in the south, of his most trusted lieutenant. He was very anxious to attempt something decisive with his own army, if he could secure the aid of a French army and fleet Two enterprises offered themselves to him—an attack upon New York, which had been greatly weakened by detachments sent from its garrison to the south, and an expedition against Cornwallis. That commander had left Wilmington, on the 20th of April, and had advanced, without encountering any serious resistance, to Petersburg, Virginia. He arrived there on the 20th of May, and was joined by the troops under General Philips, who had been plundering the country along the James river. While Washington was hesitating which would be the best course to pursue, a French frigate arrived at Newport, with the Count de Barras on board, who had come to take command of the fleet at Newport. He brought the good news that a fleet of twenty ships-of-the-line, under the Count de Grasse, having on board a considerable force of troops, had sailed for America, and might be expected to arrive in the course of a few months. Washington held a conference with the Count de Rochambeau, at Weathersfield, Connecticut, and it was resolved to attack New York. The French army was to march from Newport and form a junction with the Americans on the Hudson. A frigate was despatched to the West Indies to inform the Count de Grasse of this arrangement, and to ask his cooperation in the proposed attack.

Sir Henry Clinton, who suspected the designs of Washington, now ordered Lord Cornwallis, who had crossed the James river, and was at Williamsburg, to send him a reinforcement of troops. Cornwallis prepared to comply with this order, and for that purpose marched towards Portsmouth, followed cautiously by Lafayette and Steuben, who had with them about four thousand American troops. On the march a slight engagement occurred, near Westover, between Lafayette and Cornwallis, in which the Americans narrowly escaped a defeat. The British army crossed to the south side of the James, and a detachment was embarked for New York. At this moment a second order was received from Sir Henry Clinton, who had received a reinforcement of Hessians from England, directing Cornwallis to retain all his force, choose some central position in Virginia, fortify himself in it, and await the development of the American plans. Cornwallis should have taken position at Portsmouth, from which place his line of retreat to the south would have remained intact. In an evil hour for himself he recrossed the James, and crossing the peninsula between that river and the York, took position at the towns of Gloucester and Yorktown, opposite each other, on the York river. He had with him an army of eight thousand effective troops, and proceeded to fortify his position with strong intrenchments. A number of vessels of war were anchored between Yorktown and Gloucester to maintain the communication between those points, and to assist in the defence of the place.

During all this time the financial affairs of the republic were growing worse and more hopeless. The continental currency had become utterly worthless, one dollar in paper being worth only one cent in coin, at the opening of the year 1781. In the spring of that year Congress sought to put an end to its financial troubles by taking the control of the finances from a board which had hitherto managed them, and intrusting them to Robert Morris, whose services in behalf of the cause have been mentioned before. Morris was an experienced financier, and had opposed, with all his energy, the system of making continental money a legal

tender. He now made a return to specie payments the condition of his
acceptance of the trust imposed upon him by Congress. On the 22d of
May, 1781, Congress most unwillingly resolved: "That the whole debts
already due by the United States be liquidated as soon as may be to their
specie value, and funded, if agreeable to the creditors, as a loan upon
interest; that the States be severally informed that the calculations of
the present campaign are made in solid coin, and, therefore, that the
requisitions from them respectively being grounded on those calculations,
must be complied with in such manner as effectually to answer the purpose designed; that, experience having evinced the inefficacy of all
attempts to support the credit of paper money by compulsory acts, it is

CONTINENTAL BILLS.

recommended to such States, where laws making paper bills a tender yet
exist, to repeal the same." On the 31st of May continental bills, being
no longer a legal tender, ceased to circulate. Henceforth all transactions
were to be in hard money. The result amply vindicated the wisdom of
Morris' views. He induced Congress to establish the Bank of the
United States, at Philadelphia, with a capital of two millions of dollars
and a charter for ten years. This bank was allowed the privilege of
issuing its own notes, which it was required to redeem in specie upon
presentation. This requirement gained for the bank the confidence of
the people, and capitalists availed themselves of it for the investment of
their money. Morris used the bank freely in his public operations, and

at the same time used it so wisely that he was able to secure all the aid it was capable of bestowing without subjecting it to too severe a strain. He raised the credit of the government higher than it had ever stood before, and was able to do much towards paying the soldiers and supplying them with food and clothing. As often as the public funds failed, he pledged his own credit to supply the deficiency. No man did more to contribute to the success of the cause than Robert Morris; and no man

SCENE IN THE HIGHLANDS OF THE HUDSON.

received more ingratitude from the government and people of the Union than he.

In July Washington was joined, in the Highlands, by the French army under Count de Rochambeau, and preparations were made to attack New York. An intercepted letter informed Sir Henry Clinton of this design, and he exerted himself to put the city in a state of defence. In the midst of his preparations Washington received a letter from the Count de Grasse, stating that he would sail for the Chesapeake instead of Newport. This decision of the French admiral compelled an entire change of plan on the part of the Americans. As De Grasse would not coöperate with them, they must abandon the attack upon New York, and attempt the

capture of Cornwallis at Yorktown No time was to be lost in making
the attempt, for it was now the month of August. By a series of skilful
movements Sir Henry Clinton was induced to believe that an attack upon
New York would soon be made, and at the same time the American
army was marched rapidly across New Jersey, followed by the French.
Lafayette, who was in Virginia, was ordered to prevent at all hazards a
retreat of Cornwallis' army to North Carolina, and was directed to ask
assistance of General Greene, if necessary. The plan of Washington was
to blockade Cornwallis in the York river by means of the French fleet,
and at the same time to besiege him in Yorktown with the army. The
troops were somewhat unwilling to undertake a southern campaign in
August, but their good humor was restored at Philadelphia, where they
received a part of their pay in specie, and a supply of clothing, arms,
and ammunition, which had just arrived from France. From Philadelphia the combined armies proceeded to Elkton, at the head of the
Chesapeake, where they found transports, sent by the French admiral
and by Lafayette, to convey them to the James river

The first intimation Sir Henry Clinton had of a change in the American
plans was the sudden sailing of the French fleet from Newport on the
28th of August Supposing that De Barras's object was to unite with
another fleet in the Chesapeake, Clinton sent Admiral Graves to prevent
the junction. Upon reaching the capes the British admiral was astonished to find the fleet of the Count de Grasse, consisting of twenty ships-
of-the-line, anchored within the bay De Grasse at once put to sea as if
to engage the enemy, but in reality to draw them off and allow De Barras
to enter the Chesapeake. For five days he amused the English by constant skirmishing. De Barras at length appeared and passed within the
capes and De Grasse at once followed him. Admiral Graves was unwilling to attack this combined force and returned to New York

The movement of the American army to the south was known to
Clinton, but he supposed it was only a manœuvre to draw him off of Manhattan island into the open country. When the Americans were beyond
the Delaware and the French fleets had effected their junction in the
Chesapeake, he recognized his mistake and saw that the object of Washington was the capture of Cornwallis. It was too late to prevent it, but
in the hope of compelling Washington to send back a part of his force to
defend New England, Clinton sent the traitor Arnold with a large body
of troops to attack New London in Connecticut On the 6th of September Arnold captured that town and burned the shipping and a large part
of the town. He then took Fort Griswold, on the opposite side of the
Thames, by storm, and basely massacred Colonel Ledyard, the commander,

and sixty of the garrison after the surrender of the fort.   The militia of the State were summoned to take up arms for its defence, and responded in such numbers that Arnold became alarmed for his safety and returned to New York.   The object of his expedition failed most signally.   Washington left New England to defend herself and continued his movement against Cornwallis.

Cornwallis was very slow to realize his danger.   He believed the small force under Lafayette the only command opposed to him, and on the 10th of September wrote to Clinton that he could spare him twelve hundred men for the defence of New York.   He did not perceive his error until the French fleet had anchored in the Chesapeake and cut off his escape

BURNING OF NEW LONDON, CONNECTICUT, BY ARNOLD.

by water.   He then attempted to retreat to North Carolina, as Washington had foreseen, but Lafayette, who had been reinforced by three thousand French troops under the Marquis de St. Simon, from the fleet of De Grasse, was too active for him, and finding his retreat impossible, Cornwallis sent urgent appeals to Clinton for assistance and strengthened his fortifications.

In the meantime the American and French armies descended the Chesapeake, and took position before Yorktown, while the French fleet closed the mouth of York river.   The siege was begun on the 28th of September.   Sixteen thousand men were present under Washington's orders.   Works were erected completely enclosing those of the British, and on the 9th of October the cannonade was begun.   It was continued for four days, and the British outworks were greatly damaged, and several of their vessels in the river were burned by means of red hot shot thrown into them by the French vessels. On the 14th two of the advanced redoubts of the enemy were stormed and taken, one by the Americans, the other by the French. From the positions thus gained a very destructive fire was maintained upon the English lines, which were broken in many places, while many of their guns were dismounted and rendered useless. On the 15th Cornwallis found himself almost out of ammunition, and unable to maintain his position but for a few days longer.

In this strait the British commander resolved upon the desperate alternative of crossing the York to Gloucester, abandoning his sick and wounded and baggage, and endeavoring to force his way north-ward by extraordinary marches to New York. It was a hopeless under-taking, but Cornwal-lis resolved to make the trial. On the night of the 16th of October he crossed a part of his army from Yorktown to Gloucester, but a

LAFAYETTE STORMING THE REDOUBT AT YORKTOWN.

sudden storm delayed the passage of the river by the second division until after daylight, when it was useless to make the attempt. The first division was with difficulty brought back to Yorktown, as the boats were exposed to the fire of the American batteries while crossing the river. Nothing was left to Cornwallis now but a capitulation, as his works were in no condition to withstand an assault, and simple humanity to his men demanded that the contest should cease. He sent to Washington an offer to surrender and the terms were soon arranged. On the 19th of October Cornwallis surrendered his army of seven thousand men as prisoners of war to Washington, as commander of the allied army, and his shipping, seamen, and naval stores to the Count de Grasse, as the representative of the king of France.

Washington despatched one of his aids to Philadelphia to communicate the good news to Congress. The officer pushed forward with all speed, and reached Philadelphia at midnight, and delivered his message. Soon the peals of the State-house bell roused the citizens, and the watchmen took up the cry, "Cornwallis is taken! Cornwallis is taken!" The people poured out into the streets in throngs, and no one slept in Philadelphia that night. The next day Congress proceeded in a body to a church and gave thanks for the great victory. A national thanksgiving was ordered, and throughout the whole land rejoicings went up to God for the success which all men felt was decisive of the war.

On the 19th of October, the day of the surrender of Cornwallis, Sir Henry Clinton sailed from New York to his assistance with a force of seven thousand men. Off the capes he learned of the surrender of the British army at Yorktown, and as his fleet was not strong enough to meet that of the French he returned at once to New York.

The news of the surrender of Cornwallis was received in England with

SURRENDER OF CORNWALLIS.

astonishment and mortification. It was the second time England had lost an entire army by capture, and her efforts to subdue the United States were no nearer success than they had been at the opening of the war. The English people had never regarded the attempt to conquer America with favor, and they now became more open and energetic in their demands for peace. "Lord North, the prime minister," says an English writer, "received the intelligence of the capture of Cornwallis as he would have done a cannon ball in his breast; he paced the room, and throwing his arms wildly about, kept exclaiming, 'O God! it is all over! it is all over!'" The king and the aristocracy, however, had no thought of yielding yet to the popular pressure, and were resolved to carry on the war.

After the surrender at Yorktown Washington urged the Count de

Grasse to cooperate with General Greene in an attack upon Charleston. The French admiral declined to comply with his request, alleging the necessity of his immediate return to the West Indies. The French troops were quartered for the winter at Williamsburg, Virginia, and the American army returned northward and resumed its old positions on the Hudson. Washington, though convinced that peace was close at hand, did not relax his vigilance, and urged upon Congress the necessity of preparing for a vigorous campaign the next year, but so thoroughly was Congress carried away by the prospect of peace that his recommendations were unheeded.

In the south the British and Tories were so disheartened by the surrender of Cornwallis that they ceased active operations and evacuated all their posts but Savannah and Charleston. General Greene at once disposed his army in such a manner as to confine them closely to Charleston. In the Northern States the only place held by the British was New York.

Though active operations had ceased on the part of the two armies, a cruel and destructive warfare was continued by the Indian allies of the British against the border settlements of Pennsylvania and Virginia, and a similar warfare was maintained by the Tories and Indians along the frontier of New York. These outrages involved the Christian Delaware Indians in the punishment of the guilty savages. The Delawares had become converted to Christianity under the influence of the Moravian missionaries, and had removed from the Susquehanna to the Muskingum. They were suspected by the Americans of the crimes of their heathen brethren, and in the spring and summer of 1782 their towns were destroyed and numbers of them were slain. The war was carried into the country of the Wyandottes by the whites, but with less success. On the 6th of June a force of Pennsylvanians under Colonel Crawford was defeated by the Wyandottes. In the same summer a band of northern Indians led by Simon Girty, a Tory of infamous character, invaded Kentucky. They were met by the Kentuckians under Boone, Todd, and other leaders. A severe battle was fought at the Big Blue Lick, and the Kentuckians were defeated with the loss of nearly half their force.

In the meantime the desire of the English people for the close of the war had grown too strong to be resisted, and the king and his ministers were at length forced to yield. The impossibility of conquering America had become so apparent to the continental nations that in the spring of 1782 the Dutch republic recognized the independence of the United States, and received John Adams as envoy from that government. The king of England maintained his obstinate opposition to the wishes of his people to the last moment   On the 22d of February, 1782, a resolution was introduced into the House of Commons to put an end to the American war, and was supported by the leaders of the Whig party.   It was defeated by a majority of one, but on the 27th of February a similar resolution was introduced and was carried by a majority of nineteen. On the 20th of March Lord North and his colleagues were forced to relinquish their offices, and a new ministry was formed under the Marquis of Rockingham   Sir Henry Clinton was removed from his command in America, and was succeeded by Sir Guy Carleton, whose humane conduct of the war while governor of Canada we have related   Carleton arrived in New York in May, 1782, with full powers to open negotiations for peace.   He at once put a stop to the savage warfare of the Tories and Indians on the borders of western New York, and opened a correspondence with Washington proposing a cessation of hostilities until a definite treaty of peace could be arranged.

Five commissioners were appointed by Congress to conclude a treaty with Great Britain.   They were John Adams, Benjamin Franklin, John Jay, Henry Laurens, who had just been released from the tower of London, where he had been kept a prisoner for about a year, and Thomas Jefferson.   Mr. Jefferson was unable to leave America   Five commissioners were appointed by Great Britain to treat with "certain colonies" named in their instructions.   The commissioners from the two countries met at Paris, but the American commissioners refused to open the negotiations except in the name of the "United States of America."   This right was acknowledged by Great Britain, and on the 30th of November, 1782, a preliminary treaty was signed, which was ratified by Congress in April, 1783   This treaty could not be final because by the terms of the alliance between the United States and France neither party could make a separate treaty of peace with England   In January, 1783, France and Great Britain agreed upon terms of peace, and on the 3d of September, 1783, a final treaty of peace was signed by all the nations who had engaged in the war—by the United States, France, Spain, and Holland on the one side, and Great Britain on the other   Great Britain acknowledged the independence of the States of the Union in the following words   "His Britannic Majesty acknowledges the said United States, viz · New Hampshire, Massachusetts Bay, Rhode Island and Providence Plantations, Connecticut, New York, New Jersey, Pennsylvania, Delaware, Maryland, Virginia, North Carolina, South Carolina, and Georgia, to be free, sovereign, and independent States ; that he treats with them as such ; and for himself, his heirs, and successors, relinquishes all claim to the government proprietary and territorial rights of the same, and every part thereof." It should be observed that the treaty acknowledged the independence and sovereignty of each of the thirteen States, and not of the United States as a single nation. The independence of the States had already been recognized by several of the European powers: by Sweden, on the 5th of February, 1783; by Denmark, on the 25th of February, 1783; by Spain, on the 24th of March; and by Russia, in July, 1783.

THE BOWERY, NEW YORK, IN 1875.

Treaties of friendship and commerce were entered into between the United States and these powers.

During the year 1782 the greater part of the American army was encamped at Newburg, on the Hudson. The troops were unpaid, and were neglected by Congress and by the various States. Washington warned the government of the danger of further neglect of the army, but his warning was unheeded, and in March the patience of the army was so far exhausted that it was seriously proposed to march on Philadelphia and compel Congress to do justice to the troops. Washington appealed to the officers to remain patient a little longer, and pledged himself to use his influence with Congress to fulfil its neglected promises to the army. His appeal quieted the trouble for a time. Congress shortly after agreed to advance full pay to the soldiers for four months, and to pay in one gross sum the full pay of the officers for five years.

The condition of the country was a subject of the gravest apprehension. It was plain that the articles of confederation were not capable of continuing the Union much longer, and many persons believed that the only hope of preserving a regular government, and a permanent union to the country, lay in the establishment of a monarchy. In May, 1782,

WASHINGTON RESIGNING HIS COMMISSION.

Colonel Nicola, of the Pennsylvania line, at the instance of a number of officers, wrote a letter to Washington proposing the creation of a monarchy, and offering him the crown. Washington indignantly refused to entertain the proposition, and severely rebuked the writer of the letter.

In the spring of 1783 the news of the signing of the preliminary treaty of peace was received in America, and was officially communicated to the nation in a proclamation by Congress. On the 19th of April, 1783, just eight years from the commencement of the war at Lexington, the close of hostilities was proclaimed, in general orders, to the army at Newburg. A general exchange of prisoners followed, and large numbers of Tories were obliged to leave the country, as they feared to remain after the protection of the British forces was withdrawn. They emigrated chiefly to Canada, Nova Scotia, and the West Indies. The final treaty having been signed, the army was disbanded on the 3d of November, and the troops, with the exception of a small force, returned to their homes to enjoy their well-earned honors and the thanks of their grateful countrymen. On the 25th of November the British evacuated New York, which was at once occupied by a small force of Americans, under General Knox. In December Charleston was also evacuated by the British.

On the 2d of December Washington issued a farewell address to the army, and on the 4th of that month took leave of the officers at New York. He then proceeded to Annapolis, where Congress was in session, and on the 23d of December, under circumstances of great solemnity, resigned his commission to that body, and after receiving the thanks of Congress for the able and faithful manner in which he had discharged the task intrusted to him, retired to his home at Mount Vernon, which he had not visited for eight years, except for a few hours, while on his way to attack Cornwallis at Yorktown.

.nd
ntral
n. It
ial im-
.hich had
: same foot-
.tation in the
g States of the
ntation in Con-

CHAPTER XXXI.

THE ADOPTION OF THE CONSTITUTION—WASHINGTON'S ADMINISTRATION.

THE long war was over, and independence had been achieved; but the condition of the country was such as to excite the gravest apprehension. The country was exhausted by the sacrifices and burdens of the war, and its debts amounted to the enormous sum of one hundred and seventy millions of dollars, a sum vastly out of proportion to its resources. Two-thirds of these debts had been contracted by Congress, the remainder by the States. The articles of confederation were found inadequate to the task of enforcing the authority of the general government, and the States treated the orders of Congress with neglect. Commerce was sadly deranged for the want of a uniform system. The States entered into competition with each other for the trade of foreign nations, and articles which were required to pay heavy duties in some of the States were admitted free of duty in others. Many of the States were unable to enforce the collection of taxes within their own limits. The British merchants, at the close of the war, flooded the American markets with their manufactures at reduced prices. The result was that the domestic manufactures of the States were ruined, the country was drained of its specie, and the merchants and people of the Union were involved in heavy debts. A general poverty ensued in the Eastern States, which gave rise to much discontent. In Massachusetts, in December, 1786, a body of a thousand men, under Daniel Shays, assembled at Worcester and compelled the supreme court to adjourn, in order to prevent it from issuing writs for the collection of debts   The militia was called out, and "Shays' Rebellion" was put down, but it was evident that the sympathies of the people were largely with the insurgents   These troubles brought home to the whole country the necessity of a more perfect system of government, and measures were begun for bringing about the changes needed.

In September, 1783, delegates from five of the States met at Annapolis to deliberate upon a plan for the improvement of commerce and the revenue   They recommended the assembling of a convention to revise the articles of confederation; and, accordingly, delegates from all the States met for this purpose, at Philadelphia, in May, 1787. George Washington, who was one of the delegates from Virginia, was unanimously chosen president of the convention. The sessions of this body lasted four months, and the convention, instead of revising the articles of confederation, adopted an entirely new constitution. Each article of this constitution was discussed with care and minuteness, and with great feeling. The sessions of the convention were held with closed doors; but its proceedings were so far from harmonious that there were several occasions when it seemed likely the convention would break up in confusion, and leave its work unfinished   At length, however, through the patriotism and forbearance of its members, the convention brought its work to a close, and presented the constitution to Congress   It was submitted by that body to the several States for their approval   The State governments summoned conventions of their respective people, and submitted the constitution to them for their acceptance or rejection. By the end of 1788 it was ratified by eleven States   North Carolina did not ratify it until November, 1789; and Rhode Island held aloof from the Union until May, 1790   The right of these States to reject the constitution, and to continue their separate existence as independent States, was not questioned by any one

The new constitution was not entirely satisfactory to any party, and represented the sacrifices made by all to achieve the great end of a central government, strong enough to carry out the objects of the Union. It was a document of compromises, three of which were of especial importance   The first was a concession to the smaller States, which had feared the loss of their independence; they were placed on the same footing as the larger States by being given an equal representation in the Senate   The second was a concession to the slave-holding States of the south, and guaranteed that in apportioning their representation in Congress three-fifths of the slaves were to be included with the white population. The third was a concession to Georgia and South Carolina, and granted them permission to continue the African slave-trade until 1808. The delegates from those States refused to sign the constitution except upon this condition.

In the meantime Congress had taken a step of the highest importance in adopting the plan, presented by Mr. Jefferson, for a decimal currency. Until now the use of the English currency had been general in all the States. In August, 1786, our present system of dollars and cents was adopted by Congress, and a mint was established somewhat later. The government was so poor, however, that it could only coin a small quantity of copper cents.

The sessions of Congress were held at New York. In the session of 1787 a measure was adopted, which had the most important influence

GREAT SEAL OF THE UNITED STATES.

upon the subsequent history of the country. The treaty of Paris fixed the Mississippi river as the western boundary of the United States. This river consequently became the western limit of Virginia, Connecticut, and Massachusetts. In 1784 Virginia ceded to the general government of the United States her claim to the vast region owned by her beyond the Ohio. Massachusetts and Connecticut soon followed her example, and New York also ceded her western territory to the government. In July, 1787, Congress organized this vast region as the territory of the northwest. It was provided that slavery should never be permitted to exist in this territory, or in any of the States which might afterwards be formed out of it. This wise provision, which was the basis of the wonderful prosperity of this great region, was due to the foresight of Thomas Jefferson. The northwest being secured to freedom, emigration soon set in, and it began its great career of prosperity which has since known no slackening.

It was provided by the constitution that when it should have been ratified by two-thirds of the States, it should go into operation on the 4th of March, 1789. Eleven of the States having ratified the constitution, elections were held for President and Vice-President of the United States, and for members of Congress. New York was named as the seat of the new government. The 4th of March, 1789, was ushered in with a public demonstration at New York; but a sufficient number of members of Congress to form a quorum for the transaction of business did not arrive until the 30th of March. On the 6th of April the electoral votes were counted, and it was found that George Washington had been unanimously chosen first President of the United States, and John Adams Vice-President.

WASHINGTON RECEIVING THE INTELLIGENCE OF HIS ELECTION.

Charles Thompson, the oldest secretary of Congress, was sent to Mount Vernon to notify Washington of his election, and a messenger was despatched to Boston on a similar errand to Mr. Adams. Washington promptly signified his acceptance of the office, and, two days later, started for New York. It was his desire to travel as quietly and unostentatiously as possible, but the people of the States through which he passed would not permit him to do so. His journey was a constant ovation. Crowds greeted him at every town with the most enthusiastic demonstrations of affection and confidence; triumphal arches were erected; his way was strewn with flowers by young girls; and maidens and mothers greeted him with songs composed in his honor. In consequence of these demonstrations his progress was so much retarded that he did not reach New York until the latter part of April.

On the 30th of April Washington appeared on the balcony of Federal Hall, New York, on the site of which the United States Treasury now stands, and took the oath of office in the presence of the Senate and House of Representatives, and a large crowd of citizens assembled in the streets below. He then repaired to the Senate chamber, and there delivered an address to both houses of Congress. The organization of the government being now complete, Congress proceeded to arrange the executive department by the creation of the departments of state, the treasury, and war. President Washington appointed Thomas Jefferson, secretary of state, Alexander Hamilton, secretary of the treasury, and General Henry Knox, secretary of war. John Jay was made chief justice of the United States, and Edmund Randolph, attorney-general.

The new government found itself face to face with many difficulties, the principal of which was the payment of the national debt. This debt was in the form of notes of the government, or promises to pay for value received. These notes had been issued by the States as well as by Congress during the revolution, and had been given in payment for services

PRESIDENT WASHINGTON.

rendered the general and State governments, and for supplies. In January, 1790, Alexander Hamilton proposed to pay all these debts in full, and that the general government should assume the war debts of the States. This plan met with considerable opposition at first, but was at length adopted. It was also arranged that the revenue of the country should be divided as follows: As the control of commerce had passed into the hands of Congress the revenue derived from the duties levied upon imported merchandise was to be applied to the uses of the general government. The proceeds of the direct taxes upon real estate and other property, which could be levied only by the respective States, were to be used for the expenses of those States.

It had been for some time considered desirable to remove the seat of the federal government to some point more central than New York, and which could be brought under the supreme control of Congress. In 1790 it was resolved that the seat of government be fixed at Philadelphia for ten years, and at the end of that time be removed to a new city to be built on the banks of the Potomac. A federal district, ten miles square, was obtained by cession from Virginia and Maryland, and was placed under the sole control of the United States. The foundations of a new city, named Washington, in honor of the "Father of his Country," were laid on the left bank of the Potomac, a short distance below the falls of that river, and buildings for the accommodation of the general government were begun and pushed forward as rapidly as possible.

The general government was removed to Philadelphia in 1791, and in December of that year the second Congress began its sessions in that city. The principal measure of this session was the establishment of the Bank of the United States, in accordance with the recommendations of Alexander Hamilton. The bank was chartered for twenty years, and its capital was ten millions of dollars, of which the government took two millions, and private individuals the remainder. The measure was carried in the face of considerable opposition in Congress, but was very beneficial to the government, as well as to the general business of the country. The notes of the bank were payable in gold and silver upon presentation at its counters.

Commerce now began to show signs of a great revival from the stagnation and loss caused by the war. The duties levied upon foreign goods gave to domestic manufactures an opportunity to place themselves upon a firmer foundation. Very great improvements were made in the character of American manufactures. In New England the weaving of cotton and woollen goods was begun, in a feeble way it is true, but the foundation was laid of that great industry which has since been a constant and growing source of wealth to that section.

In 1790, the first census of the United States was taken, and showed the population to be 3,929,827 souls.

The Indians of the northwest had been very troublesome for some time. The British agents in that region incited them to hostility against the United States, and urged them to claim the Ohio as their southern and eastern boundary. They committed innumerable outrages along this river, and almost put a stop to the trade upon its waters by attacking and plundering the flatboats of the emigrants and traders which were constantly descending the river. The general government resolved to put a stop to their outrages, and General Harmer was sent against them in 1790, but was defeated with great loss. In 1791 General St. Clair, the governor of the northwest territory, was placed in command of an expedition against the savages. He set out from Fort Washington, now Cincinnati, about the middle of September, with a force of two thousand men, but near the head waters of the Wabash was surprised and defeated by an Indian force under Little Turtle, a famous chief of the Miamis. The wreck of his army fled to Fort Washington, and the frontier was once more defenceless.

President Washington now placed General Anthony Wayne in command of the forces destined to operate against the Indians. With his usual energy Wayne assembled his army at Fort Washington, and in the summer of 1794 marched into the Indian country, laid it waste, and defeated the Indian tribes in the battle of the Maumee on the 20th of August. In the summer of 1795, the Indians, cowed by their defeat, and alarmed by the withdrawal of the British from the frontier posts, met General Wayne at his camp on the Miami, and entered into a treaty with the United States by which they ceded all the eastern and southern part of Ohio to the whites, and withdrew farther westward.

In the elections of 1792 Washington and Adams were chosen President and Vice-President of the United States for a second term of four years. The disputes which had been begun by the adoption of the constitution had been continued during the first term of Washington's presidency, and had given rise to two political parties—the Federalists, or those who favor

BATTLE OF THE MAUMEE.

a strong national government, and who supported the administration; and the Anti-Federalists, who opposed the policy of the administration. Among the leaders of the Federalist party were Washington, Adams, Hamilton, and Jay; among the Anti-Federalist leaders were Jefferson, Madison, and Monroe. The differences between Jefferson and Hamilton increased with time, and soon assumed the character of a personal hostility, a circumstance which was productive of great trouble to the president, since it prevented his cabinet from acting harmoniously. As the quarrel deepened, the Anti-Federalist party repudiated that title, and took the name of *Republican*, as it better expressed their principles. The political questions entered largely into the second election, and prevented Mr. Adams from receiving the unanimous vote which was given to Washington.

Shortly after the commencement of Washington's first term of office, the French revolution broke out, and drew upon France the attention of the whole world. The events of this great struggle were watched with the deepest interest in America, for the nation cherished the warmest sentiments of gratitude to France for her aid in the revolution. The Republican party urgently favored an alliance with the French republic, but Washington and the greater part of his cabinet were resolved to maintain a strict neutrality as to all European quarrels. The excesses of the revolutionists shocked the public sentiment of America, and the events of the reign of terror cooled the zeal of many of the most ardent friends of the French republic. Still party feeling ran high upon the subject, and the disputes were yet very bitter when Mr. Edmond Charles Genet, or "Citizen Genet," as he was generally styled, arrived in the United States, in 1793, as minister from the French republic. He brought the news that France had declared war against Great Britain. He was well received by the Republicans, who were anxious that the United States should become the ally of France and thus engage in a new war with Great Britain. Washington and his cabinet were unmoved by this clamor, and a proclamation was issued declaring the neutrality of the United States in the war between Great Britain and France, and warning the American people to refrain from the commission of acts inconsistent with this neutrality. The firmness of the president in resisting the demand for an alliance with France saved the country from innumerable losses, perhaps from the destruction of the work of the revolution.

Genet, encouraged by the sympathy of the Republican party, was determined to embroil the United States with Great Britain to such an extent that they would be compelled to make common cause with France. He therefore began to fit out privateers from American ports against the commerce of England. He was warned by the government that he was transcending his privileges as the minister of a friendly power, but paid no attention to this rebuke. The Republican party now took a more active stand in favor of the French alliance, and its more ultra members assumed the name of Democrats, while others styled themselves Democratic Republicans. The determination of President Washington not to interfere in the quarrels of Europe was vehemently assailed, and the newspapers of this party went so far as to denounce the president and his supporters as the enemies of France and the friends and secret supporters of their old oppressor, the king of England.

Genet was greatly deceived by these clamors, which he mistook for the sentiment of the American people. He took a step further, and authorized the French consuls in the American ports to receive and sell vessels cap-

37

tured by French cruisers from the English, with whom the United States were at peace. He also contemplated raising a force in Georgia and the Carolinas for the purpose of seizing Florida, and another in Kentucky for the conquest of Louisiana, both of which regions were then held by Spain, a power friendly to the United States. The patience of the president having been exhausted by Genet's insolent conduct, Washington requested the French government to recall him, which it did in 1794, much to the astonishment of citizen Genet. M. Fauchet was appointed in his place. Genet did not return home, but became a citizen of the United States.

The impunity with which Genet had braved the federal government gave rise to fears that it was not strong enough to enforce its authority. Advantage was taken of this feeling in an unexpected quarter. The fertile region of western Pennsylvania, watered by the Monongahela and its tributaries, had been settled by a hardy population, chiefly of Scotch-Irish Presbyterians, who had with great labor and amid constant exposure to the attacks of the Indians, redeemed the land from the wilderness, and covered it with thriving farms and orchards. Grain and apples and peaches were their staple products; the grain was distilled into whiskey, and the fruits were made into brandies. One of Hamilton's favorite measures for the raising of a revenue was the imposition of an excise or duty upon whiskey. This tax was generally unpopular throughout the country, but especially so in the four western counties of Pennsylvania. The settlers of this region organized themselves in secret societies for the purpose of resisting this tax, and at length, in 1792, rose in rebellion against the government, refused to pay the tax, and drove off the excise officers. The best men in this section were engaged in the rebellion, and it was openly proposed to separate from Pennsylvania and form a new State. Nearly seven thousand armed men assembled, and declared their intention to resist the authority of the State and federal governments. Matters remained in this condition for about two years, and at length Washington, finding it necessary to employ force for the suppression of the revolt, sent a strong body of troops to compel the rebels to submit. Upon the appearance of the troops, the leaders of the movement fled, and the "Whiskey Insurrection" suddenly came to an end. This vigorous action of the federal government greatly added to its strength.

The fidelity with which Washington sought to discharge his duty towards England, as a neutral, was but little appreciated by the government of that country, which conducted itself towards the United States in a manner that seemed likely to result in another war. By the treaty of Paris England had agreed to surrender the frontier posts held by her forces within the limits of the United States. These were still retained, and were made by the British agents so many centres for stirring up the Indians to acts of hostility against the Americans. Orders were issued to the British naval officers to seize and detain all vessels laden with French goods, or with provisions for any of the French colonies. As the American ships were largely engaged in trade with France and her colonies, this order threatened the commerce of the States with ruin. The feeling of indignation against England, caused by these outrages, was increasing throughout the Union, and the country was rapidly drifting into a war with that kingdom. The interests of the United States demanded peace with all the world, as the country was yet too weak and unsettled to endure another war with safety. This necessity was recognized by Washington and his advisers, and the constant aim of the president was to avoid, as far as possible, all complications which might lead to war. The conduct of Great Britain could not be passed by, and if a settlement of the matter, consistent with the honor and interests of the republic could not be arranged, war was inevitable.

Anxious to exhaust all peaceful means of settlement, President Washington sent John Jay, the chief justice, to England to enter into negotiations with the British government for the settlement of all matters in dispute between the two countries. Mr. Jay was eminently qualified for the task, both by his remarkable abilities and his great and honorable services to the country since the outbreak of the revolution. He was received in England with great respect, and in the course of a few months concluded a treaty, which was submitted to the Senate of the United States for ratification. By the terms of this treaty Great Britain agreed to give up the western posts within two years, to grant to American vessels the privilege of trading with the West Indies upon certain conditions, and to admit American ships free of restrictions to the ports of Great Britain and the English East Indian possessions. On the other hand provision was made by the United States for the collection of debts due British merchants by American citizens.

This treaty did not please any party entirely, not even Mr. Jay himself; but it was the best that could be obtained from Great Britain at the time, and as such was accepted by the administration, which threw all its influence in favor of its adoption. It met with very great opposition in the Senate, and subjected the president to a great deal of adverse criticism throughout the country. After a fortnight's debate in secret session the Senate advised the ratification of the treaty. The acceptance of this treaty, imperfect and unsatisfactory as it was, secured peace to the United States for a number of years at this most critical period of its history. In 1795 treaties were also negotiated with Spain, by which the bounda-

ries between the United States and Louisiana and Florida were definitely
settled. The navigation of the Mississippi was made free to both parties,
and the Americans were granted the privilege of making New Orleans,
for three years, a place of deposit for their trade.

The commerce of the United States, which was increasing rapidly, was
confined chiefly to the New England States. A lucrative trade with the
countries of Europe bordering the Mediterranean had grown up, but was
greatly interfered with by the Algerine pirates, who sallied out from their
harbors on the African coast and captured many of the vessels engaged
in this trade, and sold the crews into slavery The European powers had
purchased exemption from these outrages by paying an annual tribute to
the Dey of Algiers. The United States for the present thought it best
to follow the universal custom, and ransomed the captive American
sailors by the payment of nearly a million of dollars. At the same
time the more sensible policy of establishing a navy for the protection of
American commerce was resolved upon, and in 1795 a bill was passed by

COAT OF ARMS OF VERMONT

Congress for the construction of
six first-class frigates. This was
the beginning of the United
States navy.

Mr. Jefferson had retired from
the cabinet at the close of 1793,
and after his withdrawal party
quarrels ran higher than ever.
The motives and conduct of the president were denounced with great bitterness by his opponents, and he was subjected to considerable annoyance
by these attacks. He continued, with firmness, the course he had marked
out for himself, trusting to time and the good sense of his countrymen for
his vindication. In September, 1796, he issued a farewell address to the
people of the United States, in which he announced his purpose to retire
from public life at the close of his second term, and delivered to his
countrymen such counsels and admonitions as he deemed suited to their
future guidance. It was the warning of a father to his children engaged
in a difficult and all-important undertaking It had a most happy effect.
It brought up the memory of the great and unselfish services of Washington, and enabled his countrymen to see him in his true light. The
gratitude of the nation, which had been long obscured by party passion,
burst forth in a mighty stream, and from every quarter came evidences
of the affection and veneration of the American people for their great
leader. Congress adopted a reply to the farewell address, expressing
the highest confidence in the wisdom and integrity of Washington, and

during the winter of 1796–97 nearly all the State legislatures adopted similar resolutions.

At the elections held in the fall of 1796 the Federalists put forward John Adams as their candidate, while the Republicans supported Thomas Jefferson. The contest was very bitter, and resulted in the election of Mr. Adams. Mr. Jefferson, receiving the next highest number of votes, was declared Vice-President, in accordance with the law as it then stood.

During the administration of President Washington three new States were admitted into the Union, making the whole number of States six-

MOUNT VERNON.

teen. They were Vermont, which was admitted on the 4th of March, 1791, making the first new State under the constitution; Kentucky, which was admitted in 1792; and Tennessee, admitted on the 1st of June, 1796.

At the close of his term of office, Washington withdrew to his home at Mount Vernon, to enjoy the repose he had so well earned, and which was so grateful to him. His administration had been eminently success-ful. When he entered upon the duties of the presidency the government was new and untried, and its best friends doubted its ability to exist long;

the finances were in confusion and the country was burdened with debt; the disputes with Great Britain threatened to involve the country in a new war, and the authority of the general government was uncertain and scarcely recognized. When he left office the state of affairs was changed The government had been severely tested and had been found equal to any demand upon it; the finances had been placed upon a safe and healthy footing, and the debt of the country had been adjusted to the satisfaction of all parties concerned in it. The disputes with England had been arranged, and the country, no longer threatened with war, was free to devote its energies to its improvement. Industry and commerce were growing rapidly. The exports from the United States had risen from nineteen millions to over fifty-six millions of dollars, and the imports had increased in nearly the same proportion. The rule of non-interference in European quarrels, and of cultivating friendly relations with all the world, had become the settled policy of the republic, and its wisdom had been amply vindicated. The progress of the republic during the eight years of Washington's administration was indeed gratifying, and gave promise of a brilliant future.

CHAPTER XXXII.

THE ADMINISTRATIONS OF JOHN ADAMS AND THOMAS JEFFERSON.

N the 4th of March, 1797, John Adams was inaugurated President of the United States, and Thomas Jefferson took the oath of office as Vice-President. Mr. Adams was in the sixty-second year of his age, and in the full vigor of health and intellect.

He made no changes in the cabinet left by President Washington, and the policy of his administration corresponded throughout with that of his great predecessor. He came into office at a time when this policy was to be subjected to the severest test, and was to be triumphantly vindicated by the trial. Mr. Adams began his official career with the declaration of his "determination to maintain peace and inviolate faith with all nations, and neutrality and impartiality with the belligerent powers of Europe."

The relations of the United States with France had been of an unfriendly nature for some time. Jay's treaty had greatly offended the French government, and the insolent conduct of M Adét, the French minister to the United States, had led to a suspension of diplomatic intercourse between the two republics. The French Directory now proceeded to manifest its disregard of the rights of America by ordering the seizure of all American vessels in its ports laden with English manufactured goods.

At the same time the American minister to France, Charles C. Pinckney, was treated with such studied insult that he demanded his passports and withdrew to Holland. Privateers were sent out from French ports, which captured American merchantmen and treated their crews as prisoners of war. France also exerted her influence with Spain and Holland to induce them to treat the United States with hostility because of the alleged partiality of Jay's treaty with Great Britain. All this while there was a considerable party in the United States which was anxious for the conclusion of an alliance with France, and which either could not, or would not, see the deliberate purpose of that country to treat with the American republic only as a dependent.

In May, 1797, President Adams called a special session of Congress and laid before it a statement of the relations with France. The announcement of the insults received by the American minister at the hands of the Directory and the increased aggressions upon American commerce, aroused

JOHN ADAMS.

a feeling of deep indignation throughout the country, and drew upon the partisans of France in America a considerable amount of deserved odium.

In the hope that a peaceful and honorable settlement might yet be had, John Marshall and Elbridge Gerry, the former a Federalist and the latter a Republican, were appointed special commissioners, and were ordered to proceed to Paris and unite with Mr. Pinckney in the negotiation of a treaty which should not conflict with those existing with other nations, and which should place beyond question the right of the United

States to maintain their neutrality. Marshall and Gerry joined Pinckney in Paris in October, 1798, and made their business known to the French minister of foreign affairs, the famous Talleyrand. He at first refused to receive the American envoys in an official capacity, and afterwards employed unknown agents to communicate with them, in order that he might be free to disavow any engagement entered into with them. It soon transpired that the object of these secret interviews was to extort money from the commissioners. They were given to understand that if they would pay Talleyrand a certain sum of money for the use of himself and his friends, and would pledge the United States to make a loan to France, negotiations would be begun without delay. The answer of the American commissioners was well expressed in the indignant words of Pinckney: "Millions for defence, not one cent for tribute." Marshall and Pinckney were ordered to quit France at once, but Mr Gerry was invited to remain and negotiate a treaty. He was nevertheless unable to accomplish anything. The correspondence between the commissioners and Talleyrand's agents was published in the United States, and aroused such a storm of indignation that the French party disappeared It never dared to make its appearance again.

About thirty thousand French exiles were residing in the United States at this time, and it was believed by the government that some of these had acted as spies for the Directory. It was known that many had abused the hospitality extended to them by seeking to induce the people of the south and west to join them in an effort to wrest Louisiana and Florida from Spain, and by endeavoring to strengthen the opposition to the efforts of the government to discharge its duty of neutrality towards the European powers In the spring of 1798, in order to remedy this trouble, Congress passed the measures known as the "alien and sedition acts," by the first of which the president was empowered to order out of the country "any foreigner whom he might believe to be dangerous to the peace and safety of the United States" By the sedition act it was made a crime with a very heavy penalty for any one to "write, utter, or publish" any "false, scandalous, and malicious writing" against "either House of the Congress of the United States or the president of the United States, with intent to defame, or to bring them, or either of them, into contempt and disrepute" These acts met with great opposition throughout the country, and the latter especially was regarded as an effort on the part of the government to destroy the freedom of the press The alien act was not executed, but a large number of foreigners left the country soon after its passage. Several persons were prosecuted under the sedition act for their severe criticisms of the government, and the result was invariably to increase the ranks of the Republican party, which steadfastly opposed the laws as unconstitutional and violative of the freedom of the people of the Union

In the summer of 1798 Mr Marshall returned from France, and his report confirmed the statements that had been made respecting the hostile intentions of the government of that country The president submitted to Congress a statement of the disputes between the two republics, and Congress, recognizing the danger of war, began to prepare for it It was resolved to create a navy, and the three frigates just completed were fitted for sea. The president was authorized to have built, or to purchase or hire twelve ships of war of twenty guns each. An army was ordered to be raised, and the prominent points on the coast were to be placed in a state of defence. Washington was made commander-in-chief of the

BOSTON IN 1873.

army, with the rank of Lieutenant-General   He accepted the position, and applied himself with energy to the task of preparing the country for defence. He gave a hearty support to the measures of the president, and used his great influence to secure for them a similar approval on the part of the people   In the winter of 1798-99 Congress appropriated a million of dollars to defray the expense of the military preparations, and authorized the construction of six ships of war of seventy-four guns each, and six sloops of war of eighteen guns each.

The energy and enthusiasm with which the Americans prepared for war opened the eyes of Talleyrand. He had not supposed they would fight, and now that he found they would, he was not willing to add to the difficulties of France by engaging in a new war. He therefore signified in an informal manner to Mr. Van Murray, the United States minister in Holland, that the French government was willing to renew diplomatic intercourse with the United States   Mr Adams, upon being informed of this, resolved to make one more effort to secure a peaceful settlement of the quarrel. He sent Oliver Ellsworth, Chief Justice of the United States, William R Davie, and William Van Murray, minister to Holland, as commissioners to treat with the French republic for a settlement of all differences between the two countries. In taking this step he greatly offended many of the leaders of his party, who insisted that overtures for peace should come from France. The most rational and probable solution of Mr. Adams' course, in the absence of direct proof, says the Hon A H Stephens, "is that he acted under the urgent private advice of Washington. Be that as it may, it proved to be one of the wisest and most beneficent deeds of his life." The commissioners were ordered by the president not to enter France unless they were assured that they would be received in a "manner befitting the commissioners of an independent nation."

Upon reaching Paris the commissioners found that a great change had taken place in the affairs of France. A revolution had unseated the Directory, and Napoleon Bonaparte was at the head of the government as first consul. Commissioners were appointed to meet the American envoys, and negotiations were begun and carried forward with such success that on the 30th of November, 1800, a treaty of peace was signed between the United States and France.

In the meantime, though war was not actually declared, hostilities had begun. More than three hundred merchant vessels were licensed to carry arms for their defence. On the 9th of February, 1799, the American frigate "Constellation" captured the French frigate "L'Insurgente," of about equal force, after a severe engagement of an hour and a quarter, inflicting upon her a severe loss in killed and wounded. Somewhat later the "Constellation" encountered the French frigate "La Vengeance," of superior force, and in an engagement of about five hours duration silenced her fire and inflicted upon her a loss of one hundred and fifty-six men in killed and wounded. The French vessel succeeded in making her escape. These successes were very gratifying to the Americans, as they showed what their navy could accomplish if given a fair trial. The news of the conclusion of peace put a stop to hostilities. The army was disbanded, but the navy was kept afloat, and the coast defences were maintained.

Before the arrival of the news of the treaty the country was called

THE SUSQUEHANNA ABOVE HARRISBURG, PENNSYLVANIA.

upon to mourn the loss of its most illustrious citizen, George Washington. He took cold while riding over his estate at Mount Vernon, and was seized with a violent sore throat, from the effects of which he died on the 14th of December, 1799, in the sixty-eighth year of his age. He was buried in his family vault at Mount Vernon, where his ashes still lie. The highest honors were paid to his memory by Congress, and by the various State governments, and in all parts of the Union a universal mourning was held for the Father of his Country. Not less sincere were the tributes paid in foreign lands to the memory of the illustrious dead. Upon the receipt of the sad news the flags of the Channel fleet of Great

Britain were placed at half-mast by order of the Admiral Lord Bridport. Napoleon, then first consul of France, caused the standards of the French army to be draped in mourning for ten days, and announced the news to the army in the orders of the day. The proudest tribute of all to the grandeur and purity of the character of Washington is the unceasing and ever increasing love and veneration with which his memory is cherished by his countrymen.

During the summer of the year 1800 the seat of the general government was removed from Philadelphia to the new federal city of Washington, in the District of Columbia. On the 22d of November, the session of Congress was opened in the unfinished capitol at Washington.

THOMAS JEFFERSON.

The elections for president and vice-president were held in the autumn of 1800. Mr. Adams was the Federalist candidate for the presidency, and Charles Cotesworth Pinckney the candidate of that party for vice-president. The Republican or Democratic party nominated Thomas Jefferson for the presidency, and Colonel Aaron Burr, of New York, for the vice-presidency. The alien and sedition laws had rendered the Federalist party so unpopular that the electors chosen at the polls failed to make a choice, and the election was thrown upon the House of Representatives, according to the terms of the Constitution. On the 17th of February, 1801, after thirty-six ballots, the House elected Thomas Jefferson President, and Aaron Burr Vice-President, of the United States, for a term of four years from and after the 4th of March, 1801.

The second census of the United States, taken in 1800, showed the population of the country to be 5,319,762 souls.

Thomas Jefferson, the third President of the United States, was inaugurated at the new capitol, in the city of Washington, on the 4th of

THE WHITE HOUSE, WASHINGTON CITY.

March, 1801. He was in his fifty-eighth year, and had long been regarded as one of the most illustrious men in America He was the author of the Declaration of Independence, had represented the country as minister to France, had served in the cabinet of General Washington as secretary of state, and had filled the high office of vice-president during the administration of Mr Adams He was the founder of the Democratic party, and was regarded by it with an enthusiastic devotion which could see no flaw in his character. By the Federalists he was denounced with intense bitterness as a Jacobin, and an enemy of organized government. He was unquestionably a believer in the largest freedom possible to man, but he was too deeply versed in the lessons of statesmanship, and was too pure a patriot to entertain for a moment the levelling principles with which his enemies charged .him. Under him the government of the republic suffered no diminution of strength, but his administration was a gain to the country

Mr. Jefferson began his administration by seeking to undo as far as possible the evil effects of the sedition act of 1798 A number of persons were in prison in consequence of sentences under this act at the time of his inauguration These were at once pardoned by the president and released from prison.

At the meeting of the seventh Congress, in December, 1801, President Jefferson, in pursuance of an announcement made some time before, inaugurated the custom which has since prevailed of sending a written message to each House of Congress, giving his views on public affairs and the situation of the country. Previous to this the president had always met the two houses upon their assembling, and had addressed them in person. A strong Democratic majority controlled this Congress, and gave a hearty support to the president. The obnoxious measures of the last administration, such as the internal taxes, the taxes on stills, distilled spirits, refined sugars, carriages, stamped paper, etc , were repealed In accordance with a suggestion of the president the period of naturalization was reduced from fourteen to five years. Measures were also set on foot for the redemption of the public debt, and it was provided that seven millions three hundred thousand dollars should be annually appropriated as a sinking fund for that purpose. Another act, of which the wisdom was not so apparent, was passed for the reduction of the army.

During the interval which had elapsed since the organization of the Territory of the Northwest, emigrants had been pouring into the southern and eastern part of it with great rapidity. In one year twenty thousand new settlers were added to the population of the Territory of Ohio The population had now become so large that the eastern part of the Northwest Territory applied for admission into the Union as a separate State. Its request was granted, and on the 19th of February it was admitted into the Union as the State of Ohio, with a population of seventy thousand.

In 1801 France by a secret treaty received back from Spain the Territory of Louisiana. The French did not occupy the country, but left it under Spanish rule. In 1803 the Spanish governor of New Orleans, in violation of the treaty of 1795, closed the port of New Orleans to American commerce. This act aroused the most intense indignation among the people along the tributaries of the Mississippi, who were thus cut off from the sea, and it was with difficulty that they could be restrained from an attempt to take possession of Louisiana.

Mr. Jefferson had long been anxious to obtain for the United States the country bordering the lower Mississippi, as he was convinced that the power holding the mouth of that river must of necessity control the great valley through which it flows. Accordingly, Robert R. Livingston, the

COAT OF ARMS OF OHIO.

American minister at Paris, was ordered to open negotiations with the French government for the purchase of Louisiana. He found this an easier task than he had expected, for Napoleon, who was on the eve of a great European war, was much in need of money, and was by no means anxious to add to his troubles by being obliged to defend Louisiana. A bargain was soon concluded by which the United States became the possessors of the whole region of Louisiana, from the Mississippi to the Pacific, embracing over a million of square miles. The United States paid to France the sum of $15,000,000 for this immense region, and guaranteed to the then inhabitants all the rights of American citizens. "This accession of territory," said Napoleon, upon the completion of the purchase, "strengthens forever the power of the United States, and I have just given to England a maritime rival that will sooner or later humble her pride."

This purchase was of the highest importance. It about doubled the area of the United States, and placed the whole valley of the Mississippi within the territory of the republic. It was naturally a most popular act, and was approved by the entire nation, with the exception of a small number of the old Federalist leaders. Congress divided this great region into two territories—the Territory of Orleans, corresponding to the present State of Louisiana, and the District of Louisiana, comprising the remainder of the purchase.

Mention has been made of the payment of tribute to the dey of Algiers by the United States during the administration of Washington. Previous to 1801 the United States expended nearly two million dollars in purchasing exemption from capture for its merchant vessels in the Mediterranean. These payments were made to all the Barbary powers, Tunis, Tripoli, Algiers, and Morocco. As the American republic lay at the other side of the Atlantic, and its ships of war were not often seen in the Mediterranean, the African pirates did not trouble themselves to comply with their agreements, and continued their outrages upon American ships in spite of the tribute paid them.

In 1801 the bey of Tripoli, dissatisfied with the tribute paid him, de-

LAFAYETTE SQUARE, NEW ORLEANS.

clared war against the United States, and a number of American war vessels were sent to the Mediterranean to protect the commerce of their country in that sea. In 1803 Commodore Preble was sent to the Mediterranean with a fleet. The frigate "Philadelphia" was stationed to blockade Tripoli, while Preble, with the remainder of the vessels, sought to punish the emperor of Morocco by an attack on Tangiers. While thus engaged the "Philadelphia" ran ashore in chasing an Algerine cruiser. In this helpless condition she was surrounded by Tripolitan gunboats and captured after a fight which lasted the entire day. Captain Bainbridge, her commander, and three hundred of her crew were made prisoners. The officers were held for ransom, but the seamen were reduced to slavery. On the 5th of February, 1804, Lieu-

38

tenant Stephen Decatur, with a picked crew of seventy-six men, entered the harbor of Tripoli in a small schooner named the "Intrepid." Placing his vessel alongside of the "Philadelphia" by night, he boarded the frigate as she lay under the guns of the castle and the Tripolitan fleet, drove the Turkish crew into the sea, set fire to the frigate in every part, and retreated from the harbor without the loss of a man. During the year 1804 the American fleet repeatedly bombarded Tripoli and did considerable damage to it. The war went on until the summer of 1805, when the bey of Tripoli asked for peace, and a treaty was made by which the Tripolitan pirates surrendered their captives on payment of a ransom, and agreed to refrain from aggressions upon the commerce of the United States in future without payment of further tribute. For some years the American vessels were safe from the outrages of the Barbary pirates.

In the fall of 1804 Mr. Jefferson was elected president for a second term, but this time Colonel Burr was dropped by his party, who nominated and elected George Clinton, of New York, vice-president in his place. Burr had at last experienced the reward of his insincerity: both parties had come to distrust him. After his defeat for the vice-presidency he had been nominated by his party as their candidate for governor of New York. He was warmly opposed by Alexander Hamilton, who was mainly instrumental in bringing about his defeat. Burr never forgave Hamilton for his course in this election, and took advantage of the first opportunity to challenge him to a duel. They met at Weehawken, on the banks of the Hudson opposite New York, on the 11th of July, 1804. Hamilton, who had accepted the challenge in opposition to his better judgment, and who had expressed his intention not to fire at Burr, was mortally wounded, and died within twenty-four hours. In him perished one of the brightest intellects and most earnest patriots of the republic. His loss was regarded as second only to that of Washington, and the sad news of his death was received in all parts of the country with profound and unaffected sorrow. A feeling of deep and general indignation was aroused against Burr, who found it expedient to withdraw from New York and retire to Georgia until the excitement had subsided.

The murder of Hamilton, for it was nothing else, closed Burr's political career. His remaining years were passed in restless intrigue. In 1805 he went west, and there undertook the organization of a military movement of some sort, which from the secrecy with which it was conducted, was generally regarded as treasonable, and intended for his own aggrandizement. In 1806 he was arrested by the United States, and after a prolonged trial, during which he defended himself with great ability, he was acquitted of the charge of treason. His subsequent career was obscure, and he died in 1836, friendless and alone. He was a man of great ability, but he failed to put his great talents to an honest use.

In the year 1807 a great change was made in the system of navigation by Robert Fulton, a native of Pennsylvania, who built and successfully navigated the first steamboat. He named it the "Clermont," and made the voyage from New York to Albany, a distance of about one hundred and fifty miles, in thirty-six hours. From this time steam navigation rapidly superseded the old system of sailing vessels in the waters of the United States, and exercised a powerful influence in the development of the wealth and prosperity of the country.

Since the beginning of the century France and England had been at war with each other, and their quarrels had drawn the whole European world into the struggle. The administration of Mr. Jefferson had continued the neutrality of its predecessors, but in a fit of mistaken economy had exhibited the greatest hostility to the navy, which had been reduced to the most inefficient state possible. The commerce of the Union had grown with remarkable rapidity, and the need of a navy for its protection was now greater than ever. The administration could not be brought to recognize this fact, however, and it regarded the navy as of no other use than to enforce the revenue laws in its home waters.

The general character of the European war had thrown the commerce of the old world into the hands of the few nations which were not engaged in the struggle. The United States obtained the largest share of this trade, but were not left long to enjoy it in peace. The efforts of Great Britain and France to injure each other caused them to extend their attacks to neutral nations. The British government, by its "orders in council," declared all vessels engaged in conveying West India produce from the United States to Europe legal prizes. This measure was intended to cripple France, and at the same time to injure the United States, which had become too successful a commercial rival to England. A number of American vessels were seized and condemned upon this pretext. Great indignation was expressed throughout the United States, but the government did nothing to remedy the trouble. In May, 1806, Great Britain declared the European coast, from Brest to the mouth of the river Elbe, in a state of blockade, thus forbidding neutral vessels to trade with any port within these prescribed limits, on pain of capture and confiscation. This high-handed measure was a direct blow to the United States. It was met on the part of France by an act equally unjustifiable. Napoleon issued his famous "Berlin decree," by which he declared the whole coast of Great Britain in a state of blockade, and forbade the intro-

duction of English goods into France, and the admission into French
ports of any neutral vessel that should first touch at an English port
In answer to this decree Great Britain forbade all trade with France by
neutral nations. Napoleon thereupon issued his " Milan decree," confis-
cating not only the vessels and cargoes that should violate the " Berlin
decree," but also such as should submit to be searched by the English.
Thus the commerce of the world was placed at the mercy of these two
nations The United States were the chief sufferers by these arbitrary
measures. Their ships were captured by both British and French cruisers,
and their remonstrances produced no cessation of the outrages It was
not possible to do anything for the protection of the commerce of the
country, as the mistaken policy of the administration had deprived it of
an efficient navy. The whole Atlantic seaboard demanded a change in
this respect, and petitions poured in upon Congress asking for the construction of more vessels of war, and for protection from the aggressions
of the European powers The only result of these petitions was a recommendation from the president to Congress to build more gunboats. It
was not possible to go to war with both England and France, and the
American government was left to make a choice as to which power it
would undertake to settle the question with. The popular feeling was
stronger against England, which, being the most active power at sea, was
the principal aggressor, and the events to be related finally turned the
scale against England.

The British government maintained the doctrine that no subject could
expatriate himself, or become a citizen of another country. This was
the opposite of the view held by the United States, which welcomed
emigrants from other countries, bestowed upon them the rights of citizenship, and in their new character of adopted citizens protected them. The
commanders of the British men-of-war were accustomed to stop American
vessels on the high seas and search them for deserters. Under this head
they included all persons born within the dominions of Great Britain,
whether naturalized American citizens or not. When found on American
vessels, these persons were removed by force and compelled to serve on
board English ships of war. The British officers did not confine these
impressments to "deserters," but seized and forced into their service
great numbers of native-born Americans, who were thus torn from their
homes and consigned to a slavery which was bitter and cruel to them.

The government of the United States addressed urgent remonstrances
to that of Great Britain against these outrages, and finally, in the spring
of 1806, sent William Pinckney as joint commissioner with James Monroe, then minister to England, for the purpose of negotiating a treaty

which should put a stop to the acts complained of. The commissioners appointed by Great Britain expressed the desire of their country not to impress American seamen, and their willingness to redress as promptly as possible any mistake of the kind. They declined to relinquish the right to search for deserters, as it would be ruinous to the English navy. The truth is Great Britain treated her seamen with such cruelty that they would have deserted by the thousand had they been assured of protection from arrest. The British commissioners declared that while their country would not relinquish the right of search and impressment, strict orders would be issued to their naval commanders to use the right with caution

A NEW JERSEY FRUIT FARM.

and moderation. The British government itself was sincerely desirous of conciliating the United States, but its naval commanders, tempted by the weakness of the American navy, paid no attention to its orders and conducted themselves with haughty insolence towards American vessels, seizing and searching them, and forcing men from their decks with the same activity as before, and rarely missing an occasion to insult the flag of the republic. Meanwhile the commissioners concluded a treaty for ten years between the United States and Great Britain. It was on the whole more advantageous than Jay's treaty, but the president was not satisfied with it, and assumed the responsibility of rejecting it, in the spring of 1807, without submitting it to the Senate.

A British naval commander now ventured upon an act which threw the relations between the two countries into a more hopeless state than ever. The United States frigate "Chesapeake," 38, under the command of Commodore Barron, was about to sail for a European station. Strict orders were issued to her officers not to enlist any British subject, knowing him to be such; but it was said that four of her crew were deserters from the British frigate "Melampus." Several British war vessels were lying in the Chesapeake bay, and one of these, the "Leopard," a fifty-gun frigate, put to sea a few hours before the "Chesapeake" sailed The latter vessel sailed before she was fully ready for sea, and the work of getting the ship in order was still in progress, when she was hailed off the capes by the "Leopard," under the pretence of sending despatches to Europe. A lieutenant of the British frigate came on board and demanded the surrender of the four men we have mentioned. Commodore Barron refused the demand on the ground that there were no such men on board The lieutenant then returned to his ship, and the "Leopard" opened fire upon the "Chesapeake" and killed three of her men and wounded eighteen others. The "Chesapeake" was utterly unprepared for resistance, and Barron struck his colors after a single gun had been fired. The four men were taken from the "Chesapeake," the "Leopard" sailed for Halifax, and the American frigate returned to Norfolk.

The news of this outrage excited the profoundest indignation throughout the country. On the 2d of July, 1807, the president issued a proclamation ordering all British vessels of war to depart from American waters, and the people were warned against holding any intercourse with them A special session of Congress was called, and the American minister at London was ordered to demand satisfaction for the outrage The British government had received information of the affair before the arrival of the American demand. The action of the commander of the "Leopard" was disavowed, and a special messenger was sent to the United States to arrange the matter. Great Britain disclaimed the right to search vessels of war, and the excitement was quieted for a time.

In December, 1806, as the outrages upon American commerce were continued, Congress, at the recommendation of the president, passed the "Embargo Act," by which all merchant vessels of the United States were prevented from leaving the ports of this country. This measure entirely put an end to the intercourse between the United States and the European nations. It was hoped by the president and the friends of the measure that it would compel Great Britain and France, by the loss of our trade, to put a stop to their arbitrary measures. Its only effects were to cause very heavy loss to the mercantile interests of this country, and to produce a general discontent throughout the Eastern and Middle States. Thousands of persons were thrown out of employment by the enforced idleness of the ships, and many of these turned their attention to manufacturing pursuits, which received a decided impetus; so that some good grew out of the embargo, after all.

In the election of 1808 Mr. Jefferson, following the example of Washington, declined to be a candidate for a third term, and the Democratic or administration party supported James Madison for the presidency, and George Clinton for the vice-presidency. They were elected by large majorities; but the effect of the embargo was seen in the casting of the electoral votes of the five New England States against the administration.

The disaffection of the New England States induced Mr. Jefferson, just before the expiration of his term of office, to recommend to Congress the repeal of the embargo act. His opinion was unchanged as to the propriety of the embargo, but he recommended its repeal as a measure of peace and conciliation. The law was repealed on the 1st of March, 1809, and in the same month Congress passed an act prohibiting trade with France and England.

At the close of his term of office Mr. Jefferson withdrew from public life, and retired to his home at Monticello, in Virginia. The wisdom and success of the general policy of his administration had far outweighed his mistakes, and he retired from office with undiminished popularity, and with the respect and confidence of the nation. Indeed his popularity was greater at the close of his administration than at the beginning—a rare and gratifying reward to a public servant. His great services in the revolution, his draft of the Declaration of

AARON BURR.

Independence, his acquisition of Louisiana, and the purity and grandeur of his character, placed him, in the public estimation, next to Washington.

CHAPTER XXXIII.

THE ADMINISTRATION OF JAMES MADISON—THE SECOND WAR WITH ENGLAND

JAMES MADISON, the fourth president of the United States, was inaugurated at Washington on the 4th of March, 1809. He was in the fifty-eighth year of his age, and had long been one of the most prominent men in the Union. He had borne a distinguished part in the convention of 1787, and was the author of the Virginia resolutions of 1786, which brought about the assembling of this convention. He had entered the convention as one of the most prominent leaders of the national party, which favored the consolidation of the States into one distinct and supreme nation, and had acted with Randolph, Hamilton, Wilson, Morris, and King, in seeking to bring about such a result. When it was found impossible to carry out this plan Mr. Madison gave his cordial support to the system which was finally adopted by the convention; and while the constitution was under discussion by the States, he united with Hamilton and Jay in earnestly recommending the adoption of the constitution by the States, in a series of able articles, to which the general title of the "Federalist" was given. After the organization of the government Mr. Madison was a member of the House of Representatives, and was regarded as one of the leaders of the Federalist party, and gave to Hamilton his cordial support in the finance measures of that minister. Towards the close of Washington's administration, however, Mr. Madison's political views underwent a great change. He was a near neighbor and warm friend of Mr. Jefferson, and

was greatly influenced by the opinions and the strong personal character of that great states- man. As the political controversies of the time deepened, he became more and more in- clined towards the Republican or "Strict Con- struction" party, and in Mr. Adams' admin- istration took his position as one of the lead- ers of that party. At the time of his election to the presidency, Mr. Jefferson having with- drawn from public life, Mr. Madison was the recognized leader of the Democratic party, as the Republican party had come to be called. In 1799 his famous report upon the Virginia resolutions of 1798 stamped him as one of the

JAMES MADISON.

first statesmen in America; and this report has always been regarded by succeeding generations as the most masterly exposition of the true prin- ciples of the constitution ever penned. During the whole of Mr. Jeffer- son's administration Mr. Madison served as secretary of state, and not only added to his great fame by his eminent services in that capacity, but prepared himself for the difficult duties of the presidency.

Mr. Madison had opposed the embargo, while sustaining the general foreign policy of Mr. Jefferson, but was in favor of the non-intercourse act, which forbade the country to trade with England and France. This act contained a clause, which provided that it should cease to apply to either or both of them as soon as they should repeal their "decrees," or "orders in council," affecting the commerce of the United States.

Mr. Erskine, the British minister to the United States, a man of noble

FALLS OF THE GENESEE, AT ROCHESTER, NEW YORK.

and generous character, was anxious that the differences between the two countries should be settled amicably, and he entered heartily into negotiations with the American government for this purpose. In accordance with the instructions he had received from England, he believed himself authorized to inform the American government that the "orders in council" of Great Britain would be revoked by that government, as far as they applied to the commerce of the United States, and to offer "a suitable provision for the widows and orphans of those who were killed on board the 'Chesapeake.'" Upon these assurances the president, on the 19th of April, 1810, issued a proclamation suspending the non-intercourse act, as to

SUPERIOR STREET, CLEVELAND, OHIO.

England, after the 10th of June following. The news was received with joy all over the country, and in the course of a few weeks over one thousand vessels sailed from the United States, laden with American products, for foreign ports. They had hardly gotten to sea when the president was informed by the British government that Mr. Erskine had exceeded his powers in promising the withdrawal of the "orders in council." The president immediately issued a second proclamation, withdrawing his first, and matters resumed their old footing. Mr. Erskine was recalled, and a Mr. Jackson was appointed in his place. The failure of the negotiation with Erskine had greatly mortified not only the president and his cabinet, but the whole nation, and Mr. Jackson was coldly

received.   That gentleman adopted a tone and style in his correspondence
with the secretary of state, which were so offensive that the president
refused to hold communication with him, and demanded his recall   All
diplomatic intercourse between the two countries thus came to an end.

The outrages upon American commerce continued.   Danish privateers almost drove the American merchantmen from the Baltic.
American ship-owners asked permission to arm their vessels for their
own defence, as the government had not a navy sufficient to protect them ;
but their petition was refused by Congress on the ground that such a
state of affairs would be equivalent to war.   The sentiment of the people
of the country was rapidly settling in favor of war, and they could see
little difference between the existing state of affairs and open hostilities.
France was equally guilty with Great Britain.   In the spring of 1810
Napoleon issued a decree by which any American vessel entering any
port of France, or of any country under French control, was made liable
to seizure and confiscation.   The decree was held back for six weeks
after its date, with the deliberate design of involving as many American
ships as possible in the ruin intended for them.   The first intimation
given to the United States of its existence was the seizure of one hundred and thirty-two American ships in the French ports.   They were
shortly afterwards sold with their cargoes, and added the sum of eight
millions of dollars to the French treasury.   The government of the
United States remonstrated against this high-handed outrage , but to no
purpose, until Napoleon's want of money induced him to adopt a more
honest course.

About the middle of the year 1810 the American minister at Paris
was informed that the Berlin and Milan decrees were revoked, and
would cease to have effect after the 1st of November of that year.   In
accordance with this information the president, on the 1st of November,
1810, issued a proclamation suspending the non-intercourse act with
respect to France, and announcing that the provisions of the act would
be continued with respect to Great Britain unless her " orders in council"
should be revoked within three months from that date.   The president
also called the attention of the British government to the repeal of the
French decrees, and as the " orders in council " were based upon these
decrees, urged their repeal.   Great Britain replied that the evidence of
the revocation of the Berlin and Milan decrees was insufficient, and that
the non-intercourse acts of Congress and the president's proclamation
were partial and unjust   This answer was regarded in the United States
as evidence of Great Britain's deliberate intention to continue her outrages upon his country and very greatly increased the popular desire for

war. England persisted in her determination to enforce her "orders in council," and even went to the inexcusable length of stationing her war vessels off the principal harbors of the United States for the purpose of intercepting our merchantmen.

While matters were in this unsettled condition the American frigate "President," on the evening of the 16th of May, 1811, encountered a strange vessel off the mouth of the Delaware. As the dusk of the evening was too deep for Commodore Rodgers to distinguish the stranger's nationality, he hailed her, and was insolently answered by a gun from her. He replied with a broadside, and after an action of twenty minutes the stranger was disabled. Rodgers then hailed again, and was answered that the disabled vessel was the British sloop of war " Little Belt " She was greatly damaged, and had thirty-two of her crew killed and wounded. The " President " was scarcely injured, and had but one man slightly wounded A different statement of the affair was rendered to his government by each of the commanding officers, and was accepted by each government. In this conflict of testimony, the matter was suffered to pass by The news of the prompt chastisement of the insolence of the British commander was received with delight in the United States, and the affair was generally regarded as, in some measure, an atonement for the disgrace of the surrender of the " Chesapeake " to the " Leopard."

The Indians of the northwest were becoming very troublesome, and their aggressions were attributed to the instigation of the British in Canada. Tecumseh, a Shawnee chief of unusual abilities, attempted to unite the Indians of the continent in a grand effort against the Americans, and for this purpose passed from tribe to tribe, from the great lakes to the Gulf of Mexico, and urged them to take up the hatchet. He was assisted by his twin brother Elskwatawa, generally called "the Prophet," who appealed to the superstitious fears of the savages by his jugglery.

The federal government determined to strike a blow at the savages before their plans for union could be brought to a successful issue. In the autumn of 1811, Major-General William Henry Harrison, then governor of Indiana Territory, was sent to operate against the tribes on the Wabash. He took with him a body of Kentucky and Indiana militia, and one regiment of regular troops On the 6th of November he arrived at the junction of the Tippecanoe and Wabash rivers near the town of the Prophet, the brother of Tecumseh. The Prophet sent several of the principal Indian chiefs to meet Harrison with offers of submission. They informed him that the Prophet would come into camp the next day, and make a treaty with him. Harrison suspected that the purpose of the Indians was simply to gain time, and that they would probably seek to

surprise him during the night, and accordingly caused his men to bivouac
on their arms that night.   His precautions were well taken.   About
four o'clock on the morning of November 7th the savages made a furious
attack on the American camp.   They were promptly received, and after
a severe conflict of several hours were put to flight.   Tecumseh was not
present in this engagement.   General Harrison followed up his victory
by destroying the Prophet's town, and building some forts for the protection of the country.   The battle of Tippecanoe quieted the Indians of
the northwest for a while, but greatly increased the desire of the people
of that region for war with England.

In view of the threatening condition of affairs the president by his

OSWEGO, N. Y., IN 1875.

proclamation convened the twelfth Congress in session a month earlier
than usual, and that body met on the 4th of November, 1811.   It was
remarkable, as was also its successor, the thirteenth Congress, for the
number of its members who afterwards took their places among the great
men of the republic.   The public men of the revolutionary period were
dropping out of political life, and new men, with new ideas, were taking
their places in the councils of the nation.   Among the new members of
Congress were Henry Clay, a native of Virginia, but a representative from
Kentucky, John C. Calhoun of South Carolina, John Randolph of Virginia, Felix Grundy of Tennessee, Josiah Quincy of Massachusetts, and

Langdon Cheeves and William Lowndes of South Carolina. There was a large administration majority in both Houses, and the prevailing sentiment of Congress was in favor of war with England. In this respect Congress fairly reflected the feeling of the country.

Under the influence of this feeling, Congress during this session voted to increase the regular army to thirty-five thousand men, and authorized the president to accept the services of fifty thousand volunteers, and to call out the militia whenever occasion might require. The vessels of the navy were ordered to be fitted for sea, and new ships were to be constructed. There was need for these measures, as the army at the time consisted of but three thousand men, and the navy of less than twenty frigates and sloops of war in commission, and about one hundred and fifty gunboats for harbor defence. The third census, taken in 1810, showed the population of the country to be 7,239,903.

During this winter the government detected and laid before Congress an effort of Great Britain to produce disaffection in the New England States, with a view to secure their withdrawal from the Union. The agent of this plot was one John Henry. The committee appointed by Congress to investigate the matter reported that " the transaction disclosed by the president's message presents to the mind of the committee

COAT OF ARMS OF LOUISIANA.

conclusive evidence that the British government, at a period of peace, and during the most friendly professions, have been deliberately and perfidiously pursuing measures to divide these States, and to involve our citizens in all the guilt of treason and the horrors of civil war."

Amid these troubles the State of Louisiana was admitted into the Union on the 8th of April, 1812. Shortly afterwards that portion of the Louisiana purchase lying outside of the limits of the State of Louisiana was organized into the Territory of Missouri.

On the 20th of April, 1805, George Clinton, the vice-president of the United States, died at Washington, at the age of seventy-three. His place was filled by William H. Crawford, of Georgia, the president *pro tempore* of the Senate.

On the 30th of May, 1812, the British minister at Washington delivered to the government of the United States the final reply of his government to the demands of this country in the questions at issue between them. This *ultimatum* was submitted to Congress by the president on the 1st of June, accompanied by a message in which he recapitulated the

CAÑON OF THE LODORE AND GREENE RIVERS, WYOMING TERRITORY.

wrongs inflicted by Great Britain upon this country, her violations of the
rights of neutrals, her impressment of American seamen, her seizures of
American ships, and her refusal to enter into any equitable arrangement
for the settlement of these questions. The determination of Great Britain
to drive American commerce from the seas was evident, and the question
was submitted to Congress whether the United States should continue to
submit to these outrages, or should resort to war to protect their rights.
After a debate of several days, an act declaring war against Great Britain
was passed by Congress, and was approved by the president on the 18th
of June, 1812. On the 19th the president issued a proclamation declaring that war existed between the United States and Great Britain and her
dependencies. Congress authorized the president to enlist twenty-five
thousand men for the regular army, to raise a force of fifty thousand
volunteers, and to call out one hundred thousand militia for garrison
duty. General Henry Dearborn, of Massachusetts, was appointed to the
chief command of the army.

The war measures of Congress were not passed without considerable
opposition. A large party, composed of some of the ablest and best men
in that body, was opposed to the war, and resented the effort to go to war
with England alone. They claimed that France had given as good cause
for war, but that nothing was said of punishing her. This was true, but
this party lost sight of the fact that the United States could not go to
war with both powers, and were compelled to direct their efforts against
the principal offender, which was clearly England. The war was regarded as an administration measure, and though it was sustained by a
large majority of the American people, there was still a strong and
respectable party, especially in the New England States, which opposed
it, and which claimed that all peaceful means of settlement had not yet
been exhausted. John Randolph, of Virginia, opposed the declaration
of war in a speech in the House of Representatives remarkable for its
boldness and vigor, and declared that he had no hesitation in saying that
he should prefer a contest with France to one with England.

Soon after the declaration of war England made an effort to settle the
controversy with the United States by negotiation. In September, 1812,
Admiral Warren, commanding the British fleet at Halifax, addressed a
letter to Mr. Monroe, the secretary of state, informing him that he was
authorized by his government to enter into negotiations for a cessation of
hostilities upon the basis of a revocation of the "orders in council." Mr.
Monroe replied that the president was willing to enter into an armistice
provided Admiral Warren had power and was willing to include in the
negotiations measures for the discontinuance of the practices of seizing

39

and searching American vessels and impressing American sailors from their decks, as experience had shown that no peace between the two countries could be lasting which did not include a settlement of these questions. As Admiral Warren had no authority to enter into these questions the president declined to proceed further, and the effort at negotiation came to an end. It has been held by many that the rejection by the president of the British overture was a grave error. John Randolph thought that all the questions at issue, save the right of a British subject to expatriate himself and receive American protection, could be settled by negotiation. That point he did not believe England would ever concede. His opinion was to some extent vindicated by the unconditional revocation of the French decrees, and the immediate repeal of the British "orders in council" upon the receipt of the news of this revocation. These measures were repealed within a month after the declaration of war by the United States. The only cause of the war remaining unsettled was the impressment question. The war thus became a struggle for the personal freedom of American sailors; and in a better cause no nation ever drew the sword

The weakness of the American navy made it impossible for this country to attempt any distant enterprise against Great Britain, and it was not believed by even the most enthusiastic Americans that we could contend with her upon terms of equality at sea. The only means by which she could be crippled by this country was by the invasion and conquest of Canada, and to this end the efforts of the United States were directed during the war It was also believed that the commerce of England could be seriously injured by the efforts of American privateers, and from the commencement of hostilities great activity was displayed in getting vessels of this class to sea

In the autumn of 1812 Mr. Madison was reelected to the presidency by a large majority Elbridge Gerry, of Connecticut, was chosen vice-president. Mr. Madison entered upon his second term on the 4th of March, 1813, some months after the war had begun.

At the outset of the war the American forces were stationed along the Canadian frontier as follows · General Dearborn, the commander-in-chief, held the right, or eastern part of the line; the centre was commanded by General Stephen Van Rensselaer; and the left was held by General William Hull, then governor of Michigan Territory The forces under these commanders were to cooperate with each other in their movements, and were to converge upon Montreal as the objective point of the campaign.

Early in July General Hull, who had seen service in the war of the revolution, collected a force of about two thousand men at Detroit. His position was very much exposed, Detroit being at that time separated from the other settlements by about two hundred miles of unbroken forest. He urged upon the government to increase his force to three thousand men, and to secure the command of Lake Erie before the British should obtain possession of it. His requests could not be complied with, and he was obliged to depend upon the force at Detroit.

Immediately upon the declaration of war the British commanders in Canada displayed great activity, seizing the most important points along the frontier. In less than a month Fort Mackinaw and other points were in their possession, and Hull's position at Detroit was surrounded

WOODWARD AVENUE, DETROIT, MICHIGAN.

and his communications with the States cut off. Hull thereupon fortified his position, and endeavored, but without success, to open communication with the country in his rear. In the meantime a strong British force assembled at Fort Malden, in Canada, opposite Detroit, under the command of General Brock, the governor of Upper Canada; and the British agents set to work to arouse the Indians of the northwest against the Americans. In these efforts they were successful. Brock erected batteries on the Canadian side of the river, in a position to command Detroit, and demanded of Hull the surrender of that place. The demand being refused, Brock crossed his forces to the American shore, about three miles below the position occupied by General Hull, on the 16th of August, and advanced to attack him. As the British army drew near the American lines they were astounded to see a white flag flying from them An officer rode up to inquire the cause The flag was the signal for a parley Negotiations were begun, and later in the day Detroit, with its garrison and stores, and the whole of Michigan Territory, was surrendered to the British by General Hull The American troops were overcome with astonishment and mortification at this shameful surrender, for the force of the enemy, to whom they were betrayed by their commander, consisted of but seven hundred British and Canadians, and six hundred Indians By the surrender of Detroit the whole northwestern frontier was exposed to the British and their Indian allies. Great Britain, unmindful of the shame she had incurred by her employment of the savages during the revolution, did not hesitate once more to devote the American frontier to the horrors of a savage war The west was greatly alarmed, and ten thousand volunteers offered their services to the government for the defence of the frontier. They were accepted, and were placed under the command of General Harrison, who was appointed to succeed Hull.

Two years later, after being exchanged, General Hull was brought to trial by a court-martial for his surrender of Detroit and his army. He was found guilty of cowardice and neglect of duty, and was sentenced to be shot He was pardoned by the president in consideration of his services during the revolution.

This was a sorry beginning for the war, and was followed by another disaster. General Van-Rensselaer, the commander of the centre of the American line, had collected a force, principally New York militia, at Lewiston, on the Niagara river At Queenstown, on the opposite side of the river, General Brock had stationed himself with a British force On the 13th of October General Van Rensselaer crossed a force, under Colonel Van Rensselaer, and attacked the British fort and captured it General Brock now arrived with a reinforcement of six hundred men, and endeavored to regain the fort, but was defeated and killed. General Van Rensselaer hastened back to the American side to bring over more troops, but his men refused to obey his orders, alleging that they could not be ordered out of their own State without their consent. The British were heavily reinforced, and the Americans were attacked and defeated, all who had crossed to the Canada side being killed or captured Among the prisoners was Lieutenant-Colonel Winfield Scott, afterwards commander-in-chief of the American army, then a young man, who had crossed over as a volunteer to aid the force on the Canada side. Utterly disgusted with the conduct of his troops, General Van Rensselaer resigned his command after the battle of Queenstown General Smyth, of Virginia, was appointed to succeed him. He made one or two efforts to enter Canada, but being each time prevented by his council of war, resigned his command

Thus closed the year 1812, and the first campaign of the war Its results were disastrous and disheartening The attempt to invade Canada had ended with the surrender of Detroit and the defeat at Queenstown. A large part of the frontier was lost, and over twenty-five hundred men had been captured by the enemy. These failures had aroused the discontent of a considerable portion of the people of the Union, and the opposition of the New England States to the war was greatly increased. Matters would have seemed hopeless had not the navy, which had been the most neglected branch of the public service, redeemed the national honor by a series of brilliant successes.

It was the intention of the government at the outset of the war to retain the vessels of the navy in the ports of the country to assist in the defence of the harbors of the United States. The fear was openly expressed that if these vessels should venture to put to sea they would certainly be captured by the British cruisers The officers of the navy were indignant at these insinuations, and as soon as the news of the declaration of war was received at New York, several of the vessels of war in that port put to sea at once to avoid the orders which their commanders feared were on the way to detain them in port, and also for the purpose of making a dash at the Jamaica fleet, which was on its way to England. They followed this fleet to the entrance to the British channel, but without overtaking it.

A British squadron sailed from Halifax to cruise off the port of New York The American frigate "Constitution," Captain Hull, while endeavoring to enter New York harbor, fell in with this squadron, and was chased by it for four days. Her escape was due entirely to the superior skill of her officers and the energy of her crew The chase was one of the most remarkable in history, and the escape of the American frigate won great credit for Captain Hull. Failing to reach New York, Hull sailed for Boston, and reached that port in safety Remaining there a few days, he put to sea again, just in time to avoid orders from Washington to remain in port

In July the American frigate "Essex" captured a transport filled with British soldiers, and a few days later encountered the British sloop of war "Alert," which mistook her for a merchantman. The "Essex" suffered her to approach, and then opened a rapid fire upon her, which soon disabled her, and forced her to surrender.

The "Constitution" sailed from Boston to the northeast. On the 19th
of August, while cruising off the mouth of the St. Lawrence, she fell in
with the British frigate "Guerrière," Captain Dacres, one of the vessels
that had chased her during the previous month. The "Guerrière" immediately stood towards her, and both vessels prepared for action. The
English commander opened his fire at long range, but Captain Hull
refused to reply until he had gotten his ship into a favorable position,
and for an hour and a half he manœuvred in silence, under a heavy fire
from the British frigate. At length, having gotten within pistol shot

COMMODORE HULL.

of her adversary, the "Constitution" opened a terrible fire upon her, and
poured in her broadsides with such effect that the "Guerrière" struck
her colors within thirty minutes. The "Guerrière" lost seventy-nine
men killed and wounded, while the loss of the "Constitution" was but
seven men. The "Guerrière" was so much injured in the fight that she
could not be carried into port, and Hull had her burned. The "Constitution" then returned to Boston with her prisoners, and was received
with an ovation. It was the first time in half a century that a British
frigate had struck her flag in a fair fight, and the victory was hailed with
delight in all parts of the country.

On the 18th of October the American sloop of war "Wasp," 18, Captain Jones, met the British brig "Frolic," 22, convoying six merchantmen. In order to give her convoy a chance to escape, the "Frolic" shortened sail, and awaited the approach of the "Wasp." The "Wasp" poured a raking fire into her antagonist, and then boarded. The boarders found the deck of the "Frolic" covered with the dead. Only one man remained unhurt, and he stood gallantly at his post at the wheel. Before the prize could be secured the British frigate "Poictiers," 74, hove in sight, and captured both vessels. The "Wasp" lost eight men in the engagement; the "Frolic" eighty.

On the 25th of October the frigate "United States," 44, Captain Decatur, encountered the British frigate "Macedonian," 49, off the Azores, and after a running fight of an hour and a half forced her to strike her colors. The "United States" lost seven killed and five wounded; the "Macedonian," thirty-six killed and sixty-eight wounded, out of a crew of three hundred men. Decatur succeeded in bringing his prize into New York.

COMMODORE BAINBRIDGE.

On the 29th of December the "Constitution," now under the command of Captain Bainbridge, captured the British frigate "Java," 38, off the coast of Brazil, after an action of three hours. The "Java" was reduced to a wreck, and as he was not able to get her into a friendly port, Captain Bainbridge caused her to be burned. The "Java" lost one hundred and sixty-one men out of a crew of four hundred; the "Constitution" lost thirty-four in killed and wounded. Among the wounded was Captain Bainbridge.

These victories aroused the greatest enthusiasm in the United States. The great disparity in the losses sustained by the respective combatants made it evident to both nations that the American ships had been better handled in every engagement. The British endeavored to account for the American successes by declaring that the United States vessels were seventy-fours in disguise, or that they carried heavier guns than their adversaries; but the thinking men of both countries saw that they had been won by the superior skill of the American officers, and that they were the plain announcement of the fact that England had found a rival capable of contesting her supremacy on the ocean.

The American privateers inflicted great damage upon the commerce of

Great Britain. During the year 1812 these vessels captured about five hundred British merchantmen, and made prisoners of three thousand British seamen. The cargoes of the captured vessels amounted to an enormous sum.

On the 8th of March, 1813, the Russian minister at Washington communicated to President Madison an offer from the Emperor Alexander of his mediation between the United States and Great Britain, for the purpose of bringing about a peace between them. The president at once accepted the Russian offer, and sent Albert Gallatin and James A. Bayard to St. Petersburg to join John Quincy Adams, then minister to Russia, as commissioners to negotiate a treaty. The British government declined the Russian mediation, and the matter was dropped.

The thirteenth Congress met on the 24th of May, 1813, and entered upon the task of providing the means of carrying on the war. The principal measure resorted to was the imposition of direct taxes and internal duties. The financial situation of the government was disheartening. The expenses of the war had greatly exceeded the estimates, and a heavy deficit had to be provided for. To meet the necessities of the occasion new loans were authorized, but they were generally paid in the depreciated treasury notes, which had been issued according to act of Congress, and did not yield much to the government. The business of the country was in a state of confusion. All the banks, save a few in New England, had suspended specie payments, and the war spirit was dying out in many parts of the Union. New England had entered into the war with great reluctance, and was a heavy loser by it. Her opposition to it was increasing daily.

The government opened the campaign of 1813 with the determination to make another effort to conquer Canada. The army of the west, under General Harrison, was stationed at the upper end of Lake Erie; that of the centre, under General Dearborn, the commander-in-chief, was posted along the Niagara river; and that of the east, under General Wade Hampton, was at Lake Champlain. Simultaneous movements were to be made from these points against the British in Canada. To oppose these forces the British stationed their armies along their frontier as follows: General Proctor was stationed with a considerable force near Detroit; General Sheaf with another force covered Montreal and the approaches from the United States by way of Lake Champlain and the Sorel river; and Sir George Prevost, the commander-in-chief, held the line of the Niagara river.

General Harrison was charged with the duty of recovering the territory lost by General Hull. Volunteers flocked to him from all parts of the west, and especially from Kentucky. A part of his force, under General Winchester, held a fort on the Maumee. In January, 1813, the British made a demonstration against Frenchtown, on the river Raisin, and Winchester sent a detachment to its relief, which compelled the British to retreat. A little later Winchester followed with the rest of his troops and took position in the open country. His whole force amounted to scarcely one thousand men. Hearing of Winchester's exposed position, General Proctor marched from Fort Malden, opposite Detroit, with fifteen hundred British and Indians, and, crossing the lake on the ice, attacked Winchester on the 22d of January, and after a desperate encounter forced him to surrender. Proctor promised Winchester that his men should be treated as prisoners of war, but in violation of his pledge set out at once

DEFENCE OF FORT MEIGS.

on his retreat to Malden, leaving the wounded Americans behind. The Indians of Proctor's command fell upon the helpless wounded men, massacred the majority of them, and carried the remainder to Detroit. Some of these they offered to release on payment of heavy ransoms; the others they held for torture. Proctor made no effort to save his reputation by protecting his prisoners, and his inhuman conduct in leaving them to the fury of the savages, in violation of his pledge, met, as it deserved, the unqualified denunciation of every honorable man. It roused a fierce spirit of revenge throughout the west.

Harrison was on his march to Winchester's assistance when he learned of his surrender. He halted at the rapids of the Maumee, and built a fort which he named Fort Meigs, in honor of the governor of Ohio.

Proctor advanced in the spring to attack this fort, and on the 1st of May opened his batteries upon it. A force of twelve hundred Kentuckians, under General Green Clay, of Kentucky, advanced to the relief of the fort, and the British and Indians were obliged to raise the siege and retreat.

General Clay was placed in command of Fort Meigs. In July Proctor again advanced and laid siege to it, but was unable to capture it. Hearing that Fort Stephenson, on the Sandusky, had a small garrison, Proctor withdrew from Fort Meigs and attacked Fort Stephenson. This fort had a garrison of one hundred and sixty men, and was commanded by Major George Croghan, a young man in his twenty-second year. He

DEFENCE OF FORT STEPHENSON.

was summoned to surrender, but answered that he should hold the fort to the last man. On the 2d of August Proctor made a determined assault upon the fort, and his regulars gained the ditch into which they crowded preparatory to attempting to scale the parapet. At this moment the only cannon in the fort, which had been doubly charged with musket-balls, opened upon them from a masked port-hole. The British were cut down by the score, and retreated in confusion. That night, fearing that Harrison would come to Croghan's relief, Proctor abandoned the siege, and retreated towards Malden.

It was clear that nothing of importance could be accomplished in this quarter as long as the British held Lake Erie. Oliver Hazard Perry, a young lieutenant of the United States navy, volunteered to win back the lake from the enemy, who held it with a small squadron under Captain Barclay. By extraordinary exertions Perry built and equipped a fleet at Presque Isle, now Erie. It consisted of nine vessels of various sizes, from one which carried twenty-five guns down to one which carried one gun. Its total armament amounted to fifty-five guns. It was manned by a small force of sailors from the east, and by a large number of volunteers from General Harrison's army. As soon as his fleet was in proper condition Perry stood out into the lake to seek the enemy. The British squadron consisted of six vessels, carrying sixty-three guns. Each fleet carried about five hundred men. The two squadrons soon encountered each other, and on the 10th of September a severe battle was fought between them at the western end of the lake. Perry at the opening of the fight displayed a flag from his vessel bearing the words of the brave Lawrence, "Don't give up the ship." It was greeted with cheers from the men. During the battle the American flag ship, the "Lawrence," was disabled, and Perry passed in an open boat, under a

DEATH OF TECUMSEH.

heavy fire, to the "Niagara," the next largest ship, and transferred his flag to her. The result was that the British fleet was defeated and forced to surrender. Perry announced his victory to General Harrison in the following characteristic message: "We have met the enemy and they are ours. Two ships, one brig, a schooner, and a sloop."

This victory was of the highest importance to the Americans. It gave them the command of Lake Erie, and opened the way to Canada. Harrison hastened to profit by it, and advanced rapidly towards Detroit and Malden. Proctor abandoned those places and retreated with his own forces and Tecumseh and his Indians into Canada. At Detroit Harrison was joined by thirty-five hundred mounted Kentuckians, under the aged Governor Shelby, one of the heroes of King's Mountain, and Colonel Richard M. Johnson. He at once entered Canada in pursuit of Proctor, and by a forced march of sixty miles came up with him on the banks of the Thames, on the 5th of October. A short but desperate battle ensued, in which Tecumseh was killed and his Indians put to flight. The British were routed, and Proctor saved himself only by the speed of his horse.

By these successes the Americans won back Michigan Territory, and for the present gave peace and security to the northwestern frontier. The Kentuckians returned home, and Colonel Lewis Cass, who was soon after appointed governor of Michigan, was left to garrison Detroit with his brigade. With fifteen hundred regulars Harrison embarked on Lake Erie and sailed for Buffalo to assist in the invasion of Canada from that quarter.

A small fleet of armed vessels was maintained in Lake Ontario by

DEATH OF GENERAL PIKE.

each of the combatants. The American fleet was commanded by Commodore Chauncey. In April General Dearborn embarked a force of seventeen hundred picked men in these vessels and sailed across Lake Ontario to attack York, now Toronto, the capital of Upper Canada. The Americans landed a short distance below the town, and advanced upon it. On the 27th of April the place was carried by assault. The British fired the magazine of one of the works from which they were driven, and General Pike, the commander of the storming party, and one or two hundred of his troops were killed by the explosion. A large amount of military stores fell into the hands of the captors. They were transferred to Sackett's Harbor.

As it was not a part of the plan of General Dearborn to hold York, the place was evacuated. Just before the withdrawal of the Americans a small building, known as the Parliament House, was burned. The British attributed this act to the Americans, who disclaimed it. The American officers believed that the house was set on fire by the disaffected Canadians, who had threatened to burn it. The burning of this building was made by the British the pretext for the destruction of the capitol and other public buildings, at Washington, the next year.

From York General Dearborn sailed to the Niagara to attack Fort George. The commander of this work, on the approach of the Americans, blew up his magazines and retreated to Burlington Heights, near the western end of the lake. Dearborn followed them in pursuit, but

ATTACK UPON SACKETT'S HARBOR.

was attacked and driven back by the British on the night of the 6th of June. Two American generals, Winder and Chandler, were made prisoners in this engagement. Dearborn fell back in haste to Fort George.

In the meantime General Prevost, having learned of Dearborn's absence from Sackett's Harbor, attacked that place, on the 29th of May, with one thousand men. He was repulsed with such vigor by the garrison, under General Brown, that he retreated to his ships, leaving his wounded behind.

Soon after this General Dearborn suffered another reverse at Fort George, and allowed a detachment of six hundred men of his army to be cut off by the British In consequence of these failures General Dearborn was removed by the president, who appointed General Wilkinson, the commander of the troops at New Orleans, as his successor.

It was proposed that General Wilkinson should enter Canada with his troops and advance upon Montreal, and that General Hampton, commanding the forces on Lake Champlain, should join him on the St. Lawrence. Wilkinson and Hampton were not on friendly terms, and neither of them were possessed of sufficient patriotism to overlook their personal differences for the good of their country. Wilkinson advanced as far as the rapids of the St. Lawrence, and sent a body of troops, under General Brown, to cover the descent of the rapids by the army. An engagement occurred at Chrysler's Farm, on the 11th of November, the British were driven back; but the Americans lost more than three hundred men. Wilkinson now sent word to Hampton to move forward to his support, but the latter answered that he had abandoned the expedition, and was going into winter quarters. Under these circumstances Wilkinson fell back to French Mills, about nine miles from St. Regis, where he went into winter quarters. Hampton prepared to pass the winter at Plattsburg on Lake Champlain Thus the expedition was ruined by the quarrels of its commanders.

In December the Americans abandoned Fort George, and retreated across the Niagara river Before doing so General McClure, the commanding officer, burned the village of Newark, in order to prevent the enemy from using it as quarters for their troops during the winter. There was no necessity and no excuse for the destruction of this village, and it was speedily avenged by the enemy About the middle of December the British crossed the Niagara river, surprised Fort Niagara, and put the garrison to the sword. In retaliation for the burning of Newark they burned every town and house that could be reached on the American side of the river, including Lewistown, Youngstown, Manchester, Black Rock, and Buffalo

The war was not confined to the northern frontier. In the spring of 1813 Tecumseh had visited the Creek tribes in the southwest and aroused their war spirit. In August seven hundred Creeks attacked and captured Fort Mims, on the west bank of the Alabama river, near the mouth of the Tombigbee. Between three and four hundred settlers, who had taken refuge in the fort, were massacred

The south was soon aroused by the news of this massacre, and in a short while a force of seven thousand volunteers was marching into the Indian country in four divisions One division, under General Andrew Jackson, of Tennessee, moved southward from Nashville; another from

East Tennessee, under General Cocke, a third from Georgia, under General Floyd; and a fourth from Mississippi Territory. In addition to these forces the lower Creeks took up arms against their brethren, and the Cherokees and Choctaws joined the Americans. The principal villages of the hostile Creeks lay on and near the Coosa and Tallapoosa rivers, and their hunting-grounds extended much farther north. The Tennessee forces, under General Jackson, were the first to enter the Indian country, and a number of unimportant encounters occurred. On the 3d of November the Indians were defeated in a bloody battle at Tallaschatche, and on the 8th of the same month at Talladega. These were hard-won victories for the Americans, and terrible blows to the savages. On the 29th of November the Georgia volunteers, under General Floyd, attacked the Creek town of Autossee, and killed two hundred warriors.

The Creeks were badly armed, but their spirit was unbroken by their reverses. Early in the year 1814 they assumed the offensive, and on the 22d of January attacked General Jackson at Emucfau. Jackson succeeded in repulsing them, but in spite of his victory deemed it best to fall back to Fort Strother. On the 25th the Indians again attacked him, and were again defeated. Soon after this Jackson, being largely reinforced, advanced into the Indian country with an army of four thousand Tennesseeans. At the Horse-Shoe Bend of the Tallapoosa the Creeks had their principal settlement, an intrenched camp, in which they had collected their women and children, under the protection of one thousand warriors. They were attacked here on the 27th of March, 1814, by Jackson's army, and their camp was carried after a desperate fight, in which six hundred warriors were killed, and two hundred and fifty women and children were made prisoners. This terrible blow put an end to the resistance of the Creeks. They sought peace, and were compelled to purchase it by the surrender of more than two-thirds of their hunting-grounds.

The year 1813 was eventful and important in the naval history of the republic, and once more the navy sustained the spirits of the country, which had been cast down by the failure of the army. On the 25th of February the American sloop of war "Hornet," Captain Lawrence, captured the British brig "Peacock," off the mouth of the Demerara river, after an action of fifteen minutes. The "Peacock" was so terribly cut up by her adversary's fire that she sank in a few minutes after she struck her flag. Captain Lawrence returned to the United States, and was promoted to the command of the frigate "Chesapeake," which was lying in Boston harbor preparing for sea. While there Lawrence was challenged by Captain Broke, of the British frigate "Shannon," which was cruising off Boston harbor Although his ship was badly manned, and his crew undisciplined, Lawrence accepted the challenge, and put to sea on the 1st of June to meet the "Shannon." The action was begun about thirty miles east of Boston Light, and lasted but fifteen minutes. The "Shannon" was in every way superior to the "Chesapeake," and the latter ship was forced to strike her flag, with a loss of one hundred and forty-six of her crew. Captain Lawrence was mortally wounded As he was being carried below his last words were. "Don't give up the ship!"—words which have since become the watchword of the service of which he was one of the brightest ornaments.

The rejoicings in England over the capture of the "Chesapeake" were very great They were highly gratifying to the Americans, and especially to the little navy of the Union, whose splendid services had won the respect of "the mistress of the seas"

In the summer of 1813 the "United States," "Macedonian," and "Hornet," while attempting to get to sea from New York through Long Island sound, were driven into the harbor of New London, and blockaded there by a British squadron In August the American sloop of war "Argus" was captured while cruising in the English channel by the "Pelican." In September the American brig "Enterprise," 12 guns, Captain Burrows, captured the British brig "Boxer," Captain Blythe, off the coast of Maine. Both commanders fell in the engagement, and were buried with equal honors.

During the summer of 1813 the British fleet of Sir George Cockburn entered the Chesapeake repeatedly and ravaged its shores. All the shipping that could be reached by the enemy was destroyed, and the towns of Frenchtown, Georgetown, Havre de Grace, and Fredericktown were plundered and burned. An attack was made on Norfolk, but was repulsed with heavy loss Cockburn then plundered the town of Hampton, and sailed to the southward The barbarities committed by this fleet along the Chesapeake and its tributaries were horrible. Neither age nor sex was spared by the British sailors and marines, and women were ravished, and old men and little children murdered, with the knowledge of the admiral, who made no effort to stop the outrages.

During the winter of 1813–14 a communication was received from the British government, stating that although Great Britain had declined the Russian mediation, she was willing to enter into direct negotiations with the United States, either at London or Gottenburg, in Sweden The president at once accepted the English offer, and Henry Clay and Jonathan Russell were added to the commissioners already in Europe. Gottenburg was at first selected as the place of meeting, which was afterwards changed to Ghent.

At this time the opposition to the war was very great in many parts of

NIAGARA FALLS.

the Union. The New England States continued bitterly hostile to it, and the legislature of Massachusetts, in a remonstrance addressed to Congress, denounced the war as unreasonable, and urged the conclusion of a
40

peace. Congress itself was more divided upon the support of the war than it had ever been. It contained many new men, some of them destined to play prominent parts in the future history of the country. Pre-eminent among these was Daniel Webster, of New Hampshire, who from the first took a high position as one of the most gifted men in Congress.

Hostilities were resumed by the Americans on the Niagara frontier with the beginning of the spring of 1814. Early in May General Brown, whose force had been increased to five thousand men, crossed the

GENERAL WINFIELD SCOTT IN 1814.

Niagara. Fort Erie surrendered to him, without a blow, on the 3d of July. On the 4th General Scott, with the advanced guard of the army, moved towards the British, who had taken position, under General Riall, at Chippewa, fifteen miles distant. Scott was joined by General Brown, with the rest of the army, on the night of the 4th, and the next day a severe engagement occurred, in which the British were defeated, with a loss of five hundred men. The loss of the Americans was three hundred.

After his defeat at Chippewa General Riall fell back to Burlington Heights, and the Americans advanced to Queenstown, but soon after withdrew to Chippewa. Being strongly reinforced by a body of troops, under General Drummond, Riall advanced from Burlington Heights to attack the Americans, followed by General Drummond's command; and at the same time General Brown, who had heard of Drummond's arrival, set out from Chippewa to attack the British. The advanced forces of the Americans were commanded by General Scott. The two armies unexpectedly met at Bridgewater, or Lundy's Lane, immediately opposite Niagara Falls, at sunset, on the 25th of July. The British occupied a strong position, and notwithstanding the lateness of the hour Scott resolved to attack them. The main body of the Americans, under General Brown, soon arrived, and the battle became general. The British had posted a battery on a hill which commanded the field, and were doing great execution in the American ranks. It was captured by the regiment of Colonel James Miller, and General Drummond, who had arrived on the field and had taken command in place of General Riall, who had been wounded and captured by the Americans, advanced to recover it. Drummond made three determined efforts to retake the battery, but was driven back each time. It was now midnight, and about eight hundred men had fallen on each side. The Americans had ex-

BATTLE OF LUNDY'S LANE.

hausted their ammunition and were dependent now upon the cartridges they obtained from the boxes of the fallen British. Finding all their efforts vain the British sullenly withdrew and left the field to the Americans. The latter were so exhausted by their hard march of fifteen miles, and five hours of constant fighting, that they made no effort at pursuit, and soon withdrew from the hill to their camp. As they had no means of hauling off the captured guns they were obliged to leave them on the field. Generals Brown and Scott were both wounded during the battle, as were nearly all of the field officers.

The victory of Lundy's Lane was particularly gratifying to the Americans. It was won, not over Canadian militia, but over veteran troops

who had served under Wellington in the wars with Napoleon. It broke
the long series of defeats sustained by the Americans since the opening
of the war, and showed what could be accomplished by American soldiers
under competent and determined commanders and in anything like a
fair fight.

General Brown withdrew to Fort Erie after the battle, and being disabled by his wounds, relinquished the command to General Gaines.
General Drummond moved forward, and on the 4th of August laid siege
to Fort Erie. On the 15th he attempted to carry the fort by an assault
at midnight, but was repulsed with a loss of one thousand men. In spite
of this reverse he pressed the siege with vigor, and in the meantime Gen-

SIEGE OF FORT ERIE.

eral Brown recovered from his wounds and resumed the command of the
fort. On the 17th of September the Americans made a sortie against
the batteries of the British, which were two miles in advance of their
camp. By a sudden dash from the fort, they stormed and carried the
batteries, spiked the guns, set fire to the magazines, inflicted a loss of six
hundred in killed and wounded upon the enemy, and retreated into the
fort, carrying with them four hundred prisoners. The American loss in
this brilliant sally was three hundred men. Drummond immediately raised
the siege and retreated across the Chippewa. In October a reinforcement
of four thousand men arrived from Lake Champlain under General Izard,
who assumed the command of the American army on the Niagara. He
was one of the old-style commanders, and at once proceeded to neutralize

the gallant achievements of Brown and Scott. He did nothing until November, when, fearing that Drummond would be reinforced, he blew up Fort Erie, and retreated across the Niagara, leaving the entire Canadian shore in the possession of the British.

General Izard had succeeded General Hampton in the command of the army on Lake Champlain. Upon his withdrawal to the Niagara, Gen-

SCENE OF THE BATTLE OF LAKE CHAMPLAIN.

eral Macomb took command of the troops that remained on Lake Champlain, and held Plattsburg with a force of about three thousand men. Hearing that General Prevost was advancing to attack him, Macomb called on the militia of New York and Vermont to come to his aid, and about three thousand of them joined him, bringing his force to six thousand men. General Prevost having been reinforced from England, advanced against Plattsburg with a force of twelve thousand veteran troops, for the purpose of invading the State of New York. Upon the approach of this force Macomb fell back behind the Saranac, a deep and rapid stream which empties into the lake at Plattsburg, and the small American squadron, under Commodore Macdonough, was moored across the entrance of Plattsburg bay. This squadron carried eighty-six guns, and was manned by eight hundred and fifty-six men. The British army was accompanied by a squadron superior in strength to that of the Americans, and upon which they depended for the control of Lake Champlain. It was commanded by Captain Downie, mounted ninety-five guns, and was manned by one thousand men.

Prevost arrived before Plattsburg on the 7th of September, and proceeded to erect batteries to cover his passage of the Saranac. On the

MACDONOUGH'S VICTORY ON LAKE CHAMPLAIN.

11th of September he made a combined attack by land and water upon the American position. The British squadron advanced to force an entrance into Plattsburg bay, and the British army at the same time attempted to force a passage of the Saranac. As the enemy's fleet advanced Macdonough called the crew of his flag-ship around him, and kneeling on the quarter-deck of his vessel prayed God to crown the American arms with victory that day. After a severe engagement of two hours and a quarter the British fleet was defeated and forced to surrender, with the exception of a few gunboats which escaped. While this battle was going on, Prevost tried repeatedly to cross the Saranac, but was driven back with heavy loss. During the night the

British army retreated in disorder, abandoning their sick and wounded and a large quantity of military stores, having lost twenty-five hundred men in the engagement.

The country had ample cause to regret the weakness of its navy during this war The exploits of those vessels which had managed to get to sea had shown what could be accomplished by this branch of the public service, and our deficiency in this respect enabled the enemy to blockade the ports of the Union, and to use the Chesapeake bay with as much freedom as if it were one of their own harbors. In the summer of 1814 a fleet of sixty British ships under Admirals Cockburn and Cochrane, having on board a land-force of five thousand men under General Ross, assembled in the Chesapeake Admiral Cochrane endeavored to induce the slaves of Virginia and Maryland to desert their masters, and offered them free transportation to the West Indies and Canada. As it was not known at what point General Ross would land his troops, General Winder of Maryland was ordered to collect a force of fifteen thousand militia from the neighboring States. He proposed to occupy a central position from which he could cover Washington City, Annapolis, and Baltimore, and was anxious to call out the militia at once; but General Armstrong, the secretary of war, decided that it would be time enough to call out the militia when the British had revealed their designs more plainly. He did not believe the British had any idea of advancing upon Washington, and thought Baltimore could defend itself. Mr Madison submitted to the decision of the secretary of war, and the national capital was left defenceless.

In the meantime, the British commanders, learning the exposed condition of the city of Washington, determined to attack it. They divided their fleet for this purpose, one portion ascending the Potomac, and another the Patuxent. The latter division conveyed the troops of General Ross, and landed them at Benedict, on the Patuxent, about fifty miles from Washington. General Ross at once set out for Washington, advancing slowly and meeting with no resistance. As he had no horses, his troops were obliged to drag their three or four cannon by hand, and the British made but about ten miles a day A few determined troops might have driven them back, and the roads might at least have been obstructed and the progress of the enemy impeded.

General Winder gathered a small force of militia, and took position at Bladensburg, on the east branch of the Potomac, about three miles from Washington. He was joined here by Commodore Barney with five hundred sailors and marines from the gunboat flotilla in the Patuxent, which Barney, unable to offer any resistance, had burned upon the approach of

VIEW ON THE GREENE RIVER AT THE CROSSING OF THE UNION PACIFIC RAILROAD, WYOMING TERRITORY.

the British fleet On the 24th of August the British reached Bladens-burg, and attacked the force under General Winder The militia fled at the first fire, but Barney and his sailors and marines stood their ground, and served their guns with vigor until their position was turned on both flanks by the superior force of the enemy, when they retreated, leaving their guns and wounded in the hands of the victors. The so-called battle of Bladensburg was little more than a skirmish

General Ross halted to rest his men, who were worn out with the heat, and towards sunset resumed his march, and entered Washington a little before dark The government had abandoned the city some hours before, and had removed the greater part of its papers and archives, and such public property as could be carried away, and only a few frightened citizens remained in the town. Admiral Cochrane had some time before announced that the British forces were ordered "to destroy and lay waste all towns and districts of the United States found accessi-ble to the attack of British armaments," and the army of General Ross now proceeded to carry out these infamous instructions They burned the capitol, and with it the library of Congress, the buildings occupied by the treasury and state departments, and plundered the president's mansion and set it on fire. A number of stores and private dwellings were also pillaged and set on fire. The navy yard, with all its contents and several vessels on the stocks, was entirely destroyed. The British afterwards attempted to excuse their shameful conduct in Washington by alleging that it was in retaliation for the burning of the parliament house at York in Canada, an act which had been disclaimed by the Americans and which the British had not been able to prove was their work. General Ross occupied Washington during the night of the 24th, and until dark on the 25th. Then fearing lest the Americans would assemble in such force as to intercept him, he retreated stealthily from Washington on the night of the 25th, and on the 29th reached Benedict and reembarked his troops The English vessels sent up the Potomac succeeded in passing Fort Washington, which made little or no effort to stop them, and on the 28th anchored off Alexandria Twenty-one vessels were captured, and the town saved itself from bombardment by paying a ransom of sixteen thousand barrels of flour and one thousand hogs-heads of tobacco.

After resting his men, General Ross ascended the Chesapeake to the Patapsco, for the purpose of attacking Baltimore, which was defended by Fort McHenry at the mouth of the harbor, and a force of Maryland militia and some volunteers from Pennsylvania. A force of eight thou-sand men was landed at the mouth of the Patapsco, under General Ross,

THE GENERAL POST-OFFICE, WASHINGTON CITY.

and on the 12th of September advanced towards the city, while the fleet
ascended the river to capture Fort McHenry and force its way into the
harbor. A small party of Americans contested the advance of the British
army, and a skirmish ensued in which General Ross was killed. A sharp
encounter followed, each side losing about two hundred and fifty men.
The American militia retired in good order, and on the morning of the
13th the British resumed their march towards Baltimore. The Americans were discovered in considerable force, occupying a line of intrenchments defended by artillery, and commanded by General Samuel Smith,

BATTLE MONUMENT, BALTIMORE, ERECTED IN MEMORY OF THOSE WHO
FELL AT NORTH POINT.

an officer of the revolution. The British commander now deemed it best
to await the result of the engagement between the fleet and Fort McHenry,
which was in progress at the time. The British fleet maintained a heavy
fire upon the fort, which replied with vigor, and soon made it apparent
to the enemy that they could not silence it or pass it. The attack on the
fort proving a failure, the British withdrew to North Point on the night
of the 13th, and reëmbarked on their ships. During this cannonade
Francis S. Key of Baltimore, who had visited the British fleet to obtain
the release of certain prisoners, and who was detained by the admiral

during the bombardment, wrote the famous song of "The Star-Spangled Banner," which has since become the national song of America

The Chesapeake was not the only part of the coast that suffered from the ravages of the British. The shores of Maine were ravaged with great barbarity. Stonington, Connecticut, was subjected to a four days' bombardment by a British fleet, but the militia repulsed every attempt of the enemy to land The foreign commerce of the country was completely destroyed The superior naval strength of the British enabled them to blockade the Atlantic ports so thoroughly, that the government ordered the lights along the coast to be destroyed, as they only served as guides to British cruisers.

The opposition of the New England States to the war, which had caused them such severe loss, increased daily, and at length the legislature of Massachusetts recommended a convention of delegates from the seaboard States to devise amendments to the Constitution for the purpose of securing them from a recurrence of such evils as they were suffering from The convention met at Hartford, Connecticut, on the 14th of December, 1814, and was composed of delegates from the New England States The convention was bitterly opposed by the advocates of the war, who charged it with the intention to make a separate peace with Great Britain, which would have been a practical secession from the Union. The convention continued in session for twenty days, and adopted an address to the country very moderate in its tone It proposed to amend the Constitution by making the representation in the lower House of Congress equal by basing it upon the free population only; by forbidding embargo and non-intercourse laws; and by making the President ineligible for a second term. The convention was for many years exposed to the bitterest denunciation of the great mass of the American people One of the results of the opposition to the war was the complete destruction of the old Federalist party which had opposed the war.

Previous to the assembling of the convention, the president, in hope of relieving the embarrassments occasioned by the opposition of New England to the war, advised the repeal of the embargo and non-intercourse acts and the abandonment of the entire restrictive system. His recommendations were carried out by Congress.

In the meantime stirring events were transpiring in the south. At this time Florida was a possession of Spain, which was supposed to be a neutral power. Great Britain had laid Spain under heavy obligations in her struggle against Napoleon, and the British had now no difficulty in entering Florida and using it as a base of operations against the south. Their fleet entered Pensacola harbor, and obtained possession of the forts. From this point they began to stir up the Creek Indians to make war on the Americans, and fitted out an expedition against Fort Bowyer, commanded by Major Lawrence, which defended the harbor of Mobile. On the 15th of September an attack was made upon this fort, and was repulsed with the loss to the enemy of a vessel and a number of men. General Jackson, having collected a force of three thousand Tennesseeans, marched to Pensacola, entered the town on the 7th of November, demanded that the British should leave the place at once, and notified the Spanish governor that he should hold him responsible for the

JACKSON SQUARE, NEW ORLEANS.

occupation of the town or the forts by the British for purposes of hostility towards the United States. The British immediately blew up a fort which they had erected seven miles below the town, and embarked in their ships.

Confident that New Orleans would be the next object of attack by the British, and knowing that the city was poorly prepared to resist, General Jackson at once sent General Coffee with the mounted Tennesseeans to that city, and followed with the rest of his troops as rapidly as possible. New Orleans was at this time a city of about twenty thousand inhabitants, less than one-half of whom were whites. The whites were principally of French birth or parentage, and cared little for the United States. They could not be relied upon to hold the city against the British. The defences were in a miserable state, and the people were demoralized and insubordinate Jackson set to work with vigor. He proclaimed martial law, and put down the opposition to his measures for the safety of the city with a firm hand. He called for volunteers to defend the city, and urged the free men of color to come forward and enroll themselves They responded in considerable numbers The prisons were emptied, and the prisoners enrolled in the ranks of the army. The services of Lafitte, a noted smuggler-chief of Barataria bay, and of his band, were accepted. The British had endeavored to secure the aid of this band as pilots, as they knew the coast thoroughly, but Lafitte and his men had refused to hold any communication with them

While Jackson was thus engaged, the British fleet arrived on the coast of Louisiana and cast anchor off the mouth of Lake Borgne, the shortest passage by water to New Orleans. It had on board a force of twelve thousand veteran troops, just released from the wars against Napoleon, and four thousand marines and sailors The British army was commanded by Sir Edward Pakenham, the brother-in-law of the Duke of Wellington, and an officer of tried ability, and under him were Generals Gibbs, Keene, and Lambert, veterans of the peninsular war.

The Americans had a small flotilla in Lake Borgne, and by extraordinary exertions, Jackson managed to collect a force of five thousand troops, only one thousand of whom were regulars. On the 14th of December the British sent their boats into Lake Borgne, and after a severe engagement captured the American flotilla, and opened the way to the city. On the 22d of December the British landed twenty-four hundred men under General Keene, who advanced to a point on the bank of the Mississippi, about nine miles below New Orleans. Jackson attacked this party on the night of the 23d with the regulars and Coffee's Tennesseans dismounted, and drove them to take shelter behind a levee. The success of the Americans in this engagement greatly encouraged them to hope for a similar issue to the final conflict.

The next day Jackson took position on solid ground behind a broad and deep trench that extended across the plain of Chalmette from the Mississippi to an impassable swamp, and covered his position with a line of intrenchments. The British, believing Jackson's force to be much stronger than it really was, made no attempt to interfere with him for several days, and he employed this delay in strengthening his line with bales of cotton. The British on the 28th of December opened a heavy cannonade upon the American line Jackson replied with energy with his five pieces of artillery, and the firing was continued without accomplishing anything definite for several hours On the 1st of January, 1815, they attempted a second cannonade, but the American guns soon silenced their fire. On the 4th of January, a body of twenty-two hundred Kentucky riflemen, who had descended the Mississippi to his assistance, reached Jackson's camp. Only one-half of them were armed. Jackson could not supply the remainder with arms, but set them to work to construct a second line of intrenchments in the rear of his first.

Having finished their preparations, the British erected a battery of six

THE PLAIN OF CHALMETTE—SCENE OF THE BATTLE OF NEW ORLEANS.

eighteen pounders on the night of the 7th of January, and on the morning of the 8th advanced to carry the American line by storm. Their centre was led by General Pakenham in person, and other columns under Generals Gibbs and Keene moved against the right and left wings of the Americans. The open space over which the enemy were obliged to pass was nearly a mile in width, and was completely commanded by Jackson's guns. The British advanced in splendid style, and were soon within

range of the American artillery, which opened on them with terrible
effect. They never wavered, but closing up their ranks firmly pressed
on. As they came within musket shot the Kentucky and Tennessee
riflemen opened a fatal fire upon them which literally mowed them down.
They wavered and broke. General Pakenham attempted to rally them,
and was shot down. Generals Gibbs and Keene were wounded while
engaged in the same attempt, the latter mortally. The command devolved
upon General Lambert, who made two more attempts to carry the line
by storm. Each time the fatal fire of the American riflemen drove
back the tried veterans of Wellington's campaigns, and at last they broke
and fled in confusion. General Lambert continued the retreat to the

BATTLE OF NEW ORLEANS.

shore of the gulf, where the British fleet lay, and about a fortnight later
embarked his troops and withdrew.

The American loss in the battle of New Orleans was seven killed and
six wounded. The British lost two thousand in killed and wounded.

The victory was of the highest importance. It saved not only New
Orleans but the mouth of the Mississippi from British control. Had
the army of General Pakenham been successful, there is good reason to
believe that England would have refused to relinquish the Mississippi,
and the war would have gone on, or peace would have been made with
the mouth of the great river under the control of England. The victory
closed the war, and was won as we shall see three weeks after the treaty
of peace was signed.

At sea the war was carried on by the few American cruisers that managed to elude the blockade of our coast. The frigate " Essex," Commodore Porter, went to sea in 1813, and made a number of captures in the Atlantic. Learning that the British whalers, which had been armed for the purpose of capturing American vessels engaged in the same trade, were doing considerable damage in the Pacific, Commodore Porter sailed around Cape Horn and entered that ocean. He captured twelve armed British whalers in the course of a few months, and then learning that the British frigate " Phœbe " had been sent in pursuit of him, Porter sailed to Valparaiso to look for her While he lay there the " Phœbe," accompanied by the English sloop of war " Cherub," arrived off the harbor. The " Phœbe " was herself a full match for the " Essex," but Porter resolved to fight both vessels As he was leaving the harbor a sudden squall carried away his main topmast, and left him at the mercy of his enemies, which at once attacked him. His defence was one of the most gallant and desperate in history, but he was forced to surrender, but not until he had lost fifty-eight of his crew killed, and sixty-six wounded

In January, 1815, the frigate " President," Commodore Decatur, managed to elude the blockade of New York and get to sea She was chased by a British squadron of five vessels, and a running fight ensued. Being entirely disabled, the " President " was forced to surrender.

In February, 1815, while cruising off the port of Lisbon, one fine moonlight night, the " Constitution," Captain Stewart, encountered two British sloops of war, the " Cyane," 24, and the " Levant," 18, and captured both of them after a short engagement These vessels were captured after peace was signed, and were restored to the British. On the 23d of March, the " Hornet," Captain Biddle, captured the British brig " Penguin " off the Cape of Good Hope The " Penguin " was so much injured that Biddle was forced to destroy her On the 30th of June the " Peacock," Captain Warrington, ignorant of the close of the war, captured the " Nautilus " in the East Indies. The latter vessel was restored to the British. Thus the war, which opened so gloomily for the Americans, closed with a series of brilliant successes for them.

In the meantime negotiations for peace had been conducted between the American and British commissioners at Ghent, in Belgium. The American commissioners had been instructed to demand the settlement of the impressment question, and at the same time to give assurance that upon the relinquishment of that claim by England Congress would enact a law forbidding the enlistment of English sailors in either the navy or merchant service of the United States. On the 14th of December, 1814, the labors of the commissioners were brought to a close, and a treaty of peace

41

between the United States and Great Britain was signed. The treaty provided that all places captured by either party during the war should be restored to their rightful possessors. Arrangements were made for determining the northwest boundary of the United States, and for settling matters of minor importance. The treaty was silent on the subject of impressments, the cause of the war. Nevertheless Great Britain ceased to exercise her claim to this right as regarded the United States, and has not since attempted to revive it, so that the object of the war, the protection of American sailors from impressment by England, was attained after all. The treaty was unanimously ratified by the Senate, and on the 18th of February peace was proclaimed by the president. A few

THE " HORNET " AND THE " PENGUIN."

days later the president recommended to Congress the passage of a law forbidding the enlistment of foreign seamen in American vessels.

The proclamation of peace was hailed with delight in all parts of the country, especially in the Atlantic cities, which had suffered heavily by the war, and the national rejoicings were intensified by the news which arrived a few days later of the brilliant victory of New Orleans.

Soon after the conclusion of peace with Great Britain, the United States were called upon to punish the insolence of the dey of Algiers. That ruler, thinking that the United States were too much crippled by their recent conflict with Great Britain to punish his insolence, suddenly made war upon it. He threatened to reduce Mr. Lear, the American

consul, to slavery, and compelled him to purchase his liberty and that of
his family by the payment of a large ransom. Several American merchantmen were captured by the Algerine pirates, and their crews reduced
to slavery. The excuse offered by the dey for these outrages was that
the presents of the American government were not satisfactory.

The government of the United States determined to compel the Barbary powers to make a definite settlement of the questions at issue
between them and this country, and in May, 1815, Commodore Decatur
was despatched to the Mediterranean with a fleet of ten vessels, three of
which were frigates. He was ordered to compel the dey to make satis-

COMMODORE DECATUR.

faction for his past outrages, and to give a guarantee for his future good
conduct. On the voyage out Decatur fell in with the largest frigate in
the Algerine service, near Gibraltar, on the 17th of June, and captured
her after a fight of thirty minutes. On the 19th another Algerine cruiser
was taken. The fleet then proceeded to Algiers, but upon its arrival
found the dey in a very humble frame of mind. The loss of his two
best ships, and the determined aspect of the Americans, terrified him into
submission, and he humbly sued for peace. He was required to come on
board of Decatur's flag-ship, and there sign a humiliating treaty with the
United States, by which he bound himself to indemnify the Americans
from whom he had extorted ransoms, to surrender all his prisoners uncon-

ditionally, to renounce all claim to tribute from the American government, and to cease from molesting American vessels in future.

The difficulty with Algiers having been satisfactorily settled, Decatur sailed to Tunis and Tripoli, and demanded of the government of each of those countries indemnity for some American vessels which had been captured by the British in their harbors with their connivance. The demand was coupled in each case with a threat of bombardment, and was complied with. About the middle of the summer Commodore Bainbridge joined Decatur with the "Independence," 74, the "Congress," and several other vessels, but the energetic Decatur had settled all the difficulties, and had so humbled the Barbary powers that they never again renewed their aggressions upon American commerce. The American fleet then visited the principal ports of the Mediterranean. The brilliant record made by the navy during the war with England secured it a flattering reception everywhere.

In the autumn of 1815 the Indian tribes deprived of the support of Great Britain made peace with each other and with the United States. The northwestern frontier was thus secured against the further hostility of the savages.

The finances of the country were in a wretched condition at the close of the war. All the banks but those of New England had suspended specie payments, and none were now in a condition to return to a specie basis. The public debt was over $100,000,000, and there was a general lack of confidence throughout the country. Mr. A. J. Dallas, the secretary of the treasury, in view of the general distress, proposed to abolish a number of the internal taxes which had been levied for the support of the war. In their place he advised the imposition upon imports from foreign countries of duties sufficiently high not only to afford a revenue, but also to protect the manufactures which had sprung up during the war, and which were threatened with ruin by the competition of European goods. The president, in his annual message, warmly recommended such a course. Another important measure was also enacted. The charter of the first Bank of the United States expired in 1811. Efforts had been made, without success, to obtain its renewal, and Mr. Madison, in January, 1814, had vetoed a bill for this purpose which had passed both Houses of Congress. In the spring of 1816 a bill was passed by Congress chartering a new Bank of the United States for twenty years, with a capital of $35,000,000, and received the president's signature on the 10th of April. It was located in Philadelphia, but had branches in other States. It gave the people a uniform currency, good in all parts of the country, and redeemable on demand in gold and silver, and thus did much to remedy the financial difficulties of the times. Somewhat later a law was passed requiring that all sums of money due the United States should be paid in gold or silver coin, "in treasury notes, in notes of the Bank of the United States, or in notes of banks payable, and paid on demand, in specie."

On the 19th of April, 1816, the Territory of Indiana was admitted into the Union as a State, making the nineteenth member of the Confederacy.

COAT OF ARMS OF INDIANA.

The presidential election took place in the fall of 1816. Mr. Madison having declined to be a candidate for a third term, the Democratic party nominated James Monroe, of Virginia, for President, and Daniel D. Tompkins, of New York, for Vice-President, and elected them by large majorities over the Federal candidates, who were: For President, Rufus King, of New York; for Vice-President, John Howard, of Maryland.

CHAPTER XXXIV.

THE ADMINISTRATIONS OF JAMES MONROE AND JOHN QUINCY ADAMS.

Inauguration of Mr. Monroe—His Tour through the Eastern States—Admission of Mississippi into the Union—Troubles with the Indians—General Jackson's Vigorous Measures against the Spaniards in Florida—Purchase of Florida by the United States—Illinois becomes a State—The First Steamship—Maine admitted into the Union—The Slavery Question—The Missouri Compromise—Admission of Missouri as a State—The Fourth Census—Re-election of Mr. Monroe—The Tariff—Protective Policy of the Government—Recognition of the Spanish Republics—The Monroe Doctrine—Visit of Lafayette to the United States—Retirement of Mr. Monroe—John Quincy Adams elected President—His Inauguration—Rapid Improvement of the Country—Increase of Wealth and Prosperity—Internal Improvements—The Creek Lands in Georgia ceded to the United States—Death of Thomas Jefferson and John Adams—The Anti-Masons—The Tariff of 1828—Andrew Jackson elected President of the United States.

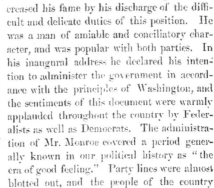

JAMES MONROE was inaugurated President of the United States, at Washington, on the 4th of March, 1817. He had served during the revolution in the army of the United States, and had entered Congress soon after the formation of the government as a representative from Virginia, and had won great credit by his services in that body. He had been secretary of state during the eight years of Mr. Madison' administration, and had greatly increased his fame by his discharge of the difficult and delicate duties of this position. He was a man of amiable and conciliatory character, and was popular with both parties. In his inaugural address he declared his intention to administer the government in accordance with the principles of Washington, and the sentiments of this document were warmly applauded throughout the country by Federalists as well as Democrats. The administration of Mr. Monroe covered a period generally known in our political history as "the era of good feeling." Party lines were almost blotted out, and the people of the country were more united than at any previous or subsequent period in the support of national measures.

JAMES MONROE.

A few months after his inauguration President Monroe made a tour through the Eastern States. He was received with marked attention everywhere, and the Federalist city of Boston entertained him with the cordial hospitality which is one of her characteristics

On the 10th of December, 1817, the western portion of the Territory of Mississippi was admitted into the Union as the State of Mississippi The eastern portion of the former Territory was erected into the Territory of Alabama, for which a government was provided by Congress.

Towards the close of the year 1817 the Seminole Indians, whose lands lay within the Spanish province of Florida, began to commit depredations along the borders of Georgia and Alabama Territory They were joined by the Creeks, and their operations soon became so important as to demand the immediate action of the federal government General Gaines, commanding the federal troops in Alabama, attempted to check the Indians, but his forces were inadequate to the task, and he was compelled to ask assistance of the government. General Jackson, commanding the southern department, was ordered to call out the militia and take the field against the Indians. He collected a force of one thousand mounted Tennesseeans, and in March, 1818, invaded the Indian country, and in a few weeks laid it waste, the villages and corn-fields were burned, and the cattle captured or killed

COAT OF ARMS OF MISSISSIPPI

Being satisfied that the Spaniards in Florida had incited the Indians to make war on the United States, General Jackson, as soon as he had punished the Indians, marched into Florida and seized St Marks, on Appalachee bay, the only fortified town of the Spaniards in that part of Florida An armed American vessel, cruising off the Florida coast, hoisted the British colors, and two prominent hostile Creek chiefs were decoyed on board, and were summarily hanged by order of Jackson In one of his forays against the Indians Jackson captured two British traders, Robert C Ambrister, or Ambrister, and Alexander Arbuthnot They were accused of aiding the Indians, were tried and found guilty by a court-martial, and were promptly hanged The Spanish governor indignantly protested against the invasion of Florida, but Jackson, unmoved by this protest, advanced in May to Pensacola, the seat of the Spanish provincial government, which place was immediately surrendered to him. The Spanish governor fled to Fort Barrancas, below the town. Jackson attacked the fort and compelled it to surrender after a brief resistance, whereupon the governor continued his flight to Havana. The invasion of Florida by Jackson drew forth an indignant protest from the Spanish government, but his conduct was sustained by a decisive majority in both Houses of Congress. The Spanish government did not press the matter, as negotiations were soon entered upon which brought about an amicable settlement of the difficulty.

The Spanish kingdom was indebted to certain citizens of the United States in sums amounting in the aggregate to $5,000,000. Spain instructed her minister at Washington to conclude a treaty with the United States ceding Florida to them as an equivalent for these claims. The treaty was arranged in 1819. Spain ceded to the United States all her claims to East and West Florida, and to the territory claimed by her on the Pacific coast north of 42 degrees of north latitude, and the federal government assumed the Spanish debt to the citizens of this country. Two years later this treaty was ratified by Spain, and on the 22d of April, 1821, the president formally announced the acquisition of Florida

by the United States. This purchase also included the territory in Oregon claimed by Spain, and embraced an area of 367,320 square miles. Florida was at once organized as a Territory, and General Jackson was appointed its first governor.

COAT OF ARMS OF ILLINOIS.

On the 3d of December, 1818, the Territory of Illinois was admitted into the Union as a State.

The year 1819 was marked by an event of great importance in the history of the world. Steam had been used for some time in the inland navigation of the Union, but it was not generally believed it could be applied to sea-going vessels. The steamship "Savannah," built in New York, but owned in the city from which she was named, made a successful voyage from New York to Savannah in the early part of 1819. In May of that year she sailed from Savannah for Liverpool, and reached that port in safety. From Liverpool she subsequently made a voyage to St. Petersburg. She was the first steam vessel that ever crossed the Atlantic, and, wherever she went, was an object of the greatest interest. The question of steam navigation on the ocean was thus satisfactorily settled by America.

On the 14th of December, 1819, Alabama was admitted into the Union as a State, making the total number of States twenty-two.

On the 15th of March, 1820, Maine, which had formed a part of

Massachusetts, but had been ceded by that State to the general government, was admitted into the Union as a State. The object of the erection of this new State was to offset the growing power of the Southern States by the creation of a new member of the Union in New England. The number of the New England States was thus increased to six.

For some years past the question of African slavery in the States had been assuming an important and alarming position in the public mind. The States of the north and west had gotten rid of such negro slaves as they had originally possessed, and had forbidden their citizens to own or bring within their limits for purposes of labor any persons of this class. The Southern States, on the other hand, comprised a region in which slave labor was particularly profitable, and it was believed by the

COAT OF ARMS OF ALABAMA.

people of this region that the industry of many parts of the south could not be properly developed by white men, as the climate was more unsuited to them than to the negroes. The production of cotton, rice, sugar, and tobacco depended on the labor of the negro, and in the States where those great staples were raised slavery was regarded as a necessity. At the period we are now considering slavery existed in the States of Delaware, Maryland, Virginia, North and South Carolina, Georgia, Alabama, Louisiana, Mississippi, Tennessee, and Kentucky. Being

COAT OF ARMS OF MAINE.

regarded by these States as necessary to their prosperity, they considered any and all plans for its removal as attacks upon their chief source of wealth.

In the non-slaveholding States the feeling that slavery was sinful had been gradually gaining ground, and there were many persons in the south who held the same views. Certain religious bodies in the country had distinctly expressed their belief that it was contrary to the teachings of Christianity to own slaves, and memorials had been presented to the legislatures of some of the States, and to the Congress of the United States, praying for the abolition of slavery.

The law for the organization of the Northwest Territory forbade the admission of slavery into the States to be formed out of that Territory, and thus secured them for free labor. Though Congress did not hesitate to legislate upon the subject of slavery in this case, it steadily refused to comply with the demands of the petitions presented to it praying it to take measures for the abolition of slavery throughout the nation. The existence of slavery within the individual States was recognized and protected by the Constitution, and Congress held that it had no right to interfere with the domestic relations of those States in which slavery, thus recognized and protected, was established.

In February, 1819, the Territory of Missouri, which was formed out

COTTON PLANTATION.

of a part of the Louisiana purchase, asked permission to form a constitution preparatory to being admitted into the Union as a State. When the bill for this purpose was presented to the House of Representatives on the 13th of February, Mr. Tallmadge, of New York, proposed to insert a clause providing " that the further introduction of slavery, or involuntary servitude, be prohibited, except for the punishment of crimes whereof the party shall have been duly convicted: and that all children born in said State, after the admission thereof into the Union, shall be free at the age of twenty-five years."

The announcement of this amendment produced a great sensation in the House, and throughout the country. It was believed by the advocates of slavery that the resolutions of the House of Representatives of 1790, in reply to the first petition presented to it for the abolition of slavery, had settled the question of the powers of the federal government respecting slavery. No effort had been made to revive the subject in the admission of Kentucky, Tennessee, Louisiana, Mississippi, or Alabama, in each of which States negro slavery existed. Many of the most determined opponents of slavery believed that, under the constitution and the Louisiana treaty with France, Congress had no right to adopt the proposed restriction upon the admission of Missouri as a State. Among these were Mr Jefferson, then living in retirement at Monticello, and John Quincy Adams, the secretary of state in Mr Monroe's cabinet. Both of these gentlemen were sincerely desirous of the abolition of slavery. Mr Jefferson believed that the States alone had power to legislate upon the subject within their respective limits. The opponents of slavery, on the other hand, contended that while Congress had no power to interfere with slavery in the thirteen original States, it had full power to legislate concerning it in the Territories, which were the common property of the States north and south. The advocates of slavery contended that, as the treaty under which the Louisiana purchase was made contained a pledge to the inhabitants of that Territory that they should enjoy "all the privileges of citizens of the United States," such a restriction as that proposed by Mr. Tallmadge would be a violation of this pledge. They claimed also that as slaves were property, and the Territories the common possession of the States, the citizens of the slaveholding States had the right to carry their property into the Territories, and that the prohibition of slavery in the Territories would be to deprive the south of her share in their enjoyment. The anti-slavery advocates replied to this, that slave and free labor could not coexist on the same soil, and that to allow slavery in the Territories would be to drive free labor out of them; and that it would be a great wrong to allow the introduction of a few hundred thousand slaves at the cost of driving millions of free men from the Territories.

The discussion of this question produced intense feeling between the Northern and Southern States, and the sectional division of the country was drawn too deep to be effaced while the cause of it remained. It was very clear to thinking men that the feelings aroused by this controversy could not be quieted until the institution of slavery should be abolished throughout the country, or should be introduced into every new State formed out of the Territories remaining to the republic. The excitement deepened daily, and at one time became so intense as to threaten the existence of the Union. Good men of all parties gave their best efforts to the task of effecting a settlement of the difficulty, but amid the storm of passion which was aroused by the debate in Congress it was hard to accomplish anything

The bill allowing the people of Missouri to form a State constitution passed the House of Representatives with Mr. Tallmadge's amendment by a small majority. It was defeated in the Senate. When Congress met again in December, 1819, the debate was renewed upon the Missouri question The House again passed the bill forbidding the existence of slavery in Missouri The Senate struck out Mr Tallmadge's amendment, and added to the House bill, as a substitute for it, a proviso offered by Mr. Thomas, of Illinois, that slavery should not exist in any part of the Louisiana Territory north of 36 degrees and 30 minutes north latitude, and west of the proposed State of Missouri, or in any State to be formed out of this Territory. The House refused to accept the Senate's amendment, and in order to adjust their differences a committee of conference was appointed by the two Houses.

Maine, whose admission we have related, was an applicant for admission into the Union at this time, and it was contended by the south that it was unjust to admit her without any restriction as to her domestic institutions, and yet to impose upon Missouri a restriction which would deprive a large part of her population of their property, and close the State against emigration from the south. The result of the committee of conference was that after long and exciting debates the amendment offered by Mr Thomas, of Illinois, was accepted. Maine was admitted as a free State It was enacted by Congress that slavery should never exist north of the line of 36 degrees 30 minutes north latitude ; and that Missouri should be admitted into the Union as a slave State upon the adoption of a constitution by her people This was regarded as an equitable settlement of the difficulty, and the measure is known as the Missouri Compromise. The act for the admission of Maine received the president's approval on the 3d of March, 1820, and the State was admitted into the Union under it on the 15th of March The separate act in relation to Missouri was approved by the president on the 8th of March, 1820 Its title shows its object. It was, "An act to authorize the people of Missouri Territory to form a constitution and State government, and for the admission of such State into the Union on an equal footing with the original States, and to prohibit slavery in certain

Territories." As we shall see the State of Missouri was not admitted into the Union under the famous Missouri Compromise

When Congress met in December, 1820, the constitution adopted by Missouri was presented to that body. It contained a clause which prevented free people of color from settling in the State "This clause," says Colonel Benton, "was adopted for the sake of peace—for the sake of internal tranquillity—and to prevent the agitation of the slave question" * It was objected to in Congress by the party that had previously opposed the admission of Missouri as a slave State This party argued that the constitution required that the citizens of one State should be entitled to the privileges of citizens in the other States; and that as some of the States recognized free people of color as citizens, this provision of the Missouri constitution was in open hostility to the constitution of the United States, since it deprived the citizens of some of the States of their rights. The friends of the compromise measure were astounded, as they had supposed that it had removed all obstacles to the admission of Missouri, which had already exercised the privileges of a State in electing senators and representatives to Congress, and in taking part in the presidential election of 1820 The subject was reopened in Congress in all its bitterness, and the country again plunged into profound agitation

At this juncture Henry Clay exerted himself with great energy to bring about a settlement of the dispute He induced the House to commit the matter to a committee of thirteen, of which he was made chairman This committee advised the admission of Missouri upon the condition that the obnoxious clause in her constitution should be withdrawn and that her legislature should pass no law violative of the rights of citizens of other States. Mr. Clay supposed that as this recommendation amply met the objection to the admission of Missouri, it would remove the last obstacle to the accomplishment of that object To his astonishment it was defeated by a vote of eighty for it and eighty-three against it The struggle now became more bitter than ever. The anti-slavery party, which had by this time obtained a definite existence, were determined that the right of the general government to control the slavery question should be acknowledged The pro-slavery party were determined to resist the exercise of that claim. Threats were freely indulged to destroy the Union by the withdrawal of the States Mr. Clay, undaunted by his failure, renewed his patriotic efforts to bring about a settlement of the dispute, and at length secured the passage of measures substantially the same as those advised by his first committee The act of Congress for this purpose was approved by the president on the 2d of March, 1821.

---

* *Benton' Thirty Years' View*, vol 1, p 8.

The Missouri legislature on the 26th of June expunged the obnoxious article from the constitution of the State, and on the 10th of August the president issued his proclamation admitting Missouri into the Union.*

The slavery question was quieted for a time by the admission of Missouri, but it was not settled. We shall encounter it again and again in the remaining chapters of this work.

In 1820 the fourth census of the United States placed the population of the republic at 9,638,191 souls.

In the fall of 1820 Mr. Monroe and Governor Tompkins were re-elected president and vice-president of the United States. Mr. Monroe received at the polls a majority of the votes of every State in the Union, and every electoral vote but one, which was one in the college of New Hampshire, and was cast for John Quincy Adams. Mr. Monroe entered upon his second term on the 4th of March, 1821.

Next in importance to the slavery question was that of the tariff, or the imposition of a protective duty in favor of home manufactures. In

COAT OF ARMS OF MISSOURI.

his inaugural address the president had recommended the imposition of such a system of duties. During the war the non-intercourse laws of Congress and the rigid blockade maintained by the British fleet entirely cut the United States off from commercial intercourse with the rest of the world, and compelled the States to depend upon their own exertions for the supply of their wants. During this period numerous manufacturing enterprises had sprung up, especially in New England, where capital was idle, and labor abundant. At the close of the war the country was flooded with European goods, which were sold at reduced prices for the especial purpose of ruining American manufactures. In their weak and helpless condition the American enterprises could not endure this competition, and

---

* "A general idea prevails very extensively that Missouri was admitted as a slave State in 1820, under an agreement with the Restrictionists, or Centralists, proposed by Mr. Clay, that she should be so admitted upon condition that negro slavery should be forever prohibited in the public domain north of 36 degrees 30 minutes north latitude. No greater error on any important historical event ever existed. The truth is, Mr. Clay was not the author of the territorial line of 36 degrees 30 minutes, incorporated in the act of 1820; nor was Missouri admitted under the provisions of that act. On the contrary, she was admitted on the 10th of August, 1821, by presidential proclamation, upon the 'Fundamental Condition,' in substance, that the State government, in all its departments, should be subject to the constitution of the United States, as all the State governments were, and are."
—A Compendium of the History of the United States. By Hon. Alexander H. Stephens, p. 329.

the tariff was proposed as the only means of saving them from ruin. The first measure of this kind was passed by Congress in 1816, and was opposed by the New England States, which were then largely engaged in commerce, and was supported by the south In 1820 the tariff was revised. The New England States, which had directed the chief efforts to manufactures since 1816, had felt the beneficial effects of protective duties, and now became the warm supporters of the tariff. The south being an agricultural section had found that its interests demanded free trade, had changed its position and resolutely opposed the tariff. In spite of the opposition to the measure, however, the duties were increased in the tariff of 1820.

For some years past Mexico and the States of South America formerly held by Spain as provinces had been struggling to achieve their independence of the mother country Henry Clay had exerted himself with enthusiasm to obtain from Congress a recognition of their independence, but such a step had been considered premature In March, 1822, however, his efforts were crowned with success, and a bill was passed by Congress, in accordance with the recommendation of the president, recognizing the independence of Mexico and the South American republics, and providing for the establishment of diplomatic relations with them The next year President Monroe declared in a message to Congress that, "as a principle, the American continents, by the free and independent position they have assumed and maintained, are henceforth not to be considered as subjects for future colonization by any European power " This claim that America belongs to republicanism, and is not to be the scene of European schemes for territorial aggrandizement, has since been known as the "Monroe doctrine," and has been regarded as one of the cardinal points of the policy of the government of the United States

The last year of Mr. Monroe's administration was marked by an event of the deepest interest to the whole country. In 1824 the venerable Marquis de Lafayette came to the United States at the express invitation of Congress, to visit the nation whose freedom he had helped to achieve. He reached New York on the 13th of August, and was received with enthusiasm He travelled through all the States, and was everywhere received with demonstrations of respect and affection, and he was given abundant evidence in all parts of the country that the nation cherished with love and pride the memory of the generous stranger who came to its aid in its darkest hour of trial. Returning to Washington during the session of Congress, Lafayette spent several weeks there. Congress, as a token of the gratitude of the nation for his services, voted him a township of land, and the sum of two hundred thousand dollars. The frigate

"Brandywine," just finished, was appointed to convey him back to France—a delicate compliment, as the vessel was named after the stream on whose banks Lafayette fought his first battle, and was wounded, in the cause of American independence. At the time of his visit to the United States Lafayette was nearly seventy years old.

In the fall of 1824 the presidential election was held amid great political excitement. The "era of good feeling" was at an end, and party spirit ran high. There were four candidates in the field, Mr. Monroe having declined a third term; Andrew Jackson, John Quincy Adams, William H. Crawford, and Henry Clay. None of these received a popular majority, and the election was thrown into the House of Representatives in Congress, and resulted in the choice of John Quincy Adams, of Massachusetts, as President of the United States. John C.

JOHN QUINCY ADAMS.

Calhoun, of South Carolina, had been chosen Vice-President by the popular vote.

On the 4th of March, 1825, John Quincy Adams was inaugurated President of the United States. He was the son of John Adams, the second president of the republic, and was in his fifty-eighth year. He was a man of great natural ability, of strong personal character, and of unbending integrity. He had been carefully educated, and was one of the most learned men in the Union. Apart from his general education he had received a special training in statesmanship. He had served as minister to the Netherlands, and in the same capacity at the courts of Portugal, Prussia, Russia, and England, where he had maintained a high reputation. He had represented the State of Massachusetts in the Federal Senate, and had been secretary of state, in the cabinet of Mr. Monroe, during the last administration. He was, therefore, thoroughly qualified for the duties of the high office upon which he now entered. He called to his cabinet men of marked ability, at the head of which was Henry Clay, who became secretary of state. The administration of Mr. Adams was one of remarkable prosperity. The country was growing wealthier by the rapid increase of its agriculture, manufactures, and commerce; and abroad it commanded the respect of the world. Still party spirit raged with great violence during the whole of this period.

The invention of the cotton gin, by Eli Whitney, in 1793, by which the seed was separated from the cotton, had so cheapened the cost of producing that great staple, that it had become the principal article of export from the United States, and a source of great and growing wealth to the whole country.

Several important undertakings were prosecuted with vigor, or were completed during Mr. Adams' term of office. The National Road, a splendidly constructed highway, built by the general government, from Cumberland, Maryland, across the mountains, was completed to Wheeling, on the Ohio, in 1820, and was carried beyond that stream during Mr. Adams' administration, the design being to extend it to the Mississippi. It furnished a broad and well-built thoroughfare between the seaboard and the west, and exerted a marked influence upon the internal trade of the country. The road from Cumberland to Wheeling cost $1,700,000.

The Erie canal, extending from Buffalo on Lake Erie to the Hudson at Albany, was projected by De Witt Clinton. The plan was at first pronounced impracticable, but Clinton succeeded in inducing the State of New York to undertake the scheme, and in 1825 the great work was completed, and the waters of the lakes and the Hudson were united. The completion of this canal secured to the city of New York the control of the western trade, and added to its wealth and importance in a marked degree.

Steam had been for some years in use as the motive power in the navigation of the rivers of the Union, and it now began to be applied to purposes of land transportation. The first railroad in this country was a mere tramway, for the transportation of granite from the quarries at Quincy to the Neponsett river, in Massachusetts, and was constructed in the year 1826. This was followed by the Mauch Chunk railway, from the coal mines to the Lehigh river, in Pennsylvania, in 1827. These were merely local works, and of but little importance, except in so far as they helped to demonstrate to the public mind the possibility and the usefulness of such enterprises upon a larger scale. Charters for roads of more importance were soon obtained in several of the States. In 1828 work was begun on the Baltimore and Ohio railroad, and in 1829 on the South Carolina railroad. In the year 1827 there were three miles of railroad in operation in the United States. In 1875 the number of miles in operation is a little over seventy thousand.

For some time previous to the entrance of Mr. Adams upon office, Georgia had been involved in a dispute with the general government and with the Creek Indians concerning the lands of the latter, which the United States had agreed to purchase for the benefit of Georgia. Twenty-five years passed after the promise was made, and the lands remained

42

unpurchased because the Indians would not sell them. A treaty was finally made in 1825 by which some of the chiefs ceded to the general government the lands in question. The majority of the Indians declared the chiefs had no authority to enter into this treaty, and called upon the United States to repudiate it. It was cancelled by the general government, but the State of Georgia determined to enforce it. The general government took the side of the Indians, and for a while it seemed that an open conflict would ensue between the State and federal authorities. The matter was settled by the Creeks consenting to sell their lands and to accept new homes in the west. The Indian lands were purchased by the United States, and the Creeks emigrated beyond the Mississippi.

On the 4th of July, 1826, died, within a few hours of each other, two ex-presidents of the republic. John Adams and Thomas Jefferson; the latter the author of the Declaration of Independence, and the former its most efficient supporter. Mr. Adams died at his home at Quincy, Massachusetts, at the ripe old age of ninety years, Mr. Jefferson at Monticello, his beautiful Virginian home, at the age of eighty-two. Both had filled the highest stations in the republic, and both had lived to see the country they loved take rank among the first nations of the globe. They died on the fiftieth anniversary of American independence.

In the year 1826 a new party made its appearance in our politics. A man named William Morgan, residing in the western part of New York, published a book purporting to reveal the secrets of the order of Freemasons. He suddenly disappeared, and it was charged that he had been seized and murdered by the Freemasons in revenge for his exposures. The affair caused great excitement in the Northern and some of the Western States, and gave rise to a political party known as the Anti-Masons, whose avowed object was the exclusion of Masons from office. It acquired considerable strength in some of the States, but in a few years died out

The tariff question now engaged the attention of the country once more. The manufacturing interests were still struggling against foreign competition, and it was the opinion of the Eastern and Middle States that the general government should protect them by the imposition of high duties upon products of foreign countries imported into the Union. The south was almost a unit in its opposition to a high tariff. Being, as we have said, an agricultural section, its interests demanded a free market, and it wished to avail itself of the privilege of purchasing where it could buy cheapest. The south and the west were the markets of the east, and the interests of that section demanded the exclusion of foreign competition in supplying these markets.

In July, 1827, a convention of manufacturers was held at Harrisburg, Pennsylvania, and a memorial was adopted praying Congress to increase the duties on foreign goods to an extent which would protect American industry. When Congress met in December, 1827, the protective policy was the most important topic of the day. It was warmly discussed in Congress and throughout the country. The interests of New England were championed by the matchless eloquence of Daniel Webster, who claimed that as the adoption of the protective policy by the government had forced New England to turn her energies to manufacturers, the government was bound to protect her against competition. The southern representatives argued that a protective tariff was unconstitutional, and was injurious in its operations to the interests of the people of the Southern States, who, being producers of staples for export, ought to have liberty to purchase such articles as they needed wherever they could find them cheapest. They declared that "duties under the protective policy were not only bounties to manufacturers, but a heavy tax levied upon their constituents and a great majority of the consumers in all the States, which never went into the public treasury." The tariff bill was passed by the House on the 15th of April, 1828, and was approved by the president a little later. It was termed by its opponents the "Bill of Abominations."

DANIEL WEBSTER.

In the midst of this excitement the presidential election occurred. Mr. Adams was a candidate for re-election, but was overwhelmingly defeated by Andrew Jackson, of Tennessee. John C. Calhoun was chosen Vice-President. The election of Jackson was regarded as a popular condemnation of the protective policy of the government.

CHAPTER XXXV.

THE ADMINISTRATIONS OF ANDREW JACKSON AND MARTIN VAN BUREN.

ANDREW JACKSON, the seventh president of the United States, was inaugurated at Washington, on the 4th of March, 1829.

President Jackson was in many respects one of the most remarkable men of his day. He was of Scotch-Irish descent, and was born in North Carolina during the controversy between the colonies and Great Britain, which preceded the revolution. He was left fatherless at an early age, and his youth was passed amid the stirring scenes of the war for independence. At the age of thirteen he began his career by taking part in the fight at Hanging Rock, under General Sumter. The home of the Jacksons was broken up and pillaged by the Tories, and the mother and her two sons became wanderers. The sons were shortly after made prisoners by the Tories, and the day after his capture Andrew Jackson was ordered by a British officer to clean his boots. He indignantly refused, and the officer struck him with the flat of his sword. The boys were at length exchanged through the exertions of their mother. Both had contracted the small-pox during their captivity, and the elder son soon died of his disease. Not long afterwards Mrs. Jackson, with some other ladies went to Charleston to minister to the wants of the American prisoners of war confined there by the British

660

A fever was raging among these unfortunates at the time, and Mrs. Jackson was soon numbered among its victims. Thus, at the age of fifteen, Andrew Jackson was left alone in the world without a relative. Though young in years, he had been greatly matured in character by his trials. Even at this early age he was generous to a fault to his friends, and immovable in his resolutions when once formed.

A few years later he removed to Tennessee, then a Territory, and upon the admission of the State into the Union was elected as her first representative in Congress. His services during the war of 1812–15 have been related. His brilliant victory over the British at New Orleans made him one of the most noted men of the day, and his prompt and decisive measures against the Spaniards in Florida during Mr. Monroe's administration greatly added to his reputation.

During the administration of John Adams General Jackson occupied a seat in the United States Senate, and gave a cordial support to the principles of Mr. Jefferson. Resigning his seat in the Senate before the close of his term, he was elected one of the judges of the supreme court of Tennessee.

ANDREW JACKSON.

The election of General Jackson to the presidency was regarded with some anxiety, for though his merits as a soldier were conceded, it was feared by many that his known imperiousness of will and his inflexibility of purpose would seriously disqualify him for the delicate duties of the presidency. Nature had made him a ruler, however, and his administration was marked by the fearless energy that characterized every act of his life, and was on the whole successful and satisfactory to the great majority of his countrymen.

General Jackson began his administration by appointing a new cabinet, at the head of which he placed Martin Van Buren, of New York, as secretary of state. Until now the postmaster-general had not been regarded as a cabinet officer. General Jackson now invited that officer to a seat in his cabinet and a share in its deliberations, and his course has since been pursued by each and all of his successors.

The first important act of the new president was to recommend to Congress the removal of all the Indian tribes remaining east of the Mississippi to new homes west of that stream. Such a measure, he contended, would give to them a broader range, and one more suited to their wants, and would relieve the States east of the Mississippi from all further apprehension of Indian wars. This removal involved considerable loss and hardship to the Creeks in Georgia, who had made an encouraging advance in civilization. A bill was passed by the Twenty-first Congress in May, 1830, for the purpose of carrying this policy into effect; but the removal of the Indians was not completed for some years afterwards.

In his first annual message to Congress, in 1829, the president took strong ground against the renewal of the charter of the Bank of the

STATE-HOUSE, AT RALEIGH, NORTH CAROLINA.

United States, which was about to expire. This was a bold step, as the bank was the most powerful institution in the United States, and had warm friends in every part of the country. The stockholders of the bank applied to the Twenty-second Congress during its first session, which began in December, 1831, for a renewal of their charter, and in the late spring of 1832 a bill renewing this charter was passed by both Houses of Congress. The president refused to sign the bill, and returned it to Congress with his objections. He held that Congress had no constitutional power to charter such a bank, and regarded it as inexpedient to continue its existence. An effort was made by the friends of the bill to pass it over the president's veto, but it failed to obtain the necessary two-thirds vote, and consequently did not become a law. The bank was therefore obliged to suspend its operations at the expiration of its charter in 1836.

In 1830 Senator Foot, of Connecticut, submitted a resolution of inquiry to the Senate concerning the disposal of the public lands. The debate upon the resolution extended far beyond the subject embraced in that document, and in the course of it Senator Robert Y. Hayne, of

STATE-HOUSE, CONCORD, NEW HAMPSHIRE.

South Carolina, a brilliant orator, declared that any State had the right, in the exercise of its sovereign power, to declare null and void any act of Congress which it should consider unconstitutional. This was a plain statement of the doctrine that the Union was simply a compact between the States, from which any of the States could secede at pleasure, and it was the first time such a sentiment had been expressed on the floor of Congress. Mr. Webster, of Massachusetts, replied to Mr. Hayne, in an oration of superb eloquence. He denied the doctrine that the Union was a compact of sovereign, independent States, from which any one of them could withdraw at pleasure; and argued that the constitution was the work of the people themselves, not as separate States, but as members of a great nation, and was designed to make the Union perpetual; that the controversies between the States and the general government were to be decided by the supreme court, the tribunal created for that purpose by the constitution, and not by the States themselves; and that any attempt on the part of the people of a State to withdraw from the Union was treason. The debate added greatly to the fame of both senators, and the sentiments of Mr. Webster were unanimously re-echoed by the north, and

SCENE IN THE MAMMOTH CAVE, KENTUCKY.

by a large majority at the south. The effect of the debate was to direct the attention of the people to a study of the principles of the constitution. Different views were maintained. The Northern and Western States regarded the Union as indissoluble, while the Southern States held that it was a compact of sovereign States, and that any State could withdraw from the Union for just cause.

During the session of the Twenty-first Congress a breach occurred between President Jackson and Mr. Calhoun, the vice-president. The former was told that Gen. Jackson, that Mr. Calhoun, while a member of

Mr. Monroe's cabinet, had endeavored to prevent the government from sustaining him in his invasion of Florida in 1818. General Jackson deeply resented this, and the breach between himself and Mr. Calhoun widened daily. Shortly afterwards Mr. Calhoun resigned the vice-presidency, and was elected to the Senate by the legislature of South Carolina in 1831. In the same year Mr. Clay was elected to the Senate from Kentucky.

On the 4th of July, 1831, ex-President Monroe died in New York, in the 74th year of his age.

In June, 1832, the Asiatic cholera made its first appearance in the United States, and swept with fearful rapidity over the whole country. Thousands of persons of all ages and conditions died of it within a few months, and a feeling of general terror pervaded the country. Its prin-

GENERAL ATKINSON'S DEFEAT OF BLACK HAWK.

cipal ravages occurred in the Northern States and in the valley of the Mississippi.

In the spring of 1832 the Sacs and Foxes, and some other tribes of Indians, inhabiting the region now known as Wisconsin, made incursions against the frontier settlements of Illinois. General Atkinson was sent by the general government with a force of troops to crush them, and with the assistance of the militia, after a series of skirmishes, drove them beyond the Mississippi. Black Hawk, a chief of the Sac nation, and the leader of the movement, was taken prisoner. He was kindly treated, and to impress him with the folly of attacking a great nation, he was taken to Washington, and then to the principal eastern cities, that he might see for himself the power of the whites.

Early in 1831 General Jackson was nominated for a re-election to the presidency by the legislature of Pennsylvania. The presidential election took place in the fall of 1832. General Jackson was supported by the Democratic party, and Mr Clay by the Whigs, for the presidency. The contest was marked by intense bitterness, for Jackson's veto of the charter of the Bank of the United States, his other vetoes of public improvement bills, and his attitude in the "Nullification" controversy between the United States and South Carolina, had created a powerful opposition to him in all parts of the country. In spite of this opposition he was re-elected by a triumphant majority, and Martin Van Buren, of New York, the Democratic nominee, was chosen vice-president

In the meantime serious trouble had arisen between the general government and the State of South Carolina. During the year 1832 the tariff was revised by Congress, and that body, instead of diminishing the duties, increased many of them. This action gave great offence to the Southern States, which regarded the denial of free trade as a great wrong to them. They were willing to submit to a tariff sufficient for a revenue, but were utterly opposed to a protective tariff for the reasons we have already stated. The States of Virginia, Georgia, and South Carolina were the most energetic in their opposition to the measure, but the first two, upon its passage, submitted to it, hoping to carry out their wishes by constitutional means at some future time.

The State of South Carolina, holding the views advocated by Mr. Hayne in the Senate, in his debate with Mr. Webster, resolved to "nullify" the law within its own limits. A convention of the people of the State was held, which adopted a measure known as the "Nullification Ordinance" This ordinance declared that the tariff act of 1832, being based upon the principle of protection, and not upon the principle of raising revenue, was unconstitutional, and was therefore null and void. Provision was made by another clause for testing the constitutionality of the law before the courts of the State. The State assumed the right to forbid the collection of the duties imposed by the tariff within its limits; and if the general government should resist the course of the State by force, the State of South Carolina was declared to be no longer a member of the Union. This ordinance was to take effect on the 12th of February, 1833, unless in the meantime the general government should abandon its policy of protection and return to a tariff for revenue only

Matters had reached this state when the presidential election occurred in the fall of 1832. The country at large was utterly opposed to the course of South Carolina, and denied its right to nullify a law of Congress, or to withdraw from the Union in support of this right. Intense excitement prevailed and the course of the president was watched with the gravest anxiety. He was known to be opposed to the protective policy; but it was generally believed that he was firm in his intention to enforce the laws, however he might disapprove of them.

Congress met in December, 1832, and in his annual message President Jackson urged upon that body a reduction of the tariff. The message gave great satisfaction to the opponents of the tariff. A few days later the president issued a proclamation against nullification, moderate in language, but firm in tone. He expressed his opinion that the course of South Carolina was unlawful and wrong, and intimated that he would exert the power intrusted to him to compel obedience to the constitution and laws of the Union. He appealed to the people of South Carolina not to persist in the enforcement of their ordinance, as such a course on their part must inevitably bring them in collision with the forces of the federal government; and told them plainly that any citizen of any of the States who should take up arms against the United States in such a conflict would be guilty of treason against the United States. Referring to the action of the convention, he said: "This ordinance is founded, not on the indefeasible right of resisting acts which are plainly unconstitutional, and too oppressive to be endured; but on the strange position that any one State may not only declare an act of Congress void, but prohibit its execution; that they may do this consistently with the constitution; that the true construction of that instrument permits a State to retain its place in the Union, and yet be bound by no other of its laws than those it may choose to consider as constitutional."

JOHN C. CALHOUN.

The leaders of the South Carolina movement were Governor Hayne and John C. Calhoun, then a senator of the United States from South Carolina. Governor Hayne replied to the president with a counter proclamation, in which he warned the people of the State against "the dangerous and pernicious doctrines" of the president's proclamation, and called upon them to disregard "those vain menaces" of military force, and "to be fully prepared to sustain the dignity and protect the liberties of the State, if need be, with their lives and fortunes." The State prepared to maintain its position by force. Troops were organized, and arms and military stores were collected.

The president, on his part, took measures promptly to enforce the law. He ordered a large body of troops to assemble at Charleston, under General Scott, and a ship of war was sent to that port to assist the federal officers in collecting the duties on imports. Civil war seemed for a time inevitable. The president was firmly resolved to compel the submission of South Carolina, and to cause the arrest of Mr. Calhoun and the other leading nullifiers, and bring them to trial for treason. The issue of such a conflict could not be doubtful.

Fortunately a peaceful settlement of the trouble was effected. Mr. Verplanck, of New York, a supporter of the administration, introduced a bill into Congress for a reduction of the tariff, and the State of Virginia sent Benjamin Watkins Leigh, a distinguished citizen, as commissioner to South Carolina, to urge her to suspend the execution of her ordinance until March 4th, as there was a probability that a peaceful settlement of the difficulty would be arranged before that time. South Carolina consented to be guided by this appeal.

Henry Clay, with his usual patriotic self-sacrifice, now came forward in the Senate with a compromise which he hoped would put an end to the trouble. He was an ardent advocate of the protective system, but he

HENRY CLAY.

was prepared to sacrifice it to the welfare of the country. He introduced a bill providing for the gradual reduction in ten years of all duties then above the revenue standard. "One-tenth of one-half of all the duties for protection above that standard was to be taken off annually for ten years, at the end of which period the whole of the other half was to be taken off, and thereafter all duties were to be levied mainly with a view to revenue and not for protection." This measure with some modifications was adopted by both Houses of Congress, and

was approved by the president on the 2d of March, 1833. The people of South Carolina rescinded their "Nullification Ordinance," and the trouble was brought to an end.*

It was generally believed that the Union had escaped from a grave peril. The firmness of the president received the approval of the nation, except in South Carolina. The action of that State was generally condemned, and the result was looked upon as a decided triumph of the national authority.

---

* "Mr. Clay, on this occasion," says Hon. Alexander H. Stephens, "had to break with his old political friends, while he was offering up the darling system of his heart upon the altar of his country. Whatever else may be said of him, no one can deny that Henry Clay was a patriot—every inch of him—a patriot of the highest standard. It was said that when he was importuned not to take the course he had resolved upon, for the reason amongst others that it would lessen his chances for the presidency, his reply was, 'I would rather be right than be president.' This showed the material he was made of. It was worthy a Marcellus or Cato."—*The War Between the States*, vol. i., p. 468.

On the 4th of March, 1833, General Jackson entered upon his second term of office. The troubles which had disquieted the country had been satisfactorily settled, and the president took advantage of the peaceful condition of affairs to visit New York and the New England States. He was received everywhere with enthusiasm.

Upon his return to the capital, the president took a step which plunged the country into great excitement once more. The charter of the Bank of the United States made that institution the legal depository of the funds of the United States. The secretary of the treasury, with the sanction of Congress, alone had authority to remove them. The president was of the opinion that the public funds were not safe in the keeping of the bank, and announced his intention to remove them from the Bank of the United States and deposit them with certain State banks. The majority of the cabinet were opposed to the measure, and the secretary of the treasury, William J. Duane, when ordered by the president to withdraw the funds, refused to obey him, as he considered the president's course "unnecessary, unwise, arbitrary, and unjust." He was at once removed from his position by President Jackson, who appointed Roger B. Taney, of Maryland, in his place. Mr. Taney issued an order to the collectors, forbidding them to deposit the public moneys paid to them in the Bank of the United States. As for the funds already in the possession of the bank, it was decided to withdraw them as they were needed for the payment of the current expenses of the government. This measure was productive of great financial distress throughout the Union, which continued for some time.

The president's course also produced open war between himself and the Senate, in which body he was opposed by Clay, Calhoun, and Webster, its foremost members. He was defended by Benton, of Missouri, and Forsyth, of Georgia, but in spite of their efforts a resolution declaring the president's course unconstitutional, and severely censuring him for it, was adopted by the Senate. The president remained firm, however. He submitted an able protest against the action of the Senate, and by the help of the House of Representatives defeated the bank on every point. The Senate subsequently recognized the propriety of the president's action, and of its own motion expunged the resolution of censure from its journal

In pursuance of its policy towards the Indians, the government attempted in 1835 to remove the Seminoles from Florida beyond the Mississippi. They were unwilling to relinquish their lands; and under the leadership of their great chief, Osceola, opposed a determined resistance to the efforts of the general government. Major Dade, with one

hundred and seventeen men, was sent from Tampa bay to the assistance
of General Clinch at Fort Drane, which was threatened by the Indians.
He was attacked on the 28th of December, 1835, while on the march,
and he and all but four of his men were massacred. On the same day
another blow was struck at Fort King, many miles away from the scene
of this massacre. Mr. Thompson, the Indian commissioner, and a party
of his friends, while dining outside of the walls of the fort, were attacked
by a band of Seminoles, led by Osceola in person, and killed and scalped.

GREAT FIRE IN NEW YORK.

General Clinch at once took the field against the savages, and on the 31st
of December defeated them at Withlacoochee, ninety miles north of
Tampa bay. In February, 1836, General Gaines won an important
victory over the savages near the same place.

The Creeks joined the Seminoles in May, 1836, and the war spread
into Georgia. The former were soon crushed by the United States troops,
and were sent west of the Mississippi. The Seminoles continued the war,
and as often as they were defeated in the open field would take refuge in
the sw   it was difficult for the whites to follow

them, and from which they maintained a constant and effective warfare upon their enemies. Osceola was always ready to make a treaty, and never hesitated to break it. At last he was conquered by his own weapon of deceit. In October, 1837, he came into the American camp under a flag of truce. He was at once seized, with all his followers, by General Jessup, the American commander. Osceola was sent as a prisoner to Fort Moultrie, in South Carolina, where he died of a fever. The war went on for several years longer.

The winter of 1834–35 was one of the coldest ever known in America. The Chesapeake bay was frozen from its head to the Capes, and on the 8th of February, 1835, the mercury stood at eight degrees below zero as far south as Charleston. On the 4th of January the mercury congealed at Lebanon, New York. On the night of December 16, 1835, a fire broke out in the city of New York, and in fourteen hours consumed the greater part of the business portion of the city, and destroyed over $17,000,000 worth of property.

In the last years of his administration President Jackson brought to a successful close a vexatious dispute with France, which had long been a source of annoyance to the

COAT OF ARMS OF ARKANSAS

country. American merchants held claims to the amount of $5,000,000 against France for the "unlawful seizures, captures, and destruction of vessels and cargoes" during the wars of Napoleon. The government of Louis Philippe acknowledged the justice of these claims, and in 1831 a treaty was negotiated between the United States and France for their payment. The Chamber of Deputies refused three times during as many years to appropriate the money for the payment of these claims, and in 1834 President Jackson ordered the United States minister at Paris to demand his passports, and advised Congress to make reprisals on French vessels. This vigorous course brought France to her senses, and at this juncture Great Britain offered her mediation for the settlement of the difficulty. The Chamber of Deputies appropriated the necessary sum, and the American claims were paid and the matter settled to the satisfaction of all parties.

Claims for similar seizures were brought against Spain, Naples, and Denmark, and were satisfactorily settled through the firmness of the president. Treaties of friendship and commerce were negotiated with Russia and Turkey.

On the 15th of June, 1836, Arkansas was admitted into the Union as a State.

One of the most important acts of General Jackson's administration was the payment of the national debt. He not only left the nation free from debt, but handed over to his successor a surplus of forty millions of dollars in the national treasury.

On the 28th of June, 1836, ex-President James Madison died at Montpelier, his home, in Virginia, in the eighty-sixth year of his age.

The presidential election was held in the fall of 1836. General Jackson having declined to be a candidate for a third term, the Democratic

party supported Martin Van Buren for President, and Richard M. Johnson, of Kentucky, for Vice-President. Mr. Van Buren was elected by a large majority; but the electors having failed to make a choice of a candidate for vice-president, that task devolved upon

COAT OF ARMS OF MICHIGAN.

the Senate, which elected Colonel Richard M. Johnson by a majority of seventeen votes.

On the 26th of January, 1837, Michigan was admitted into the Union as a State, making the twenty-sixth member of the confederacy. The original thirteen States had been doubled in number, and the Union was strong at home, and respected abroad.

At the close of his term General Jackson retired from public life, and passed the remainder of his days at his beautiful home, near Nashville, in Tennessee, which he had named the "Hermitage." He had conducted one of the most remarkable administrations in our history, and one of the most successful, and had shown himself to be an earnest, incorruptible, and self-sacrificing patriot, and a man of

MARTIN VAN BUREN.

unbending honesty and of extraordinary energy and inflexibility of purpose.

Martin Van Buren, the new president, entered upon the duties of his office on the 4th of March, 1837. He was in his fifty-fifth year, and had occupied many distinguished positions in public life. He had represented the State of New York in the Senate of the United States, and had been secretary of state. He had been minister to England, had been made secretary of state at the commencement of General Jackson's first term, and had been elected vice-president of the United States at the period of Jackson's re-election.

The extraordinary prosperity which had prevailed throughout the nation during the last year of Jackson's term came to a sudden end almost immediately after the inauguration of Mr. Van Buren. For some time past a reckless spirit of speculation had engrossed the nation, and had led to excessive banking, and the issuing of paper money to an extent far beyond the necessities of the country. The State banks, with which the public funds had been deposited by President Jackson, supposed they would be able to control these funds for an indefinite period,

MILWAUKEE, WISCONSIN, IN 1875.

as the revenue of the government was largely in excess of its expenses; and they made loans freely, and upon not the best securities, in all cases. Few of the new banks which sprang into existence had enough gold and silver in their vaults to redeem the notes with which they flooded the country. Fictitious values prevailed in every department of trade, and the banks vied with each other in affording the means for the wildest speculations.

In the midst of this excitement two acts of the general government brought matters to a crisis. The speculation mania had extended to the public lands, and in order to restrain it within manageable bounds President Jackson caused the secretary of the treasury to issue an order to the

43

collectors at the local offices to receive only gold and silver in payments for land. This order was generally known as the "Specie Circular." In the summer of 1836 a law was passed by Congress requiring the president to distribute among the States the funds on deposit in the banks. This was an unexpected measure to the banks, and forced them to call in their loans to meet the withdrawal of the government funds. The operations of the 'Specie Circular" at the same time sent large quantities of their notes back to them to be redeemed in coin. This complication of difficulties brought them at once to the end of their resources, and they were rendered powerless to extend their usual facilities to their customers. The result was that the business of the country was thrown into a state of hopeless confusion, and by the spring of 1837 the failures in New York alone amounted to one hundred million dollars. All parts of the country were affected by the financial troubles, and in New Orleans the failures amounted to twenty-seven million dollars.

Petitions were addressed to the president from all parts of the Union, praying him to take some steps to relieve the general distress, and in May a deputation of merchants and bankers from New York waited upon President Van Buren, and urged him to postpone the immediate collection of duties for which merchants had given bonds, to withdraw the treasury orders requiring sums due the United States to be paid in gold and silver, and to convene Congress in extra session for the purpose of devising measures of relief. The president complied with their request to suspend the collection of duties for which bonds had been given, but declined to take the other steps asked of him. Within a few days after his answer was known the banks of New York suspended specie payments, and their example was followed by the rest of the banks throughout the Union.

The distress of the country was very great. Hundreds of thousands of laborers were thrown out of employment, and business of all kinds was at a standstill. The government, which, a few months before, had been out of debt, and in possession of a surplus of forty millions, now found itself unable to provide funds for its ordinary expenses. The president was compelled to summon an extra session of Congress, which met on the 4th of September, 1837. The president in his message attributed the embarrassed condition of the country to the excessive issues of bank notes, the great fire in New York in 1835, and the reckless speculations of the people for several years past. He suggested no special legislation for the relief of these troubles, as he regarded such a course as beyond the constitutional authority of the general government. Indeed the gov   to restore public confidence, that was the task of the people themselves, and it was not accomplished for several years. To meet the necessities of the government, and provide a legal currency, Congress, at the recommendation of the president, issued treasury notes to the amount of ten millions of dollars. Another recommendation of the president did not give such general satisfaction. The president advised the creation of an independent treasury for the public funds, as a means of avoiding the risks assumed by the government in depositing its funds in the banks. These treasuries were to be located at certain central points, and the sub-treasurers were to be appointed by the president, and were to give bonds for the proper fulfilment of their

EASTON, PENNSYLVANIA.

duties. The president believed that the adoption of this measure would withdraw large sums of money from active circulation and so put a stop to speculation. The bill for the creation of the independent treasury was warmly opposed in and out of Congress, as it was feared by many that the withdrawal of so much gold and silver from circulation would seriously injure the business of the country. Mr. Calhoun supported the measure with all his great abilities, and Mr. Clay and Mr. Webster opposed it. The measure failed at the extra session, but became a law in 1840. In 1841 it was repealed, and in 1846 was re-enacted. It is still in force, and its wisdom and usefulness are now generally admitted.

The spirit of speculation had extended to the State governments as well as to private individuals, and State bonds had been issued to the amount of one hundred million dollars. The pretext for this excessive increase of debt was the necessity of raising funds to carry out their system of internal improvements. The panic involved the States in its effects, and eight of them found themselves unable in 1838 to pay the interest on their bonds. In course of time they made good their obligations, but the State of Mississippi and the Territory of Florida not only refused to pay the interest on their bonds, but repudiated their debts. The sale of their bonds had been made principally in Europe, and their repudiation of their debts aroused great indignation on the other side of the Atlantic, and brought disgrace upon the whole nation. The effects of this were seen a few years later, when the United States sought to negotiate a national loan in Europe. Not a bond could be sold or a dollar obtained there.

In 1837 a movement was made by the people of Canada to throw off their connection with Great Britain, and to establish their independence. It aroused the sympathies of a large number of the people of the United States, and in northern New York associations called "Hunters' Lodges" were formed for the purpose of aiding the Canadian patriots. The president of the United States and the governor of New York endeavored to suppress these illegal associations, but without success.

A body of seven hundred Canadians and American sympathizers took possession of Navy island in the Niagara river. The island is a part of Canada, and lies near the shore of that country. The force on the island employed the steamboat "Caroline" to convey men and provisions from the town of Schlosser on the American shore to the island. The British authorities in Canada determined to destroy the boat. One dark night in December, 1837, a detachment from Canada was sent to Navy island for this purpose. Not finding the "Caroline" there, they went over to Schlosser, where she was moored at her dock. The boat was captured after a short struggle in which one American was killed, and was carried out into the stream and set on fire. She drifted down to the falls, and plunged over them in a blaze. The British minister at Washington at once declared the responsibility of his government for the capture of the boat, and justified it on the ground of self-defence.

In the meantime the president had sent General Wool with a strong force to the Canadian border with orders to prevent any expedition from leaving ... the Canadians. He compelled the force on

Navy island to surrender, but the border war continued until the close of 1838, when it was put down.

In 1840 the question was to some extent revived. Alexander McLeod, a British subject residing in Canada, boasted that he had been engaged in the capture of the "Caroline," and had killed the American who fell in

RAFTING LUMBER IN MAINE.

that conflict. Shortly afterwards he visited the New York side of the river, and was at once arrested upon a charge of murder by the authorities of that State. The British government demanded his unconditional release on the ground that he had simply obeyed the orders of his government, which was alone responsible for his act. The general government of the United States also demanded the surrender of McLeod to the Federal authorities. The State of New York, however, held that the offence with which McLeod was charged had been committed on her soil, and brought the prisoner to trial. As he succeeded in proving that he was not engaged in, or present at the attack, he was acquitted. This conflict between the federal and State authority led to the passage by Congress of a law requiring similar offences to be tried before the United States courts.

In the midst of the Canadian controversy a quarrel sprang up between the State of Maine and the British province of New Brunswick, concerning the northeast boundary of the United States. Both parties prepared for a conflict, but the president sent General Scott to the scene of danger, and he, by his moderation and firmness, succeeded in maintaining peace until the matter could be settled by treaty.

The war with the Seminole Indians in Florida continued through the

BATTLE OF OKEECHOBEE.

whole of this administration. The capture and death of Osceola, which we have related, though a severe blow to his followers, did not dishearten them. On the 25th of December, 1838, Colonel Zachary Taylor inflicted a severe defeat upon the Indians at Lake Okeechobee. The war was at length brought to an end in 1842, but not until it had lasted seven years, and had cost many valuable lives and the enormous sum of nearly forty million dollars. The Seminoles were subdued, and were removed from Florida to new homes beyond the Mississippi.

The Missouri Compromise did not quiet the agitation of the slavery question. It gave to the country only a momentary respite. The Anti-slavery or Abolition party had now become one of the recognized political organizations of the country. Its avowed object was the abolition of slavery in every State in which it existed. It was argued in opposition to their principles that the constitution recognized and protected slavery in the States in which it existed, but they met this assertion by the bold declaration that they would continue their agitation until they had destroyed either slavery or the Union. They did not wish to live under a constitution which protected slavery, and which one of their principal leaders denounced as "a covenant with death, and an agreement with hell." The body embraced the extreme Anti-slavery men of the north Among its adversaries were some of the sincerest opponents of slavery, who hoped to accomplish their ends by constitutional means and by the influences of a better and more enlightened public opinion, and who deprecated and opposed the violence of the extreme Abolitionists The leader of the ultra party in Congress was John Quincy Adams, who had been returned to the House of Representatives from Massachusetts in 1831. Memorials were presented to Congress praying the abolition of slavery in the District of Columbia, and gave rise to exciting debates in that body, which affected the whole country profoundly, and did much to widen the breach between the Northern and Southern States. This agitation continued through the whole of Mr Van Buren's term of office. Early in the session of 1838–39, Mr. Atherton, of New Hampshire, offered a series of resolutions expressing the relations of the general government towards the States, and declaring the inability of Congress to interfere with slavery in those States in which it already existed, or in the District of Columbia, or the Territories. These resolutions were adopted by the House by decisive majorities, and were regarded by Mr. Clay and by the leading public men of the country as effectually disposing of the troublesome question as far as the general government was concerned The resolutions were as follows

"*Resolved*, That this government is a government of limited powers, and that by the constitution of the United States, Congress has no jurisdiction whatever over the institution of slavery in the several States of the confederacy "

The vote upon this resolution stood: 196 for it, and 6 against it.

The second resolution was in these words:

"*Resolved*, That petitions for the abolition of slavery in the District of Columbia and the Territories of the United States, and against the removal of slaves from one State to another, are a part of a plan of operations set on foot to affect the institution of slavery in the Southern States, and thus indirectly to destroy that institution within their limits "

On this resolution the vote stood: 136 for it, and 65 against it.

The third resolution was in these words:

"*Resolved*, That Congress has no right to do that indirectly which it cannot do directly;

and that the agitation of the subject of slavery in the District of Columbia, or the Territories, as a means, and with a view, of disturbing or overthrowing that institution in the several States, is against the true spirit and meaning of the constitution, an infringement of the rights of the States affected, and a breach of the public faith upon which they entered into the confederacy."

The vote on this resolution was: 164 in favor of it, and 40 against it.

The fourth of this series was in these words:

"*Resolved*, That the constitution rests on the broad principle of equality among the members of this confederacy, and that Congress, in the exercise of its acknowledged powers, has no right to discriminate between the institutions of one portion of the States and another, with a view of abolishing the one and promoting the other.'

The vote on this resolution was: 174 in favor of it, and 24 against it.

The fifth and last of Mr. Atherton's resolutions was in these words:

"*Resolved*, That all attempts on the part of Congress to abolish slavery in the District of Columbia, or the Territories, or to prohibit the removal of slaves from State to State, or to discriminate between the institutions of one portion of the confederacy and another, with the view aforesaid, are in violation of the constitution, destructive of the fundamental principle on which the union of these States rests, and beyond the jurisdiction of Congress; and that every petition, memorial, resolution, proposition, or paper, touching or relating in any way, or to any extent whatever, to slavery, as aforesaid, or the abolition thereof, shall, on the presentation thereof, without any further action thereon, be laid upon the table, without being debated, printed, or referred."

The vote on the first branch of this resolution was, 146 in favor, and 52 against it; on the second branch of the resolution the vote stood, 126 for it, and 78 against it.

As we shall see, this declaration of Congress was far from quieting the agitation upon this troublesome question. The slavery conflict had in reality just begun.

In the fall of 1840 the presidential election was held. Mr. Van Buren and Vice-President Johnson were nominated for re-election by the Democratic party, and the Whigs supported General William Henry Harrison, of Ohio, for president, and John Tyler, of Virginia, for vice-president. The financial distress of the country had been but slightly relieved, and was generally attributed by the people to the interference of the government with the currency. This feeling made the Democratic nominees exceedingly unpopular, and the political campaign, which was one of the most exciting ever conducted in this country, resulted in the election of Harrison and Tyler by overwhelming majorities.

In 1840 the sixth census showed the population of the United States to be 17,069,453.

CHAPTER XXXVI.

THE ADMINISTRATIONS OF WILLIAM HENRY HARRISON AND JOHN TYLER.

An Extra Session of Congress Summoned—Death of President Harrison—John Tyler becomes President of the United States—Meeting of Congress—The Bankrupt Law—President Tyler Vetoes the Bills to Revive the United States Bank—His Quarrel with his Party—The "Tyler Whigs"—The Tariff of 1842—The Treaty of Washington—The United States will not Tolerate the Exercise of the Right of Search—Dorr's Rebellion—The Mormons—Invention of the Electric Telegraph—Explosion on the "Princeton"—Efforts to Secure the Annexation of Texas—Early History of Texas—The Texan War of Independence—Battle of San Jacinto—Texan Independence Established—Texas Applies for Admission into the Union—Opposition to the Measure—Significance of the Vote at the Presidential Election—James K. Polk Elected President—Texas admitted into the Union—Iowa and Florida become States.

ON the 4th of March, 1841, William Henry Harrison was inaugurated president of the United States at Washington in the presence of an immense concourse of citizens from all parts of the Union. He was in his sixty-ninth year, and had spent forty years of his life in the public service. His services during the Indian hostilities which preceded the war of 1812–15, and his exploits during that war, have been related. He had served as governor of Indiana Territory, and had been both a member of Congress and a senator of the United States. He was a man of pure life and earnest character, and the certainty of a change of policy in the measures of the federal government had caused the people of the country to look forward to his administration with hope and confidence. He began by calling to seats in his cabinet men of prominence and ability. At the head of the cabinet he placed Daniel Webster, as secretary of state. The president issued a proclamation convening Congress in special session on the

WILLIAM HENRY HARRISON.

31st of May, 1841. He was not destined to fulfil the hopes of his friends, however. He was suddenly seized with pneumonia, and died on the 4th of April, 1841—just one month after his inauguration.

It was the first time that a president of the United States had died in office, and a gloom was cast over the nation by the sad event. The mourning of the people was sincere, for in General Harrison the nation lost a faithful, upright, and able citizen. He had spent forty years in prominent public positions, and had discharged every duty confided to him with ability and integrity, and went to his grave a poor man.

"Brave old Cincinnatus! he left but his plow."

Upon the assembling of Congress, that body, "out of consideration of his expenses in removing to the seat of government, and the limited means he had left behind," appropriated the equivalent of one year's presidential salary—twenty-five thousand dollars—to Mrs. Harrison.

According to the terms of the constitution, upon the death of General  Harrison, the office of president of the United States devolved upon the vice-president, John Tyler, of Virginia. Mr. Tyler was not in the city of Washington at the time of the death of his predecessor, but repaired to that city without loss of time, upon being notified of the need of his presence, and on the 6th of April took the oath of office before Judge Cranch, chief justice of the District of Columbia. Mr. Tyler was in his fifty-second year, and had served as governor of Virginia, and as representative and senator in Congress from that State. On the 9th of April President Tyler issued an address to the people of the United States, in which there was no indication of a departure

JOHN TYLER.

from the policy announced in the inaugural of General Harrison. He retained the cabinet ministers of his predecessors in their respective positions.

On the 31st of May the Twenty-seventh Congress convened in extra session. It was known as the "Whig Congress," as a large majority of its members were of that party. Had this party remained united they could have controlled the action of Congress to suit themselves, but as we shall see the policy of the executive soon divided them. The first act of this Congress was to repeal the sub-treasury bill which had been passed in 1840. The effects of the commercial crisis had involved thousands of merchants in hopeless bankruptcy, and under the old laws they had no means of recovering their lost position, as they were crushed down by their debts. Neither their creditors nor the country at large derived any benefit from this state of affairs, and Congress at once passed a general bankrupt law for the relief of persons thus situated. It was highly beneficial to the country, and was repealed, in 1843, when the necessity for it had ceased to exist.

Efforts were made to revive the Bank of the United States, and a bill was passed establishing an institution known as "The Fiscal Bank of the United States." Mr. Tyler, who was a member of the strict constructionist school, now found himself at variance with a majority of his party in both Houses of Congress. As he did not believe that Congress could constitutionally charter such an institution, he vetoed this bill. The advocates of the measure could not command the requisite two-thirds

DAVENPORT, IOWA.

majority for the passage of the bill over the president's veto, and his action was sustained. Another bill was passed by Congress, of a similar character, establishing "The Fiscal Corporation of the United States," but this also was vetoed by the president for the same reasons. His veto was sustained by Congress in this instance also. The vetoes of these measures were generally approved by the strict constructionists throughout the Union, without regard to party; but they were bitterly denounced by the majority of the Whigs, who charged the president with having violated the implied pledges upon which he was elected, and with having betrayed his party. The Whigs were for the time forgetful of the fact that at the time of his nomination to the vice-presidency Mr. Tyler was known to be opposed to the Bank of the United States. The members of the cabinet, with the single exception of the secretary of state, resigned their positions in consequence of Mr Tyler's course. Mr. Webster retained his position in order to complete the important negotiations he was at the time conducting with England. The places of the other members of the cabinet were filled by the president with prominent members of the strict constructionist school of the Whig party, who sustained the president.

The second session of the Twenty-seventh Congress met in December, 1841, and continued its sittings until August, 1842. It was noted as the longest session ever held up to this time It found the Whig party divided, and the opposing factions bitterly hostile to each other. The majority, led by Mr Clay, opposed the administration. The minority, because of their support of the president, received the name of "Tyler Whigs" The principal question agitated during this session was the tariff. According to the compromise act of 1833, the duties this year were to be regulated according to a revenue standard. The majority in Congress, however, paid no regard to the pledge given in this compromise, and a new tariff bill was passed by both Houses of Congress, regulating the duties on a strongly protective basis, and with the avowed object of reviving the protective policy. It was vetoed by the president. Another measure of a similar though slightly modified character was passed, and this was vetoed also. Congress then passed the tariff of 1842, in which the principles of the compromise of 1833 were altogether set aside, and the duties made strictly protective It required a sharp struggle in Congress to secure the passage of this bill, which received the executive signature on the 30th of August.

In the meantime Mr Webster succeeded in bringing the negotiations with Great Britain to a successful close These negotiations had grown out of the revolutionary disturbances in Canada, and the controversy respecting the northeast boundary of the United States, during the administration of Mr. Van Buren, which we have related. The boundary question was of older origin than the former controversy, and had been pending between the United States and England for fifty years. Mr. Webster, immediately upon his entrance upon the office of secretary of state, had, with the approval of the president, signified the desire of this country to terminate the controversy, and Lord Ashburton had been sent by the British government as special minister to the United States, with full power to settle all the controversies between the two countries. The treaty of Washington was concluded in 1842, and was accepted by both countries as a settlement of the questions at issue between them.

By the terms of this treaty the northeastern boundary was arranged as it exists at present; the United States obtained the free navigation of the St. John's river to the sea; and gained possession of the important military position of Rouse's Point, at the outlet of Lake Champlain. The two countries mutually agreed to surrender upon proper demand all fugitives from justice escaping from the territory of one into that of the other; and to maintain a certain number of ships of war on the African coast to aid in suppressing the slave trade.

When the treaty was completed two subjects presented themselves to the negotiators. One of these was the right claimed by Great Britain for her cruisers to stop and if necessary to search merchant vessels belonging to other nations on the high seas; the other was the impressment of seamen from American merchant vessels by British cruisers. Mr. Webster,

EVANSVILLE, INDIANA.

in a paper of great ability, addressed to the American minister at London, but intended for the British foreign minister, denied the right of search, and sustained his position by arguments that were simply irrefutable. In a letter to Lord Ashburton Mr. Webster refused to consider the impressment question, as the United States could in no case admit such a claim on the part of Great Britain, and declared that every case of impressment would be considered an act of hostility and would be repelled as such. He declared as the unalterable policy of this country the doctrine that "Every merchant vessel on the high seas is rightfully considered as a part of the territory to which it belongs;" that "in every regularly documented American merchant vessel the crew who navigate it will find their protection in the flag which is over them;" and that "the American government, then, is prepared to say that the practice of impressing seamen from American vessels cannot hereafter be allowed to take place." The tone of the secretary of state, though firm, was courteous and conciliatory, and the negotiations were conducted in the same spirit of conciliation by the British minister.

With this treaty the United States formally took their position as one of the great powers of the world. The negotiations being completed, Mr. Webster resigned his place in the cabinet in May, 1843, and was succeeded by Abel P Upshur, of Virginia.

In 1842 an insurrection broke out in the State of Rhode Island, which required the intervention of the United States for its suppression. It is known as the Dorr rebellion. The old charter of the colony, granted by Charles II., in 1663, had up to this time served as the constitution of the State It was found to be unsuited to the requirements of the people in their more prosperous condition, and an effort was made to change it. Two parties were formed, one in favor of the proposed changes, the other opposed to them. Each party nominated its candidate for the office of governor and elected him. The "suffrage party," which favored the changes, elected Thomas W. Dorr governor, took up arms, and attacked the State arsenal for the purpose of arming their followers. They were repulsed by the State militia assisted by the United States troops. Dorr was arrested, tried for treason, and sentenced to imprisonment for life He was released in 1845. The opponents of the "suffrage party" deemed it best to yield to the popular wish, however, and in November, 1842, a new constitution, embracing the desired changes, was adopted by the legislature.

About the same time a series of disturbances occurred in the State of Illinois, which were but the forerunners of a more serious embarrassment to the general government at a later period A new religious sect had sprung up some years before in the western part of New York. They called themselves Mormons, and were founded by a cunning impostor named Joseph Smith, who professed to have received a new revelation from God, written on plates of gold Among the articles of the Mormon faith is one which teaches the doctrine of a plurality of wives Feeling that the east was not favorable to their growth, the Mormons at an early day removed to the west. They settled at first in Missouri, but so exasperated the people of that State by their conduct, that they were soon driven out of Missouri.

Crossing the Mississippi, they settled in Illinois, and founded a city which they called Nauvoo, and built a temple. Their numbers increased rapidly from emigration from nearly every country in Europe The new-comers   is had part   ed   at education.

Conscious of their strength, they raised troops, and set the authority of the State of Illinois at defiance. The State endeavored to reduce them to obedience, and their conduct, as in Missouri, turned the people against them. Several conflicts ensued between the Mormons and the authorities. In one of these Joe Smith, the prophet, and his brother were seized and put in jail; and while lying there were murdered by the mob in July, 1844. This brought matters to a crisis, and the people of Illinois determined to drive the Mormons across the Mississippi. Nauvoo was attacked in 1845, and the Mormons were compelled to leave the State. In 1846 they bent their steps westward, and after a long and painful journey across the plains, reached the valley of Salt Lake, and established a settlement there. Out of this settlement grew the Territory of Utah.

MADISON, WISCONSIN.

In 1844 occurred one of the most important events in the history of the world. In 1832 Samuel F. B. Morse, a native of Massachusetts, invented the electric telegraph. He spent some years in perfecting his invention, and in 1838 applied to Congress for a small appropriation to assist him in building a line of wire to demonstrate the usefulness of his discovery. He was obliged to wait five years for a favorable answer, and it was not until he had given up all hope of receiving aid from Congress that that body, on the last day of the session of 1843, appropriated the sum of thirty thousand dollars to construct a telegraph line between Washington City and Baltimore, a distance of forty miles. The line was completed in 1844, and was successfully operated by Professor Morse This was the first line established in the world. In the thirty-one years which have elapsed since then the use of the telegraph has become general throughout the civilized world, and in the United States alone over sixty thousand miles of telegraph lines are in operation at the present time.

On the 28th of February, 1844, the president, accompanied by the members of his cabinet and a number of distinguished citizens, officers of the army and navy, and ladies, went on board the new steam frigate "Princeton," lying in the Potomac, to witness the experimental firings of a new cannon of unusual size on board that ship, to which the name of "The Peacemaker" had been given. At one of the discharges the gun exploded, causing the instant death of Messrs Upshur and Gilmer, the secretaries of state and of the navy, and several other spectators. This sad event was greatly lamented throughout the country. Judge Upshur was succeeded as secretary of state by John C. Calhoun, then a senator from South Carolina.

The last years of Mr. Tyler's administration were devoted to the effort to secure the annexation of the republic of Texas to the United States. The territory embraced within the limits of Texas constituted a part of the Spanish-American possessions, and was generally regarded as a part of Mexico. During the last century a number of forts had been erected in Texas by the Spaniards as a means of holding the province against the French, and each fort was made a missionary station, from which efforts were made to convert the Indians, but without success. The United States were, in the early part of the present century, inclined to regard Texas as rightfully a part of the Louisiana purchase, but this claim was waived when Florida was purchased.

Early in the present century pioneers from the United States began to find their way to Texas, which was then a wild country, inhabited only by roving Indians, and the garrisons of the few Spanish forts within its limits One of these emigrants, Moses Austin, of Durham, Connecticut, conceived the plan of colonizing Texas with settlers from the United States. For this purpose he obtained from the Spanish government, in 1820, the grant of an extensive tract of land; but before he could put his plans in execution he died. His son, Stephen F Austin, inherited the rights of his father under this grant, and went to Texas with a number of emigrants from this country, and explored that region for the purpose of locating his grant. He selected as the most desirable site for his colony the country between the Brazos and Colorado rivers, and founded a city, which he named Austin in honor of the originator of the colony, to whom is also owes its existence as an American commonwealth. Having seen the settlers established in their new homes, Mr. Austin returned to the United States to collect other emigrants for his colony.

During his absence Mexico and the other Spanish provinces rose in revolt against Spain, and succeeded in establishing their independence. Texas, being regarded as a part of the Mexican territory, shared the fortunes of that country. Upon his return to Texas, Austin, in consideration of the altered state of affairs, went to the city of Mexico and obtained from the Mexican government a confirmation of the grant made to his father. Such a confirmation was necessary in order to enable him to give the settlers valid titles to the lands of his colony. Mexico at first exercised but a nominal authority over the new settlements, and the colonists were

OLD FORT BENTON, MONTANA.

allowed to live under their own laws, subject to the rules drawn up by Austin. In order to encourage settlements in Texas, the Mexican Congress, on the 2d of May, 1824, enacted the following law, declaring, "That Texas is to be annexed to the Mexican province of Cohahuila, until it is of sufficient importance to form a separate State, when it is to become an independent State of the Mexican republic, equal to the other States of which the same is composed, free, sovereign, and independent in whatever exclusively relates to its internal government and administration."

Encouraged by this decree, large numbers of Americans emigrated to
44

Texas, and to these were added emigrants from all the countries of Europe. The population grew rapidly, new towns sprang up, and Austin's colony prospered in a marked degree, until 1830, when Bustamente having made himself by violence and intrigue president of the so-called Mexican republic, prohibited the emigration of foreigners to the Mexican territory, and issued a number of decrees very oppressive to the people, and in violation of the constitution of 1824 In order to enforce these measures in Texas, he occupied that province with his troops, and placed Texas under military rule. The Texans resented this interference with their rights, and finally compelled the Mexican troops to withdraw from the province In 1832 another revolution in Mexico drove Bustamente from power, and placed Santa Anna at the head of affairs as president or dictator.

Texas took no part in the disturbances of Mexico, but after the accession of Santa Anna to power, formed a constitution, and applied for admission into the Mexican republic as a State, in accordance with the constitution of 1824, and the act of the Mexican Congress which we have quoted Stephen F. Austin was sent to the city of Mexico to present the petition of Texas for this purpose. He was refused an answer to this petition for over a year, and at last wrote to the authorities of Texas, advising them to organize a State government without waiting for the action of the Mexican Congress. . For this recommendation, which the Mexican government regarded as treasonable, Santa Anna caused the arrest of Austin, and kept him in prison for over a year Texas now began to manifest the most determined opposition to the usurpation of Santa Anna, and measures were taken to maintain the rights of the province under the constitution of 1824. Troops were organized, and preparations made to resist the force which it was certain Mexico would send against them.

Santa Anna did not allow them to remain long in suspense, but at once despatched a force under General Cos, to disarm the Texans On the 2.1 of October, 1835, Cos attacked the town of Gonzalez, which was held by a Texan force, but was repulsed with heavy loss A week later, on the 9th of October, the Texans captured the town of Goliad, and a little later gained possession of the mission house of the Alamo. Both places were garrisoned, and the Texan army, which was under the command of Austin, in the course of a few months succeeded in driving the Mexicans out of Texas.

On the 12th of November, 1835, a convention of the people of Texas met at the city of Austin, and organized a regular State government. Prominent among the members was General Sam Houston, a settler from the United States. Soon after the meeting of the convention General Austin resigned the command of the army, and was sent to the United States as the commissioner of that State to this government, and was succeeded as commander-in-chief by General Sam Houston. Henry Smith was elected governor of Texas by the people.

As soon as Santa Anna learned that his troops had been driven out of Texas, and that the Texans had set up a State government, he set out for that country with an army of seventy-five hundred men. He issued orders to his troops to shoot every prisoner taken, and intended to make the struggle a war of extermination. He arrived before the Alamo late in February, 1836. This fort was very strong, and was held by a force of one hundred and forty Texans under Colonel Travis. It was besieged

FORT ALAMO—SAN ANTONIO, TEXAS.

by the whole Mexican army, and was subjected to a bombardment of eleven days. At last, on the 6th of March, the garrison being worn out with fatigue, the fort was carried by assault, and the whole garrison was put to the sword. Among the heroes who fell at the Texan Thermopylæ was the eccentric but chivalrous Colonel Davy Crockett of Tennessee, who had generously come to aid the Texans in their struggle for liberty. The capture of the Alamo cost the Mexicans a loss of sixteen hundred men, or over eleven men for every one of its defenders.

On the 17th of March, 1836, the convention adopted a constitution for an independent republic, and formally proclaimed the independence of Texas. David G. Burnett was elected president of the republic.

The fort at Goliad was held by a force of three hundred and thirty Texans, under Colonel Fanning, a native of Georgia On the 27th of March it was attacked by the Mexican army. The garrison maintained a gallant defence, but their resources being exhausted, and the Mexicans being reinforced during the night, Fanning decided to surrender his force, if he could obtain honorable terms. He proposed to Santa Anna to lay down his arms, and surrender the post on condition that he and his men should be allowed and assisted to return to the United States. The proposition was accepted by Santa Anna, and the terms of the surrender were formally drawn up and were signed by each commander. As soon as the surrender was made, however, and the arms of the Texans were delivered, Santa Anna, in base violation of his pledge, caused Fanning and the survivors of the garrison, to the number of three hundred men, to be put to death

The massacres of the Alamo and Goliad, and the steady advance of the Mexican army under Santa Anna, caused a feeling of profound alarm throughout the new republic The government was removed temporarily to Galveston, and General Houston retreated behind the San Jacinto. Santa Anna pursued the Texan forces, and at length came up with them on the banks of that stream. Houston had but seven hundred and fifty men with him, and these were imperfectly armed, and without discipline. With this force he surprised the Mexican camp, on the 21st of April, and routed the Mexican army, inflicting upon it a loss of over six hundred killed, and taking more than eight hundred prisoners. Santa Anna himself was among the prisoners. Houston at once entered into negotiations with him for the withdrawal of the Mexican forces from Texas. This was done at once, and the independence of Texas was achieved. Santa Anna also recognized the independence of the new republic, but the Mexican Congress refused to confirm this act.

Houston was now the idol of the Texan people, as the deliverer of their country from the hated Mexicans. At the next general election he was chosen president of the republic, and was inaugurated on the 22d of October, 1836. General Mirabeau B. Lamar was the third president of the republic of Texas, and entered upon his office in 1838. He was succeeded in 1844 by Anson Jones, the fourth president. The territory of the republic was sufficiently large to make five States the size of New York, and its climate and soil were among the most delightful and fertile in the world. It contained a population of about two hundred thousand, and was increasing rapidly in inhabitants and in prosperity.

On the 3d of March, 1837, the independence of the republic of Texas was acknowledged by the United States, and in 1839 by France and

England. Being young and feeble, and being settled almost entirely by Americans, the people of Texas at an early day came to the conclusion that their best interests required them to seek a union with the United States, and as early as August, 1837, a proposition was submitted to Mr. Van Buren looking to such a union. It was declined by him, but the question was taken up by the press and people of the Union, and was discussed with the greatest interest and activity. The south was unanimously in favor of the annexation of Texas, as it was a region in which slave labor would be particularly profitable; and a strong party in the north opposed the annexation for the reason that it would inevitably extend the area of slavery. An additional argument against annexation was that it would involve a war with Mexico, which had never acknowledged the independence of Texas.

In April, 1844, Texas formally applied for admission into the United States, and a treaty for that purpose was negotiated with her by the government of this country. It was rejected by the Senate.

In the fall of 1844 the presidential election took place. The leading political question of the day was the annexation of Texas. It was advocated by the administration of President Tyler and by the Democratic party. This party also made the claim of the United States to Oregon one of the leading issues of the campaign. Its candidates were James K. Polk, of Tennessee, and George M. Dallas, of Pennsylvania. The Whig party supported Henry Clay, of Kentucky, and Theodore Frelinghuysen, of New Jersey, and opposed the annexation of Texas.

COAT OF ARMS OF TEXAS.

During this campaign, which was one of unusual excitement, the Anti-slavery party made its appearance for the first time as a distinct political organization, and nominated James G. Birney as its candidate for the presidency.

The result of the campaign was a decisive victory for the Democrats. This success was generally regarded as an emphatic expression of the popular will respecting the Texas and Oregon questions. Mr. Birney did not receive a single electoral vote, and of the popular vote only sixty-four thousand six hundred and fifty-three ballots were cast for him.

When Congress met in December, 1864, the efforts for the annexation of Texas were renewed. A proposition was made to receive Texas into the Union by a joint resolution of Congress. A bill for this purpose passed the House of Representatives, but the Senate added an amendment appointing commissioners to negotiate with Mexico for the annexation of Texas, which she still claimed as a part of her territory. The president was authorized by a clause in these resolutions to adopt either the House or the Senate plan of annexation, and on the 2d of March, 1845, the resolutions were adopted. Senator Benton, of Missouri, the author of the Senate plan, was of the opinion that the matter would be left to Mr. Polk, the president-elect, to be conducted by him; and that gentleman had expressed his intention to carry out the Senate plan, as he

COAT OF ARMS OF IOWA.

hoped an amicable arrangement could be made with Mexico. Mr. Tyler, however, determined not to leave the annexation of Texas to his successor, and at once adopted the plan proposed in the House resolutions, and on the night of Sunday, March 3d, a messenger was despatched with all speed to Texas to lay the proposition before the authorities of that State. It was accepted by them, and on the 4th of July, 1845, Texas became one of the United States.

The area thus added to the territory of the Union comprised two hundred and thirty-seven thousand five hundred and four square miles. It was provided by the act of admission that four additional States might be formed out of the territory of Texas, when the population should increase to an extent which should make such a step desirable. Those States lying north of the Missouri Compromise line—36° 30′ north latitude—were to be free States; those south of that line were to be free or slave-holding, "as the people of each State asking admission may desire." To Texas was reserved the right to refuse to allow the division of her territory.

COAT OF ARMS OF FLORIDA.

On the 3d of March, 1845, the president approved an act of Congress admitting the Territories of Iowa and Florida into the Union as States.

No president has ever been more unpopular during his administration than Mr. Tyler. His administration speaks for itself, however, and bears out the truth of his memorable words: "I appeal from the vituperation of the present day to the pen of impartial history, in the full confidence that neither my motives nor my acts will bear the interpretation which has, for sinister purposes, been placed upon them."

CHAPTER XXXVII.

THE ADMINISTRATION OF JAMES K POLK—THE WAR WITH MEXICO.

THE inauguration of James K Polk, as president of the United States, took place on the 4th of March, 1845 He had served the country as governor of the State of Tennessee, and for fourteen years had been a member of the House of Representatives in Congress from that State, and had been several times chosen speaker of that body. His cabinet was selected from the first men of his party James Buchanan was secretary of state; Robert J. Walker was secretary of the treasury, William L. Marcy, secretary of war, and George Bancroft, the historian, secretary of the navy.

Two important questions presented themselves to the new administration for settlement: the troubles with Mexico growing out of the annexation of Texas, and the arrangement of the northwestern boundary of the United States

The question of the northwestern boundary had been left unsettled by the treaty of Washington in 1842. Great Britain was anxious to arrange the matter, and late in the year 1842 Mr. Fox, the British minister at

Washington, proposed to Mr. Webster, then secretary of state, to open negotiations. The British proposition was accepted, but nothing further was done until February, 1844, when Sir Richard Packenham, the British minister at Washington, proposed to take up the question of the Oregon boundary and settle it. Mr. Upshur, the secretary of state, accepted the offer, but was killed a few days later by the explosion on board the "Princeton." Six months later, Sir Richard Packenham renewed the proposal to Mr. Calhoun, who had become secretary of state, and negotiations were entered upon in earnest.

The territory of Oregon lay between the forty-second and fifty-fourth parallels of north latitude, and extended from the Rocky mountains on the east to the Pacific ocean on the west. This region was originally claimed by Spain, by whose subjects it was first discovered. At the cession of Florida, Spain ceded to the United States all her territory north

of the forty-second parallel of north latitude, from the headwaters of the Arkansas to the Pacific. Mexico, upon achieving her independence, had acknowledged by a treaty with the United States the validity of this boundary. The line of fifty-four degrees forty minutes north latitude was established by treaty between the United States, Great Britain, and Russia as the southern boundary of the Russian possessions in America.

The United States claimed the entire region of Oregon in virtue of the cession of Spain in the Florida treaty; the discoveries of Captain Gray, of Boston, who circumnavigated the globe, and in 1792 discovered to a

JAMES K. POLK.

certain extent and explored the Columbia river; the explorations of Lewis and Clarke in 1805 and 1806 of the southern main branch of the Columbia, and of the river itself from the mouth of that branch to the sea; and the settlement of Astoria planted at the mouth of the Columbia in 1811 by John Jacob Astor, of New York. Oregon was also claimed by England, who also rested her pretensions on discovery, and on the settlement made by the Northwest Company on Fraser's river, in 1806, and on another near the headwaters of the north branch of the Columbia.

In 1818 the United States and Great Britain had agreed upon the forty-ninth degree of north latitude, as the boundary between the United States and British America from the Lake of the Woods to the summit of the Rocky mountains. Mr. Calhoun now opened the negotiations by

proposing to continue this line to the Pacific. The British minister would
not consent to this, but proposed to extend the forty-ninth parallel from
the mountains to the north branch of the Columbia, and then to make
the boundary follow that stream from this point of intersection to the sea.
Mr. Calhoun at once declined to accept this boundary, and the further consideration of the subject was postponed until Packenham could receive
additional instructions from his government.

During the presidential campaign of 1844 the Democratic party adopted
as its watchword, "all of Oregon or none," and the excitement upon the
question ran high. The election of Mr. Polk showed that the American
people were resolved to insist upon their claim to Oregon, and when the
new president in his inaugural address took the bold ground that the

PORTLAND, OREGON, IN 1875—FROM EAST SIDE OF WILLAMETTE.

American title to "Oregon territory" "was dear and indisputable," and
declared his intention to maintain it at the cost of war with England, the
matter assumed a serious aspect, and for a while it seemed that party passion would involve the two countries in hostilities. President Polk, upon
a calmer consideration of the subject, caused the secretary of state to
reopen the negotiations by proposing to Great Britain the forty-ninth
parallel of latitude as a boundary. The British minister declined the
proposition, and the matter was dropped.

According to the treaties of 1818 and 1828, the joint occupation of
Oregon could be terminated by either party by giving the other twelve
months notice. The president now proposed to give the required notice,
which was done by a resolution of Congress. This put an end to the old
arrangement, and compelled the two countries to make a new settlement

of the difficulty ; and this was the object of the president in terminating
the joint occupation.

The subject was brought to the notice of the British Parliament by Sir
Robert Peel, who expressed his regret that the last offer of the United
States had been declined. The British ministry decided at length to reopen negotiations, and Sir Richard Packenham shortly after communicated
to Mr. Buchanan the willingness of his government to accept the forty-
ninth parallel as a boundary.

The time at which the joint occupation would terminate was rapidly
drawing to a close, and the president was anxious to settle the matter, but
at the same time was not willing to assume the responsibility of accept-

STREET IN OLYMPIA, WASHINGTON TERRITORY.

ing a boundary which fell so far short of the popular expectations. At
the suggestion of Senator Benton, of Missouri, he asked the advice of the
Senate as to the propriety of accepting the British offer, and pledged himself to be guided by its decision. The Senate advised him to accept it,
and when the treaty was sent to it, ratified it after a warm debate extending over two days. Thus the matter was brought to a close. By the
treaty, which was concluded in 1846, the forty-ninth parallel of north
latitude was made the boundary between the United States and the British possessions, from the summit of the Rocky mountains to the middle
of the channel between Vancouver's island and the mainland, and thence
southerly through the middle of the Straits of San Juan de Fuca to the

Pacific. The navigation of the Columbia river and its main northern branch was made free to both parties

In the meantime the Mexican difficulty had been found much harder of settlement Mexico had never acknowledged the independence of Texas, and since the defeat at San Jacinto had repeatedly threatened to restore her authority over the Texans by force of arms. She warmly resented the annexation of Texas by the United States, and a few days after that event was completed, General Almonte, the Mexican minister at Washington, entered a formal protest against the course of the United States, demanded his passports and left the country

Some years before this a number of American ships trading with Mexican ports had been seized and plundered by the Mexican authorities, who also confiscated the property of a number of American residents in that country. The sufferers by these outrages appealed for redress to the government of the United States, which had repeatedly tried to negotiate with Mexico for the collection of these claims, which amounted to six millions of dollars. Mexico made several promises of settlement, but failed to comply with them. In 1840, however, a new treaty was made between that country and the United States, and Mexico pledged herself to pay the American claims in twenty annual instalments of three hundred thousand dollars each. Three of these instalments had been paid at the time of the annexation of Texas, but Mexico now refused to make any further payment

Mexico claimed that the limits of Texas properly ended at the Neuces river, while the Texans insisted that their boundary was the Rio Grande. Thus the region between these two rivers became a debatable land, claimed by both parties, and a source of great and immediate danger It was evident that Mexico was about to occupy this region with her troops, and the legislature of Texas, alarmed by the threatening attitude of that country, called upon the United States government to protect its territory. The president at once sent General Zachary Taylor with a force of fifteen hundred regular troops, called the "army of occupation," to "take position in the country between the Neuces and the Rio Grande, and to repel any invasion of the Texan territory." General Taylor accordingly took position at Corpus Christi, at the mouth of the Neuces, in September, 1845, and remained there until the spring of 1846. At the same time a squadron of war vessels under Commodore Conner was despatched to the Gulf to coöperate with General Taylor Both of these officers "were ordered to commit no act of hostility against Mexico unless she declared war, or was herself the aggressor by striking the first blow"

At the commencement of the dispute between the two countries, Herrera was president of Mexico. Although diplomatic communications had ceased between the United States and Mexico, he was anxious to settle the quarrel by negotiation, but at the presidential election held about this time Herrera was defeated, and Paredes, who was bitterly hostile to the United States, was chosen president of the Mexican republic. Paredes openly avowed his determination to drive the Americans beyond the Neuces.

In February, 1846, General Taylor was ordered by President Polk to advance from the Neuces to a point on the Rio Grande, opposite the Mexican town of Matamoras, and establish there a fortified post, in order to check the Mexican forces which were assembling there in large numbers for the purpose of invading Texas. Taylor at once set out, and leaving the greater part of his stores at Point Isabel, on the Gulf, advanced to the Rio Grande, and built a fort and established a camp opposite and within cannon shot of Matamoras. General Ampudia, commanding the Mexican forces at Matamoras, immediately notified General Taylor that this was an act of war upon Mexican soil, and demanded that he should "break up his camp and retire beyond the Neuces" within twenty-four hours. Taylor replied that he was acting in accordance with the orders of his government, which was alone responsible for his conduct, and that he should maintain the position he had chosen. He pushed forward the work on his fortifications with energy, and kept a close watch upon the Mexicans. Neither commander was willing to take the responsibility of beginning the war, and Ampudia, notwithstanding his threat, remained inactive. His course did not satisfy his government, and he was removed, and General Arista appointed in his place. Arista at once began hostilities by interposing detachments of his army between Taylor's force and his depot of supplies at Point Isabel. On the 26th of April Taylor sent a party of sixty dragoons under Captain Thornton to reconnoitre the Mexican lines. The dragoons were surprised with a loss of sixteen killed. The remainder were made prisoners, and Thornton alone escaped. This was the first blood shed in the war with Mexico.

A day or two later, being informed by Captain Walker, who with his Texan Rangers was guarding the line of communication with Point Isabel, that the Mexicans were threatening the latter place in heavy force, General Taylor left Major Brown with three hundred men to hold the fort, and marched to Point Isabel to relieve that place. He agreed with Major Brown that if the fort should be attacked or hard pressed, the latter should notify him of his danger by firing heavy signal guns at certain intervals. He reached Point Isabel, twenty miles distant, on the 2d of May, without having met any opposition on the march.

General Arista, attributing Taylor's withdrawal to fear, determined to capture the fortification on the opposite side of the river. On the 3d of May he opened fire upon it from a heavy battery at Matamoras, and sent a large force across the Rio Grande, which took position in the rear of the fort and intrenched themselves there. In the face of this double attack the little garrison defended themselves bravely, but at length Major Brown fell mortally wounded. The command devolved upon Captain Hawkins, who now felt himself justified in warning Taylor of his danger, and began to fire the signal guns agreed upon.

Taylor was joined at Point Isabel by a small detachment, and his force

BATTLE OF PALO ALTO.

was increased to twenty-three hundred men. He listened anxiously for the booming of the signal guns from the fort on the Rio Grande, and at length they were heard. He knew that the need of assistance must be great, as the little band in the fort had held out so long without calling for help, and he at once set out to join them. He left Point Isabel on the 7th of May, taking with him a heavy supply train. The steady firing of the signal guns from Fort Brown (for so the work was afterwards named in honor of its gallant commander) urged the army to its greatest exertions.

On the 8th of May the Mexican army, six thousand strong, was discovered holding a strong position in front of a chaparral, near the small stream called the Palo Alto, intending to dispute the advance of the Americans. Taylor promptly made his dispositions to attack them. His

troops were ordered to drink from the little stream and to fill their can-
teens. The train was closed up, and the line was formed with Major
Ringgold's light battery on the right, Duncan's battery on the left, and a
battery of eighteen-pounders in the centre. The artillery was thrown
well in front of the infantry, and the order was given to advance. The
Mexicans at once opened fire with their batteries, but the distance was too
great to accomplish anything. The American batteries did not reply
until they had gotten within easy range, when they opened a fire the
accuracy and rapidity of which astonished the Mexicans. Their lines
were broken, and they fell back, and the Americans advanced steadily

DEATH OF MAJOR RINGGOLD.

through the chaparral, which had been set on fire by the discharge of
cannon, until a new position within close range was reached. Paying no
attention to the Mexican artillery, the American guns directed their fire
upon the enemy's infantry and cavalry, and broke them again and again.
The battle lasted five hours and ceased at nightfall. It was fought
entirely by the artillery of the two armies, and was won by the superior
handling and precision of the American guns. The loss of the Mexicans
was four hundred killed and wounded; that of the Americans nine killed
and forty-four wounded. Early in the battle Major Ringgold was mortally wounded, and died a little later. He was regarded as one of the
most gifted officers of the army, and to him was chiefly due the precision

and rapidity of movement acquired by the "flying artillery" of the American army, which were so successfully tested during this war.

The American army encamped on the battle-field, and the next morning, May 9th, as the Mexicans had retreated, leaving their dead unburied, resumed its advance In the afternoon the Mexicans were discovered occupying a much stronger position than they had held at Palo Alto. Their line was formed behind a ravine, called Resaca de la Palma, or the Dry River of Palms. Their flanks were protected by the thick chaparral, and their artillery was thrown forward beyond the ravine and protected by an intrenchment, and swept the road by which the Americans must advance. During the night fresh troops had joined the Mexican army, and had increased their force to seven thousand men.

Taylor formed his line with his artillery in the centre. The artillery was ordered to advance along the road commanded by the Mexican battery, and the infantry were directed to move as rapidly as possible through the chaparral, and drive out the Mexican sharp-shooters. The infantry executed this order in handsome style, but the chaparral was so dense that each man was obliged to act for himself as he forced his way through it. The Mexican battery was handled with great skill and coolness, and held the centre in check until some time after the infantry had forced their way close to the edge of the ravine At this juncture Captain May was ordered to charge the Mexican guns, and started down the road at a trot As he reached the position of the American artillery, Lieutenant Ridgely suggested that May should halt and allow him to draw the Mexican fire Ridgely opened a rapid fire on the Mexican guns, which answered immediately At the same moment May dashed at the Mexican battery with his dragoons, and reached it before the cannoneers could reload their pieces. They were sabred at their guns, and the battery was carried Captain May himself made a prisoner of General La Vega, as the latter was in the act of discharging one of the guns. Leaving the battery to the American infantry which now hurried forward to secure it, the dragoons charged the Mexican centre and broke it. The whole American line then advanced rapidly; the Mexicans gave way, and were soon flying in utter confusion towards the Rio Grande, which they crossed in such haste that many of them were drowned in the attempt to reach the Mexican shore.

General Arista, the Mexican commander, fled alone from the field, leaving all his private and official papers behind him. The Americans lost one hundred and twenty-two men killed and wounded; the Mexicans twelve hundred. All the Mexican artillery, two thousand stand of arms, and six hundred mules were captured by the Americans.

General Taylor advanced from the battle-field to Fort Brown, the garrison of which had heard the distant roar of the battle, and had seen the flight of the Mexicans across the Rio Grande.

The defeat of the Mexicans at Palo Alto and Resaca de la Palma had greatly disheartened them. They not only abandoned their intention to invade Texas, but gave up all hope of holding the Rio Grande frontier. On the night of the 17th of May their army evacuated Matamoras, and retreated upon Monterey. On the 18th the American army crossed the Rio Grande, and occupied Matamoras. General Taylor scrupulously respected the municipal laws of the town, and protected the citizens in the exercise of their civil and religious privileges. All supplies needed by the troops were purchased at a liberal price, and no plundering or disorder was allowed or attempted.

In the meantime the news of the attack upon the dragoons under Captain Thornton had reached the United States, and with it the rumor that the American army was confronted on the Texan side of the Rio Grande by a vastly superior force of Mexicans, and that its destruction was almost certain. The president sent a special message to Congress on the 11th of May, in which he informed that body that "war existed by the act of Mexico," and called upon Congress to recognize the state of war, and to provide for its support by appropriating the necessary funds, and to authorize him to call for volunteers. Under the impression that the perilous situation of Taylor's army made instant action necessary, Congress appropriated ten millions of dollars for the prosecution of the war, and authorized the president to accept the services of fifty thousand volunteers. One-half of this force was to be mustered into the service; the remainder held as a reserve. The president's call was responded to with enthusiasm all over the land, and in the course of a few weeks two hundred thousand volunteers offered their services. General Wool was ordered to muster the volunteers accepted by the president into the service.

Preparations were made by the American government to prosecute the war with vigor. At the suggestion of General Scott a comprehensive plan of operations was adopted. Two separate expeditions were to be organized. One, called the "Army of the West," was to assemble at Fort Leavenworth, on the Missouri, to cross the plains and the Rocky mountains, and to invade and conquer the northern provinces of Mexico. A powerful fleet was to be sent around Cape Horn to attack the Mexican ports on the Pacific and cooperate with the Army of the West. A second force, called the "Army of the Centre," was to advance from Texas to the city of Mexico. and, if it was thought best, was to cooperate with the "Army of Occupation" under General Taylor. As we shall see, the plan was afterwards modified, and the advance upon the Mexican capital was made from Vera Cruz on the Gulf of Mexico.

Towards the last of May the news of the brilliant victories on the Rio Grande was received at Washington, and was hailed with rejoicings throughout the Union. On the 30th of May Congress conferred upon General Taylor the rank of major-general by brevet as a reward for his victories.

On the 23d of May the Mexican Congress formally declared war against the United States, and the call of the Mexican government for

ST. JOSEPH, MISSOURI.

volunteers for the defence of that country was responded to with enthusiasm.

Thanks to the energy of General Wool, twelve thousand volunteers were mustered into the service of the United States in six weeks. Nine thousand of these were sent forward rapidly to reinforce General Taylor, and with the remainder Wool marched to San Antonio, in Texas, to await further orders.

General Taylor had been delayed at Matamoras for three months by the weakness of his force; but as soon as reinforcements reached him, he prepared to advance into the interior. His first movement was directed against the city of Monterey, the capital of the State of New Leon, where the Mexicans had collected an army. His army numbered about nine thousand men of all arms, and of these a little over twenty-three hundred men were detached for garrisons, leaving an active force of six thousand

45

six hundred and seventy men. On the 20th of August General Worth's division marched from Matamoras, and a fortnight later General Taylor set out from the Rio Grande with the main army. On the 9th of September the American forces encamped within three miles of Monterey.

Monterey is an old Spanish city, nearly three hundred years old. It lies in a beautiful valley, and is about two miles in length by one mile in breadth. The mountains approach close to it, and protect it on all sides but two. On one of these sides it is approached from the northeast by the road from Matamoras, and on the other by a rocky gorge through which runs the road connecting the city with Saltillo. The city has three large plazas or public squares, and is built like the towns of old Spain, with narrow streets, and houses of stone one story in height, with strong walls of masonry rising about three feet above the flat roofs. The city itself is enclosed with strong walls, intended for artillery. Every means of defence had been exhausted by the Mexicans. Forty-two heavy cannon were mounted on the city walls, the streets were barricaded, and the flat roofs and stone walls of the houses were arranged for infantry. Each house was a separate fortress. A strongly fortified building of heavy stone, called the Bishop's palace, stood on the side of a hill without the city walls, and on the opposite side of the city were redoubts held by infantry and artillery. The command of Monterey and its defences was held by General Ampudia, and the garrison consisted of ten thousand veteran troops.

Ten days were passed by the American army in reconnoitring the town, its peculiar situation rendering such movements very difficult. On the afternoon of the 20th of September General Worth was ordered to turn the hill on which stood the Bishop's palace, gain the Saltillo road, and carry the works in that direction. This movement was successfully accomplished, but in order to gain the desired position Worth was obliged to cut a new road across the mountain. His troops bivouacked for the night just out of range of the enemy's guns. During the night the Americans built a battery to command the Mexican citadel.

On the morning of the 21st of September the American artillery opened fire upon Monterey, and the infantry advanced to carry the Mexican works. The brigade of General Quitman carried a strong work in the lower part of the town, and at the same time General Butler, with a part of his division, forced his way into the town on the right. While these operations were in progress General Worth's division seized the Saltillo road, and secured the enemy's line of retreat. Several fortified positions along the heights were also carried, and their guns turned upon the Bishop's palace.

During the night of the 21st the Mexicans evacuated the lower part of the city, but kept their hold upon the citadel and the upper town, from which they maintained a vigorous fire upon the American positions. At daybreak, on the 22d, Worth's division, advancing in the midst of a fog and rain, carried the crest commanding the Bishop's palace, and by noon had captured the palace itself. The guns of the captured works were now directed upon the enemy in the city below.

The enemy had fortified the city so thoroughly that the Americans were not only forced to carry the various barricades in succession, but were compelled to break through the walls of the fortified houses, and advance from house to house in this way. One or two field-pieces were drawn up to the flat roofs, and the Mexicans were driven from point to point during the 22d and 23d, until they were confined to the citadel and plaza. On the night of the 23d General Ampudia opened negotiations, and on the morning of the 24th surrendered the town and garrison to General Taylor. The Mexican soldiers were allowed to march out with the honors of war. General Taylor was induced to grant this concession by his generous desire to spare the people of the city the sufferings which would have been caused by a prolonged defence.

The Mexican commander represented to General Taylor that the Mexican government was sincerely anxious for peace, and that it would respond favorably to any fair propositions upon this subject that might be laid before it. In order to afford an opportunity for such an arrangement of the war, and influenced by the scarcity of provisions—the American army having at the time but ten days' rations—Taylor agreed to a cessation of hostilities for eight weeks, subject to the consent of his government. The Mexican army withdrew from Monterey, and an American garrison, under General Worth, as governor, occupied the city. The main body of Taylor's army then went into camp at Walnut Springs, three miles distant from Monterey. The Americans lost four hundred and eighty-eight men, killed and wounded, in the storming of Monterey. The Mexican loss was much greater.

In the meantime the government of the United States had been led into a terrible blunder by its desire to bring the war to a speedy close. Santa Anna, who had been driven out of Mexico by one of the numerous revolutions in that country, was living in exile at Havana. He declared that if he were allowed to return to Mexico he would use his influence in favor of peace, and would secure a treaty for the accomplishment of that end. He was sure he could carry out this scheme, and only needed to be sustained by the United States government with the sum of three or four millions of dollars to enable him to get control of the

Mexican government. President Polk was completely duped by the "illustrious exile," and not only urged Congress to appropriate the sum of two millions of dollars to assist Santa Anna, but issued an order to Commodore Conner, commanding the American fleet in the Gulf, to permit Santa Anna to pass through his lines and return to Mexico. Santa Anna at once availed himself of this order, and landing at Vera Cruz hastened into the interior.

Once in Mexico Santa Anna thought no more of his promises to President Polk. He set to work to gain possession of the government, but not with a view to making peace. He issued a manifesto, in which he called on his countrymen to rally under his banner for the defence of their homes and country. He assured them of his undying hatred of the "perfidious Yankees," pointed to the reverses of the government of Paredes, and declared that he alone could save the country. His appeals were successful. The Mexican people rose at his call, deposed Paredes, and elected Santa Anna president. The repeated defeats of their armies were forgotten in the new enthusiasm which Santa Anna's presence and proclamations aroused, and in the course of a few months that leader found himself at the head of a well-equipped army of twenty thousand men, which was being steadily increased by the arrival of fresh recruits.

In the meantime General Wool, with a reinforcement of three thousand troops, had marched from San Antonio to join General Taylor. He had reached Monclova, about seventy miles from Monterey, when he heard of the capture of the latter place by Taylor. His route had lain across an uninhabited and desert region, in which the troops suffered greatly for want of water. He was directed by General Taylor to take position in a fertile district in the province of Durango, where he could obtain supplies for his own command as well as for the army at Monterey. General Wool conciliated the people of the region occupied by him by protecting them in their liberties and property, and paying fair prices for all the supplies furnished by them. The Mexicans were far better treated by the conquering army than they had been by their own rulers.

In accordance with orders received from Washington General Taylor put an end to the armistice on the 13th of November. On the 15th General Worth, with seven hundred men, occupied Saltillo, the capital of the State of Coahuila. Leaving a garrison in Monterey, under General Butler, Taylor moved towards the coast to attack Tampico. Upon reaching Victoria, the capital of the State of Tamaulipas, he learned that Tampico had surrendered to the United States squadron, under Commodore Conner, on the 14th of November. Victoria was occupied on the 29th of December. The troops under General Wool were now ordered to join General Worth at Saltillo, and General Taylor prepared to resume his forward movement into the heart of Mexico. At this juncture his offensive operations were suddenly brought to a close.

The plan of the invasion adopted by the government of the United States had been so far modified that the "Army of the Centre," under General Winfield Scott, was ordered to capture Vera Cruz, the principal Mexican port on the Gulf, and advance upon the city of Mexico from that point. Troops in sufficient numbers could not be drawn from the United States, and General Scott, as commander-in-chief, decided to draw the desired number of men from Taylor's army. The order for the withdrawal of these troops reached General Taylor just as he was about to resume active operations. Taylor was keenly disappointed at being thus condemned to inactivity, but like the true soldier that he was at once obeyed the orders sent him. Generals Worth and Quitman with their divisions, and the greater portion of the volunteers who had come out with General Wool, were at once despatched to the Gulf coast to join the expedition against Vera Cruz. The withdrawal of these troops left General Taylor with a very small force. During the month of January and the early part of February, 1847, reinforcements from the United States increased his army to about six thousand men. A portion of these was placed in garrison at Monterey and Saltillo, leaving General Taylor about forty-seven hundred effective troops, of whom but six hundred were regulars.

Early in January, 1847, General Scott sent Lieutenant Richey with an escort of cavalry to convey a despatch to General Taylor. Lieutenant Richey was killed by the Mexicans on the way, and his despatches were forwarded to Santa Anna, who learned from them the American plan for the invasion of Mexico. He at once resolved upon his own course. Relying upon the strength of Vera Cruz to hold Scott's army in check, he determined to attack General Taylor at once, and crush him. By the most energetic and despotic measures he silenced the opposition which prevailed in the city of Mexico, and obtained both men and money for his attempt. On the 26th of January he began his march upon Saltillo with twenty-three thousand well-armed and equipped men, and twenty pieces of artillery.

The Mexican army had reached San Louis Potosi, about sixty miles south of Saltillo, when General Wool, commanding at the latter place, learned of their approach. He at once notified General Taylor, who advanced with his whole effective force from Monterey to Saltillo. As the enemy continued to approach, Taylor left his stores at Saltillo, and moved rapidly to Agua Nueva, eighteen miles beyond Saltillo, on the

road to San Louis Potosi. His design was to secure the southern end of
the pass through the Sierra Nevada. With this pass in the possession of
the Americans the Mexican army would be compelled to fight at once, as
the country in their rear was incapable of supplying them with provisions. The reports of the reconnoitring parties made it evident that the
Mexican force was vastly superior to that of the Americans, and General
Taylor also learned that a strong body of Mexican cavalry, under General Minon, was some distance to the left of his position, which could be
turned A daring reconnoissance was made by Major M'Culloch, of the
Texan Rangers He entered the Mexican camp, passed through it, and
obtained accurate information of their numbers, and regained his own
lines in safety.

Upon receipt of M'Culloch's intelligence, and the report of the effort
of the Mexican cavalry to turn his left, General Taylor fell back from
Agua Nueva to a new position, eleven miles higher up the valley, on the
21st of February.

The withdrawal of the American army was made in good time. Santa
Anna had sent Minon with the cavalry to gain the rear of Taylor's
army, and at the same time endeavored, by a forced march of fifty miles,
to surprise General Taylor at Agua Nueva Upon arriving in front of
that place, he found to his astonishment and disappointment that Tay "
had abandoned his position Interpreting this movement as a flight, the
Mexican commander pushed on in pursuit of his adversary, and came up
with him on the morning of the 22d of February.

The position chosen by General Taylor was at the north end of the
valley known as Las Angosturas, or the Narrows, and near the hacienda
or plantation known as Buena Vista, from which latter place the battle
took its name. It was one of great strength. Its flanks were protected
by the mountains which rose abruptly from the defile, and the ground in
front was broken by numerous ravines and gullies. The American forces
were disposed so as to secure every advantage afforded by the nature of
the ground, and the road through the pass—the key to the whole position
—was swept by the fire of the artillery The troops were in high spirits.
It was Washington's birthday, and this incident was generally com-
mented upon as a good omen.

About noon a Mexican officer brought a note to General Taylor, in
which Santa Anna demanded the surrender of the American army This
demand was refused, and skirmishing at once began. During the afternoon Santa Anna sent a force under General Ampudia to ascend the
mountains and turn the American left. This brought on severe skirmishing in this quarter, but nothing definite was accomplished during the

afternoon Late in the afternoon the Mexican cavalry under General Minon, which had passed the mountains, appeared in the plains north of Saltillo Minon was ordered to halt in the position he had gained and await the result of the battle of the next day at Buena Vista His appearance caused great anxiety to General Taylor, who hastened to Saltillo with reinforcements after nightfall, as he feared Minon would seek to capture that place

During the night of the 22d Santa Anna reinforced the column under Ampudia, and opened the battle at daybreak on the 23d of February, by endeavoring to turn the American left A little later he opened fire from his artillery, and moved forward three powerful columns of attack against the American centre. The movement of the column of Ampudia was successful, the left of the American line was completely turned, but the attack upon the centre was repulsed by the splendid fire of the American batteries.

At this moment General Taylor arrived upon the field from Saltillo, bringing with him May's dragoons, several companies of Mississippi riflemen, and a portion of the Arkansas cavalry, embracing every man that could be spared from Saltillo. He had come at a critical moment, for the turning of his left flank by Ampudia had neutralized the natural advantage of the position Many of the troops were in full retreat upon Buena Vista, and nothing but the courage and constancy of those who yet remained firm could save the day By great exertions Colonel Jefferson Davis rallied the greater part of his own regiment—the Mississippi rifles—and a part of the Second Indiana, and by a rapid advance drove back a strong Mexican column in his front. He had scarcely accomplished this when he was assailed by a body of one thousand splendid Mexican lancers Davis quickly formed his own men and the Second and Third Indiana in the shape of the letter V, with the opening towards the enemy, and posted Sherman's battery on his left. The line thus formed awaited in silence the approach of the Mexican cavalry, which came on at a gallop. As they drew near the opening of this terrible V the Mexicans, who had expected the Americans to fire, when they intended to dash in upon them before the men could reload, were astonished at the silence with which they were received, and slackened their pace until they came to a walk within eighty yards of the opening of the angle. In an instant Davis gave the command, and his men took deliberate aim. Then a volley flashed from the rifles and swept away the head of the Mexican column. The next moment Sherman's guns opened upon the cavalry with grape and canister. Under this combined fire horses and lancers fell in great numbers, forming a barricade over which the enemy could not pass, and the Mexicans, seized with a panic, wheeled about and fled in confusion.

While this attack was in progress the Mexicans sent a body of cavalry under Torrejon to seize the plantation of Buena Vista. Torrejon made his attack with vigor, but was driven back by the Kentucky and Arkansas volunteers, assisted by Colonel May's dragoons. Colonel Yell, of the Arkansas regiment, was killed and Torrejon was wounded in this part of the engagement.

During all this while a steady cannonade had been in progress along the centre of the American line. The Mexicans endeavored to silence the American batteries, but without success.

Santa Anna now sent a strong force to pass around the American left

DEFEAT OF THE MEXICAN RIGHT WING AT BUENA VISTA.

and gain the rear of Taylor's line; and this force was joined by a part of Torrejon's command, which was retreating from Buena Vista. The movement was detected by Colonel May, who met it with his cavalry and several companies of Illinois and Indiana volunteers. General Taylor sent to his assistance all the cavalry he could spare and Bragg's battery. The retreat of the Mexicans, who had passed beyond the American left, was cut off, and they were driven in confusion to the base of the mountain, while Bragg's guns showered canister upon them and increased the panic which had set in among them. It seemed that the whole Mexican force, numbering five thousand men, must surrender

or be exterminated. In this emergency the Mexican commander raised
the white flag, and asked for a parley, professing to have a message from
Santa Anna to General Taylor, and the American guns ceased firing.
Before the trick was discovered the Mexican right escaped under the
cover of the flag of truce by passing along the base of the mountain to a
point from which they rejoined their main army.

Santa Anna now brought up his reserves, and late in the afternoon
made a determined attack upon the American right, which had been
greatly weakened to assist the troops engaged in repelling the attack
on the left. The Mexican column, twelve thousand strong, easily
drove back the few scattered volunteers that disputed their advance,

GENERAL TAYLOR THANKING CAPTAIN BRAGG AT BUENA VISTA.

and captured O'Brien's battery, which was without infantry support, but
not until every man had been killed or wounded. Washington's guns
now opened upon the enemy, and succeeded in holding their cavalry in
check for a moment. The Mexican infantry pushed on, firing as they
advanced, and it was evident that the crisis of the battle was at hand.
The battle had been going on for eight hours, and the American troops
were greatly exhausted by the unusual exertions they had been subjected
to; while the Mexican column, consisting mainly of their reserves, was
fresh, and four times as strong as the whole American army. Keenly
alive to his danger Taylor exerted himself in every possible way to bring
up his scattered regiments in time to save the position. The flying
rtillery of Captain Bragg was the first to reach the field. There was

not an infantry soldier near to support him, and the salvation of the army depended upon Bragg's efforts. He unlimbered his guns within a few yards of the rapidly advancing Mexicans, and poured in discharge after discharge with a rapidity which seemed wonderful. The Mexican advance was checked, and Sherman now came up and opened fire from his guns upon them. Washington's battery a little later joined in the fire. The Mississippi and Indiana volunteers now reached the field, and made a spirited attack upon the enemy's right flank. Under this terrible fire the Mexicans wavered for a few moments, and then broke in confusion and fled from the field.

The Mexicans made no further attack during the day, and that night Santa Anna, abandoning his wounded, and leaving his dead unburied, retreated rapidly towards Agua Nueva. The American loss in the battle

of Buena Vista was two hundred and sixty-seven killed, and four hundred and fifty-six wounded. That of the Mexicans was over two thousand killed and wounded, including many officers of high rank. Taylor followed the Mexican army on the 24th as far as Agua Nueva, and collecting their wounded, removed them to Saltillo, where they were attended by the American surgeons.

The victory of Buena Vista was decisive of the war. It saved the valley of the Rio Grande from invasion by a victorious Mexican army, and enabled the expedition of General Scott against Vera Cruz to proceed without delay to the accomplishment of its objects. It also greatly disheartened the Mexican people, and during the remainder of the year Taylor's army had nothing to do but to hold the country it occupied.

FREMONT.

General Taylor remained at Agua Nueva until he was satisfied that no further trouble was to be apprehended from the Mexican army, and then returned by easy stages to his camp at Walnut Springs, near Monterey, which he reached by the last of March. In the summer of 1847, leaving General Wool in command of the army, General Taylor returned to the United States, where he was received with distinguished honor.

While these events were going on in Mexico Captain John C. Fremont, of the United States army, had been engaged in prosecuting the discoveries in the Rocky mountain region, which he had begun in 1843, in which year he had explored the valley known as the Great Basin, the region of the Great Salt lake, and the valleys of the Sacramento and San

Joaquin, on the Pacific coast. In May, 1845, Fremont set out on his third expedition, and passed the winter in the valley of the San Joaquin, then Mexican territory. In May, 1846, he received orders from Washington to move into California and counteract any foreign scheme for securing that Territory, and to conciliate the good-will of the inhabitants toward the United States. Fremont had but sixty men with him, but he at once moved into the valley of the Sacramento. The Mexican

POINT ARENA LIGHTHOUSE—COAST OF CALIFORNIA.

inhabitants were seriously considering at this time whether they should massacre the American settlers, or whether, in the event of a war between Mexico and the United States, they should place California under the protection of Great Britain. Fremont was informed of these plots, and, though no war existed as yet between the two republics, he also learned that the Mexican General De Castro was advancing to drive him out of California. The American settlers flocked to Fremont's camp, with their arms and horses, and he soon found himself at the head of a considerable force. He was thus enabled to repulse De Castro's attack, and, after a few conflicts, to drive him from Upper California. By July, 1846, the Mexican authority was entirely overthrown in Upper California, and the flag of independence was raised by the settlers.

The American squadron in the Pacific was commanded by Commodore Sloat, who was ordered by the secretary of the navy to seize the port of San Francisco as soon as he was reliably informed of the existence of war between the two countries, and to occupy or blockade such other Mexican ports as his force would permit. In the early summer of 1846 the American squadron was lying at Mazatlan. A British squadron under Admiral Seymour also lay in the harbor, and the American commodore became convinced that the British admiral was watching him for the purpose of interfering with his designs upon California. He therefore resolved to get rid of him, and put to sea and sailed to the westward, as if making for the Sandwich islands. The British fleet followed him promptly, but in the night the commodore tacked and sailed up the coast to Monterey, while the British continued their course to the islands Sloat was coldly received at Monterey by the authorities. Hearing of the action of Fremont and the American settlers, the commodore a few days later took possession of the town, and sent a courier to Fremont, who at once joined him with his mounted men. California was now taken possession of in the name of the United States.

About the middle of July Commodore Stockton arrived in the harbor, and succeeded Commodore Sloat, who returned home, in the command of the squadron. The next day Admiral Seymour arrived at Monterey. He saw he was too late, and quietly submitted to what he could not prevent, though he was greatly astonished to find the town in possession of the American forces. On the 17th of August Fremont and Stockton occupied Los Angeles, the capital of Upper California.

In June, 1846, General Kearney, with the "Army of the West," numbering eighteen hundred men, marched from Fort Leavenworth, on the Missouri, across the plains to Santa Fé, the capital of the Mexican province of New Mexico. After a march of nearly one thousand miles, he occupied Santa Fé on the 18th of August. Leaving a garrison at Santa Fé, Kearney pushed on towards California, intending to conquer that province also, but upon reaching the Gila river, he was met by the famous hunter Kit Carson, who informed him of the conquest of California by Fremont and Stockton. Kearney thereupon sent two companies of dragoons under Major Sumner back to Santa Fé, and with the remainder continued his march to the Pacific coast.

Upon leaving Santa Fé, Kearney had instructed Colonel Doniphan to invade the country of the Navajoe Indians and compel them to make peace with the Americans. Doniphan set out in November, 1846, and crossing the mountains, which were covered with snow, succeeded in making a treaty with the Navajoes, by which they agreed to refrain from hostilities against the people of New Mexico. He then marched to the southeast to meet General Wool at Chihuahua.

The inhabitants of New Mexico, encouraged by the absence of Doniphan with so large a force, rose in revolt against the American forces, and murdered the American governor of the territory and several other officials on the 11th of January, 1847. Colonel Sterling Price, commanding the troops at Santa Fé, at once marched against the insurgents,

SOUTHWEST FROM SANTA FE.

defeated them in two engagements, though they greatly outnumbered his force, and suppressed the rebellion. The insurgents obtained peace only by surrendering their leaders, several of whom were hanged by the Americans.

Colonel Doniphan, in the meantime, had continued his march. His route lay through a barren region destitute of water or grass called the Jornado del Muerto—"The Journey of Death." He pressed forward with firmness through this terrible region, his men and animals suffering greatly on the march, and in the latter part of December entered the valley of the Rio Grande. With a force of eight hundred and fifty-six men he defeated over twelve hundred Mexicans at Brazito, on the 26th of December, 1846, and inflicted upon them a loss of nearly two hundred men; losing only seven men himself. On the 28th he occupied El Paso, and there waited until his artillery could join him from Santa Fé. It arrived in the course of a month, and on the 8th of February he resumed his march to Chihuahua. On the 28th he encountered and defeated a Mexican force of over fifteen hundred men with ten pieces of artillery, at a pass of the Sacramento river, a tributary of the Rio Grande. The Mexicans lost over three hundred killed and a number wounded. The Americans lost two killed and several wounded. The Mexicans were

EAST SIDE OF PLAZA—SANTA FÉ.

completely routed, and left their artillery and all their train in the hands of the Americans.

On the 1st of March, 1847, Doniphan entered Chihuahua, and raising the American flag on the citadel, took possession of the province in the name of the United States. Chihuahua was one of the largest cities in Mexico, and contained nearly thirty thousand inhabitants. Doniphan's force was less than one thousand men. He had expected to find General Wool here, and failing to meet him was in utter ignorance of the positions of the American forces. His own position, in the midst of a hostile population perilous indeed, but by his firm and just

DONIPHAN MAKING A TREATY WITH THE NAVAJOES.

measures he conciliated the inhabitants. He remained at Chihuahua for six weeks vainly expecting the arrival of General Wool, and on the 27th of April evacuated that place, and set out for Saltillo, three hundred and fifty miles distant He reached that place on the 22d of May. Remaining there but three days, he continued his march to Monterey, from which he proceeded to Matamoras. The enlistments of his men being over, they were transported to New Orleans, and there mustered out of the service.

Thus ended the most remarkable expedition on record. In less than one year a corps of volunteers, unused to the hardships of war, had marched over snow-covered mountains and across burning deserts, a distance of over five thousand miles, over three thousand of which lay through an unknown and hostile country, abounding in enemies who might have crushed them at any moment had they rallied in sufficient force.

In the meantime there had been new troubles in California. In August, 1847, Commodore Stockton appointed Captain Fremont military commandant of California, and soon after sailed from San Francisco to Monterey, from which place he continued his voyage to San Diego Soon after the departure of the fleet, Fremont learned of a conspiracy to overthrow his government. By a forced march of one hundred and fifty miles he surprised and captured the insurgent leader, Don J. Pico. A court-martial sentenced him to death, but Fremont wisely spared his life, and Pico, in gratitude for this clemency, gave him his powerful aid in his efforts to tranquillize the country.

General Kearney had continued his march from New Mexico, encountering great difficulties along the route, and suffering considerably from the repeated attacks of superior parties of the enemy. In December, 1847, he reached San Pasqual, where he was obliged to halt. His situation was desperate indeed ; his provisions were exhausted ; his horses had died on the march , his mules were disabled ; a large number of his men were sick and his camp was surrounded by the enemy, who held every road by which he could escape. In this situation three men—Kit Carson, Lieutenant Beales of the navy, and an Indian whose name is unfortunately unknown—volunteered to make their way through the enemy's lines to San Diego, thirty miles distant, and inform Commodore Stockton of Kearney's need of assistance. They succeeded in reaching San Diego, and the commodore promptly sent reinforcements to Kearney, which enabled him to drive off the enemy and reach San Diego in safety.

Commodore Stockton now directed his attention to suppressing the insurrection of the Mexican inhabitants of California, who had gotten posses-

"THE JOURNEY OF DEATH."—CROSSED BY DONIPHAN'S COMMAND.

sion of Los Angeles. Driven to extremities they surrendered the town on condition that the Americans should respect the rights and property of the citizens.

Commodore Stockton having been relieved of his civil functions by orders from Washington, General Kearney claimed the governorship of the territory by virtue of his rank. Fremont refused to recognize his authority, and was brought to trial before a court-martial, which found him guilty of disobedience of orders and mutiny, and sentenced him to be dismissed from the service. The sentence was remitted by the president on account of Fremont's meritorious and valuable services, but Fremont refused to accept the clemency of the president, and thus admit

SACRAMENTO, CALIFORNIA, IN 1875.

the justice of the sentence of the court, and resigned his commission. General Kearney remained in California as governor of that territory.

The expedition under General Scott sailed from New Orleans late in November, 1846, and rendezvoused at the island of Lobos, about one hundred and twenty-five miles north of Vera Cruz. The plan of operations for this army was very simple—to capture Vera Cruz and march to the city of Mexico by the most direct route. At length everything being in readiness, the expedition sailed from Lobos island, and on the morning of the 9th of March, 1847, the army, thirteen thousand strong, landed without opposition at a point selected by General Scott and Commodore Conner a few days before. The city and vicinity had been thoroughly reconnoitred, and the troops were at once marched to the positions assigned them by the commander-in-chief.

Vera Cruz is the principal seaport of Mexico, and contained at the time of the siege about fifteen thousand inhabitants. It was strongly fortified on the land side, and towards the Gulf was defended by the Castle of San Juan de Ulloa, the strongest fortress in America, with the exception of Quebec.

On the 10th of March the investment of the city was begun by General Worth, and the American lines were definitely established around the city for a distance of six miles. During the day, and for several days thereafter, bodies of Mexicans attempted to harass the besiegers, and a steady fire was maintained upon them by the guns of the castle and the city as they worked at their batteries. The American works being completed, and their guns in position, General Scott summoned the city of Vera Cruz to surrender, stipulating that no batteries should be placed in the city to attack the castle unless the city should be fired upon by that work. The demand was refused by General Morales, who commanded both the city and the castle, and at 4 o'clock on the afternoon of the 22d of March, the American batteries opened fire upon the town. The bombardment was continued for five days, and the fleet joined in the attack upon the castle. The city suffered terribly; a number of the inhabitants were killed, and many buildings were set on fire by the shells. On the 27th the city and castle surrendered, and were promptly occupied by the Americans. Over five thousand prisoners and five hundred pieces of artillery fell into the hands of the victors.

GENERAL WINFIELD SCOTT.

The garrison were required to march out, lay down their arms, and were then dismissed upon their parole. The inhabitants were protected in their civil and religious rights. The surrender was completed on the morning of the 29th.

Having secured the city and the castle, General Scott placed a strong garrison in each, and appointed General Worth governor of Vera Cruz. He then prepared to march upon the city of Mexico, and on the 8th of April the advance division, under General Twiggs, set out from Vera Cruz towards Jalapa. Deducting the force left to garrison Vera Cruz, Scott's whole army amounted to but eighty-five hundred men.

Santa Anna had not found the consequences to himself of the battle of Buena Vista as bad as he had expected. He had succeeded in persuading his countrymen that he had not been defeated in that battle, but had simply retreated for want of provisions, and they had agreed to give him another trial. He had pledged himself to prevent the advance of the Americans to the capital, in the event of the fall of Vera Cruz, and with the aid of those of his countrymen who were willing to support him had quelled an insurrection at the capital, and had strengthened his power to a greater degree than ever. With a force of twelve thousand men he had taken position at Cerro Gordo, a mountain pass at the eastern edge of the Cordilleras, to hold the American army in check, and had fortified his position with great skill and care.

General Twiggs halted before the Mexican position to await the arrival of General Scott, who soon joined him with the main army. The Mexican lines were carefully reconnoitred, and on the 18th of April General

BATTLE OF CERRO GORDO.

Scott, avoiding a direct attack, turned the enemy's left, seized the heights commanding their position, and drove them from their works with a loss of three thousand prisoners and forty-three pieces of artillery. Santa Anna mounted a mule, taken from his carriage, and fled, leaving the carriage and his private papers in the hands of the Americans. Besides their prisoners, the Mexicans lost over one thousand men in killed and wounded. Scott's loss was four hundred and thirty-one killed and wounded.

The brilliant victory of Cerro Gordo opened the way for the American army to Jalapa, which was occupied on the 19th of April. Continuing his advance, General Scott captured the strong fortress of Perote, situated on a peak of the Eastern Cordilleras, which was abandoned almost without a blow by its defenders, on the 22d of April. On the 15th of May Puebla, the second city of Mexico, containing eighty thousand inhabitants, was occupied. General Scott established his head-quarters at Puebla, and awaited reinforcements. The terms of the volunteers would expire in June, and they refused to re-enlist, as they were afraid to encounter the yellow fever, the scourge of the Mexican climate, the season for which was close at hand. They were returned to the United States, and General Scott was forced to spend three months at Puebla in inactivity. The force he had with him was greatly weakened by sickness, and eighteen hundred men were in the hospitals of Puebla alone.

AMERICAN ARMY ENTERING PUEBLA.

While at Puebla, General Scott was ordered by the secretary of war to collect duties on merchandise entering the Mexican ports, and to apply the money thus obtained to the needs of the army. He was also ordered to levy contributions upon the Mexican people for the use of the troops. He refused to obey this order, declaring that the country through which he was moving was too poor to warrant impressments, and that such a measure would exasperate the Mexicans and cause them to refuse to supply the army at all. "Not a ration for man or horse," he said, "would be brought in except by the bayonet, which would oblige the troops to spread themselves out many leagues to the right and left in search of subsistence, and stop all military operations." He continued to buy provisions for his army at the regular prices of the country, and by so doing greatly allayed the bitterness of feeling with which the Mexicans regarded the Americans.

Another annoyance to which the commander-in-chief was subjected arose from the ill-advised action of Mr. N. P Trist, who had been sent out to Mexico in the quality of peace commissioner. Soon after the capture of Vera Cruz, General Scott had suggested to the president the propriety of sending out commissioners to his head-quarters, who should be empowered to treat for peace when a suitable occasion should offer itself. The president selected for this purpose Mr. N. P. Trist, who had been United States consul at Havana, and who was acquainted with the Spanish language—a singular selection. Mr. Trist was furnished with the draft of a treaty carefully prepared in the state department at Washington, and was intrusted with a despatch from Mr Buchanan, the secretary of state, to the Mexican minister of foreign relations. He was instructed to communicate confidentially to General Scott and Commodore Perry both the treaty and his instructions. General Scott was informed of Trist's mission by the secretary of war, and was directed to suspend military operations until further orders, unless attacked.

Mr Trist reached Vera Cruz in due time, but instead of explaining his mission, as directed, to General Scott, he sent a note to the commander-in-chief from Vera Cruz, enclosing the letter of the secretary of war, and the sealed despatch to the Mexican minister, which he requested the general to forward to its destination. The letter of the secretary of war could not be understood by General Scott without the explanations Mr Trist was directed to give, but failed to make. General Scott very properly resented the conduct of Trist as an attempt to degrade him by making him subordinate to that personage, and in his reply to him declared that the suspension of hostilities belonged to the commander in the field and not to the secretary of war a thousand miles away. Trist thereupon wrote to General Scott, giving a full explanation of his mission, but did so in disrespectful terms. In conclusion he claimed to be the aid-de-camp of the president, and as such to possess the right to issue orders to the commander-in-chief. Scott referred the matter to the government at Washington, maintaining in the meantime his independence of action as commanding general. In due time explanations came from Washington satisfactory to the general, and Mr Trist was sharply reprimanded by the secretary of state "for his presuming to command the general-in-chief."

After the fall of Cerro Gordo, Santa Anna repaired to Orizaba, where he organized a number of guerrilla bands to attack the American trains on the road between Vera Cruz and Scott's army. He then returned to the city of Mexico, where he was coldly received by the people. The affairs of the Mexican nation were in the most hopeless confusion, and the people were utterly disheartened. Their army on which they had depended for the defence of the road to the capital had been routed at Cerro Gordo, and there was no force in existence with which to stay the advance of the victorious Americans. Had General Scott been able to advance upon Mexico immediately after his occupation of Puebla, the city would have fallen at once, and the war have been brought to an immediate close. A number of leaders contested the supremacy at the capital, and the quarrels of these factions paralyzed the efforts of the government. The most capable of these leaders was Santa Anna, and his strong qualities naturally attracted to him the largest following By his extraordinary energy he suppressed the opposition to him, secured the money he needed by forced loans from the people, and raised an army of twenty-five thousand men and sixty pieces of artillery, and fortified the city of Mexico. The three months' enforced delay of General Scott's army at Puebla gave him time to carry out these measures, and he endeavored to gain still further advantages by opening negotiations secretly with Mr. Trist, and pretending to be anxious for peace. He declared that he needed money to enable him to act with freedom in arranging a treaty, and succeeded in getting about ten thousand dollars from the secret service fund at the disposal of General Scott; but his designs were soon detected by the American commander, and the supply of money was discontinued

Reinforcements from the United States arrived at Puebla in July, and on the 7th of August General Scott resumed his advance on the city of Mexico, with a force increased to ten thousand men. The route lay through a beautiful upland country, abounding in water, and rich in the most picturesque scenery. The troops pressed on with enthusiasm, and on the 10th of August the summit of the Cordilleras was passed, and then almost from the very spot from which, more than three centuries before, the followers of Cortez looked down upon the halls of the Montezumas, the American army beheld the beautiful valley of Mexico stretching out for miles before them, with the city of Mexico lying in the midst, encircled by the strong works that had been erected for its defence.

The passes on the direct road to the city had been well fortified and garrisoned by the Mexicans, but the country upon the flanks had been left unprotected, because Santa Anna deemed it utterly impossible for any troops to pass over it and turn his position. El Peñon, the most

of subsistence, these defences, was reconnoitred by the engineers, who re-
provisions for would cost at least three thousand lives to carry it. Scott
done were determined to turn El Peñon, instead of attacking it. The city
and its defences were carefully reconnoitred, and it was discovered that the
works on the south and west were weaker than those at any other points.
General Scott now moved to the left, passed El Peñon on the south, and
by the aid of a corps of skilful engineers moved his army across ravines
and chasms which the Mexican commander had pronounced impassable,
and had left unguarded. General Twiggs led the advance, and halted
and encamped at Chalco, on the lake of the same name. Worth followed,
and, passing Twiggs, encamped at the town of San Augustin, eight miles
from the capital.

As soon as Santa Anna found that the Americans had turned El
Peñon, and had advanced to the south side of the city, he left that fortress
and took position in the strong fort of San Antonio, which lay directly in
front of Worth's new position. Northwest of San Antonio, and four
miles from the city, lay the little village of Churubusco, which had been
strongly fortified by the Mexicans. A little to the west of San Augustin
was the fortified camp of Contreras, with a garrison of about six thousand
men. In the rear, between the camp and the city, was a reserve force of
twelve thousand men. The whole number of Mexicans manning these
defences was about thirty-five thousand, with at least one hundred pieces
of artillery of various sizes

General Scott lost no time in moving against the enemy's works.
General Persifer F Smith was ordered to attack the entrenched camp at
Contreras, while Shields and Pierce should move between the camp and
Santa Anna at San Antonio, and prevent him from going to the assistance
of the force at Contreras. At three o'clock on the morning of August
20th, in the midst of a cold rain, Smith began his march, his men holding on to each other, to avoid being separated in the darkness. He made
his attack at sunrise, and in fifteen minutes had possession of the camp.
He took three thousand prisoners and thirty-three pieces of cannon.

The camp at Contreras having fallen, General Scott attacked the fortified village of Churubusco an hour or two later, and carried it after a
desperate struggle of several hours. General Worth's division stormed
and carried the strong fort of San Antonio, and General Twiggs captured another important work. The Mexicans outnumbered their assailants three to one, and fought bravely Their efforts were in vain,
however, and late in the afternoon they were driven from their defences,
and pursued by the American cavalry to the gates of the city.

These two victories had been won over a force of thirty thousand

Mexicans by less than ten thousand Americans, and a loss of four thousand killed and wounded and three thousand prisoners had been inflicted upon the Mexican army. The American loss was eleven hundred men.

Santa Anna retreated within the city, and on the 21st of August the American army advanced to within three miles of the city of Mexico. On the same day Santa Anna sent a flag of truce to General Scott, asking for a suspension of hostilities, in order to arrange the terms of a peace. The request was granted, and Mr. Trist was despatched to the city, and began negotiations with the Mexican commissioners. After protracted delays, designed to gain time, the Mexican commissioners declined the American

STORMING OF CHAPULTEPEC.

conditions, and proposed others which they knew would not be accepted. Thoroughly disgusted, Mr. Trist returned to the American camp, and brought with him the intelligence that Santa Anna had violated the armistice by using the time accorded him by it in strengthening his defences. Indignant at such treachery, General Scott at once resumed his advance upon the city.

The Mexican capital was still defended by two powerful works. One of these was Molino del Rey, "The King's Mill," a foundry, where it was said the church bells were being cast into cannon; the other was the strong castle of Chapultepec. General Scott resolved to make his first attack upon Molino del Rey, which was held by fourteen thousand

Mexicans. It was stormed and carried on the 8th of September, after a severe contest by Worth's division, four thousand strong. This was regarded as the hardest won victory of the war. The Mexicans were nearly four times as numerous as the Americans, and their position was one of very great strength. The Americans fought principally with their rifles and muskets, their artillery being of but little use to them, owing to t nature of the position. Their loss was seven hundred and eighty-seven killed and wounded—nearly one-fourth of the force engaged.

The castle of Chapultepec stood on a steep and lofty hill, and could not be turned. If won at all, it must be by a direct assault. On the 12th of September the American artillery opened fire upon it, and reduced it almost to ruins. On the morning of the 13th a determined assault was made by the Americans, and the castle was carried after a sharp struggle.

The fugitives from Chapultepec retreated to the city by the causeway leading to the Belan gate, closely followed by Quitman's division. Worth's division was moved forward to attack the San Cosmo gate, while Quitman assailed the Belen gate. The defences of the causeways were taken in succession, and by nightfall the Belen and San Cosmo gates were in possession of the Americans after a hard fight for them. The troops slept on the ground they had won

During the night of the 13th Santa Anna, with the remains of his army, retreated from the city, leaving the authorities to make the best terms they could with the conqueror. The city officials presented themselves before General Scott before daybreak, and proposed terms of capitulation. The general replied that the city was already in his power, and that he would enter it on his own terms. The next day, September 14th, 1847, the American army entered the city of Mexico, occupied the grand square, and hoisted the stars and stripes over the government buildings

Santa Anna retreated with four or five thousand men from the capital to the vicinity of Puebla, which was besieged by a Mexican force. The city contained eighteen hundred sick Americans, and was held by a garrison of five hundred men under Colonel Childs. This little force held out bravely until the arrival of a brigade from Vera Cruz, under General Lane, on its way to reinforce General Scott. Lane drove off Santa Anna's army, and relieved Puebla on the 8th of October. Ten days later Santa Anna was reported to be collecting another force at Atlixco. Lane set out immediately for that place, reached it by a forced march, and dispersed the Mexicans beyond all hope of reunion.

Immediately after the capture of the city of Mexico Santa Anna resigned the presidency of the republic in favor of Senor Peña y Peña, president of the Supreme Court of Justice, but retained his position as commander-in-chief of the army. The fall of the city was followed by the inauguration of a new government, one of the first acts of which was to dismiss Santa Anna from the command of the army. He at once left the country, and fled to the West Indies.

The Mexican government was removed to the city of Queretaro, and a new congress was elected, which began its sessions in that city. Negotiations for peace had been opened in the meantime, and the meetings of the Mexican commissioners and Mr. Trist were held at the town of Guadaloupe Hidalgo, where, on the 2d of February, 1848, a treaty of peace

CAPTURE OF THE BELEN GATE.

was signed by Nicholas P. Trist, on the part of the United States, and Senors Couto, Atristain and Cuevas, on the part of Mexico. Though Mr. Trist's powers had been withdrawn by President Polk some time before, he ventured to continue his authority on the ground that the opportunity for bringing the war to a close was too favorable to be lost. The commissioners appointed by the president to supersede him reached Mexico a little later, but found the treaty signed and sealed. It was forwarded to Washington, and was laid by the president before the Senate, which body after a brief discussion ratified it. On the 4th of July, 1848, President Polk issued a proclamation announcing the return of peace.

By the terms of the treaty the Rio Grande was accepted by Mexico as the western boundary of the United States and of Texas, and that republic ceded to the United States the provinces of New Mexico and Upper California. For this immense territory the government of the United States agreed to pay to Mexico the sum of fifteen millions of dollars, and to assume the debts due by Mexico to citizens of the United States, amounting to the sum of three and a half millions of dollars.

The treaty having been ratified, the American forces were promptly withdrawn from Mexico.

By the cession of California and New Mexico, regions as yet unknown,

HYDRAULIC MINING.

a territory four times as large as France was added to the dominions of the United States. California bordered the Pacific coast for about six hundred and fifty miles, and extended inland for about the same distance. It embraced an area of about 450,000 square miles, comprising what is now known as California, Nevada, Arizona, Utah, and parts of Colorado and New Mexico. At the close of the war it contained about 15,000 inhabitants.

In February, 1848, occurred an event destined to change the whole history of the Pacific coast. A laborer on the plantation of Captain

Sutter, situated in Coloma county, California, on a branch of the Sacramento river, while working on a mill race, discovered gold in the sands of the little stream. The precious metal was soon found to be in abundance in the neighborhood, and the news spread rapidly. It reached the United States about the time of the ratification of the treaty, and produced the most intense excitement. In the course of a few months thousands of emigrants were on their way to California to dig gold. Some went in steamers and sailing vessels around Cape Horn; some crossed the isthmus of Panama, and worked their way up the Pacific coast; and others, and by far the greater number, undertook the long and dangerous journey across the plains and the Rocky mountains, travelling generally in caravans. In a short time multitudes came flocking from every coun-

THE EMIGRANTS' CAMP ON THE PLAINS EN ROUTE TO CALIFORNIA.

try in Europe to join the throng in search of the precious metal. San Francisco was the central point of this vast emigration, and that place soon grew from a village of a few miserable huts to a city of over fifteen thousand inhabitants. Within two years after the discovery of gold the population of California had increased to nearly 100,000; two years later, in 1852, it numbered 264,000.

The influence of the discovery of gold in California was not limited to this country. It gave an impetus to the commerce and industry of the whole world.

On the 21st of February, 1848, ex-President John Quincy Adams, then a member of the House of Representatives in Congress, was stricken with paralysis in his seat in the House. He was carried into the speaker's room, where he died two days later, at the age of eighty.

On the 29th of May, 1848, Wisconsin was admitted into the Union as a State, making the thirtieth member of the confederacy.

Before the return of peace with Mexico the slavery question had been revived in the United States, and had been the cause of an agitation full of trouble to both sections. On the 8th of August, 1846, President Polk sent a message to Congress asking an appropriation of three millions of dollars to enable him to negotiate a treaty of peace with Mexico, based upon the policy of obtaining a cession of territory outside the existing limits of Texas. During the debate upon a bill to grant this appropriation, Mr. David Wilmot, a representative from Pennsylvania, made the following amendment, known as the "Wilmot Proviso:" "*Provided*, That there shall be neither slavery nor involuntary servitude in any territory which shall hereafter be acquired, or be annexed to the United

States, otherwise than in the punishment of crimes, whereof the party shall have been duly convicted : *Provided always*, That any person escaping into the same, from whom labor or service is lawfully claimed in any one of the United States, such fugitive may be

COAT OF ARMS OF WISCONSIN.

lawfully reclaimed and conveyed out of said territory to the person claiming his or her labor or service." This amendment took no notice of the Missouri Compromise line, and was opposed with great warmth by the southern members, who declared it an attempt to rob the Southern States in advance of their fair share of the territory that might be won by the joint efforts of the States. The bill failed in the Senate; but the announcement of the Wilmot Proviso reopened the slavery question in all its bitterness, and plunged the country into a state of profound excitement.

The agitation was renewed in January, 1847, when a bill for the organization of a territorial government for Oregon was reported to the House with the Wilmot Proviso incorporated in it. Mr. Burt, of South Carolina, moved to amend the bill by inserting before the restrictive clause the words: "Inasmuch as the whole of said territory lies north of 36° 30' north latitude." This was an effort to apply to the Oregon bill the principles of the Missouri Compromise; but the friends of the restriction rejected the amendment. The bill passed the House, but was defeated in the Senate. During the next session the measure was revived, and a territorial government was organized for Oregon with an unqualified restriction upon slavery.

In the fall of 1848 the presidential election occurred. The Democratic party supported Senator Lewis Cass, of Michigan, for the presidency, and General William O. Butler, of Kentucky, for the vice-presidency. The Whig party nominated General Zachary Taylor, of Louisiana, for the presidency, and Millard Fillmore, of New York, for the vice-presidency. The Anti-slavery or Free Soil party put in nomination for the presidency Martin Van Buren, of New York, and for the vice-presidency Charles Francis Adams, of Massachusetts. In the election which followed the political campaign, the candidates of the Whig party were elected by decisive majorities. The Free Soil party failed to receive a single electoral vote, but out of the popular vote of nearly three millions, nearly three hundred thousand ballots were cast for its candidates, showing a remarkable gain in strength in the past four years.

CHAPTER XXXVIII.

THE ADMINISTRATIONS OF ZACHARY TAYLOR AND MILLARD FILLMORE.

Character of General Taylor—Department of the Interior—Death of ex-President Polk—The Slavery Agitation—Views of Clay and Webster—California asks admission into the Union—Message of President Taylor—The Omnibus Bill—Efforts of Henry Clay—A Memorable Debate—Webster's "Great Union Speech"—Death of John C. Calhoun—Death of President Taylor—Millard Fillmore becomes President—Passage of the Compromise Measures of 1850—Death of Henry Clay—Dissatisfaction with the Compromise—The Fugitive Slave Law Nullified by the Northern States—The Nashville Convention—Organization of Utah Territory—The Seventh Census—The Expedition of Lopez against Cuba—The Search for Sir John Franklin—The Grinnel Expedition—Dr Kane's Voyages—Inauguration of Cheap Postage—Laying the Corner-stone of the new Capitol—Death of Daniel Webster—Arrival of Kossuth—The President Rejects the Tripartite Treaty—Franklin Pierce elected President—Death of William R King.

THE 4th of March, 1849, fell on Sunday, and the inauguration of General Taylor as president of the United States took place on Monday, March 5th.

The new president was a native of Virginia, but had removed with his parents to Kentucky at an early age, and had grown up to manhood on the frontiers of that State. In 1808, at the age of twenty-four, he was commissioned a lieutenant in the army by President Jefferson, and had spent forty years in the military service of the country. His exploits in the Florida war and the war with Mexico have been related. His brilliant victories in Mexico had made him the most popular man in the United States, and had won him the high office of the presidency at the hands of his grateful fellow-citizens. He was without political experience, but he was a man of pure and stainless integrity, of great firmness, a sincere patriot, and possessed of strong good sense. He had received a majority of the electoral votes of both the Northern and Southern States, and was free from party or sectional ties of any kind. His inaugural address was brief, and was confined to a statement of general principles. His cabinet was composed of the leaders of the Whig party, with John M. Clayton, of Delaware, as secretary of state. The last Congress had created a new executive department—that of the interior—to relieve the secretary of the treasury of a part of his duties, and President Taylor was called upon to appoint the first secretary of the interior, which he did in the person of Thomas Ewing, of Ohio.   The new department was charged with the management of the public lands, the Indian tribes, and the issuing of patents to inventors.

A few months after the opening of President Taylor's administration, ex-President Polk died at his home in Nashville, Tennessee, on the 15th of June, 1849, in the fifty-fourth year of his age.

Since the announcement of the Wilmot Proviso, the agitation of the slavery question had been incessant, and had increased instead of diminishing with each succeeding year.   It was one of the chief topics of discussion in the newspaper press of the country, and entered largely into every political controversy, however local or insignificant in its nature. The opponents of slavery regarded the annexation of Texas and the Mexican war as efforts to extend that institution, and were resolved to put an end to its existence at any cost.   The advocates of slavery claimed that the Southern States had an equal right to the common property of the States, and were entitled to protection for their slaves in any of the Territories then owned by the States or that might afterwards be acquired by them. The Missouri Compromise forbade the existence of slavery north of the line of 36° 30′ north latitude, and left the inhabitants south of that line free to decide upon their own institutions.   The Anti-slavery party was resolved that slavery should be excluded from the territory acquired from Mexico, and

ZACHARY TAYLOR.

in the Wilmot Proviso struck their first blow for the accomplishment of this purpose.   We have seen that they succeeded in prohibiting slavery, by a special act of Congress, in Oregon, although the terms of the Missouri Compromise would have excluded the institution from that Territory. Their object was fully understood by the southern people, and was bitterly resented by them.   The agitation of the subject aroused a storm of passion throughout the country, and produced a very bitter feeling between the Northern and Southern States.   In his last message to Congress President Polk had recommended that the line of 36° 30′ north latitude be extended to the Pacific, and thus leave it to the people south of that line to decide whether they would have slavery or not.   This proposition was acceptable to the south; but it was rejected by the Anti-slavery party.   The Missouri Compromise line had been limited to the Louisiana purchase, which was entirely slaveholding, and had made more

47

than one-half of it free. To extend the line to the Pacific would be to
give the south a chance to establish slavery in territory which was free
at the time of its acquisition by the United States   The north would not
listen to such a proposition.

During the last session of Congress in Mr. Polk's administration, an
effort had been made to establish territorial governments for Utah and
New Mexico, but had failed in consequence of the inability of Congress
to agree upon the question of slavery in these Territories.   In the debate
in the Senate upon these measures, Mr. Calhoun and Mr. Webster took
an active part, and each presented in a masterly manner the views of the
section he represented upon this great question.   Mr Calhoun, speaking
for the south, argued that the constitution recognized slavery, that as it
was the supreme law of the land it was superior to any territorial law or
act of Congress abolishing slavery; and that the constitution clearly and
unequivocally established and protected slavery in the Territories.

Mr. Webster, speaking for the north, declared that the constitution
was designed for the government of the States, and not for the Territories   Congress, he said, had the right to govern the Territories
independently of the constitution, and he maintained that it often exercised this right contrary to the constitution, as it did things in the Territories which it could not do in the States   He added " When new
territory has been acquired it has always been subject to the laws of
Congress—to such laws as Congress thought proper to pass for its immediate government and preparatory state in which it was to remain until
it was ready to come into the Union as one of the family of States."   He
quoted in support of his position the clause of the constitution which
declares that the " constitution and the laws of the United States which
shall be made in pursuance thereof, ... shall be the supreme law of
the land."

Congress having failed to make any provision for territorial governments for Utah and New Mexico, those Territories were left in a condition of anarchy.   One of the first duties devolving upon the new administration was the alleviation of this evil until it could be definitely settled
by Congress   President Taylor instructed the federal officers in those
Territories to encourage the people to organize temporary governments
for themselves.

California in the meantime had grown with such rapidity, and had
experienced so much trouble from its sudden increase of population and
the lack of a definite government, that its leading citizens determined to
seek admission into the Union.   In the autumn of 1849 a convention of
the people was held, a constitution formed, and a State government

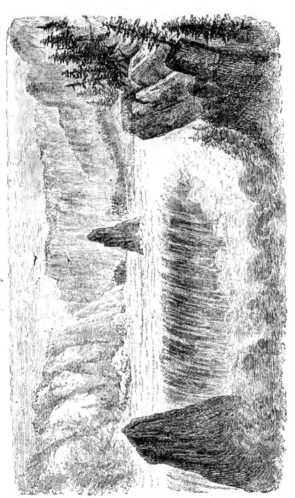

SHOSHONEE FALLS, IDAHO.

739

organized   The action of the convention was promptly ratified by the people. Upon the assembly of the Thirty-first Congress in the winter of 1849, California applied for admission into the Union as a State, with a constitution forbidding slavery within her limits

The organization of the Thirty-first Congress was delayed for three weeks   Parties were about evenly divided, and sixty ballots were taken before a speaker could be chosen.   The choice at last fell upon Howell Cobb of Georgia, who was elected by a plurality.   Partisan bitterness ran high during this struggle.

Upon the organization of the House President Taylor sent in his first and only message   He recognized the danger with which the sectional controversy threatened the country, expressed his views of the situation in moderate terms, and intimated that he should faithfully discharge his duties to the whole country.   He recommended the admission of California with the constitution she had chosen ; and advised that Utah and New Mexico should be organized as Territories, with liberty to decide the question of slavery for themselves when they were ready to enter the Union as States   A dispute having arisen between Texas and New Mexico concerning the proper boundary between them, the president recommended that it should be settled by the courts of the United States.

The other questions which demanded immediate settlement were slavery in the District of Columbia, and the demand of the Southern States for a more faithful execution of the provision of the constitution which required the arrest and return of fugitive slaves.

The south opposed the admission of California with a free constitution, and the north demanded the abolition of the slave trade in the District of Columbia, and the Northern States were unwilling to allow their officers to execute the Fugitive Slave Law within their limits   The excitement became intense, and threats to dissolve the Union of the States were freely indulged in by the extremists of both the north and the south.

On the 29th of January, 1850, Henry Clay introduced into the Senate a series of resolutions designed to settle all the points in dispute by a general compromise.   The resolutions were referred to a committee of thirteen, of which Mr. Clay was made chairman.   In due time the committee reported a bill known as the "Omnibus Bill" from its embracing in one measure all Mr Clay's propositions.   It provided for the admission of California as a free State , the organization of the Territories of Utah and New Mexico, without reference to slavery; the adjustment of the boundary between Texas and New Mexico by paving to the former ten millions of dollars · the abolition of the slave trade in the District of

Columbia; and the enactment by Congress of a more stringent and effective law for the rendition of fugitive slaves.

The Omnibus bill was warmly opposed in Congress and in the country at large. The debate in the Senate brought out the views of the leading statesmen of the country. Senator Jefferson Davis declared the bill in no sense a compromise, because it was unequal in its provisions The south he declared gained nothing by the measure, as the constitution already required the rendition of fugitive slaves He proposed, therefore, that the Missouri Compromise line should be extended to the Pacific, "with the specific recognition of the right to hold slaves in the territory below that line."

Mr. Clay replied to this that "no earthly power could induce him to vote for a specific measure for the introduction of slavery where it had not existed, either north or south of that line. . I am unwilling that the posterity of the present inhabitants of California and of New Mexico should reproach us for doing just what we reproach Great Britain for doing to us. . . . If the citizens of those Territories come here with constitutions establishing slavery, I am for admitting them into the Union; but then it will be then own work and not ours, and their posterity will have to reproach them and not us."

Mr. Calhoun was too ill to take part in the debate in person, but he prepared a speech of great ability which was read for him in the Senate by Senator Mason of Virginia He declared that the Union could be preserved only by maintaining an equal number of free and slave States, in order that the representation of the two sections of the country might be equal in the Senate.

Mr. Webster also took part in the debate, and on this occasion delivered what is known as his "great Union speech of the 7th of March," which occupied three days in its delivery. He expressed substantially the same views as those advocated by Mr Clay He opposed restriction of slavery in the Territories, and declared he would vote against the Wilmot Proviso His speech created a profound sensation throughout the country, and did much to secure the final acceptance of the compromise measures

In the midst of this discussion John C. Calhoun died, on the 31st of March, 1850. He had entered Congress in 1811, and had been in public life from that time until the day of his death He had filled many high offices, both State and national, and had discharged the duties of each and all with disinterested fidelity and admitted ability. He was one of the first statesmen this country has ever produced, and was the acknowledged leader of the south in the sectional controversy with the north. His character was above reproach, and he was a sincere and disinterested

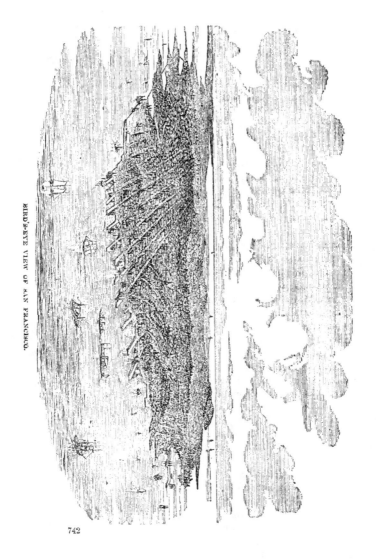

BIRD'S-EYE VIEW OF SAN FRANCISCO.

742

patriot. His death was generally lamented throughout the country, and his political adversaries joined heartily in the tributes of the nation to his many virtues and great abilities.

A few months later President Taylor was suddenly stricken down with a fever, which in a few days terminated fatally. He died on the 9th of July, 1850, amid the grief of the whole country, which felt that it had lost a faithful and upright chief magistrate. Though the successful candidate of one political party, his administration had received the earnest support of the best men of the country without regard to party, and his death was a national calamity. He had held office only sixteen months, but had shown himself equal to his difficult and delicate position. He was sixty-six years old at the time of his death.

By the terms of the constitution the office of president devolved upon Millard Fillmore, vice-president of the United States. On the 10th of July he took the oath of office before Chief Justice Cranch of the District of Columbia, and at once entered upon the duties of his new position.

MILLARD FILLMORE.

Mr. Fillmore was a native of New York, and was born in that State in the year 1800. He had served his State in Congress, and as governor, and was personally one of the most popular of the Presidents. The cabinet of General Taylor resigned their offices immediately after his death, and the new president filled their places by appointing a new cabinet with Daniel Webster at its head as secretary of state. Mr. Fillmore was in active sympathy with Mr. Clay in his efforts to secure the passage of the compromise measures, as he deemed them the best adjustment of the trouble possible under the circumstances.

The compromise measures were warmly debated in Congress, the sessions of which extended through the summer into the latter part of September. The bill was then taken up and passed, article by article, by the House of Representatives, it having previously passed the Senate. The bill at once received the executive approval, and became a law.

The clause admitting California into the Union as a State was adopted on the 9th of September, 1850.

The course of Mr. Clay in securing the passage of the compromise measures of 1850 was justly regarded as the crowning glory of his life. It won for him the love and confidence of the whole country without regard to party, and the man who "had rather be right than be president" had the proud satisfaction of seeing all the faults and mistakes of his earlier years forgotten in the confidence and gratitude with which his countrymen regarded him. He ceased now to take an active part in the questions of the day, for it was fitting that his life should close with this great service to his country. His health failed rapidly, but he continued to hold his seat in the Senate until the 29th of June, 1852, when he died at the age of seventy-five years. Honors were showered upon his memory in all parts of the Union, and he was laid to his rest amid a nation's unaffected mourning.

There were still many extremists both north and south, to whom the compromise measures failed to give satisfaction. The Fugitive Slave Law was bitterly denounced by the Anti-slavery party in the north. As the Supreme Court of the United States had decided that the justices of the peace in the respective States could not be called upon to execute the law for the rendition of fugitive slaves, a clause was inserted in the Fugitive Slave Law of 1850, providing for the appointment of United

COAT OF ARMS OF CALIFORNIA.

States commissioners, before whom such cases could be tried. The Northern States successively enacted laws for the nullification of the provisions of this law. All their jails and other State buildings were refused to the federal officers for the securing of fugitive slaves, and all State, county, and city officers were forbidden to arrest or assist in arresting or detaining any fugitive slave. In many of the States severe punishments were denounced against masters coming within their limits to claim their slaves, and such fugitives entering these States were declared free. These laws were denounced by the slaveholding States as violative of the constitution of the United States, and gave rise to great bitterness of feeling towards the north. It was maintained that these laws were direct evidence of the intention of the northern people to rob the south of its property in negro slaves.

The extremists of the south were equally dissatisfied with the compromise. They declared that the South had sacrificed everything and gained nothing by it, and boldly avowed their intention to bring about the secession of the Southern States from the Union. In the summer of 1850 a southern convention was held at Nashville, Tennessee. Its real end was the dissolution of the Union, and for that purpose it urged the Southern States to appoint delegates to a "Southern Congress." The legislatures of South Carolina and Mississippi alone responded to this invitation, but the great mass of the southern people turned a deaf ear to the appeals of the disunionists, and the convention failed to accomplish its object.

In the inauguration of a territorial government for Utah, the Mormons, whose settlement in that Territory while it was yet a possession of Mexico we have related, endeavored to frame their own government, and gave to the Territory the name of Deseret, which they declared was a word of their peculiar language meaning "The Land of the Honey Bee." President Fillmore set aside this name and carried out the act of Congress by which the Territory received its present name. Brigham Young, the Mormon leader or prophet, was appointed governor of the Territory.

In 1850 the seventh census showed the population of the United States to be 23,191,876 souls.

In the early part of President Taylor's administration, General Lopez, a Spaniard, began to enlist men in the United States ostensibly for the purpose of aiding the people of the island of Cuba to throw off their allegiance to Spain and establish their independence, but really for the purpose of driving out the Spaniards and securing the annexation of Cuba to the United States. He succeeded in inducing a number of adventurous persons to join him.

BRIGHAM YOUNG.

President Taylor, upon learning of the movement, issued a proclamation forbidding citizens of the United States to engage in it. In spite of this warning, Lopez collected a force of six hundred men, and eluding the vigilance of the United States officers, sailed for Cuba. He landed at Cardenas, but received so little encouragement that the party sailed for Key West. In 1851, Lopez again entered Cuba, this time at the head of four hundred and fifty men. His party was captured almost immediately, and he and a number of his men were put to death by the Spanish authorities at Havana.

In May, 1850, an expedition of a different character sailed from the United States. The fate of Sir John Franklin, who sailed from England in 1845, in search of the northwest passage, had long enlisted the sympathy of humane and generous souls. It was thought that the daring navigator might be confined to the Arctic regions by the loss of his ships, and that a well-executed search might either result in the discovery and relief of Franklin or settle the question as to his fate. Mr. Henry Grinnell, a wealthy merchant of New York, fitted out an expedition at his own expense, and placing it under the command of Lieutenant De Haven, of the United States navy, despatched it to the Arctic regions to search for Franklin and his men, in May, 1850 De Haven was accompanied by Dr. E. K. Kane, in the capacity of surgeon and naturalist. After a year's absence the vessels returned, the search having been unsuccessful. The general government despatched another expedition in 1851 on the same errand, and placed it under command of Dr Kane. This expedition was absent four years, and the government, becoming apprehensive of its fate, sent two vessels to search for Kane and his companions. They were found at the isle of Disco, in Greenland, having been forced to abandon their vessel in the ice. Nothing was learned by Dr Kane concerning the fate of Sir John Franklin · but the expedition resulted in the discovery of the open Polar Sea *

In the early part of 1851 Congress reduced the postage on prepaid letters to three cents to all parts of the United States, prepayment being made by means of stamps provided by the government The result was a rapid and immense increase of the postal revenue of the country.

On the 4th of July, 1851, the corner-stone of the extension of the capitol at Washington was laid by President Fillmore with appropriate ceremonies. The orator of the day was Daniel Webster His address was one of his best efforts, but was delivered under great disadvantages. His health had been failing for some time past, and his weakness was so great that he could speak only with difficulty.

This oration was one of the last public acts of the great statesman. On the 24th of October, 1852, he died at his home at Marshfield, Massachusetts, aged seventy years, and in him perished the first statesman of America. He was large and stout in frame, of swarthy complexion, and slow and heavy in movement—a man of noble and commanding appearance. His intellect was cast in the same gigantic mould as his body His language was simple and chaste, and his arguments irresistible His patriotism knew no sectional limits "I am as ready," he once said, "to fight and to fall for the constitutional rights of Virginia as I am for those of Massachusetts" Alexander H. Stephens has said of him : "He was too great a man and had too great an in-

---

* Nothing definite was learned of the fate of Sir John Franklin until 1859, when the steamer "Fox," despatched by Lady Franklin, made the melancholy discovery that Sir John Franklin died on the 11th of June, 1847, and in 1848 the "Erebus" and "Terror" were abandoned in the ice The survivors of these disasters, one hundred and five in number, died one by one from cold and exhaustion on King William's island.

tellect not to see the truth when it was presented, and he was too
honest and too patriotic a man not to proclaim the truth when he saw it,
even to an unwilling people. In this quality of moral greatness I often
thought Mr Webster had the advantage of his great contemporaries,
Messrs Clay and Calhoun Not that I would be understood as saying
that they were not men of great moral courage, for both of them showed
this high quality in many instances, but they never gave the world such
striking exhibitions of it as he did. . . Webster . often passed this
ordeal, and that he passed it with unflinching firmness is one of the
grandest features in the general grandeur of his character. Even his
detractors have been constrained to render him unwilling homage in this
respect "* His memory was honored by appropriate demonstrations in
all parts of the country, and it is said that the popular tributes on this
occasion were equalled only by those of the nation at the death of
Washington

In December, 1851, Louis Kossuth, the chief of the Hungarian insurrection of 1848, visited the United States His avowed object was to
promote the cause of his countrymen, and he made frequent addresses in
various parts of the Union, which were listened to by vast multitudes
who were charmed with his eloquence. He visited Washington, and
was granted a public reception by Congress The Austrian minister at
Washington, the Chevalier Hulseman, protested against this reception, and
his protest being unheeded, he withdrew from Washington for a while.

The attempt of Lopez upon Cuba had greatly alarmed Spain for the
safety of that island England and France, sympathizing with her, and
anxious to render the acquisition of Cuba by the United States impossible, proposed to the American government to join them in a "tripartite
treaty," in which each should disclaim any intention to seize that island,
and should guarantee Spain in her possession of it. In December, 1852,
Edward Everett, who had succeeded Mr Webster as secretary of state,
by the direction of the president, replied to the proposition of England
and France, declining to accept it "The President," he said, "does not
covet the acquisition of Cuba for the United States," but "could not see
with indifference that island fall into the possession of any European government than Spain." He stated that the situation of the island rendered
it peculiarly interesting to this country by reason of its proximity to our
coast, and its commanding the approach to the Gulf of Mexico and the
mouth of the Mississippi. The European powers were thus given to
understand that the United States would not tolerate their interference in
a question purely American.

---

* *The War Between the States*, vol 1, pp 405, 406.

The year 1852 was marked by intense excitement consequent on the political campaign which terminated in the fall in the presidential election. The Democratic party made a strong and successful effort to recover its lost power, and nominated Franklin Pierce, of New Hampshire, for president, and William R. King, of Alabama, for vice-president. The Whig party nominated General Winfield Scott for president, and William A Graham, of North Carolina, for vice-president The Anti-slavery party put in nomination John P Hale, of New Hampshire, and George W. Julian, of Indiana. The election resulted in the choice of the candidates of the Democratic party by an overwhelming majority. The Anti-slavery party on this occasion polled but 155,825 votes, or a little more than half of the strength it had shown at the previous election.

Mr. King, the vice-president elect, did not long survive his triumph. His health had been delicate for many years, and he was obliged to pass the winter succeeding the election in Cuba Being unable to return home, he took the oath of office before the American consul, at Havana, on the 4th of March, 1853. He then returned to the United States, and died at his home in Alabama on the 18th of April, 1853.

CHAPTER XXXIX.

THE ADMINISTRATION OF FRANKLIN PIERCE.

Dispute with Mexico—The Gadsden Purchase—Surveys for a Pacific Railway—The Japan Expedition—Treaty with Japan—The Koszta Affair—The "Black Warrior" seized by the Cuban Officials—The "Ostend Conference"—Dismissal of the British Minister—The Kansas-Nebraska Bill—History of the Bill—Its Passage by Congress—History of the Struggle in Kansas—Conflict between the Pro-Slavery and Free Soil Settlers—Lawrence Sacked—Civil War—The Presidential Campaign of 1856—James Buchanan elected President of the United States—Rapid increase of the Republican Party.

RESIDENT PIERCE took the oath of office at the capitol at Washington on the 4th of March, 1853, in the presence of an immense throng. He was in his forty-ninth year, and had won an enviable name by his previous services to the country. He was a native of New Hampshire, and had represented that State for four years in the lower House of Congress, and for nearly a full term in the Senate of the United States. He had also served with distinction during the Mexican war as briga-
dier-general. He placed William L. Marcy,
of New York, at the head of his cabinet as
secretary of state.

The first question of importance the new
president was called upon to settle grew out
of a dispute with Mexico concerning the
boundary between that country and the Territory of New Mexico. At the time of the
treaty of Guadaloupe Hidalgo the maps were
so imperfect that the boundary line had not
been drawn with sufficient exactness. Both
countries claimed the Mesilla valley, which
was said to be very fertile, but which was

FRANKLIN PIERCE.

more important to the United States as affording what was generally regarded as the most practicable route to California. Santa Anna was now
president of the Mexican republic again, and sent a force of Mexican
troops to occupy the region in dispute. The matter was settled by nego-

tiation, however, and the United States obtained the Mesilla valley and the free navigation of the Gulf of California and of the Colorado to the American frontier. For these concessions the federal government paid Mexico the sum of ten millions of dollars. The district thus acquired was known as the "Gadsden Purchase," and was subsequently erected into the Territory of Arizona.

The necessity of more rapid and certain communication with California had brought the nation to regard a railway between the Mississippi and the Pacific as a necessity, and as such an undertaking was considered beyond the resources of a private corporation, it was believed that it should be built by the general government, or at least that the general government should bear a part of the expense. The year 1853 witnessed the first steps towards the construction of this great work. Two expeditions were despatched under the orders of the war department to explore the best routes for a Pacific railway.

The acquisition of California brought the United States into new relations with the nations of the eastern world, as it secured for them a base upon the Pacific from which a direct trade could be conducted with China and Japan. The empire of Japan, however, was closed to foreigners, and it was very desirable to open commercial relations with it. Towards the close of Mr. Fillmore's term of office, Commodore Perry, a brother of the hero of Lake Erie, was despatched to China with a fleet of seven war steamers to negotiate a treaty with the Japanese government. He arrived in the bay of Jeddo in the summer of 1853. The natives were greatly astonished at the appearance of his steamers, the first that had ever been seen in those waters, and at his boldness in venturing into their harbors. The Japanese officials ordered him to depart, but he refused, and insisted on seeing the emperor, and making known to him the object of his friendly visit. They at length decided to lay the matter before the emperor, who consented to grant an interview to the commodore, and named the 14th of July for that purpose. On the day appointed the commodore landed, accompanied by a strong body of marines. He was received with great ceremony by the Japanese, and delivered the president's letter, to which an answer was promised. The answer of the emperor was submitted to him several months later, and was favorable. A treaty was concluded between the United States and Japan, by which the former were allowed to trade in two specified ports—Simodi and Hokadadi. American citizens were permitted to reside at these ports, and consuls were accepted for them. Thus the United States had the honor of being the first to open the rich markets of the island empire to the commerce of the civilized world. Since then the relations between the two countries have steadily grown more cordial, and Japan has shown a remarkable rapidity and facility for adopting the civilization of the west

In July, 1853, occurred an event which did much to increase the respect for our navy among the powers of the world. Martin Koszta, a Hungarian, who had taken the preliminary steps to be naturalized in the United States, happening to be in Smyrna, in Asia Minor, on business, was seized as a rebel and a refugee by order of the Austrian consul-general, and taken on board an Austrian brig The United States sloop-of-war "St. Louis," Captain Ingraham, was lying in the harbor at the time, and Ingraham was appealed to for protection for Koszta. He at once demanded his release as an American citizen The demand was refused by the authorities, and Ingraham at once called his crew to quarters and threatened to fire upon the Austrian ship if Koszta was not immediately released The Austrians at once surrendered their prisoner, and he was placed in custody of the French consul to await the action of the government of the United States The matter was settled by negotiation between this country and Austria, and Koszta was released Austria addressed to the government at Washington a remonstrance against the conduct of Captain Ingraham, but his course was warmly applauded by his countrymen and by disinterested persons in Europe.

In February, 1854, the American merchant steamer " Black Warrior" was seized by the Spanish authorities at Havana, on the pretext that she had evaded or violated some uncertain revenue law, and the ship and her cargo were declared confiscated This action of the Havana officials was regarded in the United States as unjust, and aroused a great deal of feeling against the Spaniards, and gave a sudden impetus to the national sentiment in favor of the acquisition of Cuba. The affair of the " Black Warrior " was satisfactorily settled by the Spanish government.

While the feeling aroused by the affair was at its height a conference of some of the American ministers in Europe, including Mr Buchanan, minister to England, Mr Mason, minister to France, and Mr Soulé, minister to Spain, and some others, was held at Ostend, in Belgium, and a circular was adopted recommending the acquisition of Cuba by the United States This measure attracted much attention, and elicited considerable European criticism of the alleged ambitious designs of the United States. Mr. Soulé, on his return to Madrid, was stopped at Calais by order of the emperor of the French, who had personal reasons for disliking him. The emperor, however, reconsidered his action, and allowed Soulé to pass through France to the Spanish frontier.

In 1855 Great Britain, France, Sardinia, and Turkey being engaged in a war with Russia, the agents of the British government undertook to enlist recruits for their army within the limits of the United States in defiance of the neutrality laws of this country. The matter being brought to the attention of the United States government, it was found that the British minister at Washington and the British consuls in some of the principal cities of the Union had encouraged, if they had not authorized, these enlistments The government of the United States thereupon called the attention of Great Britain to the conduct of her minister, and requested her to recall him. The queen declined to comply with this request, and the minister and the consuls were promptly dismissed by the president. The matter caused considerable irritation in England for a while, but the good sense of the English people at length perceived the propriety of the course of the American government, and cordial relations were re-established between the two countries.

The most important measure of Mr Pierce's administration was the bill to organize the Territories of Kansas and Nebraska. The region embraced in these Territories formed a part of the Louisiana purchase, and extended from the borders of Missouri, Iowa, and Minnesota to the summit of the Rocky mountains, and from the parallel of 36° 30' north latitude to the border of British America The whole region by the terms of the Missouri Compromise had been secured to free labor by the exclusion of slavery. Until the year 1850 this vast area was called by the general and somewhat indefinite name of the "Platte Country," from the Platte river, which flows through it Little was known concerning it save that it was a region of great fertility It was mainly occupied by the reservations of the Indian tribes, which had been removed from the other States to make way for the whites Across it swept the grand trails of the overland route to Utah and the Pacific. The people of the New England States were very anxious that the Indian reservations which covered the eastern part should be bought up by the general government and the country thrown open to emigration Petitions to this effect were presented to the Thirty-second Congress, but no action was taken upon them until December, 1852, when Mr. Hall, of Missouri, introduced a bill into the House to organize the "Territory of Platte." It was referred to the Committee on Territories, which in February, 1853, reported a bill organizing the "Territory of Nebraska." The bill was opposed in the House of Representatives by the full strength of the south, and in the Senate the only southern senators who voted for it were those from Missouri The Missouri Compromise, as has been stated, secured the entire Nebraska region to free labor; but notwithstanding this the southern members of Congress were resolved to oppose the organization of a new free Territory, and to endeavor to obtain a footing for slavery in at least a part of it

The matter was revived in the Senate on the 16th of January, 1854, by Senator Dixon, of Kentucky, who gave notice that whenever the Nebraska bill should be called up he would move the following amendment "That so much of the eighth section of an act approved March 6, 1820, entitled 'An act to authorize the people of the Missouri Territory to form a constitution and State government, and for the admission of such State into the Union on an equal footing with the original States, and to prohibit slavery in certain Territories,' as declares 'That, in all the territory ceded by France to the United States, under the name of Louisiana, which lies north of 36° 30′ north latitude, slavery and involuntary servitude, otherwise than in the punishment of crimes whereof the party shall have been duly convicted, shall be forever prohibited,' *shall not be so construed as to apply to the Territory contemplated by this act, or to any other Territory of the United States;* but that the citizens of the several States or Territories shall be at liberty to take and hold their slaves within any of the Territories or States to be formed therefrom, as if the said act, entitled as aforesaid, had never been passed "

The announcement of this amendment startled the country as much as the Wilmot Proviso had done years before, and produced much angry excitement It was a clear repudiation of the Missouri Compromise, which it did not even seek to repeal

Senator Douglas, of Illinois, chairman of the Committee on Territories, on the 23d of January, 1854, reported a bill which provided for the organization of the Platte country into *two* Territories. The southern portion, which lay directly west of Missouri, stretching to the Rocky mountains on the west, and extending from the thirty-seventh to the fortieth parallel of north latitude, was to be organized into a distinct Territory to be called Kansas. The remainder was to be called Nebraska, having the line of 43° 30′ for its northern boundary. Senator Douglas, in an evil hour for the country, incorporated in the bill the main features of Mr. Dixon's amendment. The bill contained the following provisions:

"SECTION 21 *And be it further enacted,* That, in order to avoid misconstruction, it is hereby declared to be the true intent and meaning of this act, so far as the question of slavery is concerned, to carry into practical operation the following propositions and principles, established by the compromise measures of one thousand eight hundred and fifty, to wit:

48

"*First.* That all questions pertaining to slavery in the Territories, and in the new States to be formed therefrom, are to be left to the decision of the people residing therein, through their appropriate representatives

"*Second.* That all cases involving title to slaves, and questions of personal freedom, are referred to the adjudication of the local tribunals, with the right of appeal to the Supreme Court of the United States.

"*Third.* That the provisions of the constitution and laws of the United States, in respect to fugitives from service, are to be carried into faithful execution in all the 'organized Territories,' the same as in the States."

The section of the bill which prescribed the qualifications and mode of election of a delegate from each of the Territories was as follows. "The constitution, and all laws of the United States which are not locally inapplicable, shall have the same force and effect within the said Territory as elsewhere in the United States, except the section of the act preparatory to the admission of Missouri into the Union, approved March 6, 1820, which was superseded by the principles of the legislation of 1850, commonly called the compromise measures, and is declared inoperative."

Mr. Dixon declared that the bill, as reported by Senator Douglas, met with his hearty approval, and that he would support it with all his ability. The debate on the bill began in the Senate on the 24th of January, and continued through several weeks   It was conducted with great ability on both sides, and engaged the earnest attention of the whole country. The Free Soil senators unanimously opposed the bill, which they denounced as a violation of the Missouri Compromise, by which the faith of the nation was pledged to the settlement then effected. The southern senators supported it with equal unanimity, as they held that the Missouri Compromise had been superseded by the compromise of 1850.

On the 6th of February Mr. Chase, of Ohio, moved to strike out so much of the bill as declared the Missouri Compromise "superseded" by the compromise of 1850, but the motion was defeated. Whereupon Mr. Douglas, on the 15th of February, moved to strike out the clause objected to by Mr Chase, and insert the following:

"Which being inconsistent with the principle of non-intervention by Congress with slavery in the States and Territories, as recognized by the legislation of 1850 (commonly called the compromise measures), is hereby declared inoperative and void; it being the true intent and meaning of this act not to legislate slavery into any Territory or State, nor to exclude it therefrom but to leave the people thereof perfectly free to form and regulate their domestic institutions in their own way, subject only to the constitution of the United States."

Mr Douglas' amendment was at once adopted, and seemed fair enough on its face. Mr Chase exposed the hollowness of it by proposing to add to it the following clause, which was promptly voted down "*Under which the people of the Territories, through their appropriate representatives, may, if they see fit, prohibit the existence of slavery therein.*"

The bill was adopted by the Senate by a vote of thirty-seven yeas to fourteen nays, and by the House by a vote of one hundred and thirteen yeas to one hundred nays, and on the 31st of May, 1854, received the approval of the president and became a law

The whole country engaged warmly in the discussion aroused by the reopening of the question of slavery in the Territories The north resented the repeal of the Missouri Compromise, and in the south a large and respectable party sincerely regretted the repeal of that settlement. By the passage of the Kansas-Nebraska bill the Thirty-third Congress assumed a grave responsibility, and opened the door to a bloody and bitter conflict in the Territories between slavery and free labor. The events now to be related were the logical consequences of the repeal of the Missouri Compromise

A few months before the final vote upon the Kansas-Nebraska bill the general government succeeded in purchasing the Indian reservations in those Territories, and removed the Indian tribes to new homes farther west. This action at once threw Kansas and Nebraska open to white settlers, and measures were set on foot in the New England States to encourage emigration thither   Kansas being a more fertile country than Nebraska naturally attracted the greater number of settlers Before anything could be done by the Free Soil men the people living on the border of Missouri passed over into Kansas, and selecting the best lands, put their mark upon them, hoping in this way to establish a pre-emption claim to them.   Their object was to organize and hold the Territory in the interest of slavery, but very few of them removed to Kansas, or had any wish to do so.

In the meantime societies had been formed in the New England States for the promotion of emigration to Kansas. As the Pro-slavery settlers had come into the Territory so slowly, and in such small numbers, it seemed certain that the northern people could secure Kansas to free labor by sending out settlers to occupy the Territory in good faith. The Pro-slavery party in Missouri determined to prevent this. In July, 1854, a meeting was held at Westport in that State, at which it was resolved that the persons taking part in the meeting would, "whenever called upon by any of the citizens of Kansas Territory, hold 'themselves' in readiness together to resist and remove any and all emigrants who go there under the auspices of the Northern Emigrant Aid Societies."

The first party sent out by the New England Aid Societies reached a point on the Kaw river, in Kansas, about the middle of July. There they pitched their tents and began the building of a town, which they named Lawrence, in honor of Amos A. Lawrence, of Boston. By the last of the month they were joined by seventy more emigrants, and the work of founding their town was pushed forward with energy. There was not a drone in the little community. They were all honest, intelli-

FIRST HOTEL IN LAWRENCE.

gent, God-fearing men and women, and they meant to succeed in the undertaking they had begun. They were in legal and peaceable possession of their settlement, and thus far had molested or wronged no one.

They were not to live in peace, however. Before they had finished building their houses, they were startled by the announcement that two hundred and fifty armed Missourians had encamped within a short distance of them for the purpose of driving them out of the Territory. The next morning the Missourians sent them a formal notice that "the Abolitionists must leave the Territory, never more to return to it." They declared their desire to avoid bloodshed; but notified the settlers that they must be ready to leave the Territory, with all their effects, at one o'clock that day. This the settlers refused to do, and prepared to defend their homes. The messengers of the Missourians found them drilling behind their tents, and reported this fact to their leaders. The firm but quiet attitude of the people of Lawrence had a happy effect. The Missourians made no effort to carry out their threat, but broke up their camp

THE PEOPLE OF LAWRENCE DETERMINED TO RESIST.

that night, and withdrew across the border, leaving the settlers in peace. Meanwhile the town of Lawrence grew and prospered, and the New England Societies continuing to send other emigrants into the Territory other towns were founded. Settlers from the Southern States came into the Territory very slowly.

The general government threw its influence as far as possible in favor of the Pro-slavery party, in the organization of the Territory, by appointing a majority of the territorial officers from the slaveholding States. A H. Reeder was appointed governor by President Pierce. He endeavored to execute the laws faithfully, and ordered an election for members of a territorial legislature, to be held on the 30th of March, 1855. On that day large numbers of armed Missourians crossed the border, and, taking possession of the polling-places in Kansas, succeeded in returning a Pro-slavery legislature.

Six districts at once forwarded protests to the governor against the elections, showing beyond all reasonable doubt that they had been controlled by citizens of Missouri. The governor, who was anxious to do justice to all parties, ordered a new election in these districts, each of which, with the exception of Lecompton, returned a Free Soil delegate. The new delegates, however, were refused their seats upon the assembling of the legislature, and the successful candidates at the original election were admitted.

The governor had summoned the legislature to meet at Pawnee City, on the Kansas river, a town nearly one hundred miles distant from the border, and supposed to be far enough away to be free from intimidation by the Missourians, but the legislature, immediately upon assembling, adjourned to Shawnee Mission, on the Missouri border. The resolution for this purpose was vetoed by the governor, but was passed over his veto and was at once carried into effect. Upon reassembling at Shawnee Mission the legislature proceeded to adopt the laws of Missouri as the laws of Kansas, and to frame a series of statutes designedly cruel and oppressive. These laws were vetoed by Governor Reeder, who was removed by the president. Wilson Shannon, of Ohio, was then appointed governor of Kansas.

In the meantime the Free Soil settlers had increased so rapidly that they at length largely outnumbered the Pro-slavery settlers. They now felt themselves strong enough to resist the outrages of the Missourians, and accordingly, on the 5th of September, 1855, held a convention, in which they distinctly repudiated the government that had been forced upon them by men who were not residents of the Territory. They announced their intention not to take part in the election of a delegate to Congress, which the territorial authorities had ordered to be held on the 1st of October, and called upon the actual residents of the Territory to send delegates to a convention to meet at Topeka on the 19th of September. This convention organized an executive committee for the Territory, and ordered an election to be held for the purpose of choosing a delegate to Congress. Governor Reeder was nominated and elected to Congress. On the 23d of October the convention adopted a Free State constitution, and forwarded it to Congress with a petition for the admission of Kansas into the Union as a State

The struggle for the possession of the Territory now passed out of the area of politics. As we have said, the repeal of the Missouri Compromise opened the way for, and was the direct cause of, the conflict between the Free and Pro-slavery settlers of Kansas. The outrages of the Pro-slavery men had forced the Free-Soilers into an attitude of direct and uncompromising resistance; and after the action of the latter, at Topeka, the struggle which had hitherto been comparatively bloodless changed its character and became an open and sanguinary war between the two parties In this struggle the Pro-slavery men were the aggressors. Bands of young men, armed and regularly organized into companies and regiments, came into the Territory from South Carolina, Georgia and the extreme Southern States, with the avowed design of making Kansas a slaveholding State at all hazards. On the morning of May 21st, 1856, under the pretext of aiding the United States marshal to serve certain processes upon citizens of Lawrence, they captured that town, sacked it, burned several houses and inflicted a loss upon it amounting to $150,000. From this time the war went on in a series of desultory but bloody encounters, some of which assumed the proportions of battles.

In the summer of 1856 Governor Shannon was removed, and John W Geary, of Pennsylvania, was appointed in his place. He exerted himself honestly to restore peace and execute the laws, and ordered "all bodies of men combined, armed and equipped with munitions of war, without authority of the government, instantly to disband and quit the Territory" In obedience to this order the Free Soil companies nearly all disbanded, but the Pro-slavery party paid scarcely any attention to it. They concentrated a force of two thousand men and advanced upon Lawrence to attack it. Governor Geary at once placed himself at the head of the United States dragoons stationed in the Territory, and by a rapid march threw himself with these troops between the town of Lawrence and the hostile force, and prevented another conflict.

Matters had reached this stage when the presidential campaign opened in 1856. The struggle in the Territories had greatly weakened the Democratic party, and had given rise to a new party which called itself Republican, and which was based upon an avowed hostility to the extension of slavery. A third party, called the American, or Know Nothing, also took part in the campaign, and was based upon the doctrine that the political offices of the country should be held only by persons of American birth. The Democratic party nominated James

Buchanan, of Pennsylvania, for the presidency, and John C. Breckenridge, of Kentucky, for the vice-presidency   The Republican nominee
for the presidency was John C. Fremont, of California, for the vice-
presidency William L. Dayton, of New Jersey.   The American party
supported Millard Fillmore, of New York, for the presidency, and
Andrew J. Donelson, of Tennessee, for the vice-presidency.   The Whig
party had been broken to pieces by its defeat in 1852, and had now
entirely disappeared.

The canvass was unusually excited   Slavery was the principal question in dispute.   Party ties had little influence upon men   The sentiment
of the nation at large had been outraged by the repeal of the Missouri
Compromise, and thousands of Democrats, desiring to rebuke their party
for its course in bringing about this repeal, united with the Republican
party, which declared as its leading principle that it was "both the right
and the duty of Congress to prohibit in the Territories those twin relics
of barbarism—polygamy and slavery."

The elections resulted in the triumph of James Buchanan, the candidate of the Democratic party.   Mr. Buchanan received 174 electoral
votes to 114 cast for Fremont.   Though a majority of the American
people sustained the action of the Democratic party, the significant fact
remained that 1,341,264 of the voters of the country had recorded their
condemnation of it by casting their votes for Fremont and Dayton.

CHAPTER XL.

THE ADMINISTRATION OF JAMES BUCHANAN.

Inauguration of Mr Buchanan—The Mormon Rebellion—The Financial Crisis of 1857—
Laying of the Atlantic Telegraphic Cable—Minnesota admitted into the Union—The
San Juan Affair—Admission of Oregon into the Union—The Kansas question—The
Lecompton Constitution—Its defeat—The Wyandotte Constitution—Admission of Kan-
sas into the Union—The John Brown Raid—Prompt action of the Government—Brown
and his Companions surrendered to the State of Virginia—Their Trial and Execution—
Presidential Campaign of 1860—Rupture of the Democratic party—Abraham Lincoln
elected President of the United States—Secession of South Carolina—Reasons for this
Act—Secession of the other Cotton States—Major Anderson occupies Fort Sumter—
Trying position of the General Government—Course of Mr Buchanan—The "Star of
the West" fired upon by the South Carolina Batteries—Organization of the Confederate
States of America—Jefferson Davis elected President of the Southern Republic—The
Peace Congress—Its Failure

JAMES BUCHANAN, the fifteenth President of the United
States, was inaugurated at Washington on the 4th of March,
1857. He was in his sixty-sixth year, and was a statesman
of great accomplishments and ripe experience. He was born in
Pennsylvania, in 1791, and was by profession a lawyer. He
had served his State in Congress as a representative and a senator, had
been minister to Russia under President Jackson, and had been a member of the cabinet of President Polk as secretary of state. During the
four years previous to his election to the presidency he had resided
abroad as the minister of the United States to Great Britain, and in that
capacity had greatly added to his reputation as a statesman. He avowed
the object of his administration to be "to destroy any sectional party,
whether North or South, and to restore, if possible, that national frater-
nal feeling between the different States that had existed during the early
days of the republic." The intense sectional feeling which the discussion
of the slavery question had aroused had alarmed patriotic men in all
parts of the Union, and it was earnestly hoped that Mr Buchanan's administration would be able to effect a peaceful settlement of the quarrel.
Mr. Buchanan selected his cabinet from the leading men of the Democratic party, and placed at its head as secretary of state Lewis Cass,
of Michigan.

761

We have in a previous portion of this work noticed the rise and growth of the Mormon sect, and their settlement in the region of the Great Salt lake, then a part of the Mexican republic. They were not at all pleased with their transfer to the United States by the cession of the territory occupied by them by the treaty of Guadaloupe Hidalgo. Their object in emigrating to Utah had been to place themselves beyond the limits of the United States, where they could enjoy without molestation their religious practices, and especially the gross and immoral institution of polygamy, to which they were attached as the foundation of their faith. They were not disturbed by the Mexican government, which was indeed scarcely aware of their existence, and thus unnoticed devoted their energies to building up the country they had occupied. Their missionaries were sent into the various countries of Europe, and converts

were made with extraordinary success and rapidity. They built up a thriving town on the borders of the great lake, to which they gave the name of Salt Lake City, and founded other towns in various parts of the Territory. By the year 1850 the population of the Territory had increased to 11,380. Being on the highway to California, the greater part of the overland traffic and travel to the Pacific passed through Salt Lake City, and was a source of considerable profit to the Mormons.

JAMES BUCHANAN.

In 1850 the Territory of Utah was organized, and Brigham Young, who had succeeded Joe Smith as the prophet or leader of the Mormons, was appointed by President Fillmore governor of the Territory. His appointment was renewed by President Pierce, and the Mormons were left during these two administrations to manage their affairs very much in their own way. Relying upon the immense distance which separated them from the States, they paid but little regard to the authority of the United States, and finally ventured openly to resist the officers of the general government, and expelled the federal judge from the Territory. President Buchanan thereupon removed Brigham Young from his office of governor, and appointed a Mr. Cumming his successor. The Mormons having declared that the new governor should not enter the Territory, General Harney was ordered to accompany him with a large body of troops and compel the submission of the people of Utah to the authority of the federal government.

MORMON TABERNACLE: ENDOWMENT HOUSE IN THE DISTANCE.

Under the leadership of Brigham Young the Mormons took up arms and prepared to dispute the entrance of the troops into the Territory. They declared that their settlement and civilization of Utah had given them the sole right to the Territory, and that they owed no allegiance to the United States. Their resistance was so formidable that the force under General Harney was largely increased, and the command was conferred upon Brigadier-General Albert Sidney Johnston, who was considered the most efficient officer in the service. General Johnston joined his troops at Fort Bridger, about one hundred miles from Salt Lake City, in September, 1857. The Mormons in heavy force occupied

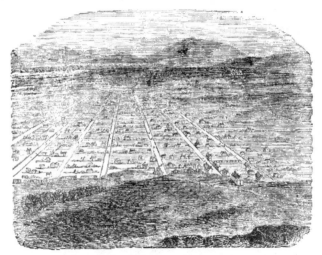

SALT LAKE CITY (FROM THE NORTH).

the passes leading to the valley of the Great Salt lake. The season was so far advanced at the time of his arrival that General Johnston concluded to pass the winter at Fort Bridger. The Mormons were very active during the winter in cutting off the trains of the federal troops.

It was General Johnston's intention to move upon Salt Lake City immediately upon the opening of the spring, but before that season arrived the matter was settled through the efforts of a Mr. Kane, of Philadelphia. He was sent out to Salt Lake City by the government, and succeeded in inducing the Mormons to lay down their arms and submit. Governor

Cumming and the federal officers then entered Salt Lake City and assumed the offices to which they had been appointed, and a force of federal troops was encamped near the city to render them such assistance as should be found necessary. President Buchanan then issued a proclamation granting a free pardon "to all, for the seditions and treasons by them committed."

In the fall of 1857 the general business of the country was thrown into confusion by a sudden financial panic, which seriously embarrassed all commercial and industrial enterprises and caused general distress. On the 26th of September the banks of Philadelphia suspended specie payments; and their example was followed by the banks of New York on the 13th of October, and by those of Boston on the 14th. The

BRIGHAM YOUNG'S RESIDENCES, SALT LAKE CITY.

failures in the United States for the year ending December 6th, 1857, are said to have reached the enormous aggregate of $291,750,000. The Western States suffered in a marked degree from the effects of this "crisis;" but the south was comparatively unharmed by it. Various causes were assigned for the panic, the principal of which were the large speculations in western lands and a heavy fall in the value of railway stocks. The New York banks resumed specie payments on the 12th of December, 1857; the Boston banks on the 14th of December of that year; and those of Philadelphia in April, 1858. Specie payments were gradually resumed in other parts of the country, but the depression of business continued until during the course of the year 1859.

In 1858 occurred an event second only in importance to the invention of the electric telegraph. For some years it had been believed possible to

connect the shores of Europe with those of America by means of a sub-
marine telegraphic cable across the Atlantic.   In 1857 an unsuccessful
effort was made by a company of American and English capitalists to
accomplish this object.   The attempt was renewed in 1858.   Two war
steamers were furnished for the work of laying the cable—the "Niagara" by
the United States, and the "Agamemnon" by Great Britain.   The two
vessels met in mid ocean, and sailed each to its own country, paying out
the cable as they proceeded on their way.   On the 5th of August, 1858,
the "Niagara" entered Trinity bay, in Newfoundland, and made fast her
end of the cable to the shore, and on the same day the "Agamemnon" reached
Valentia bay in Ireland, having successfully accomplished her part of the
work.   The great work was thus ended, and on the 16th of August a
message was received through the wires from the queen of Great Britain
and Ireland addressed to the president of the United States, who at once
returned a suitable reply.   Other messages were exchanged between the
two continents, and the practicability of the scheme was fully demonstrated.
On the first of September the laying of the cable was celebrated with

COAT OF ARMS OF MINNESOTA.

imposing ceremonies in New York,
and rejoicings were held in other
cities.   The hopes aroused by the
successful accomplishment of the
great enterprise were soon disappointed, for after a short time the
wires ceased to work, and no effort
could re-establish the communica-
tion between the two ends of the line.   The feasibility of the undertaking
had been practically demonstrated, however, and the determined men who
had carried it through to success were convinced that a new effort would
be attended with more satisfactory results.

On the 11th of May, 1858, the Territory of Minnesota was admitted
into the Union as a State.

In the autumn of 1859 a dispute arose between the United States and
Great Britain as to the ownership of the large island of San Juan lying
in the strait which separates Vancouver's island from the territory of the
United States.   General Harney, commanding the American troops in
the northwest, took possession of the island.   Governor Douglass of
British Columbia protested against this occupation, and for a while there
was danger that the two parties would come to blows.   The general
government despatched General Scott to the scene of the controversy, and
he succeeded in bringing about an adjustment of the quarrel.

On the 14th of February, 1859, Oregon was admitted into the Union
a State, the Territory of Washington being separated from it.

During the whole of Mr. Buchanan's administration the question of slavery in the Territories continued to engross the attention of the people. The struggle in Kansas went on with increased bitterness. In the summer of 1857 an election was ordered by the legislature of Kansas for delegates to a convention for the purpose of framing a constitution, and care was taken to arrange the matter so that a majority of Pro-slavery delegates should be chosen. For this reason, and others of equal force, the Free Soil men refused to take any part in the election, which consequently resulted in the choice of a Pro-slavery convention. The Free Soil party thereupon issued an address to the people of the United States, relating the wrongs they had suffered, and were still enduring.

Governor Geary now resigned his position, and President Buchanan appointed, as governor of Kansas, Robert J. Walker, a man of great eminence and ability, who was in sentiment opposed to slavery. Mr. Walker sincerely desired to effect a settlement of the quarrel, and succeeded in inducing the Free Soil party to vote at the coming election for members of the territorial legislature and a delegate to Congress. They

COAT OF ARMS OF OREGON.

did so, and a fair election was held, which resulted in the choice of the Free Soil candidates by overwhelming majorities.

In the autumn of 1857 the convention elected, as we have seen, assembled at Lecompton, and framed a State constitution. This instrument contained a clause adopting slavery, and the convention submitted this clause only to the people of the Territory for ratification or rejection at the polls. The remainder of the constitution was withheld from the popular vote. The convention also ordered that all whose votes were challenged at the polls should be required "to take an oath to support the constitution if adopted," before being allowed to deposit their ballot. The Free State men refused to take part in the vote on the ratification of this constitution, and consequently all the votes cast were in favor of it. It was declared adopted, and was sent to Congress for the approval of that body.

The discussion of the Lecompton constitution in Congress was marked by great bitterness. It was supported by the Democratic party and the administration, and was opposed with determination by the Republicans. The latter took the strong ground that the Lecompton constitution was not the work of the people of Kansas, but of a mere faction, and was distasteful to the majority of the citizens of that Territory, who were opposed to slavery. Finally, on the 30th of April, 1858, a bill was passed to submit the Lecompton constitution to the people of Kansas. This bill declared that if they ratified the constitution, they should be given certain public lands for State purposes; but that if they failed to ratify it, Kansas should not be permitted to enter the Union until it had a population of ninety-three thousand. With these strange conditions, the constitution was submitted to the people of Kansas on the 2d of August, 1858, and was rejected by them by a vote of eleven thousand three hundred against it, to seventeen hundred and eighty-eight votes in its favor.

In January, 1859, the civil strife having subsided in the Territory, and the Free Soil men having a majority in the legislature, a convention was summoned at Wyandotte. It met in July, and adopted a free State constitution, which was submitted to the people and ratified by a large majority. The "Wyandotte Constitution" was then laid before Congress, and a bill admitting Kansas into the Union as a State was passed by the lower House early in 1860. The Senate however failed to act upon the bill. At the next session the measure was revived, and on the 30th of

COAT OF ARMS OF KANSAS.

January, 1861, the opposition of the south having ceased by reason of the withdrawal of a large number of the southern representatives and senators from Congress, Kansas was admitted into the Union as a free State.

On the night of the 16th of October, 1859, John Brown, who had acquired a considerable notoriety as the leader of a Free Soil company during the war in Kansas, entered the State of Virginia, at Harper's Ferry, with a party of twenty-one companions, and seized the United States arsenal at that place. He then sent out parties to arrest the leading citizens of the vicinity, as hostages, and to induce the negro slaves to join him, his avowed object being to put an end to slavery in Virginia by exciting an insurrection of the slaves. Several citizens were kidnapped by these parties, but the slaves refused to join Brown, or to take any part in the insurrection. At daylight on the 17th of October the alarm was given, and during the morning the militia of the surrounding country was ordered under arms to put down the outbreak. Brown's force was unknown, and was greatly exaggerated.

The news of the seizure of the arsenal was telegraphed to Washington, and the government decided to recover it at once and confine the trouble to the spot on which it had originated. General Scott was absent from the capital at the time, and the president and secretary of war summoned

Colonel Robert E. Lee, a distinguished officer of the army, to consult with them as to the best course to pursue. The interview resulted in the despatching of a battalion of marines to Harper's Ferry, under the command of Colonel Lee. Orders were telegraphed to that point to suspend all operations there until Colonel Lee's arrival. He reached Harper's Ferry on the night of the 17th.

In the meantime, upon the appearance of the militia, Brown and his companions retreated to the fire-engine house in the arsenal yard. This was a strong stone building, and they barricaded the doors, and during the day maintained a desultory fire upon the town. They had taken Colonel Washington, Mr. Dangerfield, and the other citizens kidnapped by them, into the engine house with them, where they held them, in the hope that the presence of these gentlemen would prevent the troops from firing upon them.

As soon as Colonel Lee arrived at Harper's Ferry, he proceeded to surround the engine house with the marines to prevent the escape of Brown and his men, and deferred his attack upon them until the next morning, lest in a night assault some of the captive citizens might be injured. At daylight on the 18th, wishing, if possible, to accomplish the object in view without bloodshed, Colonel Lee sent his aid, Lieutenant J. E. B. Stuart, to demand the surrender of the insurgents, promising to protect them from violence at the hands of the citizens, and to hold them subject to the orders of the president. Brown refused the terms offered, and demanded to be permitted to march out with his men and prisoners, with the arms of the former, to be allowed to proceed, without being followed, to a point at a certain distance from Harper's Ferry, where he would free his prisoners. He was then willing that the troops should pursue him, and to fight if he could not escape. This proposition was inadmissible, but as a last resort, Colonel Lee directed Lieutenant Stuart to remonstrate with the insurgents upon the folly of their course. This duty Stuart performed, remaining before the engine house until his personal danger compelled him to withdraw.

Finding that nothing but force would avail, Colonel Lee gave the order for the assault, and the marines made a dash at the engine house, broke in the doors, and captured its inmates. Several of the insurgents were killed and wounded, Brown himself being desperately hurt. The marines lost one man killed, and one wounded. Fortunately none of the citizens captured by Brown were injured.

Colonel Lee took care to protect his prisoners, and there is little doubt that but for his precautions in their behalf they would have been shot down by the excited civilians. He telegraphed to Washington for

49

instructions, and was directed to deliver the prisoners to Mr Ould, the attorney for the District of Columbia, who was ordered by the government to take charge of them and bring them to trial. As soon as Mr. Ould arrived Colonel Lee turned over the prisoners to him, and being satisfied that the danger was over, went back to Washington.

As Brown and his companions had committed their chief crime against the United States, by seizing the federal arsenal and resisting the troops sent to reduce them to submission, it seemed proper that they should be tried for their offences by the general government. The attempt to excite an insurrection of the slaves, however, was a crime against the laws of the State of Virginia, and the governor of that State demanded of the federal authorities the surrender of Brown and his fellow-prisoners for trial by the State courts. The demand was complied with, and the prisoners were arraigned in the court of the county of Jefferson, the county in which their offence was committed. They were given a fair trial, and were defended by able counsel from the free States, who came to Charlestown for that purpose. Brown frankly confessed that his object was to produce an insurrection among the slaves, and then carry them off to the free States. The prisoners were found guilty of treason, murder, and an attempt to excite insurrection, and were sentenced to be hanged. Brown was executed at Charlestown on the 2d of December, 1859, and six of his companions met the same fate a few weeks later.

During his trial Brown steadily denied that he had been aided or encouraged by any persons in the north. His denial was generally doubted at the time, and it is now known that he was assisted with money and advice by some of the most respectable leaders of the extreme Anti-slavery party, and that several persons high in position knew of the designs of Brown, but failed to warn either the general government or the State of Virginia of the intended attack.*

The execution of Brown and his companions drew upon the south a storm of furious denunciation from the Anti-slavery men. Brown was regarded as a martyr to the cause of freedom, and the day of his execution was observed in many of the towns of the Northern States by the tolling of bells, prayer in the churches, the firing of minute-guns, and other public demonstrations of sorrow and respect. The conservative class in the north, however, and in this number were included some of the firmest opponents of slavery, sincerely deplored Brown's course, and acknowledged his punishment as merited. Brown was a man of many good qualities,

---

* Mr F B Sanborn, one of Brown's confederates, in a series of papers published in *The Atlantic Monthly* (vol xxxv) gives the details of this conspiracy, together with many interests   with it, which sustain the view of the case presented above

but the undertaking in which he met his fate was criminal in the extreme
Not even the intention of rescuing the slaves of Virginia from their
bondage can excuse him for seeking to excite a servile war, in which murder and violence would have been inevitable, and in which the aged and
the helpless, the defenceless women and children, would have been the
chief sufferers.

The effect of Brown's attempt upon the southern people was most
unfortunate. They regarded it as unanswerable evidence of the intention
of the people of the north to make war upon them under the cover of the
Union. Regarding this view of the case as true, they came to listen with
more favor to the arguments of the extreme class which openly favored a
dissolution of the Union, and which asserted that the only safety of the
south lay in pursuing such a course. The John Brown raid was the most
powerful argument that had ever been placed in the hands of the disunionists, and in the alarm and excitement produced by that event the
southern people lost sight of the fact that the great mass of the northern
people sincerely deplored and condemned the action of Brown and his
supporters. The voice of reason was drowned in the storm of passionate
excitement which swept over the land, and the extremists on both sides
were able to prosecute their unpatriotic work to great advantage

While the excitement was at its height the presidential campaign opened
in the spring of 1860. The slavery question was the chief issue in this
struggle. The convention of the Democratic party met at Charleston, in
April, but being unable to effect an organization adjourned to Baltimore,
and reassembled in that city in June. The extreme southern delegates
were resolved that the convention should be committed to the protection
of slavery in the Territories by Congress, and failing to control it withdrew from it in a body, and organized a separate convention, which they
declared represented the Democratic party, but which, in reality, as the
vote subsequently proved, represented but a minority of that party. The
new convention was joined by a number of delegates from the northern
and western states.

The original convention, after the withdrawal of these delegates, nominated for the presidency Stephen A. Douglas, of Illinois, and for the vice-
presidency Herschell V. Johnson, of Georgia. It then proceeded to
adopt the platform put forward by the entire party four years before at
Cincinnati, upon the nomination of Mr. Buchanan, with this additional
declaration. "That as differences of opinion exist in the Democratic
party as to the nature and extent of the powers of a territorial legislature,
and as to the powers and duties of Congress under the constitution of the
United States over the institution of slavery within the Territories, . .

the party will abide by the decisions of the Supreme Court of the United States on the questions of constitutional law."

The "Seceders' Convention," as it was commonly called, also adopted the Cincinnati platform, and pledged themselves to non-interference by Congress with slavery in the Territories or the District of Columbia. This party held to the doctrine that the constitution recognized slavery as existing in the Territories, and sanctioned and protected it there, and that neither Congress nor the people of the Territories could frame any law against slavery until the admission of such Territories into the Union as States. The regular convention held that Congress had no right to interfere with slavery in the Territories, to legislate either for or against it, that the regulation of that question belonged entirely to the people of the respective Territories acting through their legislatures. This doctrine was popularly known as "Squatter Sovereignty," and was credited to Mr. Douglas. The "Seceders' Convention" put forward as its candidate for the presidency John C. Breckenridge, of Kentucky, and for the vice-presidency Joseph Lane, of Oregon.

The Republican party took issue with both wings of the Democratic party. Its convention was held at Chicago, Illinois, and its candidates were, for president Abraham Lincoln, of Illinois, and for vice-president Hannibal Hamlin, of Maine The platform of principles adopted by the Chicago Convention declared that "the maintenance of the principles promulgated in the Declaration of Independence and embodied in the federal constitution is essential to the preservation of our republican institutions. . . . That all men are created equal ; that they are endowed by their Creator with certain inalienable rights . . . That the federal constitution, the rights of the States and the union of the States must and shall be preserved." The platform also declared that the rights of the States should be maintained inviolate, "especially the right of each State to order and control its own domestic institutions according to its own judgment exclusively." It asserted "that the normal condition of all the territory of the United States is that of freedom," and denied the right or "authority of Congress, of a territorial legislature, or of individuals, to give legal existence to slavery in any Territory of the United States."   -

A fourth party, known as the "Constitutional Union Party," proclaimed as its platform the following vague sentence : "The constitution of the country, the union of the States, and the enforcement of the laws." The convention of this party met at Baltimore, and nominated for the presidency John Bell, of Tennessee, and for the vice-presidency Edward Everett, of Massachusetts

The contest between these parties was bitter beyond all precedent. When the election took place in November, the result was as follows:

Popular vote for Lincoln, . . . 1,866,452
"   "   Douglas, ... 1,375,157
"   "   Breckenridge, . . . 847,953
"   "   Bell, ... 590,631

The electoral vote stood as follows: For Lincoln, 180; for Breckenridge, 72; for Bell, 39; for Douglas, 12.

Mr. Lincoln was thus elected by a plurality of the popular vote, which secured for him the electoral votes of eighteen States. These States were entirely north of the sectional line, and he received not a single electoral vote from a Southern State. The States which cast their electoral votes for Breckenridge, Bell, and Douglas, were entirely slaveholding. The division thus made was alarming. It was the first time in the history of the republic that a president had been elected by the votes of a single section of the Union.

The state in which the presidential election left the country was most alarming. The excitement was higher than it had been before the struggle at the polls. The Gulf States had declared at an early period of the political campaign that they would withdraw from the Union in the event of the election of a Republican president. The people of the south generally regarded the result of the election as an evidence of the determination of the Northern States to use the power of the federal government to destroy the institution of slavery. The disunion leaders exerted themselves to deepen this conviction, and to arouse the fears of the south. On the other hand, the Republican leaders took little pains to allay the excitement by declaring their intentions to execute faithfully the constitution and laws of the Union. Their declarations of fidelity to the Union were abundant, and were generally accompanied by equally plain assertions of their determination to oppose by force the withdrawal of the Southern States—declarations which were ill-suited to calm the fears of the south, or to encourage the party in that section which desired a perpetuation of the Union. A statesman of the Henry Clay school was needed at this crisis of our country's history as he had never been needed before, but, alas! statesmanship of any kind was painfully wanting.

As soon as the election of Mr. Lincoln was definitely ascertained, the legislature of South Carolina summoned a sovereign convention of the people of that State, which met on the 17th of December, 1860. This convention adopted an ordinance of secession on the 20th of December, and declared the State no longer a member of the Union. The reasons assigned for this action were thus stated by the convention:

"An increasing hostility on the part of the non-slaveholding States to the institution of slavery has led to a disregard of their obligations, and the laws of the general government have ceased to effect the objects of the constitution.   The States of Maine, New Hampshire, Vermont, Massachusetts, Connecticut, Rhode Island, New York, Pennsylvania, Illinois, Indiana, Michigan, Wisconsin, and Iowa, have enacted laws which either nullify the acts of Congress or render useless any attempt to execute them.   In many of these States the fugitive is discharged from the service or labor claimed, and in none of them has the State government complied with the stipulations made in the constitution. . . . Thus the constitutional compact has been deliberately broken and disregarded by these non-slaveholding States, and the consequence follows that South Carolina is released from her obligation.

  .   .   .   .   .   .

" We affirm that these ends for which this government was instituted have been defeated, and the government itself has been made destructive of them by the action of non-slaveholding States.   Those States have assumed the right of deciding upon the propriety of our domestic institutions; and have denied the rights of property established in fifteen of the States and recognized by the constitution , they have denounced as sinful the institution of slavery; they have permitted the open establishment among them of societies whose avowed object is to disturb the peace and to eloigne the property of citizens of other States.   They have encouraged and assisted thousands of our slaves to leave their homes ; and those who remain have been incited by emissaries, books, and pictures to servile insurrection.

" For twenty-five years this agitation has been steadily increasing, until it has now secured to its aid the power of the common government Observing the *forms* of the constitution, a sectional party has found within that article establishing the executive department the means of subverting the constitution itself.   A geographical line has been drawn across the Union, and all the States north of that line have united in the election of a man to the high office of president of the United States whose opinions and purposes are hostile to slavery.   He is to be intrusted with the administration of the common government because he has declared that that 'government cannot endure permanently half slave, half free,' and that the public mind must rest in the belief that slavery is in the course of ultimate extinction.

" This sectional combination for the subversion of the constitution has been aided in some of the States by elevating to citizenship persons who, by the supreme law of the land, are incapable of becoming citizens ; and their votes have been used to inaugurate a new policy, hostile to the south, and destructive of its peace and safety.

"On the 4th of March next this party will take possession of the government   It has announced that the south shall be excluded from the common territory; that the judicial tribunals shall be made sectional, and that a war must be waged against slavery until it shall cease throughout the United States.

"The guarantees of the constitution will then no longer exist; the equal rights of the States will be lost. The slaveholding States will no longer have the power of self-government or self-protection, and the federal government will become their enemy."

These reasons were substantially the same as those avowed by the other Southern States in support of their action, and therefore we have quoted them at length.

The example of South Carolina was followed by the other States of the far south, which summoned conventions and adopted ordinances of secession. Mississippi withdrew from the Union on the 9th of January, 1861; Florida on the 10th of January, Alabama on the 11th of January; Georgia on the 19th of January; Louisiana on the 26th of January, and Texas on the 1st of February. The forts, arsenals, and other public property of the United States within the limits of these States were seized by the authorities of the States in which they were situated, and were held by their troops, with the exception of Forts Moultrie and Sumter, in Charleston harbor, and Fort Pickens, at Pensacola.

Fort Moultrie was occupied by Major Robert Anderson, of the United States army, with a garrison of eighty men. Becoming alarmed at the rapid concentration of troops in Charleston, Major Anderson evacuated the fort on the night of December 25th, 1860, and threw himself with his command into Fort Sumter, which was built in the bay at some distance from either shore. The State troops at once occupied Fort Moultrie, and began to erect batteries of heavy guns at different points along the harbor for the reduction of Fort Sumter.

Fort Pickens was held by a garrison under Lieutenant Slemmer. The State of Florida occupied the navy yard at Pensacola and the other forts in that harbor with her troops.

The property of the general government seized by the seceded States amounted to over twenty millions of dollars in value.

The position of the general government was one of great difficulty. The president was called upon either to recognize the lawfulness of the acts of the seceded States, and thus to join in the work of dissolving the Union, or to maintain the authority of the federal government, and compel the submission of the Southern States to the constitution and laws of the land. The government was almost powerless to enforce its authority. The army, but sixteen thousand strong, was stationed upon the remote frontier, and the available vessels of the navy were nearly all absent on foreign service. Many of the most prominent federal officials, including several of the cabinet ministers, were in open sympathy with the seceded States. The president's position was unquestionably embarrassing, but he made no use of the means at his command. General Scott, the veteran commander of the army, believed that prompt action on the part of the general government would confine the evil to the six cotton States, and urged the president to act with vigor. Mr. Buchanan was sorely perplexed, and seemed chiefly anxious to postpone all definite action until the inau-

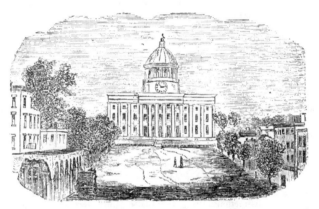

THE CAPITOL AT MONTGOMERY, ALABAMA, PLACE OF MEETING OF THE FIRST
CONFEDERATE CONGRESS.

guration of his successor. He was in favor of conceding everything but separate independence to the south, failing to perceive that the leaders of the secession movement would accept nothing but separation ; and by his timidity lost the advantages which the government would have gained by a bold, firm course.

As Major Anderson was short of supplies and needed reinforcements, the steamship "Star of the West" was despatched by the government to Charleston with provisions and a detachment of two hundred and fifty men to his assistance. She reached Charleston on the 9th of January, 1861, and attempted to enter the harbor, but was fired upon by the South Carolina batteries, and turned back.

The president was urged by the friends of the south to order Major Anderson to evacuate Fort Sumter and return to Fort Moultrie, but refused to do so. South Carolina then offered to purchase Fort Sumter from the general government for its full value, but the president refused to make the sale.

Immediately upon their withdrawal from the Union the six seceded States began to concert measures for their common protection. Delegates were elected to a convention which met at Montgomery, Alabama, on the 4th of February, 1861, to devise a plan for this purpose. The convention at once proceeded to organize a new republic, for which they adopted the name of *The Confederate States of America.* On the 8th of February, a provisional constitution having been adopted, the convention elected Jefferson Davis, of Mississippi, president, and Alexander H. Stephens, of

Georgia, vice-president of the Confederate States. The action of the convention was sustained by all the States comprising the new confederacy, and the provisional government at once entered upon its duties.

Jefferson Davis was a native of Kentucky, and was born on the 3d of June, 1808. His father had removed to Mississippi during his early childhood, and he had grown up to manhood in that State. He was educated at the West Point Military Academy, from which he was graduated in 1828, and passed the next seven years of his life in the army. He

JEFFERSON DAVIS.

served with distinction during the Black Hawk war and against the Indian tribes on the frontier. Entering into politics after his withdrawal from the army, he was soon sent to represent his State in Congress, in which body he served until the commencement of the Mexican war. During that struggle he commanded the Mississippi Rifles, and distinguished himself greatly in the battles of General Taylor's army, and especially at Buena Vista.

Upon his return home he was chosen to represent Mississippi in the Senate of the United States. Upon the inauguration of President Pierce he accepted a seat in the cabinet as secretary of war. Returning to the Senate after the close of Mr. Pierce's administration, he remained in that body until the secession of Mississippi, when he resigned his seat and returned home. He was now in his fifty-third year, and was regarded as one of the most brilliant public men in America. His election was generally looked upon in the south as a concession to the more conservative portion of the southern people, for he had not been considered as one of the original or most ultra secession leaders.

The conservative elements of both sections made great efforts to bring about a reconciliation. The State of Virginia called upon all the States to send delegates to an informal peace congress to meet in Washington. This body assembled in February. Twenty States were represented in

A. H. STEPHENS.

it—thirteen northern and seven southern—and the venerable ex-President Tyler was chosen to preside over its deliberations. Various plans of settlement were proposed, and a committee, consisting of one member from each State, was appointed to prepare a plan upon which the congress could unite. In due time it made its report to the congress, and after a careful and elaborate discussion the resolutions were adopted, and were ordered to be laid before the rival governments. The congress then adjourned. The plan proposed by this body pleased neither side. The Southern States were not satisfied with the guarantees it offered for the protection of their rights in the matter of slavery; and the Northern States were unwilling to sanction a more rigid enforcement of the constitutional provision for the rendition of fugitive slaves. The effort to close the breach between the States only served to widen it.

Matters were in this unhappy and excited condition when the administration of Mr. Buchanan came to a close. After the inauguration of his successor, he retired to his home at Wheatland, near Lancaster, Pennsylvania.

CHAPTER XLI.

THE ADMINISTRATION OF ABRAHAM LINCOLN—THE CIVIL WAR.

Inauguration of President Lincoln—His History—The Confederate Commissioners at Washington—Attack upon Fort Sumter by the Confederates—The President calls for Troops—Response of the North and West—Secession of the Border States—Opening Events of the War in Virginia—Withdrawal of West Virginia—Admitted into the Union as a separate State—Meeting of Congress—The West Virginia Campaign—Battle of Bull Run—The War in Missouri—Kentucky Occupied—The Blockade—Capture of Port Royal—The "Trent" Affair—Insurrection in East Tennessee—State of Affairs at the Opening of the Year 1862—Edwin M Stanton made Secretary of War—Capture of Forts Henry and Donelson—The Confederates fall back from Kentucky—Battle of Shiloh—Capture of Island No 10—Evacuation of Corinth—Capture of Memphis—Bragg's Kentucky Campaign—His Retreat into Tennessee—Battles of Iuka and Corinth—Battle of Murfreesboro', or Stone River—Grant's Campaign against Vicksburg—Its Failure—The War beyond the Mississippi—Battle of Pea Ridge—Capture of Roanoke Island—Capture of New Orleans—Surrender of Fort Pulaski—The War in Virginia—Johnston's Retreat from Centreville—Battle between the "Monitor" and "Virginia"—The Move to the Peninsula—Johnston Retreats to the Chickahominy—Battle of Seven Pines—Jackson's Successes in the Valley of Virginia—The Seven Days' Battles before Richmond—Battle of Cedar Mountain—Defeat of General Pope's Army—Lee Invades Maryland—Capture of Harper's Ferry—Battles of South Mountain and Antietam—Retreat of Lee into Virginia—McClellan Removed—Battle of Fredericksburg

BRAHAM LINCOLN, the sixteenth president of the United States, was inaugurated at Washington on the 4th of March, 1861. As it was feared that an attempt would be made to prevent the inauguration, the city was held by a strong body of regular troops, under General Scott, and the president-elect was escorted from his hotel to the capitol by a military force. No effort was made to interfere with the ceremonies, and the inauguration passed off quietly.

The new president was in his fifty-third year, and was a native of Kentucky. When he was but eight years old his father removed to Indiana, and the boyhood of the future president was spent in hard labor upon the farm Until he reached manhood he continued to lead this life, and during this entire period attended school for only a year. At the age of twenty-one he removed to Illinois, where he began life as a storekeeper. Being anxious to rise above his humble position, he determined to study law. He was too poor to buy the necessary books, and

779

so borrowed them from a neighboring lawyer, read them at night, and returned them in the morning. His genial character, great good nature, and love of humor, won him the friendship of the people among whom he resided, and they elected him to the lower house of the legislature of Illinois. He now abandoned his mercantile pursuits, and began the practice of the law, and was subsequently elected a representative to Congress from the Springfield district. He took an active part in the politics of his State, and in 1858 was the candidate of the Republican party for United States senator. In this capacity he engaged in a series of debates in various parts of the State with Senator Douglas, the Democratic candidate for re-election to the same position. This debate was remarkable for its brilliancy and intellectual vigor, and brought him prominently before the whole country, and opened the way to his nomination for the presidency. In person he was tall and ungainly, and in man-

ner he was rough and awkward, little versed in the refinements of society. He was a man, however, of great natural vigor of intellect, and was possessed of a fund of strong common sense, which enabled him to see at a glance through the shams by which he was surrounded, and to pursue his own aims with singleness of heart and directness of purpose. He had sprung from the ranks of the people, and he was never false to them. He was a simple, unaffected, kind-hearted man; anxious to do his duty to the whole country; domestic in his tastes and habits; and incorruptible in every relation of life. He was

ABRAHAM LINCOLN.

fond of humor, and overflowed with it; finding in his "little stories" the only relaxation he ever sought from the heavy cares of the trying position upon which he was now entering. He selected his cabinet from the leading men of the Republican party, and placed William H. Seward, of New York, at its head as secretary of state.

Mr. Lincoln was sincerely anxious to avoid everything which might precipitate the civil strife; but at the same time was determined to maintain the authority of the general government over the seceded States. In his inaugural address he declared his purpose to collect the public revenues at the ports of the seceded States, and to "hold, occupy, and possess" the forts, arsenals, and other public property seized by those States. At the time of his entrance upon the duties of his office Fort Sumter and Fort Pickens were still held by the federal forces.

The Confederate government was convinced that war was inevitable;

and since its inauguration had been preparing for the coming struggle. Nearly all the officers of the army and navy of the United States, who were natives of the seceded States, resigned their commissions in the old service, and were given similar positions in the army of the Confederate States. The forces collected at Charleston and Pensacola were reinforced

ARRIVAL OF PRESIDENT LINCOLN AT THE CAPITOL.

by troops from other States, and the command at the former place was conferred upon General Pierre G. T. Beauregard, and at the latter upon General Braxton Bragg, both of whom had been distinguished officers of the old army.

Just before the close of Mr. Buchanan's term of office the Confederate government despatched John Forsyth, of Alabama, Martin J. Crawford, of Georgia, and A. B. Roman, of Louisiana, to Washington as commissioners to endeavor to effect a peaceable adjustment of the matters at issue between the two governments, and to treat for an equitable division of the public property of the United States. Mr. Buchanan refused to receive the commissioners in their official capacity, and after the inauguration of the new administration they addressed a note to Mr. Seward, the new secretary of state, setting forth the objects of their mission, and soliciting an official interview with the president. Mr. Seward declined to receive them in their official capacity, but answered them verbally through Mr. Justice John A. Campbell, of the Supreme Court of the United States, that he was in favor of a peaceful settlement of the difficulty, and that the troops would be withdrawn from Fort Sumter in less than ten days. Mr. Seward's object appears to have been to deceive the

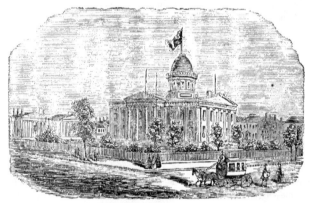

STATE-HOUSE, SPRINGFIELD, ILLINOIS.

commissioners, and lull their suspicions, in order to gain time for the preparations which had been determined upon for the relief of Fort Sumter.

In the meantime, the government having resolved to reinforce and provision Fort Sumter at all hazards, every nerve was strained to carry out this design before it should become known to the Confederates. An expedition consisting of seven ships, carrying two hundred and eighty-five guns and twenty-four hundred men, was prepared at New York and Norfolk. The southern commissioners, whose suspicions had been allayed by Mr. Seward's message, were alarmed by the rumors of these preparations, which they suspected were for the relief of Fort Sumter. They waited upon Judge Campbell to ask an explanation, and that gentleman, on the 7th of April, addressed a note to Mr. Seward asking if the assurances he had given were well or ill founded. Mr. Seward replied as follows: "Faith as to Sumter fully kept; wait and see."

In the meantime the expedition had sailed from New York and Norfolk, and was on its way to Charleston harbor. On the 8th of April, 1861, Governor Pickens, of South Carolina, was notified by the general government of its intention to relieve Fort Sumter at all hazards, and of the sailing of the fleet for that purpose. Governor Pickens at once informed General Beauregard of this notification, and the news was telegraphed by him to the Confederate government at Montgomery.

The Confederate secretary of war thereupon ordered General Beauregard to demand the immediate surrender of Fort Sumter; "and if this should be refused to proceed to reduce it." On the 11th of April General Beauregard demanded of Major Anderson the surrender of the fort.

FORT SUMTER.

The demand was refused in writing; but Major Anderson added verbally to the messenger, "I will await the first shot, and if you do not batter us to pieces, we will be starved out in a few days." Beauregard telegraphed this remark with Anderson's reply to his government, and was answered, "Do not desire needlessly to bombard Fort Sumter. If Major Anderson will state the time at which, as indicated by himself, he will evacuate, and agree that, in the meantime, he will not use his guns against us unless ours should be employed against Fort Sumter, you are authorized thus to avoid the effusion of blood. If this or its equivalent be refused, reduce the fort, as your judgment decides most practicable." The federal fleet was on its way to Charleston, and if the attack of the Confederates was to be made at all, no time was to be lost. General Beauregard, therefore, gave Major Anderson warning that he should open fire upon Fort Sumter at half-past four o'clock the next morning.

At the designated hour on the morning of April 12th, the Confederate

batteries opened fire upon Fort Sumter, which replied to them with spirit.
The bombardment lasted over thirty-two hours, and the fort was greatly
damaged, and many of the guns were dismounted   The fleet arrived off
the harbor during the bombardment, but remained in the offing, and took
no part in the engagement.   Not a single life was lost in this memorable
battle   Late in the afternoon of the 13th, Major Anderson agreed to
capitulate, and the firing ceased.   The victors granted liberal terms to
Anderson and his men, whose heroism had aroused their warmest admiration; and on the morning of Sunday, April 14th, the fort was surrendered to the Confederate forces, and Major Anderson and the garrison
embarked in one of the vessels of the fleet, which at once sailed for New
York

The attack upon Fort Sumter put an end to the last hope of peace,
and aroused the most intense excitement in both sections of the country.
On the 15th of April President Lincoln issued a proclamation calling
upon the States to furnish seventy-five thousand troops for the suppression of the rebellion, and convening Congress in extra session on the 4th
of July.   The Northern and Western States responded with enthusiasm
to the president's call for troops, and at once began to forward their
quotas to the points designated by the war department.

The enthusiasm in the south was fully equal to that of the north. The
Confederate government issued a call for volunteers to repel the threatened invasion of the federal forces, and it was responded to with alacrity.

Until now the States of Maryland, Virginia, North Carolina, Tennessee, Kentucky, Arkansas and Missouri, generally known as the Border
States, had remained in the Union, hoping to be able to effect a peaceable
settlement of the quarrel.   Their sympathies were with the Southern
States, and it was generally believed that in the event of war they would
cast their lots with those States.   Each of these States was included in the
call of President Lincoln for troops.   The governors of most of them replied by refusing to furnish the quotas required of them, and by de-
nouncing the president's demand as illegal.   Conventions of the people
were held, and all but Maryland, Kentucky and Missouri withdrew from
the Union.   The secession of Virginia took place on the 17th of April,
that of Arkansas on the 6th of May ; that of North Carolina on the 20th
of May , and that of Tennessee on the 8th of June.   These States subsequently ratified the constitution of the Confederate States, and became
members of the new republic.   Kentucky and Missouri remained neutral.

The passage of the act of secession by the Virginia convention was
kept secret for a day or two in order to give the authorities of that State
an opportunity to seize the United States arsenal at Harper's Ferry, and

the navy yard at Portsmouth. The officer in command of the arsenal, upon hearing of the approach of a force of Virginia troops, destroyed a number of the muskets stored there, set fire to the buildings, and retreated into Pennsylvania. The Virginians extinguished the flames and secured a large quantity of arms and equipments and the valuable machinery for the manufacture of arms. The commandant of the navy yard at Portsmouth, upon the approach of the Virginians, made no attempt to defend his post, but spiked the cannon, burned or sunk the war vessels lying in the harbor, set fire to the buildings, and retreated with two war

HARPER'S FERRY.

steamers. The navy yard was at once occupied by the Virginians, who secured nearly two thousand pieces of cannon, and an immense quantity of stores and munitions of all kinds. The governors of the seceded Border States issued calls for volunteers immediately upon the withdrawal of their States. Men came forward in such large numbers that arms could not be provided for all of them. The prominent points of danger in Virginia were occupied and fortified by the State troops; but the control of the military affairs in all the Border States soon passed into the hands of the Confederate government.

As it was certain that the first operations of the war would take place upon the borders of Virginia, the city of Richmond was made the capital

50

of the Confederate States, and on the 21st of May the Confederate government was removed to that city.

The western part of the State of Virginia refused to join the remainder of the State in its withdrawal from the Union. On the 11th of June, 1861, the people of the western counties met in convention at Wheeling, declared their independence of the old State, organized a State government, and proclaimed their intention to remain faithful to the Union. The action of this convention was sustained by the federal government, and on the 26th of November, 1861, another convention met at Wheeling, and adopted a constitution for the new State of West Virginia. This constitution was ratified by the people at the polls on the 3d of May, 1862, and application was made for the admission of West Virginia into the Union as a State, which was accomplished by act of Congress on the 20th of June, 1863.

In the meantime the federal government set to work with energy to prepare for the struggle before it. The call of President Lincoln for troops had been answered by three hundred thousand volunteers. On

COAT OF ARMS OF WEST VIRGINIA.

the 17th of April, two days after the president's proclamation, the Sixth Massachusetts regiment left Boston for Washington. In passing through Baltimore it was attacked by a crowd of citizens who sympathized with the south, and three soldiers were killed and eight wounded. Several citizens were killed and wounded. The regiment reached Washington the same day, and was soon joined by other troops from the Northern States. In a short time the force at the capital was sufficient to put an end to all fears for its safety. Alexandria and the Virginia shore opposite Washington were seized and fortified. Baltimore was occupied by a force under General Butler, and the communications of Washington with the north and west were made sure. On the 19th of April the president issued a proclamation declaring all the southern ports in a state of blockade; and on the 3d of May he put forth another proclamation ordering the regular army of the United States to be increased to sixty-four thousand seven hundred and forty-eight men, and the navy to eighteen thousand seamen. On the 10th of May he issued a fourth proclamation, suspending the writ of *habeas corpus* in certain localities, and authority to suspend this privilege was conferred upon the commanders of military departments soon afterward.

Under the instructions of the government these commanders now proceeded to arrest great numbers of persons in various parts of the country who were suspected of sympathizing with the south. They were imprisoned at the military posts, and were denied trial by the civil courts. John Merryman, a citizen of Maryland, was one of the persons so arrested. His friends applied for redress to the chief-justice of the United States, who held the suspension of the *habeas corpus* act by the president to be unconstitutional, and ordered the discharge of the prisoner. The government paid no attention to this decision, and held the prisoner in confinement. A little later the legislature of Maryland, which was strongly southern in its sympathies, was prevented from meeting by the sudden arrest and imprisonment of a large number of its members by order of the secretary of war.

On the 4th of July, 1861, Congress convened in extra session at Washington, in accordance with the president's proclamation. This body proceeded to give to the government a prompt and effectual support. Resolutions were introduced to legalize the extraordinary acts of the president in setting aside the writ of *habeas corpus*, in ordering the arbitrary arrest and confinement of citizens, and in assuming certain other powers which belonged to Congress. Congress refused to throw over these acts, however necessary, the sanction of the law, but in view of the necessity of prompt and vigorous action on the part of the president excused his acts on the distinct ground of the "necessities of war." Measures were adopted without delay for putting in the field an army of five hundred and twenty-five thousand men, and for equipping a powerful navy, and the sum of five hundred millions of dollars was appropriated for the prosecution of the war. During this session Congress also adopted a solemn resolution declaring "that this war is not prosecuted on our part in any spirit of oppression, nor for any purpose of conquest or subjugation, nor for the purpose of overthrowing or interfering with the rights or established institutions of those [the seceded] States; but to defend and maintain the supremacy of the constitution and all laws made in pursuance thereof, and to preserve the Union with all the dignity, equality and rights of the several States unimpaired; that as soon as these objects are accomplished the war ought to cease."

In the meantime the Confederates had collected troops at important points to resist the advance of the federal troops into Virginia. A force under Brigadier-General Garnett was stationed in West Virginia to cover the approaches from that direction; Harper's Ferry, which commanded the entrance into the valley of Virginia, was held by an army of seven thousand or eight thousand men, under General Joseph E. Johnston; a much larger force, under General Beauregard, took position near Manas-

sas Junction, about thirty miles from Washington ; and a column of several
thousand men, under General John B. Magruder, was stationed at Yorktown, on the peninsula between the York and James rivers, to cover
Richmond from the direction of Fortress Monroe at the mouth of Hampton Roads, which was still held by the federal troops. Norfolk was also
held by a strong force. With the exception of that occupied by General
Garnett's command, all these positions were carefully fortified.

The Union army at Fortress Monroe numbered about twelve thousand
men, and was commanded by General B. F. Butler. Early in June,
Magruder moved a force of eighteen hundred men and several pieces of
artillery from Yorktown, and took position at Bethel Church, about half

STATE HOUSE, COLUMBUS, OHIO.

way between Yorktown and Hampton. On the 10th of June he was
attacked by a force of four thousand troops under General Pierce, of
Massachusetts, but succeeded in repulsing the attack and maintaining his
position.

In the opposite quarter of the State, the Union forces were more suc-
cessful. In order to prevent the Confederates from overrunning West
Virginia, a strong body of Ohio and Indiana troops under General
George B. McClellan was sent into that region. McClellan set to work
at once to drive the Confederates out of West Virginia, and on the 3d of
June a portion of his command under General Kelley defeated General

Garnett at Philippi. McClellan now advanced against the main body of Garnett's forces. On the 11th of July he attacked the command of Colonel Pegram at Rich Mountain, and defeated it This defeat compelled General Garnett to fall back towards the valley of Virginia. He was pursued by McClellan and overtaken at Carrick's ford, on the Cheat river. In the battle which ensued here Garnett was killed, and the remnant of his command was driven beyond the mountains.

The United States had assembled a considerable army of volunteers and regulars at Washington under Major-General Irwin McDowell. On the 24th of May Alexandria, on the Virginia side of the Potomac, nine miles below Washington, was seized by a detachment from this army. Its commander, Colonel Ellsworth, was killed by a citizen Strong defences were erected on the Virginia shore between Washington and Alexandria, and the army was encamped within these lines Two months were passed in organizing and disciplining this force, and in the meantime the people of the Northern and Western States became impatient of the delay, and demanded an immediate advance upon the southern army and Richmond.

Preparatory to his own advance General McDowell sent General Patterson with twenty thousand men to cross the Potomac at Williamsport, and prevent General Johnston from leaving the valley and joining Beauregard at Manassas. Upon the arrival of Patterson on the upper Potomac, General Johnston evacuated Harper's Ferry and took position at Winchester. Patterson made a considerable show of force in the valley, but refrained from attacking Johnston, although the latter sought to induce him to do so. He took position about nine miles from Winchester, and remained inactive there.

In the meantime the preparations for the advance of McDowell's army were completed, and on the 17th of July he began his march from the Potomac towards Bull Run, on the banks of which the Confederates were posted. His army numbered over fifty thousand men, and forty-nine pieces of artillery. As soon as the advance of this army was known to him, General Beauregard informed General Johnston of it, and begged him to come to his assistance Johnston skilfully eluded Patterson's army, and hastened to Bull Run, arriving there with a part of his command in time to take part in the battle

The Confederate army had taken position behind Bull Run, and in advance of Manassas Junction. Including the force brought by General Johnston, who assumed the chief command by virtue of his rank, it consisted of thirty-one thousand four hundred and thirty-one men and fifty-five guns.

On the 18th of July General McDowell attempted to force a passage of Bull Run at Blackburn's ford, but was repulsed. On the morning of the 21st, the Union army advanced in force, and endeavored to turn the left of the southern line. An obstinately-contested battle ensued, which lasted from sunrise until nearly sunset. It resulted in the total defeat of the federal army, which was driven back in utter rout upon Alexandria and Washington, with a loss of between four and five thousand men in killed, wounded and prisoners, and twenty-eight pieces of artillery.

For a while the effects of this disaster upon the federal army were so great that Washington was almost defenceless; but the Confederates made no effort to follow up their victory. They were almost as badly demoralized by their success as the Union army by its defeat.

Recovering from the dismay of its first great reverse, the government went to work with vigor to repair the disaster. The levy of five hundred

dred thousand men ordered by Congress was raised promptly and without difficulty, so eager was the desire of the people to wipe out the disgrace of Bull Run. At his own request General Scott, whose bodily infirmities were so great as to render him unable to discharge the duties of his position, was relieved of the command of the army. Major-General George B. McClellan was given the chief command of the armies of the Union, and ordered to take charge of the force assembling before Washington, which was named

GEN. P. G. T. BEAUREGARD.

the Army of the Potomac. He devoted himself with success to the task of organizing and disciplining the recruits which came pouring in during the fall and winter.

The remainder of the year 1861 passed away quietly on the Potomac, with the single exception of the battle of Leesburg. Colonel Baker with a force of two thousand men was sent by General Stone to cross the Potomac at Edward's ferry, and drive back the Confederate force under General Evans from its position near Leesburg. He made his attack on the 21st of October, but was repulsed with the loss of eight hundred killed and wounded, being himself among the slain. The Confederate army held its position at Centreville through the fall and winter, and at one time its outposts were pushed forward within view of the city of Washington.

In the fall of 1861 an army of ten thousand men was sent by the Confederate government into the valley of Virginia to prevent its occupation by the federal forces. The command of these troops was conferred upon

General T. J Jackson, whose conspicuous gallantry at Bull Run had won him the sobriquet of "Stonewall Jackson," by which he was afterwards known by both armies. He established his head-quarters at Winchester.

In the meantime the war had been going on in western Virginia. After the transfer of General McClellan to Washington the command of the Union forces passed to Brigadier-General Rosecranz, an able officer. He had several indecisive encounters with the commands of Generals Floyd and Wise in the region of the Gauley and New rivers. General Robert E. Lee was sent by the Confederate government to assume the chief command in the west. He attacked the brigade of General Reynolds at Cheat mountain on the 14th of September, but was repulsed and obliged to retreat. On the 4th of October General Reynolds attacked a Confederate force under General Henry R. Jackson on the Greenbrier river, but was repulsed.

The State of Missouri took no part in the secession movements of the spring of 1861. Her people were divided, a large party sympathized with the south, but a still larger party was determined that the State should remain in the Union. These parties soon came in conflict. The governor and leading officials of the State were in favor of secession, and used all their influence to bring about the withdrawal of Missouri from the Union. A camp of the State militia was formed near St. Louis, and was called Camp Jackson in honor of the governor. It was known that the force assembled at this camp was intended to serve as a nucleus around which an army hostile to the federal government might assemble. By extraordinary exertions Colonel Francis P Blair, Jr, a member of Congress from St. Louis, and Captain Nathaniel Lyon, commanding the troops at the Jefferson barracks, near St. Louis, succeeded in collecting a force of five regiments of Union volunteers. On the 10th of May, 1861, Lyon with these five regiments suddenly surrounded Camp Jackson, and compelled General Frost, the commanding officer, to surrender his whole force, camp and equipments. By this prompt action the State forces were prevented from carrying out their plan for seizing the United States arsenal at St Louis, which contained sixty thousand stand of arms of the latest patterns, and a number of cannon, and a large quantity of ammunition. For this decisive action Captain Lyon was commissioned a brigadier-general by the president.

Satisfied that the desire of the southern party in Missouri to remain neutral was but a pretext to gain time to arm the State for a union with the Confederates, President Lincoln determined to compel all the State forces not in the federal service to disband. An interview was held at St. Louis on the 11th of June between Governor Jackson and General

ST LOUIS, 1875.

Lyon, now commanding the federal troops in Missouri. Governor Jackson demanded that no United States forces should be quartered in or marched through Missouri. General Lyon refused to comply with this demand, and insisted that the State forces should be disbanded, pledging himself to respect the rights and privileges of the State. At the close of the interview the governor returned to Jefferson City, the capital of the State, and the next day, the 12th, issued his proclamation calling fifty thousand of the State militia into active service for the purpose of driving the federal troops from the State, and protecting the " lives, liberty and property of the citizens." General Lyon at once marched upon Jefferson City, and occupied it on the 15th, the governor and his supporters having retired to the interior of the State. On the 17th Lyon proceeded to Booneville and defeated the State troops stationed there under General Price.

GEN. STERLING PRICE.

The southwestern part of Missouri is rich in deposits of lead, and valuable mines of this mineral are worked there. The State authorities were anxious to hold this region, as it was of the highest importance to them to obtain the use of these mines to supply their army with lead. A column of federal troops under General Sigel was sent by General Lyon to intercept the retreat of the State troops. On the 5th of July Sigel attacked the State troops under Governor Jackson at Carthage, but was repulsed.

The next day, July 6th, Governor Jackson was joined at Carthage by General Sterling Price, of the Missouri State Guard, and General Ben McCulloch, of the Confederate army, with several thousand men. The command of the whole force was conferred upon General McCulloch, who had been ordered by his government to advance into Missouri. The southern army, according to General McCulloch's statement, numbered fifty-three hundred infantry, six thousand mounted men, and fifteen pieces of artillery. It advanced rapidly into the interior of the State, and on the 9th of August reached Wilson's creek, near Springfield. General Lyon had taken position there with a force somewhat smaller than that of the Confederates. On the morning of the 10th he attacked the southern army. The battle lasted six hours, and was hotly contested. General Lyon was killed at the head of his troops while endeavoring to turn the left flank

MAJOR-GENERAL F. SIGEL.

of the Confederates, and his army was forced back. His body was left in the hands of the Confederates, who treated it with becoming respect.

Springfield was occupied by the Confederates the day after the battle; but McCulloch and Price being unable to agree upon the plan of the campaign, they soon withdrew to the Arkansas border. The Union army after the battle withdrew to Rolla, near the centre of the State.

A few weeks later General Price with a force of over five thousand Confederates laid siege to Lexington, on the Missouri river, which was held by about three thousand men under Colonel Mulligan. After a gallant defence Mulligan was forced to surrender on the 20th of September.

Major-General John C. Fremont was now appointed by President Lincoln to take command of the western army. He forced Price's command back into the southwestern part of the State. Arriving near Springfield, Fremont prepared to bring the Confederates to a decisive engagement, but

MAJ.-GEN. N. LYON.

on the 2d of November was removed from his command. He was succeeded by General Hunter, who abandoned the pursuit, and fell back to St. Louis. On the 18th of November Hunter was superseded by Major-General Halleck, who by a rapid advance drove Price once more towards the Arkansas border. This movement closed the campaign of 1861 in Missouri. The Union army had not only saved the State to the Union, but had confined the Confederates to the Arkansas border.

In the meantime Governor Jackson had summoned the legislature of Missouri to meet at Neosho. It assembled at that place in October, passed an ordinance of secession, and elected delegates and senators to the Confederate Congress. Though this action was merely formal, and received the support of but a small part of the people of Missouri, it was recognized as valid by the Confederate government, and Missouri was proclaimed one of the Confederate States.

The governor and State authorities of Kentucky attempted at the outset of the war to hold the position of armed neutrality between the parties to the contest; but as in the case of Missouri, this effort failed. Neither the federal government nor that of the Southern Confederacy could, in the nature of things, respect this neutrality. The federal troops were poured into Kentucky, and the Confederates seized Columbus, on the Mississippi, Bowling Green, in the centre of the State, and other positions in the western part. The southern party in Kentucky, within the protection of the Confederate lines, organized a provisional government for the State, sent senators and representatives to the Congress at Richmond, which formally recognized Kentucky as one of the Confederate States.

The force at Columbus was commanded by General Polk of the Confederate army. At Belmont, on the Missouri shore of the river, immediately opposite Columbus, a body of Confederate troops was stationed. On the 7th of November, General U. S. Grant having descended the Mississippi from Cairo, attacked the force at Belmont with his command of three thousand men. After a sharp struggle he was repulsed, and forced to retreat to Cairo.

At the outset of the war the Confederates occupied the principal ports of the south, and a number of prominent points on the Atlantic coast.

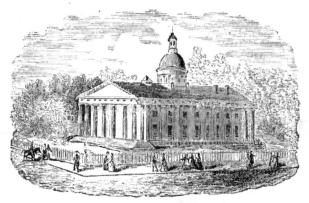

STATE HOUSE, INDIANAPOLIS, INDIANA.

These were fortified by them as well as the means at hand would permit. The general government resolved to capture these as rapidly as possible, as their reduction was necessary in order to render the blockade of the southern coast effectual. The first expedition was despatched from Fortress Monroe in August, 1861, under Commodore Stringham and General Butler, and was directed against the Confederate works at Hatteras inlet, which commanded the entrance to Albemarle and Pamlico sounds. These works were captured on the 29th of August.

The great extent of the coast to be blockaded by the navy made it necessary that a good harbor at some central point should be secured, where supplies could be stored for the fleet, and where vessels could refill without returning to the northern ports. Port Royal Harbor in South

Carolina was selected as the best place for this purpose. It was defended by Fort Walker on Hilton Head and Fort Beauregard on the opposite side of the harbor. A powerful naval and military expedition under Commodore Dupont and General Thomas W. Sherman attacked these works on the 7th of November, and reduced them after a terrible bombardment by the fleet. Port Royal was at once occupied by the expedition, and during

the war was the principal depot on the southern coast for the fleets and armies of the Union.

It was not possible, however, to render the blockade effective. Great efforts were made to increase the number of vessels employed in this duty, but the Confederates succeeded in eluding the Union cruisers almost at pleasure, and a steady communication was maintained between the southern ports and England by way of the West Indies. A number of armed vessels in the service of the confederacy succeeded in getting to sea. By the close of the year they

LIEUTENANT-GENERAL POLK.

had inflicted severe damage upon the commerce of the Northern States, and had almost driven the foreign trade of the United States from the ocean.

During the early part of the war the southern government was encouraged to hope that the governments of England and France would recognize the independence of the Confederate States, and in the fall of 1861, James M. Mason of Virginia and John Slidell of Louisiana were ordered to proceed to Europe, as commissioners from the Confederate States, to secure this recognition. They sailed from Charleston on the 12th of October, and reached Cuba in safety. There they took passage for England on board the British mail-steamer "Trent." Hearing of this, Captain Wilkes, of the United States warsteamer "San Jacinto," overhauled the "Trent" upon the high seas, boarded her, and seized the

JAMES M. MASON.

two commissioners and their secretaries and sailed with them to Boston harbor, where they were imprisoned in one of the forts.

The "Trent" in the meantime proceeded on her voyage, and upon reaching England her commander informed the British government of the outrage that had been committed upon its flag. The English government at once demanded of President Lincoln the immediate and unconditional release of the Confederate commissioners and satisfaction for the insult to its flag. It was understood that France was prepared to sustain England in her demands. The Federal government disavowed the action of Captain Wilkes in seizing the commissioners, and those gentlemen were released and allowed to continue their voyage. They reached England in due time. Mr. Mason proceeded to London and Mr. Slidell to France. Neither the English nor the French governments would receive the commissioners officially. It was understood that the United States would regard the interference of either in the American quarrel as a cause of war, and neither power cared to join in the struggle.

Tennessee seceded from the Union, as we have related, in the spring of 1861. The western and central portions of the State were unanimously in favor of joining the Southern States and gave a hearty support to the confederacy during the war, but East Tennessee, inhabited by a race of hardy mountaineers, was devoted to the Union, and was unwilling to leave it. In the autumn of 1861 the East Tennesseeans took up arms against the Confederate government, and began to destroy the railway bridges in that part of the State. This movement was full of danger to the confederacy, as the principal line of communication between Virginia and the Mississippi passed through East Tennessee. A considerable force of Confederate troops was sent into East Tennessee to hold the people in subjection and protect the railroads, but throughout

JOHN SLIDELL.

the war the hostility of the people of this region was a constant source of danger and of weakness to the Confederates.

When the year 1862 opened, the war had assumed colossal proportions. The military operations extended almost across the continent, and engaged a number of powerful armies, and a formidable navy. The call of President Lincoln for troops had been cheerfully responded to, and the opening of the year found the United States provided with a force of over half a million of men, splendidly armed and equipped, and supplied with everything necessary for the successful prosecution of the war. The north had profited by its first reverses, and was resolved that its next effort, which was to be made at the opening of the season for active operations, should find it thoroughly prepared for the task it had undertaken. A cordial support was given to the measures of the government by the people. Its wants were supplied by means of a heavy loan which was readily negotiated with the capitalists of the Eastern States. From the moment that

the despondency caused by the reverse at Bull Run had subsided sufficiently to enable the people of the loyal States to face the situation calmly,
every one saw that the work of preparation must all be done over from
the beginning, and it was done bravely and thoroughly. During the fall
and winter the army was rapidly increased ; vessels were purchased and
built for the navy.

The southern armies, on the other hand, had grown steadily weaker.
The first successes of the Confederate troops had greatly demoralized the
southern people. Volunteering soon ceased almost entirely. Even the
heaviest bounties failed to bring recruits. There was a widespread
delusion throughout the south that the war was practically ended. The
measures of the Confederate Congress steadily thinned, instead of filling
up the ranks of the southern armies, and when the new year dawned there
was grave reason to fear that the spring campaign would find the south
without an adequate army unless more vigorous measures were resorted to.
It was exceedingly doubtful whether the troops already in the service
would renew their enlistments, which expired in the spring of 1862.
During the winter the Southern Congress adopted a law granting a furlough and a heavy bounty to every soldier who would re-enlist for the
war. The furlough was to be granted during the winter, the bounty to
be paid at a later period. Many of those who went home on these fur-
loughs did so with the intention of remaining there ; and the practical
effect of the measure was to diminish the strength of the Confederate
armies. At length the Confederate Congress was driven by the necessities of the situation to adopt a most stringent and sweeping measure.
On the 16th of April, 1862, a conscription act was passed, giving to the
president of the confederacy the power to call into the military service the
entire male population of the various States between the ages of eighteen
and thirty-five years. In September, 1862, a second act was passed
extending the conscript age to forty-five years The measure was
acquiesced in by the southern people, but was never popular with them.
It served the purpose for which it was intended, however, and enabled
the Confederate government to collect a force of several hundred thousand
men in the spring of 1862, and thus to fill up the ranks of its armies in
the field, and to retain the regiments already in the service.

When the spring opened, General Halleck, whose head-quarters were at
St. Louis, held Missouri against the Confederates with a powerful army.
General Buell, with a considerable force, was stationed in central Kentucky.
In his front an inferior force of Confederates, under General Albert Sidney
Johnston, held Bowling Green and covered Nashville and the Tennessee
and Cumberland rivers They also held Columbus and other prominent

points on the Mississippi. The army of the Potomac, under General McClellan, lay along the Potomac, confronting the Confederate army of Northern Virginia, which held Centreville. A considerable force was collected at Fortress Monroe, and an army of about ten thousand Confederates, under Magruder, held a strongly fortified line extending from Yorktown across the peninsula to the James river. In addition to these forces, the Federal government had collected a powerful flotilla of steamers and gunboats at Cairo, the junction of the Ohio and Mississippi rivers, to assist in the operations of the western armies. The capture of New Orleans had been resolved upon, and a combined naval and military expedition under Commodore Farragut and General Butler was assembled for that purpose; and another expedition was organized in the Chesapeake for the reduction of Roanoke island and the forts on the North Carolina coast.

Soon after the opening of the new year, Mr. Cameron, whose administration of the war department had failed to give satisfaction to the country, was removed by President Lincoln, and sent to Russia as minister from the United States. The president on the 13th of January appointed Edwin M. Stanton, of Ohio, secretary of war. The new secretary was confessedly one of the ablest men in America, and his accession to the control of the war department infused new life into the military preparations of the government. During the remainder of the war he occupied this position, and it is not too much to say that his vigorous administration of his department was one of the chief causes of the final success of the Union arms.

Active operations were resumed earlier in the west than in the east. On the 19th of January General George H. Thomas drove the Confederates under General Zollicoffer from Mill Spring in Kentucky. The defeated force had held the right of the Confederate line in Kentucky, the centre of which was at Bowling Green, and the left at Columbus, and its reverse was a serious disaster to the Confederates.

The department of General Halleck embraced Kentucky in addition to the country west of the Mississippi. In order to hold the Cumberland and Tennessee rivers, which afforded water communication far back into the country in the rear of their line, the Confederates had built a work, known as Fort Henry, on the Tennessee, a little south of the Kentucky border, and another and a stronger work, known as Fort Donelson, on the Cumberland and a little below Nashville. At the solicitation of Brigadier-General U. S. Grant, commanding at Cairo, General Halleck determined to capture these forts, and so break the Confederate line, and compel their army to fall back from Kentucky. Fort Henry was to be first attacked. The fleet of gunboats under Commodore Foote and Grant's troops from Cairo were sent against Fort Henry, which was captured on the 6th of February after a severe bombardment by the gunboats which had ascended the Tennessee. The garrison escaped to Fort Donelson, twelve miles distant across the country.

The loss of Fort Henry compelled the Confederates to evacuate all their positions in Kentucky. General Beauregard fell back from Columbus to Corinth, Mississippi, and General Sidney Johnston slowly retired from Bowling Green upon Nashville, followed by General Buell with a vastly superior force.

After the capture of Fort Henry the gunboats returned to Cairo, and, taking on board supplies and reinforcements for the army, ascended the Ohio and entered the Cumberland, up which they passed to Fort Donelson. Grant in the meantime marched across the country from Fort Henry to Fort Donelson, and invested the latter work. The roads were so difficult that although the distance between the two forts was but twelve

ADMIRAL FOOTE.

miles, Grant spent six days in marching it. This delay gave General Johnston an opportunity to reinforce Fort Donelson. He halted at Nashville with his main army to await the result of Grant's attack on the fort. The gunboats did not join Grant until the 14th of February, and the investment was not begun until their arrival.

Fort Donelson was a stronger work than Fort Henry, and was held by a force of about thirteen thousand men, commanded by General John B. Floyd. On the 14th of February the gunboats opened fire upon the fort, and at the same time the army of General Grant, reinforced to about thirty thousand men, began to occupy the positions assigned it in the investment. The operations of the 14th ended with the repulse of the fleet, Commodore Foote being severely wounded in the engagement. Satisfied of his inability to hold the fort against the overwhelming force of the Federal army, General Floyd resolved to cut his way through, and retreat upon Nashville. On the 15th he made a gallant attempt to break through Grant's lines, but was driven back, and a portion of the southern intrenchments remained in the hands of the Union army. On the night of the 15th a council of war was held by the Confederate commanders. It was evident that escape was impossible and a surrender inevitable. General Floyd refused to surrender, and retreated from the fort with a considerable force of infantry and cavalry, with which he succeeded in reaching Nashville. General Pillow, who was left by Floyd in command, turned over the command to General Buckner, the next in rank, and joined Floyd in his flight. Being unable to offer further resistance, General Buckner, on the morning of the 16th, surrendered the fort and his troops unconditionally to the Federal army.

The capture of Fort Donelson was by far the most important success that had yet been won by the Union armies, and was hailed with rejoicings throughout the north and west. By this capture over five thousand prisoners, besides the Confederate wounded, fell into the hands of the Union forces. The Confederates also lost heavily in killed and wounded.

General Johnston, upon learning of the fall of Fort Donelson, fell back from Nashville to Murfreesboro', from which place he subsequently continued his retreat across the State, and eventually joined General Beaure-

NASHVILLE, TENNESSEE.

gard, who had taken position at Corinth, at the junction of two important railway lines on the northern border of Mississippi. Beauregard, in falling back from Columbus, had left a force at Island No. 10, which had been strongly fortified, to hold the Mississippi against the efforts of the Federal fleet and army to obtain the control of the river.

Nashville was occupied by the army of General Buell, and Grant's army was moved up the Tennessee as far as Pittsburg Landing. General Buell was ordered to march across the country from Nashville to the Tennessee, to unite his forces with Grant's, and attack the Confederates at Corinth.

General Johnston, the Confederate commander, had feared this concen-

51

tration, which would make the Federal power in this quarter irresistible, and had determined to attack Grant's army and crush it before Buell could arrive, after which he would be free to engage Buell. His plan was ably conceived, but his march was delayed by the fearful state of the roads, and he did not arrive opposite the Federal position until two days after the time fixed for his attack. Grant was encamped at Shiloh Church,

near Pittsburg Landing, with the Tennessee river in his rear. On the morning of Sunday, April 6th, his army was suddenly attacked by Johnston, and was driven steadily from its original position to the banks of the Tennessee, where it was sheltered by the fire of the gunboats. The battle was stubbornly contested, and the losses on both sides were very heavy. Late in the afternoon General Johnston was mortally wounded, and died soon afterwards. The command passed to General Beauregard, who failed to follow up his advantage. During the night the army of

GEN. ALBERT S. JOHNSTON.

General Buell arrived, and reinforced Grant. On the morning of the 7th, Grant attacked the Confederates and after a sharp fight drove them back. They retreated slowly, and returned to Corinth.

While these operations were in progress, the gunboats under Commodore Foote and a strong force of western troops under General Pope laid siege to Island No. 10, on the Mississippi. After a bombardment of twenty-three days, the Confederate works were captured, together with five thousand prisoners, on the morning of the 7th of April, the day on which Beauregard was driven back from Shiloh. The Confederates still held Fort Pillow, a strong work a short distance above Memphis. If this could be captured, the Federal forces would obtain the control of the river as far south as Vicksburg. General Pope was anxious to move against it at once, but his army was ordered to join General Halleck. Commodore Foote being

MAJ.-GEN. D. C. BUELL.

disabled by his wound received at Fort Donelson was succeeded by Captain Davis, who descended the river and took position above Fort Pillow.

General Halleck now repaired to the Tennessee, and took command of the Union armies there, amounting to more than one hundred thousand men. He moved forward leisurely towards Corinth, and laid siege to that place. Beauregard, seeing that it was impossible to hold Corinth against this greatly superior force, evacuated it on the night of the 29th of May, and retreated to Tupelo, Mississippi. The next day General Halleck occupied Corinth. The loss of Corinth compelled the evacuation of Fort Pillow, which was abandoned by the Confederates on the 4th of June. On the 6th the Union gunboats descended the river to Memphis and defeated the Confederate flotilla above that city. Memphis at once surrendered, and was occupied by the Union forces. All West Kentucky and West Tennessee were now under the control of the Union armies, which now occupied a line extending from Memphis, through Corinth, almost to Chattanooga.

The Confederates still held East Tennessee in heavy force. Shortly

MEMPHIS, TENNESSEE.

after the evacuation of Corinth General Beauregard was removed from his command, and was succeeded by General Braxton Bragg. Bragg was strongly reinforced, and it was determined to make a bold effort to drive back the Federal advance and regain West Tennessee and, if possible, Kentucky. Bragg's army was concentrated at Chattanooga, and General Kirby Smith at Knoxville was strongly reinforced. Smith was to move from Knoxville, while Bragg was to advance from Chattanooga, and the two armies were to unite in the centre of the State of Kentucky. Their combined forces amounted to over fifty thousand men, and it was hoped that this movement would compel the Federal army to abandon its advance, and fall back into Kentucky to protect that State and Ohio from the Confederates. Then by a decisive victory Bragg expected to be able to overrun and hold Kentucky and even to invade Ohio.

The division of General Smith moved forward about the middle of August, and on the 30th of August defeated a Union force under General Manson at Richmond, Kentucky, inflicting upon it a loss of six thousand

men. Smith then occupied Lexington and Frankfort, and advanced towards Cincinnati; but ascertaining that a strong force was assembling at that city, under General Lewis Wallace, he fell back to Frankfort, where he joined General Bragg on the 4th of October.

Bragg had begun his march as soon as Kirby Smith had gotten fairly started. His objective point was Louisville, and he hoped to be able to elude the army of General Buell which was at Nashville, and by a rapid advance seize Louisville before Buell's arrival. By the 17th of September

MAJ.-GEN. H. W. HALLECK.

he was at Munfordsville, Kentucky, which he captured after several slight encounters, taking forty-five hundred prisoners. Buell in the meantime had divined Bragg's purpose, and had set out from Nashville for the Ohio by forced marches. He reached Louisville before the arrival of the Confederates, and being heavily reinforced advanced to attack Bragg, who

had turned aside and occupied Frankfort on the 4th of October. Bragg fell back slowly, ravaging the country along his route; and was followed by Buell with equal deliberation. On the 8th of October an indecisive battle was fought between the two armies at Perryville. After this conflict, in which both sides lost heavily, Buell refrained from attacking Bragg again, and the latter continued his retreat leisurely into Tennessee, taking with him a wagon train forty miles in length, loaded with plunder captured in Kentucky.

GENERAL B. BRAGG.

During this campaign the Federal army under General Grant had held its line in West Tennessee, extending from Corinth to Memphis. A Confederate army under Generals Price and Van Dorn was assembled in Mississippi in front of the Union position. Grant, who was now in command of the Federal forces in West Tennessee (Halleck having been summoned to Washington as commanding General), ordered General Rosecrans to his assistance. Upon the arrival of this

CINCINNATI, IN 1875.

805

commander with his troops, Grant advanced upon Price at Iuka, and defeated him on the 19th of September. He then repaired to Jackson, Tennessee, leaving Rosecrans with nineteen thousand men to hold Corinth against the Confederates.

After his defeat at Iuka Price was joined by Van Dorn, whose troops brought the strength of the Confederate army to eighteen thousand men. They at once advanced upon Corinth, and on the 4th of October attacked that place. The battle which ensued was noted for the obstinacy with which it was contested by both sides. The Confederates were defeated

LANDING AT LOUISVILLE, KENTUCKY.

with a loss of about three thousand killed and wounded, and were pursued for about thirty miles southward. The Union loss was about five hundred and eighteen killed, wounded, and missing.

The Federal government was greatly dissatisfied with Buell's failure to intercept Bragg, and upon his arrival at Nashville he was removed from the command of his army, which was conferred upon General Rosecrans, as a reward for his victory at Corinth. Bragg had taken position near Murfreesboro', about thirty miles distant from Nashville, and Rosecrans, towards the last of December, moved upon that place to attack him. Bragg had at the same time completed his preparations to resume the offensive, and had begun his advance upon Nashville, and the two armies encountered each other at Stone river, near Murfreesboro', on the 31st of December. They were about equal in strength, each numbering about forty thousand men. The battle was fiercely disputed, but at night-fall Rosecrans was driven back with heavy loss, and Bragg telegraphed to Richmond news of a great victory. Rosecrans, however, had merely fallen back to a new and stronger position. On the 2d of January, 1863, Bragg renewed his attack, but was repulsed with terrible slaughter. On the 3d a heavy rain fell and prevented all military operations, and that night Bragg retreated from the field. He retired in good order to Tulla-homa, about thirty miles from Murfreesboro'. The losses on both sides in this battle were heavy, ranging from ten thousand to twelve thousand men in each army.

The Confederates, having lost the upper and lower Mississippi, had fortified Vicks-burg and Port Hudson, in order to main-tain their hold upon that stream, and to keep open their communications with the country west of the Mississippi. Vicks-burg had been made a post of extraordinary strength, and was garrisoned by a consider-able force of Confederate troops. Towards the last of the year General Grant deter-mined to undertake an expedition against it. He sent General Sherman, with forty thou-

MAJOR-GENERAL W. ROSECRANS.

sand men, and a fleet of gunboats, under Commodore Porter, to descend the Mississippi and attack the southern works above the city; and advanced southward from Corinth with the main army by land. Grant had accomplished fully half the distance when a strong body of Confederate cavalry, under General Van Dorn, made a dash into his rear, and on the 20th of December captured Holly Springs, Grant's principal depot of supplies. This movement compelled Grant to abandon his advance upon Vicksburg, and to fall back and re-establish his com-munications with his base. Sherman, ignorant of this disaster, left Memphis on the 20th of December, and a few days later landed his troops on the banks of the Yazoo, from which he advanced upon the Confederate works at Chickasaw bayou, on the north of Vicksburg. On the 29th of December he made a spirited attack upon them, but was repulsed. He withdrew his troops to the boats, and retired to Young's Point, on the Louisiana shore, a short distance above Vicksburg.

The Confederates were driven out of Missouri at the close of 1861, as we have seen, and retired into Arkansas. General Van Dorn was now sent by the Confederate government to take command of the forces of Price and McCulloch, which numbered about sixteen thousand men. He reached the head-quarters of this force on the 3d of March, 1862. The Federal army, under General Curtis, with General Sigel as his second in command, had taken position on the heights of Pea Ridge, around Sugar creek, in the northwestern part of Arkansas. It numbered about eleven thousand men. On the 7th of March Van Dorn attacked the Union army in this position, and after a bloody fight, which lasted for about seven or eight hours, drove it back. Curtis took up a new position dur-

LITTLE ROCK, ARKANSAS.

ing the night, and the next morning the Confederates renewed the attack, and were repulsed. After the battle of Shiloh the troops of Price and Van Dorn were withdrawn across the Mississippi to reinforce General Beauregard at Corinth. We have seen them bearing the brunt of the campaign in northern Mississippi against Grant's army. Towards the close of the summer, it being necessary to make a vigorous effort to hold the trans-Mississippi region against the efforts of the Union forces, the Confederate government sent Lieutenant-General Holmes to take command of it. The operations in this region during the remainder of the year were of an unimportant character.

The plan of the Federal government for seizing the prominent points on the coast was carried forward with great energy during the year 1862.

Between Albemarle and Pamlico sounds, on the coast of North Carolina, lies Roanoke island, famous as the scene of Sir Walter Raleigh's unfortunate attempts to colonize America, and commanding the entrance to Albemarle sound The possession of this island by the Federal forces would give them the command of the rivers entering into the sounds, place the rear defences of Norfolk at their mercy, and afford them a safe base from which to attack the towns on the North Carolina coast The Federal government having determined to obtain possession of Roanoke island, a powerful expedition against it was fitted out early in the year, under the command of Major-General Ambrose E. Burnside. The expedition sailed from Hampton Roads on the 11th of January, 1862, and after narrowly escaping being scattered by a severe storm passed through Hatteras inlet, and anchored in Pamlico sound on the 28th On the 6th of February the fleet took position off Roanoke island, and on the 7th opened fire upon the Confederate works Under the cover of this fire a force of over ten thousand troops was landed upon the island. On the 8th General Burnside attacked the Confederate intrenchments and carried them after a sharp contest. The entire Confederate force, numbering about twenty-five hundred men, fell into his hands as prisoners of war On the 10th the Confederate squadron in Albemarle sound was attacked and destroyed, or captured

Having established himself firmly on Roanoke island, General Burnside prepared to reduce the towns along the coast of North Carolina On the 14th of March Newberne surrendered to him, and on the 25th of April Fort Macon, at the entrance of Beaufort harbor, one of the strongest works on the coast, capitulated

Some important successes were won on the coast of Florida during the spring of this year. An expedition from Port Royal captured Fernandina and Fort Clinch on the 28th of February, and a little later Jacksonville, on the St. John's river, and St Augustine passed into the hands of the Federal troops. Brunswick and Darien, important places on the coast of Georgia, were captured about the same time

The most important naval expedition of the year was that which resulted in the capture of New Orleans. The Federal government had recognized from the first the importance of regaining possession of the Mississippi; and, as we have seen, a large fleet of gunboats had been prepared on the upper waters of that stream to co-operate with the army in its efforts to capture the fortified posts along the river. All these efforts, however, were useless, as long as the Confederates retained possession of the lower river or of the important city of New Orleans, the commercial metropolis of the south. It was resolved at an early period of the struggle to wrest New Orleans from the Confederates, and a fleet of forty-five vessels of war and mortar-boats was assembled for this purpose, and placed under command of Commodore Farragut, an able and experienced officer. To the fleet was added a force of fifteen thousand troops, under General B. F. Butler. The expedition rendezvoused at Ship island, near the mouth of the Mississippi, in the early part of March.

About twenty miles above the head of the passes of the Mississippi, and about seventy miles below New Orleans, the entrance to the river is defended by two strong works—Fort Jackson on the right bank of the stream, and Fort St. Philip on the left—both built before the war. The Confederates had further strengthened their position by stretching six heavy chains, supported on a series of dismasted schooners, across the river, from shore to shore, to prevent the passage of ships. Early in April the fleet sailed from Ship island, leaving the troops there to await

ADMIRAL FARRAGUT.

the result of its operations, and entering the Mississippi took position below the forts. On the 18th the bombardment of the forts was begun by the ships and the mortar-boats, and was continued with great vigor until the 24th. The results of this bombardment were most discouraging, and Farragut became convinced that the forts could not be reduced by the fire of the fleet. He therefore determined to pass them with his vessels and so neutralize them.

The chain and raft barricade across the river had been broken by a severe storm, and Farragut sent a party to enlarge the gap made in it, so as to admit the passage of the fleet. This task was accomplished with great gallantry. At three o'clock, on the morning of the 24th of April, the fleet got under headway and began to ascend the river, the commodore in his flag-ship, the "Hartford," leading the way. The fleet consisted of seventeen vessels, carrying two hundred and ninety-four guns. As the vessels came abreast of the forts the Confederates opened a heavy fire upon them, to which they responded with vigor. The forts were passed in safety at length, and a short distance above them Farragut encountered the Confederate fleet, consisting of sixteen vessels, but eight of which were armed. Two of these were iron-clads, however. A desperate battle ensued, which resulted in the total destruction of the southern fleet. When the sun rose on the morning of the 24th the forts had been passed, and the resistance of the Confederate vessels had been overcome.

There was nothing now between the Federal fleet and New Orleans, and Farragut, ascending the river slowly and cautiously, anchored in the stream, in front of the city, on the morning of the 25th. He at once demanded the capitulation of New Orleans, which had been evacuated by the Confederate troops on the previous day, and the city was surrendered

VIEW IN ST. CHARLES STREET, NEW ORLEANS.

to him by the municipal authorities. On the 28th Forts Jackson and St. Philip surrendered to Captain Porter, the commander of the mortar fleet. New Orleans being taken word was sent to General Butler, at Ship island, to hasten forward with his troops to occupy it. He arrived on the 1st of May, and at once took possession of the city. Baton Rouge, the capital of Louisiana, was occupied by the Federal forces, and Farragut pushed on up the river, and, passing the Confederate batteries at

Grand Gulf and Vicksburg, joined the fleet of Commodore Davis at Memphis.

The capture of New Orleans was a terrible blow to the south. It deprived the confederacy of the largest and wealthiest city within its limits, and wrested from it the whole of the lower Mississippi.

Another success was gained by the Union arms on the southern coast. An expedition from Port Royal, under General Hunter, laid siege to Fort Pulaski, near the mouth of the Savannah river. This fort was constructed by the Federal government previous to the war, and constituted one of the principal defences of the city of Savannah. On the 11th of April, after a bombardment of fifteen days, it surrendered to General Hunter. Its capture closed the Savannah river to the entrance of the class of vessels known as blockade runners, and deprived the south of the use of one of its principal ports.

The events of this year in Virginia were of the highest importance.

The army of the Potomac, nearly two hundred thousand strong, was ready for active operations with the early spring. General McClellan was anxious to avail himself of the superior naval strength of the United States to transport his army to a point on the Chesapeake bay, from which it could easily interpose between the Confederate army, under General Johnston, and Richmond. Suspecting such a design on the part of McClellan Johnston

MAJOR-GENERAL B. F. BUTLER.

abandoned his position at Centreville on the 8th of March, and fell back to the Rappahannock, and a little later moved back still farther to the line of the Rapidan. McClellan advanced to Centreville as soon as informed of Johnston's withdrawal, but was too late to interfere with the movements of the Confederate army.

Simultaneous with Johnston's withdrawal from Centreville occurred an incident which forms one of the most striking episodes of the war, and led to results of world-wide importance. Upon the evacuation of the Norfolk navy yard by the Federal forces, at the outset of the war, the splendid steam frigate "Merrimac" was scuttled and sunk. This vessel was subsequently raised by the Confederates, and rebuilt by them. Her upper deck was removed, and she was covered with a slanting roof. Both the roof and her sides were heavily plated with iron, and a long, stout bow was fitted to her to enable her to act as a ram. She was then armed with ten heavy guns, and named the "Virginia." Thus prepared she was the most powerful vessel afloat.

As soon as the "Virginia" was ready for service the Confederate authorities determined to test her efficiency by attempting to destroy the Federal fleet in Hampton Roads. On the 8th of March the "Virginia," accompanied by two small vessels, left Norfolk and steamed down the Elizabeth river into Hampton Roads. Her appearance took the Federal fleet by surprise, and a heavy fire was concentrated upon her from the fleet and the batteries on shore at Newport's News, at the mouth of the James river. Shot and shell flew harmlessly from her iron sides, and, firing slowly as she advanced, she aimed straight for the sloop of war "Cumberland"—the most formidable vessel of her class in the navy—and sunk her with a blow of her iron prow. The frigate "Congress," lying near by, was chased into shoal water and compelled to surrender, after which she was set on fire. The ram then endeavored to inflict a similar fate upon the frigate "Minnesota," but that vessel escaped into water too shallow for the iron-clad to venture into. At sunset the "Virginia" drew off, and returned to the Elizabeth river. She had destroyed two of the finest vessels in the Federal navy, and inflicted upon her adversaries a loss of two hundred and fifty officers and men. She was herself uninjured, and had but two men killed and eight wounded.

MAJ.-GEN. GEO. B. M'CLELLAN.

The success of the "Virginia" struck terror to the fleet in Hampton Roads, and it was by no means certain that the victorious vessel would not the next day either attack Fortress Monroe, or pass by it and ascend the Chesapeake, in which case both Washington and Baltimore would be at her mercy. During the night, however, a most unlooked-for assistance arrived. The "Monitor," an iron-clad vessel of a new plan, invented by Captain John Ericsson, entered Hampton Roads on her trial trip from New York. Upon learning the state of affairs her commander, Lieutenant Worden, determined to engage the "Virginia" the next day. On the morning of the 9th the "Virginia" again steamed out of the Elizabeth river into Hampton Roads. The "Monitor," though her inferior in size, and carrying but a single gun, at once moved forward to meet her. An engagement of several hours' duration ensued, in which both vessels were fought with great gallantry; and at the end of this time the "Virginia" drew off, and returned to Norfolk severely injured. The arrival of the "Monitor" was most fortunate. It saved the Federal fleet in

Hampton Roads from total destruction, and prevented the "Virginia" from extending her ravages to the ports of the Union. The battle between the "Monitor" and the "Virginia" will ever be famous as the first engagement between iron-clad vessels. It inaugurated a new era in naval warfare. In spite of the result of the battle, however, the presence of the "Virginia" at Norfolk deterred the Federal forces from risking an attack on that place, and prevented them from making any effort to ascend the James river with their fleet.

In the meantime the army of General McClellan had returned to its position near Alexandria, after the retreat of the Confederates to the Rapidan. General McClellan now proposed to move the bulk of his army to Fortress Monroe, and to advance from that point upon Richmond by way of the peninsula between the York and James rivers. About seventy-five thousand men were left on the Potomac to cover Washington, and the remainder, about one hundred and twenty thousand in number, were transported by water to Fortress Monroe. This movement was accomplished by the 2d of April. On the 4th the army of the Potomac began its march towards the lines of Yorktown, which were held by about eleven thousand five hundred men, under General Magruder. The Confederate commander had passed the first year of the war in fortifying his position, and had constructed a series of powerful works which enabled him, with his small force, to hold McClellan's whole army in check. On the 5th and 6th of April McClellan made repeated attempts to force the southern lines, and failing in these decided to lay siege to them. The time thus gained by Magruder enabled General Johnston to move his army from the Rapidan to the peninsula. It was in position on the lines of Yorktown by the 17th of April, making the force opposed to McClellan about fifty-eight thousand strong. The Confederates did not expect to hold their position on the peninsula, but from the first intended to move back nearer to Richmond, and occupy the line of the Chickahominy. When their preparations were completed they fell back from the lines of Yorktown, on the night of the 3d of May, just as McClellan was about to begin his bombardment of their position.

The Federal army discovered the retreat on the morning of the 4th of May, and moved forward promptly in the hope of intercepting the southern army. On the morning of the 5th the advanced forces attacked the rear-guard of Johnston's army at Williamsburg. The Confederate commander held his ground until his trains had gotten off in safety, and then resumed his retreat, and reached the Chickahominy about the 10th of May without further molestation from the Union forces. General McClellan, following leisurely, took position on the left bank of the Chickahominy, with the river between the two armies.

In accordance with General McClellan's urgent request, President Lincoln decided to order the force left to cover Washington to join the army of the Potomac, before Richmond, by way of Fredericksburg. With his force thus augmented the Union commander had no doubt of his ability to capture Richmond. Alive to this danger General Johnston directed General Jackson, who had been left to hold the valley of Virginia, to manœuvre his army so as to threaten Washington, and compel the Federal government to retain the force intended for McClellan for the defence of Washington While awaiting the arrival of this force McClellan threw his left wing across the Chickahominy, and lodged it in a position nearer to Richmond. The Federal lines now extended from Bottom's Bridge, on the Chickahominy, to Mechanicsville, north of that stream

The evacuation of the peninsula compelled the Confederates to abandon Norfolk also. They withdrew their troops from that city on the 9th of May, and sent them to reinforce General Johnston. On the 10th Norfolk and Portsmouth were occupied by the Federal forces under General Wool. Before leaving the Confederates had set fire to the navy yard, which was destroyed. The iron-clad steamer "Virginia" was taken into the James river, and on the 11th was abandoned and blown up. The loss of this steamer, which could have held the James against the whole Union fleet, left the river open to within eight miles of Richmond The gunboats, including the "Monitor," were sent up to try to force their way to Richmond, but on the 15th of May were driven back by a battery of heavy guns located on the heights at Drewry's bluff, eight miles below Richmond. They were badly injured by the plunging fire of the Confederates. The river was securely obstructed at this point to prevent a passage of the batteries by the Federal fleet.

Having been heavily reinforced, General Johnston determined to attack McClellan's exposed left wing, and on the 31st of May fell upon it at Seven Pines, and drove it back with heavy loss. General Johnston was severely wounded towards the close of the day, and was unable to carry out the plan upon which he had begun the battle. The next day there was heavy skirmishing until about ten o'clock in the morning, but nothing of a more serious nature was attempted by either side General McClellan, warned by the narrow escape of his left wing, now proceeded to fortify his position on the south bank of the Chickahominy.

While these events were in progress on the Chickahominy, General Jackson carried out with brilliant success the movements assigned him in the valley of Virginia His task required the exercise of the greatest skill and determination. He was to neutralize the forces of Fremont,

Banks and McDowell, and prevent them from rendering any assistance to McClellan. Jackson's army fell back from Winchester on the 11th of March, and retired as far as Mount Jackson. Then rapidly retracing its steps it attacked Banks' forces at Kernstown, near Winchester. Though repulsed in this engagement, it succeeded in alarming the Federal government for the safety of Washington. Banks' command was therefore re-

tained in the valley to watch Jackson, and the force under McDowell was not allowed to go to McClellan's assistance on the peninsula, lest by so doing it should uncover Washington. After the battle of Kernstown, Jackson retired up the valley, and a season of comparative quietude ensued. The Federal government even believed that his troops had been sent to Richmond. Fremont's army was ordered to move from western Virginia into the valley; Banks was directed to march to Manassas and cover

LIEUT.-GEN. T. J. JACKSON.

Washington; while McDowell, with forty thousand men, was ordered to move to Fredericksburg, from which he was to march across the country and unite with McClellan's left wing, which was thrown out far to the north of Richmond to meet him. These orders were in process of execution when Jackson, who had been reinforced by a division under General Ewell, destroyed the whole Federal plan of campaign.

Knowing that he could not possibly resist the combined forces of Fremont and Banks, Jackson determined to beat them in detail. Marching rapidly westward, he crossed the mountains, fell upon the advance guard of Fremont's army at McDowell, on the 8th of May, defeated it, and drove it back into western Virginia. Then retracing his steps with remarkable speed, he returned to the valley, and on the 23d of May attacked Banks' outlying force at Front Royal, and drove it in upon the main body at Strasburg. Banks at once broke up his camp, and fell back down the

MAJ.-GEN. N. P. BANKS.

valley, pursued by Jackson, who dealt him a terrible blow at Winchester on the 25th. By extraordinary exertions Banks succeeded in escaping across the Potomac, but left about three thousand prisoners, several pieces of artillery, nine thousand stand of arms, and the greater part of his stores in the hands of the Confederates.

This bold advance greatly alarmed the government at Washington, and the president ordered Fremont to move with speed into the valley, and directed General McDowell to suspend his movement to the assistance of McClellan, and send a force of twenty thousand men to gain Jackson's rear, and prevent his return up the valley. McDowell sent the required force under General Shields, and Fremont hurried on to gain the upper valley in advance of Jackson. These movements entirely prevented McClellan from receiving the assistance of McDowell's corps, and saved Richmond from capture.

Jackson was too good a general to be caught in the trap so skilfully laid for him. He retired up the valley with the greatest speed, and having interposed his army between Fremont and Shields, turned upon the former, and with a part of his force attacked him at Cross Keys on the 8th of June, and checked his advance. Then reuniting his forces he fell upon Shields at Port Republic on the 9th of June, and drove him back with heavy loss after one of the hardest-fought battles of the war. Having thus put an end to the pursuit of his antagonists, Jackson withdrew to a safe position, from which he could hold them in check or go to the aid of the army defending Richmond. The latter move being decided upon, he eluded the Federal forces in the valley, and marched rapidly to the Chickahominy. Before his absence from the valley was suspected, he had joined General Lee. His campaign in the valley is justly regarded as one of the most brilliant of the war. With less than twenty thousand men he had neutralized a force of sixty thousand Union troops, and prevented the execution of McClellan's carefully laid plans for the capture of Richmond.

BRIG.-GEN. JAS. SHIELDS.

Upon the fall of General Johnston the command of the Confederate army before Richmond was conferred upon General Robert E. Lee, whom subsequent events proved to be the ablest of the southern leaders. Troops were drawn from every possible point to reinforce General Lee's army, and by the middle of June his forces, including Jackson's army, amounted to ninety thousand men. The Federal army was one hundred and fifteen thousand strong. Both armies were in fine condition. General McClellan, finding it impossible to obtain the assistance of McDowell's corps, and fearing for the safety of his communications with his base of supplies, which was at West Point, at the head of the York river, prepared to move his army to the south side of the Chickahominy, and establish a new and more secure base upon the James river. Before he

52

could put this design in operation he was attacked by General Lee, who, on the 25th of June, fell upon the right of the Union line at Mechanics-ville, and forced it back upon the centre at Cold Harbor. On the 26th the position at Cold Harbor was attacked and carried by the Confederates after a desperate struggle. With great difficulty McClellan secured his retreat to the south side of the Chickahominy, and destroyed the bridges in his rear.

Having decided to retreat to the James river rather than attempt to

RICHMOND, VIRGINIA.

retain his communications with West Point, McClellan destroyed his 'stores, and on the 28th began his retreat from the Chickahominy by way of White Oak swamp. As soon as his movement was discovered pursuit was made by the Confederates, who attacked his rear guard under General Sumner at Savage Station late in the afternoon of the 29th. Sumner held his ground until the darkness put an end to the action, and during the night of the 29th withdrew across White Oak swamp, destroying all the bridges after him. On the 30th General Lee made a last effort to prevent McClellan from reaching the James, and towards the close of the afternoon the bloody battle of Frazier's Farm was fought. It was continued until nine o'clock. The Federal force at Frazier's Farm held its ground until the remainder of McClellan's army had safely traversed White Oak swamp. The object of the battle having been accomplished, McClellan resumed his retreat to the James river, and took position upon Malvern hill, within a short distance of that stream. Here he massed his artillery, and the gunboats in the James river moved up to a point from which they could throw their shells into the Confederate lines. On the afternoon of the 1st of July the Confederates made a gallant attempt to carry Malvern hill, but were repulsed with severe loss. The next morning the Federal army withdrew to Harrison's Landing on the James river. Thus ended the "Seven Days' Battles," during which the Federal army lost about twenty thousand men in killed, wounded and prisoners,

fifty-two pieces of artillery, thirty-five thousand stand of arms, and an enormous quantity of stores of all kinds. The Confederate loss was nineteen thousand five hundred and thirty-three killed, wounded and missing.

The retreat of McClellan's army threw the north into the deepest despondency. On the 2d of July President Lincoln issued a call for three hundred thousand fresh troops. The necessities of the struggle, however, made this force insufficient, and on the 4th of August the president ordered that a draft of three hundred thousand militia should be made and placed in the service of the United States for a period of nine months unless sooner discharged. The States complied with the requisitions upon them, and in the brief period of three months the enormous mass of six hundred thousand fresh troops was raised, armed, and placed in the field.

MAJ-GEN L V SUMNER

For the protection of Washington the Federal government now collected the commands of Banks, Fremont and McDowell in one army, and placed it under command of Major-General John Pope, whose capture of Island No. 10 and other points in the west had given him a fair reputation. He assumed his new command with a profusion of boasts, and promised to succeed where McClellan had failed. According to General Pope the capture of Richmond was the easiest undertaking in the world. His army towards the latter part of July advanced to the Rapidan.

To watch this force General Lee, late in July, sent General Jackson's corps to the Rapidan On the 9th of August Jackson attacked the advanced corps of Pope's army at Cedar mountain, and defeated it. This defeat suspended General Pope's forward movement General McClellan now received orders from Washington to evacuate Harrison's Landing and to reinforce General Pope with his army. He at once put this order in execution. The withdrawal of his troops was detected by General Lee, who rapidly reinforced Jackson, and finally moved with his whole army to the Rapidan. About the same time Burnside's corps, which had been withdrawn from the southern coast, and was awaiting orders in Hampton Roads, was directed to move into the Potomac and reinforce Pope. General Pope had now under his command a force of over one hundred thousand men. The Confederate army, which was concentrated upon the Rapidan by the 18th of August, numbered about seventy thousand men Its strength was greatly overestimated by General Pope, who deemed it most prudent to retire behind the Rappahannock, which he did on the 18th and 19th of August. His new position was well chosen. His right was at Rappahannock Station, and his left at Kelley's ford, some distance lower down the river.

General Lee now resolved to attack Pope before he could be joined by McClellan's troops He divided his army into two columns, and sent Jackson's corps by a circuitous route, by way of Thoroughfare gap, to gain the rear of the Federal army. This daring flank march was accomplished by Jackson, and on the 26th of August he captured Manassas Junction, Pope's main depot of supplies, with an enormous quantity of stores of all kinds, and several railroad trains loaded with supplies. Upon learning of this movement Pope at once fell back from the Rappahannock, intending to crush the isolated corps of Jackson, and at the same time Lee set off rapidly by way of Thoroughfare gap to join his endangered lieutenant. Pope's army had been reinforced by the corps of Porter and Heintzelman, and Reynolds' division of McClellan's army, and was at least one hundred and twenty thousand strong. He moved back rapidly to attack Jackson, and encountered Ewell's division near Manassas Junction on the 27th. Ewell held his ground, and at night rejoined Jackson, who moved swiftly from Manassas to a new position near the old Bull Run battle-field. This brought him nearer to Lee, and secured his retreat in case of a defeat. Ewell's resistance deceived General Pope, who had posted McDowell's and Porter's corps to hold the road from Thoroughfare gap, by which Lee must advance to Jackson's assistance Supposing that Jackson meant to make a stand at Manassas, Pope ordered these troops to move from the positions they had taken and to advance upon Manassas Junction. Manassas was reached at noon on the 28th, and then General Pope saw for the first time how he had been deceived by Jackson, and how he had blundered in leaving the road from Thoroughfare gap open to Lee. He endeavored to repair his error by attacking Jackson at once. He did attack that general in his new position late in the afternoon of the 28th, but was repulsed

with severe loss. On the same afternoon General Lee with Longstreet's corps forced the passage of Thoroughfare gap, and bivouacked that night in the open country beyond it. On the morning of the 29th he pushed forward with speed, and by noon his advanced division reached Jackson's position. By four o'clock in the afternoon the Confederate army was reunited under the command of General Lee. About three o'clock in the afternoon General Pope made a heavy attack upon Lee's position, but was repulsed. On the 30th, having reunited all the corps of his army, General Pope determined

GENERAL. R. E. LEE.

to risk the fate of the campaign upon a decisive engagement. The Confederates held a large part of the old battle-field of Bull Run, and the conflict which ensued is usually known as the second battle of Bull Run. It resulted in the defeat of General Pope, who was driven back to the heights of Centreville with heavy loss. On the 31st Jackson attacked the Federal rear-guard at Chantilly. A spirited encounter took place, and the Federal troops were slowly forced back, losing General Phil

Kearney, one of the most accomplished officers in the service. General Pope now withdrew his army within the lines of Washington. He had lost since the opening of the campaign over thirty thousand men, including eight generals killed, thirty pieces of artillery, over twenty thousand stand of arms, and an enormous quantity of stores. The Confederate loss was nine thousand one hundred and twelve, including five generals.

MAJ.-GEN. PHIL KEARNEY.

The defeat of the Union army and the presence of the Confederates on the Potomac placed the city of Washington in great danger. The government acted with vigor and decision in this emergency. The losses of Pope's army were made up by reinforcements. General Pope was relieved of his command, and General McClellan was restored to the command of the army of the Potomac. He set to work with energy to reorganize the broken masses of Pope's army into an effective force.

General Lee now crossed the Potomac and invaded Maryland, hoping to be able not only to remove the war from the soil of Virginia, but also to obtain large reinforcements from the southern sympathizers in Maryland. In this he was disappointed, as scarcely any one joined him. On the 5th of September he crossed the Potomac, and on the 6th occupied Frederick City. Harper's Ferry was held by a force of eleven thousand men under Colonel Miles, and it was necessary to reduce this post in order to preserve the communications of the Confederate army with its own country. General Jackson was despatched with his corps to capture Harper's Ferry. He promptly carried the heights overlooking the town, and on the 15th of September the town and garrison surrendered to him after a feeble resistance.

General Lee in the meantime had taken position at South mountain to await the issue of Jackson's attack upon Harper's Ferry. McClellan, advancing slowly from Washington, reached Frederick on the 12th of

MAJ.-GEN. JOHN A. DIX.

September. There he found a copy of General Lee's confidential order to his corps commanders, which had been lost by some one. This document gave the Confederate plan of operations, and enabled McClellan to act with certainty in directing his own movements. Hastening forward he attacked General Lee at South mountain on the 14th of September, and after a stubborn fight Lee fell back behind Antietam creek, and on the morning of the 17th was joined there by the troops of Jackson, who had made a forced march from Harper's Ferry.

The Confederate army numbered about forty thousand men, having been terribly reduced by the straggling of the men on the march through Virginia. The Federal army numbered over eighty thousand men, and was eager for a contest. The prolonged resistance of Harper's Ferry, and the losses of his army by straggling, had defeated Lee's plan of campaign. He was now compelled to retire across the Potomac, and he halted on the Antietam only to secure the reunion of Jackson's corps with his army and a safe passage of the Potomac. On the morning of the 17th of September General McClellan attacked the Confederate army in force, but it held its ground during the day, both armies at nightfall occupying about the same positions they had held in the morning. The Federal loss was twelve thousand four hundred and sixty-nine, including thirteen generals wounded, one mortally; that of the Confederates eight thousand seven hundred and ninety, including three generals killed, five wounded.

The 18th passed quietly away, and that night Lee silently withdrew from his position and retreated across the Potomac. He retired up the valley to Winchester. The Federal army moved to the vicinity of Harper's Ferry, and did not cross the Potomac until the 2d of November.

Upon entering Virginia General McClellan moved towards the Rappahannock with the design of interposing his army between Lee and Richmond. General Lee at once left the valley where he had been detained by the necessity of watching McClellan, and by a rapid march to Warrenton placed his army between Richmond and McClellan. The Federal army continuing to advance, he fell back to Culpepper Courthouse, and McClellan moved forward to the vicinity of Warrenton. On the 7th of November, when about to resume his advance, McClellan, whose conduct of the campaign had not pleased either President Lincoln or the people of the north, was removed from the command of the army of the Potomac, which was conferred upon General Ambrose E. Burnside.

MAJ.-GEN. A. E. BURNSIDE.

Burnside at once advanced to the banks of the Rappahannock opposite Fredericksburg, intending to pass the river at that place and move upon Richmond. Upon his arrival at Falmouth, opposite Fredericksburg, he found the Confederate army strongly posted on the heights in the rear of the latter place, prepared to dispute his advance. He crossed the Rappahannock on the 11th and 12th of December, and on the 13th attacked the Confederate position, which had been strongly intrenched. He was repulsed with a loss of eleven thousand men, and compelled to retreat across the Rappahannock. This terrible reverse greatly disheartened the army of the Potomac, and destroyed its faith in its commander; and so the year closed gloomily for the Union cause in the east.

In the fall of 1862 President Lincoln took the bold step of issuing a proclamation announcing that if the seceded States did not return to their allegiance to the Union he would declare all the negro slaves within their limits free from the 1st of January next. This proclamation was issued on the 22d of September, immediately after the battle of Antietam. The army and navy of the United States were to enforce the terms of this proclamation, and from the new year there was to be no more slavery within the limits of the Union. The proclamation was avowedly a war measure, but it was sustained by Congress by appropriate legislation during the ensuing winter.

When the year 1862 closed the Federal government, in spite of its reverses in Virginia, had great cause for hope. It had effected lodgments of its forces at important points on the southern coast, had captured New Orleans, the largest and wealthiest city of the south, and had opened the Mississippi as far as Vicksburg. West Tennessee, Kentucky and northern Missouri were overrun and held by the Union forces. A decided gain had been made, and there was reason to hope that the next year would bring more favorable results. The Confederates were greatly elated, however, by their successes in the east, which they regarded as counterbalancing their disasters in the west, and were more than ever resolved to continue the war " to the bitter end."

CHAPTER XLII.

THE ADMINISTRATION OF ABRAHAM LINCOLN—THE CIVIL WAR—CONCLUDED.

The Emancipation Proclamation—Battle of Chancellorsville—Death of Stonewall Jackson—Invasion of the North by Lee's Army—Battle of Gettysburg—Retreat of Lee into Virginia—Grant's Army crosses the Mississippi—Battle of Champion Hills—Investment of Vicksburg—Surrender of Vicksburg and Port Hudson—Battle of Chickamauga—Rosecrans shut up in Chattanooga—Grant in command of the Western Armies—Battles of Lookout Mountain and Mission Ridge—Defeat of Bragg's Army—The Campaign in East Tennessee—Retreat of Longstreet—Capture of Galveston—Attack on Charleston—Capture of Fort Wagner—Charleston Bombarded—State of Affairs in the Spring of 1864—The Red River Expedition—Grant made Lieutenant-General—Advance of the Army of the Potomac—Battles of the Wilderness, Spottsylvania, and Cold Harbor—Sheridan's Raid—Death of General J. E. B. Stuart—Battle of New Market—Early sent into the Valley of Virginia—Butler's Army at Bermuda Hundred—Grant crosses the James River—The Siege of Petersburg begun—Early's Raid upon Washington—Sheridan defeats Early at Winchester and Fisher's Hill—Battle of Cedar Creek—The final Defeat of Early's Army—Sherman's Advance to Atlanta—Johnston removed—Defeat of Hood before Atlanta—Evacuation of Atlanta—Hood's Invasion of Tennessee—Battle of Franklin—Siege of Nashville—Hood defeated at Nashville—His Retreat—Sherman's "March to the Sea"—Capture of Savannah—Battle of Mobile Bay—Attack on Fort Fisher—The Confederate Cruisers—Sinking of the "Alabama" by the "Kearsarge"—Re-election of President Lincoln—Admission of Nevada into the Union—The Hampton Roads Peace Conference—Capture of Fort Fisher—Occupation of Wilmington—Sherman advances through South Carolina—Evacuation of Charleston—Battles of Averasboro' and Bentonville—Sherman at Goldsboro'—Critical situation of Lee's Army—Attack on Fort Steadman—Sheridan joins Grant—Advance of Grant's Army—Battle of Five Forks—Attack on Petersburg—Evacuation of Richmond and Petersburg—Retreat of Lee's Army—Richmond occupied—SURRENDER of General Lee's Army—Rejoicings in the North—Assassination of President Lincoln—Death of Booth—Execution of the Conspirators—Johnston Surrenders—Surrender of the other Confederate Forces—Capture of Jefferson Davis—Close of the War

IN accordance with his proclamation of September 22d, 1862, President Lincoln, on the 1st of January, 1863, issued his proclamation of emancipation, in which he declared all the slaves within the limits of the Confederate States free from that day.

The plan of campaign adopted by the Federal government for 1863 was very much like that of the previous year. In the east the army of the Potomac was to push forward towards Richmond, and in

825

the west the army of General Grant was to capture Vicksburg, and thus
open the Mississippi, after which it was to march eastward, unite with the
forces of General Rosecrans and occupy East Tennessee, thus cutting the
communication between the Border and the Gulf States. In addition to
these operations an expedition against Charleston, South Carolina, was to
be attempted.

The army of the Potomac was greatly disheartened by its defeat at
Fredericksburg, and had lost confidence in General Burnside. That
commander, at his own request, was removed from the command, and was
succeeded by General Joseph Hooker on the 25th of January. Hooker
at once began the reorganization of his army, and soon brought it to a
splendid state of efficiency. By the opening of the spring it numbered
one hundred and twenty thousand men and four hundred pieces of artillery. General Lee had remained in his position back of Fredericksburg
all winter, and his army had been weakened by the withdrawal of Gen-

eral Longstreet's corps, twenty-four thousand
strong, by the Confederate government, leaving
him about fifty thousand men.

General Hooker, upon learning of Lee's weakened condition, determined to attack him. He
divided his army into two columns. One of these,
consisting of the Second, Fifth, Eleventh, and
Twelfth army corps, under his own command, was
to cross the Rappahannock above Fredericksburg
and turn the Confederate position. The other
column, consisting of the First, Third, and Sixth

MAJ.-GEN. JOS. HOOKER.

corps, under General Sedgwick, was to cross the river at Fredericksburg
and attack the heights. Between these forces it was believed that Lee's
army would be crushed. On the 27th of April Hooker moved off with the
first column, crossed the river on the 28th and 29th at Kelley's ford, and
on the 30th took position at Chancellorsville, on the left and in the rear
of Lee's fortified line. On the 29th General Sedgwick crossed his column
about three miles below Fredericksburg, and during that day and the
30th made demonstrations as though he intended to assault the southern
position in the rear of the town.

General Lee's situation was now critical, and demanded the most extraordinary exertions of him. Leaving a small force to hold the heights in
the rear of Fredericksburg, he moved with his main body towards Chancellorsville, where Hooker had intrenched himself with about eighty
thousand men. His only hope of safety lay in defeating this force before
Sedgwick's column could arrive to its assistance. On the 2d of May he

sent Jackson's corps to turn the Federal right, and with the remainder of his force deceived Hooker into the belief that he meant to storm the intrenched position of the Federal army. Jackson performed his flank march with success, and on the afternoon of the 2d of May made a fierce attack upon the Federal right, and drove it in upon its centre. In this attack he received a mortal wound, of which he died on the 10th of May. The next day, the 3d, having reunited Jackson's corps with his main force, Lee attacked Hooker at Chancellorsville, and drove him back to the junction of the Rappahannock and Rapidan rivers. He was preparing to storm this new position when he learned that Sedgwick had defeated the force left to hold the heights of Fredericksburg on the 3d of May, and was marching against him. His danger was now greater than ever. Leaving a part of his army to hold Hooker in check, he marched rapidly to meet Sedgwick. He encountered him at Salem heights on the 4th of May, and compelled him to recross the Rappahannock at Banks' ford. Then moving back towards

MAJ.-GEN. J. SEDGWICK.

Hooker's position Lee prepared to storm it. General Hooker, however, disheartened by Sedgwick's defeat, withdrew his army across the Rappahannock on the night of the 5th, and returned to his old position on the north side of that stream, having lost twelve thousand men and fourteen pieces of artillery in the battle of Chancellorsville. The Confederate loss was also heavy. Out of an army of about fifty thousand men, ten thousand two hundred and eighty-one were killed, wounded and captured. The victory was dearly bought by the Confederates by the death of Stonewall Jackson, who was worth fully fifty thousand men to their cause. At the moment of his success against the Federal right, he was shot down by his own men, who mistook his escort for a party of Federal cavalry.

The success of the Confederates in Virginia was more than counterbalanced by their reverses in the west and southwest. The southern government, anxious to change the course of the war by a bold stroke, decided to follow up the victory at Chancellorsville by an invasion of the north by Lee's army. This army was reinforced heavily, and by the last of May numbered seventy thousand infantry and artillery, and ten thousand cavalry. General Hooker's army on the other hand had been reduced by desertions and expirations of enlistments to about eighty thousand men, making the two forces about equal.

On the 3d of June, 1863, Lee began his forward movement, and marching through the valley of Virginia, captured Winchester, which was held by General Milroy's command, on the 14th, taking four thousand prisoners, and twenty-nine pieces of cannon. On the 22d of June the Potomac was crossed at Williamsport, and the Confederate army moved towards Hagerstown, Maryland. General Hooker had followed Lee from the Rappahannock, and had manœuvred his army so as to interpose

it between the Confederates and Washington. On the 23d the advanced corps of Lee's army under General Ewell occupied Chambersburg, Pennsylvania, and on the 25th and 26th General Hooker crossed the Potomac at Edward's Ferry, and marched to Frederick, Maryland. He was anxious to withdraw the garrison of Harper's Ferry, which had retired from that place to the Maryland heights, opposite the town, but the war department refused to allow him to do so.

LIEUT.-GEN. R. S. EWELL.

Hooker thereupon relinquished the command of the army, and was succeeded by Major-General George G. Meade, the senior corps commander, and a soldier of genuine ability. General Lee now moved his army east of the mountains, and directed his advance towards Gettysburg. In ignorance of his adversary's design, General Meade hastened forward to occupy the same point.

The invasion of Pennsylvania by the Confederate army aroused the most intense excitement in the north. President Lincoln called out one hundred thousand militia to serve for six months, unless sooner discharged, and as far north as New York preparations were made to receive the Confederate army with a stubborn resistance should it succeed in penetrating so far. Every effort was made to raise troops and forward them to General Meade in time to be of service to him.

On the morning of the 1st of July the left wing of the army of the Potomac under General Reynolds and the advanced corps

MAJ.-GEN. GEO. G. MEADE.

of Lee's army under Generals A. P. Hill and Ewell encountered each other at Gettysburg. General Reynolds was forced back and killed. General Hancock was at once sent by General Meade to assume the command of the left wing, and upon his arrival he at once recognized the importance of the position at Gettysburg, and occupied it. He was

BATTLE OF GETTYSBURG.

promptly reinforced by General Meade, and by the afternoon of the 2d of July the army of the Potomac was securely posted on the heights known as Cemetery Ridge. The Confederate army took position on the opposite hills known as Seminary Ridge. Between the two armies lay the battle-field on which the engagement of the 1st of July was fought. Heavy skirmishing prevailed throughout the day on the 2d, the advantage being with the Confederates. On the 3d of July General Lee made a general attack upon the Federal position on Cemetery Ridge, which, very strong by nature, had been rendered impregnable by intrenchments. His attack was made with determination, and was a splendid exhibition of American courage, which won for his troops the generous admiration of their adversaries; but it was unsuccessful. The grand charge of the Confederates was made in the afternoon, and was repulsed with terrible slaughter. Still Lee's position was so strong, and the morale of his army so unimpaired, that General Meade deemed it best to remain satisfied with

his victory, and not to risk its fruits by an attack upon the Confederate lines. The victory was decisive. It put an end to the Confederate invasion. On the night of the 4th of July General Lee withdrew from Seminary Ridge and retreated to the Potomac, which he crossed on the 13th and 14th without serious opposition from the Federal army. On the 15th Lee moved back to Winchester. The Federal loss at Gettysburg was twenty-three thousand, and that of the Confederates about the same.

MAJ.-GEN. J. F. REYNOLDS.

On the 17th and 18th of July General Meade crossed the Potomac below Harper's Ferry, and moving east of the Blue Ridge, endeavored to place his army between Lee and Richmond. The Confederate commander by rapid marches reached Culpepper Court-house in advance of him, however, and about the 1st of August occupied the line of the Rappahannock. The remainder of the year witnessed but one important operation by the armies in Virginia. In October General Lee made a sudden forward movement for the purpose of throwing his army between Meade and Washington, but the latter eluded him and reached Centreville in safety. Lee then withdrew to the Rapidan, and the army of the Potomac took position on the north side of that stream. Both armies passed the winter there.

In the west and southwest success crowned the Federal arms. At the opening of the year the army of General Grant lay on the Mississippi above Vicksburg, assisted by the fleet of gunboats under Admiral Porter.

VICKSBURG, MISSISSIPPI.

831

The first three months of the year were passed by the Federal army in a series of movements along the Yazoo river, the result of which was to convince General Grant that Vicksburg could not be taken from that quarter. He therefore determined upon a new and more daring plan of operations. He decided to march his army across the Louisiana shore from Milliken's bend, above Vicksburg, to New Carthage, below that city, and to run his gunboats and transports by the batteries. Should the boats succeed in passing he meant to cross his command to the Mississippi shore, and attack Vicksburg from the rear. By investing the city from the land side his flanks would rest upon and be covered by the Mississippi, and he could re-establish communication between his right wing and his base of supplies at Milliken's bend. The plan was daring in the highest degree, and required the greatest skill and resolution in its execution.

In order to retain their hold upon the Mississippi the Confederates had fortified Vicksburg with great care. Port Hudson, about two hundred and forty miles lower down the river, had also been fortified, but not so strongly as Vicksburg. As long as the Confederates held these points they were able to keep a considerable extent of the river open to themselves and closed to the Union gunboats. Thus they were enabled to cross in safety the enormous herds of beef

MAJOR-GENERAL J. A. LOGAN.

cattle which they drew from the rich pastures of Texas for their armies east of the Mississippi. A strong force held the works at Port Hudson. Vicksburg was occupied by a large garrison, and was under the command of Lieutenant-General John C. Pemberton, who, with an army of about thirty thousand men, independent of the garrison of Vicksburg, held the country in the rear of that city. Appreciating the importance of defeating the Federal army in this quarter the Confederate government, in the spring of 1863, sent General Joseph E. Johnston to take command of all the forces in Mississippi. It failed to supply him with a proper force of troops, and General Pemberton treated his orders with open defiance.

Grant having completed his preparations moved his army from Milliken's bend to a point on the Louisiana shore, opposite Grand Gulf. On the night of the 16th of April a division of gunboats and transports ran by the Vicksburg batteries, suffering severely from the heavy fire to which they were exposed for a distance of eight miles. On the night of the 22d a second division passed the batteries with similar loss. Once below Vicksburg, however, the boats were safe. They then proceeded to Grant's position on the river below. On the 29th of April the gunboats attacked the batteries at Grand Gulf, but were repulsed. The troops were then marched to a point opposite Bruinsburg, Mississippi, and the gunboats and transports were run by the Grand Gulf batteries. On the 1st of May the Federal army was ferried across to the Mississippi shore, and at once began its march into the interior. Near Port Gibson a part of Pemberton's army was encountered and defeated on the same day. This success compelled the evacuation of Grand Gulf by the Confederates. Grant now boldly threw his army between Johnston's forces at Jackson and Pemberton's army, intending to hold the former in check, and drive the latter within the defences of Vicksburg. On the 14th of May he

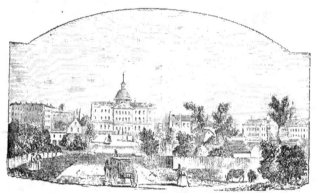

JACKSON, MISSISSIPPI.

attacked Johnston at Jackson, the capital of Mississippi, and forced him to retreat northward towards Canton. Then turning upon Pemberton he attacked him at Champion Hills, or Baker's creek, on the 16th, and inflicted a severe defeat upon him. Pemberton withdrew towards the Big Black river, and the next day met a second defeat there. He now retreated within the defences of Vicksburg, which place was promptly invested by Grant's army. On the 19th of May Grant attempted to carry the Confederate position by assault, but was repulsed with heavy loss. The assault was repeated with a like result on the 22d. There remained then nothing but a regular siege. This was pressed with vigor, and the city was subjected to a terrible bombardment, which caused great suffering to the people. While the siege was carried on Johnston's army was held back, and prevented from undertaking any movement for the

53

relief of Vicksburg. At length, reduced to despair by the steady approach of the Union trenches, Pemberton surrendered the city and his army to General Grant on the 4th of July By this surrender thirty thousand prisoners, two hundred and fifty cannon, and sixty thousand stand of arms, together with a large quantity of military stores, fell into the hands of the Union forces It was justly esteemed the greatest victory of the war.

While the siege of Vicksburg was in progress General Banks ascended the Mississippi from New Orleans and laid siege to Port Hudson. Upon hearing of the fall of Vicksburg, the Confederate commander surrendered the post and his army of sixty-two hundred and thirty-three men to General Banks, on the 8th of July.

These victories wrested from the Confederates their last hold upon the Mississippi. They created the most intense rejoicing in the Northern and Western States and a corresponding depression in the south Being simultaneous with the defeat of the southern army at Gettysburg, they were regarded as decisive of the war: as indeed they were. From this time we shall trace the declining fortunes of the southern confederacy and the gradual but steady re-establishment of the authority of the Union over the Southern States

After the battle of Murfreesboro', or Stone river, the army of General Rosecrans remained quietly in winter quarters at Nashville and Murfreesboro' Bragg's army passed the winter at Chattanooga. Towards the last of June Rosecrans moved forward from Nashville, and advancing slowly threatened Bragg's communications with Richmond. The Confederate commander had no wish to emulate the example of Pemberton at Vicksburg, and at once evacuated Chattanooga, on the 8th of September, and retired towards Dalton, Georgia. This movement, which was interpreted by Rosecrans as a retreat, was designed to secure the union with Bragg's army of Longstreet's corps, which had been detached from Lee's army and sent to join Bragg This junction was effected on the 18th, and other reinforcements arrived from Mississippi. Thus strengthened Bragg suddenly wheeled upon Rosecrans, and on the 19th of September attacked him at Chickamauga The battle was severe, but indecisive, and was renewed the next day Towards noon, on the 20th, Rosecrans having greatly weakened the other parts of his line to help the left, which was hard pressed, Longstreet made a furious dash at the weakened part, and in an irresistible attack swept the Federal right and centre from the field Rosecrans endeavored to stop the retreat, but was borne along in the dense crowd of fugitives. Only the left wing, under the command of General George H. Thomas, remained firm. Had that given way the rout would have been complete; but all through the long afternoon Thomas held on to his position with a grim resolution which nothing could shake. After nightfall he withdrew his corps in good order and retired upon Chattanooga. The Union loss at Chickamauga was sixteen thousand men and fifty-one guns; Bragg's about eighteen thousand men.

Bragg advanced at once upon the defeated army of Rosecrans, which had taken refuge in Chattanooga, occupied the heights commanding the city, and seized the communications of the Federal army with Nashville. Thus closely besieged the Union forces suffered considerably from a scarcity of provisions.

General Rosecrans was now removed from the command of the army of the Cumberland, and General Grant was appointed to the chief command of all the western armies. He at once set to work to extricate the army of the Cumberland, to the command of which General Thomas had succeeded, from its perilous situation. Hooker was sent with twenty-three thousand men from Meade's army to his assistance, and Sherman was ordered to march with the force which had taken Vicksburg along the line of the railway from Memphis to Chattanooga. The arrival of these reinforcements soon changed the aspect of affairs. On the 23d of November the army of the Cumberland made a vigorous sortie and drove the Confederates from the important position of Orchard Knob. On the 24th Hooker stormed Lookout mountain, the left of the Confederate line, and carried it after a hard fight. The investment was now thoroughly broken, and the Confederates were confined to Mission Ridge, which had formerly constituted the right of their line. On the 25th this position was assaulted by the whole strength of the Federal army, and was carried after a stubborn fight. Bragg, beaten at all points, with heavy loss, retreated into Georgia, where he was soon after removed from his command and succeeded by General Joseph E. Johnston.

During the progress of this campaign General Burnside had moved from Kentucky with a force of about twenty-five thousand men, about the time that Rosecrans began his advance from Nashville in June. The strong position of Cumberland gap was surrendered to him with scarcely an effort for its defence by the Confederates, and he moved into East Tennessee. Driving back the Confederate forces, which sought to stop his march, he occupied Knoxville. The object of his expedition was to afford a rallying point for the Union men of East Tennessee. After the battle of Chickamauga, and the investment of Chattanooga, President Jefferson Davis visited Bragg's army, and being convinced that the capture of Rosecrans' force was inevitable, decided to withdraw General

CAPTURE OF LOOKOUT MOUNTAIN.

Longstreet's corps from Bragg, and to send it to drive Burnside out of East Tennessee. Longstreet's men were in no condition to undertake such a campaign, but under their energetic commander succeeded in confining Burnside's army to the defences of Knoxville. The siege of that place was formed, and several assaults were made upon the Union works, but were each repulsed with heavy loss. Burnside's men were reduced almost to starvation, but held out with unshaken resolution. After the defeat of Bragg at Mission Ridge Grant ordered Sherman to march with his corps to the relief of Knoxville. Upon the approach of this force Longstreet, on the 4th of December, raised the siege and retreated into Virginia.

Beyond the Mississippi the war was carried on with varying success throughout the year 1863, but to the general advantage of the Federal forces. On the 3d of July the Confederates, under General Holmes, attacked Helena, Arkansas, but were repulsed. By the close of the year the Confederate forces had been pressed back as far as the Red river.

LIEUT.-GEN. J. LONGSTREET.

On the 1st of January, 1863, Galveston, Texas, which had surrendered to the Federal forces in the fall of 1862, was recaptured by the Confederates, under General Magruder. By the capture of this place the Confederates obtained one more port from which they could maintain communications with and receive supplies from Europe.

In the spring of 1863 a powerful naval expedition, under Admiral Dupont, was despatched against Charleston. On the 7th of April Dupont attempted to force his way into the harbor, but was driven back by the forts and batteries, and nine of his iron-clads were severely injured. Early in July a force of land troops, under General Gilmore, effected a lodgment on the south end of Morris' island, and secured their position by intrenchments. The Union parallels were pushed forward steadily towards Fort Wagner at the north end of the island, and a final assault of that work was ordered. Before the order could be executed Fort Wagner was evacuated on the night of the 6th of September. The Federal batteries on Morris' island now maintained a heavy and constant fire upon Fort Sumter, and reduced it to a shapeless

ADMIRAL DUPONT.

mass of rubbish on the land side. Yet in this condition it was stronger than at first, the mass of rubbish offering a more effectual resistance to shot and shell than the walls. The long-range guns on Morris' island threw shells into the city of Charleston, which was regularly bombarded from this time until its fall, in 1865. The capture of Fort Wagner enabled the Federal forces to close the harbor of Charleston effectually against blockade runners.

In spite of the victories of Chancellorsville and Chickamauga, and the invasion of the north, the close of the year found the south fairly on the downward road to final failure. Missouri was freed from the presence of the Confederate army, and the greater part of Arkansas was held by the Federal troops. The Mississippi was lost to the south, and

GALVESTON, TEXAS.

the immense supplies from the trans-Mississippi region were no longer available to the Confederate forces east of the great river. Tennessee was occupied by the Federal forces, and the invasion of the north had ended in disaster. The resources of the south were gradually becoming exhausted, and the supply of men was falling off. The north on the other hand was increasing in determination. The war had opened new channels of industry, and these had more than repaid the losses of the first period of the struggle. The north was growing richer, in spite of the war, while the south was growing poorer because of it. At the end of 1863 the Federal debt had reached the enormous total of $1,300,000,000, with the certainty of a heavy increase during the coming year. Still the people of the loyal States responded with heartiness to the heavy demands of the Federal government for men and money. Specie had long since disappeared from circulation, but a system of treasury notes, which were made a legal tender, had replaced coin as a circulating medium. The new paper money was abundant, and the north gave few outward signs of distress. Everything spoke of prosperity. The contrast between the condition of the Union and the confederacy was striking and most suggestive.

Early in the spring of 1864 an expedition was sent into that part of Louisiana known as the Red river country. It consisted of a force of ten thousand troops, under General Smith, from Vicksburg, and a fleet of gunboats, under Admiral Porter. On the 14th of March Fort de Russy was captured by the troops, and on the 21st Natchitoches was occupied. General Banks now arrived with a strong reinforcement of troops from New Orleans, and took command of the expedition. About the 1st of

BRIG.-GEN. Q. A. GILMORE.

April he set out for Shreveport, at the head of navigation on the Red river, his army marching along the shore, and the gunboats ascending the stream. The Confederates gathered in heavy force, under the command of General Kirby Smith, to oppose his advance. On the 8th of April the Confederate army attacked Banks at Sabine Cross-Roads, near Mans-

MAJOR-GENERAL E. CANBY.

field, and inflicted a stinging defeat upon him. The Union forces were rallied at Pleasant Hill, where they were attacked by the Confederates on the 9th. The Confederates were repulsed, but Banks continued his retreat, and reached Alexandria on the 25th of April. The expedition then returned to the Mississippi. Banks was relieved of the command at New Orleans, and was succeeded by General Canby.

General Steele, commanding the Union forces in Arkansas, had moved from Little Rock, on the 23d of March, towards Shreveport, to co-operate with General Banks. He was attacked by the Confederates and driven back to Little Rock, which he reached on the 2d of May.

The Red river expedition was thus a total failure, and was a source of great mortification, as well as serious loss, to the Federal government.

Early in March General Grant was raised to the grade of lieutenant-general, that rank having been revived by act of Congress to reward him

for his great services during the war. It had been held only by Washington, General Scott having been given only the brevet rank. He was
also appointed commander of all the armies of the United States. He
decided to assume the immediate direction of the campaign in Virginia,
and established his head-quarters with the army of the Potomac. At
the same time General W. T. Sherman was appointed to the command of
the military division of the Mississippi, in which were included the armies
of the Cumberland, of the Ohio, and of the Tennessee. The supreme
control of the military operations both east and west was vested in General Grant—a great gain, inasmuch as the operations in the two quarters
of the Union could now be made to assist each other. The plan of the
campaign embraced a simultaneous advance of both armies; the army of
the Potomac was charged with the task of defeating Lee and capturing
Richmond; the western army, under Sherman, was to force Johnston
back into Georgia.

The army of the Potomac numbered one hundred and forty thousand
men on the 1st of May, 1864; the Confederate army, under General
Lee, about fifty thousand General Meade retained the immediate command of the army of the Potomac, but General Grant accompanied it,
and directed its movements. On the morning of May 4th—just three
days before Sherman moved from Chattanooga—the Federal army crossed
the Rapidan, and, turning the right of Lee's position, entered the region
known as the Wilderness. General Lee determined to attack this force
and prevent it from reaching the open country beyond the Wilderness.
On the 5th of May he encountered the army of the Potomac in the
Wilderness, near the old battle-field of Chancellorsville. The attack was
made by the Federal forces, which endeavored to drive off Lee's army,
which blocked the route by which they were advancing. Lee held his
ground during the day, and that night both armies bivouacked upon the
field. The battle was renewed on the 6th, but Grant failed to force the
Confederate position. The fighting during these two days was carried on
in a thickly-wooded region, in which the artillery of the two armies could
not be used to advantage. On the 6th the Confederates suffered a serious
loss in the person of General Longstreet, who was severely wounded.
The losses in killed and wounded were very heavy on both sides, as the
fighting was of a desperate character.

On the 7th General Grant moved his army around Lee's right, and
marched rapidly to seize the strong position of Spottsylvania Court-
house, which would have placed him between the Confederates and
Richmond Lee at once divined his purpose, and fell back rapidly to
the heights around Spottsylvania Court-house, which he occupied on the

8th. Upon arriving before this position Grant found his enemy strongly intrenched in it, and at once resolved to drive him from it. On the 10th of May he made a determined attack upon the Confederate line, but failed to carry it. At daybreak on the 12th a furious assault was made by Hancock's corps upon the right centre of Lee's line, which was carried in handsome style. Grant at once followed up Hancock's success by vigorous attacks upon the other part of the southern line, but Hancock was unable to advance beyond the works he had captured in his first attack, and the other assaults were repulsed by the Confederates. It was evident that the Confederates could not be dislodged from their position without a still heavier loss to the Union army, and General Grant determined to draw them from the heights of Spottsylvania by another flank march to the right. The losses of the Union army since the opening of the campaign had been enormous, but undismayed by them, General Grant wrote to the war department, after the battle of the 12th of May: "We have now ended the sixth day of very heavy fighting. The result to this time is very much in our favor . I propose to fight it out on this line, if it takes all summer."

On the 21st of May the army of the Potomac moved from Spottsylvania to the banks of the North Anna river, and reached that stream on the 23d. Lee had marched rapidly by a shorter route, and his army was in position on the south side of the river when Grant reached the northern shore. Lee had chosen a position of very great strength in front of Hanover Junction, and had covered it with earthworks. On the 25th Grant crossed a large part of his force to the south side of the North Anna, and endeavored to force the Confederate lines, but discovering its remarkable strength, withdrew his troops to the north shore, and on the 26th moved around Lee's right in the direction of the Chickahominy. Lee followed him promptly and took position at Cold Harbor, on the north side of the Chickahominy, and within nine miles of Richmond, occupying very much the same position held by McClellan's army in the battle of Cold Harbor, on the 27th of June, 1862. He covered his entire line with strong earthworks. On the 1st of June a sharp encounter occurred between the Federal right and the Confederate left wings, and on the morning of the 3d of June Grant made a general assault upon the Confederate works. The attack was made with great gallantry, but was repulsed with a loss to the Federal army of thirteen thousand men. The losses of the army of the Potomac since the passage of the Rapidan had reached the enormous total of over sixty thousand men. The Confederate loss during the same period was about twenty thousand. Failing to force the Confederate line at Cold Harbor, General Grant drew off

BATTLE OF SPOTTSYLVANIA COURT-HOUSE.

leisurely towards the James river at Wilcox's Landing, intending to cross that river and attack Richmond from the south side of the James.

In the meantime, upon reaching Spottsylvania Court-house, General Grant had sent General Sheridan, with ten thousand cavalry, to destroy the railroads connecting Richmond with Lee's army and the valley of Virginia. Sheridan executed his orders with complete success, and went within seven miles of Richmond. On the 10th of May he reached Ashland. He was attacked there by the Confederate cavalry under General Stuart, and moved off towards Richmond. Stuart, marching by a shorter route, threw his cavalry between Sheridan and Richmond, and again encountered him at the Yellow Tavern, on the Brook turnpike, seven miles from the city. Stuart was mortally wounded, and Sheridan secured his retreat across the Chickahominy and down the peninsula. In General Stuart the Confederates lost their only great cavalry leader. Had Sheridan, instead of halting at Ashland, pushed straight on to Richmond, the Confederate capital must have fallen into his hands. On the 25th of June he rejoined General Grant.

MAJOR-GENERAL W. S. HANCOCK.

At the opening of the campaign General Butler, with a force of about thirty thousand men, known as the army of the James, was sent up the James river to attack the defences of Richmond on the south side of that river. He occupied City Point and Bermuda Hundreds on the 5th of May, and a few days later advanced up the neck of land lying between the James and the Appomattox rivers. To oppose him the Confederates collected a force of about eighteen thousand men under General Beauregard, and posted them in a fortified line extending from the James to the Appomattox, in front of the Richmond and Petersburg railroad. On the 16th of May Butler's army, having advanced within a short distance of this line, was attacked by the Confederates and driven back to Bermuda Hundreds. The Confederates then formed their lines across the narrow peninsula, and kept Butler's force enclosed between their works and the two rivers until the crossing of the James river by the army of the Potomac.

The Federal plan of campaign also included the seizure of the valley of Virginia, and of the railway connecting Virginia with East Tennessee and Georgia. On the 1st of May General Sigel, with an army of ten thousand men, advanced up the valley towards Staunton. On the 15th he was defeated with considerable loss by the Confederates under General Breckenridge at New Market, and was driven back down the valley. General Hunter was appointed in Sigel's place, and succeeded in forcing his way to the vicinity of Lynchburg. Lee, becoming alarmed for the safety of that place, sent General Early, with twelve thousand men, to its assistance. Early at once attacked Hunter, and forced him to retreat by a circuitous route into West Virginia.

In the meantime General Grant had reached the James river, where his army was reinforced to one hundred and fifty thousand men. On the 15th and 16th of June he crossed his troops near City Point, and advanced upon Petersburg. At the same time General Butler moved forward with the army of the James against the southern

MAJ.-GEN. BRECKENRIDGE. works between the James and Appomattox. On the 16th, 17th, and 18th, Grant made repeated attempts to storm the Confederate works before Petersburg and south of the James, but was repulsed with a total loss of nine thousand six hundred and sixty-five men. Being unable to carry the southern works by storm, he began the siege of Petersburg. His right rested on the James above Bermuda Hundreds, and from this point his line extended across the Appomattox, with his left thrown out towards the Weldon railroad. During the summer and fall he continued to extend his left until he had seized the Weldon road.

From this point he sought to extend his left still farther and to seize the South Side railroad, Lee's only remaining line of communication with the south and southwest. Frequent encounters occurred between the two armies during the summer and fall, a number of which attained the proportions of battles, but we have not space to relate them all. On the 30th of July a mine was sprung under one of the principal works of Lee's line, and the explosion was followed by an MAJOR-GENERAL HUNTER. assault by Burnside's corps. The attack was repulsed with a loss of over five thousand men to the Union troops. During the early autumn General Grant extended his lines across the James river, and established a force on the north side of that river to lay siege to the defences of Richmond. The right of this force was extended as far as the Williamsburg road. This was the situation of the two armies at the close of the year.

In the meantime Early had advanced into the valley of Virginia after the defeat of Hunter. The retreat of that commander into West Virginia had left the Potomac unguarded, and Washington City exposed to attack. General Lee at once reinforced Early to fifteen thousand men, and ordered him to cross the Potomac and threaten Washington, hoping by this bold movement to compel Grant to weaken his army for the protection of the capital, if not to raise the siege of Petersburg. Early moved rapidly, crossed the Potomac near Martinsburg on the 5th of July, and on the 7th occupied Frederick City in Maryland. On the 9th he defeated a small force under General Lewis Wallace at Monocacy Bridge, and advanced upon Washington. The Nineteenth army corps of the Federal army was at Fortress Monroe, where it had just arrived from New Orleans, *en route* to join Grant's army. It was at once ordered to Washington, which, until its arrival, was held by a small garrison, and Grant at the same time embarked the Sixth corps, and sent it with all speed around to the Potomac. These troops reached Washington before the arrival of Early, who appeared before the defences of that city on the 11th of July. He found the works too strongly manned to be attacked by his force. After skirmishing for several days before them, he withdrew across the Potomac on the 14th, and retreated to the neighborhood of Winchester.

MAJ.-GEN. LEW WALLACE.

Early's movement so alarmed the Federal government for the safety of Washington that a force of forty thousand men, ten thousand of which were the splendid cavalry of Sheridan, was stationed in the valley, and Major-General Sheridan was appointed to the command of this army. Had Grant been able to retain these troops with his own army, it is safe to say that Lee would have been forced to abandon his position at Petersburg in the autumn of 1864. Their absence in the valley enabled the Confederate leader to prolong his defence through the winter.

As soon as he had gotten his forces well in hand, Sheridan advanced upon Early, and on the 19th defeated him at Winchester, and drove him back to Fisher's Hill, where, on the 22d, he again defeated him and drove him out of the valley, pursuing him as far as Staunton. By the orders of General Grant, General Sheridan now laid waste the entire valley of the Shenandoah, destroying all the crops, mills, barns, and farming implements, and driving off the cattle with his army as he moved back.

Early was reinforced after his retreat to the upper valley, and about

the middle of October advanced down the valley towards the Federal
position with a force of nine thousand men and forty pieces of cannon.
The Union army lay at Cedar creek, and was under the temporary command of General Wright during the absence of General Sheridan. On
the 19th of October Early attacked this force, and drove it back for several miles.   Instead of continuing the

pursuit, his troops stopped to plunder the
Federal camp, which had fallen into their
hands.   General Wright rallied his men
and re-formed them in a new position, and
at this moment General Sheridan arrived on
the field.   He had heard the firing at Winchester, "twenty miles away," and had
ridden at full speed from that place to rejoin
his army.   He at once ordered it to advance upon Early, whose men, laden with
the plunder of the captured camp, were
driven back with terrible force and pursued

MAJ.-GEN. PHIL SHERIDAN.

up the valley for thirty miles. This success cleared the valley of the
Confederate forces, for Early was not able after this to collect more than
a handful of men, and Lee had no troops to spare him.   Sheridan's
brilliant victories cost him a total loss of seventeen thousand men.

The western army under General Sherman
was increased to one hundred thousand
men, and was concentrated in and around
Chattanooga about the last of April. Opposed to this force General Joseph E. Johnston had collected an army of fifty thousand
men at Dalton, Georgia.   The objective
point of Sherman was Atlanta, Georgia, the
key to the railroad system of the south.

On the 7th of May the Federal army began
its advance. The position at Dalton being
too strong to be assaulted, Sherman turned
it by a flank movement upon Resaca, to
which place Johnston fell back. On the 14th

GEN. W. T. SHERMAN.

and 15th of May Sherman endeavored to force the Confederate lines near
Resaca, but without success. He therefore moved around Johnston's left
again, and compelled him to fall back to Dallas. Severe fighting occurred on the 25th at New Hope Church, but Johnston maintained his
position. Heavy skirmishing ensued until the 28th, when Sherman

having turned Allatoona pass, Johnston occupied a new position, embracing Pine, Lost, and Kenesaw mountains. Between the 15th of June and the 2d of July Sherman made several attempts to force this position, which was one of the strongest yet occupied by the Confederates, and failing to carry it, again moved to the left and turned it. Johnston at once fell back across the Chattahoochee and within the lines of Atlanta.

GEN. JOS. E. JOHNSTON.

He had prepared this city for a siege, and had strongly fortified it. He had his army well in hand, and he was determined as soon as the Federal army had passed the Chattahoochee to attack Sherman and force him to a decisive encounter. He hoped to defeat him, and had purposely avoided a general battle until now. Should he succeed in his attempt the defeat of the Federal army at such a great distance from its base might result in its ruin, and at all events would be decisive of the campaign. At this juncture, however, he was removed from his command on the 17th of July by the Confederate president, who was greatly dissatisfied with the results of the campaign, and who, it was generally believed, was influenced by his personal hostility to Johnston. General John B. Hood, a gallant soldier, but unfit for the great task imposed upon him, was appointed to succeed General Johnston. In Johnston General Sherman had recognized an antagonist of the first rank, and had conducted the campaign accordingly. He regarded the appointment of General Hood as greatly simplifying the task before him. The Federal army had already paid the heavy price of over thirty thousand men for its advance to Atlanta, while Johnston had lost less than eight thousand men. The conditions were now to be reversed.

MAJ.-GEN. M'PHERSON.

On the 17th of July the Union army crossed the Chattahoochee, and advanced towards Atlanta. On the 20th and 22d Hood attacked the Federal lines on Peach Tree creek, but only to be beaten back with a loss of over eight thousand men, without inflicting any serious injury upon the Union army, which, however, lost General McPherson, one of its ablest commanders. Sherman now drew in his lines closer to Atlanta, and by a skilful movement thrust his army between the two wings of Hood's forces, thus exposing them to the danger of being beaten

in detail. This movement sealed the fate of Atlanta, which was evacuated by the Confederates on the 31st of August. On the 2d of September Sherman occupied the city. Hood retreated towards Macon. The
loss of Atlanta was a serious blow to the south. It placed the Federal
army in the heart of Georgia, and destroyed the principal source from
which the Confederate armies were supplied with military stores, which

had been manufactured in great quantities at
Atlanta. Rome, Georgia, which was captured
by Sherman's army during the campaign, was
also largely engaged in the manufacture of arms
and ammunition.

General Sherman was now anxious to march
his army through Georgia, and unite with the
Union forces on the coast, but he was unable as
yet to undertake this movement, as Hood with
an army of thirty-five thousand men lay in his
front, and his communications with Chattanooga

GEN. JOHN B. HOOD.

and Knoxville were exposed to the raids of the Confederate cavalry. He
now learned that the Confederate government had ordered General Hood
to invade Tennessee for the purpose of drawing his army out of Georgia,
and concluded to make no effort to prevent this movement. The task of
watching Hood was confided to the army of
the Tennessee, under General George H.
Thomas, who was given a sufficient force to
hold Tennessee, and Sherman set about preparing his army for his march to the sea.
Thomas was heavily reinforced from the
north.

Hood began his forward movement towards the last of October, and on the 31st of
that month crossed the Tennessee near Florence. He remained on this river until the
middle of November, and on the 19th
marched northward, forcing back the command of General Schofield, and effecting a
passage of Duck river on the 29th. Scho-

MAJ.-GEN. GEO. H. THOMAS.

field fell back to Franklin, eighteen miles south of Nashville. He was
attacked on the 30th by the Confederates and forced back to Nashville,
within the defences of which city General Thomas had collected an army
of about forty thousand men. Hood invested the city, and hastened forward his preparations to assault the Federal works. General Thomas,

however, anticipated him, and on the 15th of December attacked the Confederate army and forced it back at all points. The next day, the 16th, the battle was renewed, and Hood was completely routed. On the 17th the Union army set out in pursuit of Hood's broken columns, and followed them for over fifty miles. But for the gallantry of a small rearguard, which preserved its discipline and covered the retreat to the last, the Confederate army would have been scattered beyond all hope of reunion. Hood recrossed the Tennessee with barely twenty thousand men out of the thirty-five thousand with which he had begun the campaign. He had lost half of his generals, and nearly all of his artillery. He fell

SAVANNAH, GEORGIA.

back to Tupelo, Mississippi, and on the 23d of January, 1865, was, at his own request, relieved of his command.

In the meantime General Sherman, leaving Thomas to deal with Hood, had begun his march through the State of Georgia. Satisfied that the war was practically decided in the southwest, he proposed to march to the sea near Savannah, and thence through the confederacy to the position of General Grant's army. This movement would compel the Confederates to mass their forces in his front, and would confine the decisive opera-

54

tions of the war to the country between his own and Grant's armies, between which it was believed the southern forces could be crushed. Everything being in readiness, Sherman cut loose from his communications with Chattanooga and set fire to Atlanta. On the 14th of November he set out on his "March to the Sea," at the head of a splendid army of

sixty thousand men. He ravaged the country as he went, leaving behind him a broad belt of desolation, sixty miles in width and three hundred in length. The Confederates had not sufficient force to offer serious opposition to his march, and in about four weeks he reached the coast near the mouth of the Savannah river. On the 13th of December he stormed and captured Fort McAllister, which commanded that river. The city of Savannah was thus left at Sherman's mercy, and was occupied by his army on the 22d of December. By this suc-

MAJ.-GEN. O. O. HOWARD.

cessful march to the sea, General Sherman had not only gotten his army in a position to co-operate with Grant in the final struggle of the war, but had struck terror to the south. The most hopeful Confederate now saw that the triumph of the Union cause was inevitable and close at hand.

During the year important operations had been undertaken by the Federal forces on the coast. In July a powerful fleet under Admiral Farragut, accompanied by a strong force of troops under General Granger, was sent against Mobile. This city was one of the principal ports of the confederacy and was strongly fortified. The entrance to the bay was commanded by Forts Morgan and Gaines, two powerful works built before the war, and a number of batteries, and a Confederate fleet under Admiral Buchanan—who had commanded the "Virginia" in her fight with the "Monitor"—lay beyond the forts ready to contest the possession of the bay. On the 5th of August Farragut passed the forts with his fleet with the loss of but

ADMIRAL PORTER.

one iron-clad, and entered Mobile bay. He immediately attacked the Confederate fleet, the flag-ship of which was a powerful iron-clad ram—the "Tennessee." After one of the most desperate fights in naval annals, the entire fleet was destroyed or captured by the Union vessels. Fort Powell was evacuated and blown up by its garrison on the same day. On the 7th of August Fort Gaines surrendered to General Granger, and on the 23d Fort Morgan also capitulated. These successes made the Federal forces masters of Mobile bay, and closed the port to blockade runners; but the city, which was strongly fortified, was not taken until the next year.

Wilmington, on the Cape Fear river, was now the only port in the confederacy remaining open to blockade runners. It was defended by Fort Fisher, an unusually formidable work near the mouth of the Cape Fear. A larger fleet than had yet been employed during the war was assembled in Hampton Roads under Admiral Porter. A force of eight

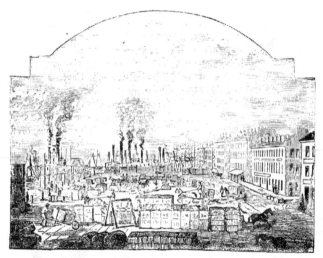

THE LANDING AT MOBILE, ALABAMA.

thousand troops under General Butler was embarked, and the expedition sailed to the Cape Fear. Fort Fisher was subjected to a vigorous bombardment, which was begun on the 24th of December, and the troops were landed; but at the last moment General Butler decided that the fort was too strong to be assaulted, and the expedition returned to Hampton Roads.

Since the opening of the war the Confederate cruisers had nearly driven the commerce of the Northern States from the ocean. These vessels were built in England, and were usually manned by crews of English seamen under Confederate naval officers. One of these, the "Florida," put to

sea in the summer of 1862, and succeeded in reaching Mobile in August
of that year. In January, 1863, she ran the blockade, and in three
months captured and destroyed fifteen merchant vessels. She was at
length seized in the harbor of Bahia, in Brazil, by a Federal man-of-war,
and taken to Hampton Roads. The Brazilian government, resenting this
breach of its neutrality, demanded the release of the "Florida," but while
the negotiations were in progress, she was sunk in Hampton Roads by a
collision with another vessel.

The most famous of all the Confederate cruisers was the "Alabama."
She was built at Liverpool, and was suffered to go to sea in spite of the
protest of the American minister at London. She was commanded by
Captain Raphael Semmes, and during her long career captured sixty-five
merchant vessels, and destroyed over ten millions of dollars worth of
property. During her entire career she never entered a Confederate port.
In the summer of 1864 she put into the harbor of Cherbourg, in France,

and was blockaded there by the United States
war-steamer "Kearsarge," Captain Winslow.
The French government ordered the "Alabama"
to leave Cherbourg, and she went to sea on the
19th of June. She was at once attacked by the
"Kearsarge," and was sunk by the guns of that
steamer after an engagement of an hour and a
quarter. Semmes was saved from drowning by an
English yacht that had witnessed the battle and
was set ashore. The destruction of the "Alabama"
was hailed with delight throughout the north.

ADMIRAL WINSLOW.

In the fall of 1864 the presidential election was held in the States
remaining faithful to the Union. The Republican party nominated
President Lincoln for re-election, and Andrew Johnson, of Tennessee, for
the vice-presidency. The Democratic party supported General George
B. McClellan for the presidency, and George H. Pendleton, of Ohio,
for the vice-presidency. Mr. Lincoln received at the polls 2,213,665
votes to 1,802,237 cast for McClellan; and the electoral votes of every
State save those of New Jersey, Delaware, and Kentucky, were cast
for him.

On the 31st of October, 1864, Nevada was admitted into the Union as
a separate State.

The year 1864 closed brilliantly for the Union cause. Though the
Confederates had gained a number of important victories during the year,
they had, on the whole, steadily lost ground. Virginia, Tennessee,
Georgia, Alabama, Mississippi, and Florida were overrun by the Federal

armies, and on the coast there was not a single port remaining open to the Confederacy save that of Wilmington, which was blockaded by a powerful fleet. It was evident that the coming spring campaign would end the war. The Federal forces had been increased to the enormous total of one million of men. The Confederates could bring into the field scarcely two hundred thousand men, and for these it was difficult to find subsistence. The vicious financial system adopted by the Confederate government had run its appointed course, and the notes of the Confederate treasury were worth scarcely three or four cents in the dollar.

The year 1865 opened with an effort to secure the return of peace without further bloodshed. In January Mr. F. P. Blair, Sr., came from Washington to Richmond, and on his own responsibility proposed to the Confederate government the appointment of commissioners to negotiate with the Federal government for the close of the war. The following commissioners were appointed by the Confederate government: Alexander H. Stephens, vice-president of the Confederate States; R. M.T. Hunter, senator from Virginia in the Confederate Congress, and John A. Campbell, assistant secretary of war. They proceeded to City Point under a safe conduct from General Grant, and were conveyed from that place to Hampton Roads in a government steamer. On the 3d of February President Lincoln and Secretary Seward having reached Hampton Roads, an informal conference was held between the president and the commissioners. The president refused to entertain any propositions which were not based upon the

BRIG.-GEN. A. TERRY.

unconditional submission of the Southern States to the authority of the Union, and as the commissioners had no authority from their government to enter into any such arrangement, the conference accomplished nothing.

In the meantime, however, Admiral Porter, undaunted by the failure of Butler to take Fort Fisher, had remained off the fort with his fleet and had asked for troops to renew the attempt. The same force that Butler had commanded, with fifteen hundred additional men, was placed under General Terry's command and ordered to join Porter. This force arrived off Fort Fisher on the 12th of January, and on the morning of the 13th accomplished its landing with success. A terrible fire was rained upon the fort by the fleet during the 13th and 14th, and on the 14th a daring reconnoissance of the Union force revealed the fact that the fort had been severely damaged by this bombardment. The trenches of the Union army were pushed rapidly through the sand to within two hundred yards of Fort Fisher in order to attract the attention of the garrison, and on the 15th a feint was made by a force of sailors and marines from the fleet in this direction. At the same time the troops under General Terry stormed the fort from the land side, and after a hard hand-to-hand struggle of about five hours, during which each traverse was carried in succession by a separate fight, Fort Fisher was captured. On the 16th and 17th the

Confederates blew up their other works at the mouth of the Cape Fear and retreated towards Wilmington. The mouth of the river was now in the possession of the Federal forces, and the last port of the south was closed. A number of blockade runners, ignorant of the capture, ran into the river and fell into the hands of the victors. Later in the month, General J. M. Schofield was placed in command of the department of North Carolina, and on the 22d of February occupied the city of Wilmington with his troops.

BRIG.-GEN. SCHOFIELD.

Sherman, after the capture of Savannah, allowed his army a month's rest on the coast, and towards the end of January moved northward through South Carolina towards Virginia. His force was sixty thousand strong and moved in four columns covering a front of fifty miles. His route was marked by the same desolation he had spread through Georgia. The roads were in a horrible condition, and in many places the men were forced to wade through the icy waters up to the arm-pits. Still he pressed on right into the heart of the confederacy. On the 17th of February he reached Columbia, South Carolina, having destroyed the railroad leading north from Charleston. General Hardee, commanding the Confederate forces at Charleston, apprehensive of being shut up in that city, which was utterly unprepared for a siege, evacuated Charleston and its defences on the 17th of February and retreated northward to join General Johnston in North Carolina. The next day

LIEUT.-GEN. W. HARDEE.

Charleston was occupied by the Federal forces. Fort Sumter was also taken possession of at the same time. The fort was a mass of ruins; the city was not much better off. It had suffered severely from the bombardment to which it had been subjected since the fall of Fort Wagner, and the Confederates upon their withdrawal had set fire to a considerable part of it.

From Columbia, Sherman moved towards Fayetteville, North Carolina,

driving back the Confederate forces that resisted his progress, and entered that place on the 12th of March. From Fayetteville he moved towards Goldsboro'.

The Confederate government, in the emergency to which it was reduced, was obliged to reappoint General Joseph E. Johnston to the command of the force assembling in Sherman's front. Johnston succeeded in collecting about thirty-five thousand troops, with which he attacked Sherman at Averasboro' on the 16th of March, and again at Bentonville on the 19th. The Confederates fought with their old enthusiasm in these encounters, but were unable to stay the progress of the Federal army, and on the 23d of March Sherman occupied Goldsboro'. Johnston withdrew towards Raleigh. At Goldsboro' Sherman was joined by the forces of Generals Schofield and Terry which had come up from the coast.

MAJOR-GENERAL H. G. WRIGHT.

The armies of Grant and Lee had lain confronting each other during the winter. General Lee had little hope of maintaining his position after the opening of hostilities. His army was growing weaker from sickness and desertion, and no more men could be obtained. The Confederate Congress made a feeble effort during the winter to enlist negro troops in its service, but with a singular recklessness refused to offer the boon of freedom to such of the blacks as would take up arms. That body believed that the negroes would fight for their own enslavement.

MAJOR-GENERAL WARREN.

Early having been driven out of the valley, General Sheridan was ordered to start from Winchester with a column of ten thousand cavalry, and cut the communications of Lee's army by railroad and telegraph north and east of Richmond. He left Winchester on the 27th of February, and defeating Early's small force at Waynesboro', broke the Virginia Central railroad at that point and moved to Charlottesville, which surrendered to him. He then divided his force into two columns and resumed his "ride" on the 6th of March. He thoroughly destroyed the railroad between Charlottesville and Lynchburg for about forty miles, and the canal between Richmond and Lynchburg shared the same fate for a considerable distance. Being unable to cross the James above Richmond on account of the high water, he moved around the north of Richmond, crossed the river at Deep Bottom, and joined Grant before Petersburg on the 26th of March. He had utterly laid waste the country along his route. The arrival of this splendid force of cavalry was of the greatest service to Grant, as we shall see.

The situation of General Lee's army was growing more critical every day. He had less than forty thousand troops. He was fully convinced of the necessity of abandoning Richmond and Petersburg, and was anxious to do so at once, and unite his army with that of General Johnston and occupy a new position in the interior of the south. In order to secure the withdrawal of his army he determined to make a vigorous attack upon Grant's right, hoping to compel him, in order to help his right, to draw back his left wing, which was in dangerous proximity to the road by which Lee wished to retreat. Could he succeed in this effort, he meant to evacu-

ate his position at Petersburg and retire towards Danville, where he hoped to unite with General Johnston. On the 25th of March he made a heavy attack upon Fort Steadman on the right of Grant's line, and captured it. The Federal forces rallied, however, and drove the Confederates from the captured works back to their own line, inflicting upon them a loss of three thousand men. Lee had now no alternative but to await the movements of General Grant, as he could not afford to make the sacrifice of men which a renewal of his efforts would require of him.

LIEUT.-GEN. A. P. HILL.

General Grant lost no time in taking the field. By the last of March his army, numbering about one hundred and seventy thousand men, including Sheridan's magnificent cavalry division, was in readiness to begin the campaign. On the 29th of March the advance of the Federal army was begun. Leaving the bulk of his army before Petersburg, Grant sent a column of twenty-five thousand men to turn the Confederate right and seize the Southside railroad, Lee's only means of communication with Johnston's army and the country in his rear. By the morning of the 30th the Federal left had gotten fairly to the right of the Confederates. On the 30th a heavy storm prevented a further advance, and Lee took advantage of the delay to reinforce his right wing with all the troops he could spare. On the 31st he attempted to drive back the Federal left, but without success. While this battle was going on, Sheridan swung around the Confederate right and seized the important position of Five

Forks. Lee then sent Pickett's and Johnston's divisions to recover this point, and they drove off the cavalry, and occupied Five Forks at night-fall on the 31st. Being joined by the Fifth corps, Sheridan attacked the Confederates on the morning of the 1st of April, and defeated them after a determined encounter, taking over five thousand prisoners.

As soon as Sheridan had secured Five Forks, Grant opened a heavy artillery fire upon the lines of Petersburg along his whole front, and continued the bombardment through the night. On the morning of the 2d of April he made a determined attack upon Lee's line, and broke it at several points. General Lee was now forced to assume a new and shorter line immediately around Petersburg. The Federal army made a vigorous effort to force its way into the city, but was unsuccessful.

The fate of Petersburg was now decided. It was impossible to hold it longer. On the night of the 2d of April General Lee withdrew his army from Richmond and Petersburg, and retreated in the direction of Amelia Court-house. His intention was to move towards Danville, and endeavor to join Johnston. His retreat was discovered on the morning of the 3d of April, and the Federal army, leaving a small force to occupy Petersburg, set off in pursuit, following the line of the Southside railroad.

On the morning of the 3d the withdrawal of the Confederates from the lines of Richmond was discovered by General Weitzel, commanding the Federal forces on the north side of the James. He at once advanced and occupied the city of MAJOR-GENERAL E. O. ORD.

Richmond, a large part of which was in flames as he entered it, having been set on fire by the Confederates upon their evacuation of it. Thus fell the Confederate capital after four long years of bloody war for its possession.

Upon reaching Amelia Court-house, General Lee found that the supplies he had ordered to be sent there from Danville were not to be had. The trains sent from Danville by his instructions had been ordered to Richmond to remove the property of the Confederate government, and had not been allowed to unload their stores at Amelia Court-house. This was a terrible blow to Lee, who was now unable to furnish food to his troops, who had eaten nothing since the commencement of the retreat. Parties were sent into the surrounding country to obtain supplies, and this consumed the whole of the 4th and 5th of April, which Lee had hoped to spend in pushing on beyond his pursuers. The delay enabled Sheridan, with eighteen thousand mounted men, to seize the Confederate line of retreat at Jetersville. This movement put an end to Lee's hope of reaching Danville and joining Johnston. A battle was impossible, for Sheridan had a force nearly equal to his own, and Grant was hurrying on with the rest of the Federal army. General Lee therefore turned off and retreated towards Farmville, hoping to be able to reach Lynchburg, but Sheridan, after passing Farmville, pushed forward again, and by a forced march reached Appomattox Station, on the Southside railroad, on the night of the 8th, and planted his force squarely across the Confederate line of retreat. The next morning Lee, when near Appomattox Court-house, discovered this obstacle in his way, and about the same time Sheridan was joined by the army of the James, under General Ord, while the army of the Potomac, under General Meade, was closing in fast upon Lee's rear. General Lee had now but eight thousand men with arms in their hands. The bulk of his forces, being too much broken down by fatigue and hunger to keep their places in the ranks, accompanied the regiments in a disorganized mass. As soon as he discovered Sheridan in his front, Lee attempted to cut his way through his lines, but failing in this effort, and being convinced that further resistance would merely be a useless sacrifice of his men, he asked for a suspension of hostilities, and went to meet General Grant.

The two commanders met at a house near Appomattox Court-house, and after a brief interview arranged the terms of the surrender. General Grant treated the beaten army with great liberality. The hungry Confederates were fed by the victors, and after laying down their arms were permitted to return to their homes. In order that the men might betake themselves as soon as possible to the cultivation of the soil, and so avoid the suffering which the failure of the harvest would entail upon the south, General Grant released all captured horses which were identified as the property of the soldiers surrendering them. The terms of the surrender were arranged on the 9th of April. On the 12th the army of northern Virginia formed in divisions for the last time, and marching to a designated spot near Appomattox Court-house, laid down its arms, and disbanded. About seventy-five hundred men with arms, and about eighteen thousand unarmed stragglers, took part in the surrender. The Federal troops treated their vanquished opponents with true soldierly kindness, and carefully refrained from everything which might seem to insult the valor that had won their earnest admiration.

The news of the capture of Richmond and Petersburg and the surrender of Lee's army was received in the north with the greatest rejoicing. Bells were rung, cannon fired, and illuminations flashed from every town and village, for it was understood that these great successes were decisive of the war.

SURRENDER OF GENERAL LEE.

In the midst of these rejoicings occurred a terrible tragedy, which plunged the country into mourning   President Lincoln, whose re-election we have related, entered upon his second term on the 4th of March, 1865, amid the congratulations of the country.   On the evening of the 14th of April he attended a performance at Ford's theatre, in the city of Washington   During the midst of the performance the report of a pistol rang through the house, and the next moment a man leaped from the president's box upon the stage, and waving a pistol over his head, shouted *" Sic semper tyrannus "* (Thus always with tyrants), and disappeared behind the scenes.   The cry was raised that the president had been killed, and in the commotion which ensued the assassin escaped. The murderer had entered the lobby of the theatre, and had fired from the door of the private box upon the unsuspicious president, who was sitting with his back to him.   Mr Lincoln fell heavily forward and never spoke again.   He was conveyed to a house on the opposite side of the street, and the highest skill was exerted to save him ; but all in vain. He died on the morning of the 15th, surrounded by his family and the leading men of the nation.   Appropriate funeral services were held on the 19th, and the body of the martyred president was conveyed through the principal cities of the north and west to Springfield, Illinois, where it was buried.   Along the entire route it was received with the evidences of the nation's grief   Cities were draped in mourning, and dense crowds poured out to greet the funeral cortege and testify their love and sorrow for the dead man   Even in the south, which had made the election of Abraham Lincoln the occasion of the dissolution of the Union, the unaffected and manly virtues of this simply great man had conquered the people, who had come to regard him as their best and truest friend.   His death was sincerely lamented there, and in the lamentation of the south Abraham Lincoln had his proudest triumph.   His death was a crushing misfortune to the whole country.   He was the only man capable of carrying out a policy of generous conciliation towards the south, and he had resolved upon such a course   He was sincerely desirous to heal the wounds of the war as soon as possible, and was strong enough to put down all opposition to his policy.   His untimely death, as well as the manner of it, threw back the settlement of our national troubles fully five years.

As he leaped from the president's box to the stage the assassin's foot caught in an American flag with which the box was draped, and he fell heavily, breaking his leg   He managed to escape, however   It was immediately ascertained that the assassin was John Wilkes Booth, a younger son of the famous actor Junius Brutus Booth.   Almost at the same time

MONUMENT TO ABRAHAM LINCOLN IN FAIRMOUNT PARK, PHILADELPHIA.

that the president was shot, another assassin, one Payne *alias* Powell, entered the residence of Secretary Seward. Proceeding to the chamber where the secretary was confined to a sick-bed, he attacked the two attendants of the invalid, and his son, Frederick W. Seward, and injured them severely, and then attempted to cut Mr. Seward's throat. He succeeded in gashing the face of his intended victim, but fled before further harm could be done.

Booth, who was most probably insane, had drawn quite a number of persons into a conspiracy, which had for its object the murder of the president and vice-president, Secretaries Seward and Stanton, and Chief Justice Chase. The plot failed through unexpected movements of some of the intended victims and the cowardice of some of the conspirators. Booth and a young man named Harold fled into lower Maryland, from which they crossed the Potomac into Virginia. They were pursued by the government detectives and a squadron of cavalry, and were tracked to a barn in Caroline county, Virginia, between Bowling Green and Port Royal. Here they were surrounded on the 26th of April. Harold surrendered himself, but Booth, refusing to yield, was shot by Sergeant Boston Corbett, and died a few hours later, after suffering intensely. His accomplices were arrested, and were brought to trial before a military commission at Washington. Payne or Powell, Atzerot, Harold, and Mrs. Surratt were condemned to death, and were hanged on the 7th of July, 1865, for complicity in the plot. Dr. Mudd, O'Laughlin and Arnold were imprisoned in the Dry Tortugas for life, and Spangler for six years. What Booth expected to accomplish by his horrible deed yet remains a mystery. It is now generally believed that he was insane; rendered so perhaps by his dissipated habits—and in this state of mind had conceived the idea that Mr. Lincoln was a tyrant, and as such ought to be put to death. He had no accomplices in the south, and his bloody deed was regarded with horror by the southern people.

HON. W. H. SEWARD.

We must now return to Sherman's army, which we left resting at Goldsboro'. Johnston's army was in the vicinity of Raleigh, and after the fall of Richmond was joined by Mr. Davis and the various officers of the Confederate government. On the 10th of April Sherman advanced from Goldsboro' towards Johnston's position, and steadily pressed the Confederate army back. On the 13th Sherman entered Raleigh. Being convinced that further resistance was hopeless, and having learned of the surrender of General Lee's army, General Johnston now opened negotiations with General Sherman for the surrender of his army to the Federal commander. The result of these negotiations was an agreement signed by the two commanders on the 18th of April. As this agreement provided for the restoration of the States of the Confederacy to their lost places in the Union, it was disapproved by the Federal government, and Sherman was ordered to resume hostilities. General Johnston was at once notified by General Sherman

LIEUT. GEN. E. KIRBY SMITH.

of this order, and on the 26th of April entered into an agreement with him by which he surrendered to General Sherman all the Confederate forces under his command, on terms similar to those granted to General Lee by General Grant.

INTERVIEW BETWEEN GENERALS SHERMAN AND JOHNSTON.

The example of Generals Lee and Johnston was followed by the other Confederate commanders throughout the south. The last to surrender was General E. Kirby Smith, in Texas, on the 26th of May. On the 29th of May President Johnson issued a proclamation announcing the close of the war, and offering amnesty to all who had participated in it

on the Confederate side, with the exception of fourteen specified classes.

Upon the surrender of Johnston's army, Mr. Davis and the members of his former cabinet endeavored to make their way to the coast of Florida, from which they hoped to be able to reach the West Indies. Some of them succeeded in doing so, but Mr. Davis was captured at Irwinsville, Georgia, on the 10th of May, and was sent as a prisoner to Fortress Monroe, where he was held in confinement until May, 1867.

JUDAH P. BENJAMIN.

The civil war was over. It had cost the country one million of men in the killed and crippled for life of the two armies. In money the north and the south had expended probably the enormous sum of $5,000,000,-000. The exact amount will never be known, as the Confederate debt perished with the government which created it.

CHAPTER XLIII.

THE ADMINISTRATION OF ANDREW JOHNSON

The New President—Return of the Army to Civil Life—The Public Debt—The Reconstruction Question—Action of the President—He declares the Southern States Readmitted into the Union—The Fifteenth Amendment—Meeting of Congress—The President's Acts Annulled—Reconstruction Policy of Congress—The Fourteenth Amendment—The Freedman's Bureau and Civil Rights Bills—The Tenure of Office Act—Admission of Nebraska into the Union—The Southern States Organized as Military Districts—Admission of Southern States into the Union—The Fourteenth Amendment Ratified—President Johnson's Quarrel with Secretary Stanton—Impeachment of the President—His Acquittal—Release of Jefferson Davis—Indian War—The French in Mexico—Fall of the Mexican Empire—Laying of the Atlantic Telegraph—Purchase of Alaska—Naturalization Treaty with Germany—Treaty with China—Death of General Scott—Death of ex-President Buchanan—General Grant Elected President—The Fifteenth Amendment

PON the death of Mr. Lincoln, Andrew Johnson, the vice-president, by the terms of the Constitution, became president of the United States. He took the oath of office on the 15th of April, and at once entered upon the discharge of his duties. His first act was to retain all the members of the cabinet appointed by Mr Lincoln.

Mr. Johnson was a native of North Carolina, having been born in Raleigh on the 29th of December, 1808. At the age of ten he was bound as an apprentice to a tailor of that city He was at this time unable to read or write Some years later, being determined to acquire an education, he learned the alphabet from a fellow-workman, and a friend taught him spelling. He was soon able to read, and pursued his studies steadily, working ten or twelve hours a day at his trade, and studying two or three more. In 1826 he removed to Greenville, Tennessee, carrving with him his mother, who was dependent upon him for support. Upon attaining manhood he married, and continued his studies under the direction of his wife, supporting his family in the meantime by his trade. He was subsequently chosen alderman of his town, and with this election entered upon his political career. Studying law he abandoned tailoring, and devoted himself to legal pursuits and politics He was successively chosen mayor, member of the legislature, presidential elector, and State senator. He was twice elected governor of Tennessee, and three times a senator of

55

the United States from that State.   Upon the secession of Tennessee from
the Union he refused to relinquish his seat in the Senate, and remained
faithful to the cause of the Union throughout the war, winning considerable reputation during the struggle by his services in behalf of the national cause. He was an earnest, honest-hearted man, who sincerely
desired to do his duty to the country. His mistakes were due to his tem-
perament, and proceeded from no desire to serve his own interests or those
of any party. In his public life he was incorruptible. A man of ardent
nature, strong convictions, and indomitable will, it was not possible that
he should avoid errors, or fail to stir up a warm and determined opposition to his policy.

The first duty devolving upon the new administration was the disband-
ing of the army, which at the close of the war numbered over a million
of men. It was prophesied by foreign nations and feared by many per-

ANDREW JOHNSON.

sons at home that the sudden return of such
a large body of men to the pursuits of civil
life would be attended with serious evils, but
both the Union and the Confederate soldiers
went back quietly and readily to their old
avocations. Thus did these citizen-soldiers
give to the world a splendid exhibition of
the triumph of law and order in a free
country, and a proof of the stability of our
institutions.

Two questions—both difficult and delicate—presented themselves for settlement by
the government. In June, 1865, the war
debt amounted to $2,700,000,000. The in-
terest on this sum was $133,000,000, and
was nearly all payable in gold. The government was called upon to
raise the latter amount to pay the interest on its bonds, and at the same
time to take measures to strengthen the confidence of the bondholders in
the security of their investments. The latter object was accomplished by
a solemn resolution of the House of Representatives, adopted with but
one dissenting voice on the 5th of December, 1865, pledging the faith of
the nation to the payment of the public debt, "principal and interest."
In order to provide for the immediate wants of the government Congress
levied additional duties on imported articles, and imposed taxes upon
manufactured articles, incomes, etc. These burdensome imposts were
cheerfully submitted to by the people, and a revenue of over $300,000,000
was raised, providing not only for the payment of the interest on the

debt, and of the current expenses of the government, but also leaving a large surplus, which was applied to the reduction of the national debt. In the year 1866, " before all the extra troops called out by the war had been discharged, the debt had been diminished more than thirty-one millions of dollars "—a striking proof of the ability as well as the willingness of the nation to discharge its financial obligations. During the remainder of Mr. Johnson's term this policy was faithfully adhered to under the able guidance of Hugh McCulloch, secretary of the treasury.

The other question demanding immediate attention was the adjustment of the relations of the States of the south to the Union. The president

CITY HALL, PORTLAND, MAINE.

held that they had never been out of the Union, but had simply been in insurrection, and had been brought back to the acknowledgment of their allegiance to the constitution and laws of the United States, which he claimed they had no power to renounce. Now that they had submitted to the authority they had formerly endeavored to reject, he claimed that they were entitled to immediate restoration to their old places in the Union. In support of his position he quoted the solemn declaration of Congress in the summer of 1861, and the assurances of Mr. Lincoln's

administration that the war was fought for the restoration of the Union,
and not for purposes of conquest. In accordance with these declarations,
provisional governments had been formed in some of the Southern States
and their representatives had been admitted to Congress during the progress of the war. A considerable party in the north supported President
Johnson in this position; but the Republican party, now the dominant
political organization of the United States, opposed his views with great
determination   The Republicans insisted that the results of the war
should be secured by stringent laws, and that the Southern States, before
their admission into the Union, should be compelled to give guarantees for
the perpetuation of these results. The Republican party, moreover, claimed
that the work of reconstructing the Union properly belonged to the legislative branch of the government and not to the president. Had the
president summoned Congress in extra session and sought the aid of that
body in the task before him, a conciliatory policy might have been agreed
upon, and the work of reconstruction have been completed without
delay

President Johnson, however, proceeded alone and without delay to the
work of restoring the Southern States to their places in the Union. On
the 29th of May, 1865, he issued a proclamation appointing a provisional
governor for the State of North Carolina, and providing for the assembling of a convention in that State for the purpose of forming a new constitution, under which the State would be recognized by him as a member
of the Federal Union. In the meantime North Carolina was kept under
military rule. A similar course was pursued by the president towards the
States of Virginia, South Carolina, Georgia, Florida, Alabama, Mississippi, Arkansas, Louisiana and Texas. The people of the ten Southern
States held conventions in accordance with the president's requirements,
annulled their ordinances of secession, renewed their obligations to the
Federal Union, adopted new State constitutions, and ratified the thirteenth amendment to the constitution of the United States prohibiting
slavery forever in all the States of the Union. They also elected senators
and representatives to Congress, and were recognized by the president as
formally restored to their places in the Federal Union.

On the 1st of February, 1865, Congress passed a resolution submitting
to the legislatures of the various States the following amendment to the
constitution:

"ARTICLE XIII *Section* 1 Neither slavery nor involuntary servitude, except as a punishment for crime, whereof the party shall have been duly convicted, shall exist within the
United States, or any place subject to their jurisdiction.

"*Section* 2. Congress shall have power to enforce this article by appropriate legislation"

On the 18th of December, William H. Seward, secretary of state, formally announced that this, the thirteenth amendment, had been duly ratified by the States, and had become a part of the constitution of the United States. The ratification of this amendment had been required of the Southern States by the president as a condition of their readmission into the Union.

The Thirty-ninth Congress met in December, 1865, and at once took measures to neutralize the reconstruction policy of the president The Republican party had a large majority in each house, and was thoroughly united in its opposition to the president. The senators and representatives of the Southern States were refused admission to seats in Congress, and the reconstruction measures of the president were treated as null and void. Congress insisted that the Union should not be "restored" as it was before the war, but "reconstructed" upon an entirely new basis. The measures of the president had made no change in the political status of the black population of the south. The negroes were secured in their freedom by the thirteenth amendment Congress now proceeded to make the negro a citizen of the United States, and to reconstruct the Union upon this basis. The following, known as the fourteenth amendment to the constitution, was adopted by Congress and proposed to the States for ratification :

"ARTICLE XIV *Section* 1 All persons born or naturalized in the United States, and subject to the jurisdiction thereof, are citizens of the United States, and of the States wherein they reside No State shall make or enforce any law which shall abridge the privileges or immunities of citizens of the United States · nor shall any State deprive any person of life, liberty, or property, without due process of law, nor deny to any person within its jurisdiction the equal protection of the laws

"*Section* 2 Representatives shall be apportioned among the several States according to their respective numbers, counting the whole number of persons in each State, excluding Indians not taxed; but when the right to vote at any election, for the choice of electors for president and vice-president of the United States, representatives in Congress, the executive and judicial officers of a State or the members of the legislature thereof, is denied to any of the male inhabitants of such State (being twenty-one years of age, and citizens of the United States), or in any way abridged except for participation in rebellion or other crime, the basis of representation therein shall be reduced in the proportion which the number of such male citizens shall bear to the whole number of male citizens twenty-one years of age, in said State.

"*Section* 3. No person shall be a senator or representative in Congress, or elector of president and vice-president, or hold any office, civil or military, under the United States, or under any State, who, having previously taken an oath as a member of Congress, or as an officer of the United States, or as a member of any State legislature, or as an executive or judicial officer of any State, to support the constitution of the United States, shall have engaged in insurrection or rebellion against the same, or given aid or comfort to the enemies thereof, but Congress may, by a vote of two-thirds of each House, remove such disability.

"*Section* 4. The validity of the public debt of the United States authorized by law, including debts incurred for payment of pensions and bounties for services in suppressing insurrection or rebellion, shall not be questioned; but neither the United States nor any State shall assume or pay any debt or obligation incurred in aid of insurrection or rebellion against the United States, or any claim for the loss or emancipation of any slave; but all such debts, obligations and claims shall be held illegal and void.

"*Section* 5. The Congress shall have power to enforce, by appropriate legislation, the provisions of this article."

This amendment was rejected by all the Southern States except Tennessee, and by several of the Northern States. Tennessee ratified the amendment, and was admitted by Congress into the Union. Congress at

CHESTNUT STREET BRIDGE OVER THE SCHUYLKILL, PHILADELPHIA.

this session enacted what is known as the "Freedman's Bureau Bill," creating a department under the Federal government for the care and protection of the newly emancipated negroes and the destitute whites of the south. This measure was vetoed by the president as unconstitutional, and was passed over his veto. It was immediately put in operation throughout the south. While the freedman's bureau did much to assist the negro in adapting himself to the duties of his new position, it was productive of an immense amount of corruption and fraud.

Another measure of Congress which was vetoed by the president upon constitutional grounds, and was passed over his veto, was the "Civil Rights Bill," which secured to the negro the rights of a citizen.

As the quarrel between the president and Congress deepened, various efforts were made by the latter to hamper the executive and impair his powers. The Thirty-ninth Congress adopted for this purpose a measure known as the "Tenure of Office Act," by the terms of which the president was forbidden to remove any person from a civil office under the government without the consent of the Senate. This bill was promptly vetoed by the president, but was passed over his veto by Congress.

On the 1st of March, 1867, a new State was added to the Union by the admission of Nebraska on an equality with the original thirteen States—four of which were at that time undergoing the process of reconstruction

In February, 1867, Congress proceeded to take extreme measures with the Southern States that had refused to ratify the fourteenth amendment. The State governments were abolished, the State officers removed, and the Southern States were organized as military districts, and placed under absolute martial law. The writ of *habeas corpus* was suspended, and the civil law was made to give place to the will of a military commander. This was done with the avowed intention of compelling the Southern States to ratify the fourteenth amendment and seek admission into the Union upon the terms prescribed by Congress The effect of the measures of Congress was to disfranchise the better class of the southern people, and to confer the unrestricted right of suffrage upon the negroes. The intelligence of the Southern States was denied any voice in their government, which was intrusted to the most ignorant and degraded part of their population The measures of Congress were regarded with bitter hostility by the south, and there were very many of the more thoughtful Republicans of the north who seriously doubted the wisdom of this method of reconstruction. The measures of Congress were vetoed by the president, but were passed over his veto, March 2d, 1867.

Upon the organization of the military districts, the commanding generals, who, as a rule, exercised their power with moderation and forbearance, caused a registry of voters to be made, and ordered elections to be held for conventions to form State governments. The conventions so elected could not in any case be said to represent the white people of the south After a bitter and protracted struggle, some of the conventions ratified the fourteenth amendment, and organized State governments. On the 24th of June, 1868, Congress passed a bill over the president's veto admitting the States of Arkansas, Alabama, Florida, Georgia, Louisiana, North Carolina, and South Carolina into the Union Virginia, Mississippi, and Texas, having refused to ratify the amendment, were denied admission into the Union

The fourteenth amendment having been adopted by the requisite

THE PATENT OFFICE, WASHINGTON CITY.

872

number of States, was formally declared a part of the constitution on the 28th of July, 1868.

In the meantime the quarrel between the president and Congress came to a decisive issue. The extreme or radical wing of the Republican party, comprising the majority in Congress, was anxious to remove Mr. Johnson from his position. Could it succeed in doing so, Benjamin Wade, of Ohio, the president of the Senate, would, by virtue of his office, become president of the United States. As Mr. Wade was one of the extreme radical leaders, this would place the whole power of the govern-

LAKE STREET, CHICAGO.

ment in the hands of that party. A quarrel between the president and Mr. Stanton, the secretary of war, furnished the occasion for this effort. On the 12th of August, 1867, Secretary Stanton was removed from the war department by President Johnson, who appointed General Grant secretary of war *ad interim*. Upon the meeting of Congress, in December, 1867, the president's course was denounced as a violation of the tenure of office act, and on the 12th of January, 1868, the Senate refused to sanction the removal of Mr. Stanton. Mr. Stanton thereupon demanded of General Grant the surrender of the war department, and the latter at once complied with the demand. On the 21st of February, President Johnson again removed Mr. Stanton, and appointed General Lorenzo Thomas, adjutant-general of the United States, secretary of war *ad interim.* He held the tenure of office act to be unconstitutional, and an invasion of his lawful powers as chief magistrate of the republic. This second removal of Mr. Stanton brought matters to a crisis, and on the 24th of February, 1868, the House of Representatives, by a strict party vote, ordered the president to be impeached of high crimes and misdemeanors *   The Senate, sitting as a high court of impeachment, met on the 5th of March, 1868, under the presidency of Chief-Justice Chase. The impeachment was conducted by managers appointed by the House, and the president was defended by able counsel.   On the 26th of May, the case being closed, the vote was taken, with the following result: For conviction, 34; for acquittal, 19.   There not being the requisite two-thirds vote for conviction, the president was acquitted.

Jefferson Davis had been confined in Fortress Monroe since his capture by the Federal forces, in May, 1865   All the Confederate officials taken by the Union forces had been released within a year after their capture on giving their parole to answer any prosecution that might be brought against them by the Federal authorities.   Mr Davis was excepted from this clemency, and remained in prison for two years   A prosecution for

---

* The charges against the president may be summed up as follows 1 Unlawfully ordering the removal of Mr Stanton from the office of secretary of war, in violation of the provisions of the tenure of office act   2 The unlawful appointment of General Lorenzo Thomas as secretary of war *ad interim*   3 Conspiring with General Thomas and other persons to prevent Edwin M Stanton, the lawfully appointed secretary of war, from holding that office   5 Conspiring with General Thomas and other persons to hinder the operation of the tenure of office act, and in pursuance of this conspiracy attempting to prevent Mr Stanton from acting as secretary of war   6 Conspiring with General Thomas and others to take forcible possession of the property in the war department   7 The president was charged with having called before him the commander of the troops in the department of Washington, and declaring to him that a law passed on the 30th of June, 1867, directing that " all orders and instructions relating to military operations, issued by the president or secretary of war, shall be issued through the general of the army, and in case of his inability through the next in rank," was unconstitutional, and not binding upon the commander of the department of Washington, the design being to induce that commander to violate the law, and obey orders issued directly from the president 8 That in a number of public speeches the president had attempted to set aside the authority of Congress, to bring it into disgrace, and to excite the hatred and resentment of the people against Congress and the laws enacted by it   9 That in August, 1866, in a public speech in Washington, the president had declared that Congress was not a body authorized by the constitution to exercise legislative powers   Then followed a specification of alleged attempts on the part of the president to prevent the execution of the laws of Congress   The impeachment articles were eleven in number   The other two were simply repetitions of some of the above charges

treason was instituted against him in the district court of Virginia, but he was not brought to trial. A number of prominent citizens of the north who had been so active in their support of the war that their motives could not be suspected, exerted themselves to procure his release on bail, and became his sureties. He was accordingly released on bail on the 13th of May, 1867. During the following year the indictment against him was quashed by the government.

During the latter part of the civil war a vexatious and bloody warfare with the Indians broke out on the frontier. It began in 1864, and extended through 1865 and 1866, and until the fall of 1868 its ravages were spread along the frontier through Southern Colorado into the Indian Territory, causing severe suffering to the settlers of this region. By the winter of 1865–'66 the war had assumed such formidable proportions that General Sheridan was sent with a considerable force against the savages. The vigorous measures of Sheridan, and General Custer's victory over the band of Black Kettle at Wacheta, brought the war to a close in the fall of 1868.

MAJ.-GEN. GEO. W. CUSTER.

While the civil war was at its height, France, England and Spain became involved in a quarrel with Mexico concerning the non-payment of certain claims due citizens of those countries by the Mexican republic, and a joint expedition was despatched to Mexico in the fall of 1861. Discovering that France was seeking to use the expedition to destroy the independence of Mexico, England and Spain settled their claims with the republic by the convention of Solidad, on the 4th of March, 1862, and withdrew their forces. The French, however, continued the war, and after a hard struggle, during which the Mexicans fought gallantly for their country, Mexico was conquered, and early in June, 1863, the French army entered the capital. The emperor of the French now proceeded to overthrow the republic, it being his intention to replace it with an empire which should be dependent upon France. An election was held, and under the intimidation of the French, resulted in a majority in favor of the abolition of the republic and the erection of the empire. Through the same influence the Mexicans chose Maximilian, archduke of Austria, emperor of Mexico, and in an evil hour for himself that amiable and high-souled prince accepted the crown.

The government of the United States had viewed the interference of France in Mexican affairs with marked displeasure, but being too much engaged in its efforts to bring the civil war to a successful close to undertake any new difficulty, simply entered its protest against the action of France. The civil war having been brought to a close, however, it took a bolder stand, and demanded of the French emperor the withdrawal of his troops from Mexico. The action of the government was sustained by the great mass of the American people, and it was believed by many that a foreign war would be a sure and speedy way of bringing about the restoration of the Union. The Emperor Napoleon hesitated for a while, but finally acceded to the American demand. The French troops were recalled at the close of the year 1866, and the Emperor Maximilian was left to face the Mexican people alone. They at once rose against him, defeated his forces, and took him prisoner. On the 19th of June, 1867, he was shot by order of the Mexican government, in spite of the efforts of the United States to save him. Thus ended the hope of reviving the dominion of France on the American continent.

The efforts of the gentlemen interested in the laying of a telegraphic cable across the Atlantic did not end with their failures in 1858. In 1865 the same company succeeded in laying a cable for about fourteen hundred miles from the Irish coast, when it suddenly parted and sank into the sea. The expedition then returned to England. Undismayed by this failure, Mr. Cyrus W. Field, of New York, to whose courage and determination the final success of the scheme was due, succeeded in persuading capitalists to make one more effort, and in July, 1866, a cable was laid from Valentia bay, in Ireland, to Heart's Content, in Newfoundland, a distance of eighteen hundred and sixty-four miles. It was found to work to the entire satisfaction of all parties, and the great enterprise was now an accomplished fact. The fleet then sailed from Newfoundland to the spot where the cable of 1865 had parted in mid-ocean, and proceeded to grapple for it. It was recovered and raised from a depth of over two miles, and was then spliced to the coil on board the "Great Eastern," the ship employed in the undertaking. The huge steamer then put about, and completed the laying of the cable to Heart's Content, thus giving the company two working lines. The completion of the work was hailed with rejoicings in both America and Europe.

On the 29th of March, 1867, a treaty was concluded between the United States and Russia, by which the latter power sold to the United States for the sum of seven million two hundred thousand dollars, all of the region in the extreme northwestern part of the American continent known as Russian America. The treaty was ratified by the Senate on the 9th of April. The new territory added to the area of the United States a district of about five hundred and seventy-seven thousand three hundred and ninety square miles. In July, 1868, Congress extended over this region the laws of the United States relating to customs, commerce and navigation, and established a collection district. In August, 1868, the military district of ALASKA was organized, and attached to the department of California. With the exception of about ten thousand whites, the inhabitants were, at the time of the purchase of Alaska, all Indians. The region is chiefly valuable for its furs and fisheries, and for its harbors, which afford a safe retreat for the American whalers in the Pacific.

In 1868 a treaty was negotiated between the United States and the North German Confederation, by which the latter power recognized the right of German emigrants to the United States to renounce their allegiance to the countries of their birth, and become citizens of the United States by naturalization.

In the same year a treaty was negotiated with China, through an embassy from that country, which visited the United States under the charge of Anson Burlingame, formerly the American minister to China. It was the first instance in which that exclusive nation had ever sought to negotiate a treaty of commerce and friendship with a foreign nation. Liberty of conscience to Americans residing in China, protection of their property and persons, and important commercial privileges were secured by this treaty.

In 1866 the Fenians, a secret society organized for the purpose of delivering Ireland from British rule, invaded Canada in large numbers from Buffalo, New York, and St Albans, Vermont. President Johnson at once issued his proclamation declaring the Fenian movement a violation of the neutrality of the United States, and sent General Meade with a sufficient force to the border to execute the laws. This decisive action put an end to the hopes of the Fenians of embroiling this country in hostilities with Great Britain, and after some slight encounters with the British troops in Canada they abandoned the expedition.

During President Johnson's administration, two distinguished public servants passed away. On the 29th of May, 1866, Lieutenant-General Winfield Scott, the veteran conqueror of Mexico, died at the age of eighty years. On the 1st of June, 1868, ex-President James Buchanan died at his home at Wheatland, near Lancaster, Pennsylvania, in the seventy-eighth year of his age.

In the fall of 1868 the presidential election was held. The Republican party nominated General Ulysses S. Grant, the commanding-general of the army, for the presidency, and Schuyler Colfax, of Indiana, for the vice-presidency. The Democratic party nominated Horatio Seymour, of New York, for the presidency, and Frank P. Blair, of Missouri, for the vice-presidency. The election resulted in the choice of General Grant by a popular vote of 2,985,031 to 2,648,830 votes cast for Mr. Seymour. In the electoral college Grant received two hundred and seventeen votes and Seymour seventy-seven. The States of Virginia, Mississippi and Texas were not allowed to take part in this election, being still out of the Union.

In February, 1869, the two houses of Congress adopted the fifteenth amendment to the constitution of the United States, and submitted *it* to the various States for ratification by them. It was in the following words: "The right of the citizens of the United States to vote shall not be denied or abridged by the United States, or any State, on account of race, color, or previous condition of servitude."

CHAPTER XLIV.

THE ADMINISTRATION OF ULYSSES S. GRANT.

Early Life of President Grant—Completion of the Pacific Railway—Death of ex-President Pierce—The Fifteenth Amendment Ratified—Prosperity of the Country—The Enforcement Act—The Test-oath Abolished—The Constitutionality of the Legal Tender Act Affirmed—Death of Admiral Farragut—Death of General Lee—The Income Tax Repealed—The Alabama Claims—Treaty of Washington—The Geneva Conference—Award in favor of the United States—The San Juan Boundary Question settled—Efforts to annex St Domingo—Burning of Chicago—Forest Fires—The Civil Disabilities removed from the Southern People—Re-election of General Grant—Death of Horace Greeley—Great Fire at Boston—The Modoc War—Murder of General Canby and the Peace Commissioners—Execution of the Modoc Chiefs—The Cuban Revolution—Capture of the "Virginius"—Execution of the Prisoners—Action of the Federal Government—The Panic of 1873—Bill for the Resumption of Specie Payments—Preparations for the Centennial Exhibition.

ULYSSES S. GRANT, the eighteenth president of the United States, was inaugurated at Washington with imposing ceremonies on the 4th of March, 1869 He was born at Mount Pleasant, Ohio, on the 27th of April, 1822. His father was a tanner, and wished him to follow his trade, but the boy had more ambitious hopes, and at the age of seventeen a friend secured for him an appointment as a cadet at West Point, where he was educated. Upon graduating he entered the army. Two years later he was sent to Mexico, and served through the war with that country with distinction He was specially noticed by his commanders, and was promoted for gallant conduct Soon after the close of the war he resigned his commission, and remained in civil life and obscurity until the breaking out of the civil war, when he volunteered his services, and was commissioned by Governor Yates colonel of the twenty-first Illinois regiment. He was soon made a brigadier-general, and fought his first battle at Belmont His subsequent career has already been related in these pages He selected the members of his cabinet more because of his personal friendship for them than for their weight and influence in the party that had elected him. Hamilton Fish of New York was made secretary of state.

The most important event of the year 1869 was the opening of the Pacific railway from the Missouri river to the Pacific ocean. The eastern

879

division of this road is known as the Union Pacific railway, and was begun at Omaha, Nebraska, in December, 1863, and carried westward. But little progress was made in the work until 1865, when it was pushed rapidly forward. The western division, known as the Central Pacific railway, was begun at San Francisco near about the same time, and carried eastward across the Sierra Nevada. The two roads unite at Ogden, near Salt Lake City, in Utah, and the union was accomplished on the 10th of May, 1869, on which day the last rail was laid. The Union Pacific railway, from Omaha to Ogden, is one thousand and thirty-two miles in length; the Central Pacific, from Ogden to San Francisco, eight hundred and eighty-two miles; making a total line of nineteen hundred and fourteen miles, and constituting by far the most important railway enterprise in the world. By the completion of this great road, to the construction of which the general government contributed liberally in

ULYSSES S. GRANT.

money and lands, Portland, Maine, and San Francisco, the extremes of the continent, are brought within a week's travel. The long and difficult journey across the plains has been dispensed with, and the traveller may now pass over this once terrible and dangerous route with speed and safety, enjoying all the while the highest comforts of the most advanced civilization. The east and the west are no longer separated, and the rapid development of the resqurces of the rich Pacific slope has more than repaid the enormous cost of the road. A direct trade with China and Japan has been opened, and the wealth of the Orient is beginning to pour into America through the portals of the Golden Gate. The shortest route to India— the dream of Columbus and the old mariners—has indeed been found.

On the 8th of October, 1869, ex-President Franklin Pierce died, at the age of sixty-five years.

The fifteenth amendment, having been ratified by the necessary number of States, was formally proclaimed by Hamilton Fish, secretary of state, a part of the constitution of the United States, on the 30th of March, 1870.

In the year 1870 the ninth census of the United States was taken, and showed the population of the country to be 38,558,371 souls.

The country had now attained a marked degree of prosperity. Gold fell to 110, and during the first two years of President Grant's administration, $204,000,000 of the national debt were paid. The effects of the war were being rapidly overcome, and the bitter feelings engendered by the struggle were giving way to a more friendly intercourse between the north and the south. The manufacturing industries of the country had nearly doubled since 1860, and the five years that had elapsed since the war had witnessed a marked improvement in the condition of the south,

PRESIDENT GRANT LEAVING THE WHITE HOUSE TO BE INAUGURATED.

which was gradually adjusting her industry upon the basis of free labor, and entering upon new and profitable enterprises of manufacture and commerce.

The work of reconstruction was concluded in the year 1870. On the 8th of October, 1869, the State of Virginia ratified the fourteenth and fifteenth amendments, and on the 26th of January, 1870, was readmitted

56

CHEYENNES RECONNOITERING THE FIRST TRAIN ON THE PACIFIC RAILROAD.

882

into the Union   On the 11th of January, 1870, Mississippi ratified these amendments, and was readmitted into the Union on the 17th of February, 1870.   Texas was the last to return to the Union, but came in during the year, having ratified the amendments to the constitution

The political troubles in the south, however, did not end with the return of the States to the Union   A great deal of lawlessness prevailed in many of the Southern States, and considerable suffering was experienced by the negroes, whose sudden endowment with the rights and privileges of citizenship was resented by a lawless class of white men   The Federal government undertook to remedy these troubles rather than leave them to be dealt with by the States   In the spring of 1871 Congress passed a measure known as the "Enforcement Act," or the "Kuklux Act of 1871," which gave to the Federal officials absolute power over the liberties of the citizens of the States in which these troubles occurred.   The president carried out the terms of the act with promptness, and on the 17th of October issued a proclamation suspending the writ of *habeas corpus* in nine counties in South Carolina, in order that the law might be enforced without the interference of the courts of the State   The evils which these severe measures were intended to remedy were unquestionably very great, but the enforcement bill was nevertheless a dangerous departure from the principles of free government as understood in this country.   A free people cannot too jealously guard their liberties.

On the 31st of January, 1871, Congress repealed the test oath law, which required all applicants for civil offices to swear that they had not participated in the secession movement.   As few southern men could take this oath, this law excluded the genuine inhabitants of the Southern States from office under the general government, and threw the political power of those States into the hands of a class of adventurers, who had been drawn to the south since the war by the hope of obtaining office   The repeal of this law by Congress restored the control of the Southern States to the legitimate citizens and tax-payers thereof

In 1870 the Supreme Court of the United States decided that the act of Congress making "greenbacks," or the notes of the Federal treasury, a legal tender, was unconstitutional as regarded the payment of debts contracted prior to the passage of that act.   As this decision had been given by a majority of but one justice, Mr Hoar, the attorney-general, moved to reconsider it   The case was heard again, and the decision of the court was reversed by a vote of five to four, on the 18th of January, 1871.   Thus the constitutionality of the legal tender act was affirmed.

In 1870 died Admiral David G. Farragut, on the 14th of August,

THE BUREAU OF AGRICULTURE, WASHINGTON, D. C.

aged sixty-nine, General George H. Thomas, "the Rock of Chicka-mauga," and the defender of Nashville, on the 28th of December, aged fifty-three, and General Robert E. Lee, the commander of the Confederate army of northern Virginia during the civil war, on the 12th of October, aged sixty-three.

On the 26th of January, 1871, Congress repealed the income tax It had been retained long after the necessity for it had passed away, and had become odious to the nation, which had only submitted to it at first because of the urgency of the need for it

Immediately upon the opening of President Lincoln's second term of office, Mr. Charles Francis Adams, the American minister at the court of St. James, was instructed to call the attention of the British government to the depredations committed upon American commerce by Confederate cruisers, built, equipped, and manned in England, and to insist upon the responsibility of Great Britain for the losses thus incurred by American ship-owners. Mr Adams discharged this duty in a communication addressed to the British government, on the 7th of April, 1865. This led to a correspondence which continued through the summer of that year. Great Britain refused to admit the validity of the American claim, or to submit the question to the arbitration of any foreign government. The "Alabama question" remained unsettled for several years, and occasioned a considerable amount of ill-feeling between the two countries. Both governments regarded it as full of danger, but to Great Britain it was especially so, as in the event of a war between that country and any foreign power, the United States, following the example of England, might and doubtless would allow cruisers to be sent out from their ports which would seriously cripple, if they did not destroy, the British commerce. After Mr Adams' return from England, his successor, Reverdy Johnson, was directed by the president to reopen the matter. He negotiated a treaty with the Earl of Clarendon on behalf of the British government, in 1869, but this arrangement was unsatisfactory to the Senate, which body refused to ratify it. Two years later the matter was revived. and in 1871 a joint high commission, composed of a number of distinguished public men, appointed by the American and British governments, met at Washington, and arranged a settlement known as the treaty of Washington, which was ratified by both governments This treaty was ratified by the Senate on the 24th of May, and provided for the settlement not only of the Alabama claims, but of all other questions at issue between the United States and Great Britain

The Alabama claims were referred by the treaty of Washington to a board of arbitration composed of five commissioners selected from the neutral nations. This board met at Geneva, in Switzerland, on the 15th of April, 1872, and the American and English representatives presented to it their respective cases, which had been prepared by the most learned counsel in both countries. On the 27th of June, the board announced its decision The claims of the United States were admitted, and the damages awarded to that government were $16,250,000 These were paid in due time.

In our account of the administration of Mr. Buchanan we have related the dispute between the United States and Great Britain concerning the possession of the island of San Juan, growing out of the uncertainty as to the true course of the northwestern boundary of the Union. This had been an open question all through the civil war. By the thirty-fourth article of the treaty of Washington the two countries agreed to refer this dispute to the friendly arbitration of the emperor of Germany. Soon after the award of the Geneva conference was made, the boundary question was decided by the Emperor William in favor of the United States, into the possession of which the island of San Juan accordingly passed. Thus were these delicate and dangerous questions satisfactorily adjusted by peaceful methods, and not by the sword.

In 1870 the republic of St Domingo, comprising a large part of the island of Hayti, applied for annexation to the United States President Grant was very anxious to secure the annexation of this island, and to accomplish it went to the very verge of his constitutional powers—going farther, indeed, than many of his friends believed he had the right. Measures were introduced into Congress for the purpose of securing this union, but were warmly opposed. A commission of eminent gentlemen was appointed by the president to visit the island and examine into its condition. They reported favorably, but after a warm debate in Congress the measures for the annexation of the Dominican republic were defeated by a decisive majority.

On the night of Sunday, October 8th, 1871, a fire broke out in the city of Chicago, and raged with tremendous violence for two days, laying the greater part of the city in ashes. It was the most destructive conflagration of modern times The total area of the city burned over was 2124 acres, or very nearly three and one-third square miles The number of buildings destroyed was 17,450. About 250 persons died from various causes during the conflagration, and 98,000 persons were rendered homeless by it The entire business quarter was destroyed. The actual loss will never be known As far as it can be ascertained, it was about $196,000,000.

Almost simultaneous with this disaster, extensive forest fires swept

THE BURNING OF CHICAGO.

over the woods of Wisconsin, Minnesota, and Michigan. Whole villages were destroyed by the flames, which travelled with such speed that it was often impossible for the fleetest horse to escape from them. Over fifteen hundred people perished in Wisconsin alone.

These terrible calamities aroused the generous sympathy of the rest of the country, and aid in money, clothing, and the necessities of life was liberally extended to the sufferers in Chicago and the other afflicted communities. The telegraph flashed the news across the Atlantic, and in an almost incredibly short time liberal contributions in money came pouring in from England and continental Europe, and even from the far-off cities of India.

HORACE GREELEY.

On the 29th of May, 1872, Congress passed an act removing the disabilities imposed upon the southern people by the third section of the fourteenth amendment to the constitution. From this general exemption were excepted all persons who had been members of Congress, officers of the army or navy, heads of departments under the general government, or ministers to foreign countries, who had resigned their positions and joined the secession movement. By this act at least one hundred and fifty thousand men of capacity and experience, whose services were greatly needed by the south, were restored to political life.

In the fall of 1872 the presidential election occurred. The canvass was marked by the most intense partisan bitterness. The Republican party renominated General Grant for the presidency, and supported

Henry Wilson for the vice-presidency. The measures of the administration had arrayed a large number of Republicans against it. These now organized themselves as the Liberal Republican party, and nominated Horace Greeley of New York for the presidency, and B Gratz Brown of Missouri for the vice-presidency. The Democratic party made no nominations, and its convention indorsed the candidates of the Liberal Republican party The election resulted in the triumph of the Republican candidates by overwhelming majorities.

The elections were scarcely over when the country was saddened by the death of Horace Greeley He had been one of the founders of the Republican party, and had been closely identified with the political history of the country for over thirty years He was the " Founder of the New York *Tribune*," and had done good service with his journal in behalf of the cause he believed to be founded in right He was a man of simple and childlike character, utterly unaffected, and generous to a fault In his manner and dress he was eccentric, but nature had made him a true gentleman at heart His intellectual ability was conceded by all. His experience in public life and his natural disposition induced him to favor a policy of conciliation in the settlement of the reconstruction question, and, influenced by these convictions, he signed the bail-bond of Jefferson Davis and secured the release of the fallen leader of the south from his imprisonment This act cost him a large part of his popularity in the north He accepted the presidential nomination of the Liberal party in the belief that his election would aid in bringing about a better state of feeling between the north and the south He was attacked by his political opponents with a bitterness which caused him much suffering, and many of his old friends deserted him and joined in the warfare upon him Just before the close of the canvass, his wife, to whom he was tenderly attached, died, and his grief for her and the excitement and sorrow caused him by the political contest broke down his firmness and unsettled his mind He was conveyed by his friends to a private asylum, where he died on the 29th of November, 1872, in the sixty-second year of his age. The country could ill afford to spare him

On the 9th of November, 1872, a fire occurred in Boston, and burned until late on the 10th, sweeping over an area of sixty-five acres in the centre of the wholesale trade of the city, and destroying property to the amount of seventy-eight million dollars. As this fire was confined to the business quarter of the city, comparatively few persons were deprived of their homes.

On the 4th of March, 1873, President Grant was inaugurated a second time at Washington with great pomp. Twelve thousand troops took part in the procession which escorted him to the capitol.

Early in 1873 a troublesome war began with the Modoc Indian tribe on the Pacific coast These Indians had been removed by the government from their old homes in California to reservations in the northern part of Oregon. They at length became dissatisfied with their new location, which they declared was unable to afford them a support, and began a series of depredations upon the settlements of the whites, which soon drew upon them the vengeance of the Federal government Troops were sent against them, but they retreated to their fastnesses in the lava beds, where they maintained a successful resistance for several months. The government at length reinforced the troops operating against them, and General Canby, commanding the department of the Pacific, assumed the immediate command of the troops in the field At the same time a commission was appointed by the government to endeavor to settle the quarrel with the Indians peaceably This commission held several conferences with Captain Jack, the head chief of the Modocs, and the other Indian leaders, but accomplished nothing. At length the commissioners and General Canby agreed to meet the Indians in the lava beds a short distance in advance of the lines of the troops. They went unarmed and without an escort While the conference was in progress the Indians suddenly rose upon the commissioners, and killed all but one, who managed to escape with severe wounds General Canby was shot down at the same time, and died instantly

The Indians at once fled to their strongholds amid the rocks. The troops, infuriated by the murder of their commander, closed in upon them from all sides, and shut them in the lava beds. Their position was one which a handful of men might defend against an army, and they held it with a desperate determination. They were dislodged finally by the shells of the American guns, and such as were not killed were captured Captain Jack and his associates in the murder of General Canby and the commissioners were tried by a court-martial and sentenced to death. They were hanged in the presence of their countrymen and of the troops on the 3d of October, 1873.

For many years Cuba had been growing dissatisfied with the rule of Spain In 1868 a revolution broke out in that island, having for its object the expulsion of the Spaniards and the establishment of the independence of Cuba. The patriot army was able to win numerous successes over the Spanish troops, and for several years maintained its position against every effort to dislodge it. Very great sympathy was manifested for the Cuban patriots by the people of the United States, and repeated

PRESIDENT GRANT PASSING THROUGH THE ROTUNDA TO TAKE THE OATH OF OFFICE.

891

efforts were made to induce the government of this country to recognize the independence of Cuba and assist the patriots, or at least to acknowledge their rights as belligerents. The government, however, faithfully observed its obligations as a neutral power, and forbade the organization or departure of all expeditions from this country for the assistance of the Cubans The Cuban agents were prevented from shipping arms or military supplies to their forces, and several vessels intended to serve as cruisers against the Spanish commerce were seized and detained by the Federal authorities.

In spite of the precautions of the government, however, several expeditions did succeed in getting to sea and reaching Cuba One of these embarked on the steamer "Virginius," in the fall of 1873. When off the coast of Jamaica, the Spanish war-steamer "Tornado" was sighted. She at once gave chase, and though the "Virginius" was on the high seas and was flying the American flag, overhauled her and took possession of her on the 31st of October The "Tornado" then carried her prize into the port of Santiago de Cuba, which was reached the next day. Captain Fry, the commander of the "Virginius," and the crew and passengers of the vessel, were thrown into prison. After a mock trial, in which the simplest forms of decency were disregarded, Captain Fry and a number of the crew and passengers of the "Virginius," about thirty-five or forty in all, were shot by order of the military authorities. The other prisoners were held in a most cruel captivity to await the pleasure of the Spanish officials at Havana The consul of the United States at Santiago de Cuba made great exertions to save Fry and those condemned to die with him. He was treated with great indignity by the Spanish officials, and was not allowed to communicate with Havana, from which point he could consult his government by telegraph.

When the news of the seizure of the "Virginius" at sea under the American flag reached the United States, it aroused a storm of indignation. Meetings were held in all the principal cities, and the press unanimously sustained the popular demand that the government should require satisfaction for the outrage upon its flag. The general sentiment of the people was in favor of instant war, and it was openly declared that a better opportunity would never arise to drive the Spaniards out of Cuba and obtain possession of the island.

The government acted with firmness and prudence. Several vessels of war were sent to Santiago de Cuba to prevent the execution of the surviving prisoners taken with the "Virginius;" the fleet in the West Indies was reinforced as rapidly as possible, and the navy was at once put on a war-footing in order to be ready for any emergency. The president was urged to convene Congress in extra session, but he declined to do so,

THE LAVA BEDS.

knowing that that body would be most likely to yield to the popular demand for war, and he was anxious to settle the difficulty by peaceful means if possible   General Sickles, the American minister at Madrid, was ordered to demand of the Spanish government the arrest and punishment of the officials implicated in the massacre of Captain Fry and his associates, a suitable indemnity in money for the families of the murdered men, an apology to the United States for the outrage upon their flag, and the surrender of the "Virginius" to the naval authorities of the United States   These demands were at once submitted to Señor Castellar, the president of the Spanish republic   In the critical situation in which Spain was then placed by her internal dissensions, Castellar had no choice but to submit to the American demands.   Orders were at once transmitted to Cuba to surrender the "Virginius" and all the prisoners to the American naval forces.

The orders of the Spanish government were at first disregarded by the officials at Havana, who blustered a great deal, and declared their willingness to go to war with the United States.   They were brought to their senses, however, by the warning of Captain General Jovellar, who told them that their refusal to obey the orders of the Madrid government would certainly involve them in a war with the United States, in which Spain would leave them to fight that power without aid from her   The Havana officials therefore yielded an ungracious obedience to the orders of the home government.   The survivors of the "Virginius" expedition, who were in a most pitiable condition in consequence of the cruelty with which they had been treated during their imprisonment, were released, and delivered on board of an American man-of-war in the harbor of Havana   On the 12th of December the "Virginius," which had been taken to Havana by her captors some time before, was towed out of that harbor and delivered to an American vessel sent to receive her.   She was carried to Key West, from which port she was ordered to New York.   On the voyage she foundered at sea in a gale off Cape Fear, on the 26th of December   At a later period the Spanish government paid the indemnity demanded by the United States.

In the fall of 1873 a severe commercial crisis known as the "Railroad Panic" burst upon the country   It was caused by excessive speculation in railway stocks and the reckless construction of railways in portions of the country where they were not yet needed and which could not support them   The excitement began on the 17th of September, and on the 18th, 19th and 20th several of the principal banking firms of New York and Philadelphia suspended payment   The failure of these houses involved hundreds of other firms in all parts of the country in their ruin   The

SCENE IN THE NEW YORK STOCK EXCHANGE DURING THE PANIC OF 1873.

excitement became so intense that on the 20th the New York Stock Exchange closed its doors and put a stop to all sales of stocks in order to prevent a general destruction of the values of all securities. The banks were obliged to resort to the most stringent measures to avoid being drawn into the common ruin.

President Grant and the secretary of the treasury hastened to New York to consult the capitalists of that city as to the proper measures to be taken for the relief of the business of the country. Various measures were urged upon them. A strong appeal was made to the president to lend the whole or the greater part of the treasury reserve of forty-four million dollars of greenbacks to the banks to furnish the Wall street brokers with funds to settle their losses and resume business. He at once declined to take so grave a step, and, thanks to his firmness, the credit of the United States was not placed at the mercy of the reckless men who had caused the trouble. The government as a measure of relief consented to purchase a number of its bonds of a certain class at a fair price, and thus enable the holders who were in need of money to obtain it without sacrificing their securities. On the 22d the excitement in New York and the eastern cities began to subside. The trouble

NEW YORK STOCK EXCHANGE.

was not over, however. The stringency of the money market which followed the first excitement prevailed for fully a year, and affected all branches of the industry of the country, and caused severe suffering from loss of employment and lowering of wages to the working classes.

The panic showed the extent to which railroad gambling had demoralized the business and the people of the country. It showed that some of the strongest and most trusted firms in the Union had lent themselves to the task of inducing people to invest their money in the securities of enterprises the success of which was, to say the least, doubtful. It showed that the banks, the depositories of the people's money, had to an alarming extent crippled themselves by neglecting their legitimate business and making advances on securities which in the hour of trial proved worthless in many cases, uncertain in most. The money needed for the use of the legitimate business of the country had been placed at the mercy of the railroad gamblers and had been used by them. The funds of helpless and dependent persons, of widows and orphan children, had been used to pay fictitious dividends and advance schemes which had been stamped with the disapproval of the public. An amount of recklessness and demoralization was revealed in the management of the financial interests of the country that startled even the most hardened. The lesson was severe, but it was needed. The panic was followed by a better and more healthful state of affairs. The business of the country slowly settled down within proper channels. Recklessness was succeeded by prudence;

extravagance by economy in all quarters. The American people took their severe lesson to heart, and resolutely set to work to secure the good results that came to them from this harvest of misfortune.

COAT OF ARMS OF COLORADO.

In January, 1875, Congress passed an act providing for the resumption of specie payments, and requiring that on and after January 1st, 1879, the legal tender notes of the government shall be redeemed in specie. In the meantime silver coin is to be substituted for the fractional paper currency.

On the 4th of March, 1875, the Territory of Colorado was admitted into the Union as a State, making the thirty-eighth member of the confederacy.

The political troubles in Louisiana and Arkansas assumed a most serious character during the year 1873, amounting to civil war in both States. The president in view of the serious nature of the disturbances intervened with force in each State, and compelled the rival parties to refrain from additional hostilities, and the quarrels were settled in the course of the year without further bloodshed.

The year 1875 completed the period of one hundred years from the opening of the revolution, and the events of 1775 were celebrated with appropriate commemorative ceremonies in the places where they occurred. The centennial anniversary of the battles at Lexington and Concord was celebrated at those places on the 19th of April with great rejoicings. On the 17th of June the centennial of Bunker Hill was celebrated at Charlestown Vast crowds were present from all parts of the country. One of the most gratifying features of the celebration was the presence and hearty participation in the ceremonies of a large number of troops from the Southern States Nearly all of these had served in the Confederate army, and their presence in the metropolis of New England was an emphatic proof that the Union has indeed been restored The memory of the common glory won by the fathers of the republic has already done much to heal the wounds and obliterate the scars of the civil war May the good work go on.

As early as 1872 measures were set on foot for the proper observance of the one hundredth anniversary of the independence of the United States It was resolved to commemorate it by a national exposition to be held at Philadelphia, in 1876, in which all the world was invited to take part. As these pages are passing through the press, the preparations for this great celebration are being carried forward with success. The exhibition will undoubtedly be one of the most notable events of the century

CHAPTER XLV.

CONCLUSION.

E have now traced the history of the republic from its settlement through the first century of its national existence, and from the point we have reached may look back over the long period we have traversed, and mark the results accomplished by the nation and the lessons which our history teaches

In material growth our country has surpassed every nation upon the globe. At the beginning of the Revolution, nearly two centuries after the settlement at Jamestown, the population of the thirteen colonies was a little more than three millions By 1790, the year after the inauguration of the republic, it was 3,929,827 In 1870 it had reached the enormous figure of 38,517,229. In 1776 the area of the States comprising the Union was less than one million square miles, embracing only a narrow strip of country along the Atlantic from Georgia to Canada It has grown by successive additions until it is now nearly four millions of square miles, and stretches from the Atlantic to the Pacific, and from the Gulf of Mexico to the Arctic ocean

In 1776 but a few wretched roads connected the distant parts of the country. Now all points are brought into close and intimate relations with each other by lines of railway and canals. Splendid steamers navigate our bays, lakes and rivers, and the feeble and precarious trade of colonial days has expanded into a mighty and growing system of commerce which is rapidly enriching the country In 1872 there were about sixty thousand eight hundred and fifty-two miles of railway in operation in the United States The telegraph was unknown at the commencement of our existence. Over sixty thousand miles of wire are now in operation in this country.

In 1776 the manufactures of the country were few, and were limited to one or two necessary articles. In 1870 there were 252,148 establishments in the United States, employing a capital of $2,118,208,769, and producing manufactured articles to the value of $4,232,325,442 annually.

In 1790 the tonnage of the United States engaged in foreign trade was only a little over half a million In 1860 it exceed d six millions It

926

fell off during the war, in consequence of the depredations of the Anglo-Confederate cruisers, but it is now rapidly reviving, and ranks next to that of Great Britain. In 1870 the total value of goods imported into the United States from foreign countries was $315,200,022; the total value of exports for the same year was $254,137,208.

In 1790 the cultivation of cotton was just being introduced in the south. In 1860 the cotton crop amounted to 5,198,077 bales, and constituted the principal article of export at that period. In 1870 the crop amounted to 3,011,996 bales.

Besides the larger crops, the value of orchard and market garden pro-

SCENE ON THE HUDSON RIVER IN 1875.

ducts in 1870 was $68,054,418. In the same year the value of home-made articles was $23,433,332; the value of slaughtered animals, $398,956,376; the cash value of farms, $9,262,803,861; and the value of farming implements and machinery, $336,878,429.

The inventive genius of the country has supplied every demand which its rapid development has created. To Americans the world owes the application of steam to navigation, the invention of the electric telegraph, the sewing machine, the cotton gin, the reaping machine, the discovery of the use of ether as an anæsthetic, and the great improvements in the steam-engine and the printing-press. "The States were behind us in invention," says Mr. Charles Reade. "They soon advanced upon us, and caught us, and now they head us far. . . Europe teems with the material products of American genius. American patents print English newspapers, and sew Englishmen's shirts. A Briton goes to his work by American clocks, and is warmed by American stoves, and cleaned by American dust-collectors. . . In a word America is the leading nation in all matters of material invention and construction, and no other nation rivals nor approaches her."

Nor is it only in material wealth that the improvement of our country

ST. PAUL, MINNESOTA.

has been so remarkable. In the higher departments of intellectual effort it has kept pace with its growth in riches.

In 1800 there were but two hundred newspapers published in the United States. In 1870 the number of newspapers and periodicals was five thousand seven hundred and seventy-five, and their circulation amounted to 28,492,655 copies.

At the opening of the century there were few libraries in this country, and these were chiefly in the hands of private individuals. In 1870 there were in the United States 164,815 public and private libraries, containing 45,528,938 volumes.

In 1790 there were not more than a dozen colleges in the Union, and the common schools were confined to the New England States In 1870 there were 2454 colleges and professional and scientific schools in the United States, with an attendance of 255,190 pupils The private schools in the same year numbered 14,025, with 726,688 pupils, and the free public schools 125,059, with an attendance of 6,228,060 pupils. The total income of all these establishments in 1870 was $95,402,726. In the same year there were but 748,970 white males and 1,145,718 white females, of twenty-one years and over, who could not read, among the inhabitants of the United States The public schools exist now in every State, and liberal provision is made for their support, in order that the blessings of education may be diffused among the entire population

At the beginning of the century the number of churches was limited, and in many communities there was not a single religious establishment. In 1870 there were 63,082 religious edifices in the Union, with sittings for 21,665,062 worshippers. In this year the value of church property was $354,483,581

Such are some of the results of a century of free government. Few persons, one hundred years ago, would have believed them possible The American republic was an experiment, and its establishment and first steps were watched with the keenest anxiety by the friends of human freedom in all parts of the world Even the founders of our system of government were painfully apprehensive of the future, while from monarchical Europe came hosts of predictions of failure. The wisest statesmen of Europe had grave doubts whether a nation established upon principles such as ours could long endure. They predicted that in a short time we would be involved in wars with foreign powers, that our government, unable to give security to life and property, would end in anarchy, and that we would at last be driven into monarchy as the only solution of the troubles that would afflict us before the end of the century.

Time, the great solver of all problems, has demonstrated the wisdom of the fathers of the republic, and has confounded the predictions of their opponents Republican institutions have been tested, and have been found sufficient to all the wants of a free people.

Let us compare the predictions of our adversaries at the commencement of our existence with the actual facts as they have occurred

It was predicted that we would be involved in ruinous foreign wars, as our weakness would tempt stronger nations to acts of aggression. We have had but two foreign wars—one with England and the other with Mexico—from both of which we have emerged successfully and with increased strength In the same period England has engaged in four

VIEW ON THE COLORADO RIVER.

foreign wars, besides her wars in India, China and Persia   France has
had ten, Prussia six, Russia ten, Austria five, and Italy six foreign wars
in the same period of time.   With the exception of England every one
of these nations has been beaten in some of its wars   Thus it appears
that republican institutions have not only given us success in war, but
have secured for us a longer period of unbroken peace than any European
power has enjoyed.

It was predicted that we would be torn by internal dissensions, and
that our government would end in anarchy.   During the entire period of
our national existence we have had but one serious internal disturbance—
the civil war—which has been happily overcome, and the wounds of
which are being healed by the virtues of our free institutions.   During
this same period England has had two insurrections, Prussia one, Austria
two of great severity, Russia one, France seven revolutions, each of which
has been accompanied by a change in the form of government, and Italy
and Spain an indefinite number.   Our government has been strong
enough to put down the most formidable civil war of history, and yet at
the same time to preserve the institutions of the republic unimpaired
The result has shown that we are less inclined to civil wars and revolutions than monarchical Europe.

Our government has never been overthrown, while those of many
European states have been overturned by revolutions since the establishment of our own.   France has never been able to maintain a system of
government for a quarter of a century since the great Revolution.   In
Austria, Bavaria and Greece, the sovereign has been forced to abdicate,
and in France he has several times been driven from the throne and
country   Even Prussia has been forced to submit to the demands of the
revolutionary spirit, as when in 1848, she changed her form of government from an absolute to a constitutional monarchy

Our confederation of States has never been broken up.   Germany has
witnessed the destruction of the Holy Roman Empire, the downfall of
the system established by Napoleon, and the destruction of the German
confederation   The Austrian state has been several times overthrown.
Italy has been changed from a kingdom to a collection of detached states,
and then to a kingdom again   France has lost her possessions of Holland
and Belgium and the Rhine provinces.   During this period our government has prospered and grown great, and at the same time the various
States, as many in number as all the countries of Europe, have retained
their independence and the sole management of their internal affairs.

We have gained ground steadily   Our territory has increased rapidly
by conquest, purchase, or cession, and we have never at any time parted

with a foot of land belonging to the republic During this period scarcely a state of Europe has failed at some time or other to lose a material part of itself Thus republican institutions have enabled us not only to retain our original possessions, but to aggrandize ourselves beyond the wildest dreams of any European monarchy.

Our growth in material wealth and in the higher departments of civilization has been shown It was argued at the commencement of our existence that our republican ideas would lead us to run into licentiousness and infidelity To-day we have more churches than any nation in Europe, and our people are a more practically religious people than any European nation. Foreign writers often admit that this is the only country whose civilization is based on personal religion. Yet we have no state religion or religious laws, but leave matters of conscience to be settled between the man and his Creator Our benevolent institutions are equal to those of any European country in number, efficiency and the liberality with which they are supported Crime is not more frequent here than in other lands, and it is a notorious fact that our criminal and pauper classes are almost entirely composed of foreigners.

Thus we have proved to the world that republican institutions can make a country as great, as strong at home and respected abroad, as prosperous and as stable, as enlightened and as virtuous as the most powerful monarchy, and by far freer and happier

Such a destiny could not be worked out by any but a free people The supremacy of the law in this country leaves the citizen free and untrammelled We have dispensed with large standing armies, which eat up the life of states, and the safety of the republic and our institutions is intrusted to the whole body of citizens, each of whom is vitally interested in maintaining it. We have no class interests to array our people in hostile divisions Church and state are separate, neither intrudes upon the domain of the other, and the result is to the advantage of each All men are equal before the law, and personal merit is the only badge of distinction among us Men are trained to regard themselves as free citizens of a free land, a title more precious than all princely rank.

Such a state of society can exist only among an educated people An ignorant man can never be a good citizen This was the deep conviction of the Pilgrim fathers, and it led them to undertake the great experiment of educating the people at the expense of the state, in order that they might properly discharge their obligations of citizenship. Their descendants have continued their work, and have extended the work begun by them throughout the entire country, and have wisely made the free school the basis of our whole political system There free from sectarian influence or teachings, the young citizen receives the training which fits him to appreciate and enjoy in after years the blessings secured to him, and to labor for their perpetuity. If any man seek the reason of the remarkable prosperity of our country, he will find it in the general intelligence of our people. As a whole our people are more intelligent than those of European states. The education of our women is higher than that of any other nation. For this we are indebted to the free school.

If, then, the story of our first hundred years teaches us any lesson, or conveys any warning, it is that we should guard with jealous care our system of free public education, and resist any and all efforts to impair its usefulness, or to give to it a sectarian character. It is the most precious heritage that has come down to us from our fathers—the corner-stone of republican liberty. It is worth fighting for, worth dying for, if need be.

APPENDIX.

THE CENTENNIAL EXHIBITION.

AS the close of the first century of the independence of the United States drew near, it was generally regarded as the duty of the nation to celebrate it in a manner worthy of the great fame and wealth of the republic. Various plans for accomplishing this object were suggested, but none met with a national approval. In 1866, a number of gentlemen conceived the idea of celebrating the great event by an exhibition of the progress, wealth, and general condition of the republic, in which all the nations of the world should be invited to participate. The honor of originating and urging this plan upon the public belongs to the Hon. John Bigelow, formerly minister from the United States to France, General Charles B Norton, who had served as a commissioner of the United States at the Paris exposition of 1867, Professor John L Campbell, of Wabash College, Indiana, and Colonel M. Richards Muckle, of Philadelphia The plan proposed by these gentlemen was not generally received with favor at first. It was argued in opposition to it that the great exhibitions of Europe were the work of the government of the countries in which they were held; that under our peculiar system the government could not take the same part in our exhibition, and that it would thus be thrown into the hands of private parties and would result in failure The city of Philadelphia was designated as the place at which the exhibition should be held. This feature of the plan aroused considerable opposition growing out of local jealousies It was argued by the friends of the scheme that Philadelphia was fairly entitled to the honor, inasmuch as it had been the scene of the signing of the declaration of independence; and that the city was also admirably located for such an exhibition, being easily accessible from all parts of the Union and from Europe

The friends of the scheme labored hard to overcome the objections urged against it, and had the satisfaction of seeing their plans become more popular every day. The matter was ably discussed in the press of the country, and at length was taken in hand by the Franklin Institute

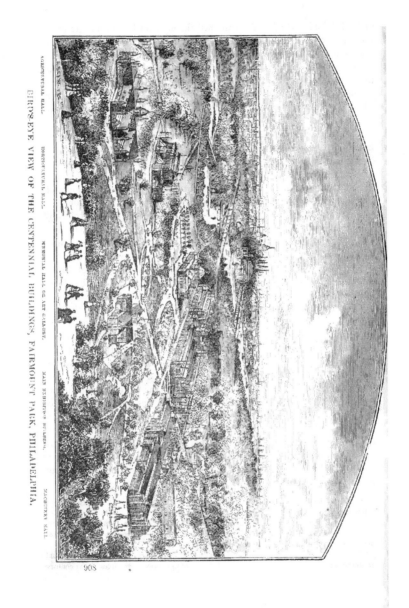

AGRICULTURAL HALL.   HORTICULTURAL HALL.   MEMORIAL HALL OR ART GALLERY.   MAIN EXHIBITION BUILDING.   MACHINERY HALL.

BIRD'S-EYE VIEW OF THE CENTENNIAL BUILDINGS, FAIRMOUNT PARK, PHILADELPHIA.

of Philadelphia, which body petitioned the municipal authorities to grant
the use of a portion of Fairmount Park for the purposes of a centennial
celebration. This petition was laid before the select council by Mr John
L Shoemaker, one of that body, who offered a resolution providing for
the appointment of a joint commission of seven members from each
chamber to take the subject into consideration. The resolution was
adopted, and Mr. Shoemaker was appointed president of the joint commission

After a careful consideration of the subject, the commission decided to
lay the plan before Congress The legislature of Pennsylvania now came
to the assistance of the commission, and adopted a resolution requesting
the Congress of the United States to take such action as in its judgment
should seem wise in favor of an international celebration in the city of
Philadelphia of the one hundredth anniversary of American independence. The legislature also appointed a committee of ten to accompany
the Philadelphia commission to Washington to present a memorial upon
the subject to Congress. The memorial of the committees was presented
to Congress by the Hon. W D Kelley, a representative from Pennsylvania, who urged its adoption by that body, and the selection of Philadelphia as the scene of the celebration, as that city had witnessed the
adoption, signing, and proclamation of the declaration of independence.

Early in March, 1870, Mr Daniel J Morrell, of Pennsylvania, presented a bill in the lower House of Congress, making provision for the
proposed exhibition. The bill was several times amended, and was
finally adopted by Congress on the 3d of March, 1871. It provided for
the appointment by the president of the United States of a commissioner
and alternate commissioner from each State and Territory of the Union,
who were to be nominated by the governors of the States and Territories
from which they were appointed. Philadelphia was selected as the place
at which the exhibition should be held ; and it was expressly declared that
the United States should not be liable for any of the expenses attending
the exhibition. In the preamble to this act, the following reasons were
given for the selection of Philadelphia as the place, and of an International exhibition as the means, of celebrating the centennial of our
national existence :

"*Whereas*, The declaration of independence of the United States of America was prepared, signed, and promulgated in the year 1776, in the city of Philadelphia, and

"*Whereas*, It behooves the people of the United States to celebrate, by appropriate ceremonies, the centennial anniversary of this memorable and decisive event, which constituted
the fourth day of July, 1776, the birthday of the nation, and

"*Whereas*, It is deemed fitting that the completion of the first century of our national
existence shall be commemorated by an exhibition of the national resources of the country

and their development, and of its progress in those arts which benefit mankind in comparison with those of older nations, and

"*Whereas*, No place is so appropriate for such exhibition as the city in which occurred the event it is designed to commemorate, and

"*Whereas*, As the exhibition should be a national celebration, in which the people of the whole country should participate, it should have the sanction of the Congress of the United States; therefore,' etc

The president having approved the bill, it became a law During the year 1871 he appointed the commissioners provided for by the act of Congress They were invited to assemble at Philadelphia on the 4th of March, 1872, and on that day commissioners from twenty-four States, three Territories and the District of Columbia met at the Continental Hotel, in Philadelphia A temporary organization was effected by the election of David Atwood, of Wisconsin, as chairman, and J. N Baxter, of Vermont, as secretary The commissioners then repaired in a body to Independence Hall, where they were officially received and welcomed by Mayor Stokley. General Joseph R Hawley, of Connecticut, responded to this address on behalf of the commissioners, who then repaired to the chamber of the common council After a prayer by the Rev. Dr. Hutter, the commissioners proceeded to business On the 5th, a permanent organization was effected, officers were elected, nine standing committees were appointed, and the *United States Centennial Commission* was definitely organized.

Several changes have been made since 1872, and at present the commission is constituted as follows:

PRESIDENT—Hon Joseph R Hawley

VICE-PRESIDENTS—Hon Alfred T Goshorn, Hon Orestes Cleveland, Hon John Dunbar Creigh, Hon Robert Lowry, and Hon Robert Mallory

SECRETARY—Professor John L Campbell.

DIRECTOR-GENERAL—Hon Alfred T Goshorn

COUNSELLOR AND SOLICITOR—John L Shoemaker

The members of the Centennial Commission for 1875 are·

ALABAMA—James L Cooper

ARIZONA—Richard C McCormick, John Wasson.

ARKANSAS—George W Lawrence, Alexander McDonald.

CALIFORNIA—John Dunbar Creigh, Benjamin P Kooser.

COLORADO—J Marshal Paul, N C Meeker.

CONNECTICUT—Joseph R Hawley, William Phipps Blake

DAKOTAH—J A Burbank, Solomon L Spink

DELAWARE—Henry F. Askew, John H Rodney

DISTRICT OF COLUMBIA—James E Dexter, Lawrence A Gobright.

FLORIDA—John S Adams, J T Bernard

GEORGIA—George Hillyer, Richard Peters, Jr

IDAHO—Thomas Donaldson, C W Moore

ILLINOIS—Frederick T Mathews, Lawrence Weldon

INDIANA—John L Campbell, Franklin C Johnson.
IOWA—Robert Lowry, Coker F Clarkson
KANSAS—John A Martin, George A Crawford
KENTUCKY—Robert Mallory, Smith M Hobbs
LOUISIANA—John Lynch, Edward Pennington
MAINE—Joshua Nye, Charles P Kimball
MARYLAND—James T Lile, S M Shoemaker
MASSACHUSETTS—George B Loring, William B Spooner
MICHIGAN—James Birney, Claudius B Grant
MINNESOTA—J Fletcher Williams, W W Folwell
MISSISSIPPI—O C French
MISSOURI—John McNeil, Samuel Hayes
MONTANA—J P Woolman, Patrick A Largey
NEBRASKA—Henry S Moody, R W Furnas
NEVADA—William Wmt McCoy, James W Haines
NEW HAMPSHIRE—Ezekiel A Straw, Asa P Cate
NEW JERSEY—Orestes Cleveland, John G Stevens
NEW MEXICO—Eldridge W. Little, Stephen B Elkins
NEW YORK—N M Beckwith, Charles H Marshall
NORTH CAROLINA—Samuel F Phillips, Jonathan W Albertson
OHIO—Alfred T Goshorn, Wilson W Griffith
OREGON—James W Virtue, Andrew J Dufur.
PENNSYLVANIA—Daniel J Morrell, Asa Packer
RHODE ISLAND—George H Corliss, Samuel Powell
SOUTH CAROLINA—William Guincy Archibald Cameron
TENNESSEE—Thomas H Coldwell, William F Prosser
TEXAS—William H Parsons, John C Chew
UTAH—John H Wickizer, William Haydon
VERMONT—Middleton Goldsmith, Henry Chase
VIRGINIA—Walter W Wood, Edmund R Bogwell
WASHINGTON TERRITORY—Ellwood Evans, Alexander S Abernethy.
WEST VIRGINIA—Alexander R Boteler, Andrew J Sweeney
WISCONSIN—David Atwood, Edward D Holton
WYOMING—Joseph M Carey, Robert H Lamborn

EXECUTIVE COMMITTEE—Daniel J Morrell, Pennsylvania, Alfred T Goshorn, Ohio; E A Straw, New Hampshire, N M Beckwith, New York, James T Earle Maryland, George H Corliss, Rhode Island John G Stevens, New Jersey, Alexander R Boteler, West Virginia, Richard C McCormick, Arizona, John Lynch, Louisiana, James Birney, Michigan, Charles P Kimball, Maine, Samuel F Phillips, North Carolina

In order to provide the necessary funds for the exhibition, Congress, on the 1st of June, 1872, adopted a bill creating a "Centennial Board of Finance," who were authorized to issue stock in shares of ten dollars' each, the whole amount issued not to exceed ten millions of dollars The commissioners adopted rules for the organization and government of this board, and directed that the books for subscriptions to the stock should be opened on the 21st of November, 1872, and should remain open for one hundred days. At the same time the president and secretary of the Centennial Commission issued an address to the people of the

United States, setting forth the objects of the exhibition, and asking their support and assistance in carrying the enterprise through to success

The Centennial Board of Finance is at present (1875) composed of the following gentlemen ·

PRESIDENT—John Welsh, Philadelphia.

VICE-PRESIDENTS—William Sellers, Philadelphia, and John S Barbour, Virginia

DIRECTORS—Samuel M Felton, Daniel M. Fox, Thomas Cochran, Clement M Biddle, N Parker Shortridge, James M Robb, Edward T Steel, John Wanamaker, John Price Wetherill, Henry Winsor, Henry Lewis, Amos R Little, John Baird, all of Philadelphia Thomas H Dudley, New Jersey; A S Hewitt, New York, John Cummings, Massachusetts, John Gorham, Rhode Island, Charles W Cooper, and William Bigler, Pennsylvania; Robert M. Patton, Alabama, J B Drake, Illinois, George Bain, Missouri

SECRETARY AND TREASURER—Frederick Fraley, Philadelphia

ENGINEERS AND ARCHITECTS—Henry Pettit, Joseph M Wilson, H J. Schwarzmann

The members of the Centennial Board of Finance were appointed by the stockholders at a meeting held in April, 1873 A majority of the members of the board were chosen from Philadelphia in order that, these gentlemen being residents of the city, there might always be a quorum for the transaction of business present at the meetings of the board. The board was authorized to issue bonds to an amount not to exceed the capital, to be secured upon the exhibition buildings and other property in possession of the commission, and upon its prospective revenues. The board was also ordered to begin at once the work of preparing the grounds and erecting the necessary buildings for the exhibition.

On the 4th of July, 1873, the commissioners of Fairmount Park formally surrendered to the Centennial Commission the area of four hundred and fifty acres that had been set apart by the city government for the purposes of the exhibition. The transfer was made in presence of an immense throng of citizens, and with imposing ceremonies in which the military and civic organizations of Philadelphia took part. The ceremonies were opened with a prayer by Bishop Simpson of the Methodist Episcopal Church, after which Hon Morton McMichael, president of the Park Commission, formally surrendered the grounds to General J. R Hawley, president of the Centennial Commission, who accepted them in an appropriate address As he closed his address, General Hawley exclaimed, "In token that the United States Centennial Commission now takes possession of these grounds for the purpose we have described, let the flag be unfurled and duly saluted" The stars and stripes were then raised, and at the same moment the trumpeter of the City Troop gave a signal which was answered by a salute of thirteen guns from the Keystone Battery. A grand military review succeeded these ceremonies, and the festivities were closed by a display of fireworks at night.

On the 3d of July 1873, the president of the United States issued a proclamation in which, after stating the action of Congress with reference to the exhibition, and declaring that he had received official notice that the grounds had been secured and that the buildings would be immediately commenced, he declared. "Now, therefore, I, Ulysses S. Grant, President of the United States, in conformity with the provisions of the Act of Congress aforesaid, do hereby declare and proclaim that there will be held, at the City of Philadelphia, in the State of Pennsylvania, an International Exhibition of Arts, Manufactures, and Products of the Soil and Mine, to be opened on the 19th day of April, Anno Domini eighteen hundred and seventy-six, and to be closed on the 19th day of October in the same year.

"And, in the interest of peace, civilization and domestic and international friendship and intercourse, I commend the celebration and exhibition to the people of the United States; and in behalf of the government and people, I cordially commend them to all nations who may be pleased to take part therein."

On the 5th of July, the secretary of state of the United States forwarded the president's proclamation to the various foreign ministers residing in the United States, together with an official note, from which we make the following extract:

"The president indulges the hope that the government of ———— will be pleased to notice the subject, and may deem it proper to bring the exhibition and its objects to the attention of the people of that country, and thus encourage their co-operation in the proposed celebration And he further hopes that the opportunity afforded by the exhibition for the interchange of national sentiment and friendly intercourse between the people of both nations may result in new and still greater advantages to science and industry, and at the same time serve to strengthen the bonds of peace and friendship which already happily subsist between the government and people of ———— and those of the United States."

In order that the Federal government shall be fully represented in the exhibition, the president of the United States, on the 23d of January, 1874, issued an order that there should be displayed in the exhibition such objects appertaining to the executive departments of the government as should "illustrate the functions and administrative faculties of the government in time of peace and its resources as a war power, and thereby serve to demonstrate the nature of our institutions, and their adaptations to the wants of the people." To carry out the requirements of this order the president directed that each of the departments participating in the exhibition should appoint one person to take charge of its property and arrange for its proper display and safe-keeping

58

On the 5th of June, 1874, Congress adopted a resolution requesting the president to extend, in the name of the United States, "a respectful and cordial invitation to the governments of other nations to be repre-

sented and take part in the Centennial Exposition." In accordance with this resolution the invitation was extended by the president, and was accepted by nearly all the European governments.

On the 16th of June Congress passed a bill authorizing the Centennial Commission to cause to be prepared and struck at the Mint at Philadelphia, medals commemorating the one hundredth anniversary of the declaration of independence. The said medals were to be furnished to the commission

CENTENNIAL MEDAL—OBVERSE.

by the Mint "upon the payment of a sum not less than the cost thereof."

On the 18th of June, 1874, Congress passed an act for the admission, free of duties, of all articles from foreign countries intended for the International Exhibition.

The work upon the buildings and grounds of the exhibition was begun immediately after the transfer of the grounds to the Centennial Commission, and has been pushed forward steadily since then. The enterprise has received the cordial indorsement and hearty support of the people of the United States, and ample funds have been provided to insure its success.

The grounds appropriated to the exhibition comprise four hundred and fifty acres situated within the well-known and beautiful Fair-

CENTENNIAL MEDAL—REVERSE.

mount Park, the total area of which is three thousand acres. They extend from the foot of George's Hill almost to the Schuylkill river, and north to Columbia bridge and Belmont mansion. The principal buildings are located on the level space known as the Lansdowne plateau, at the intersection of Elm and Belmont avenues. From this spot a noble view can be had of the city and surrounding country, with the beautiful Schuylkill winding through the landscape The site is commanding and in the midst of a region famed for its beauty.

The principal buildings are five in number, and consist of the Main Hall of the exhibition, the Memorial Hall or Art Gallery, the Agricultural Hall, the Horticultural Hall, and the Machinery Hall. These cover a total area of about forty-eight acres, and constitute the principal edifices only Besides these there will be a large number of smaller edifices devoted to the exhibition of special departments of industry, and to the use of the commissions from the various States and Territories of the Union and from foreign countries. The largest of these will be the building devoted to the uses of the government of the United States

The *Main Exhibition Building* is a parallelogram in shape, 1880 feet in length by 464 feet in width and 70 feet in height, with central towers 120 feet high. Including its towers and projections, it covers an area of twenty-one and a half acres. At the centre of the longer sides are projections 416 feet in length, and in the centre of the shorter sides or ends of the building are projections 216 feet in length In these projections, in the centre of the four sides, are located the main entrances, which are provided with arcades upon the ground floor, and central façades extending to the height of 90 feet The building is of iron and glass, and in the interior shows a grand hall 70 feet in height, with a central pavilion rising to a height of 96 feet. A magnificent central avenue 120 feet wide extends through the entire length of the building, and there are two side aisles of equal length and 100 feet wide Three transepts or cross avenues intercept the three long avenues, and divide the plan into nine open spaces, free from supporting columns. A number of lesser aisles traverse the building The latter are 48 feet in width.

In this building will be displayed the greater part of the articles comprising the exhibition The arrangement is simple, and is based upon common sense, but is a departure from the strictly scientific method which has prevailed in other exhibitions " Each country occupies a compact space. Within the territory of each the objects displayed will be grouped so as to make the most attractive appearance, keeping the different classes together as much as possible, but there will be no attempt to form belts of like objects extending from country to country throughout the building. The most advantageous positions are assigned to the four leading nations, the United States, England, France, and Germany These nations will divide equally the lofty central pavilion, and each possess one of the four towers The proximity to each other of these great competitors for the trade of the world will stimulate rivalry and make the portion of the building where their territory is exceedingly attractive. Here the most costly and beautiful articles will be displayed, and here will be the central point of attraction of the whole exhibition.

"The area assigned to the United States is more than one-fourth of the entire floor space, stretching from the centre to the west portal of the building. That this space will be filled is not doubted. England, Germany, and France have all applied for additional space since the first allotment, and will crowd their enlarged areas with their best products. The self-interest, if not the patriotism of the American manufacturers, ought to induce them to make great efforts to equal if not surpass their foreign rivals.

"Several weeks ago the system of classification adopted last year was materially modified in order to have each of the principal exhibition buildings contain one or more complete departments. This departure from a strictly scientific system to a more practical and convenient one reduced the number of departments from ten to seven, only three of which go into the Main Building These, with their subordinate groups and the number of classes composed in each, are as follows:

I.—Mining and Metallurgy

Classes	Groups
100—100 ...	Minerals, Ores, Stone, Mining Products.
110—119. .	Metallurgical Products
120—120	Mining Engineering

II.—Manufactures

200—205	Chemical Manufactures.
206—216 .	Ceramics, Pottery, Porcelain, Glass, etc
217—227	Furniture, etc
228—234 ...	Yarns and Woven Goods of Vegetable or Mineral Materials.
235—241	Woven and Felted Goods of Wool, etc
242—249	Silk and Silk Fabrics
250—257	Clothing, Jewelry, etc
258—264	Paper, Blank-Books, Stationery
265—271	Weapons, etc
272—279 ..	Medicine Surgery, Prothesis
280—284 ..	Hardware, Edge Tools, Cutlery and Metallic Products.
285—291 .	Fabrics of Vegetable, Animal, or Mineral Materials
292—296	Carriages, Vehicles, and Accessories

III.—Education and Science

300—309	Educational Systems, Methods and Libraries
310—319	Institutions and Organizations
320—329 .	Scientific and Philosophical Instruments and Methods.
330—339 ..	Engineering, Architecture, Maps etc
340—349	Physical Social and Moral Condition of Man

AGRICULTURAL BUILDING—INTERNATIONAL EXHIBITION.

820 feet in length, and 540 feet in width.

917

"This arrangement leaves for the Art Hall not only sculpture and painting, but also engraving and lithography, photography, ceramic decorations, mosaics, etc. At Vienna most of the articles in these classes were put in the Industrial Palace. The limited capacity of the Art Hall will probably make it necessary to erect two wooden annexes—one for photographs and the other for engravings. The character of the exhibit that will be made by foreign countries in the Main Building can already be pretty definitely ascertained from information in possession of the commissioners representing them here, and of the Centennial Commission. England will show a full representation of her textile fabrics and of her multiform iron and steel products. The Wedgewood, Minton, and other potteries, that have for years excelled the French establishments in producing graceful forms and beautiful ornamentation, will make striking displays, and one may expect specimens of the London silversmiths and jewellers. So of the 'Brummagem' bronze foundries, that it is said turn out heathen gods for the Chinese, antique statues for the Italian venders of vertu, and church ornaments for home use with equal readiness.

"In the German section one may expect to see an immense variety of articles, of which the ruling characteristic will be utility and cheapness rather than beauty. Unique displays will be made by the toymakers of Nuremburg, the clockmakers of the Black Forest, by Krupp's Cannon Foundry, and by several other special industries, and the educational department will be of great interest. In the department of mining and metallurgy it is thought that the German exhibit will far surpass that of any other European nation. It will include not only specimens of ores and metals, but a large collection of models, charts, and engravings, showing the methods of working mines and of smelting, refining, etc., the various metallic products of the empire.

"The French section will, no doubt, as at previous exhibitions, surpass all others in systematic and tasteful arrangement, and in the profusion of rich and beautiful objects displayed. Sevres porcelain, Gobelin tapestry, Paris bronzes and jewelry, the silks and velvets of Lyons, costly furniture of rare inlaid woods, and a countless multitude of other objects to delight the eye, will assert the supremacy of French taste.

"The special feature of the Austrian section will be Bohemian glassware, Moravian cloths, and the many manufactures of Russian leather, amber, meerschaum, and ivory, for which Vienna is famous. In the variety of fancy goods shown Austria will probably be second only to France, and she will be pretty sure to display also, and with some pride, the results of the protected iron industries recently developed in the provinces of Styria and Carinthia. Hungary will have a separate section, and make the most of the young industries of Buda-Pesth and Presburg—industries not peculiarly distinctive, except when producing the curious semi-Asiatic costumes and ornaments of the peasantry of the country, but of growing importance

"Belgium, next-door neighbor to France in the exhibition as on the map, will show, as the most prominent features in her section, the most delicate and the most substantial of manufactures—the laces of Brussels and Mechlin and the iron products of Liège and Namur A complete catalogue of the contributions of this busy little country to all departments of the fair has already been published In the Main Building her display will include glass, wood, marble, steel, iron, cotton, linen, and woollen wares, perfumeries, toys, military goods, paper-hangings, sacred vestments, precious stones, hair ornaments, etc.

"Holland's principal products will go into the Agricultural Hall, but she will have a variety of manufactured articles to put in the Main Building of no striking merit, perhaps, but serving to illustrate her diversified industry The curious and often beautiful fabrics of her vast East Indian possessions will also be exhibited. It is to be hoped that we shall also have an opportunity of studying by the help of models the remarkable system of engineering by which the water of innumerable canals and rivers is kept in circulation above the general level of the land and below the level of the sea

"Italy will be officially represented, the cabinet at Rome reconsidered its determination, and it is likely that a number of Italian manufacturers will be permitted to exhibit their goods in a corner of the space reserved If so, one may look for a goodly array of Venetian glass, Naples and Genoa coral work, and mosaics from Florence and Rome

"Switzerland will excel in watches, mathematical and surgical instruments, laces, and carved wood work Denmark will show a variety of excellent domestic manufactures little known outside of her own borders. Sweden's chief export products, and consequently those which will be most prominently exhibited, are iron and steel, furs, and friction matches. Her educational exhibit will be made in a model school-house, and if she makes an exhibit of her fisheries it will probably be in the Agricultural Hall, which is to be the grand receptacle for all food products Russia has not yet consented to take part in the fair. Greece also will not send articles. Spain and Portugal will both be represented. Neither manufactures extensively, but their fabrics of cotton, woollen, and silk, and their tools, pottery, and domestic utensils, will be all the more interesting from the fact that they are rarely seen in the markets of the world. Cuba

HORTICULTURAL HALL.—INTERNATIONAL EXHIBITION.

383 feet in length, and 193 feet in width.

and the other Spanish colonies will exhibit with the mother country; but most of the articles they send will go into Agricultural Hall.

" The Turkish and Egyptian sections promise to be among the most attractive in the exhibition. By their display of costumes, arms, household furniture, equipages, etc , they will afford a vivid picture of oriental life, and on the part of Egypt this characteristic view of the manners of Mohammedan countries will be contrasted with evidences of the remarkable enterprise and progress introduced by the wise and vigorous policy of the Khedive The quaint and ingenious wares of Japan and China will fill a good deal of space Siam and Persia have not yet signified an intention of being represented, but if they should come in at the last moment room will be made for them if possible

" Most of the nations on the American continent will make their best display in the Agricultural Hall, their products being chiefly those of the soil Canada will fill a large space in the Main Building with general manufactures , but with the exception of the products of the Mexican and Peruvian mines and a few rude fabrics, it is not easy to see, under the classification adopted, what the lands to the south of the United States will have to display in this building. As they will want to be represented there, they may obtain such a modification of the rules as will enable them to duplicate the display of national products which they will make in the Agricultural Hall. It is to be hoped, however, that whatever articles they do make will be shown, even if crude and imperfect, to illustrate, if not in a way flattering to themselves, the condition of the industrial arts among them "

The *Art Gallery or Memorial Hall* is located north of the Main Exhibition Building. It is situated on the most commanding portion of the Landsdowne plateau, 116 feet above the Schuylkill river, and looks down over the lower park and the city It is built in the style of the modern renaissance It is intended to remain as a permanent art gallery after the exhibition is closed, and is therefore constructed in the most substantial manner. The materials are granite, iron, and glass, no wood being used, in order that the edifice may be as nearly fire-proof as possible. The building is 365 feet long, 210 feet wide, and 59 feet high. From the central portion of the roof a graceful dome rises to a height of 150 feet The dome is surmounted by a colossal ball upon which stands a figure of Columbia with protecting hands At each corner of the base of the dome stands a gigantic figure typifying one of the four quarters of the globe

In the centre of the south or principal front of the edifice is situated the main entrance, consisting of three colossal arched doorways of equal proportions. At each end is a pavilion connected with the centre by arcades. The main entrance is approached by thirteen massive steps 70 feet wide. The entrance is by three arched doorways, each 40 feet high and 15 feet wide, opening into a hall. Between the arches of the doorways are clusters of columns terminating in emblematic designs illustrative of science and art. The doors are of iron, and are relieved by panels of bronze having the coats of arms of all the States and Territories of the Union. The coat of arms of the United States is in the centre of the main frieze. The cornice is handsome in design, and is surmounted by a balustrade with candelabra. At each end is an allegorical figure representing science and art. In the front of each pavilion is a window 30 feet high and 12 feet wide. Each pavilion is also ornamented with tile work, wreaths of oak and laurel, thirteen stars in the frieze, and a colossal eagle at each corner. The arcades are designed to screen the long walls in each gallery, and give an air of lightness and grace to the front. They consist of five groined arches and four promenades looking outward over the grounds and inwards over open gardens which extend back to the main wall of the building. These garden flats are each 90 feet long, 36 feet deep, and are ornamented in the centre with fountains. They are designed for the display of statuary. From the gardens a stairway leads to the upper line of the arcades, where there is a magnificent promenade 35 feet above the ground. It is protected by a balustrade ornamented with vases and designs for statues. The building covers an acre and a half of ground.

The main entrance opens into a hall decorated in the renaissance style, 80 feet long by 60 feet wide. The sides form two long galleries over 200 feet in length. The cost of this superb edifice will be $1,500,000. The hall will be seen to most advantage after the exhibition is over, when the other structures are cleared away, and its main front is seen across a broad level lawn covered with verdure and flowers.

The *Machinery Hall* is west of the intersection of Belmont and Elm avenues, on a line with the principal building and 542 feet from it. The building consists of the Main Hall 1402 feet long by 360 feet wide, and an annex of 208 by 210 feet. It contains about fourteen acres of floor space. The principal portion of the edifice is one story in height. The main cornice is 40 feet from the ground. The aisles are 40 feet in height in the interior, and the height of the central avenue is 70 feet from the floor to the ventilators. The main entrances are finished with handsome façades rising to a height of seventy feet. The building is constructed of glass and iron. Along the south side is the boiler-house and other buildings. A special room is set apart for the display of steam and rotary pumps and turbine water-wheels. "There will be eight lines

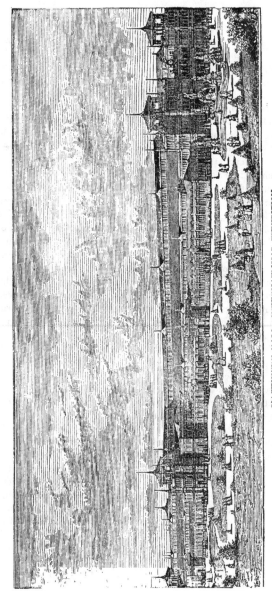

MACHINERY HALL—INTERNATIONAL EXHIBITION.

1402 feet in length and 360 feet in width.

923

of shafting extending lengthwise, seven to have a speed of 120 revolutions and one of 240 revolutions per minute. Steam and water power will be supplied gratuitously to exhibitors. They will be required, however, to furnish such pulleys, counter-shafts and belts as they need at their own cost, and to pay for erecting foundations for their machines The latter must be finished by the 1st of March, 1876 A space will be reserved for steam-hammers in operation, and for heating and working metals."

The *Horticultural Hall* is the property of the city of Philadelphia, at the cost of which it was built It will remain as a permanent ornament of the park It is situated on the Landsdowne plateau, a short distance north of the Main Building and Art Gallery, and is built in the style of architecture of the twelfth century, and chiefly of iron and glass. Its length is 383 feet; its width 193 feet, and its height to the top of the lantern 72 feet Flights of steps of blue marble lead to the east and west entrances from terraces 80 by 20 feet, in the centre of which stands an open kiosk or summer house 20 feet in diameter. The angles of the main conservatory are adorned with eight ornamental fountains. The central conservatory occupies the main floor It is 230 feet long by 80 feet in width and 55 feet in height, and is surmounted by a lantern 170 feet long, 20 feet wide, and 14 feet high A gallery five feet in width runs entirely around this conservatory at a height of 20 feet from the floor.

The *Agricultural Hall* lies north of the Horticultural Building, on the eastern side of Belmont avenue It is constructed chiefly of wood and glass, and consists of a long nave crossed by three transepts, nave and transepts being all composed of truss arches of Gothic form The length of the nave is 820 feet, its width 125, and its height from the floor to the point of the arch 75 feet The central transept is of the same height and is 100 feet wide. The two end transepts are 70 feet high and 80 feet wide.

"It has not yet been decided whether the exhibitions of horses, cattle, sheep, and swine will be held on the restricted grounds near the Agricultural Building or in some ampler area outside of the park The date for opening the show of horned cattle is fixed for September 20, 1876, and it will last fifteen days From a circular issued by the chief of the Bureau of Agriculture I learn that it is assumed that 700 head will cover all desirable entries, and upon that basis will be calculated the number of stalls which will be apportioned each breed. The scale divides the aggregate number into ten parts, and of these four-tenths are assigned to Shorthorns, two-tenths to Channel Islands, one-tenth to Devons, one-tenth to Holsteins, one-tenth to Ayrshires, and one-tenth to animals of other pure breeds The exhibition in each breed will comprehend animals of various ages, as well as of both sexes. Draft and fat cattle will be admitted irrespective of breed

"Ground for the competitive trial of reapers and mowers has been secured on the line of the Pennsylvania railroad, between Philadelphia and Trenton, near Schenck's Station, an excellent site on account of direct rail communication with the Centennial grounds American reapers and mowers have excelled at all competitive trials in Europe, and have control of the markets of the world; it is therefore scarcely probable that foreign machines will be sent here to compete with them on their own ground In the steam-plowing matches, however, the English will have the field to themselves. Three or four prominent manufacturers are expected to make the most of this opportunity to introduce their machines, which are admirably adapted for western prairies."

The arrangements for transporting visitors to the Centennial grounds are of the amplest and most satisfactory character Horse railways from the city will extend to the main entrance; and the Pennsylvania Railroad Company will prolong their line to the same point, where they will establish a depot, thus enabling them to convey travellers from all parts of the Union to the doors of the exhibition This connection is in the form of a circle, by which all trains from the north, east, south, and west, arriving over their road and carrying visitors to the exhibition, are run at once into the Centennial depot, in which there are four tracks Passengers can be arriving and departing at the same time without confusion, and the arrangement is such that a train can be received and despatched every three minutes, furnishing transit facilities at this depot alone for sixteen thousand people per day. The other railroads entering Philadelphia will make similar connections.

THE END.

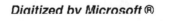

CPSIA information can be obtained
at www.ICGtesting.com
Printed in the USA
LVHW050800070723
751368LV00051B/274

9 781018 171395